Sociology:
An Interactive Approach

Nik Jorgensen
John Bird
Andrea Heyhoe
Bev Russell
Mike Savvas
with
Shaun Best

Collins
Educational
An imprint of HarperCollinsPublishers

Published by Collins Educational
An imprint of HarperCollins*Publishers* Ltd
77–85 Fulham Palace Road
Hammersmith
London W6 8JB

© HarperCollins*Publishers* Ltd 1997

First published 1997

ISBN 0 00 322443 0

A catalogue record for this book is available from the
British Library.

Commissioned by Emma Dunlop
Production managed by Hugh Hillyard-Parker
Edited by Ros Connelly, Abigail Concannon
Index compiled by Ian Kingston
Cover by Moondisks
Cover image: Mountain High Maps, copyright 1993 Digital Wisdom, Inc.
Page design by Hilary Norman
Typesetting by Hugh Hillyard-Parker and Liz Gordon, Cambridge
Cartoons by Martin Shovel (unless otherwise attributed)
Printed and bound by Rotolito Lombarda, Italy.

Contents

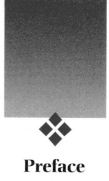

Preface

The aim of this textbook is to provide you, the student, with a clear introduction to sociology. Our approach as authors is to enhance your knowledge and understanding through activity and involvement.

We hope that you will find the material we have included clear, interesting and accessible. As well as working with the text, we advise you to be 'interactive' by carrying out as many of the activities and coursework suggestions as possible. In this way you will come to understand what being a sociologist is all about!

Acknowledgements

We are pleased to acknowledge that writing this book has been very much a team effort which has gone beyond the five co-authors and the contributory author, Shaun Best. The project was initiated back in 1994 by Patrick McNeill who successfully guided us through the early stages. Particular thanks go to our Commissioning Editor, Emma Dunlop, who since the beginning of 1995 has been an invaluable source of unstinting support and guidance, keeping our wilder suggestions on a sound footing through sometimes gritted teeth! Emma has been ably assisted at Collins Educational by the ever cheerful Victoria Ingham and Rachel Haggaty. Hugh Hillyard-Parker has done a marvellous job as Editor coordinating the difficult task of drawing together a team of authors in a highly successful manner. Our thanks also go to Hugh's colleague, Rebecca Green.

The authors and editors would also like to acknowledge their gratitude to the many sociologists who read the manuscript and advised in a constructive way. Particular thanks are due to Tony Breslin, Calvin Taylor, Pip Jones and Patrick McNeill.

❖ *Nik Jorgensen:* thanks the staff of the libraries at Lancaster University and Blackburn College for their support. More indirectly, a number of staff in the sociology departments of Lancaster and Salford Universities provided stimulation and maintained enthusiasm. On a personal note, Jan, Gabbie and Lucy have helped and supported in their own inimitable ways.

❖ *John Bird:* many years of teaching in the Sociology School at the University of the West of England have given me an awareness of how difficult introductory sociology can be. Colleagues have endlessly helped me to develop strategies to make sociology approachable. Hopefully, these are clear in this book! Personally, grateful thanks to Margaret.

❖ *Andrea Heyhoe:* thanks the many staff of Marlwood School who gave support, encouragement and valued contributions. Special thanks to Year 12 and 13 students for their cooperation and enthusiasm. Without Simon's patience and understanding, the writing of my chapters would have been far more difficult.

❖ *Bev Russell:* acknowledges what she has learned from introducing sociology to all her 'Access to HE' and A-Level students over the years. They have been a constant support and inspiration to her. Bev also acknowledges and thanks Russ Russell for his support and encouragement.

❖ *Mike Savvas:* wishes to thank the sociology staff at Filton College who helped develop his ideas over a period of time. On a personal note, Mike wishes to thank his parents, Nick and Anthony for their support and love over the years.

Finally, the contribution of our students must also be recognised. Their frame of reference has been a guiding influence in developing our ideas of what is required of a newcomer to this demanding discipline. We hope that we have provoked thought and debate in an accessible, interesting and simulating manner, encouraging you to be a truly 'interactive' sociology student.

April 1997

The table below shows which theories and theorists are relevant to each of the main chapters in the book. The position of each name indicates the degree to which they were influenced by different theories. Where names go across columns, it indicates cross-influences.

Chapter	THEORIES EMPHASIZING		
	Function	Structure	Social action
2 Culture and identity	Parsons	Bauman Bourdieu Hall Giddens Elias	Mead Garfinkel Goffman
3 Families and households	Parsons Murdock Goode	Laslett Giddens Young & Willmott Ariès	Berger & Kellner
4 Education and training	Parsons Douglas	Troyna Young Cicourel Keddie Bernstein Bourdieu Willis	
5 Work, organzations, unemployment and leisure		Braverman Goldthorpe Beynon Gilroy Castles & Kosack	Goffman
6 Stratification and differentiation	Parsons Davis & Moore Saunders	Halsey Goldthorpe Goldthorpe & Lockwood Bradley	
7 Theory and methods	✓	✓	✓
8 World sociology	Parsons Rostow	Frank Giddens Warren Sklair Wallerstein	
9 Community and localities	Castells Harvey	Young & Willmott Giddens Willis Goldthorpe & Lockwood Newby Park Rex & Moore	
10 Health, poverty and welfare	Parsons	Illich Navarro Wilkinson Townsend Le Grand	Blaxter Goffman Szasz Lewis
11 Deviance, crime and social control	Merton	A. Cohen Taylor Hall	Matza Plummer Young
12 Mass media		Hall Gramsci Fiske S. Cohen M. Barker Ang	
13 Power and politics	Habermas	Mills Poulantzas Giddens Goffman Miliband Pareto Gramsci Etzioni	
14 Religion	Parsons	Bruce Wilson Wallis E. Barker Troeltsch Turner Berger Heelas	

	FOUNDERS				CONTEMPORARY SOCIAL THEORY		
	Durkheim	Max	Weber	Freud	Feminism	Poststructuralism	Postmodernism
2	✓	✓	✓	✓	Oakley Sharpe	Foucault	Baudrillard
3	✓	✓		✓	Barrett Dobash & Dobash Abbott & Wallace	Foucault Donzelot	Beck
4	✓	✓			Sharpe Spender		
5	✓	✓	✓		Bruegel Duncombe & Marsden Crompton		Veal Urry
6	✓	✓	✓		Barrett Millett Walby		Hall
7	✓	✓	✓	✓	✓	✓	✓
8	✓	✓	✓		Foster-Carter		Beck
9	✓	✓	✓				Lash & Urry Bauman Beck Keith & Pile
10	✓	✓			Graham Clark	Foucault	Baudrillard
11	✓	✓			Stanworth McRobbie & Garber Carlen	Foucault Davies	
12	✓	✓			Skeggs Meehan Morley	Foucault Fairclough	Jameson Beck
13	✓	✓	✓		Abbott & Wallace Lovenduski & Randall		Bauman Lyotard Beck
14	✓	✓	✓	✓	Watson Bruce		

Chapter 1

Introduction: Getting started

❖ Preview

In this chapter we shall be looking at:

- ❖ what it is that sociologists do
- ❖ the skills that sociologists need in their work
- ❖ what is required of sociology students
- ❖ the demands of assessment for A-level sociology and how to prepare yourself for it
- ❖ how to make the most of this book as you study for your A-level sociology.

❖ Introduction

One of the most difficult things at the start of a course is defining the subject you are studying. Sociologists themselves often find it difficult precisely to define sociology when asked – particularly, when people who are not sociologists ask them!

What we will *not* do in this introduction is give you a definition – what we *will* do is say what sorts of things sociologists do. We will also introduce you to some of the more well-known sociologists and some of the concepts and methods sociologists have used. Finally, we will provide ideas about how you – as students – should study sociology in order to gain good grades.

Only at the end of the chapter will we ask you to develop a definition of sociology.

At this moment, as you are starting your course, there are about 31,000 other people starting A-level sociology. Also, there are 22,000 starting GCSE sociology, and another 22,000 beginning introductory sociology courses in universities and colleges of higher education. Finally, there are 2,500 or so sociologists teaching or doing research in universities. Sociology, for example at A level, has expanded very rapidly: in 1965, just eight students took sociology with the AEB. Between 1979 and 1995, just over 409,000 students studied the A-level course. Sociology is clearly very popular.

What sociologists do

Common sense and sociology

If we examine a common-sense view of an important social issue such as crime, we can show that sociology is not simply common sense and – at the same time – give some idea of what sociologists actually do. Look at Table 1.1.

There is a very important message here. We all have common-sense views on things; however, as you begin to challenge these assumptions, you are on the way to being *sociological*. Sociology is fascinating for precisely that reason: it is prepared to question 'received wisdom' and assert that the reasons for what happens in society lie below the surface of most people's everyday understanding.

What do sociologists do?

The sorts of jobs that someone with a degree in sociology might be doing include:

❖ teaching
❖ research
❖ working for central or local government
❖ health and social welfare professions
❖ personnel management
❖ computing
❖ tourism and leisure
❖ journalism and the media
❖ the police and the legal professions.

In this sense, sociologists are not unusual or unique. Put another way, sociology is a good route into lots of jobs and, as we will see later, it helps develop skills which are useful for many things other than passing examinations and getting certificates.

Studying society

Sociologists *study society*. This fact is basic to all sociology, although sociologists do disagree over what society is. Society includes structures (industry, the education system, the family and so on) as well as people, their ideas, their cultures and their interests.

Table 1.1 Comparison of views on crime

Common sense	Sociology
Crime is on the increase.	We don't know how much crime there really is, we only know how much is reported. Reported crime may be only a small proportion of the total amount of crime that goes on. Therefore, measuring increases (or decreases) in crime is problematic. Alternatively, it may seem as if crime is on the increase because of the mass media's concentration on criminal activity.
Crime is caused by lack of rules and inadequate punishment of criminals.	Criminal legislation and sentencing have changed from decade to decade without seeming to make a difference to the statistics on crime. Some politicians will claim that harsh punishment of criminals will reduce the crime rate. Sociologists may choose to concentrate on the unreliability of official statistics and the difficulty of 'proving' a direct link between harsher punishment and its deterrent effect.

❖ Activity 1 ❖

You can try either or both parts of this activity.

1 Draw a picture of society. Include four words that indicate what society is. If possible, compare your pictures and word lists with other students.

2 A group of 200 people has crash-landed on a desert island. There are men, women and children from many different backgrounds and nationalities. There is no chance of them being rescued and so they have to think about how they will live together; in other words they will have to form some sort of society. How will this group deal with the following questions?

- Who will do the various jobs required for survival?
- How are decisions going to be taken?
- How are decisions going to be enforced?
- How will childcare and the production of children be organized?
- What will be done about those who break the rules?
- How will food and other commodities be produced and distributed?
- What sort of society will develop?

You can do this exercise in groups and then compare the different answers.

Try Activity 1. This should give you some idea of what society is and help you to feel that asking 'What is society?' is not a strange question to ask.

Studying in a reasoned and disciplined way

Sociologists study society in a *reasoned and disciplined way*. In other words, they have particular methods for studying society; they don't make things up and they don't lie about their results. We will return to sociologists' methods later (in Chapter 7).

One of the most important figures in the early history of sociology, the German Max Weber (1864–1920), saw sociology as a vocation – something that you feel called to do. It needs careful, hard work and a professional attitude if you are going to discover things that are important, challenge preconceived views and argue for social change.

In other words, sociologists don't just find things out, e.g. the causes and extent of poverty in Britain. They can also advise and assist in the development of policies directed towards eliminating poverty.

Studying social behaviour

Sociologists *study social behaviour*. This behaviour turns out to be regular and often predictable – even though we all think we are individuals who take our own decisions. Put another way, we may think we are always doing what we want, but we are also controlled by society.

As an example, we can take marriage. In the West, most people decide for themselves whom they will marry. This contrasts with some cultures where marriage is arranged by the family who try to ensure that the chosen partner is of similar educational status and social background. However, when looking at 'Western' marriages, sociologists have found that when it comes to selecting a partner, it makes little difference whether individuals have free choice or not: most people choose partners from the same social background and group as themselves. This is perhaps not surprising (generally speaking, we meet people who are like us), but it does mean that the idea of choice and free will is not all that it seems to be. Whatever individuals decide to do, there are social patterns. Sociologists study these wider social patterns.

Comparing types of society

As the example of marriage shows, sociologists compare types of society and, in so doing, look at forms of social behaviour which look unusual and different. There are two ways of dealing with those differences:

❖ We can treat them as intolerable and dangerous and say people ought to give them up.

❖ We can be more tolerant and accept that different social groups behave differently.

Sociologists do the second of these much of the time. They have given this a name: *relativism*. Relativists treat other people's ways of life in a tolerant and open-minded way, and try to make sense of those ways of life. In the context of marriages arranged by parents, these still occur widely for example amongst the aristocracies and monarchies of Europe where marriage may have more to do with increasing a family's economic power than securing a love match.

In conclusion then, we can say that sociologists:

❖ study society in a careful and disciplined manner

❖ discover regularities in social behaviour which often defy common sense

❖ study society in a tolerant fashion.

Good sociology also develops what the American sociologist C. Wright Mills calls a sociological imagination:

'The sociological imagination enables its possessors to understand the larger historical scene in terms of its meaning for the inner life and the external career of a variety of individuals ... The sociological imagination enables us to grasp history and biography and the relations between the two in society. This is its task and its promise.' (Mills 1970, pp. 5–6)

Famous names, important concepts and useful theories

The people who provided the foundations for sociology mostly wrote in the nineteenth and early twentieth centuries. Subsequent sociologists have developed and extended their original ideas.

You will find a 'timeline' in Chapter 7 which not only gives you a list of the major sociologists, but also places them in their historical context and lists a few of the concepts which each used. It is worth, however, identifying some of the key founders and developers here.

The early founders

Among the most important early sociologists are the following:

❖ Auguste Comte (French)

❖ Karl Marx (German)

❖ Georg Simmel (German)

❖ Emile Durkheim (French)

❖ Max Weber (German)

❖ Sigmund Freud (German)

❖ George Herbert Mead (American).

You will come across these people and their ideas in later chapters. There are, however, several interesting things that we can observe about this group:

❖ They are mainly from Western Europe.

❖ None of them is English.

❖ They are all men.

❖ They are all white.

❖ Four of them are Jewish.

Between them they provided the basis for most of the schools of sociology that you will find in this book, including functionalism, structural functionalism, structuralism, conflict theory, interactionism, and ethnomethodology.

In the early development of sociology, women and black people played a marginal role. There are, however, women and black people who produced sociological writing in the nineteenth centuries but these people are rarely mentioned in introductory textbooks. These include Harriet Martineau (English), Helen McFarlane (English), Marianne Weber (German), W.E.B duBois (black American) and Eleanor Aveling-Marx (German). Two of the themes of this book – the analysis of gender and race and the systems of discrimination which these produce – will help to explain why so few women and black sociologists are now highlighted in introductions to sociology.

Later developers

The original theories and writings of the founders of sociology have been developed further by a huge number of sociologists, indicating how widespread and important sociology has become. There is probably at least one major sociologist corresponding to each letter of the alphabet! To prove this, try Activity 2 now.

Three themes

Three themes can be identified that feature in the work of sociologists:

❖ the distinction between *traditional* and *modern* societies

❖ the *nature* of modern societies – what the modern world is like

❖ the *direction* in which the modern world is going.

❖ **Activity 2** ❖

Using this book and other books try to identify the name of one sociologist for each letter of the alphabet. Identify whether they are men or women, what country they come from, where they did their work and if they are white or black. Give their date of birth and, where appropriate, date of death.

Does this activity suggest that there is a 'typical' sociologist? If so, what is he or she like?

Traditional and modern societies

The majority of sociologists are committed to the idea that there are traditional and modern societies and that, increasingly, traditional societies are under threat. They use different terms to describe traditional and modern societies – see Table 1.2.

It is important to realize that the boundaries between subjects is arbitrary. Although sociology tends to study the modern world and how it developed, there are other disciplines which study society, e.g. social anthropology which tends to study small-scale, pre-modern societies. There are also disciplines which study modern societies from a different viewpoint – economics, for example, looks at how goods and services are produced and distributed to people.

Table 1.2 Describing different types of society

Traditional	Modern	Postmodern
rural	urban	urban
subsistence	surplus	surplus
pre-capitalist	capitalist	post-capitalist
pre-industrial	industrial	post-industrial
simple	complex	complex
traditional	post-traditional	post-traditional

The founders of sociology in particular were interested in the transition from traditional to modern society, that is, with how the modern world came about. Also, they were generally convinced that this development of modernity involved progress – modern societies were better than traditional ones, e.g. in producing more food, in being more scientific, in being more democratic.

What the modern world is like

As Table 1.2 shows, modern societies tend to be large, complex and predominantly urban. They are also industrial, with complex mixtures of corporations producing goods and services. They have what Durkheim calls a complex division of labour, with people specializing in particular things – teaching, selling food, making cricket balls, and so on. Because we specialize, we are dependent on other people. As a teacher or cricket-ball manufacturer, for example, you cannot produce your own food, so you rely on other people to do that.

A variety of words are used to distinguish between types of modern society: industrial, capitalist, socialist, post-industrial, postmodern and so on. These will all be explained in this book.

Where the modern world is going

Many of the founders of sociology believed that modern societies were not only more complex but were in many senses actually (or, at least, potentially) *better* than other forms of society. They were committed to the idea of progress and improvement.

Those who have developed sociology have either kept that progressive stance or have argued that all we can say is that societies are *different*. In addition, they have been concerned about whether the modern world is changing, for example, as a result of the global impact of the mass media. Sociologists in fact disagree about whether the world of the late twentieth century is distinct; some talk of globalization, others of late modernity and others of postmodernity.

What makes sociology particularly interesting, but sometimes confusing to people who are new to it, is that when sociologists study the same thing – family, social class, education – they will come up with different explanations. In other words, they often disagree, even though each has studied long and hard to come to reliable and interesting conclusions. The reason they disagree is because they disagree over which theoretical tradition is the most useful and reliable.

Look at the list of founders on p. 4 and your alphabetical lists of those who have developed sociology. If you accept what Marx has to say, then you are likely to see social class and the inequalities associated with social class as more important than anything else. On the other hand, if you agree with Weber, then you will give more attention to social status and how that is important in having power in society. If you are interested in the social position of women, you will, like some of those who have developed sociology, be very critical of the founders for saying very little about women. Finally, if you consider issues of race and ethnicity to be important, the founders can also be criticized for saying very little about issues of race discrimination and for not criticizing some of the things – imperialism and nationalism – which are central to the development of that discrimination.

In looking at these three important issues – the distinction between traditional and modern societies, the nature of the modern world and where the modern world is going – sociologists have developed and used a wide range of concepts. We can list some of the most important as being:

❖ social class

❖ gender

❖ race and ethnicity

❖ status

❖ power

❖ the state

❖ the family.

Notice that these concepts are also used by many people who are not sociologists. What sociologists try to do is to use the concepts very precisely and in a way that is sociological. This is something that you may not be able to do immediately, but by the end of the book you should be well on the way to understanding sociological concepts and to using them sociologically.

❖ Activity 3 ❖

Look through the book and write short notes on each of the items given in the list at the bottom of p. 6. Write no more than 25 words on each of the items.

'Doing sociology': sociological skills

We have looked at what sociologists do and considered some of the key sociologists and sociological ideas and concepts. We are now going to look at the skills you need to become a good sociologist and how you can do well in your sociology courses.

Academic and intellectual skills

The Associated Examining Board assesses students at GCE A Level on three skill areas. These are broadly similar to the skill areas required for for higher courses at an introductory level, e.g. first-year sociology degree courses in universities and colleges of higher education. The skill areas are:

1 *Knowledge and Understanding* – This includes knowledge and understanding of the central theories and concepts of sociology outlined above and discussed, particularly, in Chapter 7. In short, you must show that you correctly understand the subject matter.

2 *Interpretation and Application* – As well as knowledge of subject content, you need to be able to apply your knowledge correctly to the question set and to make your answer relevant. As you work through this book, you will increasingly develop the ability to interpret what sociologists say and apply it to a range of social issues.

3 *Evaluation* – This is the ability to weigh debates and arguments, theories and research findings and make judgements about their effectiveness in explaining a social phenomenon. This is a most important skill in sociology, as you will soon find that there is a range of answers to any question. In this sense sociology has been described as an 'argument' subject which is closer to philosophy than science. You will discover that every area of sociology involves issues of definition, such as what is meant by 'religion' or 'the family'.

There are competing theories which allow you to answer such questions. As already suggested, the debate about the family is a very different debate if you follow what Marx says rather than what later feminist theorists say.

Evaluation is about the ability to steer your way through such differences and assess them in a reasoned manner. For this reason, evaluation is more than a matter of your own opinion.

The varying definitions, competing theories and conflicting perspectives in sociology mean that you must develop an informed and critical stance towards whatever you read, see or hear. This is the main challenge of sociology to new students, but it is also what makes sociology interesting and exciting. Sociology demands imagination, and you will really begin to exercise your own imagination in taking up this challenge.

Of the three skills listed above, the first is the one most students are best at. Here we have the traditional idea of an exam as a memory exercise, where you try and recall as much subject content as possible and write it down. Such an approach will not rate highly. To do well in sociology you must develop the remaining two skills. Always make sure you answer the question set (2 above) and develop the ability to make academic judgements about competing views and arguments (3 above). In assessment, the ability to answer the question set and evaluate effectively can offset weaknesses in content. Ideally, you should aim to be good at all three.

Developing transferable skills

The previous section on the skills required for sociology may have given some idea of their relevance to wider fields. Taking an A level in sociology can show that you have:

- *knowledge* – It is useful to be knowledgeable about a subject which has such a wide application.

- *communication skills* – You will have demonstrated that you are able to express yourself clearly, either orally or in written form. Activities such as seminars and report presentation can show oral skills. Writing coursework assignments develops written communication ability. Information technology has a variety of applications in analysing data, presenting coursework and research.

- *analytical and evaluative skills* – What you show here is that you can solve problems.

- *data-handling skills* – Throughout your course you will be handling statistics, graphs and tables; understanding what they represent and using them as

evidence for and against particular points of view.

- *the ability to work independently* – This can be shown particularly through coursework projects where the need to research and work on your own is required. Doing coursework and preparing for exams requires concentration and independent effort.

- *the ability to work in teams* – Class activities such as groupwork can indicate cooperative and leadership abilities.

- *sensitivity to the complexities of society and people's lives* – Virtually all occupations involve working with people. The study of sociology enhances this by helping to develop an understanding of individuals and groups of people within the social context of how they live and their experiences of life.

- *awareness of self in relation to society* – An understanding of the social forces that are around us, such as social class, gender, ethnicity, age, health, physical and mental abilities, sexuality, and local, regional, national and international identities, helps us to understand ourselves and others better.

- *the ability to achieve* – Gaining good grades and passing exams is an indication of your hard work, motivation and organization as well as your academic and intellectual ability.

Many of these skills are transferable into the next level of your studies. Once developed, these skills will prove useful time and again. Whatever you go on to do, whether starting a university degree course or moving directly into employment, many of these skills will be invaluable to you.

Being a sociology student

Resources for sociology

As sociology involves the study of society, the subject matter is all around you. In this sense resources are limitless. Here are some suggestions as to some of the most useful resources:

❖ *An introductory textbook such as this one –* Textbooks like this give you a comprehensive introduction to the subject matter, key terms, concepts and theories.

❖ *Dictionaries of sociology –* Dictionaries are useful for looking up new words and terms. Do not be over-reliant on dictionaries. Try and familiarize yourself with the jargon and concepts in the context of the subject you are currently working on.

❖ *A sociology reader –* 'Readers' are collections of articles and extracts by a range of sociological authors. They supplement textbooks, giving you a chance to engage with some original works and readings. There are many examples but two good ones are O'Donnell (1993) and Giddens (1992).

❖ *Topic books –* These deal with a range of sociological topics in more detail, with a range of activities and exercises which encourage a 'doing' approach. An excellent series of topic books is the *Sociology in Action* series which includes titles by Nik Jorgensen (1995) *Investigating Families and Households,* and Paul Trowler (1996) *Investigating Mass Media.*

❖ *Original works and studies –* These can broaden and deepen your knowledge, e.g. Emile Durkheim (1897/1952) *Suicide,* Ann Oakley (1972) *Sex, Gender and Society,* and Heidi Mirza (1992) *Young, Female and Black.* You will find many other original works and studies in the References section of this book.

❖ *Journals –* These contain up-to-date articles which add breadth and depth to your reading. Useful journals are Sociology Review; British Journal of Sociology and Sociology. The former is specifically written for A-level candidates, the latter two are academic journals and may be more demanding for the students who are new to sociology.

❖ *Syllabuses, past examination papers and examiners' reports –* These are very useful in guiding you through how you are to be assessed and can be obtained from the various examination boards.

❖ *Newspapers –* You should keep up with current affairs and topical issues to develop your knowledge. Look out for reports on areas such as crime rates, marital trends such as divorce rates, changing patterns of work and other relevant issues which feature regularly. Always keep your own record of such materials.

❖ *CD-ROM back issues of newspapers* such as *The Times, The Guardian* and *The Independent* are now available. These are particularly useful for project research when seeking up-to-date information. Information searches can be carried out when topic areas are keyed in.

❖ *Television and radio –* These media regularly feature documentaries, discussion programmes and features on a wide range of sociological topics.

❖ *The internet –* This global network of computer terminals contains massive amounts of information on all conceivable subjects.

❖ *Your own experience and observations –* These can be a useful source to supplement all the other resources. Care needs to be taken when citing such experience, but if it is relevant, it can be useful as a further illustration of a topic, showing good 'sociological imagination', as in the following example:

'The nature of obligations and responsibilities within the family as highlighted by Finch and Mason's study has relevance in my own family: although she lives thirty miles away, my elderly grandmother is visited regularly by different members of my family. This brings into question the so-called "isolation of the nuclear family" highlighted by Parsons.'

This list is not exhaustive but gives some indication of the wealth of resources that are available. Do not see sociology as a 'one textbook' subject – the more you read and research, the greater your knowledge and enjoyment will be.

❖ Activity 4 ❖

In your school, college or local library make a list of how many of the above resources are available. If any are not available directly, find out how to get hold of them, for example by using the Inter-Library Loans Service.

Study skills

Being aware of the resources available to you is only the start; you also need to know how to work with them. The study of any academic subject needs a certain level of skills to make effective progress. Some are general and personal, such as the ability to concentrate on material that is often demanding and to organize an effective study programme and timetable. Other study skills include the ability to:

❖ carry out effective research – using libraries, resource centres and information technology

❖ read effectively

❖ make notes – in linear and/or diagrammatic form.

Assessment can involve writing essays, reports, using stimulus-response materials and doing coursework projects. Most courses also have examinations. Below we focus on some of the key study skills required for effective progress in sociology.

Effective reading

At times, you may find some of the reading you have to do heavy going, but don't worry as this applies to widely experienced sociologists as well as beginners. Do not attempt to read too much at one go. Take on manageable amounts (five to ten pages or a section of a chapter), and as soon as concentration lapses, take a break. A simple reading 'system' is as follows:

❖ *Scan and skim* – Read the section quickly to get the 'gist'. Skate over words and terms you do not understand and then briefly note what you think the passage is saying.

❖ *Concentrated reading* – Read the section again, noting headings, key points/arguments/debates. Make notes (see below) so you have an easily accessible record of what you have read. A difficult section might mean rereading before you can clearly identify the main themes. Be prepared for this.

❖ *Recall/review* – Summarize mentally the reading you have done. If necessary, prompt yourself with your notes. When you are satisfied that you have understood the section, carry on with another or, if necessary, take a break.

Note-taking and making

You should never read anything or use resources without making a record of what they are. This includes taking notes from classes, lessons, lectures, seminars and reading, but also from television, radio and newspapers. At the time of reading, listening or watching you may think that you have understood everything and can remember the key points, but your course will involve a large amount of information which you will need to draw on at a later date. Remembering everything is impossible. This is why a simplified record in the form of your own notes is essential. Good notes can give you a quick overview and act as a prompt for previous work. You may need to return to the original source for clarification of detail but your notes mean you are not 'starting from scratch'. Here are some examples of note-taking strategies:

❖ *Linear notes* – These are the most familiar and come in the form of headings, sub-headings and numbered or lettered key points. The key emphasis is on *accessibility*; so indentation, underlining, abbreviations and diagrams are necessary to make the notes as visually easy to take in as possible. Figure 1.1 give an example of how you might take linear notes on secularization.

❖ *Pattern notes*, e.g. spray or spider web – These are more diagrammatic than linear notes and are useful when an overall summary of a topic is required or for revision when brainstorming can be used. Figure 1.2 shows an example of notes in this form.

Pattern notes, being pictorial, may register more effectively, but linear notes tend to be more appropriate for complex information and notes from a lecture or reading. Adapt your note style to the situation and topic.

A common problem with making notes is knowing what to include and what to omit. Poor notes are often slightly shorter longhand versions of the original. You will

Figure 1.1
Example of linear notes on secularization

SECULARIZATION

DEFINITION: Process through which religious thinking, practice and institutions 'lose their social significance' (Wilson).

THEORETICAL LINK: Weber – as society becomes increasingly industrialized, rational and scientific ideas would sweep away traditional and irrational sources of authority and belief.

PRO-SECULARIZATION ARGUMENTS (BRYAN WILSON)

1 Decline in religious practice and participation in advanced societies. Church attendance falls. Less involvement in organized religion.

2 Decline in religious belief – less interest in religion.

3 Church less important and influential in society. Religion replaced by other agencies, e.g. mass media, schools, welfare state.

4 Church less a place of worship, more secular, i.e. church used for playgroups, youth clubs, etc. Church becomes a social rather than religious centre.

ANTI-SECULARIZATION ARGUMENTS (DAVID MARTIN)

1 How do you measure religiosity (the degree of religious feeling)? Church attendance statistics may be unreliable indicators (see arguments about suicide statistics). Church attendance may be low but belief in God may be high (New Society survey, 1985).

2 Church attendance not equated with being religious. Other sources, e.g. TV's *Songs of Praise*.

3 Sects growing in number and membership, e.g. the Moonies (Eileen Barker).

4 Historical evidence – no golden age for religion in the past. 40 per cent attended church regularly in 1851.

5 Cause and effect – industrialization 'caused' secularization or, as Weber argued, Protestant ethic 'caused' the industrial revolution?

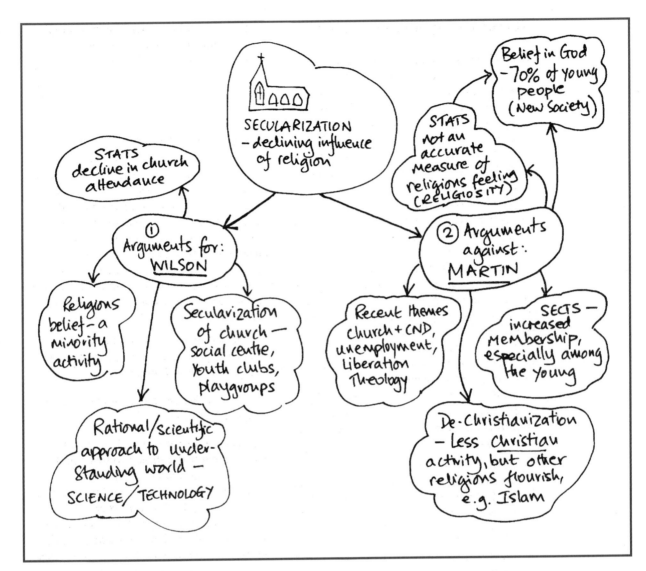

Figure 1.2
Example of pattern notes on secularization

need to concentrate on your reading so you develop the skill of extracting information and presenting it in note form, without losing the most important points.

File organization

Once you have made notes, make sure they are kept in order in the relevant sections of your sociology file. That will make the information easier to retrieve.

 Assessment

Assessment refers to those situations where you are given the opportunity to show your skills as a sociologist. In the A-level examination, this takes several forms:

❖ stimulus-response questions

❖ essay questions

❖ coursework.

Stimulus-response questions

Examples of this type of question are included at the end of several of the chapters. Stimulus-response questions developed as an assessment method in the early 1990s, as an alternative to the standard examination essay. One of the main GCE Advanced Level boards, the AEB, includes such questions in Paper 1 and essays in Paper 2.

The first point to note is that you are given the marks available for each question. Be guided by this – give appropriate time and detail to each question. Do not write too much for short questions, i.e. those worth 1 to 4 marks. Only give brief, precise pieces of information. For example, if asked for a percentage, write the percentage only, rather than a full sentence with detailed explanation. Higher-mark questions (i.e. worth over 7 marks) usually require a short essay (see below).

In the exam, you have approximately 45 minutes to one hour to complete each stimulus-response question. You need to do the following:

❖ Read the items quickly, noting or underlining the main points. Some items are in the form of diagrams, tables or statistics (see below for guidance on this)

❖ Read all the questions.

❖ Identify points in items that are relevant to the questions set.

❖ Plan your answers by rough notes or brainstorming sprays (as above). It is important to cover and plan all the questions before you start the answers. This helps you to avoid the possibility of overlapping answers.

❖ Write your answers. Bear in mind that you will probably have about 40 to 55 minutes for this. If you have planned well and know what you are doing, this is enough time to gain good marks. Don't think that you have to write for the whole of this time. You need, for example, to leave time to read what you have written and make any changes that are necessary.

A very useful book with more examples and guidance on stimulus-response questions is Kirby *et al.* (1993).

Writing essays

An essay can be defined as a continuous piece of writing set out in paragraph form which addresses a set question. Coursework essay titles may be given a few weeks in advance so you can research and read; exam essay titles, however, are unseen.

One of the most common mistakes in tackling essays is failing to address the question set. Many students write essays which don't address the question set and so are not given many marks. Consider the following title:

'The selection and presentation of the news depends more on practical issues than on cultural influences.'

Critically discuss the arguments for and against this view.

A good essay on this topic might, for example, cover the three academic and intellectual skills discussed on p. 13, i.e. knowledge and understanding, interpretation and application, and evaluation. A less successful essay will be knowledge-driven and will probably present a 'catch-all' type of answer based on common sense and/or media sources, rather than sociological approaches to the mass media.

Avoid writing in a haphazard, 'write-all-I-know-about' manner, but aim to show a clear, reasoned response to the question set. Table 1.3 summarizes what your approach should be.

At its most basic, an essay can be divided into three parts: an introduction, a main body and a conclusion.

❖ *Introduction* – This is where you address the full title directly. If there is a quote, explain it briefly. Set the agenda for your essay by covering the issues you plan to address. Avoid simply listing, point by point, what you are going to cover. Correct question analysis is vital and will be

Table 1.3 Strategy for answering exam questions

Show that you have:	Skill	Place in essay
1 ... understood the question you have answered	analysing, decoding or dismantling the question	introduction
2 ... collected material in a conscientious manner	research, ability to look more widely than textbook; library work – variety of sources	research for main body
3 ... made a plan from this material	planning, good preparation	before essay writing begins
4 ... sorted out (and organized) material appropriate to the essay	organization, structure	main body
5 ... written a clear and cohesive answer, which is well structured, has appropriate content and shows a good style of presentation	written communication, logical thought, grammar, spelling and punctuation	throughout the essay
6 ... appraised and evaluated your material and made clear its relevance to the essay title.	critical thought, presentation of arguments for and against – weighing and making judgement of arguments presented in essay	conclusion

rewarded. A sound introduction can set you well on the way to a safe pass mark.

A good answer to the media question above will have an introduction which explains the question and says how you will answer it. It will refer to sociological studies of how the news is constructed by journalists, how the professional ideology of journalism effects what news is, and will mention studies of how people interpret the news.

❖ Main body – Here you develop in detailed paragraphs the key points and issues, comparing and contrasting, explaining strengths and weaknesses, outlining arguments for and against – preferably supported by appropriate sociological evidence from studies and research.

In the mass media essay, you would write in detail about the various sociological studies of news. This means mentioning the authors, their arguments, the concepts and theories they use. In addition, a good essay will say something about which studies of news are the most sociologically convincing.

❖ Conclusion – Round off your essay discussion with a sound, concluding section. This should be more than a summary of your main points; it should have an evaluative dimension to it. Return directly to the essay title and explain your answer to it in the light of your main discussion. Draw a conclusion where you make judgements about the strongest arguments and evidence presented and say why this is so. You will be rewarded for this.

In the conclusion to the media essay, you would need to say whether, on balance, cultural or practical issues determine what news is and how it is reported. The judgement here is, as suggested above, on the basis of the quality of the arguments and evidence which the sociologists use.

Many students find the introduction and, particularly, the conclusion of an essay to be the hardest parts. This is because they have to present their own thoughts and ideas, rather than the more second-hand material in the main sections. Writing good introductions and conclusions is a skill you need to develop.

It is crucial to indicate at the end of an essay the details of the reading you have done. This also applies to research and project work. In addition to this, essays and similar assignments at degree level require a referencing system where you provide details of sources cited in your work. Below is an example of how to present a reference

Jorgensen, N., Bird, J., Heyhoe, A., Russell, B. and Savvas, M. (1997) *Sociology: An Interactive Approach*, London: Collins Educational.

If you quote from that book in an essay, then after the quote put (Jorgensen *et al.* 1997, p. 240) where '240' refers to the page from which the quotation comes.

What you are doing in the bibliography is not only showing what you have read but also how your work relates to existing sociological material. Note that bibliographies and referencing are not required in examinations.

Coursework

Most A-level sociology examination boards offer coursework as part of their assessment. This represents 20 per cent of the total examination for the AEB and Interboard, and 16 per cent for the NEAB. Many other courses require what are called projects or dissertations and the points discussed below are likely to apply equally to these.

Beginning coursework

Make sure you know exactly what is expected of you and the manner in which you will be assessed. For example, the AEB recommends approximately 5,000 words, judged by the criteria of knowledge and understanding, interpretation and application, and evaluation (see p. 8).

At this stage, it is very important to listen carefully to your tutor's advice and to refer to the syllabus, mark schemes and exemplars provided by your exam board.

Choosing a topic

Above all, you need to choose something that is 'do-able' and that you find interesting. There are a number of other factors to consider when choosing a topic.

❖ Your topic does need to be syllabus relevant.

❖ The project must be legal and ethical. It is important to look at the guidelines provided by your assessment body. Sensitive topics, such as domestic violence, mental illness and crime, need very careful thought. A direct approach is unlikely to be acceptable, although a survey of the public's attitude to such issues could be within reason. Whatever your topic, you must respect the people who assist you. This means considering confidentiality and negotiating tactfully throughout your coursework. You must also be aware of your own bias and recognize its significance.

❖ You will need to consider practical constraints. Time and cost will be important factors, so don't be over-ambitious. At an early stage ensure you have access to the people, secondary sources and background material that you will need.

❖ Deciding upon a title can be difficult when choice is so flexible. Some coursework ideas are given at the back of most of the chapters in this textbook. A good starting point is to follow through the questions in 'Starting Out' below and then complete a copy of the 'Coursework Outline' which can then be discussed with your tutor.

Starting Out

1 Topic area interested in?

2 The specific area within this topic that you are interested in?

3 What are likely to be the key issues to consider in this topic?

4 Suitable hypothesis/aim?

5 Subhypotheses/sub-aims?

6 What methods?

   (a) Is the project mainly concerned with people's experience, perceptions, attitudes, their viewpoint?

   This would require methods that are largely qualitative – unstructured interviews, observation, documents of life, diaries, qualitative content analysis.

   (b) Is the project mainly concerned with discovering information for a larger group of people? To make comparisons? To correlate things?

   For example, the greater the involvement of women in paid work, the greater domestic equality in the home. This would require methods that are largely quantitative – questionnaires, structured interviews, quantitative content analysis, official statistics, documents, social surveys.

   (c) Both of the above? In which case use combined methods.

7 Group of people relevant to study? (Think of size and characteristics of group).

8 What secondary sources may be needed?

9 Any ethical issues to consider?

10 Any predicted problems?

Coursework Outline

Aim or hypothesis

Sub-aims or -hypotheses

Methods

Sample

Sources

Doing the project

❖ *Planning* is very important if your project is to be enjoyable and manageable. A last minute rush will inhibit you achieving your potential.

❖ Keep a *project diary* or *note book*. This can be used to keep a list of all the sources and addresses you have used. It will be much more time consuming to complete your bibliography at a later date. Your sources should be recorded as: Author, (date), title, place published, publisher. You may also need to list material produced from IT sources, such as the Internet, SECOS and CD-ROM software. Use you diary to jot down ideas as they come to you. All coursework involves a retrospective evaluation, so record problems, solutions and things that have gone particularly well as they occur rather than risk forgetting them.

❖ Set realistic *deadlines* and interim deadlines for key stages of the project. It is advisable to discuss these with a supervisor and draw on their expertise as much as possible.

Writing up the results

Your results can be based on primary, secondary, quantitative or qualitative data, or a combination of these. Whatever method you use to produce the results, it is important to present them in a clear and direct manner.

Quantitative techniques are usually well dealt with by tables, bar graphs, pie charts, histograms, pictograms and line graphs. These should all be titled and labelled. Avoid graphs and tables that are too complicated – these can detract from your study.

Qualitative material is normally delivered as prose and it is important that you faithfully report the words of your respondents.

As you present your material, it is necessary to provide a written commentary using your sociological insight to interpret the findings. You should then summarize your main findings and analyse them as a conclusion.

Finally, you will need to discuss the relative success of your project and its methodology; this includes discussing the limitations of the methods you have used. You should consider what changes you would make with hindsight and offer possible new directions for your research.

Coursework in sociology can be extremely rewarding, providing an opportunity for you to work independently. However, good organization and seeking sound advice are vital for success.

Some useful additional resources are listed at the end of this chapter.

The marking of your work

Wherever you are studying, your work will be assessed and often given a percentage mark. This will have an important role to play in the grade you get for your A level or your university course. A-level grades and grading at university are not quite the same, but the reasons behind the marks are similar.

A-level grading

Here is a brief explanation of what grades mean for an essay:

❖ *Grade A* (approximately 70 per cent +, or 18+ marks out of 25)

All sections outstanding. Evidence of wide reading, analysis in depth to support arguments. No arguments unsubstantiated. Reading and material from class well integrated. Issues clearly understood. Content, interpretation and evaluation excellent throughout. High standard of organization and presentation. Effective and stimulating communication. All major points covered. No irrelevant material. Evidence of original thought. Correct and complete referencing throughout bibliography.

❖ *Grade B* (approximately 64 to 69 per cent, or 16 or 17/25)

All sections very good. Wide reading, interpreted intelligently, issues understood. Some independent thought. Sensibly organized and well presented. Reading and material from class integrated. Major points covered. No irrelevant points. Effective communication. Content, interpretation and evaluation balanced and to a good standard. Evidence of research from references and bibliography.

❖ *Grade C* (approximately 55 to 63 per cent or 14 or 15/25)

Most sections good. Wider reading than basic sources incorporated in text effectively. Analysis adequate though not original or in depth. Presentation and organization mostly clear. Most but not all major points covered. Some unnecessary and irrelevant material included but most appropriate. Some substantial points and arguments. Content, interpretation and evaluation inadequately balanced. Some references. Some grammar, spelling and presentational weaknesses.

❖ *Grade D* (approximately 48 to 54 per cent, or 12 or 13/25)

Some quite good sections. Reliance mainly on basic sources and class materials. Some vagueness and lack of clarity in parts. A tendency to irrelevance in some sections. Some analysis but patchy. Content, interpretation and evaluation imbalanced and weighted towards the former. Several major points and issues explored but in a basic manner showing little evidence of wider reading. Communication ineffective in some sections.

❖ *Grade E* (approximately 40 to 47 per cent, or 10 or 11/25)

Heavy reliance on basic sources indicating little attempt to research more widely. In the main the question is answered but in a predictable manner. Significant amount of irrelevant material. Tendency toward simplistic and descriptive account. Sometimes difficult to follow. Organization and presentation unsatisfactory in parts. Content thin, interpretation patchy, little analysis or evaluation. Insufficient writing and material provided to develop points and arguments.

❖ *Grade N* (Marginal fail, approximately 35 to 39 per cent, or 9/25)

Some attempt made to address the question indicating a very basic understanding, but lacking in most areas. Evidence of rushed and badly thought out approach. Class materials and basic sources not used effectively. Significant amount of irrelevance and misunderstanding. No evaluation. Communication and presentation problems.

❖ *Grade U* (34 or less, or 8/25 or less)

Fail grade. No evidence of understanding of question set. Lacking in all areas.

University grading

❖ First Class – 70 per cent +
❖ Second Class, Upper (2.1) – 60 to 69 per cent
❖ Second Class, Lower (2.2) – 50 to 59 per cent
❖ Third Class – 40 to 49 per cent
❖ Fail – 39 per cent and below

Using this book

This book is to be *used*. You will find plenty of exercises and activities which encourage you to *do* sociology. We have also included plenty of material on the concepts and theories of sociology in each chapter. The chart on p. vi shows you where each of the major theoretical perspectives in sociology is discussed most fully. In each of the main chapters we also discuss some of the most important issues in sociology – gender, race and ethnicity, age.

The index at the end of the book will also help you find information you are looking for.

Finally, this book is being published only three years before the new millennium starts. Sociology, like other subjects, is developing and moving forward. It is a very different subject from what it was at the start of the twentieth century. We cannot guess what sociologists will be talking about in the year 2100, but there are some new issues being discussed now which will certainly not go away. These include discussions of identity (who we are), of globalization (that all societies are becoming modern), of postmodernity (whether the world we are living in is totally different from the world of the founders of sociology). All of these issues at the 'sharp end' of sociology are discussed.

Chapter summary

One of the aims of this chapter was to identify some sort of useful definition of what sociology is. A lot of what we have done in this chapter is to look at what sociologists *do*. To complete your work on this chapter, try Activity 5.

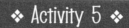

❖ Activity 5 ❖

In small groups try and produce a short definition of sociology. Compare your definition with other groups and identify the major similarities and differences.

Further reading

Two books that provide excellent guidance on sociological research and coursework are:

Bailey, V. (1996), *Essential Research Skills*, London: Collins Educational.

Howe, N. (1994) *Advanced Practical Sociology*, London: Nelson.

Chapter 2

Culture and identity

❖ Preview

In this chapter we shall be looking at:

- ❖ what sociologists mean by the term identity, including:
    - historical views of identity
    - sexed and gendered identities
    - disability and identity
    - the social construction of identity
- ❖ sociological approaches to culture, including:
    - dominant ideologies
    - culture and prejudice
    - culture and social structure
- ❖ ideas of socialization, value, norm and their limitations

- ❖ relationships between culture and identity, including:
    - ethnic identity
    - new racism
    - identity and consumption
    - projects of the self
    - identity and the self in work
- ❖ the politics of culture and identity, including:
    - élite, mass, popular and folk culture
    - subcultures of resistance
    - new social movements and identity politics.

❖ Introduction

Culture and identity have been important issues for many for sociologists from the founding of the discipline in the nineteenth and early twentieth centuries. Many of those who developed sociology – Marx, Weber and Durkheim – had theories of culture and identified what, for sociological study, counts as culture. They recognized that there is a great diversity of things which make up culture and that all societies have things that count as culture – language, beliefs and values, art, clothing, ways of cooking and so on. They also recognized that people's culture is very important in how groups identify themselves as groups; national identity is, for example, closely tied to aspects of culture.

Issues of culture are important for ordinary people in many ways, for example in the controversy over modern art (see *In Focus* on next page). However, issues of culture and cultural identity play a part in everyday life way beyond debates and discussions about what is good and bad art.

In Focus

◆

Art and culture

In the 1980s Carl Andre exhibited a pile of bricks and in the 1990s Damien Hirst exhibited a dead sheep in formaldehyde (see right). There was considerable discussion and controversy over these as works of art. In particular, people were concerned that they were not really works of art at all and should not count as serious aspects of culture. In this debate the sociological meaning of culture gets mixed up with an élitist view which claims that only some things count as

art/culture. Sociologists would see these things as aspects of culture even though they might deny that they are art.

For example, 'Britishness' is often defined by reference to something called 'British culture'. The point for the sociologists is that people do not seem to agree on what is meant by British culture.

❖ Activity 1 ❖

Identify what you think are the central features of British culture.

To what extent do you think it possible to get one, agreed definition of British culture?

If we can arrive at an agreed definition, then it may not be a definition that everyone in this country accepts. This will be the case even if being British *is* defined in terms of acceptance of a common culture. In other words, people with different cultures who live in Britain may find that particular definitions of British culture ignore and devalue their culture. For example, many Muslim citizens of Britain argue that their culture is unrecognized and devalued in the school system (see Chapter 14). This devaluing of other cultures is a common feature of all societies and can lead to people of another culture being removed or exterminated, as the example of ethnic cleansing in the former Yugoslavia shows.

Issues of culture and identity are, therefore, central in defining:

❖ who we are as *individuals*

❖ who we are as *communities*

❖ whom we do *not accept* as part of 'us'.

Put another way, any claim to a culture or an identity can become a political claim and a way of distinguishing between social groups. Sociologists are interested in investigating situations in which cultural differences become the basis for conflict and comparing them with situations where culturally different groups coexist peacefully.

Identity

I'm not **RITA HAYWORTH**

...And happy to be me.
And with the new Lux range,
there's always something just right
for me... whatever my mood,
whatever my needs I can choose
from a range of sensations in
shower gels, foam baths, beauty
bars and liquid soap. Whether
it's soothing relaxation, renewal
vitality, or beautiful refreshment,
the choice is mine. Each leaves
my skin feeling beautiful, so I
feel beautiful. And can't imagine
wanting to be anyone else.

I am ME.

NEW *Lux* RANGE. BRING OUT THE STAR IN YOU.

In this section, we will explore the idea of identity, particularly with reference to issues of gender and disability. In particular, we will look at sociological and social psychological approaches to the self.

❖ **Activity 2** ❖

How would you answer the question 'who am I?'. Note down the factors you would include. Discuss these definitions of identity in small groups.

The issue here is what makes us who we are and involves answering the questions 'Who am I?' and 'Who are we?'

People tend to see identity as simple, fixed and unitary. This is indicated in the *Oxford English Dictionary* definition of identity:

'*Identity*: the sameness of a person ... at all times or in all circumstances; the condition or fact that a person or thing is itself and not something else; individuality, personality' (OED 1970, p. 1368).

This implies that individuals have one identity which is easily acquired and does not change. Even the question 'Who am I' seems to many people an odd one. If they give an answer it will either refer to a name – 'I am John' – or to a relationship – 'I am someone's brother/lover/employer/teacher'. Sociologists, however, are likely to view identity formation as more complex than this, seeing identity as related to the society in which people live. In other words, people are, in part, *socialized* into their identities.

In Focus

◆

Bali's birth order names

Some of the most interesting and challenging material on identity comes from studies of small-scale societies by social anthropologists. They suggest that different societies have very different ideas about identity and the self. For example in Western societies, we see our names as central to our identities, as making us the unique individuals that we are, whereas the people of Bali have personal names which are unimportant, arbitrary and like nonsense syllables (Geertz 1975). However, they also have important names that are used to indicate birth order. There are four of these and when a fifth child arrives, the sequence repeats itself. These birth order names do not, in any sense, stress the uniqueness of the person who has them. Our Western way of naming suggests the importance of the individual; traditional Balinese names emphasize that the social groups is more important.

Historical views of identity

Stuart Hall (1996) argues that identity is one of the most important issues for sociologists but that, until recently, the problem of identity has often been ignored. Hall (1992a) provides three views on identity – what sociologists often call the subject – all of which provide a basis for answering the question 'Who am I'.

- ❖ In the seventeenth and eighteenth centuries, the dominant view was that human beings were unified individuals with consciousness and the ability to reason about things. Your identity as an individual stayed the same throughout life and did not change with social circumstances.

- ❖ Later sociologists, such as George Herbert Mead (1934), argued that the self is developed in interaction with society, with what he called 'significant others'. The first significant others include parents and carers. If there is a 'real me', it is modified and developed in a dialogue with other people and with social institutions. We might feel that our identity, our self, is inside us and part of us, but it is in fact social.

- ❖ The idea that we now live in a postmodern world has lead to a third approach to the self. Identity is no longer fixed, but is continuously being changed, for example, through the ability to consume different products. As we will see below, lifestyle shopping is increasingly important and is a way in which people can buy new identities through the things they consume. In addition, people can have several, contradictory identities at the same time without that being a sign of illness or making social life difficult.

Sexed and gendered identities

For sociologists, there is an important distinction to be drawn between sex and gender, which in turn affects how we understand identity. 'Sex' deals with what are often biological differences, while 'gender' is about a socially constructed role. Therefore, the labels 'woman' and 'man' are about both biological *and* social differences.

Biological determinists

A lot of sociological debate is about the relationship between the biological and the social. At one end of the debate are those who see activity such as sexual behaviour as entirely about biology – they are called *biological determinists*. They argue that there is a biological basis for things like child-rearing and different sexual orientations. They also claim that there is a maternal instinct that leads women to want children, so that women who reject maternity are flying in the face of instinct.

In Focus

◆

Multiple personalities

Historically, there has been interest, especially from psychologists, in people with multiple personalities; that is, people who seems to have more than one 'self'. The first case of multiple personality was identified in 1791 and, for a long period, multiples had two personalities. Increasingly in the twentieth century, multiples have had many personalities – as many as 30. The issue for psychologists and sociologists is who the real person is. If someone has many personalities, is one of them their true identity? Whereas sociologists are likely to recognise personality is not stable and unitary, many discussions of multiples by psychologists and psychiatrists have suggested that they are, in one way of another, ill. For example, it is sometimes argued that multiple personalities may arise because of abuse in childhood. Hacking (1995) provides a history of multiple personality.

❖ Activity 3 ❖

Spend a few minutes thinking about the following questions. If possible, discuss them with other sociology students:

- What is human nature?
- Is it the same in every society?
- If it varies between societies, then why does it vary?

By 'instinct', biologists are referring to biological and preprogrammed behaviour which it is very difficult for the animal to stop. So, a cat that is hungry will miaow even if food is not there, because its instinct makes it do this. One of the debates between biologists and sociologists is the role that instincts play in human behaviour. If, for example, there is a survival or a maternal instinct, then what is interesting to the sociologist are the variations between ways in which people survive and deal with children in different societies. There are similar issues with the idea of human nature.

The alleged central importance of biology is used by Robin Fox (1967) in a study of kinship, marriage and the family. For Fox there are four biologically based rules which determine both sexuality and also family structure:

- ❖ Women have children
- ❖ Men impregnate women.
- ❖ Close kin avoid sexual relationships.
- ❖ Men control women.

Even though we may think that some of these are *socially* determined (e.g. men controlling women), Fox claims they are biologically determined. For Fox, these rules set limits to women's special status and also imply that some sort of family structure is necessary if these biological rules are to work. By implication, certain sorts of family structure and certain sorts of gender relationship are inevitable.

Social constructionists

At the other end of the scale are the social constructionists who see sexual and other behaviour as entirely socially constructed. They argue that biology is effectively irrelevant in matters of gender and sexual orientation. They would contradict Fox's views in two ways:

- ❖ They would argue that some of his rules are not rules at all – e.g. there is no biological basis for men controlling women.
- ❖ They would challenge the idea that having children is a basis for a particular type of family and for women's second-class status in many past and present societies.

As with many 'either/or' positions, it is increasingly clear that things like sexuality have biological foundations *and* are socially constructed. This is the only way we can explain the wide variations in sexual behaviour across societies, within any one society and over time.

Social anthropologists usually study small-scale, traditional societies and have provided considerable evidence of the cross-cultural variability in sexual behaviour and values. They agree that there seem to be universals – women have children – but also agree that diversity is common. As Malinowski showed in his study of the Trobriand Islanders of Melanesia (1932), societies vary in degrees of sexual repression, in the frequency of sexual activities and in what people find normal and pleasurable. This diversity is difficult to explain if sexuality is simply instinctual and simply to do with reproducing the human race. The variability is also noticeable within societies. As Weeks (1986), suggests, some sexualities are seen as normal and others seen as pathological – for example, heterosexuality compared with homosexuality; there is then the tendency to see the pathological sexuality as biologically determined rather than as socially constructed.

In everyday life, there is an interaction between sex and gender. For example, a male manager might refuse to appoint women because of a worry that they are less likely, as child-bearers, to be reliable workers. Here, something about the biology of women is being used to discriminate – covertly or overtly – against women in employment.

In her book *Sex, Gender and Society* (1972), Anne Oakley argues that gender roles are culturally determined. Therefore most of the things that we might see as natural for women – with the possible exception of childbirth – are cultural. This means two things:

❖ that assumed biological factors need not bar women or men from particular social roles

❖ that assumptions about the biological basis of social roles do not need to imply differences of status.

In others words, situations where women have lower status than men are a result of social factors not biological ones.

Feminism, sex and gender

It is now generally recognized that issues of sexuality and gender were placed on the agenda of sociology by women, in particular those women who developed feminist theory.

❖ Activity 4 ❖

Using your school college or local library, identify four women who have contributed to a sociological understanding of gender relationships. Briefly identify their main ideas.

Many feminist theorists set out to challenge the dominance of men within sociology and to establish an important place for women both in the subject matter of sociology and the profession of sociologists. Most, like Anne Oakley, were social constructionists. Most saw that the major issue for women was patriarchy, that

is, a system in which power rests with men. Importantly, these women argued not only that men occupied the significant power position in society but that within sociology there were many ideas that served to maintain that power-base. A good example here is the distinction that Parsons (1951) draws between *instrumental* and *expressive* roles.

❖ Expressive roles are about caring and, for Parsons, are best done by women.

❖ Instrumental roles include working for money – something best done by men.

As many women sociologists argued, this tends to prescribe and maintain a particular family structure – the nuclear family, discussed in Chapter 3. As social anthropologists and social historians suggest (Anderson 1980, Mair 1971), there is no one family structure found in all societies and at all times, nor is it always the case that men perform instrumental roles, leaving the expressive ones for women. What Parsons is doing is something which sociologists should be wary of: describing a particular way that social roles are distributed in *one* type of society and prescribing that distribution for *all* societies.

Some idea of the complexity of sex and gendered identity can be gained from looking at two examples:

❖ the definition of the sex of athletes in the Olympic movement

❖ ethnomethodological studies of gender identity.

The Olympic movement's definition of sex

The simple view that there is *one* way of determining sex and that gender is more *complex* is thrown into question by how the Olympic movement has defined the sex of athletes. What seems to be an obvious thing – sex – has been defined in a variety of ways: by physical appearance, by hormones, by genetic make-up. These overlap but do not match totally: someone may be genetically of one sex and hormonally of another. Relying on appearance seems an obvious marker of the sex of a person until we realize that things like facial hair are not accurate markers but constitute part of the social definition of what makes a man a man.

This example also tells us a lot about sex and gendered identity as an issue associated with power. The need to define someone's sex accurately in the Olympic movement is to stop cheating, that is, stop people who are really men competing as women and having an unfair advantage.

This discussion raises the rather odd question of whether there are only two sexes. Biologists suggest that there are conditions which make a person's sex ambiguous and difficult to determine – hermaphrodites have the sexual organs of both sexes. However, society is not willing to admit such an intermediate position, but 'forces' people to be either male or female. This process is discussed in a detailed documentary record of a hermaphrodite by Michel Foucault (1980). In early life in a village, there was no attempt to assign Barbin a sex. When he came to the attention of doctors they were only willing to see Herculine Barbin as having one sex, in this case, female. This identity came to dominate Barbin's whole life.

Sexual identity is also legally defined. When a baby is born, there is a certain amount of time in which to register the birth. Central to that process is the allocation of a sex; on the certificate it says the baby is either male or female. If you are defined as a man at birth, there is nothing you can do to change this identity even if you subsequently see yourself as female and undergo a sex change operation. This, then, has serious implications if a person who has changed their sex wants to marry. If a man who has changed sex wishes to marry a man, in legal terms this involves two men marrying which is, at present, illegal.

The question of how many sexes there are, and the related one about what gender is, has received much attention from biologists. Many ordinary people, as well as many sociologists, feel that someone's sex is clear and unambiguous, but biologists argue, on the basis of hormones, that there is some ambiguity. Both men and women have male and female hormones. For the sociologist, the lesson here is important. In more or less all societies, people are expected to be one sex or the other; there are, socially, no acceptable and normative intermediate positions. This does not, of course, prevent people from asserting the value of non-normative sexualities and of intermediate positions. This is what is happening in the demand for gay rights, and when people assert the right to bisexuality and androgyny.

❖ Activity 5 ❖

Many sociologists argue that gender is socially constructed, in that gender identity varies between societies and within societies. With this in mind, take an A4 sheet of paper and draw up a table with the column and row headings shown in the diagram below.

In each column, note down examples of the roles which men and women perform.

Does what you have written in the table support the view that gender is socially constructed?

	Biologically Based	Socially Based
Men's roles		
Women's roles		

Ethnomethodological studies of gender identity

Garfinkel's (1984) work suggests two things about gendered identity.

❖ It is about exhibiting certain signs of identity and managing that identity. As such, we assume that we know what gender someone is by how they look, what they do. We know the rules of the gender game and assume that other people play them. What is important here is that we may get it wrong and misread the signals that people are giving us.

❖ Gendered identity *is* about role-playing. It is about learning to do something and convincing others that we are doing it right.

Kessler and McKenna (1978), identify a number of factors which indicate what gender a person is and which can be 'managed' to give the impression that someone is of that particular gender. These include:

❖ physical appearance in public

❖ content and manner of speech

❖ information about one's life

❖ managing the private aspects of the body.

All of these provide opportunities and difficulties for people experiencing gender ambiguity, e.g. transsexuals. A male-to-female transsexual, for example, may:

❖ disguise the maleness of the body by removing hair

❖ use more facial expression than men normally do

❖ avoid swimming baths.

In general, therefore, sociologists suggest that gender identity is socially constructed, i.e. what counts as femininity and masculinity varies between societies. In fact, sociologists go further than this and argue that in any complex society, there are likely to be *several* femininities and masculini*ties*. For instance, what someone from a middle-class background sees as typical of femininity and masculinity may not be the same as that recognised by someone from a working-class background. There are likely to be similar sorts of difference associated with age and ethnicity. As we shall see later, some men and women see body-building as central to their gendered identity; however, it is unlikely that the majority of people would see the sorts of bodies which body builders have as typical of masculinity or femininity.

The recognition that there are many masculinities and femininities should not disguise the fact that some are dominant. As Bob Connell's studies of masculinity suggests, there is a hegemonic masculinity which marginalises other masculinities and also has implication for women (Connell 1996, p. 77):

In Focus

◆

Garfinkel's study of Agnes

Agnes was born a boy and classified as such. However, she became convinced that she was a girl, developed breasts at puberty and, at the age of 20, had surgery to remove the male sex organs and construct female organs. The crucial issue for Garfinkel is how Agnes passes as female:

> 'The work of achieving and making secure her rights to live as a normal, natural female, while having continually to provide for the possibility of detection and ruin, carried on within

socially structured conditions, I call Agnes' passing.' (Garfinkel 1984, p. 137)

'Passing' involves managing identity and, if the choice was between passing as female and some other social activity (say, getting a job), then the former took precedence. Managing this identity became a matter of planning, e.g. getting a job close to home that does not involve driving in case she has a car accident, falls unconscious and is unmasked in the hospital emergency room as not really a woman.

'Hegemonic masculinity can be defined as the configuration of gender practice which embodies the currently accepted answer to the problem of the legitimacy of patriarchy [male dominance and power over women] ... which guarantees ... the dominant position of men and the subordination of women. ... So the top levels of business, the military and government provide a fairly convincing corporate display of masculinity, still little shaken by feminist women or dissenting men.'

Sue Sharpe's studies of how girls see femininity (1994) also suggest that there is more than one idea of femininity, but that some definitions of what is feminine are dominant.

❖ Activity 6 ❖

Think about the following questions and if possible, discuss your ideas with other sociology students:

- What do you consider to be the essential elements of 'femininity' and 'masculinity'?
- How have ideas about these changed over time?
- Do your lists of essential elements agree with other people's lists?

Disability and identity

The works of Erving Goffman (1969, 1970) suggest that we manage our identities and present them in everyday life. Being normal is crucial here and many people have to work hard at presenting themselves as normal, as fitting in with society's values. In some sense, everyone has to work hard at doing this. Teachers, for example, manage their presentation of self in order to try and maintain power and control in the classroom. For sociology teachers and lecturers, there is a complex process of managing identity which includes being familiar with the latest sociology books, always knowing more than the students, using phrases like 'Research has shown ...' and putting books they have written on reading lists. For Goffman this is, in part, habitual and, in part, cynical.

Spoiled identities

There are people whose identities are likely to be 'spoiled' – they have disabilities, disfigurements and suchlike. For these people there is a contradiction between virtual social identity – how they see themselves – and actual social identity – how others see them. Others tend to see only their disability and view their disability as influencing everything they do. Therefore their presentation of self is more problematic than for people socially defined as 'normal'. Managing spoiled identities becomes an acute problem and there is a range of strategies available including normalization and resistance.

- ❖ *Normalization* involves trying to appear as normal as possible by managing – hiding, disguising – the spoiled identity, e.g. using makeup to cover up a scar.
- ❖ *Resistance* involves not hiding the problem but using it, e.g. as the basis for forming a community of others with the same problem.

In Focus

◆

The pride or shame of scars

Spoiled identities are themselves culturally specific. In many societies, having scars is a sign of status and honour – for example amongst some social groups in seventeenth- and eighteenth-century Germany where having scars as a result of duelling was something that was made very visible. Wearing scars proudly sometimes occurs following warfare as a sign that you have been brave. However, in other situations – e.g. following the US defeat in the Vietnam War – showing the visible signs of having fought was frowned upon.

The social construction of identity

Some of the questions that sociologists ask about the self are:

❖ Is the self simply the totality of the roles that I play?

❖ If so, who is my real self?

❖ If I have a lot of roles and therefore a lot of selves, who am I?

What sociologists hold in common is the idea that identity and selfhood are related to the societies in which we live, i.e. are socially constructed. This is the view of Durkheim (1952, originally 1897) in discussing the problems of anomie in industrial societies. Social rules are what make us what we are. *Anomie* involves a social situation in which the rules and norms which govern what we do break down and leave people without clear guides to what they ought to do. This can occur when, as in an economic boom, our expectations are exceeded and also, as in an economic slump, when our expectations are difficult to meet. This lack of clear rules leads to anomie and increased rates of suicide.

For Cooley (1969), our self is developed through interactions with other people; it is a looking-glass self in which we see ourselves mirrored back to us by those with whom we interact. The implication here is that if people present a difficult image to a person – for example, the image of a disruptive child in a school – that person may fit into that picture. As we will see in Chapter 4, *Education*, this provides a basis for labelling theory which aims to explain how people become rule-breakers by looking at how other people treat them and behave towards them.

For Mead (1934), we develop our sense of self in interaction with others; because we interact in many different social contexts, we have many different selves. I might be a controlling person at work and a relaxed and democratic person at home and these different selves develop because the social situation is different. Mead is sometimes difficult to follow, but he makes an important distinction between '*I*' and

'*Me*'. Both are elements of what most of us would see as the '*self*'. The '*I*' is that aspect of the self which thinks and acts; it also judges things. '*Me*' is that aspect of the self which '*I*' think about, reflect on and judge. In other words, we recognize that we have a wide range of selves – father, mother, friend, employee, music-lover – but we also see ourselves as one '*I*'. Who I am remains, as far as I am concerned, the same over long periods of time. The process of socialization involves the '*I*' seeing the self as others see the self, as becoming what Mead calls a *generalized other*. This is how we become social and moral beings.

Berger and Kelner (1977) develop these ideas and argue that stable identities require stable social relationships in which to develop. If social relationships are not stable, then people will not develop mature and stable identities. This will then become the root of a wide range of social problems. For Berger and Kelner stable identities are tied closely to stable marriage relationships. Marriage provides order and allows people to make sense of their social situation. What marriage provides is a small number of people – what they call 'significant others' – who can validate our place in the world. As they put it:

'Every individual requires the ongoing validation of his world, including ... the validation of his identity ... Just as the individual's deprivation of relationship with his significant others will plunge him into anomie, so their continued presence will sustain [that feeling of being] at home in the world.'
(Berger and Kelner 1977, p. 29)

❖ Activity 7 ❖

How would you define a stable social relationship?

What helps to make social relationships stable?

How valid is Berger and Kelner's idea that marriage is an important basis of stable identity?

In Focus

◆

Total institutions

The importance for our sense of identity of the social institutions in which we live is developed in a very interesting way in Goffman's studies of *total institutions* (1961). These are social institutions which look very different – asylums, monasteries, public schools, prisons – but which have in common the fact that they take total control of the lives of people who live in them. Entry into such institutions requires an individual to give up his or her previous identity; this occurs through *mortification of the self*. This may involve giving up your clothes, having you head shaved, loss of possessions, wearing a uniform. Essentially, the total institution can make us take on a particular identity – as criminal, mad – and that is, in the end, what the total institution, as a bureaucracy with its own rules, is for. The way that total institutions operate then has implications for the reform of prisoners and the cure of those with psychiatric illness. As Rosenhahn (1975) suggests, it is relatively easy to get into a mental hospital, but often difficult to get out of it precisely because this sort of hospital 'rewards' behaviour which indicates psychiatric disturbance. In other words, in this setting behaviour which indicates psychiatric illness is more acceptable than that which suggests normality.

Marriage stabilizes identity as the partners come to know, through dialogue and discussion, who they are and how they fit into wider social networks.

In many cases, our selves and identities are structured around cultures and cultural issues; they also relate to the various aspects of social differentiation – class, age, region, gender, ethnicity and so on. At particular times, some aspect of a person's identity may be seen as more important than the others. If a black woman is facing racial harassment, she may feel that it is her ethnic identity which is being threatened; if she faces sexual harassment at work, then her gender identity may be the main focus of concern. To take another example, a person may have strong feelings of identity with workmates, but may feel separated from them if the football team he has supported since childhood is different from theirs.

How are you today?

WHO am I today?

What the hell will I be?

I.M.D.P.

❖ Activity 8 ❖

Try the 'Who am I?' exercise again (Activity 2). Is your perception of who you affected by the following:

- your social class
- your region/locality
- your ethnicity
- your gender
- your age
- your sexuality?

Is any of these who you really are?

One conclusion to the 'Who am I?' exercise is suggested by Stuart Hall:

'If we feel we have a unified identity ... it is only because we construct a comforting story or "narrative of the self" about ourselves ... The fully unified, completed, secure and coherent identity is a fantasy.' (Hall 1992a, p. 277)

Two cloned sheep at the Roslin Institute, Edinburgh. Scientists' increasing skill at cloning mammals raises important questions about individuality and identity

This is why Harriet Bradley (1996) entitles her book on social inequalities *Fractured Identities*. We all belong to social class groups, ethnic groups, gender groups, age groups and so on and each of these provides us with an identity. These identities are rarely unified. In fact, the idea that we do have many identities is part of the complexity of the modern world which most sociologists have tried to analyse.

In concluding this section, it is important to remember what sociologists are committed to: in some sense, all aspects of our lives are socially constructed, and this will apply to very fundamental issues like who we are, which gender we are and what we believe. In the debate about the relative importance of the biological and the social in what people do and believe, and in the formation and understanding of their identities, sociologists lean towards the social.

In Focus

◆

The genes debate

The idea that what we do is caused by society is one which raises major moral and political questions. If I am deviant because of my social position, then:

1 Am I responsible for my deviance?

2 Should I be punished for it?

3 How can society control deviance?

There are similar problems when it is argued that what we do is biologically and genetically determined. Steve Jones (1996) cites a number of cases where people convicted of murder have claimed that they are murderers because they have inherited a gene from their parents. The important point for Jones is that there is no evidence that criminality can be inherited. As Phil Webster suggests in 'Sociology and the genes debate' (1996), the idea that social behaviour has a genetic basis is becoming more and more prominent with ideas that intelligence is inherited, that we are all robots operated by 'selfish genes', and that gender divisions are genetic. This is despite Jones' argument that there is no such genetic basis. Increasingly, sociologists reject such genetic determinism although they rarely go as far as denying any biological element to social behaviour. Webster also tries to explain this pre-eminence of genetic determinism. On the one hand there is a large and powerful biotechnology industry with a financial interest in the idea. On the other, if a lot of social problems – poverty, for example – are a result of genetic factors, then governments cannot be blamed if these problems continue to exist.

Sociological approaches to culture

In this section we will outline some sociological approaches to culture and look at how we learn about our culture through processes of socialization. We will develop an approach to socialization which suggests that we do not just passively accept what we are told to accept.

Definitions

We can start with a quotation that provides the basic sociological approach to culture:

> ' ... when sociologists deploy the concept of culture, they are seeking to explain the symbolic, socially patterned nature and form of individual thought and action.' (Sugrue and Taylor 1996a, p. 10)

We need to look more closely at what is meant by 'symbolic' and 'socially patterned'.

Symbolism

Most sociologists would agree that culture includes a whole range of things that are about signs and symbols – language, values, beliefs, religions, ideologies, art, literature and so on. These are what we use to define our membership of a social group or a community.

In important ways, symbols stand for much more than they appear to. For example, the language I use not only indicates which country I come from, but also (through accent and dialect) which part of a country I am from. In addition, people will learn about my education through the way I talk and write. So language is clearly about symbols – the words I use refer to many of the things in the world around me – but it also says much about my background, education, job and so on. To take another example. If I give a present to someone it is clearly a real object – a box of chocolates, a CD, a ring, a computer – but it is also symbolic of my relationship with that person. Certain gifts are appropriate and others are not.

Appropriateness itself relates to who is giving and who is receiving the gift:

- ❖ Age is important: only certain gifts are given to children and you would not give the same gifts to adults.

- ❖ Gifts that are appropriate to lovers would be odd if given to total strangers.

- ❖ Social status is also crucial. In Japan, for example, there is an elaborate set of rules concerning how gifts are wrapped which are really about the status of the giver and the receiver.

We might change the common view that, when a gift is given, 'It's the thought that counts' to 'It's the social relationship that counts'.

❖ Activity 9 ❖

Schoolchildren often give gifts to teachers.
- What is the symbolic role of these gifts?
- Does it matter if the gift is wrapped or not?
- Should the teacher reciprocate?

There is a very important point here: even hard, material things like books, flowers or CDs have a symbolic role and a symbolic significance. This indicates that culture is more than ideas, language, values and beliefs; it is also material things and forms of social behaviour.

Social patterning

In common with a lot of the things that sociologists study, cultures are socially patterned. This means two things:

- ❖ Cultures are what is called *socially determined* – for example, when you are born, you are born into an existing symbolic order; you don't choose the culture into which you are born.

Everything we do is socially patterned. This applies even to things which we might think have little social significance, such as food. Sociologists and social anthropologists have been interested in food for two main reasons:

❖ Food shows that there is patterning which varies between societies. The English pattern of breakfast–lunch–dinner is culturally and historically specific. We expect certain things of specific meals. Think about how odd it would seem if someone gave you a meal in the evening which had ice-cream, then cereal, followed by soup. This might be perfectly nutritious but would seem peculiar and inappropriate.

❖ Food does much more than satisfy hunger – what we eat has a great social significance. Vegetarianism is a very good example here.

❖ Cultures are *patterned* in that they form relatively coherent packages of signs and symbols. It is this patterning which allows people to learn their culture and to transmit it over time.

❖ Activity 10 ❖

How many people do you know who are vegetarian?

Find out:

• why they are vegetarian

• why they came to reject meat

• whether their relatives and friends are vegetarian.

Some sociological writers – e.g. Adam (1990) – suggest that vegetarianism is to do with gender differences and that it tells us a lot about gender relationships. For Adam there is a link between masculinity and the violence that is part of preparing meat for human consumption. In addition, she argues that men who give up meat are seen as effeminate. The work of others – e.g. Norbert Elias (1978) – allows us to relate vegetarianism to the development of modern societies. For Elias, the modern world is one that is generally safer than the premodern world and one in which there is greater state control and greater predictability of life. Meat-eating is a reminder of the violence of the premodern world; vegetarianism is a likely outcome of the relative stability of life in the modern world. Eating implements may be indicative here: people use knives less and less and other, less threatening implements more.

Dominant ideologies

Most societies consist of different groups, each having its own culture around which identities are constructed. Societies vary in their complexity and some tend to have less variety of culture than others. This is partly what Durkheim (1947) meant in distinguishing between 'mechanical solidarity' and 'organic solidarity'. In simpler societies – called by him 'mechanical' – there is likely to be one set of beliefs which people generally accept. In more complex, 'organic' societies, there is likely to be a plurality of cultures with no one culture able to remain dominant for long. This contrasts, for example, with Marx's approach to what he called ideologies, where, even in complex societies, one ideology is dominant and maintains its dominance through the mass media, education and suchlike. This ideology serves to hide the real sources of power in society and, in that sense, encourages people to be law-abiding and compliant. For Marx, the ruling class in a capitalist society maintains its control through its ownership of property, its control over employment opportunities and its control of ideas and culture.

Abercrombie *et al.* (1980) suggest that the idea of a dominant ideology, which is central to social order and the power of ruling classes, is misleading. For them, many people who do not own wealth and property reject many of the things which those in power say and do. For example, they reject the value of schooling and the hidden curriculum in school. The question then becomes: if theirs isn't a dominant ideology and if people see through the dominant ideology, then why is there social order? The answer for Abercrombie and colleagues is that fear of unemployment, job insecurity, poverty and so on are what keep people in order, even though they do not accept any dominant ideology.

Bourdieu (1977) takes a different view. For him, things like education do reproduce the culture of dominant groups. The more people accept the dominant culture, the more they have *cultural capital*, and this

becomes a basis for success, for example, in the education system. He also developed an approach to lifestyles based on access to economic and cultural capital (1984). Bourdieu indicates some of the differences in cultural preference based on studies in France, shown in Table 2.1.

Bourdieu suggests that each group has its own sets of tastes and preference, but goes further than that and argues that, as lower groups take on the tastes and preferences of higher groups, the latter change their lifestyles.

Often, higher groups develop tastes for things that are in short supply and hence expensive. Crucially, those with lots of cultural capital – intellectuals and academics – may have considerably less economic capital than industrialists. A group which is dominant economically (because it has most property and income) may not be dominant culturally. These

Table 2.1 Differences in cultural preferences between social groups

Preferences	High economic capital	High cultural capital	Low economic/ cultural capital
	e.g. industrialist	*e.g. higher education and school teacher*	*e.g. semi-skilled worker*
1 Art	impressionism	abstract art	'art is nice, but difficult'
2 Classical music	Vivaldi	Mozart	'don't like Bach'
3 Language*	some accent	no accent	strong accent
4 Leisure activities	photography/records	photography/records	DIY
5 Clothes	chic	clothes that suit personality	value for money
6 Cooking	exotic business meals	chinese food	simple food/ cheap wine
7 Books	historical novels	classics/political & philosophical essays	thrillers
8 Games/sports	tennis/water-skiing	chess	football

* *Interpretation by interviewer*

Source: based on Bourdieu (1984, pp. 128–9 and 526–45)

issues are explored further in Chapter 6 on social stratification.

❖ Activity 11 ❖

Do you think there is a dominant ideology is Britain? If so:

1 How did you identify that ideology?

2 What are the features of that ideology?

Any rejection of the idea of a dominant ideology suggests that in real societies:

❖ there is likely to be a variety of cultures

❖ people will not accept every culture or every aspect of a culture

❖ if you ask people what they believe, they are unlikely to provide a coherent answer.

The last point is important: people hold *contradictory* beliefs. They accept the importance of equality, but discriminate against people. They accept the importance of the welfare state, but are against one-parent families.

Culture and prejudice

The idea that people hold contradictory beliefs is evident in sociological studies of attitudes. The annual *British Social Attitudes* (Jowell *et al.*) regularly asks people if they, or other people, are racist and discriminate against minorities. It is noticeable that most people say that they are not racist, but also say that other people are racist. Of course, both of these cannot be true. In addition,

Billig *et al.*'s work (1988) shows the inconsistencies and contradictions in how people talk about prejudice. Most people distinguish between 'reasonable' prejudice – what they do – which is justified by them, and 'unreasonable' prejudice. The latter is what others – the *real* racists – do. This distinction is shown in *prejudiced talk*. A common ploy is to say 'I am not prejudiced, but ... '. Here the 'but' can stand for anything: minorities don't want to fit in, they work harder/less hard than we do, they demand special treatment. These ploys mean that, in the end, the person *is* prejudiced, either because there is no evidence for the assertions about minorities that are being made, or because there is no reason to assume that everyone should be the same.

❖ Activity 12 ❖

Look at some newspapers and listen to some TV interviews. Find examples of the 'I am not prejudiced, but ... ' kind. They might also be of the 'I am tolerant, but..', 'I am in favour of equality, but ... ' kind.

Who is using these examples? What are they really saying? Why are they saying these things?

Reasonable prejudice becomes acceptable in contrast to the violent hatred and enmity of those who are 'really' prejudiced. Contrasting reasonable prejudice with more obvious hatred becomes a way of making it legitimate. In particular, reasonable prejudice includes the idea that it is not based on error and misunderstanding.

In Focus

◆

Election campaigns and hate speech

In a study of US Presidential election campaigns, Whillock (1995) suggests that violent hate speech has often been used to mobilize political support without any claim that this hate speak is reasonable. In other words, overtly hateful political campaigns can be a way to gain electoral support. These electoral campaigns often include the claim that there is a rational reason for hatred, for example, that some group which we hate is threatening our job opportunities.

Culture and social structure

Many of the issues we have discussed in this section relate to one of the big theoretical issues in sociology: what is the relationship between culture – values, attitudes, dress styles, sexual rules – and social structure? There are, in effect, three answers to this question.

❖ The first answer is provided by those who stress the importance of social structures. Marx and Durkheim are both *structuralists* because they argue that the structure of society – the system of production for Marx, the division of labour for Durkheim – is what gives rise to culture. They would expect to find only certain types of culture in particular types of social structure, for example the literary form of the novel in capitalist societies.

❖ A second answer is provided by those who argue that culture is either partly or totally unrelated to social structure. The best word for this view is *culturalist*.

❖ Finally, there is a view – for example, in the work of Giddens, where it is referred to as duality of structure –that structures and systems of ideas are interrelated in a complex manner.

These views are summarized in Fig. 2.1. Chapter 7, on sociological theory, looks at some of these ideas in more detail.

Figure 2.1
A summary of sociological positions in relating culture to social structure

STRUCTURALISTS

Difficulties with this view

Groups develop their own cultures and identity; they feel that they create them; people do contradict the dominant culture

CULTURALISTS

There are dominant cultures; people cannot just create any culture and identity; some cultures thrive is some social structures and not in others.

DUALITY OF STRUCTURE

The possibility of ignoring the fact that, although people make their cultures and identities, they do so with limits and constraints that are partly structural ones.

The socialization debate

The socialization debate is focused on what makes us social. Studies of what are called feral children – that is, children isolated from a very early age from human contact – provide insights into this area (see *In Focus* on the next page).

The idea of socialization is used by sociologists to explain how people learn a particular culture and become functioning individuals. The process of socialization is therefore a way of explaining the relationships between culture and identity, and between the biological and the social.

We can distinguish between a simple theory of socialization and a complex one.

When Itard (Malson and Itard 1972) found and took Victor, the 'Wild Boy of Aveyron', into his family, he provided the basis for a continuing debate about the social and the natural. Victor could not feel pain and could not talk. Possible explanations for this included the idea that he was physically damaged as a result of living in the wild or that he had perhaps not been socialized to experience pain and to talk.

Itard eventually trained Victor to talk and to feel pain, but his speech always remained undeveloped. Now, most sociologists and psychologists would argue that socialization plays an important part of language learning and that there is an ideal time when children learn to speak. If children do not hear speech during that time, they may have great difficulty in learning to speak. See Maclean's work for more on feral children (1977).

A simple view of socialization

The simple view suggests, correctly, that newborn babies are dependent upon the adult world and learn a lot from it. It goes further than this and argues that there is a one-way relationship between the baby and the social world: the baby passively receives socialization and becomes what its parents, and what society, wants. Once this *primary socialization* has happened, there is a range of institutions which develop *secondary socialization* which backs up what happened in the family – media, education, peers and so on. This process of socialization makes us social by providing us with the *values* and *norms* of our social groups or society. The extent to which we accept these values and norms determines our social status.

The combination of primary and secondary socialization will tend to produce a vast majority of people who accept the values of their society. There is an implication here that every society has its own basic set of values which all people recognize and can accept. According to Parsons (1951) who is a functionalist

(see Chapter 7), socialization involves the internalization of norms and values and, by internalizing these, we are able to perform our various social roles.

❖ Activity 13 ❖

Identify the main institutions of primary and secondary socialization. How do they, in practice, socialize people? What happens if people resist the pressure to be socialized?

This simple view of socialization has great difficulty is explaining change, as you may have realized from Activity 13. How do people change if everyone is socialized by the last generation? In addition, how do values and norms change if each of us learns them through agents of socialization like teachers and parents? This view is only able to explain deviance by saying that this generation was wrongly socialized by its parents, who were wrongly socialized by

Although the terms norm and value are central to what is called functionalist sociology (see Chapter 7), they are very difficult to define precisely. The closest we can get to a clear meaning is probably this: norms are about

correct and proper behaviour, whilst values are principles and standards of behaviour. Note that most norms and values do not have legal backing, but still many people accept them and behave accordingly.

theirs. There is, in consequence, a debate about what is correct socialization which then leads to all sorts of political debate about the family and whether the family is to blame for such social changes as rising crime rates and levels of illegitimacy (see Chapter 3).

❖ **Activity 14** ❖

Identify the norms and values of any group of which you are a member.

The final implication of this view is that there is a structure of society which individuals passively absorb; that socialization is a form of cultural programming. Giddens (1976) sees this view as part of a long-standing debate in sociology about the relative importance of structure and of what individuals do – what he calls 'agency'. This is discussed in Chapter 7, but we can quote briefly from Giddens here:

'The realm of human agency is bounded. Individuals produce society, but they do so as historically situated actors, and not under conditions of their own choosing. Structures must not be conceptualized as simply placing constraints upon human agency, but as enabling.' (Giddens 1976, pp. 160–1)

This suggests that there are limits to what individuals can do; they may think they are acting freely but, in fact, much of what they do happens within strict limits. However, these limits are not as restrictive as the simple view of socialization implies; people are not, as this simple view implies, robots. On the one hand, therefore, we have the view that we are robots and, on the other, the view that we are totally free. Sociologists like Giddens argue that we are somewhere in the middle, constrained by the society in which we live but still free to do things. Some of the limits on what we can do are biological, e.g. we cannot fly unaided, and some are social, e.g. generally we should not attack other people.

A complex view of socialization

This leads us to a more complex, but sociologically more useful, view that socialization is about an interaction between individuals and the society in which they live. To take newborn babies again, they are undoubtedly dependent upon adults and that is to do with the relative immaturity at birth of their brains and bodies. However, newly born infants are not passive; rather they interact with their environments and have done so since before they were born. This lack of passivity means that a child socialized by a family of criminals will not necessarily become criminal; it also means that criminals may come from perfectly 'normal' families!

The study of infants and how they learn raises two issues which bridge the gap between the biological and the social. The first issue is whether we have preprogrammed, biological instincts. If we do have them, then they may limit the role that socialization plays in our development, and suggest, as we saw in the discussion of Fox's work, that some of our social roles and social institutions have a biological basis.

The second issue was raised by John Bowlby (1978). Bowlby wanted to know whether infants needed attachment to a primary carer, that is, a mother. His conclusion that mothers were important and that infants denied attachment would suffer has had important sociological and political implications. For the sociologists, the importance of early attachment is that infants are not preprogrammed by instincts to survive. Politically, the need for primary carers – usually mothers – has been criticized by feminist theorists. The issue here becomes whether women need to be primary carers and whether that should adversely effect their economic and political power.

The final point on the socialization debate is that what becomes customary and habitual is learnt only after serious effort. As Goffman suggests, part of what we have called socialization is learning to manage ourselves and this applies to even the most routine of social activities. He puts it very interestingly:

' ... almost every **activity** that the individual easily performs now was at some time for him something that required serious mobilization of effort. To walk, to cross a road, to utter a complex sentence, to wear long pants, to tie one's own shoes, to add a column of figures – all these routines were attained through an acquisition process whose early stages were negotiated in a cold sweat.'
(Goffman 1971, p. 248)

For Goffman, learning to be what we are is not easy and includes an element of danger if we get it wrong. It also includes,

as with the teacher and lecturer example earlier, an element of conning people into believing that we are normal people performing the roles into which we were socialized.

❖ Activity 15 ❖

If you have just started either A level sociology, first year sociology in a university, or some other sociology course, describe how you were socialized into the new role of sociology students.

The relationship between culture and identity

This is a very important issue for sociologists and has, as we will see, become a central theme in discussions of postmodernism. Essentially, who we are is closely tied to the culture(s) with which we identify.

Ethnic identity

The term 'ethnicity' is now widely used and raises issues about community, community values and belonging to a community. Britain is, and always has been, a society with many ethnic groups; that is, one with people from a variety of ethnic backgrounds. This is made clear in Peter Fryer's work (1984), where he traces the history of the black and Asian presence in Britain.

Statistics for 1992 provide us with one perspective on the complexity of the British population (see Table 2.2).

These figures indicate why the *British culture* exercise was so difficult. First, the overwhelming majority of the people in the groups listed in Table 2.2 are British citizens, even though they have a variety of cultures and cultural traditions. Second, the group that is called 'white' is, itself, diverse and includes English, Scottish, Welsh, Irish, Cornish, Polish, German, French, American, Jewish, Roman Catholic and so on. Notice the difficulty here: ethnicity can include where you live (e.g. British), where you come from (e.g. Polish) and your religion (e.g. Jewish). And it can be a mixture of these things – Afro-Caribbean and British.

In Focus
◆
Terminology

There is considerable controversy over the terms which we should use to describe the various minority ethnic groups in Britain, e.g. the use of terms like 'black' and 'Asian'.

Black has been used in two main senses:

❖ to distinguish a whole range of minorities from white people

❖ to identify a range of minorities that have a common experience of oppression and powerlessness.

Neither of these makes any simple identification between the term 'black' and a particular colour. In other words, some people may call themselves black because they see themselves as victims of racial oppression even though, to a white person, they may not look black.

Table 2.2 British population by ethnic origin

White	**94.3%**
Non-white	**4.5%**

of which:		
	Indian	30%
	Pakistani	17.6%
	Afro-Caribbean	17%
	Mixed origin	11%
	African	5%
	Bangladeshi	4%
	Arab	2.4%

Source: adapted from Social Trends (1992)

❖ Activity 16 ❖

Carry out an ethnic census of your class or group. Ask people how they define their ethnicity and ask for information on the ethnic origins and identities of parents and grandparents.

What does this information tell us about:

- what we mean by ethnicity?
- how multi-ethnic Britain now is?

The United Kingdom: a multi-ethnic, multicultural society

There does seem, however, to be a popular version of British culture: democracy, fair play, tolerance and equality. This contrasts with the reality of structures of discrimination which disproportionately affect some minority ethnic groups. We will see throughout this book that there is discrimination against many minorities – in particular, black and Asian people – in employment, education, policing, health and access to housing. In addition, we will see that this discrimination persists despite the widely held view that we live in a fair and tolerant society and despite the aims of the Race Relations Acts to eradicate discrimination (see *In Focus*).

In Focus ◆ **Race Relations Acts 1965, 1968, 1976**

The Race Relations Acts of 1965, 1968 and 1976 attempted to end discrimination. The 1965 Act made illegal direct and overt discrimination in public facilities, including hotels, restaurants and transport. The 1968 act extended this to employment, housing and commercial services. For example, it outlawed advertisements which said that black people need not apply for a particular job. Similarly, it said that people who were letting flats could not put notices in their windows saying that only white people need apply.

The 1976 Act attempted to outlaw indirect discrimination, which is more difficult to identify. Anything which looks fair and yet discriminates against some minority is unlawful. For example, people of Afro-Caribbean origin are – like many women – underrepresented in managerial jobs, and so asking for managerial experience in a job advert could be indirectly discriminatory against those groups. Another example would be a job advertisement which said that only people born in the UK should apply.

continued on next page

In Focus

◆

Race Relations Acts (ctd)

In these situations, many people of Afro-Caribbean, Asian and African descent cannot compete on fair and equal terms. Jenkins (1986) has shown, however, that the employer can still discriminate by using culturally specific acceptability criteria in deciding who gets a job. These might include whether a person will fit in to an existing work group or whether a person makes eye-contact at interview. In Jenkins' study, many employers had negative stereotypes of black and Asian people and these linked to the acceptability criteria. For example, some employers saw Asians as very hardworking and said this would threaten the existing all-white work groups who were less committed to very hard work!

New racism

Barker and others have drawn attention to a new way of thinking and talking about cultural differences which developed in the 1950s and 60s. Barker (1981) calls this the *new racism*. In the eighteenth and nineteenth centuries, racial theory emphasized the biological inferiority of certain social groups and said that this biological inferiority also produced social and cultural inferiority. This has now been proved to be false and there is no evidence that biological differences between different groups of human beings – in features such as skin colour or hair type – have any effect at all on social life and social behaviour. There is now a powerful language which talks about cultural *differences*. Several things are distinctive about this new racism.

❖ The claim is made that the existence of racism is exaggerated and that most people are, in fact, not racist.

❖ New racism talks about 'difference' rather than 'inequality' and claims that difference is a problem, especially where people with different cultures live in the same location.

❖ It asserts that people have a natural attachment to their own culture and, therefore, find other cultures dangerous and threatening. These natural attachments are powerful and emotional and are, therefore, difficult to control and legislate against.

❖ It claims that other cultures are the root-cause of social problems.

❖ Finally, it is a view which claims to be common sense. Common sense then comes to have a very powerful role to play in that anyone who disagrees with the common sense view is easily defined as irrational and dangerous.

What is happening here is a process of pathologizing other cultures and blaming them for the problems which 'our' culture faces. This produces a view of ethnic minorities as 'the enemy within' and becomes the basis for policies which try to control immigration as a condition for peaceful 'race relations' at home. Part of the process of pathologizing involves misunderstanding what other cultures are like and presenting them in a stereotypical fashion.

Zygmunt Bauman (1989), in a study of the links between the modern world and the Holocaust of Jews, gypsies, the mentally ill and the disabled in Nazi Germany in the 1930s and 1940s, developed the idea that different cultures and ways of life are seen as threatening in two directions:

❖ Seeing other ways of life as threatening can lead to calls for their extermination and policies of extermination.

❖ This extermination was part of a modern, bureaucratic society. As Bilton *et al.* put it:

'Bauman sees the Final Solution [the exterminations] as a telling illustration of the way institutions of modernity distance people from moral responsibility for their actions. It demonstrates the ethical blindness of rational bureaucracies whose members can argue that "I was only following orders". ...

In Focus

◆

**Prejudice,
discrimi-
nation and
racism**

Sociologists commonly distinguish between prejudice, discrimination and racism.

❖ *Prejudice* involves prejudging a group of people to be inferior or otherwise different in the absence of evidence. Prejudice is common and can occur between any groups of people. An example would be the belief held by many English people that German people lack a sense of humour.

❖ *Discrimination* occurs when groups of people are treated as inferior and/or different. Individuals can discriminate for example, by shouting offensive terms to someone they see walking down the street. Institutions can discriminate by excluding those who want to enter them from an equal chance of entry even when those people are suitably qualified. This may, for example, be why there are so few women in senior positions in the armed forces.

❖ *Racism* is that form of discrimination which treats people as inferior and/or different on the basis of physical characteristics or aspects of their culture. Examples of racism could therefore include racist name-calling and the high rates of exclusion of Afro-Caribbean boys from primary and secondary schooling.

The Holocaust also shows the terrible potential for harm which lies in the state's claim to be able to do anything it wishes within its sovereign territory.' (Bilton 1996, p. 44)

The danger, therefore, lies in the combination of hatred of others, the technology available to kill people and claims by the state and its inhabitants that outsiders are a problem that needs controlling.

The logic of the new racism is that cultures different from the dominant one must assimilate the dominant culture. This is argued for because people feel that other, minority cultures are threatening and dangerous, even though there is no evidence that they really are.

This is an extremely important issue for sociology. Sociologists spend a lot of time finding evidence for things. They use this evidence as the basis for rational discussion and often to promote social changes. Studies of racism indicate that the issue is not only one of evidence but of feelings and emotions. The problem is that the evidence rarely gets rid of such racist feelings.

Sociologists have, in fact, had little difficulty in recognizing and describing the mutual fear which people from different cultures have of each other. However, they have been less successful in explaining *why* there is that fear and often hatred. Social anthropologists, like Mary Douglas (1966) have tried to develop explanations of antipathy to other people. Put simply, different cultures do not fit into our systems of classification and things that do not fit in must be dealt with; in other words, societies do a lot of things to maintain clear boundaries including excluding and demonizing those who are defined as outsiders.

In Focus

◆

**The 'cricket
test'**

In the 1980s Norman Tebbitt, then a leading member of the Conservative party, developed the idea of a 'cricket test'. If you were British, you should support the English cricket team. Therefore, people who migrated to England from the Caribbean or India must, if they are to count as British, change their sporting allegiances. In other words, you cannot simultaneously support the West Indian or Indian cricket teams and count as British.

What is noticeable is a shift in emphasis in discussions of ethnicity. In particular, there has been an increasing interest in what Stuart Hall (1989) has called *new ethnicities*. The central issue for Hall is that we *all* have ethnicities; they are not just restricted to minorities. In this sense, every group with some form of culture and identity is an ethnic group. This has two implications: the old idea that ethnicity applies only to non-white people and that ideas of ethnicity are to do with ideas of race and nation need to be abandoned. In addition, these new ethnicities cut across previous definitions of ethnicity; so, for example, Rap music and other elements of black culture appeal to, and are increasingly being adopted by, white working-class boys. As Back suggests (1993), this sharing of cultural traditions does not in fact get rid of racial discrimination. Back's work shows that white working-class and Afro-Caribbean boys do socialize together, with the white boys taking on aspects of black culture, including style of language. The white boys still have racist attitudes and indulge in racist behaviour, including name-calling. Together, the white and black boys harass, negatively stereotype and discriminate against other minorities in the area, particularly refugees of Vietnamese origin. Vietnamese boys are seen as weak and effeminate, thus combining elements of race and gender stereotyping.

For Hall (1992a) many minorities face distinct issues because they have been displaced. This displacement is a result of processes of migration which had an economic rationale. People from areas including the Caribbean and the Indian subcontinent were subject to push and pull factors that saw them moving to Britain, e.g. in the 1950s. Pull factors included the demand for labour in Britain. Push factors included the increasing poverty and unemployment which resulted from colonialism (see Chapter 8, *World sociology*).

Hall gives a picture of the effects of this process on how those people who were displaced feel about who they are and where they belong, i.e. their identity.

'[There are] the millions of displaced peoples, dislocated cultures and fractured communities of the south, who have been moved from their "settled communities", their "placeable feelings", their "whole ways of life". They are products of the new diasporas [migrations and dispersals], obliged to inhabit at least two identities, to speak at least two cultural languages, to negotiate and "translate" between them. In this way, though they are struggling in one sense at the margins of modernity, they are at the leading edge of what is destined to become the truly "late-modern" experience. They are the products of cultures of hybridity. They bear the traces of particular cultures, traditions, languages, systems of belief, texts and histories that have shaped them. But they are also obliged to come to terms with and to make something new of the cultures they inhabit, without simply assimilating to them. They are not and never will be unified in the old sense, because they are inevitably the products of several interlocking histories and cultures, belonging at the same time to several "homes" – and thus to no one, particular home.' (Hall 1992b, p. 8)

❖ Activity 17 ❖

What do you mean by 'home'?

What do your parents mean by 'home'?

To what extent is home a community, rather than simply the building you live in?

National identity and nationalism

One of the central points about the new racism is that it stresses national identity and a feeling of belonging to a nation. The emphasis on the nation and its cultural heritage takes the place of more overt emphasis on race. This is very close to nationalism which involves the idea that a culturally homogenous group of people inhabits a territory which is its own. There is, in fact, a range of types of nationalism:

❖ the nationalism which characterizes the debate in Britain about the European Union and the extent to which membership of the EU is threatening British culture and British sovereignty

❖ the nationalism that was associated with decolonization, for example, in Africa, where movements of national unity became the basis for removing colonial governments

❖ the form of nationalism which Smith (1995) calls 'ethnic nationalism' – which makes claims about the importance of often small national groups within larger nations.

As Giddens (1995) suggests, there are common roots of nationalism – for example, the collapse of communities – but nationalism is also double-edged:

> 'On the one hand, nationalist sentiments are often associated with trends towards democracy – this was true, for example, of the 1989 events in Eastern Europe. On the other hand, however, nationalist feelings equally often inspire antagonism, and have inspired some of the most destructive conflicts of the nineteenth and twentieth centuries.' (Giddens 1995, p. 343)

Britain is a multicultural society, but it is also seen as a nation. The two can come into conflict. The debate about assimilation suggests that some people see a conflict between being a nation and being multicultural. However, this flies in the face of history. As Peter Fryer (1984) shows, Britain has been multicultural for a very long time indeed.

Material culture and ethnic identity

There is an important role for material culture – that is, everyday commodities like clothes and food – in the construction of ethnic identities. Note the word 'construction' here. We no longer assume that ethnic identity is given and fixed; rather it is made by people actually doing things. This is made very clear by Shaun Hides (1995) in a study of Asian communities in Leicester. For Hides anything may convey a sense of identity; in this case clothing is particularly important.

Clothing becomes a way of developing identities along three axes: gender, age and context. The gender dimension is the most obvious. Across religions – Hindu, Muslim and Sikh – women are much more likely to wear traditional clothing than are men. While many would see this as a sign of the oppression of women, there is much more to it than that. For example, the home is an arena in which, in racist societies, people feel safer and more able to express their cultural identities. Therefore, as women are more likely to be in the home, it is they who are more likely to wear traditional dress. Age and context interact with gender here. Older people are more likely to wear traditional clothes and all people are more likely to wear them in certain contexts, particularly in life-cycle ceremonies like weddings and funerals. Older people are also concerned that younger people do not easily accept traditional clothing.

The problems of ethnic identity indicate something very important about relationships between culture and identity. Cultural identity is one of the ways in which social solidarity and social order come about and are maintained. This is something that, for example, Durkheim emphasised in his discussions of social solidarity (1893/1960; see Chapter 7).

Identity and consumption

As we said earlier, the sociological interest in identity and culture has been given a boost by ideas of postmodernity.

Sociologists, in fact, disagree not only about what postmodernism is, but also about whether it is something new. Some say that the world we now live in is postmodern, suggesting that it has replaced modernity, while others, including Giddens, argue that the world we now live in is better called 'late modern' or 'post-traditional'.

In Focus

◆

Terminology

The terms 'postmodernity' and 'postmodernism' are both used in all sociological writing on the topic. Postmodernism tends to apply to aspects of culture, while postmodernity refers to a type of social structure and/or a new historical epoch. However, you will often find the terms used interchangeably.

In effect, it is different from traditional, rural societies but also has all the features of modernity (see Chapter 7). What is clear is that for a long time sociologists – e.g. Simmel, writing around the turn of this century – identified something new about modern societies. For example, people have briefer and shallower contacts with each other that are more instrumental than in the past, that is are more to do with what people can get out of contacts with others than the intrinsic merit of the contacts. They also have a diversity of roles to occupy which tends to produce a fragmented identity. Therefore, whether we see the world we now live in as late modern or postmodern, it is certainly very different from the past.

One of the areas that is central to postmodernism is the study of lifestyle shopping: how we make and change our identities through consumption and how we can now consume things from a variety of cultural backgrounds. We live, it is argued, in a culturally hybrid world in which our identities can be both bought and changed regularly. This is part of the process of globalization which is discussed in Chapter 8. The global economic system we live in can provide us with commodities from the whole world with its diversity of traditions. However, it is also possible that this global economic system is destroying many traditions and making the whole world more uniform. This may be one of the lessons of the near-universal availability of Coca-Cola.

Q: What do you get if you cross a member of the Mafia with a postmodernist?

A: An offer you can't understand.

In Focus

◆

Giddens on Postmodernity

Giddens provides a useful definition of postmodernity:

'What does postmodernity ordinarily refer to? Apart from the general sense of living through a period of marked disparity with the past, the term usually means one or more of the following: that we have discovered that nothing can be known with any certainty, since all pre-existing "foundations" ... have been shown to be unreliable; that "history" is devoid of teleology [of a direction] and consequently no version of "progress" can plausibly be defended; and that a new social and political agenda has come into being with the increasing prominence of ecological concerns and perhaps new social movements generally.' (1990, p. 46)

❖ Activity 18 ❖

When you go to a local super/hyper-market or shopping mall, see how many different food traditions can you identify. Are any of these traditions your own?

Something in you wants to pick up the art of over 300 cultures from the sidewalk.

Indonesia, a world of art and craft.

One street in Jakarta, Indonesia's capital, offers a crash course in the archipelago's 17,000 islands and 300 cultures. A stroll down Jalan Surabaya might reveal a length of batik cloth with a handpainted Garuda, once reserved for nobles on the island of Java. A scene from Hindu myth painted on wood, from the island paradise of Bali. A filigree silver

Part of an advertisement from the Indonesia Tourism Promotion Board

There is a new social organization of lifestyle shopping in the form of the shopping mall. Rob Shields gives a flavour of the mall:

'"Malls" are typically more grandiose than shopping centres ... In the malls, the plan becomes more complex ..., everything is larger, the architecture more monumental (expensive finishes such as marble, skylit arcades, soaring ceiling heights, dizzying mezzanines ...), the major "anchor stores" multiply and functions increase with the addition of cinemas, hotels, zoos, recreation complexes ..., churches – in short almost any urban activity one can imagine ... The mall forms the centre of an urban constellation and a social community is born ... The elderly walk from the nearby apartments and the adolescent "mall jammers" migrate from schools in the vicinity to match wits with security personnel, in search of less controlled areas than the schoolyard. Others arrive by car or on buses ... Parking space and waiting areas [are] patrolled by the mall owners' security guards ... Ease of access, controlled climate and reduced prices based on a higher market volume are the functional attractions of the mall ... These benefits are [however] quickly outstripped by the symbolic and social value of the mall as a site of communication and interaction ... Purchases often represent very minor expenditures (for example, a cup of coffee) and the spending of money is not required in any case ... It is [in the mall] that groups meet, that face-to-face communication if not community is a practice for a huge number of people ...' (Shields 1992, pp. 4–6)

One of the major theorists of these ideas is Jean Baudrillard (1988) who claims that shopping is what makes us what we are. Baudrillard suggests we have a society in which, because you shop, you become a person. You shop, therefore you are a particular type of person. This implies that we consume both material things *and* cultural things.

One of the central features of postmodernity is the shift from a concern with production of goods to their consumption. Shields' image is of everyone being able to participate in the life of the mall. However, for the owners of the mall the imperative is still selling commodities for profit. In this sense, the emphasis on the buying of life styles which you can change regularly is partly, if not predominantly, dependent on income and wealth. Whereas we can all visit the mall, buying the new life style is still something that only some groups of people can do.

The roles of the mall as the new place where people spend their leisure time and as the palace of consumption may also conflict with each other. Malls now employ security guards, one of whose roles is to police undesirables; these include young people who use the mall as a place to meet even though they may spend very little. This policing of the shopping mall is part of general concern with disorder in the city and with the development of surveillance.

Thus, the idea that, in the postmodern world, we are free to choose our identities and freely indulge in the pleasures of consumption, is open to criticism from two directions.

❖ The work of Foucault (1977) and Lyon (1994) suggests that there is a vast extension of systems of surveillance which monitor and control our outer behaviour and inner feelings. These include the proliferation of cameras in public places and the increasing use of discount and other forms of 'loyalty' card in shops. Both of these allow the careful and continuous monitoring of what we do. Your Tesco loyalty card simultaneously gives you money back but also allows Tesco to know exactly how you consume and to tailor its provision to your needs.

❖ There are also material conditions which affect people's ability to participate in mall culture; for example, you are likely to need a car to get to the mall in the first place.

What we see here is one of the central debates in sociology: how far our behaviour is determined by our social position and how much of it is up to us as individuals. In the postmodern world it is claimed that much of our behaviour is freely chosen and entered into. What Foucault, Lyon and others suggest is that the degree of freedom may be strictly limited; we may think we are free but we are, in fact, constrained in what we do. Not only are the poor excluded from the new world of consumption, but the prosperous are much less in control of that system than they might like to think. Our identities and cultures are continually being shaped by commercial corporations. However, we may still resist those commercial pressures. We may refuse to consume. We may buy things and customize them. For example, it was common in the 1980s to buy Levi jeans and fray them at the knee and fade them with bleach. The producers rapidly recognized this trend and started to manufacture pre-washed and faded jeans!

Projects of the self

There is more to the self in the postmodern world than shopping. Giddens and others argue that the self is itself something we work on and try to improve. This includes working hard on our bodies to make them more desirable and socially acceptable. Part of this process of working on the self is shown in diet and fitness regimes. There has been a tremendous expansion in the last thirty years in the number of health clubs, exercise videos and books on dieting. The best evidence for this expansion comes from the USA:

'Over the past couple of decades national surveys ... have documented a widespread and growing interest among middle and upper class Americans in the pursuit of fitness. Health clubs grossed $5 billion in 1987, exercise equipment $738 million (up from $5 million ten years earlier), diet products grossed $74 million, and vitamin products $2.7

billion ... Frequently throughout the 1980s, exercise video cassettes have appeared on weekly *Billboard* lists of the top ten selling home video products ... approximately 50,000 US corporations made available exercise, diet, and other "wellness" programs to their employees in hopes of reducing insurance, absentee, and inefficiency costs at a time when many were "downsizing" their work-forces.' (Glassner 1989, p. 180)

Part of the promise of all this is to turn us into fit and healthy people, i.e. to make us stay young for a long time. It is possible that fitness and dietary regimes are trying to deal with some of the most fundamental problems that people face – problems about ageing, disease and death. As Chapter 14 discusses, these are issues which have, traditionally, been dealt with through religion.

In all societies people alter their natural bodies. In Britain, large amounts of money are spent on things like hair products, ear-piercing and breast implants. Across all cultures similar things go on. We might think that what other people do, e.g. foot-binding in prerevolutionary China, or tattooing and scarring in some traditional African societies, is odd, or even horrific, but outsiders might also see what we do as strange and frightening. What is going on is that the natural body, the one we are born

with, is being altered to make it social. For example, the way we do our hair may confirm our membership of a particular group of people; a Rastafarian's dreadlocks may express religious and cultural beliefs.

The sociological significance of what we do to the body is indicated in what some consider to be extreme forms of bodily cultivation. We will take two examples here: body building and cryonics (see *In Focus* on next page).

'Shape of things to come... most men want to look more like Stallone'
Source: The Guardian, 11 June 1996

Is this the female form of the future?

Sam Fussell (1991) provides a personal insight into body building:

'There was a beautiful simplicity about it. The harder I worked, the better I felt. My routine brought order amid chaos. I knew just where to shuffle and when: deltoids followed pecks, hamstrings followed quads ... And if I wasn't strong, I could make up for it by continuing to exercise long after others had padded off to the showers. Set after set. Ninety minutes straight. Week after week ... I took 6,666% of the daily minimum requirement of vitamin B1, 5,882 percent of B2, 1,333 per cent of E, 1,000 per cent of C, and so on ... I supplemented my supplements with desiccated and defatted beef-liver tablets to help my liver and kidneys process the overload. (Fussell 1991, pp. 43 and 82)

Once he entered competition, the routine of training became more complex. Fussell had to look right:

'The aim of [the] diet was to keep my fat and sodium levels to a minimum, while juggling my carbohydrate to protein ration ... If I timed it right, on the day of the contest my skin would look tight as a drum. Bodybuilders call it the "shrink-wrap" fit.' (p. 186)

'Mark Muhlstein ... earns a tidy $100,000 a year as a computer analyst. He has an adoring wife, Judy, 43, and between them they share eight kids, three cars and a roomy Spanish-style stucco house with a pool in north Tucson, Arizona. But Muhlstein is not content with his slice of the American Dream; he wants more. He wants to live forever ... Muhlstein is a happy man, for he believes he has found the key to immortality. When his final hour comes, a team of technicians will be poised at his side, ready to pack his body in ice and inject him with organ-preserving fluid as soon as legal death is pronounced. Laid in a rubber "mobile rescue cart", his corpse will be rushed by ambulance to a laboratory, where it will be drained of blood and pumped with glycerol. His head will be cut off with a bone saw and deep-frozen alongside others in a concrete vat of liquid nitrogen. It will be stored at minus 196°C indefinitely, until the day – which Muhlstein believes will come – when the technology to revive him is in place. Then he will be reanimated, and the good life, the all-American life, need never come to an end ... the Muhlsteins' life-insurance policy secures the freezing of their heads only ... Those who opt for 'whole body' suspension pay a total of $120,000 ... In a whole-body suspension, the corpse is sewn up after being perfused with glycerol, immersed in a silicone oil bath and left to soak for 36 hours. By the time it is fished out, the body temperature is minus 78°C. Frozen and desiccated, it is strapped into a body bag lined with aluminium foil, hoisted in the air and gently lowered into a liquid-nitrogen-filled vacuum flask ... to await the call to eternal life.'

Source: Sunday Times colour supplement, 7 July 1996)

Cryonics involves freezing the body (or head) at death in the hope that it can be revived in the future. It is a minority interest, but is still sociologically of some significance.

To many people, body building and cryonics may seem odd – even horrific or mad. However, these are things that people are doing and things that challenge the sociologist. What is going on in these examples and in diet and exercise regimes, and what do they tell us about the sociological significance of our bodies and our identities?

❖ Activity 19 ❖

Do you, or your friends or parents, do regular exercise and diet? Design a small questionnaire to assess the motivation behind such activities. (Chapter 7 gives guidance on questionnaire design.)

As sociologists, we can interpret what is going on here in a number of ways:

❖ Body building and cryonics are industries. They cost money, employ people and have their own technology and consumer products.

❖ Body building says something about gender. It started as a male preserve, but now increasingly attracts women. Many female body builders see the attainment of a muscular body as something profoundly feminine and as challenging the idea that men have the monopoly of muscle power.

❖ There is a moral aspect: in particular, in body building there is the idea that the outer body says something about the inner body. Having a strong, muscular body, one that is fit and trained, is a sign of your inner worth, that you are a disciplined person. This has wider implications which include the increasing relationship between fitness and employability, i.e. the extent to which people in senior management positions have to appear fit and healthy because that says something about the fitness and health of the company for which they work.

❖ Body building and cryonics tell us something about attitudes to disease and death. The desire to be fit and healthy has much to do with the fear of ageing, which itself relates to how we deal with death. In modern societies ageing is often seen as a problem and those who grow old are marginalized. One function of body building and fitness regimes is to stay young-looking for as long as possible and to suppress the signs of ageing.

All societies have to deal with death and, despite the interest in cryonics, death seems to be inevitable for everyone. Death is, in the modern world, increasingly hidden. Most people die in hospital away from their families. Their death is controlled by experts and there is a whole bureaucracy of death – certificates, insurance policies to cover the cost of funerals, undertakers. There has, however, been a reaction to this in the hospice movement. There is therefore a contrast between death in the modern world and death in traditional societies, where it was often common, occurred at all ages, was a public thing and involved families and the wider community. In the modern world, only the deaths of famous people retain similar social dimensions and are public property.

Identity and the self in work

The idea that our identities are tied up with the work we do was central to Marx's ideas. The concept of *alienation* described a situation where workers lack control over work, are isolated from other individuals, do not own what they produce and do not fulfil themselves in work. This alienation is characteristic of capitalist societies where there is a complex division of labour and in which one group owns and controls capital. It is obvious that the work we do influences the sort of person we are; we spend many hours each day and many years of our lives working and working is, often, what produces the means to consume things.

Marx's view of the alienated worker is of a worker who is not fulfilled in work. Part of the solution for Marx lies in workers organizing in trade unions to challenge the power of those who own capital. There is, however, now evidence that trade unions are less powerful than in the past and that the nature of work and employment has changed. In particular, work is less secure and workers can no longer expect to have the same job for all their lives; they increasingly work in organizations where there is a stress on team work and where there are flatter structures, that is, there are less layers of workers with different status and prestige. Casey (1995) in a study of what she calls the Hephaestus Corporation looks at how self-identity is related to work. For Casey there is a corporate culture which produces designer employees. In particular, the corporate culture stresses teamwork in an environment in which there is less distance between managers and workers. The team is a two-edged thing: it rewards those who fit in, work hard, deliver and do not speak out, but it punishes those who do not fit in or deliver. In that sense, the team is like the image of an old-fashioned, Victorian family.

Employees often feel ambivalent about fitting in with this corporate culture. Often they have difficulty in fitting into it and then being different people when they are at home; corporate cultures often impinge on family life. What employees do is interesting. Some become defensive, others collude and a third group capitulates. Workers with a *defensive self* feel generally unhappy with work, will give examples of how badly they are treated but never fully revolt; they go in for small-scale resistance. For example, Case cites a worker, Jerry, who suffered a heart attack because of overwork says that what the company produces is the best but is critical of what work is doing to him. *Collusive workers* comply, are manipulable and often totally dedicated. Actually, they

compulsively collude and are unworried that the corporate culture is taking over their whole lives. Finally, the *capitulated worker* is one who is cynical about the company as a way of denying the total commitment which the new corporate culture requires.

❖ **Activity 20** ❖

Ask your teacher/lecturer how their identity and sense of self relate to the work they do.

Do they fit into the categories identified by Casey: defensive; collusive; capitulated?

The discussion of ethnic identity, of bodies and of the self in work raises the issue of whether we have moved from a society in which identity is based on social class to one in which identity is mainly based on status. Clarke and Saunders suggest (1991) that we now live in societies in which identity based on social class is less important than it used to be, noting the declining role of trade unions, as well as the decline in references to social class in party political broadcasts and manifestoes. Instead, they argue, social status becomes central for defining identity and as a basis for collective action. In other words, people increasingly define themselves by reference to status categories – gender, age, ethnicity – and these become the basis for collective action. As we will see later this leads to new form of politics, a politics of social movements.

The politics of culture and identity

Issues of culture and identity are often political ones. Who I am and which group I belong to are not neutral questions. They also have implications for others who are different from us and belong to different social groups. Some of the problems in the former Yugoslavia relate to issues of

ethnicity and what happens when people of different ethnic origin no longer want to occupy the same territory. For sociologists, these issues raise very important points.

❖ They force us to recognize that power feelings play a central role in who people think they are.

❖ They show how people who used to live peacefully together, can rapidly come into conflict with each other.

❖ They indicate the central role that violence can play in the lives of individuals and communities.

These negative aspects of culture and identity mean that we have to recognise that communities of people who accept the same culture and define their identity in terms of that culture may be violently opposed to outsiders and those who are different. When people nostalgically look back to a time when we had strong communities, they often ignore this dark side of community.

Edward Said extends this idea (1985). He shows how we get a lot of our cultural identity and derive much of the strength of our community by seeing other cultures and communities as negative. If we see ourselves as progressive, democratic and open, we define other cultures and communities as antiprogressive, antidemocratic and closed. As is discussed in Chapter 14, this is what happens in Western perceptions of religious fundamentalism.

In this section, however, we will concentrate on three issues:

❖ what we mean by élite, mass and popular culture and how that is a political debate

❖ the sociological study of subcultures as cultures of resistance

❖ the development of new social movements that stress the importance of identity and develop forms of political action that link people of different social class, gender groups, ethnic groups, geographical locations and ages.

Elite, mass, popular and folk culture

The debate about the national curriculum in schools is, in part, a debate about cultural value. There are certain books which you must read because they are quality books; they are part of what makes up what has been called élite or high culture. This includes, for instance, Shakespeare, Milton and Jane Austen, and excludes others, such as comics or rap music. The latter are part of mass or popular culture.

The distinctions between folk, élite, mass and popular culture are not easy to understand, partly because the terms are used imprecisely and in ways that sociologists do not accept. Elite culture is, as the name implies, the culture of a minority that has the power to define what it is. Such culture is seen to have value – something which is called aesthetic value. Certain words attach themselves to élite culture: tradition, skill, good, quality, beauty, form, content.

Mass and popular culture are what élite culture is *not*. They are culture for the majority. However, that majority is characterized in different ways by those who identify a mass culture and those who identify a folk or popular culture. There is a historical dimension here. As Peter Burke (1988) and others argue, popular culture has often been seen as a threat by those in power. Carnivals and fairs were cultures of the majority and often included overt criticism of those in power. Folk and popular culture came to be seen as particularly threatening when, in the seventeenth and eighteenth centuries, there was a movement of people from rural to urban areas. What was seen as acceptable in the country – regular fairs and carnivals where the powerful were mocked – was seen as uncivilized and dangerous in the city, and was also seen as a distraction from the discipline of hard work in factories. This distrust of what the élite saw as the masses was common; it included ideas that the masses were dirty, violent and sexually promiscuous and that crowds of any kind were dangerous. This view has continued to effect both sociological and non-sociological views of popular culture.

There are two dimensions to the élite/mass/folk/popular distinction:

❖ folk and popular culture as made *by* many people versus mass culture as made *for* many people.

❖ folk and popular culture as the culture of a number of organized communities versus mass culture as culture for a mass of mainly isolated individuals.

As we will see, there is also debate about how folk and popular culture becomes mass culture by being taken over by the culture industry. This relates to different forms of cultural production.

Table 2.3 below summarizes the distinctions between élite, mass and popular culture.

Table 2.3 The distinctions between élite, mass and popular culture

	Elite culture	Mass culture	Folk/popular culture
The culture	High quality	Low quality	High quality
	Produced for/ by a few	Mass produced/ reproducible/ commercial	Mass produced/ reproducible/ commercial
The society	Elite and masses	Atomized (i.e. made up of isolated individuals)	Organized/structured
		Few communities	Communities with links: class, gender, age, ethnicity, etc.
The individual	Not manipulable	Isolated/manipulable	Member of a community and therefore less manipulable

In Focus

◆

The War of the Worlds

The debate about folk, élite, mass and popular culture can be illustrated by referring to a notorious example of how the mass media can influence what people do. On 31 October 1938 (Halloween), Americans heard a report that the USA had been invaded by aliens from Mars. Some fled their homes and there was chaos and concern across the USA. What had happened was the radio broadcast of a play based on H.G. Wells' novel *The War of the Worlds*, directed by Orson Welles. The play had used what seemed to be a normal non-fiction format with regular interruptions for new items of explosions on Mars, strange things seen in the sky, landings of strange craft and sightings of hostile aliens. This news format, combined with fears of war and considerable interest in science fiction, led people to misinterpret fiction as fact. The worry was that the mass media could influence what people do and what they believe. This concern was increased as a result of the powerful role that propaganda had played in the rise to power of Hitler in Germany. Both these produced what has now been called the mass manipulative view of the mass media (see Chapter 12). In this view the audience for the mass media is isolated, atomized and therefore very easily to manipulate. The mass-manipulative model is, in fact, claiming that the folk and popular cultures developed by organized groups of people in communities is being undermined.

Whether we decide that we have mass or popular culture, it is important to recognize that, in the modern world, we have a culture industry. This may, as in the work of Herbert Marcuse (1964), be seen as repressive and as making people less able to criticize the society they are in, or it may be seen as potentially liberating and challenging. One example here is the extent to which the singer and actress Madonna successfully challenges gender stereotypes and images of femininity.

Virtually all cultural products are mass produced for a very big market. Whereas it is fairly certain that when John Milton wrote *Paradise Lost*, he knew many of the people who would read it and it was not produced in large numbers, a novel by Salman Rushdie is produced in huge numbers for a market with which he has little contact. Even popular culture is mass produced. For many Marxists, this means that cultural items are produced to make a profit rather than because they have a use or have some intrinsic value. There are two important conclusions for us:

❖ It is likely that even independent and small-scale cultural production will get taken into the mass market – this has, for example, been the fate of many independent record companies.

❖ Although many people think that mass production is a problem, that it devalues and waters down the quality of what is produced, sociologists are more likely to recognize the diversity of what is produced and be less worried about quality.

Before reading on, try Activity 21 below.

Subcultures of resistance

As we have seen, societies contain many and diverse cultures. Some of these are devalued and some defined as good, dominant and correct. The obvious issue for us now is how the dominant and the subordinate cultures relate to each other and in particular, how subcultures become ways of resisting the demands of dominant culture(s).

Much of the early sociological work on subcultures related to studies of crime and delinquency, particularly amongst those who were working class and who, in various ways, rejected society's norms and values (see Chapter 11). Subsequently, the idea of resistance has been applied to studies of the workplace, of gender, of ethnicity, of education and of politics generally. The idea of resistance – that people do not accept the situations they are in – is of vital

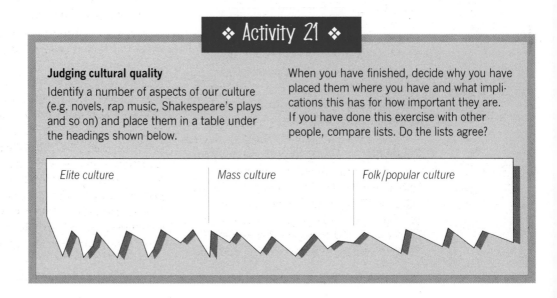

❖ Activity 21 ❖

Judging cultural quality

Identify a number of aspects of our culture (e.g. novels, rap music, Shakespeare's plays and so on) and place them in a table under the headings shown below.

When you have finished, decide why you have placed them where you have and what implications this has for how important they are. If you have done this exercise with other people, compare lists. Do the lists agree?

Elite culture	Mass culture	Folk/popular culture

importance for sociologists. It suggests that our behaviour is not just a product of the society in which we live and that power is not just something which dominant groups use to control subordinate ones.

Sociological studies of power tend to fall into two camps: those which see power as being monopolized by the few, as in Marxist studies of the state, and those which see power as more diffused and distributed. Perhaps the most interesting version of the second view is contained in the works of Michel Foucault (1977) who saw power as diffused – that there is a struggle between a disciplinary society in which people's lives and identities are continually being policed and the fact that people always resist this. For him, we live in a disciplinary but not a disciplined society. Part of this discipline is the way that identities are forced on us – criminal, sick, teacher – and become everything that we are; so, the role of teacher is seen to determine everything the individual does. For Foucault, part of living in the modern, disciplined world, is to resist being tied to one identity which takes you over. Power and resistance go together.

Studies of subcultural resistance in education (Willis 1977), work (Beynon 1975), criminality (Cohen 1955), identity formation (Sharpe 1994, Kettle and Hodges 1982), have a number of things in common:

❖ Subcultures *are* resistances. From the outside they may look odd, dangerous or meaningless, but a lot of what goes on within subcultures makes sense for those in them. As with most of social behaviour, subcultural behaviour has its own rules and rituals. In Beynon's study of car factories, he found sabotage including putting screws inside door panels which would then rattle. In one sense this is meaningless, but in another sense it is an expression of how workers felt about the alienating, boring and repetitive work they had to do.

❖ Subcultures include an element of style. Each one has its own culture, including styles of dress, language, behaviour in public and so on. This culture will be unlike that of the wider society, but may contain elements of that wider culture combined in new ways.

❖ Following from the style, the subculture excludes people from participation in 'normal' society – that is its point and members are actively eliminating themselves from the wider society by, for example, refusing to do well in school or wearing particular sorts of clothing.

❖ Finally, the subculture often gives people a status which is denied in the wider society.

Power is always resisted
Source: Fillingham (1993, p. 145)

If there is no one in charge of power, no one to blame, is there any way to resist power?

Yes, but resistance does not exist outside of the system of power relations. It is, instead, inherently part of the relation. In modern-day normalizing power relations, this tends very much to isolate and individuate resistance into a series of 'special cases' which do not allow generalization

In Focus
◆
Sociologists and subcultures

Studies of subcultural resistance by sociologists are often rejected by politicians on the basis that they are justifying something that may be violent and aggressive. There is, however, a difference between explaining something and justifying it. In the case of gang violence, sociologists have been able to explain what is going on through an understanding of the role of subcultures and how they are about resisting things that the wider society is demanding. This does not mean that sociologists are justifying gang violence. What the explanation may provide the basis for is doing something to limit or eradicate a problem. This is why there is sometimes a close relationship between what sociologists do and what those who develop and use social policy are doing.

New social movements and identity politics

A lot of what has been discussed in this chapter suggests that identity has, itself, become a political issue, that people now feel that they have a right to have a certain identity. Chapter 13 looks at sociological approaches to power and politics, but this section focuses on what has come to be called *identity politics* and the politics of new social movements.

Sociologists have always been interested in social movements, that is, movements which aim to pursue some common interest through collective actions. Aberle (1966) distinguishes between two pairs of movements.

❖ *Transformist/reformist movements* – These are groups which aim for change in society. *Transformist movements* tend to be revolutionary and desire total change in the social structure, whereas *reformist movements* are more likely to want small-scale changes to some part of society.

❖ *Redemptive/alternative movements* – Other movements argue for changes in how people live in society, rather than changes in society itself. *Redemptive movements* – many of which are religious – attempt to save people from a society which is seen as evil by requiring them to change their whole lives. *Alternative movements* only require change in one or two aspects of life, for example, eating habits.

As we will see in Chapter 6, *Stratification and differentiation*, social class divisions have always been extremely important in modern societies and a lot of political behaviour is related to social class location. Political parties provide examples of social movements based on social class location. However, many social movements have nothing to do with social class; these have been called *new social movements*. Not only are they more likely to develop from within particular social groups – rather than being imposed from above – but they tend to focus on particular issues. These include national identity (Welsh Nationalism), sexual identity (gay rights), citizenship rights (civil rights movements), animal rights (anti-vivisection movements), the environment (Greenpeace), peace movements (CND). Notice, the focus is on identity and on rights.

In Focus

◆

The Newbury bypass protest

The Newbury bypass protest had many of the features of a new social movement. It included people from a wide range of social locations – middle class, older people, young people, the unemployed. It was focused on a single issue, opposition to the building of a bypass. It involved people with a range of other political interests – anti-car, ecology/environment. It also involved forms of direct action – lying in front of contractors' vehicles, living in trees.

Two features of new social movements were not present in the Newbury bypass protest:

❖ acknowledging complex identities
❖ challenging experts.

Acknowledging complex identities

Foucault argued that identity is a complex thing. It is something that we all have and want, but it can also be a way that we are controlled and denied rights. Many new social movements are about asserting an identity which is often denied in the wider society. For example, gay and lesbian people not only assert their civil rights to live as gays and lesbians, but also argue that there is more to a person than just sexuality – a point which rarely has to be made about heterosexual people.

The same thing occurs for criminals – their whole lives are understood through the lens of criminality as if they cannot be perfectly normal in their family lives, their support for football teams or their diet.

Challenging experts

Many new social movements challenge the right of experts to decide what happens in society. Opposition to nuclear power includes a challenge to the information that experts provide and to the idea that such issues are purely technical ones.

More and more, the monopoly over truth that experts have claimed is being undermined. This has been the case, for example, with the scare over bovine spongiform encephalopathy (BSE or 'Mad Cow Disease'). Not only do experts disagree with each other, but ordinary people do not accept what experts say. This seems to be a feature of what some sociologists, e.g. Beck (1992), have called a 'risk society' – a society which seems to have increasing elements of risk. These risks are associated with the development of society itself and are often global, such as risks to the environment and to health. These risks challenge how we see experts and how much trust we place in them.

The uncertainties over the BSE crisis have shaken many people's faith in the reliability of 'experts'

Chapter summary

❖ This chapter has focused on what sociologists mean by 'culture' and 'identity', and the relationship between the two.

❖ Sociologists increasingly see identity as socially constructed and reject the idea that people are socialized into their identities passively.

❖ People get their identities from a range of social factors: their work, their ethnicity, what and how they consume.

❖ Sociologists recognize that the societies they study have a range of cultures and that one culture may be dominant. There are also likely to be a number of subcultures which allow people to resist the dominant culture.

❖ Sociologists who argue that we live in a postmodern society emphasize the importance of identity politics and the politics of new social movements.

Coursework

There are enormous possibilities for coursework in this area. In part this is because many of the issues associated with culture and identity are very interesting and very popular in the wider society. In addition, there are lots of issues that can be the basis for small-scale pieces of research or project work which can then form the basis for coursework essays.

❖ What do sociologists mean by an ethnic group? Identify the ethnic groups which make up British society?

❖ Why has there been an increase in concern with fitness and diet?

❖ What do sociologists mean by élite, mass and popular culture? Give examples of each of these.

❖ How do sociological approaches to socialization explain how people's behaviour, norms and values change over time?

❖ Identify three examples of subcultures. Why do people join subcultural groups?

❖ What do sociologists mean by new social movements? What do such movements do and what sorts of people join them?

Most of these allow you to do some small-scale research. For example, you could investigate the ethnic make-up of the your class or seminar group. To tackle the question on fitness and dietary regimes, you could ask people whether they diet, and if so, how. Also, you could use material from newspapers and television to tackle the question about new social movements and about élite, mass and popular culture.

You will find guidance on how to design questionnaires and interview schedules, how to administer them and how to interpret the data you get in Chapter 7, *Theory and methods*.

Stimulus–response question

Using the information from this chapter and the stimulus items below, answer the following questions:

1 In Item A, how does Debbie define her white identity?

2 In Item B, how does Denise define her black identity?

3 With reference to Item C and other sources, what do these statistics tell us about ethnicity in Britain?

4 Referring to all the items, what is meant by 'ethnic identity'?

5 With reference to Item D and other sources, assess whether Britain is characterized by multiculturalism or ethnic absolutism, i.e. the attempt to impose one culture on all people.

Item A One woman's experience

Debbie, a 19-year-old white woman of Italian and German parentage:

'I mean I went through a stage when I was 14 or 15 when I wanted to be black. I mean I wasn't really accepted by the English people and I wasn't really accepted by the black people because I was white. So I thought I could change my skin colour then I would be all right ... I used to cuss off white people. It didn't matter where they were from. It didn't matter if they were English or whatever – "Look at that white person".'

She came to reject this identification as black:

' ... they [her black friends] taught me the value of who I am – my German-ness, my Italian-ness. It's important, you have to have an identity, right. I mean it's hard for me, right, because English people say I am not white ...'

Source: Back 1996, pp. 137–8

Item C The British population: 1991

White	94.5
Black Caribbean	0.9
Black African	0.4
Black Other	0.3
Indian	1.5
Pakistani	0.9
Bangladeshi	0.3
Chinese	0.3

Source: Teague (1993)

Item B '... the way I am ...'

'Of course I am black. I can't escape it. But I'm not black in colour, very few people are actually black or close to it. It actually doesn't describe the way I look but it's the way I am. It is like I haven't actually felt discrimination myself, I don't feel it every day because I live in an area where there are a lot of black people, no, not me personally but I don't have to feel it every day to know that it is there – you know what I mean?'

Black girl, Denise, *quoted in* Back 1996, p. 146

Item D Changing cultures

'The vision of an ethnically pure nation sharing a common way of life has always been a myth – albeit a potent one. The great migrations of the post-war period have, however, openly challenged notions of unified, shared national cultures not only in Britain but across the Western world ... There is a growing multiplicity of religions, languages and ways of life within and across national borders ...

An influential way to express the growing cultural diversity of Western societies is to talk the language of *multiculturalism* – dividing up societies into neatly homogenous traditions or communities. This approach has serious limitations, not least because it shares many assumptions with the New Racism about fixed, immutable differences between ethnicities ...

The realities of contemporary life are more interesting than proponents of *'ethnic absolutism'* contend; what is striking are the variety of [identities] and the complex patterns of cultural change currently emerging ...

Examples of cultural change and hybridity [i.e. mixing of cultures] are important because they illustrate the ways that identities are actively constituted and negotiated ... [there] has been the revival (perhaps redefinition would be a better word) of local identities and ethnic differences ... [this] ethnic revival can in part, be understood as a defensive response on the part of migrants in the face of discrimination and disadvantage ... the ethnic revival is [also] a symptom of the greater awareness of difference which springs from increased contact between ways of life and the growing pace of cultural change ... Hybridity is one response to these developments but just as significant are the ways people attempt to deal with problems of identity by proclaiming absolute, fixed, ethnicities.'

Source: Bilton *et al.* 1996, pp. 257–8

Essay questions

1 What do sociologists mean by socialization? How far do people resist and negotiate the processes of socialization?

2 What are the main difference between mass, élite, popular and folk culture? Illustrate your answer with examples of each.

3 What does Stuart Hall mean by 'new ethnicities'?

4 'Gender identity is not as simple as it seems.' Discuss with reference to *EITHER:*

 (a) ethnomethodological studies of gender, *OR*

 (b) sociological studies of femininity and masculinity.

Further reading

This is a new area of sociology and a new area for many syllabuses. That means that there is, as yet, no basic textbook which covers all the issues associated with culture and identity. The most recently published book on the subject is:

Taylor, P. (1997) *Investigating Culture and Identity*, London: Collins Educational.

Some of the most interesting material is found in articles. In *Sociology Review* you will find the following:

Craib, I. (1994) 'Going to pieces or getting it together: Giddens and the sociology of the self', *Sociology Review*, November, pp. 12–15.

Hides, S. (1995) 'Consuming identities', *Sociology Review*, November, pp. 30–3.

Sugrue, B. and Taylor, C. (1996) 'Cultures and identities', *Sociology Review*, February, pp. 10–13.

Two books that are good on particular aspects of this subject are:

Goffman, E. (1969) *The Presentation of Self in Everyday Life*, Harmondsworth: Penguin.

Kessler, S. J. and McKenna, W. (1978) *Gender: An Ethnomethodological Approach*, New York: Wiley.

Chapter 3

Families and households

❖ Preview

In this chapter we shall be looking at:

❖ what is meant by the term 'family'

❖ why we have families

❖ whether the family is essential for social stability

❖ comparative approaches to the study of family and marriage

❖ whether the term 'household' is more relevant to the diverse way people live in modern societies

❖ sociological theories of the family

❖ contemporary trends in marriage, families and households

❖ relationships between women, children and men in family settings

❖ the future of personal relationships, families and households.

❖ Introduction

The previous chapter deals with issues of self and personal identity focusing on the question, 'Who am I?' A very important part of our identity is formed within our family. Who we are is closely bound up with our upbringing within families and households.

❖ Activity 1 ❖

Working either in pairs or on your own, briefly answer the following questions:

• Why do human societies have families?

• What is a family?

• What is a household?

• Why do you think some people are critical of the family?

• Do you think the family is declining or in crisis?

Compare and discuss your answers.

What is the family?

The family is a social institution that affects all our lives at the deepest personal level. Our experience of such a personal and private institution means that objective academic study is difficult. Bear this in mind as you work through this chapter.

Some sociologists have divided the modern social world into the public and the private, a distinction that was less in evidence in former times. The family is the social institution that is most often associated with the private world, so when people refer to an 'invasion of privacy' it is often associated with their home and family life.

However, it needs to be noted that family life is not always regarded as private. There are many instances where the family becomes an area of public concern. For example, child abuse and single-parent families have become part of a public debate in recent years. Sometimes the boundaries between the private and public worlds are blurred, as in those cases where disruptive behaviour of pupils in schools is linked to bad parenting.

The universality of 'family' experience

Why do we have families? As with many areas of sociology, the first response might be one of common sense – families are natural, human beings need families – but being good, tenacious sociologists, we continue to ask 'Why?' The next response in this imaginary dialogue might be that human beings need to raise children and have sexual relationships in a stable setting. However, the case studies in the *In Focus* show that there is in fact a range and diversity of options available throughout the world. These options lead us to issues of how we might define 'family'. The family can be defined as a group of people related by blood, marriage (or equivalent option such as cohabitation), or adoption, occupying the same household who share the main responsibility for reproduction and caring for its members.

❖ Activity 2 ❖

Read the article below (see *In Focus*) and then think of some more examples of:

- private aspects of families
- public aspects of families
- recent examples where the public and private boundaries are blurred.

In Focus

◆

Children at risk?

'It is common sense that young children left unsupervised, especially at night, are vulnerable and at risk. If parents are unable or unwilling to protect them, then 'society' must step in. We get calls to our charity from parents of children bullied by gangs of 8- and 9-year-olds in their own neighbourhoods. These parents keep their own children in but say that the other children are out until all hours and are out of control.

I have seen children out at night on Queensway in London grabbing handbags from unwary foreign visitors and have myself been targeted by 8-year-olds who have attempted to pickpocket me at 10 p.m. Some of these children have been recruited by drug dealers and thieves. They are the victims of neglect and for the rest of us to pretend it isn't happening and to ignore the problem is intolerable in a caring society.'

(Dr) Michele Elliott, Director, Kidscape
(Letter to the Editor, *The Guardian*, 5 June 1996)

Sociologists move further than the above definition and raise issues of classification by reference to types, forms and structure of families such as the nuclear family, extended family, reconstituted and single-parent family. So definitions of 'the family' can range from the very broad to the more scientific and specific classifications of family type.

The majority of the world's population experience a form of family life for most of their lives but this can involve a wide variety of options (see *In Focus* below).

❖ Activity 3 ❖

Take each of the examples in the *In Focus* below and explain why such behaviour patterns might not be approved of or seen as strange in your own society. Some people might see such practices as 'unnatural'. Why?

As the *In Focus* shows, the family can be an extremely complex and diverse phenomenon and the authors question whether one particular form or type of family (in the case of our culture often taken to be the nuclear family, comprising parents and children) is the only natural or desirable way to live within our personal relationships. Our lives within families and households can involve a variety of experiences and attitudes ranging from the highly positive to the highly negative.

Many 'experts' including psychologists and sociologists claim that our experiences in families and households makes us what we are in the deepest possible sense. Loss of, or breakdown within, our family can cause lifelong personal problems. The family is an institution of great depth and complexity both within society and in its relation to ourselves personally.

Sociologists hold a variety of views on the family ranging from positive to negative.

Positive views

❖ The family is a haven in a heartless world.

❖ The family is like a warm bath that we can sink into at the end of the day.

❖ The family benefits children, husbands and wives.

❖ The family is the most basic and vital institution of society.

❖ In an increasingly impersonal world, the family gives a sense of belonging and identity.

In Focus

◆

A comparative perspective on family and marriage

❖ In the Toda culture of southern India, a woman may be simultaneously married to several men. Fatherhood is not always connected with biology: any husband may establish paternity by presenting a pregnant woman with a toy bow and arrow.

❖ In some Western societies, such as Britain and America, some couples have an 'open marriage' where each partner may have sexual relationships with a number of other people.

❖ The Balinese of Indonesia permit twins to marry each other because they believe that twins have already been intimate in the womb.

❖ In Britain a number of gay couples have applied to adopt and raise children.

❖ In the Banaro culture of New Guinea, the husband is forbidden to have intercourse with his wife until she has borne a child by another man chosen for that purpose. Once the wife has proved that she can bear children, the husband is allowed to have sexual relations with her.

Source: Leslie and Korman (1989), pp. 15, 30, 39

Negative views

❖ The family is a source of tension and conflict.

❖ The family exploits women and represses children.

❖ The family is inward looking and cares only for its own members.

❖ The family is a violent institution and the main victims are women and children.

Perspectives on the family

Broadly three sociological stances on the family can be identified:

❖ traditional

❖ liberal

❖ antifamily.

Traditional

Such an approach refers to the 'Sociology of the Family'. In this context 'the family' often implies the stereotypical nuclear family of bread-winning husband, dependent wife and children. This view is supported by traditional functionalist perspectives such as those of Parsons (1959) (see p. 72) and, more recently, of the New Right (see p. 95). Traditional Marxist approaches influenced by Engels (see p. 75), tend to revolve around the nuclear family model. Moralists and Conservative politicians attack single parents and emphasize the necessity of marriage and stable parenthood for the well-being of children and for the good of society as a whole. The mass media, particularly advertising, often portrays a 'cereal packet' image of stereotypical nuclear families.

❖ Activity 4 ❖

A small piece of research

Use the following descriptions of households as the basis of a survey. Ask a variety of people (friends, relatives) to rank each in the terms of their closest correspondence to a family. You can then construct tables or graphs to highlight similarities or differences. You can take the work further by organizing follow-up interviews, asking respondents the reasons for their ranking. If a wide age range and social background is included in your survey you can make comparisons, for example, do older people have more rigid attitudes than younger people? Women compared to men? Working class compared to middle class? If possible, include a variety of ethnic groups to add another comparative dimension. This could be developed into a more detailed survey for eventual submission as a coursework project concerning people's ideas about families (see Chapter 7, *Theory and methods*).

Please rank the following households in order of their closest correspondence to a family. Rank the closest as 1, the next closest as 2, and so on.

A an elderly widow living alone

B a remarried divorcee, her husband and children from their former marriages

C a homosexual couple with adopted children

D a married couple whose adult children have left home

E a single parent with two dependent children

F a married couple with dependent children

G an unrelated group of friends/students who live together

H a divorcee living alone

J an unmarried couple with two dependent children

K a young person living alone.

Give reasons in each case.

Are there any central themes that emerge concerning dominant views of what a family is? For example, how important is the role of marriage or having children within the relationships accepted as families?

Liberal

This approach emphasizes the variety of different family forms and structures and the diversity of ways in which people live together. The range of family types includes extended, nuclear, single-parent, reconstituted or homosexual families, cohabiting parents and so on. Diversity is seen as desirable and a feature of an open, tolerant, pluralistic society. To focus on one type as more desirable or more natural than any other (as in the traditional approach above) is disapproved of.

The antifamily perspective

This sees the traditional and liberal perspectives, which emphasize 'family' or 'families', as ideological and in Barrett and McIntosh's terms, 'antisocial' (1982). They refer to *familial ideology*: a set of ideas and beliefs centring around the supposed ideal or naturalness of the nuclear family in Western societies. This ostracizes large numbers of people who may not wish to live in a conventional family or who may have alternatives to heterosexual or monogamous relationships. Such relationships or simply living alone, as many do, is stigmatized. Instead of one dominant type or a diversity of family types, it is argued that there is a diversity in the way people live their personal lives and all should be equally acceptable. This view suggests that the preferred term for the study of this area is 'households'.

Radical feminism supports this approach. One of the key debates concerns patriarchy (see p. 76), and whether men and women can live together in a form of family that does not oppress women. The antifamily perspective denies this. Any kind of family unit inevitably exploits women and favours men. Some of these views go even further and say that all relationships of any kind between men and women involve men's gain and women's loss (for further development of these points see the section on feminist perspectives, pp. 75–84).

❖ Activity 5 ❖

Which of the three stances seems most plausible to you? Briefly give reasons.

Comparative sociological approaches

Emile Durkheim, a key figure in the development of sociology, was a strong advocate of the comparative method in sociology (1938). Making a comparison of groups within societies, such as between the middle and working classes or women and men, is a useful research tool. Another is to compare different societies, because this helps to avoid *ethnocentrism*, the placing of your own group or society at the centre of explanation, thereby implying that other groups or cultures are in some way inferior to your own.

The *In Focus* on p. 64 offers some insight into different forms and structures of family and household and indicates the degree of diversity to be found in lifestyle and personal relationships both historically and geographically. Historians provide evidence for this and anthropological studies highlight the variety of family forms and ways of having personal relationships in non-industrial cultures and societies.

A world trend to monogamy and nuclear family patterns?

George Peter Murdock

Murdock raised the issue of such a trend in the 1940s as a conclusion to his study of 250 societies throughout the world (1949), covering a wide range of types from tribal to industrial. He found that the family was a universal institution, with the monogamous nuclear family the dominant type, and that this would increasingly be the option for most people in most world societies.

William J. Goode

In *World Revolution and Family Patterns*, Goode (1963), an American sociologist, echoes the views of Murdock. Industrialization and modernizing influences on a world scale were behind the trend. Forms of polygamous (marriage to several partners) relationships and large networks of kin and extended families were only appropriate for agricultural societies where labour intensive work was carried out, often at a subsistence level. However, it needs to be noted that William Goode was an American sociologist writing about such issues in the 1950s when functionalism was dominant in American sociology. A key influence was Talcott Parsons. Parsons' work (1959) suggested that the evolution of the family towards the stereotypical nuclear model would best 'fit' the needs of an advanced industrial society that required geographical and social mobility among its population (see Fig. 3.1 below).

Giddens and changes in family patterns worldwide

Giddens (1993) supports the views above, seeing such changes in family structure occurring in most parts of the world as a result of the impact of modern industry and urban life. He summarizes the trends as follows:

1 the *breakdown of clans* and *corporate kin groups* as exampled in the Chinese Tsu system, which was broken up when the Chinese communists came to power

2 the move towards *individualism* and *romantic love*, leading to free choice of spouse rather than an arranged marriage controlled by the extended family

3 *increased freedom for women* in choosing a husband and having power within the family, driven by women's increased participation in the labour market

4 the *decline in the importance of kin networks* as a basis for marital choice, either outside the immediate clan (exogamy) or within the immediate clan (endogamy)

5 *greater sexual freedom* in societies which once were repressive – This has not all been one way, however. Religious fundamentalism has reversed this trend in some societies such as Iran (in the late 1970s) and, more recently, among the Christian, Right-influenced 'moral majority' in the USA. In the latter case, a number of young Americans are taking virginity pledges until marriage.

6 the *development of children's rights* in societies where traditionally they had none and could be liable to exploitation and abuse – In some societies arranged child marriages were common. Such practices are gradually disappearing.

The above factors are some indication of tendencies that are leading to the globalization of Western marriage and family patterns, but Giddens admits that most societies still have extended families (see the definition in the *In Focus* on the next page) as the norm and there is still much

Figure 3.1
The functionalist view of the evolving family

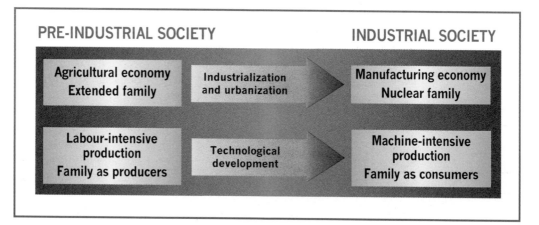

PRE-INDUSTRIAL SOCIETY   INDUSTRIAL SOCIETY

Agricultural economy
Extended family

Industrialization and urbanization

Manufacturing economy
Nuclear family

Labour-intensive production
Family as producers

Technological development

Machine-intensive production
Family as consumers

In Focus

◆

The extended family – a declining family type?

An extended family is defined as more than two generations living in the same house. So, as well as parents and children, other older relatives such as grandparents occupy the same residence. In modern industrialized societies this is uncommon, but if other relatives live nearby and are closely involved with the nuclear family (for example, childminding or shopping), this is now referred to as the modified extended family. Such a family structure was identified in Wilmott and Young's classic study of a working-class community in the 1950s.

Source: Wilmott and Young (1961)

❖ Activity 6 ❖

How closely involved have your grandparents been in your family? For example, did they look after you when you were young? If so, what were the reasons for this?

Give other examples of the involvement of your extended family.

Compare your experiences with those of others.

This could develop into a survey focusing on whether the extended family still plays a key role in people's lives.

What image is presented in the photo below?

evidence of diversity. Where poverty still exists, extended families are still important for support and in Britain grandparents still have involvement through childminding when both parents are working. Hollinger and Haller (1990) point to the rejuvenation of the extended family in Poland as a result of the increased numbers of parents of both sexes going out to work.

A recent study (Devine 1992) returned to the same area of London as studied by Wilmott and Young in the 1950s. It challenges several assumptions about the decline of the family network. The area is still predominantly working-class and, as expected, there have been some changes, particularly concerning more unstable employment, more dual earner households, higher divorce rates and single-parent households. However, what has not changed significantly since the 1950s is kin contact and association; there is still much evidence of the importance of the extended family.

The effects of industrialization and urbanization on the family

'Sociologists in particular argued that, in pre-industrial societies, the dominant household form had contained an extended family, often involving three co-resident generations, and that the 'modern' family, characterized by a nuclear family household structure, family limitation, the spacing of children, and population mobility, was the product of Industrialization.' (Hareven 1994, p. 14)

Figure 3.2
The Marxist view of
the evolving family

	Agricultural revolution →	Industrial revolution →	Political revolution →	
	Primitive	Feudalism	Capitalism	Socialism
Production	Hunter–gatherer bands	Landowners and serfs	Owners and workers	Common ownership
Stratification	Classless society	Aristocracy & peasantry	Bourgeoisie & proletariat	Classless society
Authority	Matriarchy	Patriarchy	Patriarchy	Equality
Context of reproduction	Group marriage	Extended family	Nuclear family	Community family

As a family historian, Hareven takes issue with the historical accuracy of traditional sociological views which have developed from the evolutionary perspective of early sociologists going back to Durkheim. A similar view is contained in the Marxist perspective as espoused by Engels in *The Origin of the Family, Private Property and the State* (1884/1985).

The child as miniature adult A portrait of a boy aged 4 and a girl aged 3, with a small dog, by Hendrick Munnichhoven (c. 1630–64)

Rafael Valls Gallery, London/Bridgman Art Library, London

He linked the emergence of the modern nuclear household and the exploited housewife role to the development of capitalism. Such processes are linked to the family, as shown in Fig. 3.2 above.

Support for the traditional evolutionary views

Studies of the historically changing nature of childhood, such as that of the French historian Phillipe Ariès, have indirectly supported the idea of key changes in family life taking place over time. Ariès suggests that the modern concept of 'childhood' is different from its previous context, when children were, in effect, miniature adults who worked with and alongside adults from an early age. This is similar to much that occurs in Third World countries today. So the idea that childrearing involves years of nurturing (usually by the mother at home) did not really exist. People lived in larger-group households which often contained related and unrelated occupants and children were a part of this more fluid arrangement.

The 'invention' of childhood was first exposed by Philippe Ariès, a French demographer and historian. His classic study, *Centuries of Childhood* (Ariès 1960/1973), changed the way many thought about children, although many of its lessons appear not to have filtered through to a wider public. It makes interesting reading for those who hark back to a golden age of childish innocence, and condemn the horrors and 'new sexuality' of modern children.

Aries shows how, in medieval days, 5-year-olds would go to school armed, handing in their swords or sticks before lessons; and how their brothers of 10 were sexually active ... the diaries of Henry IV's physician, Heroard, on the young life of Louis XIII, show how the future king would have the court in fits by lifting his robe, playing with himself and making everyone file past to kiss his penis. He was 1 year old. This was not a quirk of royalty, but an earthy attitude prevalent through society.

For many centuries, in a society described as 'carnival', children would fight, steal, copulate, learn, travel, find homes and work, just as small adults; free of protection, certainly, but also free of the constraints of adult control which, as time went on, took increasing territory from them. During the seventeenth century, two things changed the perception of children: the Jesuits taught them guilt, seeing them as characters who could be winnable for God ('give me the child and I'll give you the man'), while in art and the rest of society, parents were beginning to venerate the 'childish things' and enjoy their children as something akin to toys. The idea of an age of innocence had arrived. It grew fast, benefiting children through safety but robbing them of long-held traditional freedoms, until, by the Victorian age, the idea had arrived that children should be seen and not heard.

Source: adapted from *The Observer*, 9 June 1996

❖ Activity 7 ❖

'Children today are far worse than they have ever been'. Use the extract above to provide a counter-argument to this view of childhood in the past and present.

Adult and child relationships began to change in Britain during the nineteenth century when legislation prevented child labour in industry. The 1870 Forster Education Act introduced compulsory state schooling which meant children became more dependent on adults and, in particular, their parents. Correspondingly, legislation restricted women's working opportunities so, increasingly, women stayed at home as housewives and mothers, supported by a bread-winning male – the basis of the twentieth century stereotypical nuclear family household.

Laslett: Arguments against the evolutionary perspective

Peter Laslett (1972) was one of the first to question 'conventional wisdom' concerning family and household life in former times. His Cambridge Family History Group carried out detailed demographic studies of several European countries in earlier centuries, using historical documentary records such as parish registers and population census data. It was found that, contrary to the traditional sociological view, the extended family had not been a dominant household type in the past. This was found to be particularly true for Western Europe, where the nuclear family household was more prevalent and the size of households on average was not significantly different from ours today. Laslett points out that part of the explanation for this was a high mortality rate and low average life expectancy, which meant that older relatives often died prematurely. Another factor, as highlighted by the historian Alan McFarlane (1978), was the nature of ownership, together with property and land inheritance, which, through primogeniture, passed on to the eldest son. This meant that in several parts of Europe, including England, the extended family and wider kin networks, centred on *communal* inheritance of property, were less important.

Wally Secombe (1992) has recently taken issue with some of the earlier historical studies such as Laslett's, mainly because of the somewhat oversimplified picture of family life presented. Secombe argues that European family structures have been subject to greater changes and diversity than is often supposed and that the state of 'flux' and instability highlighted in the modern context is nothing new. He sees what we now refer to as the 'traditional family' as a recent invention; the product of a period of exceptional stability and uniformity in family relations that lasted up to and including the 1950s. We may now have returned to a more 'normal' situation where variability and diversity in family structures prevail.

Michael Anderson: The extended family in industrial society

Another perspective from historical study comes from Michael Anderson (1981) who carried out a study of a Lancashire textile area in the nineteenth century. He found that extended family households were common in working-class communities, one reason for this being that low wages, insecurity and poverty meant that it was advantageous for all family members to live together for support. For example, older members could look after the young who, in turn, could look after the elderly. Anderson found households sometimes taking in lodgers and orphans who also contributed, to mutual benefit.

Community studies of working-class neighbourhoods in the twentieth century have echoed Anderson's findings concerning extended families. Peter Wilmott and Michael Young's famous study (1961)

❖ Activity 8 ❖

In the nineteenth century there were large numbers of single-parent households. What do you think was the most likely cause then as compared to single-parent families today?

of Bethnal Green in East London in the 1950s, Dennis *et al.*'s study (1956) of a Yorkshire mining village and Jeremy Tunstall's study (1962) of Hull trawler men in the 1960s all featured similar portraits of extended family life and support.

More recently, there is clear evidence of the importance of extended families in ethnic minority communities, particularly those originating from South Asia. Cultural and religious factors underpin the extended family but there are also similar features to those found in Anderson's work. These concern the mutual economic benefits to extended family members among groups on low incomes and in insecure employment. An added dimension for ethnic minorities is the experience of racism, which can make a larger extended family network more important in terms of support and protection. Hareven (1994) has suggested that the extended family network can be functional for an industrial society, as work opportunities can be found through relatives and a network of kin can be the basis of a stable workforce.

Rather than industrialization leading to changes in family structures, Harris (1983) has suggested that the nature of inheritance based on primogeniture (to the first-born son), in societies such as Britain, actually provided the impetus for industrialization. Any subsequent offspring had to survive independently, thus promoting a drive to create wealth through industry along with accompanying geographical and social mobility.

It may be argued that increased prosperity for many in the second part of the twentieth century has meant that the nuclear family has become the dominant form of household. Evidence supports this, but the studies cited above can be used to counteract the traditional sociological view which connects the process of industrialization to the development of the nuclear family in a simple and straightforward sense. Detailed historical evidence has been a useful corrective to such an oversimplified evolutionary approach. It can also be noted that a form of extended family is still evident in a number of communities and that the modified extended family, where members occupy separate residences but have regular contact, is experienced by many.

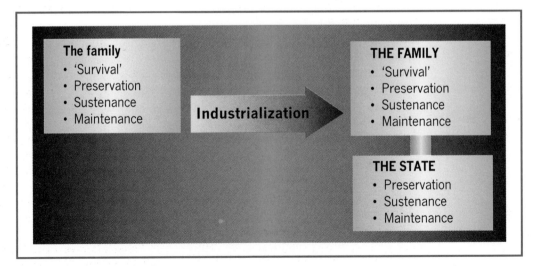

❖ Activity 9 ❖

Summarize the arguments for and against the view that industrialization led to the demise of the extended family and the development of the nuclear family.

Functionalist sociological approaches

The functionalist approach is most often associated with American sociology and one figure in particular, Talcott Parsons (1902–79), formerly a Professor of Sociology at Harvard University. Functionalists see the family as the basic social unit and the core institution of society. Functionalist sociologists offer the most positive view of the family within society. Their view can be linked to the more recent approaches of the New Right (see p. 95), particularly with their emphasis on the benefits to society of the stereotypical nuclear family of married parents raising children. Other theoretical perspectives are more negative about the emphasis on this family type.

Our family of origin influences us in many ways, e.g. by:

❖ placing us in an economic and class structure

❖ governing our religious affiliation and political allegiance

❖ affecting how long we remain in the education system.

Parsons' work on the family can be linked with evolutionary approaches of earlier sociologists, connecting industrialization with social changes leading to the nuclear family (see Fig. 3.3). Parsons was influenced by P.I. Sorokin (1959), one of the first sociologists to make a connection between urban life, modern industry and a smaller family unit. Parsons then argued that the nuclear family best 'fits' the needs of an advanced industrial society which requires a geographically and socially

Figure 3.3
Changing functions of the family

The family	Industrialization	THE FAMILY
• 'Survival' • Preservation • Sustenance • Maintenance		• 'Survival' • Preservation • Sustenance • Maintenance

THE STATE
• Preservation
• Sustenance
• Maintenance

mobile workforce. The extended family prevented such mobility. Another emphasis was on the male as breadwinner with a dependent wife and children. Parsons assumed differences between men and women which accepted that men were better able to cope with their role as a breadwinner in the expressive, rational world of work and women as being better in the affective, emotional, caring sphere which home-making and childrearing required.

Parsons also pointed to the changing functions of the family as society advanced, suggesting that the modern nuclear family has been stripped of many of its former functions. Traditional functions of the family had been:

❖ reproduction – bearing children

❖ stable sexual relations within monogamous partnerships

❖ economic maintenance – providing necessities for all family members, i.e. food, clothing and shelter

❖ welfare – looking after and taking care of all family members 'from the cradle to the grave'

❖ socialization and education of the young

❖ a sense of identity and belonging within stable communities.

With the rise of state welfare systems, schooling and other features related to modernization, the family now has to fulfil fewer functions for its members (see Fig. 3.3). Parsons identified two broad remaining functions:

❖ *primary socialization of children* – Children are raised in their early years by parents who pass on core norms and values, and help them learn to distinguish right from wrong. However, their future lives at work and in the economic sphere are dependent on years of schooling.

❖ *stabilization of adult personalities* – This accords with the 'warm bath' theory espoused by a number of sociologists. According to this view, the family provides a haven in a heartless world which is symptomized by demanding work, pressures from bosses, striving for

promotion and other features of the 'rat race'. In such a world, the family can provide an individual with a reason for living and a sense of belonging and purpose. Increased impersonality at work means that one can only be oneself within the family. In an increasingly stressful and impersonal world, the family becomes the main (and only?) source of satisfaction and self-fulfilment.

The isolated and private nuclear family?

The functionalist approach to the family presents an image of the family which involves:

❖ isolation from wider kinship groups

❖ ideas concerning rising incomes and standards of living

❖ the support for the nuclear family from the welfare state

❖ distance from kin because of the mobility required by labour markets in industrial societies

❖ the provision of childcare by non-family agencies such as playgroups, nurseries and eventually school.

Associated with the view that the family is isolated is that of the privatization of the family. This presents the modern family as a home-centred, inward-looking unit which has little contact with neighbours and community. Those who were once work-mates have now become colleagues, a more neutral relationship, and the dominant emotional and affective focus becomes the family. The private world is centred on the home and, for many, their world revolves around this. A survey of car workers in the 1960s presaged this, quoting from one respondent who said, 'my family is my hobby' (Goldthorpe *et al.* 1968). Similarly, in the 1980s, homes were described by the British Prime Minister, Margaret Thatcher, as 'entertainment centres' and a 'little bit of heaven here on earth'.

Today's houses are full of products such as TVs, videos, CD players, multi-media computers and similar gadgetry which means that the family need never go out for entertainment, as they did in the past. Fewer adult males visit pubs regularly, as drinking and eating have increasingly become home-based activities. Home improvement and DIY indicate further dimensions of the 'privatized' family.

❖ Activity 10 ❖

Consider some of the views presented above and compare them to your own homes and families.

- Are families today more private?
- Add further examples to illustrate the private nature of the home.
- What are (a) the positive and (b) the negative aspects of the 'privatized' family?

Ronald Fletcher

Ronald Fletcher, a British sociologist who was broadly in agreement with the functionalist approach, disagreed with the view that the functions of the family in advanced societies had diminished (1966). He argued that, if anything, they had increased.

He listed the following modern functions of the family:

❖ regulating sexual behaviour

❖ providing a responsible basis for procreation and the rearing of children

❖ caring for dependent members, whether young or old

❖ acting as the earliest and most powerful socializing agency

❖ teaching family members the roles they will play in society, and helping them to accept the rights, duties and obligations linked to those roles.

Such functions were still a part of family life which meant that the family was still a core social institution.

Evaluation of functionalist approaches

Most sociologists accept that social institutions such as the family are interdependent on other social institutions, such as the education system, and that these institutions have purposes for human life. In this sense, most sociology is 'functionalist'. However, disagreement can occur over the nature of the function of particular social institutions and, more importantly, over the functionalist assumption that such functions work to preserve stability and equilibrium in the wider social system.

Parsons' critics see his view of the family as predominantly white and middle class, favouring males and ignoring the female perspective. They argue that Parsons assumes housewives and mothers are content with their lot, an issue that has been a target of feminist writings for a number of years. His family model was also set in the context of mid-twentieth century America, implying that such an institution, and key norms and values of American society, were a desirable goal for all. Issues of rising divorce rates and marital instability were not a part of functionalist theorizing, except to refer to such issues as 'dysfunctional', which is hardly a satisfactory explanation. Proponents of diversity in family forms and structures point to the variety of family types that exist; the stereotypical nuclear family being only one option that people may choose to live by.

However, despite such criticisms there are some who would suggest that a form of nuclear family is the dominant family structure. Robert Chester (1985) puts forward the idea of the 'neo-conventional family' which takes into account working wives and mothers and is, in effect, a modified version of the nuclear family. When most people's life course or biography is examined, nuclear family residence is a significant proportion of a lifetime.

Marxist approaches to the family

Early Marxist work: Engels

The *Origin of the Family, Private Property and the State*, was first published not long after Karl Marx's death in 1883, by his lifelong friend and collaborator, Friedrich Engels. Engels presented what is now regarded as the first Marxist account linking the evolution of the bourgeois nuclear family with a breadwinner male wage slave, dependent wife and children. Engels followed up Marx's review of a work by Lewis Henry Morgan (1963), which presented an evolutionary view of changes in society from the prehistoric era to modern times. Morgan's approach was to link economic and technological changes to changes in family and sexual relationships. Engels suggests that early human beings lived as hunter gatherers based on cooperation. There was no concept of property, everyone shared everything. Correspondingly, there was no need to establish paternity of children. Sexual relations were promiscuous and women were more powerful than men, a matriarchal society.

The development of property ownership through agriculture led to the need to establish paternity of children so that inheritance rights could be established. This shifted the balance of power from women to men and led to a patriarchal system. Industrialization, the development of capitalism and its associated technologies of machine production meant that men were now required in the workplace and became exploited wage slaves. Women were forced into the home to look after children for longer periods of time. The male children would be raised as the next generation of wage slaves. Thus women had become homemakers and carers rather than workers alongside men. In this sense, capitalism led to the exploitation and oppression of women in the home. Their unpaid labour in serving their wage slave husbands enabled capitalism to make greater profits.

Marxist-feminism

Engels' work is today viewed as an early version of Marxist-feminism which sees the overthrow of capitalism as necessary to create equality between women and men. More recently, some feminists (Hartmann 1981) have objected to the dominance of Marxism over feminism in this approach.

Feminist Marxists attempt to redress this imbalance by suggesting that the family under capitalism is an ideological as well as an economically exploitative institution, that it passes on pro-capitalist values through the generations of family members. Such values include individualism, competitiveness and what is expected of a woman in terms of housewifery and motherhood – the 'ideal' home with 'perfect' children and so on.

The key aspect of Marxist-feminism is that the overthrow of capitalism and the establishment of a socialist society will result in a changed family structure where State involvement in the provision of childcare will result in equality for women alongside men in the economic sphere.

Women as a reserve army of labour

A more recent addition to Marxist-feminist perspectives on family life is the recognition that women not only provide domestic labour and childrearing in support of capitalism, but are also a readily available source of cheap and exploitable labour. The constraints of domestic and childcare activities in terms of time and availability mean that many women have to take whatever is on offer, regardless of their talents and abilities. So low-paid work which offers part-time and/or flexible hours is the only option for many. Since the 1950s, the dramatic expansion of service and distributive industries has resulted in a large female labour force, many of them married women receiving low pay in such occupations as shopwork.

❖ Activity 11 ❖

Give examples of jobs that wives and mothers take up which illustrate the previous section. Conduct research among your family, friends and acquaintances to investigate whether women are forced to accept whatever is on offer, often resulting in low-paid, low-status employment.

Socialist feminists

Socialist feminists have recognized some of the weaknesses of Marxist versions of feminism, particularly the over-concentration on capitalism as the sole source of women's oppression. They are unconvinced that the overthrow of capitalism will create a society and family structure where women and men are equal. Nickie Charles (1993) reviewed studies of the USSR carried out prior to its break up and found that women had made gains such as paid maternity leave and workplace childcare but that, overall, they were far from equal with men. Apart from this, empirical studies of communist or socialist societies, such as Hilda Scott's study (1976) of women in socialist Czechoslovakia, showed the persistence of inequalities between women and men in the wider society as well as in the context of the family, with most domestic labour and childcare being carried out by women.

Socialist feminists would use such evidence to point to the inadequacy of the Marxist view, i.e. that under socialism men and women would be equal. They highlight the concept of patriarchy where men have power and authority in all walks of life. As a result, they do see the need for the ending of capitalism to help create equality, but also stress that in the personal sphere of relationships between women and men, patriarchy needs to be confronted and challenged. In this sense, as some feminists have said, 'the personal is the political' – i.e. it is no good having a socialist society where women and men are equal at the 'Macro' level of politics and work, (for example, there being equal numbers of female to male politicians or managers) if, at the personal level, men continue to dominate and exploit women in the home and in personal relationships generally (see *In Focus*).

Socialist feminists advocate a two-pronged attack on capitalism and patriarchy in order to bring about real fairness and justice for women. They point out that the relationship between capitalism and patriarchy is a complex and interdependent one which needs to be recognized by all feminists.

❖ Activity 12 ❖

What image of traditional male attitudes is presented here?

In Focus

◆

'Husband told to avoid wife'

'A husband who told a jury that his angry wife made a false rape complaint because he criticized the Sunday dinner, was warned to stay away from her by an Old Bailey judge yesterday. After the man had been cleared of rape, Judge Valerie Pearlman took the unusual step of keeping him in the dock until he promised not to go near his wife.

He denied having sex with his wife and said she had "cried rape" after a violent row when he got home from a fishing trip. He said she had promised him roast chicken with all the trimmings. "All I got was a bit of pie and a potato. I threw it out of the window. If she had made an effort or bothered about the meal I wouldn't have been upset," he told the jury. "While I was fishing, she had been out to a night-club."'

Source: The Guardian, 13 June 1996

Liberal and radical feminist approaches

Some versions of feminism discount Marxist-influenced views that capitalism is the key factor in the oppression of women in society and, in particular, within the family. Such approaches place patriarchy at the centre of any explanation, using empirical studies of socialist societies (such as those cited above) as evidence of inequality between men and women in all types of society, ranging from capitalist to communist, and from industrial to tribal. Broadly, two such approaches can be identified: liberal feminism and radical feminism.

Liberal feminist

Liberal feminists offer more optimistic accounts of relationships between women and men in families. They point to the advances that have been made in societies such as Britain throughout the twentieth century, such as women's political freedoms (e.g. voting rights) and legislation covering women at work (e.g. equal pay and antidis-criminatory laws). Recent legislation has made marital rape a crime and domestic violence a serious criminal offence. This has been one part of wider social changes that have meant greater freedom and equality for all women. Not only have women gained from such improvements; men have also benefited, as they are more involved with their families and can express the caring and sharing aspects of their natures that were previously suppressed. The increased number of working wives has meant an improved standard of living for the family and less pressure on men to play the lone bread winning role.

Within families and households the context of gradual social change has meant the increased involvement of men in domestic labour and childcare. As a result, developments such as the symmetrical family (see p. 79), as identified by Young and Wilmott (1961), where women and men increasingly share household responsi-bilities, has become a feature of family life on a significant scale. Husbands and fathers are today more family-centred than in previous generations. The family has become a focus for shared activities such as leisure and shopping.

However, it needs to be noted that liberal feminists are not complacent about the gradual improvements that have occurred. They still recognize that there are many further things that need to be done on behalf of women, but that this can be carried out through persuasion and an appeal to both men and women's sense of fairness and justice in the context of a liberal democratic society. This, in turn, can be supported by legislation upholding equal opportunities for women and men.

Evaluation

The liberal feminist view of gradual improvements for all women, both in society generally and, specifically, in family life, has attracted criticism. Critics suggest that the extent of change has been less sweeping and that there are still key structural inequalities between women and men in all walks of life including the family. The majority of wives and mothers now work, but women's average earnings are still around 70 per cent of men's – because many women are in part-time, low-paid work. So, women are a long way from economic equality. In the family, if women work fewer hours on average and earn less, this becomes a factor in their carrying out the majority of household and childcare tasks. In the late 1980s, the statistical review *Social Trends* suggested that wives and mothers who worked part time had 'the worst of both worlds'.

Furthermore, critics point out that even when women are in full-time work, they are still expected to do most domestic labour. An example of this was Elston's 1980 study of husbands and wives who were both doctors, which discovered that wives invariably carried out more household tasks (Elston 1980). This indicates that, even in the higher-educated, professional classes where it may be expected that feminist ideals of equality are influential, housework is still seen as a woman's responsibility.

In Focus

◆

A 1950s image of 'How to be a Good Wife'

◆ **HAVE DINNER READY:** Plan ahead, even the night before, to have a delicious meal on time. This is a way of letting him know that you have been thinking about him and are concerned about his needs. Most men are hungry when they come home and the prospect of a good meal is part of the warm welcome needed.

◆ **PREPARE YOURSELF:** Take 15 minutes to rest so that you'll be refreshed when he arrives. Touch up your make-up, put a ribbon in your hair and be fresh looking. He has just been with a lot of work-weary people. Be happy and cheerful and a little more interesting. His boring day may need a lift.

◆ **CLEAR AWAY THE CLUTTER:** Make one last trip through the main part of the house just before your husband arrives, gathering up school books, toys, paper, etc. Then run a dust cloth over the tables. Your husband will feel he has reached a haven of rest and order and it will give you a lift too.

◆ **PREPARE THE CHILDREN:** Take a few minutes to wash the children's hands and faces (if they are small), comb their hair and, if necessary, change their clothes. They are little treasures and he would like to see them playing the part.

◆ **MINIMIZE ALL NOISE:** At the time of his arrival, eliminate all noise of the washer, dryer, dishwasher or vacuum. Try to encourage the children to be quiet. Be happy to see him. Greet him with a warm smile and be glad to see him.

◆ **SOME DON'TS:** Don't greet him with problems or complaints. Don't complain if he's late for dinner. Count this as minor compared with what he might have gone through that day. Make him comfortable. Have him lean back in a comfortable chair or suggest he lie down in the bedroom. Have a cool or warm drink ready for him. Arrange his pillow and offer to take off his shoes. Speak in a low, soft, soothing and pleasant voice. Allow him to relax and unwind.

◆ **LISTEN TO HIM:** You may have a dozen things to tell him, but the moment of his arrival is not the time. Let him talk first.

◆ **MAKE THE EVENING HIS:** Never complain if he does not take you out to dinner or to other places of entertainment. Instead, try to understand his world of strain and pressure, his need to be home and relax.

◆ **THE GOAL:** Try to make your home a place of peace and order, where your husband can renew himself in body and spirit.

Source: adapted from an American home economics paper 1952

The domestic division of labour

The debate about the domestic division of labour came to the fore in the early 1970s with the publication of two studies, each with very different conclusions about women's and men's involvement and contribution to domestic tasks and family life in general.

❖ Activity 13 ❖

What does Table 3.1 tell us about the division of labour? Summarize the changes that have taken place.

What is the significance of the difference between 'actual allocation' and 'how tasks should be allocated'?

Table 3.1 Division of household tasks[1], Great Britain 1983 and 1991

| | Actual allocation of tasks (%) | | | | | | How tasks should be allocated (%) | | |
| | 1983 | | | 1991 | | | 1991 | | |
	Mainly man	mainly woman	Shared equally	Mainly man	mainly woman	Shared equally	Mainly man	mainly woman	Shared equally
Household shopping	5	51	44	8	45	47	1	22	76
Makes evening meal	5	77	17	9	70	20	1	39	58
Does evening dishes	17	40	40	28	33	37	12	11	76
Does household cleaning	3	72	24	4	68	27	1	36	62
Does washing and ironing	1	89	10	3	84	12	–	58	40
Repairs household equipment	82	6	10	82	6	10	66	1	31
Organizes household money and bills	29	39	32	31	40	28	17	14	66
Child rearing[2]									
Looks after sick children	1	63	35	1	60	39	–	37	60
Teaches children discipline	10	12	77	9	17	73	8	4	85

[1] By married couples or couples living as married
[2] Data for 1983 relate to 1984.

Source: Social Trends (1995)

Michael Young and Peter Wilmott (1975) suggested an evolutionary portrait of family change in *The Symmetrical Family*. They charted the development in the second half of the twentieth century towards greater equality between husbands and wives in terms of their contribution to family life.

This differed from previous generations, when men were predominantly bread-winners and women were housewives. Such men had little involvement in household tasks and childcare; in essence husbands and fathers were shadowy figures. Young and Wilmott point to the growing development of egalitarian attitudes throughout society which inevitably impinged on family relationships. Increased numbers of working women helped to erode the traditional male breadwinner image; the growth in ideals of domesticity, the rise of the privatized family and increased space and comfort in homes meant that men have increasingly shared household activities with their wives.

This does not necessarily mean that role reversal, i.e. women carrying out traditional male activities and vice versa, has taken place. Domestic work can still be 'gendered', with men decorating and maintaining and women cooking and ironing. Symmetry or balance in marital relationships is reflected in the broadly

equal time and commitment both husbands and wives have to family life.

Ann Oakley (1975) arrived at very different conclusions from those of Young and Wilmott. She interviewed 40 housewives in London to ascertain attitudes to domestic work and how this related to female and male roles and identity. A picture emerged of the continuance of women's predominant involvement in housework and, importantly, a significant proportion of women who did not wish men to be involved, because as one respondent put it, 'I like a man to be a man'. This raises issues of identity and what women associate with femininity and masculinity in relation to housework, as well as the expectations of husbands and wives, fathers and mothers.

Figure 3.4
Trends in domestic work

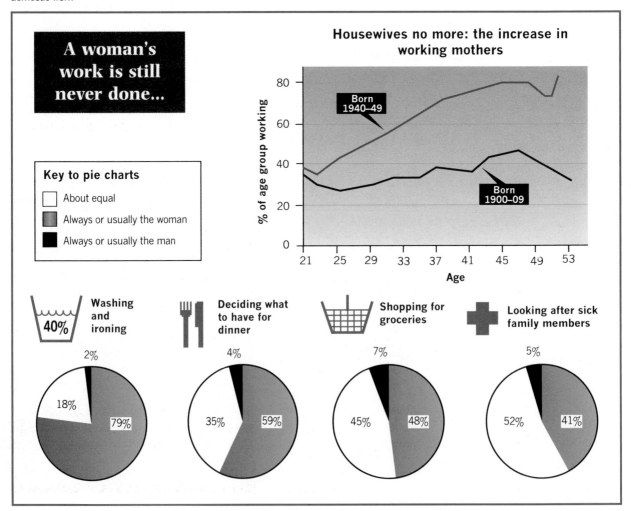

❖ Activity 14 ❖

Explain Oakley's findings further, giving appropriate examples. Are the views she encountered old-fashioned and are they disappearing? Conduct further research via a small survey. This could be developed into a larger coursework project on gender identity through the generations.

The two studies above are over twenty years old. Questions need to be asked as to which is most applicable today. Evidence from more recent research shows considerable support for Oakley's findings, i.e. that the majority of household tasks are still carried out by women. Family studies by Ray Pahl (1984) and Melanie Henwood (1987), recent British Social Attitudes reports and other, similar studies point to the continuance of inequality in the domestic division of labour, even when wives and mothers are in paid employment.

However, an international study covering Canada and a number of European countries by Jonathan Gershuny (1992) lends some support to egalitarian trends. He found that men are carrying out the more routine domestic activities to a greater degree than formerly. This is particularly evident where wives/partners go out to work. Nevertheless, Gershuny does point out that women's total working hours including domestic activities still remain greater than men's. Despite this, he concludes on an optimistic note by saying that, 'there is evidence of a really very substantial social change over the last couple of decades – and (trends) provide the basis for a not unhopeful view of the future of the household.'

In summary, two positions can be identified:

❖ There is a significant trend towards a more egalitarian future in relationships, marriages and households. This is the symmetrical family and liberal feminist position.

❖ The changes that have occurred have been relatively insignificant and have made little impact on the unequal burden of domestic labour and childcare borne by women. This is the position adopted by Ann Oakley and the radical feminists.

Women continue to have a predominant involvement in housework, despite going out to work in increased numbers

❖ Activity 15 ❖

Use popular magazines to find examples of links between notions of femininity, gender roles and housework and childcare. Other sources for research can be used, such as television advertising, soap operas or sitcoms.

Use your own family, friends and acquaintances as a source for further research into the division of domestic tasks.

Use your research findings as a basis to address the following: 'In comparison with former times, modern relationships, families and households are characterized by a much greater degree of equality and sharing of tasks'.

The New Man of the 1980s has failed to make it into the 1990s. Among couples, eight out of ten women still always or usually do the washing or ironing, only 35 per cent of men share the job of deciding what to have for dinner, and while men and women share shopping more equally, it is still men who are overwhelmingly likely to do the repairs around the home.

Women spend eight hours more per week on housework, cooking and shopping even when they are working full time – and as a result, men in full-time work tend to have two hours' more free time at weekends than their working partners. But some things change: the proportion of women doing home improvements in their free time rose to 30 per cent.

And while men remain more likely than women to take part in sport or other physical activity, the gap between the genders has narrowed. In 1993–94, 57 per cent of women took part in at least one activity in the four weeks preceding a survey, against 72 per cent of men.

Source: Nicholas Timmins, *The Independent*, 25 January 1996

❖ Activity 16 ❖

1 What trends are featured in Table 3.1, Fig. 3.4 and the *In Focus* above?
2 How do such findings relate to the 'symmetrical family' debate?

Radical or pure feminism

Radical feminism covers a range of views, but a common focus is a disagreement with Marxist feminism as to whether the replacement of capitalism by socialism will result in equality between men and women. Radical feminists see patriarchy (see p. 76) as a pervasive force in most world societies, whether capitalist or socialist, tribal or industrial. Within the family, men, as husbands, brothers and sons, are seen to gain at the expense of women as wives, sisters and daughters. For example, most domestic work is carried out by the women of the household (see Table 3.1 on p. 79).

The family is therefore an exploitative institution. Some radical feminists see relationships between men and women as being endemically oppressive and that this is found in a heightened form in the nuclear family. The family is, in Barrett and

McIntosh's terms, 'antisocial' because it not only oppresses women, it also excludes people who do not live in families and who wish to pursue different lifestyles (Barrett and McIntosh 1982). Hard or ultra-hard versions of radical feminism (sometimes referred to as *separatists*) see no scope for change in men – they therefore advocate the abolition of the family and women's separation from men in order to lead fuller, non-exploited lives. They focus on 'familial ideology' (a dominant set of beliefs and ideas centring around the desirability and normality of the nuclear family) as a key part of society which persuades people that the only 'natural' way to live is in a family. People who live alone or in non-familial households are seen as unusual and sometimes as deviant.

Another issue highlighted by the harder version of radical feminism is that of domestic violence, usually perpetrated by men on women and children within the family. Such issues raise doubts about how 'safe' and 'secure' the family is, particularly for its most vulnerable members. Portrayals of the family as a 'haven', offering security and support, are challenged by the growing evidence from criminal statistics of the degree of violence within households. Most murders are committed within the context of a family, often of wives by husbands, and there is a continuing catalogue of lesser crimes of violence which has only recently become a serious focus of police attention. Until the 1990s, such incidents were invariably classed as 'domestic' and not dealt with as criminal occurrences, except in the case of more extreme levels of violence involving serious injury or death.

Less strong versions of radical feminism are less 'anti-male' and less anti the family, seeing some scope for change within conventional family structures. They echo some aspects of liberal feminism in the belief that it is possible to change and coexist with men, but they are not as complacent about the degree of gradual change that has occurred and the willingness of men to change by 'friendly persuasion'. Women have to fight for their rights in areas such as employment and politics as well as within the family, because it is unlikely that men will voluntarily give up their dominant position. In the 1980s, an example of the sort of action which reflects this perspective was the 'Wages for Housework' campaign. This argued (unsuccessfully) for housewives to be paid an economic wage from the state which would be deducted as a form of tax on their husband's salary. More recently, women such as Helena Kennedy QC have been active in pressing for legislation to criminalize marital rape and domestic violence, with successful results. Such changes have not come about gradually as implied by liberal feminists, but as a result of direct action on the part of women. It is possible, therefore, in this view for women to coexist with men, but there is much to be done and no scope for complacency.

❖ Activity 17 ❖

What is 'familialism' and how does it relate to radical feminism? (Think about familial ideology as defined above.)
In what ways can familialism be seen as similar to racism and sexism?

Evaluation

Radical feminism has contributed a great deal to debates in sociology about vital aspects of women's position in society. It would seem that their case against Marxism is supported by empirical studies of socialist societies which find little evidence of major differences in women's oppression from capitalist societies such as ours. Criticisms of the harder or separatist versions of radical feminism can be made concerning the possibility of men and women leading separate non exploitative lives. Such views seem utopian and have been linked to the advocacy of lesbianism as a viable alternative to free women from patriarchal structures. In the 1980s, the Leeds Revolutionary Feminist Group argued that only lesbians can be true feminists. Defenders of such views point to the possibility (through advances in reproductive technologies such as egg transplants and artificial insemination) that women can be separate from men and raise children without men.

The reality in the current context is that many women are heads of single-parent households and do not need men for support. However, the majority of women seek relationships with men and it is still the case that most people desire to live in conventional family settings and raise children. It is in this context that softer versions of radical feminism say that the struggle for women's equality must be carried out. Whether such desires for 'conventional' families and relationships are a result of free choice or a pervasive familial ideology presenting only limited options for relationships, is the subject of continuing debate. An example of a recent contribution to this is described in the *In Focus* on p. 84.

'An unprecedented war of words has erupted among a group of feminist academics about whether the majority of women prefer to stay at home and look after children rather than go to work. Catherine Hakim, a senior research fellow at the London School of Economics, has caused uproar among feminists by saying that only a small number of women were truly career minded. Challenging a long-standing feminist assumption that given a level playing field most women would opt to work, she claimed most did not want to work at all. "The unpalatable truth is that a substantial proportion of women still see homemaking as women's principal activity and income earning as men's principal activity in life," she wrote.

Those who tried to combine career and family still accepted that the domestic chores were more their responsibility than their male partner's, whose role is to be the breadwinner. "The proportion of women who accept the homemaker role varies from half to two-thirds."

Yesterday Dr Hakim was forced to defend her views, published in the *British Journal of Sociology*, after the publication of a critique signed by 11 eminent academics.

She said that her paper, entitled 'Five myths on women's employment', showed that not all women had the same aims and would not benefit from the same policies. "Most women still go along with the sexual division of labour, many actively preferring it and colluding with men, others are not sufficiently inconvenienced by it to make a stand," she argued.

She cited a survey in 1988 which showed that two-thirds of British men and women believe that being a housewife can be as fulfilling as paid work. Dr Hakim insisted that the female population is polarizing into careerist women and home-centred women, often with conflicting interests.

'The former Employment Department sociologist admitted that her views had made her unpopular and that some academics had refused to talk to her. The 11 sociologists have written a reply in which they criticize her for failing to document or give evidence for her arguments. "Hakim's feminist is, of course, a caricature," they say. The critique, also published in the *British Journal of Sociology*, further accused Dr Hakim of not taking into account economic influences. Irene Bruegel, of the University of the South Bank in London, said: "The myths about women and work are all of her making." Another critic, Ceridwen Roberts, director of the Family Policies Study Centre, said, "I regret that Catherine has made a media fight over what is an academic discussion. In the process the subtleties of the debate are now getting lost."'

Source: Angella Johnson, *The Guardian*,
29 March 1996

Critical theory

Radical psychiatry

Critical theories of the family are strongly negative about its effects on individual members and see the family as a seething mass of various discontents which are destructive and oppressive for all concerned.

The earliest accounts in this tradition come from what became known as 'radical psychiatry'. The two leading protagonists of this view, R.D. Laing and David Cooper, were both former psychiatrists who had become critical of their profession.

From a critique of psychiatry and its medical model of mental illness, they developed a more environmental perspective which saw mental illness as a product of social forces surrounding the individual. Laing (1970) suggested that mental illness was a product of a 'sick' society rather than a condition that could be explained in terms of individual failings. In this sense they brought a sociological dimension to an area which had, for the most part, previously been dealt with at the individual and psychological level. Laing also turned his attention to the psychodynamics of the family and a sociological explanation of the mental illness schizophrenia. He saw this as a confusing term for a crisis of identity which could be explained and dealt with more effectively as such, than as an individual 'illness' dealt with by conventional means such as drugs. He cited a number of case histories of schizophrenia whose causes could be linked to the family circumstances of the individual concerned (Laing and Esterson 1970). A commonly occurring factor was that of an adolescent young woman, an only child, who had a diagnosed schizophrenic breakdown.

Laing advocated examining the family circumstances, suggesting that tensions involved parents and child in a complex web of conflicting emotions. The daughter was on the brink of adulthood and the parents might try to control and restrict her life excessively, perhaps because of subconscious jealousy on the part of one or both parents. Such issues can be linked to the psychoanalytic approach deriving from the work of Sigmund Freud (see Chapter 7). If the social pressures become too much, a form of identity crisis 'breakdown' may result which is then referred to medical experts who diagnose schizophrenia. Laing disagreed with this medicalizing of the individual and advocated that the whole family should be treated as 'schizophrenogenic' (schizophrenia-producing). The root causes were the tensions and emotional pressures between all the members of the family which should be brought to the surface through family therapy. Laing developed family therapy clinics and centres which have become an established form of treatment for a range of disorders previously dealt with at the individual level.

David Cooper (1972) follows Laing's attack on the family and highlights the way children can be denied any scope for individuality and freedom of identity by parents who act in a psychologically and emotionally suffocating way. This serves the interests of a society that exploits its members and demands subservience and obedience. Cooper says that the family is 'an ideological conditioning device in an exploitive society'. Although he is not a Marxist, Cooper echoes several concurrent themes which contain criticisms of the oppressive and exploitative nature of capitalism.

Evaluation

Radical psychiatry could be seen as one of the most negative approaches to the family. In its simplest form the approach seems to be saying that relationships in the family are the 'sick' outcome of a 'sick' society. Critics point out that most families do not suffocate people in the way that radical psychiatrists suggest. Laing and Cooper were in fact dealing in their professional work with a tiny minority of dysfunctional families with damaging interpersonal dynamics. To build an antifamily theory on such a limited and untypical sample is dubious to say the least. Most families are relatively free from such high levels of emotional tensions and some would say that the best forms of family dynamics are psychologically healthy for the individual. A contented family life is a desirable goal for a large number of people, and physical and personal well-being can be linked to happiness in one's family. Laing himself remarked in 1977 that he had enjoyed his own family life.

'Clare Rayner, the advice columnist, described smacking children as "somewhat barbaric". "It's bad family politics. If you get really mad I would slap the table to express your rage. It's even worse when they are very young. Tiny children don't misbehave; they don't know what it means to be naughty. You should simply remove a child from the scene and say 'No'."

Baroness David, Labour spokeswoman in the Lords, said in 1992, "If we want to produce self-discipline and reduce violence in a society we must give parents a clear lead.

The first step towards changing the current culture of British parenting, which all too often relies on smacking or beating, is for the Government to give a lead and quite explicitly discourage all physical punishment."

The Heritage Secretary, Virginia Bottomley, has regularly supported parents' right to use physical force.

"When my children were younger," she told a childcare conference in 1994, "there were occasions when I had to give them a smack. I agree that parents should smack their children if they want to, and if a childminder is looking after a child and is well known and trusted by the parents and the parents are willing for her to administer a mild smack, she should be allowed to do so." Mrs Bottomley declined to comment further yesterday.

Cary Cooper, professor of psychology at UMIST, said that never smacking a child was unrealistic. "We should try and constrain ourselves as much as possible but sometimes we may give a small smack. People always feel guilty about it, and in a way you are telling the child that you cannot control the situation. But if it's by way of venting your aggression that's a different matter." '

Source: Owen Bowcott, *The Observer*, 1996

Domestic violence and abuse: the dark side of family life

If, as the antipsychiatrists suggest, children are emotionally 'abused' within families, it may not seem surprising that physical abuse can also occur. One issue concerns defining abuse. For example, in 1996 there was controversy in Britain over the smacking of children by parents (see *In Focus* above and Activity 18).

Emotional tensions, rivalries and jealousies can develop into serious physical and sexual abuse for some. Fathers are the most common perpetrators of abuse of all kinds, which may vindicate feminist concerns about men and personal relationships within the family. However, whether abuse is a structural feature and an outcome of patriarchal family structures, as the stronger forms of radical feminism advocate, has yet to be demonstrated. Exposure in the 1990s of the extent of the

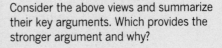

❖ Activity 18 ❖

Consider the above views and summarize their key arguments. Which provides the stronger argument and why?

abuse of children in care suggests that removing children from damaging family circumstances to the care of the State is not always the answer.

Violence against women

Radical feminists highlight the scale and amount of adult male violence on wives and partners in studies such as those of Dobash and Dobash (1979). However, it has been pointed out that not all violence is male on female – it can be the other way round, albeit in a minority of cases.

However, a BBC *Panorama* programme in November 1996 controversially suggested a hidden level of female on male violence in families which is not reflected in the statistics because of underreporting. Psychologist Dr. Ann Campbell of Durham University stated that a higher proportion of domestic violence was committed by women than men. Unsurprisingly, such views attracted much opposition from those who see women as the main victims of such violence. Read the *In Focus* on p. 88 and try Activity 19.

❖ Activity 19 ❖

1 What reasons can be given for rising violence from women?
2 Why might abused men not report offences to the police?
3 Is this a relatively minor issue in comparison with the far greater amount of domestic violence against women?

In Focus

◆

A survey of domestic violence against women

'Surrey County Council has taken the unusual step of producing a comprehensive survey of domestic violence in its region. Of the women surveyed, 31 per cent had experienced violence from a known man, a disturbing 24 per cent had been beaten up, 9 per cent had their lives threatened and 5 per cent had been attacked by a weapon. More than a fifth of the women interviewed said they had suffered psychological abuse – such as being prevented from seeing their friends.'

Source: The Guardian, 22 January 1996

❖ Activity 20 ❖

1 Why might reports such as the one described in the *In Focus* above indicate that statistics are misleading?
2 What is the problem in defining 'psychological abuse'?

❖ Activity 21 ❖

1 In the case described below (see *In Focus*), what justification has the judge given for the leniency of the sentence?
2 What image of family life does he hold?

In Focus

◆

Five years for killing wife

'A butcher was jailed for five years at the Old Bailey yesterday for slashing his wife to death with a boning knife and attacking her boyfriend after he discovered they were having an affair. Graham Barrie, aged 58, had admitted manslaughter and was cleared of murder after a retrial when the first jury could not agree on a verdict.

June Barrie staggered bleeding on to the pavement outside the couple's butcher shop in Bromley, south London, on December 16 after her husband stabbed her several times. As a number of people gave her first aid Barrie went out and stabbed her another four or five times, the court was told.

"It is clear your wife was having some sort of affair," said Judge Gerald Gordon. "I accept that the discovery of it and the events which followed had a devastating effect. It is right for me to take into account provocation and diminished responsibility."

Mrs Barrie's friend, Kenneth Williams, aged 59, recovered from a punctured liver.

Source: The Guardian, 21 October 1995

'Men in Sweden are on the receiving end of an upsurge in violent assaults by their wives and girlfriends, according to figures published yesterday. Some 300 men lodged official complaints last year after suffering domestic attacks by their partners, confirming a growing incidence of violence by women against men, the Stockholm daily newspaper *Expressen* reported. One complainant, Magnus Eriksson, aged 22, has launched criminal proceedings against his former girlfriend after allegedly being physically battered while being ejected from the flat the couple shared.

"She hit me twice, hard in the face, and spat on me," he said. The woman, described as "older and athletic", then allegedly knocked him over and pinned him down. "She screamed as loud as she could in my left ear. I constantly hear a beeping noise in it now."

Mr Eriksson, who claims the injury has impaired his musical career, said not all men had muscles like Rambo or Arnold Schwarzenegger, and many felt embarrassed to report violence against them by women.

"I am not seeking revenge. But I must exercise the right that so few Swedish men in our land of equality choose to exercise," he said.

Sweden, with almost equal numbers of men and women in work, is renowned for its equality. But researchers say many male battery victims are too ashamed to report cases.

Mikael Rying, of the National Crime Prevention Board, said: "It is a bit like incest. Once you start to talk about it, more and more comes up to the surface."'

Source: *The Guardian*, 6 February 1996

Michel Foucault's critical theory

'The judges of normality are present everywhere. We are in the society of the teacher-judge, the doctor-judge, the educator-judge, the 'social-worker'-judge; it is on them that the universal reign of the normative is based; and each individual, wherever he may find himself, subjects to it his body, his gestures, his behaviour, his aptitudes, his achievements.' (Foucault 1975, p.304)

The work of Foucault (1926–84), a French philosopher and historian, has attracted considerable attention in the social sciences since the 1980s. He suggested that the social world is constructed through language or, in his terms, discourse. With reference to families and personal relationships, he made a number of points concerning power which differed from conventional structuralist approaches such as Marxism. Power is diffused throughout society as a characteristic of social relationships, including the family. It can also be found in the knowledge base of society and exercised by 'thought police', such as teachers, doctors, counsellors, psychiatrists and social workers. The language or discourse of such professionals echoes this; for example, the use of the term 'problem families' in relation to deprivation and poverty may focus on individual families rather than more general issues of the structural causes of their situation.

This is quite different to liberal welfare views that present state agencies and their professional representatives in a supportive role, helping to keep the family intact. Foucault, on the other hand, sees them as having more to do with power and control in the sphere of personal relationships. The law, social work, the social security, tax and welfare systems are in fact controlling and intervening in family life. He referred to these as 'regulations through the family'. Society supports a particular kind of family life that is based on a monogamous nuclear family with a breadwinner husband, dependent wife and children. Any deviation from this stereotypical norm can be corrected by laws (for example, bigamy is illegal in Britain), social workers (who can remove children from families) and similar 'corrective' agencies.

One theme in Foucault's work is the way conventional ideas of motherhood are reinforced. Mothers of young children who wish to work face difficulties in arranging satisfactory childcare, so their opportunities are restricted in comparison to men's. In Foucault's terms, the 'message' that is being conveyed to such mothers is that going out to work is not 'normal'. Many such women experience guilt and stress which can be indirectly related to the 'social disapproval' they encounter.

Another feature of Foucault's work that is relevant to family life concerns historical change in the nature of sexuality, which has increasingly become a focus for attention and intervention in modern societies. There is an emphasis on 'discipline', meaning the ability to conform to a norm of performance and behaviour, and 'confession', which, in the modern world, means confessing to 'experts' such as counsellors, doctors, psychologists and psychiatrists about one's performance 'inadequacies' (see *In Focus* below and Chapter 10).

Foucault also highlighted historical changes in the controls that society exercises over the formation of families. In the past, the main concern (especially of the upper classes) was with marriage alliances between lineages, but in recent times there has been a shift towards two forms of 'power over life' which have had implications for contemporary families:

❖ There are social controls of the body's biological and psychological life forces – examples being the emphasis on reproduction within monogamous marriage and the condemnation of homosexuality as a 'perversion'. Such social controls integrate individuals into the economic, political and social systems of an exploitative and repressive society. Such a view seems to be very similar to Marxism but Foucault was doubtful about any possibility of change and offered a gloomy view of the future rather than a revolutionary one resulting in the establishment of socialism.

❖ The power of nation states depends upon the demographic characteristics of national populations – here, birth-rate trends, life expectancy and levels of physical and mental wellbeing are important factors in stabilizing and

In Focus

◆

Strains within marriage – poor sexual performance

A man facing redundancy already has financial problems. As a result of sexual dysfunction he is referred by his doctor to a psychosexual counsellor. The counsellor deals with the sexual dysfunction as the key problem, i.e. his performance is not complying to 'normal' standards. Attempts through therapy, and possibly drugs, are made to 'cure' this problem. Issues of his work and financial situation are seen as secondary or unimportant.

This is an example of how power works through discourses such as the medicalization of what may be a politically or economically caused problem, i.e. the 'patient's' sexual dysfunction could well be a result of his work and financial circumstances, so the 'cure' may well be different to that advocated by the counsellor. Such performance indicators are controlled and set by the powerful, who can shape the private world of relationships by implementing their version of normality on others. The boundaries around behaviour are clearly set, incorporating monogamous heterosexuality within a nuclear family framework. Anyone who strays outside such parameters is deviant and in need of 'treatment' by an array of counsellors, therapists, and similar professions, whose job is to steer the person back to 'normality'.

strengthening such power. In this context, homosexual parenting, which has recently been seen as a cause for concern in the media, can be seen as a challenge which the establishment must address.

Morgan (1985) makes the following points concerning Foucault's views on sexuality:

❖ Greater openness about sex in modern societies is a superficial liberation. While controls are more diffuse and apparently non-repressive, a sexual yardstick has been established against which one is expected to measure one's own performance, and now there is an obligation to work at and enjoy sex.

❖ The learning of sexual techniques requires teachers, counsellors, sexologists and related 'experts' as well as a whole sex industry of manuals, videos, magazines, books and literature within a network of clinics and therapy centres.

❖ There is an overlap between sex, truth and confession. Confession to 'experts' (doctors, therapists) about 'problems' such as sexual dysfunction, parallels the idea of religious confession as the path to truth.

❖ There is an 'artificial unity' of 'sex' linking a diversity of concerns, practices and theories. The emotional, the biological, the interpersonal and the moral are merged so that 'sex' becomes a taken-for-granted 'fact of life' tied into

marriage and the family. Morgan sees this trend as important in the development of individualization and the depoliticization of people's lives.

Clearly Foucault's views are controversial but some of the latter points could well be agreed upon by the public. His original writings are difficult and demanding to read but this does not detract from a very lively and stimulating thinker who has contributed much to our understanding of social life.

The French Marxist Jacques Donzelot (1980) follows Foucault's tradition in his portrayal of the family in the modern world as an institution under siege from various agencies of the State. A variety of experts, professionals and counsellors intervene in the supposedly secure private world of family life, effectively to control and supervise it.

❖ Activity 22 ❖

Examine further the role of such experts as social workers:

- What negative role might they play in family life?
- What positive arguments are offered for the intervention of social workers?

Use newspapers, media reports, CD-ROM to help illustrate with appropriate examples.

Table 3.2 The two sociologies

	Structuralist	Interpretist
Focus	Macro – large-scale study	Micro – small-scale study
Unit of analysis	Society	Interaction
Research	Social surveys, quantitative techniques	Qualitative, observational, in-depth techniques
Key theme	The role of the family in society in relation to other social institutions	What occurs in families and how family life, roles and responsibilities are negotiated and understood.

Interpretive approaches to the family

The approaches to the family and its role in society covered so far are macro or large-scale theories; i.e. they explain the family in terms of its relation to the wider society. For example, feminist theories look at the family in relation to a general theory about the oppression of women throughout society.

When research is carried out to substantiate such theories (see Chapter 7, *Theory and methods*) large samples are used. Interpretive sociology has a different methodology. The theoretical emphasis is on the everyday social world focusing on interaction between people in their daily lives. Studies are small-scale or micro in approach and involve small research samples and case studies. The aim is to gather qualitative data (again, see Chapter 7) which explores the way people attribute meaning and understanding to their interactions with others. A key theoretical and methodological difference between this approach and macro or structuralist studies is that different questions are asked about the topic of study and there is a different stance with respect to matters of causation. For example, functionalists and Marxists both approach the family in terms of its role in society, attempting to answer such questions as: 'What caused the family to be in the form it is? What purpose does the family serve for society?' Depending on the perspective, answers such as 'The family is a key socializing agency' or 'The family serves the interests of capitalism' are offered.

Interpretivists approach their subject matter using a different frame of reference. Instead of asking causative questions as outlined above, they approach the topic from a 'how' rather than a 'why' stance. So, study of the family involves examining how people make sense of and understand their lives within families. David Morgan (1991) gives the example of a wife, husband and child sitting at a breakfast table. The wife says, 'I must remember to get some more marmalade' and everyone laughs. An outsider, unaware of the social context, would see such a scene as puzzling, but to the family concerned their behaviour is quite rational.

Although apparently trivial, such events in the everyday social world are seen by Interpretivists as important indicators of the complexity of interaction and are therefore the proper subject of study. A focus on conversation, speech and talk in family settings is a vital part of such work, because it is in this way that meaning and social reality is expressed. The family is an arena for negotiation and sense-making in a complex manner which the sociologist aims to explain. More 'macro' structural themes such as class and gender in relation to the family cannot be properly understood without such 'micro' understanding.

In this sense, the everyday world of life within families and households is not trivial or mundane and is a proper subject of study for the sociologist. Indeed, an understanding of such everyday matters is a vital aspect of the sociological task.

Interpretive studies

The following are some examples of the sorts of study engaged in by interpretive sociologists. It is useful to compare the topics of such studies and the way research is carried out, so that you gain a greater understanding of issues relating to theory and method.

Berger and Kellner (1964)

The essay, 'Marriage and the construction of reality', by the two American sociologists Berger and Kellner (1964) was one of the earliest examples of interpretive work within the sphere of personal relationships. They examined marriage and the relationships, roles and interactions between husbands and wives from the point of view of meaning – what it is to be a husband or a wife, and how such behaviours are social constructions centred on mutual expectations, obligations and negotiations between marital partners.

❖ Activity 23 ❖

What might some of these 'mutual expectations, obligations and negotiations' involve? .

Construct a role play where a newly married couple sort out issues of who does what around the home, e.g. washing, ironing, shopping, cleaning, cooking. What influences are at work in such interactions?

Despite the micro emphasis of such studies, wider structural issues such as power and gender are linked to the interpretive themes. Morgan (1985) points out that the so-called 'gap' between interpretive and structuralist approaches may not be as wide as is often assumed. More recent studies illustrate such issues.

Mansfield and Collard (1988)

Penny Mansfield and Jean Collard looked at the processes of becoming a married couple in a sample of first marriages which included the early years of marriage. They examined such issues as:

❖ living arrangements covering matters of where to live, type of accommodation and related themes

❖ how decisions were made about the division of labour in the home

❖ how paid employment and domestic life were balanced

❖ wives' and husbands' responses to conflicts and differences of opinion within marriage.

In terms of methodology, Mansfield and Collard used the in-depth interview, which they described as 'a conversation with a purpose'. Their aim was to develop something as close to natural conversation as possible. A total of 130 two- to three-hour interviews were carried out by an all-female research team with both partners.

Unlike more large scale studies, which aim for generalizations based on large samples, such studies do not aim for 'findings' in this sense, but some descriptive generalizations. For example, could the fact that over half the sample started their married lives in their own accommodation be linked to a discussion of the importance of starting out married life independently?

This study points to the dynamic processes of change and development that are part of married life. These are not as predictable as implied by the use of the term 'career' because behaviour and accepted patterns of interaction can change through time.

A common finding concerning the division of labour was a 'neo-traditional' pattern in which both partners are in paid employment but the female does most of the domestic labour. The husband 'helps' as necessary.

❖ Activity 24 ❖

1 What gender issues are highlighted by the use of the word 'helps' above?

2 In what ways does this raise questions about Young and Wilmott's symmetrical family thesis (see p. 79)?

Traditional views about the greater importance of the husband's work were upheld; some couples had arrived at a sort of symmetrical understanding in that they expected a shared or balanced burden of household responsibilities despite housework being the majority task for wives.

Such research uses qualitative methods to illustrate and examine important facets of the 'how' and the 'meaning' associated with marital behaviour which would not be disclosed in more conventional survey-type research.

Charles and Kerr (1988)

Until recently food and the family meal have not been a subject for sociological study but food, and issues surrounding its preparation and consumption, can be seen as a central and dominant part of family life. Food can be related to social class and lifestyle, as a source of women's oppression and as an indication of care and nurturance within the family.

Warde and Abercrombie (1994) reinforce this when they state, 'Food habits tell a great deal about the texture of family relations, the generation and reinforcement of gender divisions in the household, and social distinctions between people belonging to different categories.'

Most British households spend approximately one-fifth of their budgets on food. Food preparation and family meals take up a significant proportion of family time and tell us a lot about key aspects of life in families and households. Communal eating and sharing food are sometimes central to the definition of a household.

Nickie Charles and Marion Kerr (1988) carried out their study, *Women Food and Families*, using in-depth interviews with a sample of 200 women, each of whom had at least one pre-school child, so the sample was relatively young. As is typical in this sort of research, open-ended questions and verbatim responses were used as a basis for detailed qualitative data. In addition to the interviews, each respondent kept a diary, recording what every household member ate and drank.

Charles and Kerr's findings pointed to the continuing tradition of the 'proper meal' – hot meat and vegetables at least once a day – and this was associated (in terms of meaning) with the 'proper family' and familial harmony. Family meals were also important features of the socialization of young children into accepted cultural habits and manners. Food and family meals also have strong emotional associations and are regarded as indicators of a happy family life. Charles and Kerr found class differences were evident, with the middle classes emphasizing the importance of taking the family meal at table, rather than while watching television.

It emerges overwhelmingly that women are the prime providers and preparers of food and meals, and this activity is invariably geared to the needs of their husbands and children. Women make a strong emotional investment in such matters, and consider it very important when meals are refused or a particular dish is not liked.

❖ Activity 25 ❖

You could carry out a survey investigating some of the issues raised by Charles and Kerr, possibly using your own family's eating arrangements as a starting point to compare with a sample. This sample might incorporate a wide age range and differing social backgrounds.

Finch and Mason (1993)

Janet Finch and Jennifer Mason (1993) used a multi-method approach. This involved a large-scale survey, as well as an in-depth qualitative study, to consider whether families in contemporary Western societies are becoming smaller; more inward looking; less rooted in traditional kinship relationships; and less connected with other related families or the local community.

A key aspect of their work examined obligations, which are the ways in which family members feel obliged to provide help and assistance to other family members. The qualitative part of the study looked at how beliefs (reflected in the survey data) translated into actual behaviour.

Finch and Mason's study clearly shows the danger of oversimplifying from assumptions made about the privatization of the family. They found that people still have an idea of family responsibilities and quite complex ways of negotiating and dealing with them. Rather than having detailed sets of rules about such matters, people more often subscribe to guidelines concerning reciprocity, the balance of independence and dependency, and related issues. These confirm how important and persistent family relations are in a supposedly isolated, privatized, inward-looking nuclear family world.

❖ Activity 26 ❖

Referring to Table 3.3, what conclusions would you draw about the following questions:

1 Which is the most help parents give to children?
2 Which is the least?
3 Which is the most help children give to parents?
4 Which is the least?
5 Write a sentence giving an example to illustrate each of your answers to the above questions in more detail.

Criticisms of interpretive approaches

Critics of interpretive approaches to the family make the following comments:

❖ Such small-scale studies based on possibly unrepresentative samples make generalizations about family life difficult.

❖ The close subjective involvement of the researcher in the lives of the people studied might result in a distorted or overly sympathetic account of what is going on.

❖ Large-scale or macro issues of social class, gender, ethnicity, the changing nature of work and occupations and new technologies at the structural level may not be addressed. All of these are inextricably linked with changes in family life. In this sense, interpretive perspectives present the family within a social structural vacuum.

Table 3.3 Examples of who gives help to whom

	Parents to children	Children to parents	Other (e.g. grand-parents)
Financial help	89	10	37
Providing a home*	25	18	8
Practical help	10	27	37
Emotional support	35	13	44
TOTALS	159	68	126

*This excludes 21 young adults who had never left the parental home, but might well do so.

Source: Finch and Mason (1993, p. 31)

New Right approaches to the family

'I work from the premise that the traditional monogamous marriage, with children, is in reality, on average, in the long run, the most satisfying way to live a human life.' (Charles Murray, *Sunday Times*, 22 May 1994)

The New Right is not a coherent socio-logical theory but instead covers a range of ideas and philosophies developed in the 1980s by social scientists such as Charles Murray, a controversial American intel-lectual (quoted above), politicians, journalists and writers. They can be linked to dominant political trends of that time which included Thatcherism in Britain and Reaganism in the USA. Their campaigns and concerns have ranged from antiabortion, to law and order and the eradication of pornography. A common theme is that society today has deteriorated in comparison with the past.

❖ Activity 27 ❖

1 What particular family type are politicians such as those quoted below most critical of?

2 Which is the 'best' family type?

3 Give some examples of things that were supposedly better in the past

The family and its apparent decline has become a central issue for the New Right. The growth of single parenthood in particular is the object of concern. Murray has carried out research in both the USA and Britain, focusing on the underclass in deprived and run-down areas of the inner cities. He sees single parenthood, illegit-imacy and marital instability to be rife and

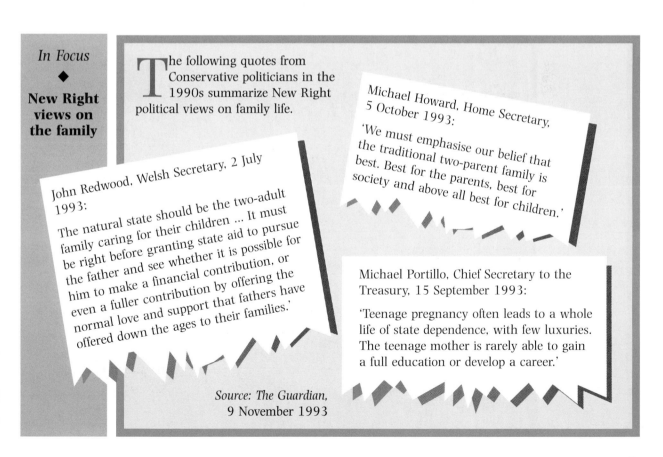

In Focus

◆

New Right views on the family

The following quotes from Conservative politicians in the 1990s summarize New Right political views on family life.

John Redwood, Welsh Secretary, 2 July 1993:

'The natural state should be the two-adult family caring for their children ... It must be right before granting state aid to pursue the father and see whether it is possible for him to make a financial contribution, or even a fuller contribution by offering the normal love and support that fathers have offered down the ages to their families.'

Michael Howard, Home Secretary, 5 October 1993:

'We must emphasise our belief that the traditional two-parent family is best. Best for the parents, best for society and above all best for children.'

Michael Portillo, Chief Secretary to the Treasury, 15 September 1993:

'Teenage pregnancy often leads to a whole life of state dependence, with few luxuries. The teenage mother is rarely able to gain a full education or develop a career.'

Source: The Guardian,
9 November 1993

a major factor behind the growth of social problems in such neighbourhoods. Very young children roam the streets unsupervised and quickly become involved in drug taking, vandalism and criminality. There are few 'father figures' to maintain discipline and young mothers lose control, in particular of their male offspring.

In the USA a controversial element in Murray's work is that the 'underclass' he describes is predominantly Afro-American black, which has led to accusations of racism from liberal commentators. This is less so in his brief studies of British inner cities, where he visited areas such as the North East and South Wales where the majority of the population is white. Murray and other New Right thinkers see the growth in single parenthood as a key factor in under achievement in schools, truancy, poor health and instability in relationships in adulthood.

Support for and criticisms of the New Right

Support for such views has come from outside the New Right. Brigitte Berger (1993) an American sociologist of the family has defended the 'bourgeois family' – in essence the stereotypical nuclear family – from attacks by Marxists and leftist political critics. She sees such a family as a positive feature of modern society fostering a range of desirable values such as enterprise, decency, common sense, politeness, respect for others and a general sense of fairness.

❖ Activity 28 ❖

Read the *In Focus* below.

1 What image of the role of fathers is featured in this report?
2 Make a table summarizing the opposing arguments offered.

In Focus

◆

Absent fathers 'main cause of crime'

'The main cause of crime and violence among young people is the absence of a father at home, it was claimed yesterday. Dr Frederick Goodwin told a US conference on the possible link between genetic background and crime that children of two-parent households were less likely to offend: "That cuts across all races and classes." Dr Goodwin claimed there were proportionally more blacks in US prisons because a corresponding number of families in that ethnic group were fatherless. Twelve per cent of Americans are black but the group accounts for 45 per cent of arrests for violent crime. Sociologist, Dr Brenda Cohen, supported Dr Goodwin's view. "Children, especially boys, who grow up without a responsible man in the house, without a role model, have great difficulty accepting authority," she said.

But in Britain, child psychologist Richard Woolfson said having a father at home was not necessarily an advantage. "There are many cases where the presence of a father might be causing the child psychological difficulties," said Dr Woolfson. Professor John Pearce, of Nottingham University said there was "certainly an association" between absent fathers and crime but poverty, schooling, IQ and temperament could all play a part. One suggestion was that genes and childhood experiences affected the likelihood of a child turning to crime. "For example, the genetic make-up of the father may have led him into criminality which creates the environment for the child." Dr David Comings, of Duarte, California, said: "There is certainly no gene for criminal behaviour. But there are genes which put people at greater risk."'

Source: Lorraine Fraser, The Mail on Sunday, 24 September 1995

Two British sociologists who are not conservative and describe themselves as 'ethical socialists', A.H. Halsey (1992) and Norman Dennis (1993), have supported key aspects of New Right views. Along with Murray they identify problems emanating from single parenthood and absent fathers which are becoming particularly prevalent in inner-city areas. Unemployment among young working-class males has meant they have no clear 'breadwinner' role as they had in the past when traditional heavy industries, such as mining and shipbuilding provided employment. As adults they may be rejected by the mothers of their children as they are not a source of financial support, so relationships are often transitory and short lived. The drift into crime and drug abuse becomes almost inevitable.

As Halsey explains, a key issue in such debates is whether the 'cause' of delinquency among children of single parents is the absence of a financially supportive father and male role model who can exert discipline and stability on his offspring, or more structural factors such as unemployment and poverty. It is clear that a lack of money and job opportunity is a predominant issue in any explanation of criminality. Halsey admits that it has not been resolved whether the key causal factor is an absent father or unemployment and poverty. New Right thinkers associate delinquency with the former explanation, and see the 'answer' as a return to stable families and family values. Critics of the New Right, for example Marxists, turn to the latter definition and advocate the need for economic structural change to eradicate poverty if the social problems described are to be addressed (see *In Focus* below).

Abbott and Wallace's criticisms

Pamela Abbott and Clare Wallace (1992) criticize the New Right from a socialist-feminist perspective. They take issue with the desirable family model that is presented, pointing to the exploitation of women in families and the degree of unhappiness and frustration experienced by many in such circumstances. The high incidence of depression and related illnesses provides evidence of this. Another issue is the extent and seriousness of violence perpetrated by husbands on wives and children, which does not seem to be recognized by the New Right.

The aspects of New Right ideals they criticized include the following:

❖ homemaking and childcare as the key elements of a woman's role

---

In Focus

'Homes Study Explodes Single Mothers Myth'

'The idea of teenage mothers who deliberately get pregnant to jump the housing queue is a myth, according to a new report. In fact, only 10 per cent of the "small minority" of women who became mothers without forming any bond with the father, were living alone with their child in social housing six months after the birth, said the Economic and Social Research Council's centre on microsocial change. Rather, almost half these young mothers were still living with their parents six months later.

Professor John Ermisch, author of the report said: "The phenomenon of young single mothers entering social housing is exaggerated by the media and popular discussion.

While early motherhood increased the chances substantially that young woman's first major tenure is social housing, the young mothers usually entered social housing with a partner. Young single motherhood is not therefore a major force in creating social housing tenants."'

Source: Glenda Cooper, *The Independent*, 8 February 1996

❖ the stress on role models of a breadwinner father and homemaker mother for girls

❖ the claim that children should be brought up at home by two loving, heterosexual parents

❖ the New Right opposition to:

- easy availability of divorce

- cohabitation, which is seen as a sign of instability and impermanence

- abortion, since they hold that foetuses have a right to life

- feminism, which they hold responsible for unhappiness and the disruption of family life

- single parenthood

- homosexuality, which they believe to be 'deviant' and a sign of moral decadence.

Abbott and Wallace take issue with all the above points. They favour tolerance and

❖ Activity 29 ❖

Discuss with a partner the New Right views above and explain each in more detail. Present arguments for and against.

diversity in the way people live together, and advocate a variety of options in the way people live their personal lives. These include:

❖ living alone

❖ living as homosexual couples

❖ single-parent households

❖ female breadwinners with househusbands caring for children.

In the 1990s New Right views have attracted widespread media attention and been supported by moralist religious leaders and politicians.

Communitarianism

The basic ideas of communitarianism centred around the work of the American sociologist, Amitai Etzioni, are outlined in the Chapter 9, *Community and localities*. It is clear that the family is a central part of the communitarianist strategy because it is within the family that the earliest transmission of values occurs. Strong family support networks will mean strong communities. Community support for childrearing and family life would be advocated through neighbourliness, e.g. childminding for working parents by older neighbours or grandparents. The community would look after its members, controlling or reporting wrongdoers, and family connections and links would be important in this. However, this has led to accusations of the encouragement of 'net curtain twitching nosiness' or spying.

More recently, Francis Fukuyama (1995) has added another dimension to the communitarianism debate by using the example of Far Eastern family structures that contribute to the dynamism of their economies. This goes against conventional functionalist views on the extended family, which imply that it is a barrier to economic development and that the nuclear family structure is necessary for a society which needs a fluid, mobile labour force. Fukuyama places the Eastern extended family structure in the context of dynamic and supportive business communities with the valuable, far-reaching links, connections and social contacts necessary for business success. Such views were previously presented in Brigitte Berger's defence of the traditional 'bourgeois' family.

Postmodernist approaches to the family

Ulrich Beck (1992), a German sociologist, identifies five key turning points in relation to women and men's relationships and the modern family and household structures:

1 *increased life expectancy* – Women have experienced a demographic liberation which has meant that childrearing is a small proportion of their adult lives compared to earlier times.

2 *restructured housework* – Technology has led to the rise of labour-saving devices which, while not necessarily lightening the housework burden, has made it 'left-over' work after paid employment. The 'de-skilling' of housework has directed women towards work outside the home in search of a 'fulfilled' life.

> ❖ **Activity 30** ❖
>
> From your knowledge of the majority of jobs that women do, do you agree with this last point? How might women's class position be a factor?

3 *birth control* – Children and motherhood no longer constitute a 'natural fate' and there is scope for all children to be wanted and motherhood to be intentional and voluntary.

4 *rising divorce* – This highlights the fragility of marital and family support. Women are just a husband away from poverty, so an established career and economic security from their own earnings becomes essential.

5 *equal educational opportunities* – This is related to the above point. Women have greatly benefited from increased educational opportunities in modern societies.

As a result, Beck argues that women have been liberated from their traditional lives and their relationships with men and within families has altered irrevocably (Beck 1992).

Postmodernists highlight the trends identified by Beck. Family life and relationships are becoming increasingly fragmented and unstable, making traditional models such as the stereotypical nuclear family increasingly untenable. Norman Denzin (1987) emphasizes the fact that the modern nuclear family, in which two children are cared for by two parents within a protective and emotionally secure environment, is no longer the norm in America. He puts forward a definition of a new type of family for the postmodern period:

> 'It is a single-parent family, headed by a teenage mother, who may be drawn to drug abuse and alcoholism. She and her children live in a household that is prone to be violent.' (Denzin 1987, p. 33)

In addition, Denzin refers to two aspects concerning the connections that family members have with the social environment:

❖ He suggests that increasing numbers of children are now cared for by someone other than a parent. How this occurs clearly has an impact on the child.

❖ The presence in virtually every household of a television, which can be on for seven or more hours a day, means that children can interact more with it for longer periods than they spend in school. Television has become an important agency of socialization where children gain knowledge of cultural myths and particular views about the social world.

> ❖ **Activity 31** ❖
>
> Give three examples of childcare that is not provided by a parent.
>
> Describe the sorts of knowledge that television passes on to children and what sort of effects this may have.

Denzin sees television offering a view of the world which involves an excess of cultural products. This can cause confusion, as when fictional characters are seen to be 'real'. In this way, the distinction between the 'private' and 'public' becomes increasingly blurred, as television and the media generally invade and disclose intimate details of private lives. A good example of this in the 1990s is the exposure of the marital problems of the British Royal family, notably the Prince and Princess of Wales, who have both confessed adulterous relationships in television interviews. Other dimensions are in the realm of the ideological reinforcement of stereotypical notions of male-dominated, married, heterosexual couples raising children. The result of this for children who do not live with such parents can lead to a confusion about identity with respect to the self, parents and gender, which has been described as 'the death of the subject'.

Daytime, non-parental childcare also raises concerns about children's emotional development, which may be affected by a professional carer who is more emotionally detached from the child than a parent. This can result in the child becoming as similarly emotionally detached as the adult, which could be seen as a worrying trend for the stability of relationships and parenting in the future.

Evaluation

Postmodernism has been increasingly influential in sociology in recent years and the approach to families has echoes in empirical reality and trends which emphasize diversity in relationships. Whether such diversity is a 'good' or a 'bad' thing can depend on the perspective followed.

❖ Activity 32 ❖

Which perspectives see postmodern developments as a 'good' thing and which as a 'bad' thing? Explain why.

Increased trends in childlessness

If their prognostications are correct, the future could be seen as a gloomy one, with children being the losers. It could also mean a greater number of people questioning the need to bear children; there is some evidence of this emerging already, with a significant increase in the numbers of adult women remaining childless. In the early 1990s, it was estimated that 20 per cent of young adult females would never have children. The equivalent figure for their mothers' generation was 10 per cent, so the trend of childlessness appears to be growing.

❖ Activity 33 ❖

Summarize and explain the trends indicated in the two articles that follow (see *In Focus* below and on p. 101).

In Focus

◆

'The clock in the waiting womb'

'Last year, a study by the Family Policy Studies Centre suggesting that one in five young women will remain childless was received with consternation. Was feminism responsible for this recalcitrant, self-obsessed generation? The FPSC is now conducting more research, asking women aged between 35 and 39 why they have chosen "voluntary childlessness". Studies in Canada and America suggest that "voluntary" may not be quite the right word.

"When they've interviewed those people," says Fiona McAllister, FPSC research officer, "they've found it's not so much that they're radically opposed to parenthood, that they think it's a terrible

continued on p. 101

thing, but they've got quite strong reverse ideas, about the sacrifices of parenthood ... They were talking to people who had high standards in all areas of their life and they couldn't see how they would be the sort of mother they would most like to be – as well as being the kind of professional, or the kind of wife, or whatever.'

Typically, those who defer motherhood are educated women. A recent study showed that women who have O levels and above are twice as likely as those with no qualifications to say they expect to have no, or no more, children. A report from the Rowntree Foundation reached the unsurprising conclusion that teenage mothers are often low educational achievers from impoverished homes. For them, a child may seem the only thing they have the power to create. And if, as some religious leaders claim, a child is the greatest gift a woman can give, then these young mothers are superior to educated women who plan ahead, master the arts of contraception, take control over their lives and evaluate their actions.'

Source: The Guardian, 20 February 1996

'At least one in five women now in their 20s and 30s will have no children, government statisticians predicted yesterday as they set out how Britain's population will start to fall for the first time since records began. The proportion of women who remain childless is expected to double compared with those now in their 40s and 50s, as growing numbers decide to put careers first.

Apart from a blip in 1983, Britain's population has been growing for hundreds of years and may not have been on a downward trend since the Black Death in 1347–51. Officials of the Office for National Statistics (ONS), expect that the United Kingdom's population, now more than 58 million, will start falling after 2025 and drop to about 55 million by 2075. The birth rate is already below the level necessary to replenish the population, but totals are being sustained by the swelling ranks of pensioners and the large number of women born in the 1960s who are of child-bearing age. Birth rates are dropping in much of Europe, and Germany already has a falling population. According to ONS forecasts, more than 20 per cent of women born since 1964 will have no children. Latest figures show that 61 per cent of those born in 1969 were childless at 25, as were 23 per cent of those born in 1959 at 35.

The forecast of 20 per cent childlessness by the age of 45 among those born since 1964 compares with 10 per cent of women born in 1944 and 13 per cent of those born in 1949.

Bob Armitage, an ONS statistician, said: "It is a problem. We are likely to have a population more heavily weighted to the elderly." The birth rate among women aged 25–29, the peak age for having babies, fell last year to its lowest since 1941. The rate among women aged 30–34 is higher than that among those aged 20–24, indicating that women having children are increasingly doing so after establishing a career.

A new analysis of abortion data shows that women in the south-east are much more likely than average to terminate a pregnancy. In 1993, the abortion rate in inner London was 35 per cent, while in most of greater London it was 26 per cent. Overall, one in three pregnancies outside marriage was aborted, compared with fewer than one in 10 of those of married women.'

Source: *David Brindle, The Guardian,* 14 June 1996

Contemporary trends in families and households

Choice of marital partner

Romantic love

In Britain and other Westernized societies, marriage is becoming less popular but there are still significant numbers marrying each year, as photographs in your local papers show. The dominant pattern of choosing a partner is by romantic love, which is assumed to be based on the 'free' choice of the two people involved. We are assumed to 'fall in love' in a random, magical or mysterious fashion which cannot be explained in a reasoned manner. Sociologists question this and point out that the apparent 'randomness' of 'Cupid's Dart' is in fact much more predictable and can be subject to scientific enquiry.

❖ Activity 34 ❖

Carry out some research among friends and relatives to see if their choice of partner is socially determined. Are the backgrounds of your sample similar along lines of social class, race/ethnicity, religion, education, income and wealth?

An arranged marriage

Arranged marriage

This is most often associated with people from the Southern Asian subcontinent and involves the extended family in the choice of marital partner. From a Western perspective, a common stereotype is of a reluctant young woman being forced to marry someone she hardly knows by her older relatives. In fact the picture is more complex than this, with increasing evidence of negotiation and choice for the couple concerned. There are still some traditional Asian communities where the couple have little or no say in their choice, mostly those that adhere to fundamentalist religious practices and traditional cultural norms. Such marriages tend to be called forced marriages and, in Britain, their numbers are declining through the generations.

A further complication is that the term 'Asian' covers a wide variety of people and backgrounds:

- ❖ *country of origin* – India, Uganda, Pakistan, Malawi, Bangladesh, etc., are very different societies and cultures.

- ❖ *religion* – In Britain the majority of the 'Asian' population are Muslim, but there are also Hindus, Sikhs and Buddhists, all with different cultural norms and values.

- ❖ *regional location* – People from more remote rural areas tend to be more conservative than those from urban areas (towns and cities).

- ❖ *length of residence* – People who have arrived in the Western society more recently tend to adhere to traditions more than second or third generation residents.

- ❖ *education* – Higher levels of education can lead to a loosening of traditional ties and the questioning of traditional practices.

- ❖ *social class* – The higher the social class, the more likelihood of Westernized attitudes to marriage; for example, African Asians tend to come from business and professional backgrounds and their children are highly likely to go to university, where questioning is encouraged. This group tend to have a higher proportion of inter-ethnic marriages.

The dominant pattern for such a diverse group of people tends to be for an arranged marriage which involves much more choice and negotiation between couples and their families than is usually supposed. A young woman can confide with her parents (usually her mother) and refuse if she does not like a prospective partner. Further meetings will be arranged with other approved-of partners until eventually a mutually suitable choice has been made. The extended families on both sides are still involved, so the 'choice' is not completely free. Most young Asians will marry someone of very similar cultural and religious background, but they may well negotiate and refuse several partners before a final choice is made.

The situation with contemporary arranged marriages can be seen to have parallels with the Western system of romantic love as a basis of supposedly 'free' choice. Most people tend to marry partners who are socially similar to themselves. In addition, advocates of arranged marriages (where it is assumed that 'love' develops

after marriage as the result of families being involved in a wise choice of partner), could well point to the dramatically high divorce rate in societies where it is supposed that love 'will conquer all'.

❖ Activity 35 ❖

Examine the arguments for and against arranged marriages. What are the problems with over-generalizing about such a complex social phenomenon?

Number of partners

In Western societies such as Britain, the practice of monogamy, i.e. marriage to one partner, is legally enforced and the penalties for bigamy can be severe. However, there are a number of societies throughout the world where marriage to more than one partner, polygamy, is permissible, e.g. a number of African countries such as Kenya, as well as some Muslim societies. There is evidence that as these societies modernize, polygamy is becoming less popular. It can certainly be difficult for women and it

Table 3.4 Changing world patterns in marriage and family life

Area	Move away from	Move towards
Social organization/ideology	Patriarchy/matriarchy	Egalitarian
Family type	Extended	Nuclear, symmetrical
Number of partners	Polygamy	Monogamy
Partner choice	Arranged	Romantic love
Treatment of children	Sent to work at early age	Protected, nurtured
Role of children	Producers	Consumers
Domestic labour	Female	Shared

appears that they are behind the move toward monogamy as they become increasingly economically independent.

William J. Goode (1963) and Anthony Giddens (1993) have both identified a world trend toward monogamy as described in Table 3.4 on p. 103.

Marital stability and divorce

Dramatic changes in marital patterns have clearly been occurring in many societies during the second half of the twentieth century. In the USA and Europe, divorce rates have risen (see Table 3.5) and there are signs that cohabitation is becoming established as an alternative to marriage.

❖ Activity 36 ❖

1 Which two countries had the largest decrease in marriage rates from 1981 to 1993?

2 Two countries had an increase in marriage rates. Why is this surprising?

3 Which two countries had (a) the highest and (b) the lowest divorce rates?

4 How would you explain the different divorce rates between some of the European countries?

Table 3.5 Marriage and divorce rates in the EC, 1981 and 1993

| | Rates per 1,000 population | | | |
| | Marriages | | Divorces | |
	1981	1993	1981	1993
United Kingdom	7.1	5.9	2.8	3.1
Denmark	5.0	6.1	2.8	2.5
Finland	6.3	4.9	2.0	2.5
Sweden	4.5	3.9	2.4	2.5
Belgium	6.5	5.4	1.6	2.1
Austria	6.3	5.6	1.8	2.0
Netherlands	6.0	5.8	2.0	2.0
France	5.8	4.4	1.6	1.9
Germany	6.2	5.5	2.0	1.9
Luxembourg	5.5	6.0	1.4	1.9
Portugal	7.8	6.9	0.7	1.2
Greece	6.9	6.0	0.7	0.7
Spain	5.4	5.0	0.3	0.7
Italy	5.6	5.1	0.2	0.4
Irish Republic	6.0	4.4	–	–
EC average	6.1	5.3	1.5	1.7

Source: Social Trends (1996)

Divorce rates are increasing in most societies, with the highest rates in the USA; in California more than half of marriages end in divorce. The highest rates in Europe are in Britain and Denmark, with lower rates in Catholic countries where religion may still have influence. In Britain, divorce is low amongst some ethnic minorities, e.g. Muslims. In Britain about 4 in 10 contemporary marriages will end in divorce, whereas the overall rate for all marriage age groups is about 1 in 7.

A variety of explanations have been offered for the dramatic increase in divorce which has noticeably escalated in the last 25 years:

❖ *increased liberalization of the divorce laws* – There was a sharp increase in divorce after 1970. This was a result of the 1969 Divorce Reform Act which shifted the grounds for divorce from matrimonial guilt (where a partner had to prove wrongdoing on grounds such as adultery, cruelty or desertion) to irretrievable breakdown, where divorces could be granted after a period of separation (two years if both consent, five years if only one partner consents).

❖ *increased social acceptance of marital breakdown and less stigma for divorced people* – The mass media often feature divorce as a common aspect of the lives of the rich and famous, most notably in recent times the Royal family.

❖ *changes affecting women's lives* – The majority of divorce petitions are now made by women, which could be a reflection of their increased discontent with men who have refused to recognize that wives work in paid employment. Women wish to have a more equal partnership based on shared domestic labour and childcare and involving companionship and compatibility.

Women of all social classes are educated to higher levels and now the majority of wives and mothers work, which can make them more financially independent. So if a relationship is unsatisfactory it can be ended where, formerly, women were economically trapped in 'empty shell' marriages where there was little love or emotional attachment between husband and wife.

Not only are increased numbers of women in paid employment, significant numbers are in demanding professional occupations which may not be recognized and appreciated by a husband with traditional male attitudes, who sees his own work as more important than that of his wife.

In Focus

◆

Changing times

'Norwich vicar is holding special services for divorcing couples to mark the end of their relationship. They are asked to sell their rings to raise money for Christian Aid.'

Source: The Guardian, 24 April 1996

❖ Activity 37 ❖

What does the newspaper snippet (see *In Focus* above) tell us about changing attitudes to divorce?

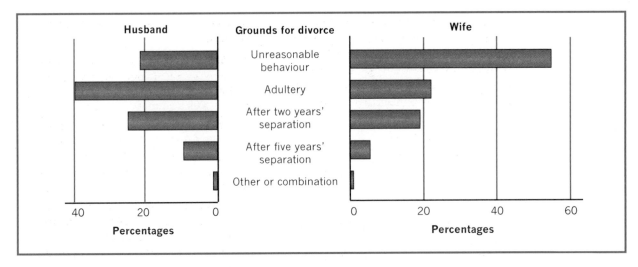

Figure 3.5
Divorces granted to spouses: by ground, England, Wales and N. Ireland, 1993

❖ **Activity 38** ❖

1 Explain the different grounds for divorce between husbands and wives.
2 Who gets granted divorce most? Explain why.

The privatization of the family

If the family has become a 'haven in a heartless world' or equivalent to a 'warm bath' as some sociologists have suggested (see p. 73), there is a cost. The increased search for privacy and intimacy as a counter to pressures in the outside world of work becomes focused on a small group of two or three people in the nuclear family. This can mean that families become a hotbed of emotional intensity and tensions which can result in divorce. In the past, the extended family and possibly the neigh-

❖ **Activity 39** ❖

Can marital advisory agencies such as Relate provide equivalent 'wise counsel'?

Conduct some research to find out more about the activities of Relate in your area (the Citizens' Advice Bureau can provide details).

bourliness of community could act as a safety valve, i.e. if marital difficulties were encountered, wise counsel from an older relative was never far away and could help to ease tensions.

Who divorces?

Several factors such as age, social class and occupation, ethnicity, religion, divorce experience in the family, and status differences between partners can be noted:

❖ *age* – The younger age groups, notably teenage marriages, have higher divorce rates. Young people change as they mature, so couples can 'drift apart'. Often their financial or employment circumstances are insecure, which can be a source of tension. If the reason for marriage was pregnancy, the divorce chances are much greater: over half such marriages break down.

❖ *social class and occupation* – Despite the impression conveyed by the media, the middle classes tend to have lower divorce rates than the working class, with the highest rates being among the unemployed. Some middle-class occupations which involve long periods of living separately, e.g. actors, authors, artists, company directors and hotel keepers also have higher than average divorce rates.

However, the general picture is that economic well-being, job security and a good standard of living are associated with marital stability. Evidence to support this comes from couples who commonly cite financial difficulties as a cause of tensions within their marriage.

❖ *ethnicity* – Overall divorce rates are lower among ethnic minorities; one factor for this may be cultural attitudes where marriage is highly valued and divorce unthinkable.

The planning and foresight that is part of the arranged marriage system (see below) may be seen as a contributory factor. It may be that there are significant numbers of 'empty shell' marriages because divorce is not approved of in tight-knit communities where a wide network of kin can register strong disapproval of marital failure.

❖ *religion* – Similar points to the above can be made; strong religious affiliation can mean that divorce would never be considered. In the recent past, devout Catholics would never divorce because of their religious beliefs, so the 'empty shell'

marriage or separation were the only options.

❖ *family experience of divorce* – You are more likely to divorce if your parents divorced; a phenomenon referred to as 'the divorce inheritance'. Several reasons have been offered for this, among them being the possibility that psychological insecurity and instability among children of divorced parents produces divorce-prone adults. Nicky Hart (1976) argues that within divorced families there may be greater acceptance by offspring of divorce as a solution when they themselves eventually experience marital difficulties.

❖ *social and status differences between partners* – The greater the social distance between couples along lines of class, occupation, ethnicity, religion or age, the more the likelihood of divorce. In some circumstances, e.g. inter-ethnic marriage, the social disapproval from kin and the wider society can be a source of instability for the couple. The children of such relationships can add to tensions as they grow older and may experience confusion as to their ethnic identity.

Table 3.6 Divorce: by duration of marriage, United Kingdom

	1961	1971	Percentages 1981	1991	1993
0–2 years	1	1	2	9	8
3–4 years	10	12	19	14	14
5–9 years	31	31	29	27	28
10–14 years	23	19	20	18	18
15–19	} 14	13	13	13	12
20–24		10	9	10	10
25–29	} 21	6	5	5	5
30 years+		9	5	4	4
All durations (=100%) (thousands)	27.0	79.2	155.6	171.1	180.0

Source: Social Trends (1996)

❖ Activity 40 ❖

1 Referring to Table 3.6, summarize the key changes in divorce by duration of marriage between 1961 and 1993.

2 How would you explain any significant changes?

Consequences of divorce

The effects on children

Reference has been made previously to New Right views on single-parent families and their relationship to increasing social problems such as delinquency, poor educational achievement and rising crime rates. Sociologists such as Dennis (1993) and Halsey (1992) (see p. 93) have highlighted similar trends in association with 'fatherless families'. Traditionally, there was little emphasis on the effects of divorce on children, a common assumption being that the divorce of one's parents had little effect in the longer term. This view has been increasingly questioned in recent years. A number of studies in Britain and the USA have indicated worrying trends and patterns in the lives of the children of divorced parents.

As adults, when compared with those from non-divorced backgrounds, such children are more likely to:

❖ get divorced themselves

❖ underachieve educationally

❖ experience unemployment and poverty

❖ suffer poor health, mental illness and commit suicide

❖ become criminals.

All the above effects remain when account is taken of class, economic circumstances and related variables.

However, William J. Goode (1993) points out that it is difficult to disentangle the effects of divorce from the undoubted prior tensions during the marriage. He says: 'Many if not most of the problems exhibited by children of divorce were visible in their families long before the legal dissolution took place' (Goode 1993, p. 179).

In the early 1990s, a study in Exeter by Cockett and Tripp (1994) supported the negative findings as outlined above. They found that children in 'reordered families' (their term for families involving remarriages and new step relationships) experienced great difficulties of adjustment and were more likely to experience social problems in adult lives as well as during their school years. A common theme was that such children would have preferred to remain with their original parents even when relationships had been strained and involved tension and feuding. Such findings counter earlier views that a marriage involving tension is bad for children. It seems from the Exeter study that children adapt and survive in relationships that might be seen as damaging to an outsider. What children seem to want is their original families to remain intact whatever the circumstances (see *In Focus* on p. 109). The best way for them to cope with the dramatic changes incurred by their parents' divorce is for their experience of loss to be recognized and dealt with appropriately.

A more positive view concerning the effects of divorce on children is that, for some, divorce of parents can mean insights into relationships that give a more mature outlook on potential problems in marriage. As a result, relationships are entered into with understanding and a desire for stability. A key factor contributing to the emotional health and stability of a child with divorced parents is the degree to which both parents have helped the child understand the divorce process, i.e. accepting that their mother and father have to separate but making it clear that the child is not to blame and should not feel guilt. Such issues are increasingly being recognized in legislation concerning divorce, where children's needs, experiences and rights are considered along with the parents.

Another positive view on divorce comes from the Norwegian sociologist, Kari Moxnes (1989), who suggests that rather

In Focus
◆
Children's loyalty to family of origin

Children's loyalty was graphically illustrated in the aftermath of the multiple murder conviction in 1995 of Rosemary West, whose husband Fred West committed suicide while in prison awaiting trial. Accounts from their children indicated their experience of appalling levels of physical and sexual abuse, brutality and depravity. Despite this, when two of their children were interviewed on television after their mother's trial, they disclosed their love of their parents and the wish that their father was still alive. Stephen West related an account of an early investigation by the NSPCC after a teacher had reported his physical injuries after a beating from his mother. The investigation was discontinued after Stephen withdrew his allegations because he did not want his family to be broken up. Tragically this occurred before a number of further murders had been carried out. Such an extreme and unusual case indicates the degree of loyalty some children display in appalling circumstances. It may be an indication of how powerful the ideology of family and biological parenthood is within our society.

than seeing divorce as the loss or break up of a family, it involves instead the creation of a new 'bi-nuclear' family where there are benevolent connections between old and new partners and children. This might be seen as an overly optimistic view, considering many divorces involve bitterness and jealousy between former partners, but it is interesting to see if present social policies involving conciliation and mediation within divorcing families can aid such desirable goals as raised by Moxnes.

Loss of contact with the father

Another consequence in the aftermath of divorce is the eventual loss of contact with the father. Over half of divorced fathers make no contact with their children within two years of divorce. From a feminist perspective this may at first be seen as further evidence of the heartlessness of men, but the factors involved are complex. If a wife moves away, geographical distance can be an obvious barrier to contact. If access is for a day or a weekend on a monthly basis, the brief meeting and parting can be distressing for the child and the father. If one or both parents are in new relationships, tensions can arise with the children being involved in divided loyalties. The pressure group 'Families Need Fathers' took up such issues and highlighted them in the 1980s.

As suggested above, recent divorce legislation has recognized such complexities and has attempted to foster access agreements which are more amicable and satisfactory for all involved. A child's needs are investigated through professional experts such as Court Welfare Officers who provide advice and guidance through the divorce courts.

❖ Activity 41 ❖

Examine the views on the consequences of divorce outlined above. What would you suggest could be done to alleviate the painfulness of divorce on families?

Cohabitation

The increase in cohabitation suggests a change from previous patterns, when cohabitation was usually a trial or temporary phase prior to marriage. Today, increased numbers of cohabiting couples raise children in stable relationships. In Britain and a number of European countries, there is growing evidence that long-term cohabitation is growing in popularity. This is less the case in countries such as Ireland, Italy and Portugal where marriage continues to be popular.

Table 3.7 Percentage of women cohabiting: by age and marital status, Great Britain, 1993–94 to 1994–95

	Single[1]	Separated	Divorced	Widowed	All non-married women
					Percentages
16–24	14	8	–	–	14
25–34	33	17	29	–	30
35–49	18	7	25	14	19
50–59	6	5	12	3	8
All aged 16–59	20	10	24	6	19

[1] Never married

Source: Social Trends (1996)

❖ Activity 42 ❖

1 Referring to Table 3.7, summarize the differences between (a) age groups and (b) marital status.
2 How would you explain the differences?

Coleman and Salt (1992) suggest a considerable erosion of traditional assumptions and attitudes which could be linked to the declining popularity of marriage in Britain. The traditional assumptions include:

❖ Marriage confers on a woman a secure, settled income and a status and role based on raising children and keeping house; tasks around which most of the rest of her life will revolve.

❖ Marriage lasts for the rest of an increasingly long life.

❖ Marriage is the setting for almost all childbearing and sexual cohabitation.

Changes have occurred and there are newer ideas, laws, economic roles for women and more reliable forms of birth control, all of which challenge the assumptions above.

❖ Activity 43 ❖

1 Explain what these changes might be, giving examples.
2 How might such changes undermine the popularity of marriage?

Cohabitation has always been an option and in previous centuries many people did not have a formal wedding because of the cost. Living together was acceptable for many in the lower social classes, with marriage being associated with the higher social classes. The change in the twentieth century from cohabitation being a temporary phase to a long-term choice can be explained in several ways:

❖ Marriage is becoming less fashionable; cohabiting media role models influence opinion.

❖ Marriage is expensive, e.g. a wedding dress can cost hundreds of pounds.

❖ The influence of religion is declining (see Chapter 14, *Religion*) and increasing numbers question the purpose of a religious ceremony when they have no belief in it.

❖ Growing economic and employment insecurity may make people wary of commitment to long-term relationships. There is evidence of this particularly among young men who have increasing

difficulty in finding work – a basis for 'settling down' and marrying.

❖ Awareness of, or experience of, high divorce rates make people more cautious about marriage.

❖ Activity 44 ❖

1 After reading the previous text, Table 3.8 and the *In Focus* below, what does this information tell you about attitudes to cohabitation between (a) different age groups and (b) men and women?

2 How may this explain rising levels of cohabitation?

Table 3.8   People who feel cohabitation[1] is wrong: by gender, 1994

| | | *Percentages* |
Year of birth	Males	Females
1960–1978	7	6
1950–1959	10	8
1940–1949	16	14
1930–1939	23	22
Before 1930	40	34
All	17	16

[1]Percentage agreeing with the statement that living together outside marriage is always wrong.

Source: Social Trends (1996)

There is some evidence that cohabiting relationships are less stable than marriages. A 1994 Economic and Social Research Council report found that couples living together were four times more likely to separate than married couples. However, this study did not distinguish between couples with children and couples without, so a wide range of circumstances could be aggregated together in the results. For example, young cohabiting couples such as students may well not be committed to a longer term relationship. Also, the stronger position of women in cohabiting relationships could mean they are less willing to tolerate a male partner who is not participating in the relationship on an equal basis.

In Focus

◆

Changing times

Increased acceptance from the establishment for cohabitation

'I think there are degrees of wrong. Promiscuity is far worse, sexual abuse is far worse. Within a cohabiting relationship, there is at least commitment and there may well be as serious a commitment and as serious an intention to stay together as there is in marriage, which has been legally settled, and I think therefore one has to have some sort of sliding scale in one's mind.'

Source: John Hapgood, Archbishop of York, quoted in the *Daily Mail*, adapted by *The Guardian*, 22 June 1995

❖ **Activity 45** ❖

Does marriage 'bind' people together in stronger ways than cohabitation?

Debate the arguments for and against this view.

Living alone

If increasing numbers are choosing to cohabit because of increased instability in marriage, another option that is increasing is for people to live alone. In 1996, just over 25 per cent of households were occupied by one person and this proportion is forecast to continue rising. As would probably be expected, a significant proportion are the elderly widowed, usually women, and divorced or separated men and women. However, a rapidly growing proportion are single people of either sex who are opting to live alone.

It would seem that increasing numbers of young professionals are opting for independent living. They may have relationships, but they desire to live alone rather than cohabit or marry. Their work can involve long hours and commitment which means that childrearing becomes impossible and in any case they question the necessity of having children in an insecure and uncertain world.

❖ **Activity 46** ❖

Why do people have children? What factors may lead to increased questioning of the need to have children in the future?

In an essay in *The Observer*, 11 February 1996, Anthony Giddens suggests that living alone as an option will increase. Rather than seeing single people in a negative light, almost as lonely 'outcasts' subject to social derision or pity, he suggests that living alone will become a valued option,

offering benefits of choice and independence that are not available in more conventional family settings. He suggests that a person on their own may, in fact, have *more* contact with a wider network of relatives and kin than the conventional married couple, whose 'coupledom' could be a more isolated experience.

❖ **Activity 47** ❖

Refer back to the section on the 'isolated nuclear family' (p. 73) and give examples of how a person living alone may have more contact with other relatives.

What are your views on a future where more people may opt to live alone?

Conduct a small survey covering a variety of people to ascertain attitudes to 'living alone'.

Single parenthood

As Fig. 3.6 shows, there has clearly been a dramatic increase in the proportion of single-parent households in Britain and other Western societies in the last two decades. Contrary to the popular media stereotype, which gives the impression of a high number of feckless teenage mothers, the largest number of such households are occupied by women in their late twenties and early thirties. Until recently the largest proportion were divorcees, but in the early 1990s the greater proportion became households headed by a woman who had never married, in a similar age group. Teenage motherhood has declined and many in this category live with their parents. This counteracts media impressions that deliberate pregnancy is used to jump council housing waiting lists while living off state benefits; a theme much beloved by New Right thinkers and conservative politicians (see p. 95)

The high proportion of single-parent households headed by an older woman is probably explained as part of the rise in

Figure 3.6
Families headed by lone parents as a percentage of all families with dependent children

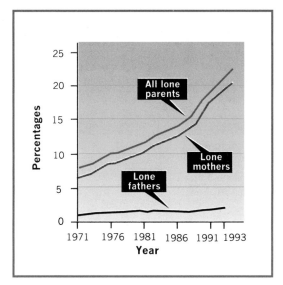

involve both male and female divorcees bringing children from their previous marriages.

Reconstituted families involve relationship complexities which can be an additional source of tension. This may lead to instability; divorce rates are higher for second marriages. One cause of this can be financial difficulties where previous relationships involving children include maintenance payments.

Step-parenting

Other factors can centre around the step relationships between both parents and siblings. Tensions can develop along the lines of 'you can't tell me what to do; you're not my real father'. If the couple are fairly young, further children can result in jealousy and a feeling of rejection among older siblings. Studies of step-parenting indicate the potential for conflict with children, the sad outcome of this being the high proportion of abused children who are the victims of stepfathers.

Step relationships as a norm?

It is to be expected that, as the rate of divorce and relationship breakdown continue to rise, and approximately one in three marriages is a remarriage, the proportion of reconstituted families will grow. If Moxnes views on the 'bi-nuclear' family (see p. 108) can be developed, this could be beneficial to all concerned.

The changing age structure and effects on family members

Childhood

Phillipe Ariès' views on childhood have been referred to previously (see p. 70). He sees the concept of childhood (in the sense of the child's world being separate from the world of adults) as a recent phenomenon in modern societies. Reasons for this are evident in the length of compulsory schooling and the illegality of child labour.

cohabitation, examined above. Rather than irresponsibly having children outside a stable relationship with a man, it is more likely that there was a period of stable cohabitation which eventually broke down – not dramatically different from a marriage that ends in divorce. It is still not clear whether cohabiting relationships involving children are more likely to break up than those of married parents with children. Common sense and the older generation may assume that cohabitation is less stable than marriage, but if there has been a change to a stronger sense of commitment within cohabiting relationships, particularly where there are children, then the chances of break up will be similar to those of married couples.

Reconstituted families (blended, step or reordered families)

These are families formed as a result of the remarriage of one or both partners and they constitute a rising proportion of households as divorces increase. One in three marriages now involve a remarriage for one or both partners. A significant number will have children from former marriages. It is more likely that women rather than men will have custody of children after divorce, so only a small proportion of reconstituted households will

The result has been a lengthened period of a child's dependency on his or her parents. Whereas in the past the child could contribute as a 'small adult' to the family budget through work, making the family a 'production unit', today the family with children has become more of a 'consumption unit'. Companies such as Mothercare and Toys Я Us have recognized the business potential of the large 'childhood' market. 'Cereal packet' images of families abound in advertising where parents are exhorted to buy the best products for their child's well-being.

Adolescence

As childhood dependency has increased from the nineteenth century, the late twentieth century has seen an increase and extension of adolescent dependency within families. In Britain the school leaving age is 16, but very few go straight to full-time work because of the unavailability of jobs and apprenticeships. Further and higher education from 16 years onwards has become a majority experience and, if higher-level qualifications are taken at university, the age of adolescent dependency has risen for many to the early 20s. Added to this are cuts in grants to and funding for students, meaning that a combination of loans, low-paid, part-time work and, inevitably, financial and related support from parents extends many young adults' period of dependency (see *In Focus* on p. 115).

Such a situation clearly has the potential for tension as the young adult is fully developed in a physical, maturational sense but is still classed as a dependant within the family and the wider society. One outcome can be an increase in familial stress, particularly where financial hardship is experienced. In some circumstances, divorce may result as parents and children become locked into emotional turmoil and confusion.

Such factors, together with the decreased availability of State benefits to young people, have been used to explain the increase in homelessness among the young and, for increasing numbers, the inevitable drift into drugs and crime.

❖ Activity 48 ❖

1 What possible strains in families may occur when young men live at home?
2 Looking at Fig. 3.7 on p. 115, what do you think might explain the differences between the proportion of women compared to men who live at home.

The elderly

Average life expectancy has increased throughout this century. In Britain, by the year 2000, the average life expectancy for women will be 80 years and for men 75 years. In simple terms, this means increased numbers of elderly people in the population. In contrast to this is the trend towards smaller families and childlessness because of increased numbers of working women. The result is a shift in the age structure of the population toward the older age groups.

Increased length of life means that disability and ill-health are likely to be experienced by more people. Medical advances have meant that many formerly life-threatening conditions can be managed and life sustained for longer periods (see Chapter 10, *Health, poverty and welfare*). In the context of cuts in public expenditure affecting state provision of care for the elderly, the question arises as to who has to look after the old. The obvious answer is the family, and some see this as the right and only option. Such views are summarized in Margaret Thatcher's notorious statement that, 'there is no such thing as society, there are individuals and there are families, and nothing else'.

It is not just conservatives who present such views; many see that family responsibilities and obligations have a moral basis to them, e.g. functionalist sociologists would see such mutual ties as strengthening the family as a core social unit.

However, regardless of such values and ideals, a number of difficulties emerge in the light of current social trends. A key question is that, if the elderly are to be

'Family life is changing in thousands of homes as more young men choose to remain living with their parents rather than flee the nest for marriage, cohabitation or independence.

Experts yesterday said that while this could lead to rises in family tension and even violence, it may improve relationships by giving children the chance to see their parents as independent adults rather than just as parents.

The Survey of English Housing, based on interviews with 20,000 households and published by the Office for National Statistics, showed significant rises over the past four years in the proportion of adults aged between 20 and 34 staying put. There were fewer young couples forming households, while figures for under-35s opting for a single life remained static.

This may be partly a reflection of the recession and poor private housing prospects in the early 1990s. But the trend towards later marriage may also be an important factor. Well over half of men aged 20 to 24 live with their parents, as do nearly a quarter of men aged 25 to 29. Four in ten of students – who traditionally went away to college – live with their parents.

Alan Cooklin, a consultant in family psychiatry and an academic at University College, London, said: "In our culture we tend to think of maleness and adulthood in terms of separation, particularly in moving away from home and mother. You tend now to get more problems and more potential for violence, between mothers and sons particularly. I see a significant number of these."

Relate, the marriage guidance organization, said it had dealt with many couples for whom the departure of children had been "quite a shock" as they discovered they needed serious work on their own relationship.

Julia Cole, Relate's press officer, said there may be gains in having children around for longer "after the storm of teenage tantrums", allowing all those involved to see the others as independent adults rather than mothers, fathers, sons or daughters.

Other experts said yesterday the stay-at-home trend among younger unmarried people would be unlikely to affect significantly government projections that another 4.4 million homes would be needed over the next twenty years. The explosion in older people living alone after divorce or their partner's death was likely to continue.

One other finding could provide fresh ammunition for opponents of new housing benefit restrictions on unemployed people aged under 25. The report said the benefit was not a factor in encouraging young single people to leave home for private accommodation. Even those entitled did not claim.'

Source:
James Meikie,
The Guardian,
12 April 1996

Figure 3.7 Percentage of men and women still living with their parents

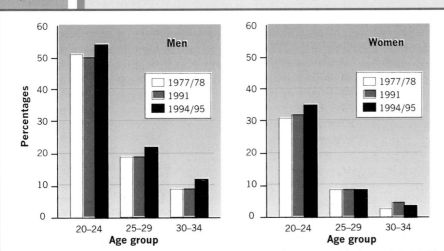

cared for within families, who does the caring? It has been pointed out elsewhere that it is inevitably seen as the female's responsibility. Given that the majority of wives and mothers now work, the fact that women comprise half the labour force, and that there is a rising trend towards having children later, there is clearly a problem. If state support for the elderly is not provided then it is likely to add to the previ-ously identified 'dual burden' of work: women having to manage both work and childcare responsibilities with little support from men or the state. Christina Hardyment (1990) recently referred to the 'Tricycle of care' involving women throughout their adult lives. This covers the raising of babies and children, the care of elderly parents and, eventually, the care of an elderly husband.

Social policy and the family

Social policy issues, such as the effects of divorce and the future care of the elderly have been addressed in previous sections of this chapter. A point to note is that in Britain, unlike other European countries such as Sweden and Germany, there have never been direct family social policies as such. Instead, social policies (e.g. on divorce) have indirectly impinged on families. The cultural and historical reason for this is the much sharper delineation in British society between the 'public' and the 'private'. The latter 'private' domain is clearly associated with the family and the political assumption of freedom and non-interference by the state in the private world of individuals and families. It is not seen as the job of govern-ments or the state to interfere in the private world of families and individuals. Once you close your front door, what happens behind it is for you and your family only.

There are obviously problems with this and there are clear indications that the government and the state does 'interfere' in family life in a variety of ways, some of which can be seen negatively, some positively. Foucault (1979) highlights some of the negative dimensions with his views on state 'thought police', such as social workers and counsellors who impose their, supposedly, superior versions of correct family life and behaviour on the more vulnerable members of the population. Donzelot (1980) refers to such aspects as the 'policing of families'.

On the positive side, most would agree that where abuse and harm to family members is involved, governments and the state should 'interfere' through social work agencies and legislation.

Future developments in social policy will probably focus on a number of areas of family life covering divorce, children's rights, women and employment, pensions and care of the elderly. Governments of either persuasion will probably adhere to the notion of non-interference in the 'private' domain as an ideal, but in practice will indirectly affect family life through their political policies.

The future of families and households

'... in the past twenty-five years we have witnessed: the demise of the male bread-winner family economy, with the mass employment of married women outside the home; skyrocketing rates of divorce and remarriage; birth rates dipping to unprece-dented levels, well below replacement rates; the proliferation of single-parent house-holds, mostly female-headed; and a sharp rise in the proportion of adults living alone.' (Secombe 1992)

The key distinction that emerges from the debates covered in this chapter lies between the idea of a majority experience in a nuclear form of family and the advocates of diversity in households and family structure. Within this polarity are aspects of political and moral views about the ideal way to live, to have personal relationships and to raise children.

Arguments for the conventional nuclear family

Functionalists, New Right thinkers and conservatives highlight the desirability and naturalness of stereotypical nuclear families for social stability and order. The supposed breakdown of such families is seen to be responsible for increased social problems, such as crime and drug abuse among the young. In social policy terms, marriage and family life must be strengthened.

Liberalization of divorce laws, cohabitation and homosexual families are disap-

proved of and seen as undermining 'conventional' marriage and family life – seen as the basis of a 'healthy' society. The increase in AIDs and HIV-related illnesses is presented as evidence of the need to return to conventional, heterosexual, monogamous families.

New Right thinkers suggest that the Welfare State has weakened the family by creating a 'culture of dependency' where family members opt out of responsibility for one another and rely on state support.

❖ Activity 49 ❖

Look at Table 3.9 and Fig. 3.8 on p. 118

1 Summarize the trends from 1972 to 1994–95 for (a) couples, (b) lone mothers and (c) lone fathers.

2 What explanations can be given for such trends?

3 Make some predictions about trends in the future.

Table 3.9 Percentage of dependent children living in different family types

| | Percentages | | | | |
	1972	1981	1986	1991	1994–95
Couple					
1 child	16	18	18	17	16
2 children	35	41	41	37	37
3 or more children	41	29	28	28	27
Lone mother					
1 child	2	3	4	5	6
2 children	2	4	5	7	8
3 or more children	2	3	3	6	6
Lone father					
1 child	-	1	1	-	1
2 or more children	1	1	1	1	-
All dependent children	100	100	100	100	100

Source: Social Trends (1996)

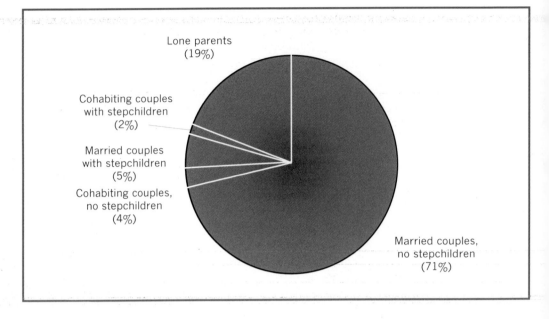

Figure 3.8
Families with dependent children: by family type, 1991

Lone parents (19%)

Cohabiting couples with stepchildren (2%)

Married couples with stepchildren (5%)

Cohabiting couples, no stepchildren (4%)

Married couples, no stepchildren (71%)

Arguments for diversity

Advocates for diversity see variation and choice in relationship and childrearing options as a vital ingredient in an open, democratic, tolerant and pluralistic society. Morality is relative and non-judgmental; there is a wide range of relationship options and no one option should be valued more highly than another. Social problems cannot be directly linked to diversity in relationships. Rather, it is the stigmatization of 'non-conventional' lifestyles that may cause some to become 'outsiders'. So, from this perspective, increased tolerance of diversity will result in a more harmonious society.

Using statistics

The debate between those who argue for the conventional nuclear family and those arguing for diversity is a good example of how values are often featured in sociological arguments. This does not stop us from seeking 'facts' about families and households, and statistics can help us to gain some purchase on what these facts are. However, difficulties remain, as statistical findings have to be interpreted within a framework where values also emerge.

❖ Activity 50 ❖

Study Tables 3.10 and 3.11 opposite.

1 Which table could you use as the basis of an argument that there is a broadly nuclear family structure in Britain?

2 Which table could you use to emphasize diversity in domestic arrangements?

❖ Activity 51 ❖

'Most adults still marry and have children. Most children are reared by their natural parents. Most people live in a household headed by a married couple. Most marriages continue until parted by death. No great change seems currently in prospect.' (Chester 1985)

This statement was made in 1985. In the light of some of the trends indicated in this chapter, can Chester's views still be upheld? Present arguments for and against.

Table 3.10 Households: by size, Great Britain

	1961	1971	1981	1991	1994–95
			Percentages		
One person	14	18	22	27	27
Two people	30	32	32	34	34
Three people	23	19	17	16	16
Four people	18	17	18	16	15
Five people	9	8	7	5	6
Six or more people	7	6	4	2	2
All households (=100%)(millions)	16.2	18.2	19.5	22.4	23.1

Source: Social Trends (1996)

Table 3.11 Types of household: Great Britain, 1961 to 1994–95

	1961	1971	1981	1991	1994–95
			Percentages		
One person					
Under pensionable age	4	6	8	11	12
Over pensionable age	7	12	14	16	15
Two or more unrelated adults	5	4	5	3	6
One family					
Married couple[1]	2	4	5	7	8
No children	26	27	26	28	25
1–2 dependent children[2]	30	26	25	20	20
3 or more dependent children	8	9	6	5	5
Non-dependent children only	10	8	8	8	6
Lone parent[1]					
Dependent children[3]	2	3	5	6	7
Non-dependent children only	4	4	4	4	3
Two or more families	3	1	1	1	1
All households (=100%)(millions)	16.2	18.2	19.5	22.4	23.1

Source: Social Trends (1996)

1 See Appendix, Part 2: Households.
2 Other individuals who were not family members may be included.
3 May also include non-dependent children.

A good example of this is Robert Chester's conception of the neo-conventional family, which he inteprets from the statistics of household composition. Chester (1985) envisages the future of family lives remaining much the same as at present, with most people experiencing 'modified' nuclear family relationships for a significant proportion of their lives.

In support of Chester's views, the Family Policy Studies Group in 1994 projected that the year 2000 would see 75 per cent of children still being brought up by their parents to adulthood. It must, of course, be noted then that 25 per cent of children would probably experience the separation or divorce of their parents.

Reproductive technologies

Another dimension of the future of families and households is the changing nature of parenting. It is clear that increasing numbers of couples in stable, long-term relationships will remain childless, so ideas and definitions of 'family' which include children will have to be reconsidered. The age of first motherhood will probably continue to rise, so in the future motherhood in the late teens or twenties will become more unusual. An interesting development concerning reproductive technologies centres around the case of a 62-year-old Italian woman who received

hormone treatment and gave birth to a boy in 1994.

A number of actresses and media personalities have attracted publicity as a result of having children in their 40s. If this trend develops, a future possibility is the deferral of motherhood until after early retirement at around 50 years old. This may be seen as a possible answer to childcare problems. So a woman's life course could be as shown in Table 3.12.

The end of marriage?

There is clear evidence that cohabitation is becoming an established alternative to marriage in a number of European societies. In Sweden and Denmark, more children are raised by cohabiting parents than married ones. The evidence on the comparative stability of marriage to cohabitation is still unclear, but it seems clear that parents with children have a sense of long-term commitment. The debates surrounding the 1996 Divorce Bill legislation in Britain have included concerns about the possible weakening of marriage, but historical trends in divorce inexorably move toward liberalization. Whether this is arrested depends on how influential New Right politicians are in exerting their wishes to strengthen marriage and family life. Such issues are obviously irrelevant to the growing numbers of cohabiting couples.

Table 3.12   A woman's life course

Infancy/childhood	▶ Dependency
Adolescence	▶ Dependency
Young adulthood	▶ Partial dependency/ Early career
Adulthood	▶ Career
Middle age	▶ Retirement/Parenting
Old age	▶ Dependency on offspring

Chapter summary

❖ The subject matter of this chapter is clearly a complex phenomenon involving a wide range of sociological views. On balance these views tend towards the negative, particularly when the stereotypical nuclear family is presented as the norm and ideal for everyone.

❖ Sociological 'facts' and investigations into how people actually live their personal lives and construct their relationships show that many either do not wish to or cannot attain this 'norm'.

❖ Diversity in relationships must be a central feature of modern life and sociological research. However, the statistically-backed household composition arguments of Chester's 'neo-conventional family' must be considered. The majority of the population do tend to experience a form of nuclear household for a significant part of their lives. Whether this is a result of 'familial ideology' and a cause for discontent is the subject of continuing sociological debate.

❖ A final question is that if a new version of family is to be substituted, what will it be like? Studies of 1960/70s communes and the Israeli *kibbutz* system tend to indicate instability, so such alternatives are unlikely to become widespread. It would seem that most people, for the foreseeable future, will seek out relationships involving some sense of stability and commitment but within more varied and flexible boundaries than the standard model of married, heterosexual parents raising children. Historical evidence tells us that this has probably always been the case.

Stimulus–response question

Using the information from this chapter and the items given on p. 122, answer the following questions:

1 By how many points has the percentage of women remaining unmarried by the age of 50 increased between 1971 and 1987 (Item C)?

(1 mark)

2 With reference to Item B and other sources, identify four characteristics of the 'normal' or 'cornflake packet family'.

(4 marks)

3 To what extent is it true that sociologists 'have neglected the emotional or expressive side' of marital relationships? Support your argument with appropriate examples (Item A).

(5 marks)

4 Using information from the items and elsewhere, discuss sociological reasons for the 'decline in the popularity of marriage' (Item C).

(7 marks)

5 With reference to the Items and elsewhere, assess the contribution made by feminist sociologists to an understanding of the changing structure of the family in modern society.

(8 marks)

AEB June 1996, Paper 1, Question 2

Item A

Recent sociological research on marriage and the family has focused on inequalities in who does the housework and childcare, and on how couples arrange their finance. These might be called the 'instrumental' or task-orientated aspects of marital and couple relationships. However, although such approaches have been very fruitful, sociologists have neglected the emotional or expressive side of relationships – in particular, the experiences of love and intimacy which many people say they regard as the most important thing in their lives. Increasingly, the message from the mass media is that everyone should be in a relationship.

The move from traditional marriage as an 'institution' to modern marriage as a 'personal relationship' has brought not only rising expectations of this relationship, but also increasing instability. However, as well as continuing dissatisfaction with gender inequalities in domestic tasks and finance management, many women now express unhappiness with what they perceive as men's unwillingness or inability to have intimate or emotionally close relationships.

Item B

Like many other ideologies, 'family values' are often only vaguely defined, but four main aspects of such values can be identified.

❖ 'Family values' are founded on the view that there is a 'normal' type of family, sometimes referred to as the 'cornflake packet family'.

❖ Supporters of 'family values' often celebrate what they regard as the traditional pattern of hierarchy, deference and division of labour within 'normal' family units. The disciplines of patriarchal control are assumed to be vital to the development of law-abiding and stable adults and children.

❖ The use of the term 'family values' is often code for the belief that family members have the duty to provide for one another and that they should be given a free hand in doing so.

❖ 'Family values' often entail broad opposition to liberal social codes with respect to sexuality and sexual reproduction.

Source: adapted from Jewson (1994)

Item C

Marriage is a normal and expected part of women's lives in Western society. However, although the vast majority of women will expect to marry at some time and at least once, in recent years there has been some decline in the popularity of marriage. In 1971 only 4 per cent of women remained unmarried by 50, but by 1987 the proportion had grown to 17 per cent. Women today are marrying older and marrying less and the trend may foreshadow other changes in household organization and family formation. Marriage is important in all women's lives, whether they are married or not, and this social status seems to symbolize the 'wholeness' of what it is to be a woman. The structure of the female labour market contains the assumption that working women are married. Also, the couple is the essential unit of household organization and domestic economy for adults who do not live alone.

Essay questions

1 'The "cornflake packet" image of the family does not represent the reality of family life in a modern society.' Discuss.

2 Examine the view that modern marriage is a partnership of equals.

3 How have feminists explained modern family life?

4 'Diversity has always been a feature of family structures both in the present and in the past.' Discuss.

5 How have changes in the lives of women this century affected marriage and family lives?

6 Is the family in crisis?

7 Do families need fathers?

 ## Further reading

Barrett, M. and McIntosh, M. (1982) *The Anti-Social Family*, London: Verso.

A socialist feminist critique of the conventional family in particular. The authors argue for a much wider range of possibilities for people to live together or alone.

Berger, B. and Berger, P.L. (1983) *The War Over the Family*, London: Hutchinson.

Two American sociologists defend the 'bourgeois', i.e. nuclear family and stress its desirable qualities for children and parents, emphasizing stability, loyalty, decency and trust.

Delphy, C. and Leonard, D. (1992) *Familiar Exploitation*, Cambridge: Polity Press.

A more recent contribution from feminist sociology, highlighting the inbuilt exploitative aspects of conventional families in which men gain and women lose.

Drake, M. (ed.) (1994) *Time, Family and Community*, Oxford: Blackwell.

An interesting collection of historical articles on various aspects of family life and women's and men's lives in the past, useful for our understanding of how families are as they are today.

Finch, J. and Mason, J. (1993) *Negotiating Family Responsibilities*, London: Routledge.

This highlights the complex web of ties and mutual obligations that family life entails, using examples such as the care of the sick and the elderly. The feminist emphasis highlights the key role played by women.

Morgan, D. (1985) *The Family, Politics and Social Theory*, London: Routledge.

One of Britain's foremost experts on the sociology of the family examines the relationships between theory and structural forces in society and its political impact on the family.

Warde, A. and Abercrombie, N. (eds) (1994) *Family, Household and the Life-Course*, Lancaster: Framework Press.

An interesting collection of articles summarizing key aspects of a range of recent studies which have examined dimensions of families and households.

Chapter 4

Education and training

❖ Preview

In this chapter we shall be looking at:

- ❖ key changes in the educational system of the United Kingdom over the last one hundred years

- ❖ wider social and political changes that have influenced these changes and set the agenda of research activity, for instance into the meritocracy ideal and comprehensive schools

- ❖ the methodology and focus of particular studies, including the influence of social theorists

- ❖ how educational performance is differentiated by other aspects of social structure and social processes, such as class background, ethnicity and gender

- ❖ how current day political and educational debates relate to wider social issues, such as unemployment and vocational training, and see their connections to the research agenda

- ❖ how to evaluate studies and evidence against the agenda issues.

❖ Introduction

Why study education?

Education, socialization and learning are three different, but related, concepts. *Education* is usually understood to mean what goes on in schools, colleges and universities. If we ask what happens in these institutions, the answer usually includes some such concept as *learning*. We can see from this that education is about 'learning' or *'socialization'* – it is a continuation of the socialization that starts in the family. But learning can take place anywhere and does not have to be in a school. In many societies a child may learn how to plant crops, build a hut, cook or make clothes from their mother or father, aunt or uncle. They may learn how to dance from watching and copying, and by listening to the comments on their performances as their skills grow. In complex Western societies there are a great many other sources of socialization that are more formal but are outside the family. These sources include books, television and other mass media.

Education takes place in a set of organisations. It is a set of social institutions, of social processes, fulfilling certain social functions, and illustrating social tensions and conflicts. It takes place in a collection of buildings and with specific personnel. It is something that everyone experiences, as it has been made compulsory by the state. There are massive legal and state structures to ensure that everyone is required to experience it. Clearly, education must be seen as a key process of social control.

All the sources of learning and socialization, other than in the educational system, are important and are discussed in this book. But it is as a continuation of socialization in schools that the state feels it must support, guarantee, structure and determine what goes on. The educational system is large, expensive and connected to the central structures of power in society. It is, therefore, of great interest to sociologists.

Most people agree that there is a close connection between the structure and success of the economy and the skills that people acquire in the education system. The precise nature of the relationship of the economy to the education system is something which needs to be established sociologically, if only because citizens and politicians also expect educational institutions to be concerned with other broader aspects of socialization into wider cultural values as well as the success of the economy.

Furthermore, most people believe that the kind of work people do (and their chances in life generally) depends on what kind of education they get. Where an individual ends up in society depends both on where they start (their family) and on the educational processes they experience. In other words, questions of social mobility are linked to a study of the educational system.

Rewards are not evenly distributed in our society, but despite this most people believe that everyone should have a fair and equal chance to get on in the educational system. This is a statement of values and preferences, but it is a statement that has a high level of acceptance among the general public and has, in many ways, been a guiding thread for the educational policies of governments for well over fifty years. If we are to understand the way our society works, we must look at exactly who succeeds in our educational system, and why, and the connection of that to wider social values. There is, for example, a common assumption that effort and hard work should be rewarded with greater access to education. Put another way, a combination of ability and hard work should be rewarded with better access to the better paid work in our society.

Schools also stand out as the first organizations that people attend *on their own*. Moreover, they do it for nearly seven hours at a time, for day after day. The experience of being at school comes to be for individuals the model for all subsequent organizations they join. It is their first and forming experience of organizations.

To sum up:

❖ Education is a continuation of the socialization that starts in the family.

❖ The educational system is large, expensive and connected to the central structures of power in society.

❖ There is a close connection between the structure and success of the economy and the skills that people acquire in the education system.

❖ The kind of work people do (and their chances in life generally) depends on what kind of education they get.

❖ We must look at exactly who succeeds in our educational system and why and the connection of that to wider social values.

❖ The experience of being at school comes to be for individuals the model for all subsequent organizations they join.

The development of Britain's educational system

Early beginnings

The idea of schooling really began in England during the later part of the fifteenth century and many of the 'grammar schools' founded then are still running. For hundreds of years these few schools continued, mostly in small towns, teaching the small number of children whose parents could afford not to have their children working alongside them. All others learnt to read and write in more informal settings: at home, at Sunday schools, at 'Dame-schools' organized in a room of a house belonging to a woman who could at least read and write. The better-off parents hired governesses and tutors to teach their children at home. Not until quite late in the nineteenth century did it become normal for the rich to send their children away to boarding schools. Until 1832 the state had no part in education – it was an entirely private matter.

From 1800 onwards, all countries in Europe experienced a steady, if slow, expansion in the number and range of schools. Parents and the public authorities generally took more of an interest and tried to ensure a steady stream of sufficiently educated people for the economy. The state was always concerned to keep the economy healthy, while most parents wanted to help their children to gain secure and rewarding employment. More than that, the idea of educated citizens became almost a political requirement. If increasing numbers of the population could read, demand the vote and organize themselves, then the state might intervene, structure and control the schooling and its curriculum to help produce a more amenable population, willing to take orders (the term used at the time was 'biddable').

The long-term, close association of schooling with the church was dealt with in France by its Republican governments. Often hating Catholicism, they sought to ensure that state education would be strictly agnostic. England proposed a different solution. Because there were many Christian Churches in England, the state (through the national government) would give equally to the School Associations of the various Churches to enable them to build and run schools. This started in 1832 and continued to expand rapidly thereafter. By 1870 the system was seen by the national government to be insufficient, particularly in the newer industrial towns where the traditional churches were rather weak. But the tradition of not having schools run by the national government had been well established. In 1870 the government therefore established local authorities to build and run schools, filling up the gaps left in the church system. The national government, in this new system, did not deny that it had an overall responsibility. It only expressed the opinion that, if other partners were funded, structured and encouraged, the tasks were better carried by them than by the state. The notion of partnerships between the national state, local government and the churches was clearly articulated in this period and came to dominate all thinking on educational provision until the late 1980s.

A three-storey Board school built by the School Board of London in the period 1880–1900

By 1902 the system was recognizable as very similar to the modern system and it largely remained the same for a further ninety years. There were multipurpose, elected local government organizations, funded in part by national government. These local authorities ran the elementary schools, secondary schools, technical colleges (colleges of further education), teacher training colleges, polytechnics and similar degree-level colleges. The church schools were largely incorporated into the local authority system for everything, except that they retained extra minor powers over their curriculum and staff appointments. Within this system the schools themselves had tremendous powers over themselves and their curriculum. Schooling was compulsory and free from the ages of 5 to 13 (raised to 14 in 1918), although the average leaving age was about a year greater than that. The country was getting towards literacy rates of over 90% of the population.

It is worth noting that Britain remained almost unique in Europe. It was virtually the only country where the national state *did not* run schools, hire and appoint teachers, decide the curriculum, set examinations or award certificates. The changes since 1988 should be seen in this context.

The 1944 Education Act and after

The Second World War saw a tremendous shift of policy. In order to sustain the morale and effort of the population, planning for a much better future began in earnest. Politically, and possibly also economically, it became impossible to sustain a system whereby only elementary education was free and compulsory, while secondary education was charged for and available only to a minority. The national government had to intervene. The 1944 Education Act promised that secondary education would be free, compulsory for all, and would (eventually) be for a full five years from the

ages of 11 to 16. Although many large towns had already made significant moves in this direction, there was still a lot to be done in 1945. The new Labour Government set about this in various ways:

❖ by requiring plans from the local education authorities (LEAs) as to how this was to be achieved

❖ by supporting building plans

❖ by funding

❖ by raising the school leaving age to 15.

A major problem was that there was no clear agreement as to what 'secondary education for all' might look like. The traditional grammar schools for the most academically able were understood. So were the technical schools that many LEAs had. It was believed that these two forms of secondary education would not be appropriate for all pupils. To provide for the rest, the third type of school was added: the secondary modern school. This system of three types of schools was usually called the tripartite system. Not all liked the tripartite system, but it was a system that had been thought-out and largely agreed before 1939. Butler (a Conservative party member of the National Coalition Government), the President of the Board of Education who put the 1944 Education Bill to Parliament, refused to impose the system on the LEAs and drafted the Bill accordingly. Butler knew that many Labour-controlled LEAs wished to introduce what they called 'multilateral schools', where all three types of education would be available in the one school (this type of school later became known as 'comprehensive'). In internal memoranda in the Board of Education he described the imposition of a single system as a *'gleich-geschaltet'*, a term that the Nazi party used to describe their control of local government in Germany after 1933 (Barber 1994).

IQ and the meritocratic ideal

It was widely believed that the problem of the allocation of pupils to the three types of schools could be solved. Many psychologists, and Cyril Burt in particular, claimed that

Modern schools for young children are much smaller, less intimidating and more child-centred than in the past. Children are expected to develop rather than be dominated.

they had developed good standard 'Intelligence Tests' that could be given to any pupil that had mastered the basic skills of reading and writing. These tests would clearly indicate an 'intelligence quotient' (IQ) for any pupil, which would be free from the influence of home background, school coaching or any factor other than the child's natural ability. If administered at about the age of 10 or 11, they claimed, the declared IQ would be an accurate predictor of what kind of school the child was suited to.

We mentioned earlier the idea that success ought to relate to some combination of effort and ability. This idea is usually called the 'meritocratic ideal'. Michael Young (1961) summed up the idea with the provocative and simplistic formula of 'IQ + Effort = Merit'. Young believed that this value was widely held and fed not only into education, but also into a wide range of social policies and attitudes. The whole IQ notion is central to the 'meritocratic' formula: ability can be *measured* and then *encouraged*. If the state ensures that secondary schools are free and easily accessible, there is a 'level playing field' on which pupils can compete, providing they put the effort in. The state will also have fulfilled its obligations to its citizens and the economy. The business of what goes on in schools becomes the business of professional educators and is less and less influenced by what takes place outside. Was the educational system, established in 1944 and lasting until 1988, going to work for meritocracy? The system was also supported by:

❖ free transport to secondary schools if the pupils lived more than three miles from the school

❖ grants to poor parents to purchase uniforms where schools required them

❖ generous grants to children of poor parents if the child achieved a place in a university.

This system of schooling, and the meritocratic ideal set the research agenda for the next thirty, even fifty years. A good deal of research was oriented to a conflict or Marxist perspective and was to describe the ways in which the overall power structures

❖ Activity 1 ❖

School buildings

Look at four or five school buildings close to where you live or study. Try to identify when they were built and for what sort of school.

Architects always try to design a building that reflects its use. They have differing images of a primary school and a secondary school for example. All buildings are a statement about the relationship of the organization it contains to other organizations in the community. Buildings also establish a relationship between the organization and its clients.

The buildings themselves and the detail of their construction are symbols carrying messages about relationships. The clients of a school are the parents and teachers.

- What messages are implicit in the buildings you look at?
- Does the school look powerful and dominant, or helpful and friendly?
- Are the boundaries open or closed?

Analyse what you see and discuss it with colleagues.

in a society were seen to be preventing a simple meritocratic system. Similarly, research from an interactionist perspective focused on the causes in the classroom which prevented a simple meritocratic system. The 'official view' that the structures were fair (or meritocratic), which set the agenda, was challenged many times.

Comprehensive schools

Comprehensive schools are a response to the belief that the tripartite and IQ system would not work in achieving the open, liberal, meritocratic ideal. Even in 1945 some LEAs decided to introduce comprehensive schools (although they were sometimes called 'multilateral' schools). They were to make a comprehensive provision for all types and levels of ability in one school. Above all, they avoided the loss of self-esteem and the associated loss of enthusiasm for learning that would be associated with 'failing' the so-called 11+ exam (the IQ test) – 'failure' it was, since the grammar schools retained their ancient prestige as the highest or best type of school.

By 1964, there had accumulated significant evidence – such as that by Douglas (1967) – that the tripartite system was failing to identify talent and create a meritocratic system. When the Labour Party came back to office they determined to bring in secondary schools that were 'comprehensive' in the range of abilities they provided for. The Labour Government used their powers under the 1944 Act to request all LEAs to submit new plans for secondary education, to reorganize their schools to be 'broadly comprehensive in character' (plans could include some non-comprehensive schools). This marginal openness seemed to generate a good response and nearly all LEAs responded very quickly. When a Conservative government came back to power in 1970, it chose to let the reforms go ahead, although it allowed LEAs to back-track on their plans if they wished to. Few did so.

At the time, very few LEAs wished to change their plans: the comprehensive ideal had been quickly accepted. The mood had changed. No longer was policy about favouring the most able; it was about developing the talent and ability available in every individual for a complex, industrial, technologically advanced society.

The sociological research agenda was changing. The old agenda – the methodology of positivism and survey methods concerning the influence of non-IQ factors – remained. To it, though, was added an agenda which focused on school practices:

Traditional grammar schools (such as the one shown below) expect to educate 'leaders' and exhibit traditional values in their buildings. Comprehensive schools (such as the one on the right) are designed to create an open and modern feel.

❖ How did the schooling system itself interact with pupils to create differentiated achievement?

❖ What did it mean to encourage the development of all talent and ability?

From within the educational system this tended to mean a more open and liberal curriculum: one that encouraged all types of learning and skill as appropriate instead of sustaining the weight of the traditional academic curriculum. A 'new sociology of education' developed, as we shall see in the next section. From outside the schooling system, however, the policy agenda became more economic in orientation: how can the children all get better jobs and serve the needs of the economy in an increasingly competitive environment?

In addition, the examination structure for pupils changed. With comprehensive secondary schools, the primary schools became freer from the constraints that the 11+ selection imposed on them. They became freer to decide what to teach, and how to teach it and in what groups to teach. For the secondary schools, a new set of examinations had been made available in addition to the General Certificate of Education (GCEs) Ordinary Levels, which had been designed only for the most able 40% of the population. These new examinations were the Certificate of Secondary Education (CSEs) and with them the examination structures were available to more pupils.

As a consequence of these changes, the sociological research agenda from 1968 onwards was changing. Once more it was felt that the structure of the school system created good equal opportunities. So research began more specifically to address problems that could be dealt with within the schools. The old agenda of the influence of the family background remained, but in a new way. The new agenda focused on teachers and school practices: How did the schools and teachers themselves interact with pupils to create differentiated achievement? What did it mean to encourage the development of all talent and ability?

'The Great Debate'

The debate about the curriculum and purpose of education began, from a policy point of view, with a speech by the then Prime Minister, James Callaghan. He intended, he said, to start a 'great debate'. In order to emphasize this desire, he made the speech in 1976 at Ruskin College in Oxford – not one of the main colleges of Oxford University, but an adult education college established to provide a basic full-time course for trade unionists who wished to improve their education. It was a venue calculated to start a debate inside his own party (The Labour Party).

❖ Activity 2 ❖

Your relatives' educational experiences

This may be difficult, but ask your grandparents or other relatives, going back two generations if you can, what schools they went to. Ask them the following questions:

• How did they see the purpose and character of these schools at the time?

• Were they aware of other types of school existing then?

• How do they describe the other types of school and how did they feel about them?

• Can they remember political discussion about schools when they were younger?

If the opportunity arises discuss this with other students.

If your relatives were educated outside Britain, try to get as much information about this as possible. Were their schools modelled on a British system?

For many years, very little happened. Neither the Labour government nor the Conservative governments that followed the general election of 1979 chose to break into the traditions that had been established between 1944 and 1976. One tradition was that the national government largely stayed out of the curriculum and examinations, and that the LEAs ran the schools and colleges. Indeed, the only significant policy decision put into action between 1976 and 1988 was the last acceptance of comprehensive education: the creation of the GCSE. The GCSE combined the 'Ordinary Level' of the General Certificate of Education, an examination designed for grammar school pupils, and the Certificate of Secondary Education, an examination designed for secondary modern pupils. The introduction of the new GCSE made schools as comprehensive as they could be.

But a new major change was about to impact on the schools. Following the general election of 1979, radical Conservative governments began reforming a whole range of state institutions, including local government, housing, the health service, transport and public utilities. One central approach to the reform of these institutions was an attitude that those that ran the services had got a little too 'cosy' in their relationship with the state and generally gave advice that served their own interests as service providers rather than the interests of the consumers or the wider society. It was, therefore, imperative to reduce their power and to initiate radical reform. Only in this way could the needs of the community be met.

The National Curriculum and the new vocationalism

There then followed a series of government actions in education based on two priorities:

❖ to establish a National Curriculum with the 1988 Education Act

❖ to make the schools more obviously vocational in their purpose.

We can label these initiatives as a move towards 'vocationalism' in the school curriculum, especially the secondary school curriculum. They included systems of making pupil activities more manifestly orientated to the economy and its productive activities. The initiatives included:

❖ the Technical and Vocational Education Initiative (TVEI) – a scheme of the Department of Employment (DE) to give money to schools to help make their curriculum more relevant to work

❖ School-Compacts (also DE funded) which were agreements between local schools and local employers that the employers would guarantee initial work and training to some pupils.

The Government, in collaboration with the Confederation of British Industry, also looked at the 'core' skills that industry needed and tried to identify what could be done inside schools to develop these. As a result they developed a number of new educational awards, the General National Vocational Qualifications (GNVQs), that could be taught and assessed in schools. They also merged the Employment Department and the Department for Education and Science in 1995 – a merger which expresses a belief in the common purposes of the activities, coordinating school, college and training provision.

The term 'vocationalists' (and thus the new 'vocationalism') has been defined as:

> 'those who wish to argue that education should be made more relevant to the needs of the economy in opposition to a traditional "liberal-humanist" view that education should be seen as a end in itself or as a means to realizing human potential for its own sake.'
> (Hickox 1995, p. 153)

This definition differs sharply from a useful definition of 'vocational educators' given by Tom Phillips (1995) who suggests that vocational educators are those who help a young person come to a specific vocational identity.

The new 'vocationalism' as a movement or set of ideas, however, sat a little uneasily alongside the main priority of the 1988 Act, that of developing a National Curriculum that all schools were to work to. This priority, that came to dominate what schools do, derives from a desire to create a standard curriculum in all schools, based on traditional subjects, and on firm and certain moral attitudes. This approach has been called 'cultural restorationism' by Stephen Ball (1994a, p. 28). Ball identifies this movement with a desire to ensure that the current population should not see education as leading to a self-identity in which they are empowered to change social values or structures. Instead the curriculum:

'replaces the uncertainties of change with cosy, sepia images of family, nation and school which are tied into an ensemble of nostalgia.' (Ball 1994a, p. 46)

Stephen Ball's assertion of an emphasis on the past and nostalgia does not accord with the modernity of the new vocationalism and *its* emphasis on adaptability and being ready for change. But it is interesting to note that the more highly regarded an educational programme (e.g. A Levels), the less it is penetrated by modernity and vocationalism. Modern reform is apparently more for the working class. Restoration of traditional texts and histories dominates the changes for the elite streams of education.

School organization

In the late 1980s and the 1990s the Government initiated major policies in regard to control over schools. By 1988, the Government had taken major initiatives in introducing a centralization of the curriculum. At the same time it wished, as it had done with the curriculum, to reduce the control of local government over the organization of the schools. There were three main components to this drive:

1 The government developed new 'city technology colleges' (CTCs) – secondary schools that were selective in entry, orientated to a technical curriculum, and founded and, in part, funded by a variety of private organizations. They received from central government vastly more funding than local education authority schools.

2 A policy was introduced of encouraging schools to break away from their local authorities and to receive their funds directly from central government. These schools are called 'grant maintained schools' (GMSs).

3 The government created new rules whereby LEAs could only fund their schools on a strict formula basis (with the formula based mainly on enrolments), while the schools themselves 'locally managed' their funds and activities. These schools (i.e. the majority) are called 'locally managed schools' (LMSs).

In total, these new organizational and curriculum initiatives set a new agenda for the sociology of education.

Sociological theory and research in education

The meritocratic agenda and research

The House of Commons elected in the UK in 1945 represented a landslide victory for the Labour Party and the whole idea of social improvement and reform. The scale of the victory probably took even the Labour Party by surprise as it began the tasks that had been set by the destruction of war. Social scientists of all sorts and persuasions saw that this was the time to start mapping and researching the extent to which the ambitious goals of the social programme could be achieved. We will discuss a few of the researches on the education aspects of these wider social policies.

Cover of Michael Young's book *The Rise of the Meritocracy*

the rise of the MERITOCRACY

I. Q. + effort = MERIT

MICHAEL YOUNG

which concepts of economic production and occupation determine most aspects of society: that is a form of Marxist class and conflict theory. The model was not initially seen as problematic and it fell within the traditions of what is sometimes called the 'political arithmetic' tradition (see *In Focus*). This tradition refers to the old idea that one could contribute significantly to a social debate by simple counting, without a careful conceptual analysis of what it might be that could be counted.

The best way to describe this political agenda in education is as the 'meritocratic agenda'. This was an attempt to shift society towards meritocracy, a system where intelligence and hard work (and not 'accidents' of birth) would lead to the rewards available. This formula was expressed a little while afterwards by Michael Young in a famous (part-serious, part-satirical) book entitled *The Rise of the Meritocracy* (1961). At the time, the policies were also described as the creation of an 'equality of opportunity'. The educational policies were specifically about reducing the effects of the occupational background of children's parents on the educational achievements of the young. This would also then reduce the effects of class origins on occupational success and achievement.

So successful was the creation of this political agenda that it is one of the few aspects of that radical government unchallenged in the 1990s. Even John Major, the Conservative who became Prime Minister in 1990, was moved to say that it was one of his main political goals.

The sociological model underlying these notions assumes that parental occupation, the educational achievement of their children, as well as the children's social advantage and occupational achievement, are so closely structured that they are causally related. In addition, from a point of view of sociological theory, we are implying a particular model of the social structure in

❖ Activity 3 ❖

Read the following passage from Douglas:

'In this study, the level of the parents' interest in their children's work was partly based on comments made by the class teachers at the end of the fourth primary school year, and partly on the records of the number of times each parent visited the schools to discuss their child's progress with the Head or class teacher. Parents are said to show a 'high level of interest' if the teachers regarded them through-out the primary school period as very interested in their children's work and if they had also taken the opportunity to visit the primary schools at least once a year to discuss their children's progress. They show a 'fair level of interest' if they fall short on one of these counts, and a 'low level of interest' if they fall short on more than one.'

Source: Douglas (1967, p. 83)

Comment on the adequacy of this measure of parental interest. Do you think there are other ways of measuring the concept of 'parental interest'?

The categories and procedures for intelligence testing were seen as a little more problematic than the questionnaire design, but not for serious discussion, only for resolution by other experts. It was known that there was a wide variety of testing procedures available and used in the

In Focus

◆

The work of J.W.B. Douglas

One most remarkable study was that organized by J.W.B. Douglas in 1945. The team's intention was to study the health and early development of very young children and their mothers as part of the mapping and preparation for the introduction of a National Health Service. Cooperation was obtained from almost every Medical Officer of Health in the local arrangements of the time and they agreed to provide free the services of the health visitors as interviewers for this important national survey. In the event nearly all women who had borne a child in one week in March 1946 agreed to take part. Nothing like a work of this scale and comprehensiveness has been attempted since.

A second remarkable feature was that the advisory committee to the research quickly realized the potential of setting up a very large-scale, longitudinal study of the children involved (that is, a study which follows up the same people, at intervals over a long period of time).

The work eventually became orientated towards the 'meritocratic agenda'. The main publication arising out of the study was called *The Home and The School* (1967). It had followed the sample through secondary school and looked closely at the interaction of home and school, comparing actual performance with performance predicted by intelligence tests. It remains a classic example of the work of the times in its methodology and theoretical analysis.

The research criteria (the size of the sample and the procedures for drawing it randomly) were exemplary. Having picked their week in March, they made contact with virtually the whole population to be studied, and sustained their contact over many years.

In the Douglas studies there appears to be a consensus about the purpose of the research, the methodology and the funding. The director of the research was a medical doctor with little experience of sociology. The research reports make few references to wider sociological theory. The theoretical assumptions are simple: that social behaviours are structured and behaviour in one sphere of an individual's life is linked to another. If we ask the 'right questions' and analyse the mathematical relationship between the results, we can approach the causation clearly and easily. The researchers seem to imply that the subtleties of human interaction need not detain us too long. It is almost as if 'the facts can speak for themselves'.

In as much as they were aware of sociological theory, they could be said to be operating in a clear, positivist analytic framework, which is what political arithmetic is. The approach is also *structural* in that it relates statistics on different aspects of social behaviour in a structure.

In the Douglas surveys, the interviews and questionnaire completion were all done by intermediary staff of schools, health services and so on. The main writers felt very little need to engage themselves in extensive field interviewing. With a research population of that size evenly distributed across the country, they could only have undertaken a small number of interviews themselves. Yet they chose not to add to their questionnaire design and its results with direct, open-ended interviews by the researchers. Their approach is in part revealed in the selected title, *The Home and The School*, when it might have been called *Parents and the Learning their Children Achieve*. In this approach parents as multifaceted people, or even just a role, are reduced to 'The Home'. The home itself can be reduced to a number of 'factors', such as the father's occupation, the place of the child in the family or the parents' interest in their children. For example, the family of each child was placed in one of three categories by a procedure described in Activity 3.

LEAs. The procedure adopted was really to subcontract the task to 'the experts' in the National Foundation for Educational Research. They devised some robust, uncomplicated tests that could be easily administered by any school teacher.

There is no doubt that over the years the research became more and more orientated towards the meritocratic agenda and was much influenced by the work of some young sociologists, A.H. Halsey and Jean Floud (Halsey *et al.* 1961). Although from the perspective of modern sociological theory, Douglas's study looks very unsophisticated, it was thoroughly acceptable at the time. It was rigorous, covered the complete population by a large, well-structured sample, and was undertaken and written in a confident, almost magisterial, style. It demonstrated that the occupational background of the parent remained a prime cause of achievement. The structural and financial reform of schooling (by intelligence testing and free places at grammar schools) had not, on its own, achieved a meritocracy.

The Chair of the Population Investigation Committee that steered the research of the Douglas team through most of its educational work was Professor D.V. Glass. He was himself engaged in parallel research of other aspects of the same problem. He was interested in social mobility and, with his colleagues, conducted the first large scale research on adult males. The base date-line for the research was 1949 and the survey was of over 3,400 people. The key questions were very simple:

❖ What is your occupation now?

❖ What occupations have you had?

❖ What was your father's main occupation?

❖ What other occupations did he have?

From this simple question and answer set, Glass and his colleagues could construct measures of mobility from one class to another over the previous thirty years. The study was not longitudinal, as the Douglas studies were, but more of a snapshot. However, he was creating a base-line in time for further, later research. As already stated,

the assumed close relationship between educational achievement and occupational achievement is what links the areas together.

Brian Jackson and Dennis Marsden, in the Institute of Community Studies, undertook a study (1962) of the experience of working-class children in grammar schools in one town in the north of England. This study contrasts in method with that of Douglas in that it was local to one town and was of only eighty-eight children, but the researchers did directly discuss the experiences of the ex-pupils and their families with them. By doing that, the work comes closer to explaining and describing how it is that aspirations of able pupils can be progressively weakened and eroded. This study is successful despite the fact that it concentrates on pupils who were in fact successful. With even these the tensions are revealed. This kind of study was pointing away from social policy and into the education process itself.

By the time that Douglas' second (main) volume was published in 1967, there were few who believed that the schooling system was precisely selecting and retaining 'the most able'. It was also clear that there was a massive wastage of the talents and abilities amongst the broad range of pupils excluded from the grammar schools (and even some wastage within them). The works of many sociologists and educationalists, including those of Halsey and Floud, had brought this realization about. The second volume of Douglas helped to weaken the anti-comprehensive school arguments fatally.

It was also time for a new school of thought in the sociology of education. The positivism, structuralism and social policy orientations (leading to large-scale positivist studies such as that of Douglas and his team) were thought not capable of describing and explaining satisfactorily what was going on. It was accepted (rightly or wrongly) that the institutional structure of all schools had to be comprehensive if the social goals were to be attained. But it was felt that more detailed study of school processes would be needed.

❖ Activity 4 ❖

Discuss the following with fellow students:

The term 'comprehensive' is normally only applied to secondary education, but primary education is also 'comprehensive' if it is non-selective. Why is this so rarely recognized and why does it not appear as a conscious, cultural alternative that we could have selective primary schools?

But there was more to the need for a new sociology: it was becoming necessary to look at the interaction of school culture with home culture, to look at the different valuations placed on ideas, to look at direct interaction in the class-room. 'Culture', 'values' and 'ideas' had to be analysed as problematic categories and not just observed, measured and recorded. The 'new sociology' arose not in the sociology and social policy sections of the traditional universities, but in the schools and in the institutes and departments of education of the universities and colleges, amongst practising teachers and those working with them.

The 'new' sociology of education

It is probably wrong to think of the studies of education from the mid-1960s as a single school of thought. There are a number of connected threads that mark a sharp change of perspective at that time. Principally, the new sociology took a closer look at the actual interactions between pupils and the school, particularly what we might call classroom interactions.

Language codes

The work of Basil Bernstein (1990) in the London Institute of Education focused on the language used in the families of pupils. It explained differential performance in terms of the relative resonance (or lack of it) between the language of the home and that of the school. This marked a major shift of emphasis since what he was researching, language, was a deep expression of culture and not directly connected to the occupational structure or to the economy. Bernstein proposed that one might describe language in terms of 'codes' that are seen to be appropriate to certain situations and social uses.

'Restricted codes' are appropriate only for communications in a relatively limited set of social settings where the structures and meanings available are already well understood. These are often connected to class culture and understandings. They are also used, often unconsciously, as identifiers in class situations. Communication in restricted codes is often in short, grammatically simple, unelaborated, often unfinished sentences. So much is taken as understood that there is no need to be more elaborate. All families have their own particular codes and these are slight variations of wider, often class-based, codes. The meanings expressed are particular to the situation.

There is also an 'elaborated code' that exists in the wider business and academic culture. It takes little for granted and exists explicitly to express meanings in a precise way. This code was seen by Bernstein as universalistic, in that all meanings can be expressed within the code. Of course, there are also codes restricted to specific situations in business, universities, churches and so on. These are codes in which the meanings expressed are given in short cues and clues, but can be fully expressed and explained when necessary (to clients or other outsiders, for example).

Bernstein's main point, in terms of explaining differential performance, is that the speech within middle-class families in ordinary situations moves *more* frequently between the elaborated code and the restricted middle-class codes than conversation in working-class households moves between elaborated code and working-class restricted codes. When children in middle-class families ask questions, they may be given answers, not necessarily in terms of the most elaborate versions of the language, but in ways which bring the child to better understanding of the complex grammar and syntax of the elaborated code. Bernstein suggests that there are three aspects to this:

❖ Adult family members are more directly engaged in work or academic situations where the elaborate codes are used, and so they unconsciously move into and out of the code at home.

❖ These adults also move consciously into elaborated codes as part of their deliberate child-rearing practices, to help their child learn the appropriate ways of speaking in school, and work.

❖ Middle-class families, whose relationships are more negotiated and explained than in working-class families, negotiate in the elaborated code. In working-class families, Bernstein asserts, the power relationships between parents and children are more often asserted with 'because I say so'. In middle-class families, they will also resort to 'because I say so', but usually after more discussion in elaborated speech patterns.

The work of Bernstein proved both interesting and provocative. It seemed to provide a model that explained the mechanisms of differential educational performance. However, Bernstein's model was challenged on a number of grounds. Harold Rosen (1974) pointed out that the model varied from one paper of Bernstein's to another. Sometimes Bernstein talked of the 'lower working class', sometime of a single group. Sometimes he emphasized the educational background of parents and sometimes their occupational background. Moreover, Bernstein presents rather patchy evidence concerning the actual relationships of class-based speech patterns in school, home and work. While we see some of the evidence through the tested performances of children and interviews with parents, the actual examples given of typical family interactions are rather scarce – they appear to be manufactured as illustration by Bernstein, rather than taken from detailed observational notes. For Rosen, too much is presumed. He does not challenge the model or the theory, but finds its support inadequate. Underlying his criticisms is a feeling that working-class language is criticized as culturally deficient and he attacks the whole body of research. Labov (1973) makes that point more explicitly and points out that non-standard variants of English can carry much the same meanings as the elaborated codes. The main point of Bernstein, however, remains: if children are living in homes where the dominant means of communication is not the standard English version of the elaborated code, then they will remain disadvantaged in examinations, tests and teacher-interactions, given that these are couched in, and specifically designed to test competence in, the standard elaborated code.

The poem below, written by Tom Leonard and intended to be recited in a broad Glasgow accent, attacks the notion that only standard, middle-class English carries enough authority to convey 'the truth'.

this is thi
six a clock
news thi
man said n
thi reason
a talk wia
BBC accent
iz coz yi
widny wahnt
mi ti talk
aboot thi
trooth wia
voice lik
wanna yoo
scruff. if
a tokaboot
thi trooth
lik wanna yoo
scruff yi
widny thingk
it wuz troo.

jist wanna you
scruff tokn.
thirza right
way ti spell
ana right way
ti tok it. this
is me tokn yir
right way a
spellin. this
is ma trooth.
yooz doant no
thi trooth
yirsellz cawz
yi canny talk
right. this is
the six a clock
nyooz. belt up.

from *Unrelated*
Incidents
by Tom Leonard

At the same time as Bernstein was working, other approaches to improving school performance were being developed, particularly in the United States. The presumptions were very much like that of Bernstein: that the home in some ways failed to support the school. In one particular series of projects in the United States, Moynihan, as a social analyst and thinker, proposed that certain schools should be singled out to give children a 'Head Start'. Inner-city areas that experienced multiple deprivations would be selected and the schools funded appropriately. Their research evidence seems to show that work of this sort at any early age had a lasting effect on educational performance. In England, the review of research by Rutter and Madge (1976) seemed to support this idea and a similar programme was started under the name of 'Educational Priority Areas'.

Schools labelling pupils

These social and educational programmes were based on an analysis of the interaction of home background with the school, but tended to take for granted the way the schools operated and what they tried to achieve. Sociologists were also becoming aware of the inadequacies of this aspect of

the two-way relationships between the pupil and the school (see *In Focus* below).

❖ Activity 5 ❖

- Have you heard your own educational or occupational potential being discussed? If so, what advice have you received?
- Have you heard the potential of others being discussed? If so, in what terms?
- How would you describe yourself in terms of your educational or occupational potential?

Try to list all the words, phrases and categories that pass between individuals and their advisers that become labels or self-fulfilling prophesies when accepted by the person to whom they are applied.

The study by Cicourel and Kitsuse was part of a great American tradition, often seen as based in Chicago, of direct observation and interpretation of the reality of social interactions. One aspect of this way of thinking is usually called 'symbolic interactionism' and another is called 'ethnomethodology'. Even now, one of the

---

In Focus

◆

Cicourel and Kitsuse's study of high-school counsellors

Aaron Cicourel and John Kitsuse (1963) conducted a study of high-school counsellors in an American school. Counsellors are very important in the high-school system because they strongly influence what happens to students. They, in effect, decide on what courses students work their way through the optional programmes of the high schools. Entry to higher education is largely determined on entry to and success in the key 'academic courses'. Because of this the counsellors can be regarded as 'the educational decision-makers', the title of Cicourel and Kitsuse's study. In making their decisions, the

counsellors used IQ tests and grade performances, but also discussion with the young people and a range of reports and interactions with the teachers. Cicourel and Kitsuse mapped closely the language patterns or 'labels' that the counsellors and others applied to the pupils. It became clear that a range of non-academic factors influenced the decisions taken. These included students' appearance, manner, dress, and so on. The result was that there was not equal access for those of equal ability. Access was mediated by assumptions about social potential and the likelihood of higher education completion.

great classic texts on the methodology in observation still comes from this approach and school: Glaser and Strauss' *The Discovery of Grounded Theory* (1967).

High-status and low-status knowledge

In the late 1960s, the new British sociology of education became very interested in approaches such as that of Cicourel and Kitsuse, as it moved from the large-scale survey and an engagement with public policy into the actual mechanisms. Centrally, the sociologists of education became interested in what the pupil brought to the school. Teachers, educationalists and sociologists were moving towards an easier acceptance of what was called 'cultural relativism': a situation in which all cultures are regarded as relatively equal in value.

To many radical thinkers it seemed that the social policy approach to research had too readily accepted the 'official' view of what was to be valued and what counted as an educational achievement.

❖ Activity 6 ❖

1. Read the quotation from Giddens (see *In Focus*) and examine the differences between:
   - being knowledgeable and being educated
   - learning and schooling.
2. Discuss what types of knowledge are valued in school and what are not valued.

In Focus

◆

Jean-Paul's knowledge

'Imagine you are in the shoes – or the wooden clogs – of Jean-Paul Didion, a peasant boy growing up in a French farming community about two centuries ago. Jean-Paul is fourteen years old in 1750. He cannot read or write, but this is not uncommon; only a few of the adults in his village have the ability to decipher more than the odd word or two of written texts. There are some schools in nearby districts, run by monks and nuns, but these are completely removed from Jean-Paul's experience. He has never known anyone who attended school, save for the local priest. For the past eight or ten years, Jean-Paul has been spending most of his time helping with domestic tasks and working in the fields. The older he gets, the longer each day he is expected to share in the hard physical work involved in intensive tilling of his father's plot of land.

Jean-Paul is likely never to leave the area where he was born, and may spend almost his whole life within the village and surrounding fields, only occasionally travelling to other local villages and towns. He is aware that he is "French", that his country is ruled by a particular monarch, and he is aware that there is a wider world beyond even France itself. But he has only a vague awareness even of France as a distinct political entity.

Although in modern terms Jean-Paul is uneducated, he is far from ignorant. He has a sensitive and developed understanding of the family and of children, having had to care for those younger than himself since he was very young. He is already very knowledgeable about the land, methods of crop production and modes of preserving and storing food. His mastery of local customs and traditions is profound, and he can turn his hand to many tasks other than agricultural cultivation, such as weaving or basket making.

Jean-Paul is an invention, but the description above represents the typical experience of a boy growing up in early modern Europe.'

Source: Giddens (1993, pp. 24–25)

The new sociology wanted to achieve several goals:

❖ to identify what was seen as the structure of knowledge to be valued

❖ to relate it to a specific social formation or milieu

❖ to challenge the structure of knowledge in schools and to advance alternatives.

Some knowledge was regarded as high-status knowledge and some as low-status knowledge.

Keddie's research into labelling

Schools were seen to be about labelling children and differentiating access to the knowledge the school offered according to those labels. The work of Cicourel and Kitsuse became well known at about this time and the general theme of labelling also pervaded the work of Nell Keddie (1971). She examined closely the development of new curricula and new methods of assessment in a South London comprehensive school. The school was very innovative. It tried to write its own curricula and obtain an assessment structure that was wholly in the hands of the teachers (this system, now abolished in the National Curriculum Reforms, was called a 'Mode 3' form of syllabus development). All pupils were divided into three broad 'bands' of ability and for the Humanities courses that formed the centre of the study, the classes were mixed across the range of ability in those broad bands. The same formal syllabus and materials were available to all, reflecting the desire of the teachers to treat all pupils equally. Keddie's way of researching included:

❖ direct (naturalistic) observation of teachers working with classes and individual pupils

❖ discussion between teachers

❖ discussions between teachers and the researcher.

Keddie did not explore how pupils came to be placed by teachers in a mental category called 'C stream', but explored what this categorization meant in terms of classroom action and teacher discussion. Late on in the school-life of pupils, such categories as 'C stream' become more related to predicted job-opportunities than they do to parental class. What happens in interaction is that teachers scan what they hear from pupils for meanings and understandings. According to Keddie, they are far more likely to perceive good understanding and good questions in an A stream pupil than in a C stream pupil. However, C stream pupils are actually more likely to challenge or question the ideas put to them by teachers or in teacher-prepared materials. What is not clear is whether this represents a lower ability or not. One very telling example, used by Keddie, is that A stream pupils could say that 'the course allowed them to question what the teachers say'. When asked for an actual example of when they had questioned the categories or concepts given, the pupils could not give one. Keddie asserts that the description of the course is just one adopted from the teachers, but not operated by the A stream pupils in practice. C stream pupils, who do challenge the meanings, do not *experience* the course as allowing them to do that, but only as being confusing. Keddie sums the work up as follows:

> 'By their characterization of C stream pupils as "that kind of child" and "these children", teachers feel that C stream pupils are unlike themselves. By inference, teachers feel that A stream pupils are more like themselves, at least in ways that count in school. Teaching A stream pupils seems to be relatively unproblematic for teachers: they take the activities in the classroom for granted ... The assumption is that C stream pupils disrupt teachers' expectations and violate their norms of appropriate social, moral and intellectual pupil behaviour.'
> (Keddie 1971, p. 134)

Sociological theorists

Another aspect of the work of the new sociologists of education was their very wide interest in and focus on sociological theory. This was markedly different from the social policy orientations that assumed the validity of the positivist approach and the apparent non-problematic nature of measurement, as in the Douglas study. The new focus on theory led them to seek inspiration in the more theoretically orientated writers from other countries, particularly the USA, France and Germany, because much of the earlier writings in Britain on the sociology of education focused very much on the British social structure and process. They drew attention to writings of C. Wright Mills, Alfred Schutz, Herbert Marcuse, Jurgen Habermas, Harold Garfinkel, Louis Althusser and also Pierre Bourdieu. Rather later, they drew into the debate the works of Michel Foucault, a pupil of Althusser. You will find that all these writers are referred to elsewhere in this textbook. They represent a variety of Marxist, ethnomethodological, symbolic interactionist and postmodernist schools. It is this variety of theory and perspectives that came to be a main concern of sociology and remains so, at A Level as well as in postgraduate research.

The work of Bourdieu (see *In Focus*) was very influential and much used in explanations of differential performance. However, his work is not all about school practices, and where it is, it is about French

---

In Focus

◆

Bourdieu and cultural reproduction

ourdieu and his colleagues in Paris (1977) developed the twin concepts of cultural reproduction and of cultural capital. 'Cultural reproduction' refers to the processes whereby a dominant culture penetrates many educational institutions (secondary schools and universities) and is reproduced in the minds, values and activities of dominant groups in the wider society. Culture, or the dominant culture, is not separate from these wider organizations and sources of power. In the processes of social reproduction (i.e. the reproduction of society through the socialization of new members), those that can be recognized as being of the same culture are accepted into the class and power positions available. This culture may contain elements of what might be called 'high' or artistic culture, or simply ways of speaking and behaving at a level of social interaction. Each individual may be described as living in a social 'habitus' that is made up of ways of thinking, ideas and symbols of value. A habitus is both structured and structuring; it is at once a system of 'taste', a scheme of perception and a system of generating classifiable practices and works. Every social act, every social perception has the effect of classifying the actor in the eyes of the other actors. Every social act or perception contains elements of claiming and achieving a class position and of advancing (or not) both the individual and the social group.

The range of interests of Bourdieu and his colleagues is broad and they applied their form of cultural analysis to nearly all aspects of social life: from clothing to table manners, and even what, how and when one eats. Each social group has its own 'culture', but the powerful groups have a dominant culture that infuses the educational system.

Those individuals that possess this dominant culture, Bourdieu and his colleagues argue, use it as a form of 'capital' in that it is turned into positions of power and income. In school situations, pupils whose background helps them achieve this are recognized by the teachers, selected and encouraged. Similarly, those same pupils are tuned in to receive, decode or understand the messages emanating from the teachers. All this goes on in an overall ethos of equal opportunity, so the process is a slow and interactive one in which less able pupils, those with less cultural capital or from the lower classes, are edged slowly to a position where they seem to fail or they voluntarily depart.

Differing homes provide differing 'cultural capital'

'The difficult thing to explain about how middle-class kids get middle-class jobs is why others let them. The difficult thing to explain about how working-class kids get working-class jobs is why they let themselves.'

He conducted an ethnographic study of a small number of:

'non-academic working class lads ... attending a boys-only, non-selective secondary modern school ... The main group was studied intensively by means of observation and participant observation in class, around the school and during leisure activities; regular recorded group discussions; informal interviews and diaries.'

Willis followed the main sample into work: 'Fifteen short periods of participant observation were devoted to actually working alongside each lad in his job.' Willis brought to his study a conflict perspective. He explicitly states that instead of seeing a gradual shading off of ability from the middle classes to the working classes, 'we must conceive of radical breaks represented by the interface of cultural forms'. He goes on to emphasize that the decision to become a manual labourer is taken in the milieu of a working-class counter-culture, a culture that is actively expressed as an opposition to the middle-class ethos (or milieu) of the school. Nor does Willis attribute this wholly to a lack of ability but sees that to some extent it is a matter of choice.

'Furthermore, it was by no means only the least able who were involved in the counter-school culture. Some of its central members were highly articulate, clear-sighted, assertive and able across a wide range of activities.'

This should perhaps be related to the work of Nell Keddie in the early 1970s, which remained more teacher-focused than that of Willis in the later 1970s.

Perhaps central to the Willis study is that it was conducted in the last years when most young men could be sure of getting fairly well-paid, manual jobs. This was the

schools. The use of the work in Britain may require some modification. Initially the work of Bourdieu was used mainly in providing direct explanations of differential performance within schools, but its use more recently has also been in policy and organizational studies of schools.

A sociology of vocational education

The new sociology of education led to close ethnographic studies of what went on in schools. One such study looked at how working-class boys acquired their distinctive culture. Paul Willis (1977) conducted the study that was amongst the most widely read and influential of its time. He developed an empirical basis for studying the processes whereby the working classes in particular manage to cut themselves off voluntarily from the school-learning processes well before they actually leave school. They become socialized to enjoy or look forward to their leaving of school. Willis described his starting point as follows:

situation from 1945 through to 1979. Almost immediately after Willis finished writing, the economy went into a rapid decline for many reasons. At the same time, the number of young people entering the labour market was rising. The British economy, along with all economies in Western Europe, struggled to cope with the problems of incorporating the young into the economy. The massive rise in youth unemployment from 1979 to 1984 led to a significant restructuring in the thinking about the whole business of vocational training.

The policy approach of the government was primarily to create the huge Youth Training Scheme (YTS), that guaranteed two years of training to any school leaver that applied. Each year many hundreds of thousands – up to 30 per cent of the age cohort – did so. Studies of vocational education and training took two main approaches. The main line of most studies has been to follow the approach of Willis and undertake a series of ethnographic and similar studies of groups of trainees. We will look at these later in this chapter. The other approach was to pursue a sociological study of the process of policy creation and the outcomes of the policies themselves.

A sociology of policy studies

The changes in school curriculum, in school organization, in vocationalism and in vocational education were brought about by a series of Acts of Parliament, as well as administrative acts and the creation of new organizations (such as the Schools Curriculum and Assessment Council) to implement them. The state re-emerged as a major organization capable of structuring and controlling society. Sociologists turned their attention back to these problems, many of them well schooled in conflict theory and the neo-marxism of Louis Althusser and the theories of power control and social-reproduction of Pierre Bourdieu and Michel Foucault. So different was the new context of their work to what had

existed before that it even became necessary to establish a new journal to carry the material and develop the ideas, the *Journal of Education Policy*, founded in 1988. The new shift of focus was back to national policies. The 1988 Education Act had brought the national government back into the schools and their curriculum as a major player.

Stephen Ball and his colleagues at King's College, London, have been very instrumental and to some extent at the centre of this movement. Ball (1994a, p. 1) has said that:

> 'Three epistemologies or analytic perspectives fight to be heard in this theory-work. At times they clash and grate against one another but the resultant friction is, I hope, purposeful and effective rather than a distraction. They are: critical policy analysis, post-structuralism and critical ethnography.'

Ball, then, recognizes and uses three different perspectives and their particular languages and ways of thinking, analysing and proceeding:

❖ Critical policy analysis starts with the policy documents of government and with speeches, newspaper articles and pamphlets from the key actors on the political scene. To these it applies reflexive approaches as well as interpretation of the moral order of reform.

❖ Post-structuralism applies the ideas of power and discourse and the location of values in structures of values, class and power.

❖ Ethnography is applied mainly at case-study level. In the case of Ball, this has been mainly within individual grant maintained schools where he explores the policy effects of the policy-in-implementation, for he is not content to stay at the level of critical analysis, but must see what actually happens.

Some of these studies by Ball and colleagues are reviewed later in this chapter.

◆ Differential achievement

Intelligence as an explanation of school performance

There are two common explanations of the differential performance of children in schools. One is that, in a very basic or biological way, some children are more intelligent than others. Quite what this means is still uncertain, but enormous effort has been put into refining the concept, particularly through ways of measuring it. 'Intelligence' has come to mean some generalizable ability in reasoning that can be applied to all types of learning. Thus, someone who is very able will automatically show this ability in a wide range of learnings: in concept formation, logical deductions, seeing connections and detecting patterns. This is held to apply to all types of learning, mathematical, spatial, verbal and so on.

The other assumption is that, eventually, as children progress, they will develop their abilities in one area more than another. The presumption is that suitable tests can be devised that test ability across a wide range of types of ability and learning and that from that, the basic general intelligence can be deduced and expressed as a quotient or percentage of the average.

There are clearly some questions about these assumptions.

❖ Does this quotient or factor remain stable in an individual over time?

❖ Is it subject to variations that derive from different learning situations or teaching programmes?

❖ How easy is it to devise tests that will reach through what the individual has already learned, to measure this basic ability? For example, someone who cannot read cannot take pencil and paper tests. We must ask what assumptions are built into the tests.

❖ Activity 7 ❖

Look back at the *In Focus* on p. 139. How do you think that the fictional Jean-Paul might get on with such a test as he would take in Britain today? What would be the problems in devising a test for him?

There is an underlying assumption that the basic ability that is called 'intelligence' is genetically determined and biologically inherited. It is also clear that some of the difference is determined by the kind of learning and the encouragement of learning that takes place at home and is structured by the parents. Thus it becomes difficult to determine when one is testing genetic inheritance and when social inheritance.

The construction of the tests also raises interesting issues. Each test consists of a number of questions or items. These are selected so that when given to a large number of people, they yield a distribution pattern called a normal distribution curve (see Fig. 4.1).

The construction of nearly all tests tends to make an assumption that the ability is genetic and the test items are selected to yield a 'normal' pattern of distribution. Most socially distributed patterns, such as income or wealth, are severely skewed or asymmetric patterns (as in Fig. 4.2), but no intelligence test is devised to show this kind of pattern.

Figure 4.1
A normal distribution curve

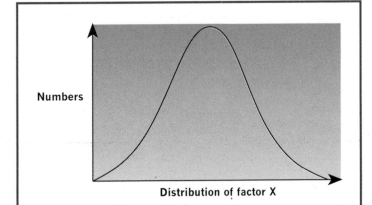

Numbers

Distribution of factor X

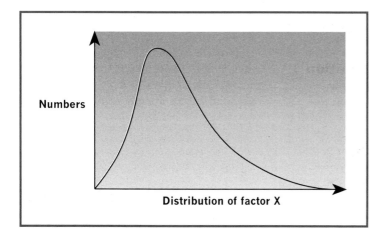

Figure 4.2
A 'skewed' distribution curve, typical of social distributions such as income

Good tests must work through assumptions about standardized learning opportunities that the young will have experienced. Yet as sociologists, we know that the experiences of children will always vary. Different parents play or work with their children in different ways. We would be surprised if the differences were merely random and not in some way structured to the previous education of the parents, to their work, to their social class, their ethnic origins and cultural background. The more heterogeneous our society becomes, the more difficult it is to obtain a standard test that is in any way free or independent of a specific subculture. Only such a test can measure some 'basic ability' through the varied structural opportunities for learning that have been experienced in the cultural heterogeneity. Yet the need for such a test is increased.

Schools performance and class background

The relationship between these factors is an important area of study. Most survey studies come to some correlation between performance of children in school and the class background of pupils. What varies a good deal is the precise aspects of what counts as class background and the sorts of explanation for the ways in which schools deal with this.

Douglas's famous longitudinal study published in 1967 provided a quite devastating critique of the idea that performance in schools was linked primarily to some basic (or genetic) factor called intelligence. Central in the study were two intelligence tests, the most culture-free that could be devised, which were independently administered to the children at the ages of 8 and 11. School performance was then compared to factors including the occupation of the parents and their attitudes to schooling. What was clear was that when the children were placed into broad ability bands (as defined by these ability tests), school performance was correlated in significant ways to the other factors as well. At every stage from 5 years old to 16, groups of children of high ability but low social class, performed less well than children of the same ability but higher social class. The cumulative effect from birth was virtually impossible to measure and calculate, particularly using the techniques of the study.

Most centrally, the stability of the measured ability was called into question. At the time, it was common for primary schools to be 'streamed', i.e. classes were organized within a year group so that children defined as having a similar ability (whether high or low) were placed together in a class. Douglas found that where children whom the survey found to be of high ability were placed in a low-stream class they actually *lost* measured ability between the ages of 8 and 11. This finding actually casts very severe doubt on what it is that intelligence tests are measuring. It did not look like some immutable, genetically determined factor.

Douglas proposed that the main variable was not the direct influence of the occupation of the parents but the expression of parental encouragement and the children's attitude and behaviour. In other words, he was expressing the idea of a working-class subculture which did not value or know how to contribute to educational success and which became the main determinant of differential performance.

In essence, the ideas of Bourdieu discussed earlier (see p. 141) express this

In Focus

◆

Bourdieu and the art of living

'The art of eating and drinking remains one of the few areas in which the working classes explicitly challenge the legitimate art of living. In the face of the new ethic of sobriety for the sake of slimness, which is most recognized at the highest levels of a social hierarchy, peasants and especially industrial workers maintain an ethic of convivial indulgence. A *bon-vivant* is not just someone who enjoys eating and drinking; he is someone capable of entering into the generous and familiar – that is, both simple and free – relationship that is encouraged and symbolized by eating and drinking together, in a conviviality which sweeps away restraints and reticence.'

Source: Bourdieu (1984 , p. 179)

phenomenon but analyse it at a more directly cultural level. Implicit in Douglas' approach is that the working-class subculture may be actually hostile to the main academic culture, an idea also strongly expressed by Willis (see p. 142). Bourdieu, on the other hand, is more concerned with the degree of fit between individuals and the dominant culture – in other words, how much cultural capital they can bring to bear on their own behalf. While Bourdieu acknowledges the counter-culture idea, it is rather less dominant in his thinking. Generally he assumes that a successful dominant culture induces almost a guilt feeling in those who do not share it, rather than any positive challenges, which remain rare. One of Bourdieu's more surprising examples of the 'rare challenge' is described above (see *In Focus*).

❖ Activity 8 ❖

Think about the interaction of cultures in school activities and behaviours. Can you think of cultural activities in schools in which pupils directly challenge the official dominant culture?

Discuss this question and ask how direct challenges interact with the perception that teachers have of individual pupils.

Typing, labelling and self-identification

Culture is a process. At one level we can describe the values and preferred behaviours in a culture, but it is also very important to see that there has to be a process whereby individuals are drawn into, or away from, incorporating those values into their own attitudes. Every social act is an expression or actualization of culture and a cultural process in its own right. We also need to analyse the way in which these values get perpetuated in a process of cultural reproduction. Schools are defined as places of learning and what goes on is not just confined to the particular content of lessons. Pupils gradually acquire an identity for themselves and that identity will be based on their interactions with others in the school.

In the process whereby pupils acquire a school identity for themselves, the teachers lead the way. They make initial, but not equal, responses to all pupils – that is, the teachers respond to certain signals and come quite quickly to label pupils. Hargreaves *et al.* (1975) have studied this in the entry of pupils into two secondary schools. Their methods included a variety of techniques, including classroom observation and interviews with teachers. Teachers distinguished pupils according to:

❖ their appearance

❖ how quickly they conformed to discipline

❖ their enthusiasm for work

❖ their relationships to other pupils

❖ their negative or disruptive behaviours.

How would you describe these individuals? (See Activity 9)

in which, as far they the school was concerned, they became 'delinquescent', i.e. they adopted attitudes and behaviours in conflict with those of the school. The studies of Paul Willis (1977) confirm all this and one has to observe that it is difficult to see how it could be otherwise. The labour market demands certain types of people to fill certain types of jobs. It should come as no surprise that the school system produces personality types that are appropriate to the jobs and individuals who know where they are heading. It is very striking that in the works of Hargreaves and Willis the individual identity is, for the individuals concerned, a question of marking themselves off from the other available types. The language words, codes and symbols will vary over place and time (and with enormous speed), but the principles will remain the same. In Willis's study those heading for manual labour called themselves '*the lads*' and labelled the others as the '*ear'oles*'.

The teachers in the survey, as all teachers everywhere, said that their initial estimates were just that – initial estimates that they would modify as time went on. But they were working hypotheses, the frameworks around which observations were made and the evidence gathered. Gradually of course, these observations became stabilized and the pupils come to adopt the appropriate responding behaviours.

In earlier studies Hargreaves (1967) had found that over the first three or four years in secondary schools (and in particular secondary modern schools), a group of pupils came to reject all that school could offer and set themselves on a 'school career'

❖ Activity 9 ❖

Try to recall for yourselves the kind of words and language with which groups of pupils marked themselves off from others during the first four years of secondary school (see also the photograph above). Relate this both to the school culture and to wider cultural frameworks.

In Focus

◆

School conformists and 'The Lads', by David Willis

'It is essentially what appears to be their own enthusiasm for and complicity with, immediate authority which makes the school conformists- or "ear'oles", the ... great target for "the lads". The term "ear'ole" itself connotes the passivity and absurdity of the school conformists for "the lads". It seems that they are always listening, never doing: never animated with their own internal life, but formless in rigid reception. The ear is one of the least expressive organs of the human body: it responds to the expressivity of others... Crucially, "the lads" feel superior to the "ear'oles". The obvious medium for the enactment of this superiority is that which the "ear'oles" apparently yield; fun, independence and excitement: having a "laff".'

Source: Willis (1977, p. 14)

Gender and differential achievement

Most societies have traditionally contained widespread differential cultural expectations for women and for men. Women and men are expected to have different attitudes and different values, to dress differently, to behave differently and to engage in the labour market differently. These differences have led many observers to see the negative effects on the ability of both women and men to lead fulfilling lives. Over the last twenty or so years, there have been vigorous attempts and campaigns by many in Western society to increase the similarity of expectations of women and men in the educational system and in the labour market. These campaigns and the people involved in them are usually called the feminist movement.

Part of feminist campaigning has been the careful research and analysis of the differential performance of boys and girls in schools. In as much as the campaigning is successful, the attention drawn to differential practices leads to modifications in practice which in turn makes the research out of date. Indeed, without in any way advocating complacency, campaigning has been particularly successful in the area of gender differentiation, more so than in class differentiation. In the early 1970s, girls performed less well than boys in every educational performance indicator after the age of 15. By the mid-1990s, this situation had been reversed in the majority of key indicators and research might now reasonably be made to explain why boys perform so badly! But simple performance statistics, like the average number of 'good grades' at GCSE, are not the whole picture.

For many years few individuals considered it as important or desirable for women to perform well in the educational system as for men. Girls and young women generally conformed to the images presented to them. Although there were many girls and young women who clearly focused their developing identity on a career in the economic system, many more focused on a career as a girlfriend, wife, mother and home-maker. The result was a relative invisibility of women in the educational system and in educational institutions themselves.

Sue Sharpe (1976, 1994) has studied by a variety of techniques 'how girls learn to be women' (the subtitle of her book). One of her main techniques was to interview young women who were heading mainly for working-class occupations in London, and discuss their hopes and aspirations for the future. She found that their concerns were 'love, marriage, husbands, children, jobs and careers, more or less in that order' (1976, p. 46). In this context they could scarcely have high educational aspirations for themselves. Not all young women are like this, but there were enough to create a gender-based differential in educational performance.

Michelle Stanworth (1983) interviewed a number of A Level teachers and asked them to describe the students that they taught. Both male and female teachers expressed the same problems in that they could recall and describe the young men (boys) rather better than they could the young women (girls). In particular, quiet young men could be recalled and described in some detail, including their hobbies. But quiet young women could not be recalled. This attitude also existed amongst the students. The young men, when interviewed, disliked the young women who were described as being either too colourless and docile, or as speaking out too aggressively and hogging the limelight. The students also reported that the young men spoke four times as often as the young women, were twice as likely to seek help and twice as likely to be asked questions by the teachers.

In sections of Stanworth's interviews, the teachers displayed a series of stereotypes when trying to describe which careers the students would be suited to. Few women were seen as having much potential for academic careers, and in most cases marriage was mentioned for the young women, but not for the young men.

Dale Spender (1983) wrote an excellent study using a wide range of sources from literature, official statistics and many other sociological studies. She analyses carefully many studies of classroom behaviour and finds that the boys always dominate and that the girls are, relatively excluded from the classroom discussions and activities. Girls rapidly learn this passive role and the boys learn theirs. So firm is this expectation that Dale Spender herself found it hard to overcome. She tape-recorded her own lessons in which she tried to achieve the explicit aim of an even balance. She reports:

> 'At the end of the lesson I have felt that I managed to achieve that goal – sometimes I have even thought I have gone too far and spent *more* time with the girls than the boys. But the tapes have proved otherwise... the maximum time I spent interacting with girls was 42 per cent and on average 38 per cent, and the minimum time with boys 58 per cent. It is nothing short of a substantial shock to appreciate the discrepancy between what I *thought* I was doing and what I actually *was doing*.'
> (Spender 1983, p. 56)

Gay Randall and Sarah Delamont have pointed out that they have failed to find such blatant reported sexism as Stanworth and Spender found. Such disagreements are in the nature of case studies. What Stanworth and Spender saw may be similar to that experienced by Randall and Delamont, but the latter researchers do not describe it the same way. Or on the other hand, what they saw may be different and if Randall and Delamont had seen it, they may have agreed that it was best described in different language. Nevertheless, the tendency to sexist behaviour and interpretation by teachers, is reported by nearly all systematic observers and researchers. Stanworth reports a male teacher who listed all his male pupils, with a description, and concluded by saying that 'the rest are girls'. This is clearly a kind of sexist behaviour but may not represent the fact that he cannot recall them. It may indicate only that, in an unforgivable sexist way, he wishes to challenge Michelle Stanworth with a confronting behaviour. It is probable that he expresses negative

attitudes to his female pupils, but without more direct observation we cannot know exactly what the remark implied. Such behaviours were probably much commoner in the 1970s and 1980s than they are now, but it is difficult to estimate the degree of change.

What is clear is that in the late 1990s, girls, despite whatever negative experiences they have in school, out-perform boys in GCSE and A Level. There seem to be three principal reasons for this:

❖ The Women's Movement and the associated campaigns have made unacceptable blatantly discriminatory behaviour amongst teachers and the whole structure of expectations has changed.

❖ Girls and young women have responded generally to the campaigns and no longer accept low expectations for themselves.

❖ Changes in the structure of marriages and their relative uncertainty have made girls and young women plan their careers around at least the possibility that they may at some point be single parents and need a well-paid job in order to support themselves.

Ethnicity and differential performance

If the differential expectations brought about by cultural processes affect young people through class cultures or gender-based cultures, we would expect the impact of ethnic cultural processes to be rather greater in differentiating educational achievement.

The patterns are rather complex and at present only partly researched. There are a number of reasons for this. One is that data on precise ethnic origin are rarely gathered and when this is done, it is often in crude geographic categories such as: 'Indian subcontinent' or 'African'. There is an enormous number of cultures in the Indian subcontinent, and the attitudes they display to education and the value they place on it vary enormously. Similarly, a large number of people of language and cultural origins best described as 'Indian' migrated to England from East Africa in the 1960s and 1970s and might appear in official statistics as 'African'. Small-scale studies can use forms of 'obvious' ethnic labelling for direct observation and interview that may be inaccurate or even offensive to those being studied. It is now clear that only a voluntary self-identification in broad ethnic-cultural categories produces any useful data looking at differentiation of performance and selection.

Bernard Coard in 1971 wrote a short study of schooling in England and detailed all the racist attitudes he saw in the system. Famously, that study was entitled *How the West Indian Child is Made Educationally Sub-normal*. Coard mapped out all the ways in which West Indian culture and language was ignored or treated as second-rate and not fit for any interaction in schools. He recorded the attitudes expressed in many text-books of the time and noted the racist attitudes of many teachers. That study was itself part of a movement of black consciousness and black pride, and those movements, like the women's movements, have had a great impact in the intervening decades. Such blatant racism as Coard observed is now less often found in schools.

❖ Activity 10 ❖

Investigate your school or college library. Look at the books in the fiction and history sections (in a school you may prefer to look at the sets of teaching books used for the ages 11 to 16). In a group, allocate the books to individual readers in your group and quickly scan or read the books, noting positive and negative images of peoples that have come to form ethnic minorities in Britain, and at images of the history and cultural achievements of those peoples. This content analysis can review any symbols, images, words or value statements. Report to each other what you find.

It is also clear that many of the communities that have grown up in Britain around a base of migrants, do in fact place very high value and expectations on education and have high aspirations for their children to succeed. One might expect this: after all, people that are ready to leave their homes and travel thousands of miles to achieve something, clearly have high expectations for themselves. Migrants, unless they are forced to move, are always a self-selecting sample of the general population from which they come. One would expect them to be, on average, more ambitious for themselves and their children.

Despite this reasonable expectation of high achievement, at the age of 16 there would appear to be fairly systematic, and frequently reported, lower levels of achievement in terms of GCSE 'scores' amongst pupils of ethnic minority populations than amongst the white majority (Troyna and Carrington 1990). This is especially noticeable in the case of African-Caribbean pupils, particularly boys.

Young British pupils with Afro-Caribbean parentage and minority ethnic backgrounds frequently have parents who have working-class or lower level occupations. What then becomes unclear is how much of the differential performance can be attributed to their parental background and how much to their ethnic background as such. This is a common problem in social sciences (see *In Focus* on the next page). We might want to determine the proportion of differential performance that may reasonably be associated with occupational class and that which is associated with ethnicity. While we lack both sets of data from a single study, we cannot even begin the analysis. But whatever the conclusions of such studies, it is clear that there are questions of explanation of differentiated performance that need answering.

Trevor Jones (1993) from the Policy Studies Institute has reworked many figures available from the Labour Market Surveys of the statistical branch of the (then) Employment Department. His conclusion is that the staying-on rates for all ethnic minorities are higher than for the white

When two variables correlate statistically we still have to postulate some causative mechanism that is plausible if we wish to explain this correlation. When three or more variables are found to correlate (which is usually the case in social sciences), the problem is greater.

Statistical techniques such as regression analysis, or multi-level analysis have been developed to deal with these problems and analyse which patterns of correlation in a network are strongest. If you wish to look at regression analysis and multi-level analysis you could study the works of Kerlinger and Pedhazur (1982) and of Goldstein (1995). If you are embarking on any sociological study yourself or are also studying psychology, you may find a study of such techniques interesting and well worthwhile.

populations. In addition, ethnic minorities have higher participation rates in part-time study and, by the time they are 24 years old, they generally have higher levels of qualifications than their white counterparts in similar jobs. These findings are quite consistent both with the ideas of ambitions in the parental groups and with the ideas of negative interactions of teachers and ethnic minority pupils. There are (at least) two possible explanations for this and both might apply:

❖ Parents have high expectations for their young children and these expectations are accepted by their children.

❖ Staying on may be preferable to unemployment because they have very poor employment prospects. Faced with a real and sustained discrimination in the labour market, people from ethnic minorities react in a rational way.

The explanations of the initial poor performance are difficult to make. The curriculum in schools is very much focused on the achievements of a white, European culture and in no useful way acknowledges the multicultural facets of Britain, except in some aspects of primary education in some inner cities. This was true before 1990 and, since then, the compulsory National Curriculum documents coming from central government agencies have, according to many critics, increased the tendency to focus the curriculum on the traditional culture of the white middle and upper classes. Troyna, with a number of

colleagues, has analysed and recorded the implicit racism in the state educational system (Troyna 1993, Troyna and Carrington 1990, Gill *et al.* 1992). Young people from ethnic minorities must generally feel rather isolated and set on one side of the dominant culture, no matter how hard they, or their teachers, try.

However much the teachers, and school actions and behaviours have improved, there are many aspects of British culture that remain very racist. It is clear that in many schools, racial harassment is a daily experience for young people from ethnic minorities, as are persistent racist attacks on the way to and from schools (Commission for Racial Equality 1988). In the more extreme cases, pupils have been stabbed to death, as have teachers attempting to intervene (Macdonald *et al.* 1989).

As far as the official curriculum is concerned, the UK seems to have been through three phases:

1 From 1944 to the mid 1970s, the assumptions were those of assimilation. In other words, no attempt was made in the definitions of the curriculum to recognize the differing cultures increasingly represented in the school population.

2 From the mid 1970s until 1990, there were systematic attempts to create a multicultural curriculum in which most cultures received some form of recognition. Multiculturalism also had its critics, who saw it as being isolated into

unimportant aspects of the curriculum and generating a view of the ethnic minorities as exotic species.

3 From 1990 onwards, the creation of a National Curriculum tended to put the situation into a reverse. The National Curriculum prioritizes a British perspective on history, the use of a standardized English and Christianity in Religious Education. It has been described as a National*ist* Curriculum (Gillborn 1990).

One result of this is that pupils from ethnic minorities tend to adopt various survival strategies which are centred round a sort of isolation from many, but not all, aspects of the school and its culture. Mairtin Mac an Ghaill (1988) has pointed out from his ethnographic studies that Afro-Caribbean girls tended to band together for mutual support, often helping each other with school work, but marking themselves off with behaviour to the teachers and the school culture that is as 'provocative' as they dare, e.g. by not conforming to school rules on dress or behaviour. For such girls, the core of 'school-work' seems well carried out in this form of isolation. There now seems evidence that Afro-Caribbean boys' patterns of resistance are similar, but less acceptable to teachers. Certainly they are over-represented in school exclusions and studies of truancy. More recent studies have suggested that there can be particular effects resulting from the internal organizational aspects and attitudes of different schools. When comparing schools of very similar ethnic populations, they are often found to have quite different results in terms of educational achievements (Smith and Tomlinson 1989, Gillborn 1990). This

should not be taken to mean that overall, there is no systematic or institutionalized disadvantage. On the contrary, the studies tend to reinforce the idea that such disadvantages are deeply institutionalized and need radical efforts to remove them.

The studies also suggest that teachers continue to have low expectations of ethnic minorities, in that they do not seem to be very proactive or interventionist in obtaining the best from these pupils. As a result, ethnic origin plays a strong part in constructing differentiated performance within the school system.

At levels of continuing, further and higher education there is no such evidence. As part of public policy, the centralized national admission systems for entry to higher education undertook routine monitoring of applications to HE, using the techniques of voluntary identification (there were, in Great Britain, two separately funded and recognized systems for entry to HE until 1993). Comparisons of entry to HE with national census data led to the conclusion that Asian ethnic minorities were slightly over-represented compared to their general representation in the general population, while African and Caribbean minorities were represented proportionally according to the admissions systems for colleges and universities. All of this is consistent with the other information and research that people from ethnic minorities, in order to find employment commensurate with their ambitions, tend to need higher qualifications than their white counterparts. It tells us little about the details of interaction of their cultural patterns with the educational system, except that the notion of disadvantage or deprivation becomes harder to use and analyse at the tertiary level.

The labour market, industrial change and training

Our changing world

The detailed study of the transition from school to working life is something that has only really begun since the mid-1970s and

only gained any momentum from the mid-1980s. This is somewhat surprising since the connections between the schooling systems, and the formation of adult attitudes about work and society, are clearly most likely founded in what happens to young people between the ages of about 15 and 20, i.e. the period of the transition and the period of their first and most formative experiences of work. It remains a sociological and historical problem to decide why this arena was previously so little studied or drawn attention to.

A partial explanation for this neglect may lie in the fact that until the 1990s, there was no university base in England for the training of further or vocational education teachers and no university base for the training of trainers in industry (there was a small University base in Wales). Universities have always put a great value on research and publication and a great value on research from a critical viewpoint, independent of government and specific groups. Careers in universities are built on this. But the absence in universities of a group of academics concerned with training for vocational education and training has meant that until recently, there was no group of academics dedicated to the pursuit of research in this area. This is as much a cultural and sociological explanation as an economic one.

The reasons why the period of transition came so clearly to be a focus of concern are simple and reduce to almost one: the political questions raised up by the rapid rise of youth unemployment, accompanied by structural and institutional disruption in the formal provisions for vocational education and training. Behind that lie some simple demographic and economic facts.

Demography and economic change

During the 1950s and early 1960s, the whole of Western Europe went through a sustained economic development and boom in employment and living conditions. The birth rate rose from the early 1950s and reached a peak during 1964. From there it fell significantly, almost certainly as a principal response to a bio-technological innovation: the introduction of a cheap and efficient contraceptive pill.

This steady rise in the birth rate led turn to a steadily rising number of school leavers

some seventeen years later (the average interval between birth and leaving school). Unfortunately, this took place almost simultaneously with a major economic restructuring. The sharp rises in the price of fuel and oil in the early seventies, the drastic retooling and changes in manufacturing production as the result of technological changes (particularly in manufacturing industries) brought about by automation, computerization and robotics, all coincided with this rise in the school leaver rate. The traditional structures for incorporating school leavers into the economy, all across Europe, were in a state of near collapse. The rate of youth unemployment rose sharply and all governments sought ways to deal with the new situation, some more successfully than others.

One thing was very clear: all industry and commerce was shedding labour and was reluctant to recruit youth. In the UK, officially registered unemployment rose from one and a half million to well over three million in less than five years (1979 to 1984), the precise years when the number of school leavers rose from about 600,000 a year to over 900,000 a year. The result was close to catastrophic for the young. Opportunities for either work or systematic training within industry collapsed. Youth unemployment rose, and parents and young people wondered what to do for the best.

One feature of all booms and slumps since 1979 in the UK has been that those still in work in core jobs or the core parts of the economy continued to be fairly prosperous with rising wages. The period since then has been a period of rising wage differentiation. Of course, those in work responded to the situation of their own young children by encouraging them to stay on at school or try to find some vocational education in a college of further education. An understandable response was to delay the decision to enter the work force and eventually to enter better equipped with skills, qualifications, certificates and diplomas.

Parallel with this was a significant change in the economic structure of the UK. In particular, employment opportunities in the fields of manufacturing or construction contracted very quickly. There was some compensatory growth in the service sectors, but this actually contained few employment opportunities offering systematic training for young people. This was important because, during the period 1964 to 1984, manufacturing and construction had been great sources of apprenticeships and systematic training for young men (but alas not for young women). It seemed clear that the trends in future employment were towards higher skills, especially in areas of business and finance, and towards the service trades in general. These new areas of employment are sometimes thought of as dominated by the handling of information and by the related information technology. Most analysts and politicians think that mass employment in manufacturing is now a thing of the past and since many people in employment have changed jobs or careers, this trend will increase. They argue that what is called for is broad-based vocational education. This way of thinking encourages the move from job-specific training in industry to broad training in colleges and schools.

Government training schemes

The government of the UK responded to the problems and to the perceived causes of the problem by developing an ever changing and ever more bewildering variety of 'schemes' to provide beneficial activity and training for young people. These were funded by the state and as closely associated as possible with the employers who were showing themselves so reluctant to fund training for themselves. The government also provided funding for some significant and serious expansions of the provisions for further and higher education. These extra provisions forced the Conservative government of the 1980s to think carefully about how to tackle the enormous challenges it was facing. There was a fluidity of policy that seemed to derive from the political needs of government and career needs of junior ministers. Both needed, every two years or less, to be seen to be

making a new initiative, another contribution or innovation to the collection of schemes that already existed. But in addition, the government undertook some very drastic rethinking of educational policy and came up with some radical changes in the educational system that are likely to persist. For nearly ten years the training schemes had a temporary character, but by 1990 it was accepted by most politicians and analysts that only acceptance of the structural changes in the location and types of training would work in the provision of a skilled work force.

Structural changes

Although the politicians have seen the driving force for change as lying with the social and economic problems of possible youth unemployment, they have nevertheless looked also at the school system. The argument seems to run: 'If our young people cannot get jobs, then there must be something lacking in the skills that they have.' A second line of argument is: 'If there is something lacking in the skills that young people have when they leave school, there must be something wrong with the schools.' It is these lines of thought that have driven the changes.

Compared to the attention paid to schools and colleges, little attention has been paid to the employers who during this period have withdrawn from supporting training for 16- to 19-year-olds and almost abandoned the policy of recruiting 16-year-olds. Where this is seen as a problem by government, it is one for persuasion and for encouragement with subsidy funding. For schools the policy remedies are legislative, regulatory and structural.

The principal changes to the educational system have been in accordance with the Conservative administrations' overarching policy preferences which have been applied to all (previously) public services. They sought to strengthen the regulatory framework at national level while giving decision-making to the providing institutions themselves rather than local government or other intermediary organizations. They created structures within which these providing institutions compete to provide the services required, believing that this competition would improve quality and lower cost.

One strong element in the background to this was the responses of young people themselves and their parents. Within the previous structures, there had been an accepted freedom for young people to leave school or college when they wished after the age of 16. A response to youth unemployment was to increase the staying-on rate. Fewer and fewer left at 16 to seek work or training, so that during this period those continuing their education became a majority for the first time.

The changes in the system were:

❖ For the first time, the national government took legal powers to determine a National Curriculum that had to apply to all pupils between the ages of 5 and 16. This curriculum has been difficult to implement and has changed a number of times within its first ten years, but it was a key instrument for regulating the schools and had a potential for measuring school performance.

❖ Schools were given more independence from their Local education Authority (LEA) in financial matters and in their own governance.

❖ New forms of school that were independent of the LEA were developed, in particular the system of grant maintained schools. All schools were asked to consider whether they wished to become independent of their LEA, with a ballot of parents to be the key deciding factor. They became funded directly by the national government through a funding agency.

❖ Parents were given greater powers to request that their children should go to particular schools, and since schools are all funded basically on a formula in which pupil numbers predominate,

schools would compete for the finance represented by each child.

❖ The government set about establishing a National Council for Vocational Qualifications (NCVQ), to improve and enhance the qualifications already available to colleges, employers and training-scheme managers. This Council drew up two types of award: the National Vocational Qualifications (NVQs) to be mainly work-based and General National Vocational Qualifications (GNVQs) to be mainly based in schools and colleges.

❖ All colleges of further and higher education were removed from local authority control and turned into independent corporations funded directly by the government through funding councils.

❖ The government continued the schemes for the training of unemployed young people, made the schemes more permanent and tried to enhance their status and image by naming their preferred scheme 'Modern Apprenticeships'.

❖ For the management of training locally and for the encouragement of enterprise in small firms, the government established a network of Training and Enterprise Councils (TECs) across the country. Each of these was funded by the government but, like the colleges, was to be controlled by local private business people who would nominate their successors.

Research responses

This restructuring of the educational system took place with a number of pieces of legislation and administrative acts but the bulk of the action was in the five-year period 1988 to 1993 and in total constitutes the greatest restructuring since the 1944 Education Act. Few of these structural reforms are likely to be changed in the foreseeable future, whatever government is in office. How has the sociological research community responded to these changes?

There have been three main lines of research:

❖ a growth of interest in how young people form a vocational identity and other aspects of their mature adult personality

❖ studies of the social processes of policy formulation and the political processes generally, often accompanied by an exploration of the value consequences of the changes

❖ interest in studies of the organizational processes within the independent, grant-maintained schools.

Vocational identity

We have already described the seminal study of Paul Willis and we have already commented that it took place when it was easy for school leavers to obtain reasonably paid employment as labourers.

The focus of Paul Willis's study was in school and shortly afterwards. He also focused on a group who were prepared for and sought tough, demanding jobs but jobs that carried no particular career identity. Since the time of Willis's study a growing volume of studies have, amongst other things, mapped the rapidly changing routes and patterns of transition from school to working life. This has included a massive growth of full-time vocational courses in

Official publicity increasingly emphasizes work roles

both schools and colleges and also the Youth Training Schemes (now just called Youth Training).

A major research initiative by the Economic and Social Research Council (led by Professor Blythe of the City University) funded a number of empirical studies and seminars and has formed the base for much work, not all of which has been wholly funded by the ESRC. One research approach has been that of the case study of a course group. Inge Bates (1988), for example, has studied groups of trainees from Youth Training Schemes that were intended to lead to careers in caring. Her research methods were classroom observation and extensive interviewing of the trainees themselves. They had joined the programme because they initially thought that they could become carers for children. Over time it became clear to them that there were very few jobs in this type of work and that they were likely only to find work in caring for the elderly. This work was not what they had intended and was not initially part of their identity. The work was often traumatic, with the elderly who were sometimes aggressive or violent, sometimes incontinent. The young people often had to confront death and mortality in new ways. In the face of these circumstances their vocational identity grew around the fact that they could survive, that they were not 'bleeding whining minnies'. Gradually they came to accept their roles and even saw them in terms of a positive choice rather than a mere circumstance: they had survived, and decided to stay and commit themselves.

Bates (1989) also studied students on two-year fashion courses at a local college. In this case the girls had aspirations to find work as fashion designers and lead a metropolitan, jet-setting life style. The reality was that most would find work as pattern cutters, machinists, in the buying departments of shops or even just working in shops. They hung on to their role-ideals, progressively distancing themselves from what they were actually doing, thinking of their actual occupations as actually temporary or even 'trash' jobs.

Karen Evans from Surrey and Walter Heinz from Hamburg (1994) conducted some medium-term, comparative studies in various towns in England and Germany, following young people through the transition from school to work over a number of years. They interviewed the young people in their sample population a number of times and decided that the individuals created their own idea of their personalities (individualization) through the decisions they made at the time of transition. They observed, however, two models of this process: one active and one passive.

❖ In the *active* model, young people conformed to what is often seen as a model-dominating careers guidance. Early on, young people formed a career goal and then worked towards it, e.g. wanting to be a doctor or a teacher.

❖ In the *passive* model, the decisions were circumscribed and narrow. The structure of the situation seemed to be accepted through passive individualization. Inge Bates' care assistants exhibit this trend.

Both Evans and Heinz (1994) and Roberts (1995) have found that the active model tends to exist or even dominate primarily in a few high-status occupations such as doctor or architect. For nearly all other occupations, most entrants are in the passive mode of engagement. This actually makes the system very flexible in that individuals are prepared to transfer between, as well as within, the segments of the labour market (see *In Focus* below).

The study of both the acquisition of a work identity and of the parallel processes of individualization have now got well under way in the UK, largely as a response to the threats of large-scale youth unemployment and of the policy responses to it. We must now look at the study of the policy responses.

❖ Activity 11 ❖

Examine the *In Focus* below. How could you design research to test the hypothesis that most young people delay entry to the labour market to fulfil their aspirations?

Policy studies

Many sociologists would be very uncertain about the position of policy studies as a part of sociology. The principal technique of policy studies is a close analysis of policy statements, journal articles, electoral manifestos, speeches and other representations of political opinion. These are examined for values and purposes and relate to other social debates and changes.

| *In Focus* ◆ **Underskilled or overqualified?** | 'I have been consistently sceptical towards claims that the UK's methods of vocational preparation are less capable of delivering the workers required by a modern world-class economy than education and training in other parts of Europe. If these criticisms of the UK's education and training were valid, one would expect employers to be experiencing persistent difficulties in recruiting enough young people capable of being trained up to the standards that the firms require. There is in fact no such evidence of any such widespread | problems. There is far more evidence that young people have to delay their entry into employment for longer than they would prefer, of them being unable to obtain jobs that match their qualifications, skills and aspirations and then face working lives in which they will be underemployed relative to their capacities. If Britain's economy is weaker than its European or North American competitors, there are more likely explanations than deficiencies in the country's education and training.'

Source: Roberts (1995, p.124) |

What makes policy studies sociological is the character of the relationships within the social structure drawn out and the interconnections within the value structures and the cultural systems and processes.

Salter and Tapper have argued that 'significant structural change in education is preceded by a period of ideological conflict' (1988, p. 57). They have analysed the growth of influence of the 'New Right' on educational policy. They quote Sir Keith Joseph (later Lord Joseph) speaking in 1975. Joseph was a leading Conservative politician who went on to become the longest serving Conservative Minister of Education. His argument was that for too long the Conservatives had had no distinct policy of their own. The result was that each time the left made a change or innovation, the right left it alone, creating a sort of 'left-wing ratchet' in which policy always shifted to the left and never back. Joseph determined that when in office, the Conservatives should apply a right-wing ratchet in a very deliberate way, creating measures that would be hard to reverse. Salter and Tapper identify four main components of right-wing policy for education:

❖ a particular desired social order of individual or local choice

❖ the education and production of individuals to support that order

❖ educational institutions ordered and managed by those principles

❖ a clear conception of human nature that limits both what is educationally desirable and possible.

The implementation of policy by Conservative administrations is quite clear and can now be seen clearly to follow these lines. Joseph did not himself introduce the National Curriculum, nor grant-maintained schools, but they conform to policies of the sort he intended. Local management of non-grant-maintained schools places more power in the hands of the parents, but the new governing bodies are freed from their previous dependence on teachers and the educational establishment for understanding what might be in the curriculum, as everyone has to follow the National Curriculum. Unless teachers can perform well against this standard, they will lose influence even locally. As Whitty (1989) explains, these policies have the character of a right-wing ratchet because they are both hard to undo in administrative terms and create anxiety in opponents, as policies to reverse them seem potential vote-losers.

In addition to Salter and Tapper, there is the work of Stephen Ball and his colleagues. Ball has made an important contribution not only to studies in this field but also to the methodologies used and the theoretical orientations. He has emphasized the relevance of the more general and theoretical work of Bourdieu and of Foucault. In Ball's (1994b) account of

The big players in educational policy-making: parliament, the Department for Education and Employment, and local government. *Where does the power lie now?*

Foucault, the key concepts are the intertwining of power and knowledge in a symbiotic coupling. In actual discourse in a social network, in addition to the other coercive powers that individuals hold, they dominate through their use of knowledge and language that relates to cultural power. Foucault also points out that in any power relationship, there is the possibility of resistance and it is important to be aware of this possibility if one wishes to avoid complete domination. This analysis of power and resistance to power lies at the heart of Ball's purposes.

Grant maintained schools

Grant maintained schools have only been with us for a few years, and, at the time of writing, most studies have been by those involved with the movement, are largely descriptive and are in no sense impartial. Nevertheless, they reveal a good deal about the organizational processes within the schools.

In their 1992 work, Davies and Anderson attempted to provide commentary on what was clearly a very radical policy initiative. Several chapters in the book are contributed by those who experienced the process and its immediate aftermath first-hand, and it is these that provide some interesting insights. Roger Perks (1992), as headteacher of a Birmingham school, depicts the importance of developing and establishing a strong school ethos, particularly for his inner-city school. In the

shift from being an LEA school to GMS, it was essential that the leadership articulated its educational philosophy in clear and precise terms.

In a study published a year later, Halpin et al. (1993) set about 'testing' empirically the claims and predictions made by both the critics and advocates of the GM schools policy. This study is particularly useful for two reasons:

❖ Much of the work was done after the 1992 General Election. The election had created a degree of uncertainty over the policy. This uncertainty was lifted with the Conservative victory and lead to a spate of applications for GM status.

❖ Much of the work draws useful comparisons and provides insights to the effect of the policy in other areas of the state sector. Some interesting discoveries were made with regard to the scale, distribution and pace of 'opting out'. They find that 'Predictions that, if one school becomes grant maintained, others in the same locality may be tempted to do so, are beginning to be borne out in practice.' (Halpin et al. 1993)

Some areas of the country had been hardly touched by the policy, irrespective of political control of the LEA, whilst in other areas there was a 'concentration' of GM Schools. The indication being perhaps that in some way GM status would provide an 'edge' that other schools felt necessary to follow. Other interesting figures showed that there was a strong presence in the GM sector of academically selective, single-sex schools and institutions offering post-compulsory options (i.e. 6th-form courses), compared to LEA-maintained secondary schools. The results are shown in Table 4.1.

For none of these institutions, however, did the change to GM entail a change in their character and what they offered the educational market place.

The impact of the GM policy on the rest of the system has been substantial. With regard to the LEAs the schools were opting out from:

Table 4.1 Comparison of types of schools in grant maintained and LEA-maintained schools

	Grant maintained sector	LEA-maintained secondary schools
Academically selective	23%	4%
Single sex schools	29%	13%
Offering 6th-form courses	75%	45%

'There was hardly an LEA and not one local authority organization which welcomed the policy.' (Halpin *et al.* 1993)

This was irrespective of political persuasion, because those who were not opposed in principle found that, in practice, the opportunity for a school to 'opt out' would have huge implications for their capacity to develop sensible plans for the rationalization of school provision. Because the LEA were also not allowed to know which parents had chosen GM schools, it made it difficult to the point of impossible to plan the size of provision they should make. Therefore, because of their legal obligation as last recourse for provision, the LEAs would be:

'forced to maintain a large surplus of capacity in their schools, thus adding considerably to the cost of running their education services as a whole.' (Halpin *et al.* 1993)

It was also discovered that where LEAs were in full negotiation for a rationalization of provision with 'every conceivable vested interest', a school threatened with closure, amalgamation or redesignation would apply for and obtain GM status as a last resort. The LEA plans would be thwarted and they would be left with little option than to identify other schools for closure who could then pursue the same route. The result being that plans were frequently having to be abandoned.

The rare change of character permissible and restrictions of the National Curriculum for schools which opted out led Halpin *et al.* (1993) to state that: 'All schools do not constitute an expansion of alternatives from which parents can choose.' However, that is not to say that the policy was to have no impact on the market place. Their research was to show that the grant maintained factor seemed to have little influence on parental choice; rather that the choice tended to be dominated by unofficial reputation and factors such as proximity to home, exam results and ethos. The impact of GM schools on the market place is not realized through the provision of a 'new'

kind of school but rather through increased resourcing and independence to define and emphasize a particular image. Increased resourcing has given the ability to pay attention to decorative order to help foster positive impressions and augment school recruitment. The authors of the study also drew attention to other subtle areas of reputation management: pupils frequently stating there had been increased emphasis placed on their appearance and behaviour as indicators of 'good' schooling. In all research, pupils reported a tightening up of the dress code. Whilst such 'marketing techniques' can be pursued with a greater freedom by GM schools, they are not exclusive and they can also be seen in LMSs. The impression that marketing techniques are being pursued with greater vigour in GMSs than LMSs does not hide the fact that this is largely image-building exercise and does not represent a substantial increase in choice for parents.

Gewirtz *et al.* (1995) have also studied the processes of selection of the intake for fourteen schools and the parents of 140 children. Their work was informed by the thinking of Bourdieu but the focus was on entry to secondary schools. The process is viewed in their studies often from the viewpoint of the parent as chosen. However much it might desire to get the best pupils, a school still has to persuade the parents of the best pupils to 'choose' their school. As the authors put it:

'Our contextual analysis of choice and class goes to the heart of the ideology of the market and the claims of classlessness and neutrality. Choice emerges as a major new factor in maintaining and indeed reinforcing social-class divisions and inequalities... post-1988, the strategies of competitive advantage are now ideologically endorsed and practically facilitated by open enrolment, the deregulation of recruitment and parental choice.' (Gewirtz *et al.* 1995, p. 23)

The authors go on to create a typology of choosers: privileged and skilled choosers;

semi-skilled choosers; and disconnected choosers. While not exclusively related to social and occupational class, these three categories are related in many ways. The acts of finding the information, making the evaluation, selecting the schools, applying and then being interviewed are acts in which the possession of cultural capital reigns supreme. Individuals possess varying abilities to participate in or benefit from the culture of choice: that is, to 'decipher and manipulate complex structures' (Bourdieu and Passeron 1990, p 73). When parents apply to a school, they will be interviewed by the school. The school will then select the kind of parents that can offer the kind of cultural support the school wants and needs to make the pupils successful in examinations in the dominant cultural codes. But before the selection process can operate, the parents have differentially entered into a culture of self-selection and of self-exclusion.

What marks this out from the older system of selection for Grammar schools is its partiality. In the older systems, intelligence tests were administered to all, precisely to identify the 'most able', whether their parents were skilled in the application processes or not. The culture of the market proceeds without any care for the losers in the system. It becomes the fault of the class itself if it cannot work the system; it is not the responsibility of those that design or run the system. The market, as it is structured now, cannot result in an equal distribution of educational chances. Indeed it should not. As Jonathon points out:

> 'Since education has exchange value as well as intrinsic value, and since its value in exchange, like that of any other currency, depends on the amount of this good that an individual holds *relative to others*, then a more favourable experience – in exchange value terms – secured for one child, entails a less favourable experience in those terms for some other child or children.' (Jonathon 1990, p. 19)

The final irony that Jonathon points out is that, winners or losers, all have to pay for the schools through their taxes. The market is not being applied to goods wholly paid for by the parents themselves, but by the whole community.

Chapter summary

❖ The agenda for sociological research in education is closely linked to the political agenda.

❖ Survey work and educational achievement dominated the research before 1970.

❖ After 1970 the agenda shifted to the internal processes of schools.

❖ From 1970 to 1988 the agenda was the way in which the schools themselves set the targets and research into classroom processes. Concepts such as 'labelling' were key factors.

❖ Since 1988 the political agenda has shifted back to the centre and central decision-making. Sociological research has refocused on policy-making in national government and inside the schools.

❖ Since the rise in unemployment, the political and research agendas have shifted to a concern with vocationalism and vocational education.

Coursework

Small-scale surveys can be carried out on populations within larger 11-to-18 schools or FE Colleges that focus on specific aspects of the educational process. Such work can be supported by ethnographic observations and studies and by open-ended interviews. This work might be group or individual work. Generally, there is in the literature very little about the procedures for group work in ethnographic studies and observations, although the basic stages identified by Glaser and Strauss (1967) for the operational discovery of grounded theory might be adopted and adapted. The methodological discussion should prove very valuable. Topics might include:

1 the processes of choice-making at the transition from Year 11 in schools and the kind of alternatives at 16+ that were actually made – these can be seen simply as processes or added to by more systematic study of structured differentiation by gender, by parental occupation or by parental educational achievement

2 the processes of adopting vocational identities in FE Colleges, by students in specific course groups (see Bates 1989)

3 an analysis of either the library or sets of teaching texts for the images and values implicit in the books, and a comparison of these with the values held by parental groups to consider their appropriateness.

Essay questions

1 Examine sociological explanations of differences in educational achievement.

2 Compare and contrast two major theories of the role of education in society.

3 How significant has comprehensive schooling been for the British educational system?

4 Use sociological and policy studies to examine the proposition that Grant Maintained Schools will lead to a more selective system of secondary education.

5 'The National Curriculum does not reflect the reality of schooling for many.' Discuss.

6 Give sociological explanations for how 'working-class kids get working-class jobs'.

Further reading

Mackinnon, D., Statham, J. and Hales, M. (1995) *Education in the UK: Facts and Figures,* London: Hodder & Stoughton.

A very useful book and a good source of reference if you need further information, or facts and figures for further study.

Cantor, L., Roberts, I. and Pratley, B. (1995) *A Guide to FE in England and Wales,* London: Cassel Educational.

A good reference source on further Education.

Trowler, P. (1995) *Investigating Education and Training,* London: Collins Educational.

This general text contains many good ideas and references for further study.

For more specific sociological focuses, look to more general sociology books. For example, if interested in ethnicity and education, the general text below is both illuminating in itself and contains many good references to follow up.

Mason, D. (1995) *Race and Ethnicity in Modern Britain,* Oxford: Oxford University Press.

Chapter 5

Work, organizations, unemployment and leisure

❖ Preview

In this chapter we shall be looking at:

❖ the distinctions between work, non-work and leisure

❖ the changing nature of work

❖ the ownership and control of work

❖ sociological concepts and theories of work: alienation, technology and determinism, de-skilling

❖ the changing workplace

❖ conflict at work

❖ inequality at work: class, gender, ethnicity, age and physical ability or disability

❖ the growth of organizations

❖ unemployment: the causes and consequences of lack of work

❖ leisure

❖ current trends: 'downshifting', 'downsizing', 'outsourcing' and TQM

❖ the future of work and leisure.

❖ Introduction

Work and identity

'What do you do for a living?' – 'Where do you work?' – Such questions are common openings to conversations between strangers. If we are told that someone is a doctor, or a bus driver, or a secretary, or a bricklayer, or an advertising executive, we make assumptions about what kind of person they are and the kind of lifestyle they have. Once we know somebody's occupation, we feel that we can make a good guess at their educational background, income, political leanings, even their choice of newspaper, although we may, of course, be proved wrong.

❖ Activity 1 ❖

Briefly describe what some of the assumptions might generally be about people in the following occupations: accountant, carpenter, social worker, telephonist.

This chapter covers a topic that can be seen as being as important in human lives as our families and personal relationships, our gender, our religion and our class position. As the activity above indicates, our work is a significant part of our identity (see Chapter 2, *Culture and identity*).

Our work can be so central to our identity that losing our job can result in mental and health problems, marital breakdown and even suicide. Conversely, getting a job or being promoted can be a cause of celebration and give us a great sense of pride and wellbeing. As the nineteenth-century Scottish essayist and historian, Thomas Carlyle wrote: 'Work is the grand cure of all maladies and miseries that ever beset mankind.'

Throughout human history the nature of work and occupations has changed dramatically as societies have changed. At present it could be argued that we are on the brink of the most significant changes ever, leading sociologists and others to question the need for work in the conventional sense. Questions about the centrality of work to our lives and issues of where technology might take us in the future, lead us on to deeper philosophical questions concerning the meaning and purpose of life. Many earlier philosophers and sociologists, including Karl Marx, saw the need to work as a part of our human nature. His collaborator Engels saw work as being the thing that separated humans from animals. In other words, without work we cease to be human. This connects with the point made above about the centrality of work to many people's identity. Along with this go feelings of belonging to society and having self-

❖ Activity 2 ❖

In general terms, do you think that men and women view their work as equally central to their identity? If not, why not? Do you think the position is changing? What might the feminist perspective on this issue be?

Do you think that there are differences between older and younger people's attitudes to the importance of work?

You could conduct a small-scale survey to investigate this issue further with regard to age and gender (see Chapter 7, *Theory and methods*, for guidance on conducting surveys).

worth (see Activity 2). Our occupational status enables us to locate ourselves in relation to other people in terms of social class and status. So, what is work?

Defining what is and what is not work is not straightforward and in the first part of this chapter we will look at this issue as well as the associated issues of workplaces and organizations, unemployment and leisure. We will also examine the dramatic changes that have taken place concerning work and occupations and how these relate to the wider economic, political and technological environment. Social scientists have made a key distinction between Fordism and post-Fordism to highlight the changes in manufacturing from the early to the end of the twentieth century. They have theorized, conceptualized and explained these changes in different ways, some highlighting the cooperative nature of human work and the advantages of the division of labour (Durkheim), others highlighting the conflicts that have arisen from the changes (Marx).

Three key sociological concepts associated with work are the division of labour, alienation and de-skilling. Sociologists have sought to find out whether work in industrial society is inevitably a negative experience for the majority of people, and to this end have examined people's experience of work, to see whether it is of mind-numbing boredom and leads to clockwatching, or alternatively provides creativity, excitement and a sense of purpose. Sociological research has also investigated work along class, gender and ethnic lines.

Workplaces and unions

The *places* in which we work are important. We can all identify factories, offices, schools, universities and so forth as places in which people work, but in the final years of the twentieth century an increasing number of people are working from home. If this increase in home-working is attributable to advances in technology, we would expect this figure to increase in the next century: the traditional workplaces we recognize today might become as obsolete as Lancashire cotton mills. Another feature of the twentieth century is that workplaces have grown in size and scale, a trend first highlighted by Max Weber. Whether such bureaucracies, as they came to be known, make work more or less efficient has been the subject of sociological investigation for many years.

If workplaces are arenas for conflict, as some sociologists claim, what part do trade unions and similar organizations play in this? It is useful to examine whether in Britain the dominance of New Right political policies during the 1980s and 1990s has significantly reduced the power of trade unions. Certainly the number of strikes and related industrial disputes has declined throughout the 1980s and 1990s. At the time of writing, the British Labour Party, which has always been linked to the trade union movement, is arousing controversy because of its moves to remove such ties. This could be seen as further evidence of the declining influence of trade unions on people's working lives. The growth in non-manual and professional occupations since the 1960s has led to a large increase in white-collar unions and professional associations. Sociologists have asked

whether these new unions perform a similar role to the more traditional manual trade unions, i.e. do the *new* unions concentrate on pay and conditions and the protection of workers' rights?

The sociological study of unemployment has increased in recent years. Sociologists examine patterns and variations in it based on to age, regions, ethnicity, gender and social class. It is commonly assumed that, like death, unemployment is the 'great leveller' affecting all social groups equally, but closer study reveals that this is not the case.

Unemployment, non-work and leisure

If work in industrial societies has become increasingly unavailable, boring and tedious, can our non-work or leisure time be seen as a compensation? A person's job in the factory or office might be unfulfilling, but at least the money they earn can be used to buy material goods such as TVs, CDs, cars and sports equipment which make life more interesting and varied. We will examine arguments about the compensatory potential of leisure, as well as opposing arguments that highlight the differential access and inequalities associated with leisure.

A feature of many societies throughout the world is the development of sport, which is now much more than a simple leisure pursuit and which has become a major industry in terms of entertainment, merchandising and media interests.

If Karl Marx were alive today he might say that sport, rather than religion, is the 'opiate of the people', diverting attention away from the stresses and strains of degrading work under capitalism. Non-Marxist sociologists highlight democratization through the increased availability and access to sport and leisure, which are now consumer items from which people can choose a wide variety of options.

An advert for the Manchester United VISA card – part of the multimillion pound Manchester United leisure industry

Defining work, non-work and leisure

What is work? Our vocabulary for work includes the words 'occupation', 'profession', 'toil', 'labour', 'career' and 'vocation'. Some of these terms reveal a negative and some a positive attitude towards work.

❖ Activity 3 ❖

1 Try to find further examples of the words associated with work. Which are positive and which negative? Explain why there might be such a range.

2 Consider the following quotes:

   'Work is love made visible. And if you cannot work with love but only with distaste, it is better that you should leave your work and sit at the gate of the temple and take alms of those who work with joy.' (Kahlil Gibran, Syrian poet)

   'If any would not work, neither should he eat.' (*The Bible*, Thessalonians 2, 3:10)

   '[Work is] the supply of physical, mental, and emotional effort to produce goods and services for own consumption, or for consumption by others.' (Gordon Marshall 1984)

   In the first two statements, human work seems to take on a moral or spiritual dimension linked to a philosophical or religious stance. Karl Marx, who is associated with a non-religious view of the world, saw work as an essential part of human nature or, as he put it, our 'species being'. Gordon Marshall's definition is closer to that of the dictionary.

   Do you think Marshall's definition is satisfactory? Does it cover all types of work in all circumstances?

3 How would you define work? Try to do so now in no more than 50 words.

The problem with a clear definition of work is that different people can define the same activity in different ways. Take gardening, for example: one person might dislike it intensely, describing it as hard work and a chore, whereas another person might regard gardening as a leisure activity and describe it as uplifting and invigorating.

Definitions of work often include the idea of an *economic reward*. However, this is not always accurate: what about a man looking after his elderly parents or a woman bringing up a young family – would they receive money for this kind of work? Neither are all leisure activities unpaid: someone fishing as a hobby may receive economic reward if they sell their catch to workmates or to a local restaurant.

Most people in industrial societies would associate a definition of work with a specific *workplace* such as a shop, an office, a factory or a room given over to work within the home.

❖ Activity 4 ❖

How do you think people in non-industrial societies would regard this idea of a workplace?

A similar point can be made about work time: industrial societies see work time in separate blocks from other periods of time in the day, week or year. Stanley Parker (1971), a British sociologist, drew attention to the time dimension as part of our understanding of the distinction between work, non-work and leisure. He identified as 'non-work time' those periods when we are not engaged in work or leisure, which includes getting ready for and travelling to work. Even eating a meal can be seen in this way, as feeding is necessary for us to work effectively. Parker devised the categories shown in Fig. 5.1.

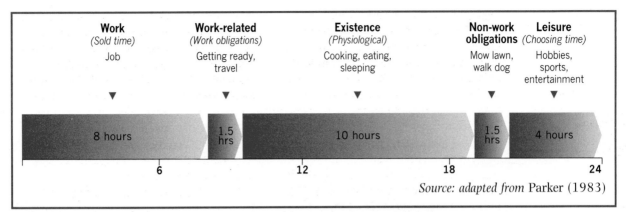

Work (Sold time) Job	**Work-related** (Work obligations) Getting ready, travel	**Existence** (Physiological) Cooking, eating, sleeping	**Non-work obligations** Mow lawn, walk dog	**Leisure** (Choosing time) Hobbies, sports, entertainment
▼	▼	▼	▼	▼
8 hours	1.5 hrs	10 hours	1.5 hrs	4 hours

6   12   18   24

Source: adapted from Parker (1983)

Figure 5.1
Dividing time:
work, non-work
and leisure

❖ **Activity 5** ❖

Fill in three examples of work, non-work and leisure in a table similar to the one below.
Briefly explain why you put each in the category chosen.

Work	**Non-work**	**Leisure**

In industrial societies our lives and time periods are fragmented and compartmentalized into separate 'blocks' more than in any other type of society. For example, if you asked a medieval peasant or a Kalahari bushman about time they 'work' and what time they have as 'leisure', they would probably have no idea what you were talking about. They would probably describe themselves as 'living' or doing things which are not separated into time blocks. So, beating a drum is indistinguishable from cooking a chicken – they are all part of doing life things.

> 'Work ... does not exist in a non-literate world. Where the whole man is involved there is no work. Work begins with the division of labour.' (McLuhan 1964)

The historian E.P. Thompson (1986) highlighted the time dimension of work when he made the distinction between 'task-oriented' work and 'time-oriented' work.

❖ *Task-oriented work* is that which occurs in former and present agricultural societies. People work according to the seasons and hours of daylight. So, for example, in a farming community long hours will be worked during the summer months and particularly during harvest. This is offset during the winter months when shorter daylight hours and inclement weather mean that there is much less to do. It is often assumed that in the past (at least before the Industrial Revolution), people worked far longer hours than they do today, but historical research indicates that this was generally not so. There were *periods* of the year when there were long working days, but there were longer periods when there was not much to do. There were also far more feast days and holidays in medieval Britain than there are public and bank holidays today.

❖ *Time-oriented work* is where people work in specific time periods. For example, an office worker may work from nine in the morning until five in the afternoon, Monday to Friday. If your job is of this kind, you finish at five regardless of what tasks there are left to complete. Sometimes this can be a cause of conflict when a boss asks an employee to finish off a task before going home and the worker responds by pointing at the clock.

❖ Activity 6 ❖

1 In the situation described above, explain the different points of view of (a) the boss and (b) the worker. Do they view work in different ways?

2 What factors influence the different work times of the nine-to-five office worker and a farm worker at harvest time?

3 Construct a table with two columns to compare and contrast work that is task-oriented or time-oriented.

In short, work can be seen as something we 'have' to do to earn money, something that may be regarded with resignation by some ('It's only a job'), or with outright hostility by others ('I hate work'), or for a lucky few as an interesting and creative activity – 'I do not see football as work, I would play football for nothing if necessary' (Kevin Keegan, when a player in the 1970s).

Although work is seen in a negative way by many, it is often assumed that leisure can in some way compensate: we can fulfil ourselves in leisure time by engaging in interesting hobbies and sports. Some people even regard carrying out what might be disagreeable or demanding work as necessary in order to appreciate leisure time fully – 'It is impossible to enjoy idling thoroughly unless one has plenty of work to do' (Jerome K. Jerome).

Non-work time, such as eating and travelling to work, is seen in a more neutral way, as something that is necessary without being bad or good.

❖ Activity 7 ❖

What do you think about the idea that to appreciate and enjoy our leisure fully it is necessary to 'suffer' work? If our work was more pleasurable, would we enjoy our leisure less?

Types of economy

Work is often associated with the wider economy: we go out to work to contribute to the economy and receive a salary as a reward. Sociologists such as Pahl and Gershuny (1980) find this unsatisfactory as many people work without receiving a formal wage. They feel that this must be recognized as part of total economic activity. They distinguish three types of economy:

❖ the *formal* economy – People work 'officially' for a living and contribute to the nation's gross national product.

❖ the *informal* or *hidden* economy – Work is carried out 'unofficially' in a variety of forms, some of which are fraudulent or illegal. Examples range from being paid cash in hand to avoid paying VAT (a fairly regular practice in the building trade, for instance), to working unofficially and claiming unemployment benefit. In his study of the Isle of Sheppey in Kent, Pahl (1984) found a form of community or barter economy where neighbours and relatives did jobs for each other on an exchange basis, e.g. an electrician would do some unpaid work for a motor mechanic in return for his car being repaired. Economists have estimated that the informal economy could add significantly to the gross domestic product if there was some way of officially recording it. Tax inspectors estimate that it causes losses in tax revenue worth millions of pounds.

❖ the *domestic* or *household* economy – Work such as housework and childcare, usually carried out by women, is seen as unpaid labour. Marxist feminists have consistently highlighted this important dimension of women's oppression in the domestic labour debate. Ann Oakley's (1974) study of housework found the drudgery and tedium associated with housework to be worse than factory assembly-line work.

The changing nature of work and occupations

In tribal societies where people live at the subsistence level, the types of activity which we see as work change little through time, so anthropologists' discoveries of previously unknown tribes who still use simple tools and technology are often described as 'Stone Age' tribesmen and women in media reports. Ways of hunting, gathering and fishing may change little for thousands of years and education often consists largely of learning these techniques from the older generation (see Chapter 4, *Education and training*).

In modern societies, however, work has changed constantly, with the most dramatic changes occurring in those that have been industrialized. The key to any explanation of the changed nature of work is technology

and its development. For example, compare the spade, which was once seen as effective 'technology' for digging holes, to the giant machines and borers that dug underneath the sea to complete the Channel Tunnel (see below). Such technological changes not only mean that more gets done quicker but also that occupations change qualitatively. Different and, in many cases, more complex skills are involved as technology advances (note that Harry Braverman (1974), writing from a Marxist perspective challenges this, see p. 180). The downside is that often fewer workers are needed, so unemployment rises. The optimistic view is that such changes are temporary, and that workers can be retrained to use newer technologies to make new products (so people employed to make horse-drawn carriages switch to car production).

The division of labour

Durkheim (1947) highlighted the increased division of labour (see p. 165) that industrialization brought about. The classical economist Adam Smith (1776) described how the manufacture of a pin could be broken into at least 40 different processes from the raw material stage to the completed pin. Smith thought that the manufacturing process was most efficient when each task was

Table 5.1 Ideal types of production system

	Fordist	*Post-Fordist*
1 *Technology*	• fixed, dedicated machines	• micro-electronically controlled, multi-purpose machines
	• vertically integrated operation	• sub-contracting
	• mass production	• batch production
2 *Products*	• for a mass consumer market	• diverse, specialized products
	• relatively cheap	• high quality
3 *Labour process*	• fragmented, few tasks	• many tasks for versatile workers
	• little discretion	• some autonomy
	• hierarchical authority and technical control	• group control
4 *Contracts*	• collectively negotiated for the job	• payment by individual performance
	• relatively secure	• dual market: secure core, highly insecure periphery

repetitive factory jobs. In some cases, consumer choice and diversity has resulted in newer forms of repetitive work in different locations. Food and catering is a good example of this with multinational hamburger and fast-food firms vying in every high street for hungry consumers. Such firms have introduced manufacturing-style production methods into mass catering and have become multi-million pound global empires with branches in all the world's major cities from Moscow to Melbourne, New Delhi to New York.

What is it like working for a global fast-food company? For the type of work offered – part time with flexible hours – the pay and conditions can be reasonable, hence the attraction for young workers, students and women with children. Labour turnover can be high but replacement employees are quickly trained. All the products are processed and part cooked in centralized factories and distributed to the retail outlets for the final simple stages of heating and preparing for the customer. Technology is used to simplify tasks wherever possible so the skills requirement is low. Employees are trained in American-style, customer-care techniques which involve smiling and good wishes: 'Have a nice day' and 'Enjoy your meal' can be heard in a variety of languages and accents throughout the world, although the smile could well be backed by gritted teeth! The division of labour linked to the division of production is applied to the simplest of tasks and precise amounts of production: Big Macs have exactly the same amount of relish wherever they are bought.

Ritzer (1993) suggests that there has been a 'McDonaldization' of society where such production methods, managerial style and employee behaviour have affected all types of work situation from pubs to rail travel, from teaching to social work. Precise documentation in official manuals of the tasks and procedures to be followed is happening in virtually every major industry in the world. The emphasis on welcoming behaviour and customer care is also prevalent.

Increasing complexity of work

Some see the McDonaldization analysis as too sweeping; they point to the increased complexity of a large number of jobs. As science and technology have advanced, so people have had to specialize (this links back to the earlier division of labour debate). Consider an agricultural society: the farmer will have to use many skills – in animal rearing, the growing of crops, effective land usage, etc. – in order for the farm to be effective. Compare this to a modern industrial society such as Britain where many jobs are much more specialized. A database operator, for instance, may have the complex skills needed to use a single database package, but may be unable to use any other package without further training.

Durkheim used the terms 'mechanical' and 'organic solidarity' to illustrate the difference between agricultural and industrial societies:

❖ In *mechanical* societies, roles are diverse and there is little division of labour, as in the case of the farmer described above.

❖ In *organic* societies, roles are clearly defined and there is a complex division of labour associated with this.

❖ Activity 10 ❖

Compare work on a farm with work in a car factory. Write down under separate headings the sorts of activity each involves and make a list of job titles associated with each work setting. Which has the most workers and why?

The physical requirements of work

Another aspect of the change in work and occupations that can be linked to technology

❖ Activity 11 ❖

Do you agree that work today involves less physical input for most people? If you have experience of work, even if it is only a Saturday job, note down those activities you have observed which still require physical strength. Who does them and why?

is that many areas of work require less physical strength than formerly. The fork lift truck and the mechanical digger – both machines operated by a single person and replacing many manual labourers – are just two of many examples that could be given. One view is that this development enabled more women to enter occupations such as factory work because male physical strength was no longer required (see Activity 11).

However, the situation is more complex than this. Historically, women's opportunities have been restricted for reasons other than the supposed lack of physical strength, as has been indicated in the chapters on families (the home and childrearing has been seen as women's prime responsibility) and education (girls' education has been seen as less important than boys'). In the nineteenth century, women did hard physical labour in mines, often working in the narrower coal seams because of their smaller size. In modern factories, men may operate machinery like fork-lift trucks but it is often women workers who do still do much of the repetitive, physical work such as packing boxes. In many less affluent countries, women carry out the hard manual work of fetching and carrying where men are more likely to be operating the machinery and supervising. In developed countries at least, fewer jobs today involve backbreaking physical toil for either men or women. A typical employee today is more likely to work in a shop or office and use non-manual skills rather than sheer physical strength.

The ownership and control of work

Marx's theories of ownership

Marx saw the origins of a class society as rooted in the change in agriculture. He suggested that in the earliest forms of society, people were hunter–gatherers. In this situation, which he referred to as 'primitive communism', nobody owned property – the land belonged to everyone and each took only what they required; food-gathering was a cooperative activity and everything was shared. This arrangement is described in Marx's famous statement, 'From each according to his ability, to each according to his needs' (*The Communist Manifesto* 1848). With the development of more sophisticated agricultural techniques in crop-growing and animal-rearing, the notion of communal land changed. Ditches and hedges became the way property boundaries between fields were marked and some people became more powerful than others by acquiring and controlling land. The powerful became even more so by employing soldiers and guards to protect their property and fight battles to acquire more land. So, an increasingly powerful few owned the land and property, and the rest worked for them. This development signalled the beginnings of a class system. This was the feudal structure.

The next key stage after this feudal structure was the industrial revolution. The industrial revolution resulted in a change whereby ownership of agricultural land became less important than the ownership of business and industry (Marx refers to the 'means of production' to describe such things as factories, plant and machinery – anything which manufactures goods for wealth creation). This capitalist society was based on the acquisition of the majority of the wealth by the few owners who relied on the workers to produce the goods which made the profits. This contrast between increasingly wealthy factory-, mill- and mine-owners and exploited, impoverished workers has been most commonly associated with the nineteenth century.

Marx used this picture as a basis to predict the downfall of capitalism and its replacement by socialism where, as in hunter–gatherer societies in the early stages of history, there is common ownership of the means of production. More detailed accounts and criticisms of this view are provided elsewhere in this book (see Chapter 7), but it is relevant to note that a significant part of the criticisms highlight the changes in the twentieth century in the way industry is owned and structured. In the nineteenth century there was a broad two-class model:

1 the *owners* – also known as capitalists or the bourgeoisie

2 the *workers* – also known as the proletariat.

Fragmentation of ownership

The simple Marxist model has altered dramatically this century with the appearance of a vast range of new occupations and the fragmentation of ownership in ways never envisaged by Marx.

The key debate between neo-Marxists and non-Marxists concerns whether these two changes, first in the way industry is owned and managed and secondly in the range of occupations and layers in industry, is a qualitative one that negates both Marx's conflict perspective and his vision of the eventual downfall of capitalism. What *is* clear is that the way in which business and industry is owned and managed is very different today from in Marx's time. Who owns the means of production and whether there is still an identifiable capitalist or ruling class is an issue that continues to occupy today's sociologists.

James Burnham (1943), writing in the early years of the twentieth century, was one of the first to note the change in ownership and control of industry: he described this as the 'managerial revolution'. It was a revolution because salaried managers had taken over the day-to-day running of firms which had previously been carried out by the owners. Ideologically, salaried managers were different from the traditional owners: they ran the company as a job like any other, the company was not their personal pride and joy in the way it was for the owners. Critics like Useem (1984) disagree with this analysis and point out that, in effect, managers and capitalists are on the same side. Many senior managers have shares in their companies and their salaries are linked to company profitability via bonuses and fringe benefits. Pahl and Winkler (1974) found little difference in attitude between managers and owners about the importance of keeping labour costs down.

Shareholding

Another issue was the question of share-holding in companies. It has become rare, particularly in the case of large companies, for businesses to be owned by one person or one family as had been the case in the past. Today most large companies are owned by

the shareholders. A shareholder can be anyone who buys shares (the shareholder's stake can cost a few pounds or a few million pounds). In the 1980s, Margaret Thatcher proudly boasted that through her policies of privatization of public utilities, Britain had become a nation of capitalists. She also pointed out that in this period the number of shareholders in the country outnumbered the members of trade unions.

In reality this situation is more complex, with a few individuals owning very large numbers of shares and having a significant say in running a company as compared with the isolated individual holding just a few shares. Scott (1986) referred to control by a 'constellation of interests' including directors, majority shareholders, and others with benefits to gain from successful profit-making.

❖ Activity 12 ❖

Investigate a local firm to see if you can identify the complexities of its ownership.

Sociological concepts and theories of work

We have already encountered some socio-logical views on the way work can be defined and how it has changed. We will now look at some of the key sociological concepts in more detail.

Alienation

'For men must work, and women must weep, and there's little to earn, and many to keep.' (Charles Kingsley, *The Three Fishes*)

The Collins English Dictionary defines alienation as 'the state of being an outsider or the feeling of being isolated, as from society'. This dictionary definition conjures up imagery of detachment and personal isolation; Karl Marx also adapted such themes to develop his critique of capitalism.

The exploitative nature of work in capitalist society means that workers lose all sense of creativity and involvement in what they are doing. Not owning the means of production results in a loss of a sense of identity in work; people feel divorced from the products of their labour. They have little involvement or pride in what they do.

Marxist view of alienation

A key difference between the Marxist and non-Marxist view of alienation is that for Marx, alienation is not just associated with one's work situation, it is a feature that is endemic to all aspects of life in a capitalist society. Put simply, the alienation produced in the capitalist work situation spills over into the whole of life itself – it permeates the whole of society. Marx saw this as a key dimension to the revolutionary potential of the working class. Workers not only endure exploitation through low wages and backbreaking toil, they are psychologically detached from their work, which in turn affects their lives outside work. This for Marx would be bound to create a sense of dissatisfaction that would increase as the quest for ever-increasing profits made conditions worse, until eventually there would be a rising up of the working class, the overthrow of capitalism and the establishment of a socialist society. In such a society, the common ownership of the means of production would mean the end of alienation and the establishment of a new classless society.

Non-Marxist view of alienation

A different view of alienation is that it relates solely to the workplace and is produced by boring, monotonous work. The cause of this is not capitalism and non-ownership of the means of production but other more concrete factors such as technology and machinery. These have increasingly removed the craft and skill from work, so that the worker has become a mere appendage to the machine.

To highlight the differing views involved, consider two car-factory workers both assembling doors to cars. Outwardly this may seem to be a repetitive uninteresting job for both workers. However, one works in a socialist society, the other in a capitalist society. Under the Marxist view of alienation outlined above, only the worker in the capitalist society is alienated, as the worker in the socialist

society has a stake or involvement in the work. For the non-Marxist, both workers are alienated because their work is the same, the work situation produces the alienation not capitalism. The compensation for such unrewarding work would have to be fulfilment outside work, in leisure activities.

❖ Activity 13 ❖

Write down two or three sentences covering examples and points to support the Marxist and non-Marxist views of alienation.

Technology

Technology is a key dimension in work satisfaction. At its simplest level, technology can be described as the use of tools or machinery to make work easier or more effective. Both a hoe and a lathe can be regarded as technology. For sociologists examining work in industrial societies, a distinction has been made between mechanization and automation:

❖ *mechanization* – the use of machinery to help people carry out their work more effectively, for example a mechanical digger operated by a person.

❖ *automation* – where machines take over and replace workers altogether, for example, robots doing up nuts and bolts on a washing machine assembly-line.

Table 5.2 Societies and technology

Low technology	*Medium technology*	*High technology*
Pre-industrial	Industrial	Post-industrial
Simple implements	Tools and simple machinery	Computers and robots
Satisfaction	Craftsmanship	Alienation
Labour intensive	Machine intensive	Unemployment

❖ Activity 14 ❖

Write two paragraphs summarizing the information in Table 5.2, using appropriate examples as necessary.

Technological determinism

Sociologists who see technology as the key to explaining attitudes and involvement in work are called 'technological determinists'. They see attitudes to work as determined by the technology used. An early example of such an approach was that of an American sociologist, Robert Blauner (1964). In the late 1940s, he studied a variety of work situations to examine the relationship between alienation and work satisfaction. He carried out research using social surveys of workers in the four industries: printing, textiles, car manufacture and chemicals. He saw alienation as having four dimensions:

❖ powerlessness – where there are feelings of lack of control and influence in the work situation

❖ meaninglessness – where there is no sense of purpose in what is done

❖ isolation – where workers are separated from each other and there is little social interaction

❖ self-estrangement – where the previous dimensions combine together to give the worker an overall feeling of detachment from the self, a sense of not belonging to the social or individual realm.

Blauner's studies in the 1940s found high degrees of dissatisfaction and alienation on assembly lines in car factories. He linked this to the degree of mechanization, which allowed little scope for craft skills. He found a different situation among printworkers, where craftsmanship and a high level of skill resulted in high levels of satisfaction. Machine-minding in the textile industry was fairly high on alienation, but workers gained satisfaction from other aspects of their lives such as the close personal contacts in the tightly knit textile communities of that time.

Blauner saw cause for optimism in what were the developing automated plants of the chemical industry, where he found much lower levels of alienation. If such industries were portents of future developments, then alienation would be expected to decline. However, more recent commentators such as Braverman (see p. 180) have highlighted the increased mechanization and automation of industry – printworkers now have much less craft skill in their work and developments have been more along the car-industry model, resulting in increased alienation for all.

Grint (1992) gives five criticisms of Blauner:

❖ His data sources were dubious: they were gathered for other purposes, were already dated, and involved questions on job satisfaction which are problematic.

❖ Not all workers in a single industry are using the same technology or operating in the same way, so to generalize about all printworkers, for example, is misleading.

❖ He assumes that issues of ownership and major decision-making powers are unimportant when in fact they can be seen as key dimensions of alienation at work.

❖ His study of textile workers suggests that the alienation effects of the technology used are countered by strong community bonds. This is an external factor, whereas Blauner's theory centres around the role of technology, an internal factor.

❖ His arguments concerning women workers undermine his own view on technology as a deciding factor in work satisfaction. He recognizes their dual role as textile and domestic workers and argues that this (and not technology) is the key factor in fatigue and in affecting women's level of work satisfaction.

Social determinism

A famous example of a counter approach to that of technological determinism is the British study of Vauxhall car workers carried out by Goldthorpe et al. (1968) in the

1960s. This approach has been described as 'social determinism'. Goldthorpe *et al.*'s work has relevance to a wide number of sociological areas, including the changing working class and political attitudes in the postwar period. They used interviews and questionnaires to ascertain car workers' attitudes to their work situation.

Rather than technology being a key factor in work satisfaction (an *intrinsic* or internal factor) – as suggested by Blauner – Goldthorpe *et al.* found that it was the attitudes that workers bring to the workplace from outside (an *extrinsic* or external factor) that were the key to understanding such issues. The question is that if work is as unsatisfying as the technological determinists suggest, why then don't the workers concerned leave? (Note that their study was carried out in the 1960s, a time of full employment, so explanations offering fear of unemployment were not so relevant then). Goldthorpe *et al.* found that car workers, who at that time were earning high wages, did not have great expectations about their work and gained satisfaction in *instrumental* ways, e.g. from the money they earned which gave them a reasonable standard of living. Many workers placed a high value on their home and family life, a good annual holiday and a decent car and these factors offset the tedium of their job. So, in contrast to Blauner – who optimistically thought that technological developments could make work more interesting – Goldthorpe *et al.*'s work focused on the low

expectations that manual workers have of their work. This implied that attempts to make work more interesting and satisfying might not necessarily be attractive, particularly if the pay were less than in other industries (see Activity 15).

Variations in technological and social determinism

Wedderburn and Crompton's study (1976) attempted to bridge the gap between technological determinism and the instrumental, social-determinist view. They studied a variety of industries and found that levels of job satisfaction varied between industries as expected, but also that technology could mean more satisfaction if skills were also used. In other industries instrumental orientation applied, so managerial attempts to make work more interesting were resisted, particularly if the workers felt pay and bonuses from monotonous work were being threatened.

Duncan Gallie (1978) carried out a comparative study in the 1970s of four oil refineries, two in Britain and two in France. This was an interesting study as the workplaces concerned used similar technologies so, according to the technological determinist view, levels of job satisfaction should have been similar. This was not what Gallie found: there were differences between the British and French workers, with higher levels of satisfaction among the former than the latter. Gallie concluded that the differences could be explained through cultural and political differences between Britain and France. The culture and history of France involved a major political and economic revolution and this has resulted in a more politically conscious and oppositional working class than in Britain. Evidence for this can perhaps be seen in newspaper reports of industrial unrest in France in the 1990s (see *In Focus* on p. 180). Gallie found the cultural differences resulted in a more politicized and union-minded workforce in the French refineries. The French workers were more likely to see managers and workers in oppositional, 'them-and-us' terms than the British workers. As would be

❖ Activity 15 ❖

1 Is money rather than job satisfaction the principal reason why people work?

2 If you have a part-time job, explain why you do it. Place the reasons in the order of their importance to you. How high up the list is money?

3 List the things that are satisfying and dissatisfying about your job? Compare your list with other people's. Include full-time workers because they may have different priorities.

France again faces winter of discontent over job cuts

'France braced itself for a harsh winter of industrial discontent yesterday, with 20,000 workers from armaments industries marching through Paris over the weekend in advance of crippling strikes planned for Thursday.

Yesterday's march – which echoed last year's industrial strife – crammed the streets of the capital. The marchers were protesting against government proposals to close arms factories and shipyards.

Thursday's planned action across France is backed by civil servants, transport workers, defence industry workers and doctors.'

Source: Alex Duval Smith, *The Guardian*, 14 October 1996

expected, levels of job satisfaction were lower among the French workers than the British, who accepted their situation and felt that good wages were compensation for less than perfect conditions.

Serge Mallet (1963), a French neo-Marxist, saw the future of automated industries differently from Blauner. He recognized that the oil and chemical industry workers were more highly skilled in their work with complex technology, but saw this in terms of empowerment of workers. They worked in isolation from managers and employers and Mallet saw this as helping to develop a 'them-and-us' proletarian consciousness. This could develop into demands for a socialist society where large groups of similar workers would be involved in the ownership and control of their workplaces. So automation could eventually result in workers realizing that they were a 'class for itself'. This is a neo-Marxist variant on Blauner's technological determinism.

Wedderburn and Crompton's study of a number of work organizations found variations in work satisfaction which could sometimes be explained in terms of social factors and sometimes by technological factors.

The de-skilling debate

One of the most influential books of the 1970s dealing with what has become known as 'labour process theory' was Harry Braverman's *Labour and Monopoly Capital: The Degradation of Work in the Twentieth*

Century (1974). Braverman himself never used the term 'de-skilling'. preferring instead to use the word 'degrading' (the word has a double meaning – work is degrading for the worker and work itself has been degraded or de-skilled). Writing from a Marxist perspective, he examined the development of capitalism in the USA over the last two centuries. He challenged the conventional view that as technology became increasingly complex, so work became correspondingly more demanding in the skills required from the workforce. Braverman argues that in fact in the nineteenth century, the artisans and craftsmen were more highly skilled and correspondingly more powerful in their relations with employers than workers today. He highlights the role of managerialist social science, such as Taylorism (scientific management) and the human-relations school, as attempts to improve productivity and de-skill workers, thus making managers and employers more powerful. The ruling class had used technological advances such as mechanization to take the power away from such craft workers. There are many examples of this in industry, ranging from automated looms and weaving machinery to the computer-aided design and manufacture of many of today's goods. Replacing skilled workers with semi- and unskilled workers operating machinery is profitable for the capitalist as wages are lower and workers can easily be replaced, particularly if they are unionized and pressing for rises. In effect, the skills of the worker have been built in to the machine, hence Braverman's use of the second meaning of degrading.

In *Working for Ford* (1973), a study of Ford's Halewood plant on Merseyside, Beynon found a very bleak view of work in a car factory: assembly-line work was grinding people down, causing ill-health and in extreme cases even death (Beynon reported the machine which pushed workers to the limits, nicknamed the 'Heart Attack Machine'). Despite advances in technology and optimistic accounts of the use of robots in car production to replace boring jobs, more recent studies have shown that even with such developments, building cars is a pressurized and low-skill job where the technology drives the pace of work and managers can speed up the pace to increase productivity.

Living with Capitalism (1977) is an account of a study of the chemical industry in the North East of England. This is the industry cited by Blauner as one where more highly skilled workers working with complex technology were least alienated. Nichols and Beynon interviewed a manager who divided work into 'scientific work' done by a few and 'donkeywork' done by the majority. Much of what they observed was heavy labouring, loading and unloading large sacks. One area of a plant was nicknamed 'the Black Hole of Calcutta' because of the constant gloom from dark, thick clouds of dust that permeated the atmosphere. Workers in control rooms which supervised complex technological operations were doing little more than observing dials and monitoring dysfunctions in the production process. So despite the outward appearance of complexity, the work itself was unfulfilling.

There are two classic empirical studies that have been used to see if there is evidence for the conclusions of Braverman or those of non-Marxist optimistic technological determinists such as Blauner (see *In Focus* above). They tend to give support to Braverman and question the more optimistic views of Blauner.

Conclusion: de-skilling or more highly skilled work?

While there is much in Braverman's analysis that is plausible and logical and can be supported by empirical evidence, his broad, sweeping approach has been the subject of a number of criticisms. It is certainly true that many jobs are less skilled today and that machines have replaced many skilled workers; the car industry is a clear example of that. However, closer examination of a number of occupations and industries suggest that Braverman can be accused of over-generalization. Some critics point out that rather than de-skilling, many jobs have been subject to 'enskilling' or 'reskilling'. For example, the typist who thirty years ago would have operated a manual typewriter will now be working at a sophisticated computer/word-processor. Similarly with advances in medical science, the nurse today has to be far more knowledgeable, as well as being able to use computers.

❖ Activity 16 ❖

Explain briefly how the following occupations might have been 'enskilled' or 'reskilled' in the last thirty to forty years: police officer, teacher, pilot, car mechanic.

Are there any problems associated with reskilling?

A historical criticism made of Braverman is that he overemphasizes the amount of craft and trades workers in the nineteenth century, implying that they were more dominant and substantial in the labour force than they were. There were also many unskilled workers, labourers and casual workers who lived under very insecure employment conditions and had little power or control in the workplace.

In the modern context, a number of empirical sociological studies have been carried out to investigate Braverman's thesis. Penn (1984) looked at the paper industry and found little support for Braverman, as there was a decline in the number of unskilled labourers, who had been replaced by more skilled and semiskilled workers such as fork-lift truck drivers. Feminist sociologists such as Beechey (1982) have pointed to the greater impact of de-skilling on women workers in comparison with men. Men are invariably involved where technology demands more highly skilled work. Sometimes employers exploit gender divisions by employing less unionized, unskilled women in preference to unionized, skilled male workers. Another dimension that Beechey refers to is the problem of clearly defining 'skill', which she sees as socially constructed to favour men. She suggests that 'skill' is far from clear in many occupations. In practice, many jobs described as 'skilled' are done by men and those deemed 'unskilled' are done by women. In the 1980s a female cook in a shipyard won an equal opportunities case when it was adjudged that her skills and training as a cook were equivalent to the more highly paid, male shipyard workers.

Gallie (1994) argues that 'skill polarization' is occurring: those jobs with high-level skills are becoming more complex, those with low-level skills becoming further de-skilled or being replaced. In other words, there is a process of 'selective de-skilling' which is adding to the existing divisions in society.

Crompton and Jones (1984) examined clerical work and found clear evidence that the lower-grade occupations mainly done by women were being de-skilled and that higher-grade skilled work in banking and insurance was dominated by men.

Evaluating Braverman

Despite such criticisms, which are important matters of empirical evidence, there is much in Braverman's work which can be supported. There *are* machines which have taken over the skills of many workers, the computer being a good example. Unemployment *has* risen in most capitalist economies and there is widespread insecurity about jobs among a cross-section of the population, including formerly 'secure' professions such as banking, the civil service, law and management.

❖ Activity 17 ❖

Coursework suggestions

There are a number of issues raised by Braverman's work which could be developed into coursework projects involving your own research. Employment statistics from the Department of Employment and *Social Trends* could be used to examine the changing structure of jobs in relation to skills. Is there any evidence of reskilling or de-skilling? Check unemployment levels among various types of worker. You could conduct a social survey to examine people's experiences of such issues, for example do they consider their job more or less skilled than 10–20 years ago? Use as wide a sample of job types as possible. Find out if there are empirical studies that have investigated the de-skilling thesis.

The changing workplace

As well as what our work is, where we work is an important part of the experience of work. Working knee-deep in a hole in the ground with water up to the waist is very different from working in a plush office with nice furniture, carpets, iced water and drinks machines. The *conditions of work* can be related to social class: the more comfortable conditions are associated with middle-class occupations, whereas many working-class jobs involve discomfort, noise and sometimes physical danger (see *In Focus*).

In early history the home and workplace were indistinguishable, all recognizable

In Focus

◆

Danger at work

Agony of man who saw friend die: horror accident at work

'A factory worker has relived the moment he saw his friend fall to his death in the jaws of a paper crushing machine. John Brown told a Blackburn inquest how he watched in horror as his workmate Fred Smith fell from a stationary conveyor belt into the paper compactor at a recycling plant last September.

The fatal accident happened when the pair climbed on to the conveyor belt to help clear a pile-up of cardboard which was preventing the machine from working. Their efforts ended in tragedy when Fred Smith, 34, plunged into the machine and was instantly crushed. The jury returned a verdict of "accidental death".'

Source: Lancashire Evening Telegraph,
10 July 1996

work taking place in the home or its immediate environment. The agricultural revolution resulted in the field being the workplace, but still there was a close proximity to home. The industrial revolution led to the growth of the factory as a workplace for many, but it was not until the development of efficient transport that home could be separated by distance from work. Earlier this century many factory workers lived within cycling or walking distance of their work. Now greater distances are travelled by bus, train or car. This century has been marked by the rise of the office as a place of work, as the high-rise buildings and skyscrapers of any major modern city testify.

The rush-hour traffic jams in every city are also evidence of the massive numbers of people who work in offices today. One prediction is that the computer has provided a new possibility for many people to work from home. The internet, fax machines and modems have meant that swift and rapid communication and information-gathering can be done from home rather than the office. Some see such developments as beneficial, particularly in the light of city traffic volume and pollution levels.

Looking back with a historical perspective, the period of human history when people have gone out to work and travelled great distances to work has lasted for about 100 years, a very small proportion of human history. Working from home could, therefore, be seen as more usual practice than going out to work, which is symptomatic only of our age.

❖ Activity 18 ❖

List some of the (a) benefits, and (b) disadvantages of working at home.

Would you prefer to be at home with computer links to fellow students and tutors? Give reasons for your preference.

Conflict at work

If, as previous sections suggest, work for many is a negative experience involving boredom, monotony and low pay, with employers wanting to increase profits, it is not surprising that there is conflict at work. Often there are specific factors that lead to conflict at work:

❖ harassment of workers

❖ discrimination – because of gender, ethnic origin, age, sexual orientation, etc.

❖ lowering wages or increasing working hours

❖ changing conditions of employment without consultation.

Trade unions and, in more recent years, professional associations have traditionally been the institutionalized agencies supporting workers in conflict with their employers. Conflict at work can take several forms:

- ❖ low productivity
- ❖ absenteeism and high labour turnover
- ❖ industrial sabotage
- ❖ work to rule
- ❖ use of mass media to foster public awareness
- ❖ strikes.

Low productivity

Uninterested workers do the bare minimum required by the employer, who cannot raise productivity levels. Various expressions, some going back to sailing ship days such as 'swinging the lead', 'going through the motions', are well-known in many industries. Employers have tried various strategies to combat this, such as job enrichment to make boring tasks more involving and interesting.

Absenteeism and high labour turnover

When work lacks any inherent interest, sickness and related absenteeism can be high. In some industries there is high absenteeism, particularly on Mondays, for this reason. A similar indicator is high labour turnover, where workers cannot stand the type of work and leave at the earliest possible moment. Employers do what they can to rectify these situations, as both are costly, the former because of lower productivity, the latter because of the costs of training new workers

Industrial sabotage

This occurs when workers deliberately destroy or undermine aspects of their work such as the machinery they use ('the spanner in the works') or the product they make (in the 1970s when there was a lot of industrial unrest in the car industry, the term 'Friday car' was used for poorer quality

cars often resulting from deliberately slipshod work). Some examples of industrial sabotage have been seen as amusing and have taken on the status of folk legends, such as the swear words (F*** Off!) put into a batch of seaside rock by disgruntled employees. More typical forms of sabotage are the 'accidental' breaking down of a machine causing a temporary respite. Such activities would be clear evidence from a conflict perspective of the oppositional nature of worker and employer relations in capitalist workplaces.

Work to rule

This is a practice which seems illogical on first consideration. Workers in a dispute with an employer work to rule by only carrying out the prescribed duties in the exact manner as laid down in the company regulations, which often slows work down. For example, a bus company may stipulate a full safety check involving tyre pressures, oil level, brakes and steering before any vehicle can leave the depot. In practice such checks may be skimped over so buses can leave on time. In a work to rule dispute, carrying out such checks as prescribed results in buses being late.

Use of the mass media

This is a more recent strategy used when workers conflict with employers. Several unions now appoint public relations and press officers as they recognize the importance of public support in an industrial dispute. Letters explaining the workers' grievances are sent to newspapers, television appearances are made and leaflets are handed out in shopping precincts explaining the workers' position. Marches and demonstrations can perform a similar function.

Strikes

A strike is the most high-profile and well-known manifestation of industrial conflict – often described as a weapon of last resort when all other negotiating procedures between managers and workers have been exhausted. The 1960s and 1970s are

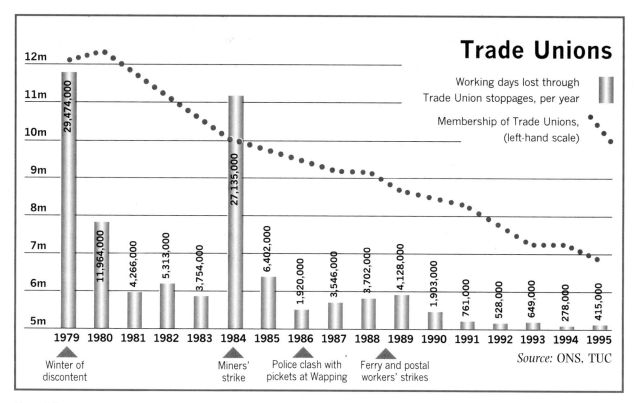

Trade Unions

Working days lost through Trade Union stoppages, per year

Membership of Trade Unions, (left-hand scale)

12m
11m
10m
9m
8m
7m
6m
5m

29,474,000
11,964,000
4,266,000
5,313,000
3,754,000
27,135,000
6,402,000
1,920,000
3,546,000
3,702,000
4,128,000
1,903,000
761,000
528,000
649,000
278,000
415,000

1979 1980 1981 1982 1983 1984 1985 1986 1987 1988 1989 1990 1991 1992 1993 1994 1995

Winter of discontent

Miners' strike

Police clash with pickets at Wapping

Ferry and postal workers' strikes

Source: ONS, TUC

Figure 5.2
Trends in trade unionism

❖ Activity 19 ❖

Make two or three points summarizing and explaining the trends illustrated in Fig. 5.2.

associated with high strike records in Britain. The low strike records since the early 1980s (see Fig. 5.2) have been associated with the success of the New Right political philosophy espoused by Margaret Thatcher.

Legislation has severely curtailed unions' ability to use the strike as a weapon in an industrial dispute. Newer aspects of union law include:

❖ banning of secondary picketing

❖ introduction of postal ballots of workers before strike action (see *In Focus*)

❖ notice to employers well before any strike action

❖ providing employers with a full list of union members in a firm prior to a strike.

In Focus
◆
'Court out' – college bosses block strike bid

'Accrington and Rossendale College management pulled the plug on union strike action by taking it to the High Court. On the eve of the planned strike – aimed to coincide with college inspections – a judge at the High Court in London declared a postal ballot of lecturers invalid. NATFHE members voted two-to-one in favour of industrial action in opposition to 341 staff redundancies and the introduction of Nottingham-based employment agency ELA. The NATFHE branch may conduct another strike ballot if an agreement with management cannot be met. A NATFHE spokesman said: "Lecturers are sad and angry that the college has spent thousands of pounds on using the law to prevent them from exercising their democratic decision."'

Source: The Blackburn Citizen,
3 October 1996

Any breach of this legislation is likely to result in High Court action and a ruling banning the proposed strike.

From a Neo-Marxist perspective, Richard Hyman (1984) sees strikes as involving the following:

❖ Workers cease to work, so production halts completely (unlike the other forms of conflict shown above).

❖ Strikes are temporary stoppages. The majority do not last long, though there have been notable exceptions such as the 1984 miners' strike.

❖ Striking workers act collectively and are guided and organized by trade union officials. This collective action results in a feeling of solidarity in the struggle against the employer.

❖ Strikes involve action by employees and are a reflection of their discontent about pay and/or conditions at work.

❖ Striking workers have goals, such as the desire to settle their grievances through pressure on the employer to negotiate.

The mass media often portray negative images of striking workers by focusing on alleged violence on picket lines and the

unreasonable demands of the strikers. Attempts have been made to counteract such views, but despite this, striking workers are often displayed negatively, with news stories concentrating on inconvenience to the public and the disruption and cost of striker's actions (see Activity 20).

Union membership

Since 1979 there has been a political attack on the power of the trade unions to influence governments and employers by their actions through strikes and industrial

---

❖ **Activity 20** ❖

1 Collect mass media reports of recent strikes. Do such reports support the view of a negative image of strikers?

2 Write a sample letter to your local newspaper explaining why students are demanding higher grants. Write some replies from politicians from different parties, as well as a lead article for the newspaper.

Table 5.3 Trade union membership as a percentage of the civilian workforce in employment: by gender and occupation, Autumn 1994

	Males	Females	All persons
Managers and administrators	20	21	21
Professional	39	59	47
Associate professional and technical	33	53	43
Clerical and secretarial	35	24	27
Craft and related	29	27	29
Personal and protective services	38	24	29
Sales	13	10	11
Plant and machine operatives	44	32	41
Other	30	23	26
All in employment	31	29	30

Source: Social Trends (1996)

disputes. Whether this is a good or a bad thing depends on your political perspective. Legislation curbing workers' abilities to stop the production process is now deeply embedded and all the current main political parties recognize and accept this. In the late 1990s, the Labour Party leadership has stated that it does not wish to return to the 'bad old days of high numbers of strikes and secondary picketing'. Critics from leftist perspectives protest at this 'capitalism has won' view. They point out that employers are free to exploit workers to maximize profits with little restriction. The growth of part-time, low-wage and low-skill jobs is seen as evidence for the sort of de-skilling predictions made by Braverman in the 1970s. Trade unions have been unsure how to respond. Membership has fallen dramatically in the last twenty years and many of the most exploited workers do not belong to unions (see Table 5.3).

Nevertheless, there are still examples of conflicts where workers are resisting some of the trends. In the late 1990s there have been strikes by civil servants, postal workers, firefighters and railway workers. Three hundred Liverpool dockers were locked out of their jobs in an extended dispute with their employer. College and university teachers mounted one-day strikes in protest at education cuts. Unions have played an active role in all these disputes. Some employers, such as Sainsburys, are openly in favour of a minimum wage to help the low-paid and wish to maintain union membership in their firms.

Keith Grint (1991) disagrees that the lower numbers of strikes since 1979 are solely the result of the Conservative government's policies. He points out that the statistics indicate falling rates prior to 1979. Also, in the last twenty to thirty years, strike rates have been falling in most industrial countries, whatever their type of government. It could be that with rising standards of living, workers are less willing to engage in a strike and see it as a last resort when all other negotiating procedures fail. Also, employers may be much more flexible in a highly competitive business climate, fearing the damaging effects of a stoppage of production.

Another issue is the familiar one of interpreting official statistics. There are complex procedures to be followed before employees' actions can be defined as a strike. Some employers are willing to report strikes officially, possibly to influence politicians to enact anti-union legislation. Others, who do not report strikes, may wish to conceal negative information about their company from competitors. International comparisons are also difficult as different countries can have different definitions of what comprises a strike, may ban trade unions, and may wish to portray themselves as strike-free in competitive global markets.

It does appear that protracted disputes, as in the car and mining industry in the 1960s and 1970s, are less likely in the future. It remains to be seen whether the result will be a compliant, cowed labour force who feel themselves lucky to have a job. There is also an increased recognition of the global aspects of industrial economies. International companies now have enormous power in terms of their ability to move factories and production on a global basis to low-wage and non-unionized economies. Workers recognize this and there are international labour organizations which aim to establish global links between workers to counteract the power of such companies.

White-collar unions and professional associations

A feature of the changing nature of the occupational structure is the large rise in white-collar and professional workers. Such workers are now a large proportion of the workforce and in the last thirty years have experienced increasingly similar work conflicts to those of manual workers. Previously secure, reasonably well-paid jobs such as in banking and the civil service are now far less secure, and there are threats of large-scale redundancy among all types of workers. One outcome has been a rise in union membership among white-collar workers. Among professional groups, professional associations have come to act increasingly like conventional manual trade unions. Since the 1970s, there has been increased militancy among such groups, with teachers, bank workers, nurses and civil servants taking part in industrial action over a range of concerns including threats of redundancy, working conditions, pay and public expenditure cuts.

Inequality at work: class, race, gender, age, disability

'Which of us ... is to do the hard and dirty work for the rest ... and for what pay? Who is to do the clean and pleasant work, and for what pay?' (John Ruskin, *Sesame and Lilies*)

Inequalities at work broadly reflect wider structural inequalities along familiar lines:

❖ social class

❖ gender

❖ ethnicity

❖ age

❖ physical ability or disability.

Social class

Manual jobs, which are regarded as working-class positions, usually pay less than non-manual, middle-class jobs (see Activity 21). Such jobs generally involve physical activity and are likely to be monotonous and repetitive, involving noisy, dirty conditions, e.g. on building sites, in factories, mills and mines.

Non-manual work is associated with the middle class and in general pays more than manual work (see Fig. 5.3). However, as lower-level work, such as shopwork and

❖ Activity 21 ❖

Use the data in Figure 5.3 to answer the following questions.

1 Which is the highest paid occupation?

2 Which is the lowest paid?

3 Summarize what this tells you about levels of pay in relation to class.

4 Summarize the occupational and pay differences between men and women.

Figure 5.3
Average weekly earnings, professional and manual workers

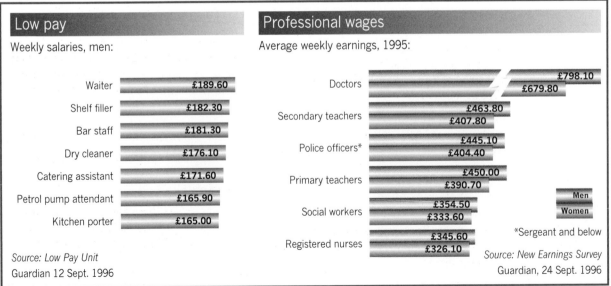

Low pay
Weekly salaries, men:

Waiter	£189.60
Shelf filler	£182.30
Bar staff	£181.30
Dry cleaner	£176.10
Catering assistant	£171.60
Petrol pump attendant	£165.90
Kitchen porter	£165.00

Source: Low Pay Unit
Guardian 12 Sept. 1996

Professional wages
Average weekly earnings, 1995:

	Men	Women
Doctors	£798.10	£679.80
Secondary teachers	£463.80	£407.80
Police officers*	£445.10	£404.40
Primary teachers	£450.00	£390.70
Social workers	£354.50	£333.60
Registered nurses	£345.60	£326.10

*Sergeant and below

Source: New Earnings Survey
Guardian, 24 Sept. 1996

catering in the service and distributive industries, has expanded, there are proportionately larger groups of low-paid, non-manual workers. Many such workers are females working part-time. Non-manual work usually involves pleasanter conditions than manual work, taking place in offices and often with reasonable environments.

Gender

'The sociology of work has until recently been about men ... assuming that relations between capital and labour is one between bosses and men ... and neglecting gender relations whether at work or at home.'
Cockburn (1991)

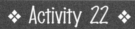
❖ Activity 22 ❖

Take each of the five signs mentioned in the *In Focus* below and suggest what may happen in the next 20 years.

This book consistently highlights women's lack of opportunity in comparison with men. There are complex interrelationships between socialization, male–female roles, family and domestic life, education and work, which have always restricted women's opportunities in comparison with men. Things have slowly improved: women are now about half of the workforce and increased numbers are pursuing careers with promotion and higher managerial

prospects. In 1997, a high-flying woman financial consultant earning £1 million per year made newspaper headlines. Despite such examples, we can see from Figs 5.4 and 5.5 that there are glaring employment inequalities along gender lines.

❖ Activity 23 ❖

What trends are revealed by the data given in Figs 5.4 and 5.5 on p. 190?

Patriarchal theories

A number of explanations have been offered for women's unequal work opportunities. You should by now be familiar with the concept of patriarchy. Women are denied equal opportunity in seeking out work, in the workplace and in work prospects by the dominance of men in positions of power. They are also denied equal opportunity through sexism of all types, including bullying, ridicule and stereotyping, and in lack of availability of childcare, if they are mothers.

Duncombe and Marsden (1995) describe women's 'triple shift': paid work, domestic labour and emotion work. 'Emotion work' relates to male–female relationships and the parenting role. Male heterosexuality involves a suppression of emotions in personal relationships. This gap is filled by women whose emotion work involves their partner, children and sometimes disabled and elderly relatives. So, as well as coping

---

In Focus

◆

Five tell-tale signs that you're a woman

❖ You do the same job as your colleague for 79% of the pay.

❖ You get fired from the armed services when you become a parent.

❖ You cannot hear confession or celebrate Mass in the Roman Catholic church.

❖ As you hit middle age you have seven hours less leisure time than your partner.

❖ You have a 3 per cent chance of being a machine operative but an 86 per cent likelihood of being a nursery school teacher.

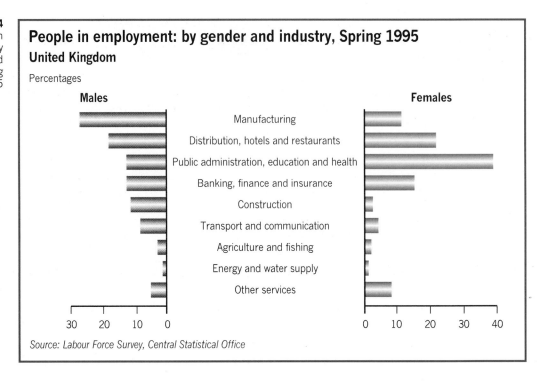

People in employment: by gender and industry, Spring 1995
United Kingdom

Source: Labour Force Survey, Central Statistical Office

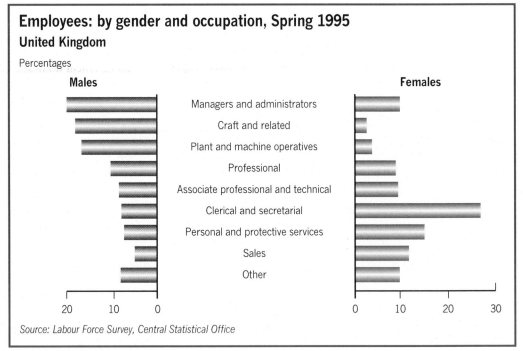

Employees: by gender and occupation, Spring 1995
United Kingdom

Source: Labour Force Survey, Central Statistical Office

with the demands of paid work, many women have two extra shifts in comparison with men. Another dimension is that women's 'emotional skills' are applied to their work in a range of caring occupations such as air hostesses, nannies, receptionists, and nurses. Senior women teachers often have pastoral care as their area of responsibility, another aspect of emotion work.

❖ Activity 24 ❖

Consider the following:

- A surgeon was killed and his son was critically injured in a tragic road accident in bad weather. An emergency operation was necessary to save the son's life, but on seeing the patient's name, the surgeon on duty declared, 'I cannot operate, that is my son'. Explain.

- The lawyer has a brother who goes to sea, but the brother who goes to sea has not got a brother. Explain.

As a good sociology student, you should have immediately guessed that in both cases a woman was involved, not least because you are reading about gender issues! Try these exercises on a variety of friends and relatives to see the types of answers offered. It would be surprising if all immediately guessed correctly.

You could make this into a fuller research exercise to see how wide-ranging gender stereotyping of occupations is.

Occupational segregation

Occupational segregation is where there are 'men's jobs' and 'women's jobs'. Its rationale is summed up in the following quote:

> 'Job segregation by sex ... is the primary mechanism in capitalist society that maintains the superiority of men over women, because it enforces lower wages for women in the labour market. Low

wages keep women dependent on men because they encourage women to marry. Married women must perform domestic chores for their husbands. Men benefit, then, from both higher wages and the domestic division of labour. This domestic division of labour, in turn, acts to weaken women's position in the labour market. Thus, the hierarchical domestic division of labour is perpetuated by the labour market, and vice versa.' (Hartmann 1982)

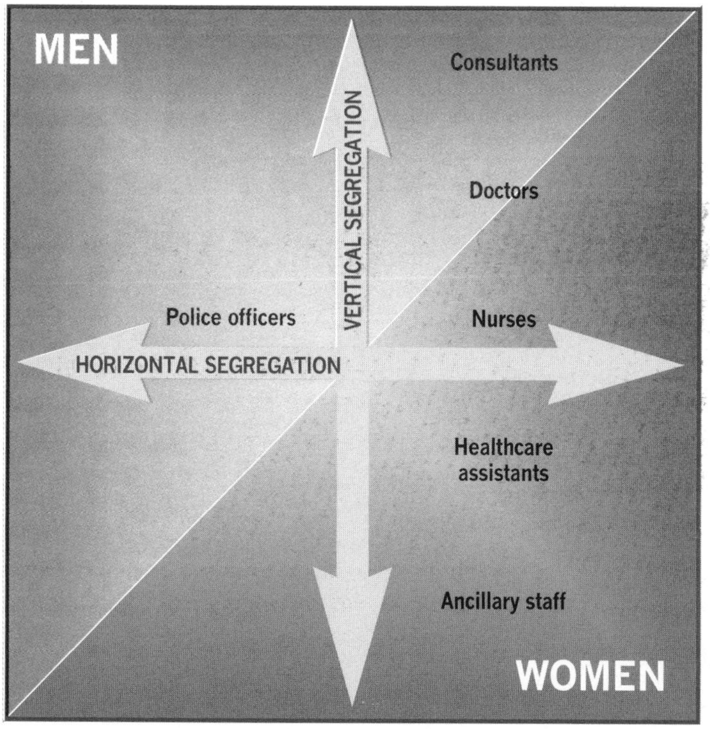

There are a number of ways in which we can analyse gender stereotyping in terms of occupation, e.g. by horizontal or vertical segregation (see Fig. 5.6):

- ❖ *horizontal segregation* – Men and women traditionally do different jobs, but the job is of equivalent status, e.g. men become police officers and women become nurses.

- ❖ *vertical segregation* – In the same occupation, women are in the lower levels or less prestigious positions,

Figure 5.6
Analysis of gender stereotyping in occupations: horizontal and vertical segregation

❖ Activity 25 ❖

Fill out your own version of Fig. 5.6 with five more examples.

Is there more progress towards gender equality in some occupations than others? Explain why you think this is the case.

e.g. men are sales *directors* while women are sales *representatives*. It hardly needs to be said which is the higher salaried specialism (see Activity 25).

In addition to patriarchal theories, there are two major theoretical explanations of such female–male inequalities: labour market theory and the reserve army of labour theory.

Labour market theory

This was devised by Barron and Norris (1976) and explained inequalities in terms of there being two labour markets for workers:

❖ The *primary labour market* comprises larger firms who can offer high salaries, full-time skilled jobs, secure employment, promotion prospects, good conditions and fringe benefits. Such firms' employees tend to be male, white and married with dependants. They are unionized, usually with a good relationship between management and union representatives.

❖ The *secondary labour market* comprises smaller 'back street' firms who offer lower pay, part-time and temporary unskilled work, with few prospects and poor conditions. Many of the employees are female, from ethnic minorities, older and from poorer neighbourhoods. Not surprisingly trade union membership is low.

Critics point to the somewhat over-generalized model of the two labour markets. There is no really satisfactory explanation of why women may be employed in the secondary labour-market firms apart from their restricted opportunities resulting from family and household commitments.

Reserve army of labour

Karl Marx's original writings pointed to capitalism's need to have a reserve supply of labour who could be drawn in to the labour force during times of boom and high profits. Because of the cyclical nature of capitalist demand, booms turn to slumps with low profitability. Here the low-paid and low-skilled reserve supply of labour can be easily

discarded and drawn upon again when conditions improve. Another benefit to capitalism is that such workers can be used to keep wage costs down by replacing more skilled workers who might be demanding higher wages. Marxist-feminists such as Irene Bruegel (1979) have applied this analysis to the situation of women. They are trapped and restricted in their opportunities to work by child and domestic responsibilities, so unskilled, part-time, low-paid work is often the only option.

The imbalance of opportunities between men and women still clearly exists. The 1992 general election resulted in around 60 female MPs out of a total of 650 – and politics is no exception. Most walks of life at senior levels are dominated by men: at the time of writing, there are:

❖ two women High Court judges out of 90

❖ only one woman university professor for every 30 men

❖ one female managing director on the board of the top 200 British companies

❖ one female editor of a major national daily newspaper.

This situation still persists despite the much-heralded Equal Opportunity Acts concerning equal pay and opportunity for women, seen as such a breakthrough in the mid-1970s (see the *In Focus* on p. 193).

However, the picture is not all doom and gloom. Changes in attitudes and legislation since the 1970s *have* improved the prospects for many women.

Some recent changes

❖ 1970   Barbara Castle's Equal Pay Act is passed – the most important advance for women since gaining the vote. Right to equal treatment where men and women do the same or broadly similar work.

❖ 1971   The first national women's liberation demonstration for equal pay, equal education and job opportunities, nurseries, free contraception and abortion on demand.

When women do make it to senior positions, the glass ceiling effect often applies. This refers to the situation facing many senior women managers who get so far, but never reach the very top position which is occupied by a man. For example, a woman becomes a college vice-principal, but the principal is a man.

❖ *management* – Only 8 per cent of the 144, 000 managers in large companies are women.

❖ *public appointments* – The ratio of men

to women holding public appointments is 3 to 1.

❖ *education* – Women make up 46% of all university students, but only 3 per cent of professors and senior academics.

❖ *medicine* – Half of all medical students are female, but only 15 per cent of medical consultants are women.

❖ *engineering* – There are only 25,000 qualified female engineers out of a total of 537, 000.

Source: adapted from Employment News, February 1993

❖ 1974   With a shortage of male drivers, London Transport Board persuades unions to accept women bus drivers.

❖ 1975   Sex Discrimination Act introduced. Sex discrimination is made unlawful in employment, training, education, and the provision of housing, services, goods and facilities to the public. Equal Opportunities Commission set up.

❖ 1980   Social Security Act: equality of entitlement to most social security benefits.

❖ 1983   Equal Pay (Amendment) Regulations: equal pay for women for work of equal value.

❖ 1992   Church of England Synod votes for women priests.

In the 1990s, large numbers of young women are entering lower managerial and professional occupations – a percentage of them have a good chance of making it to the top. There are now, for example, more women under 30 training to be solicitors than men and this applies to a number of equivalent occupations. If note is taken of the way females are out-performing males in educational qualifications (see Chapter 4, *Education and training*, p. 148), then the future may well be 'female'.

❖ Activity 26 ❖

Write a short essay (up to 500 words) on the following: When considering current trends in employment, it seems that 'the future will be female'.

It will be useful to look up the sections on education and patriarchy to help you to answer this question.

Ethnicity

A similar picture to the position of women can be identified for ethnic groups. In Britain, a key factor in discrimination is skin colour (see Chapter 6, *Stratification and differentiation*), with certain groups, such as those of African and Afro-Caribbean heritage, experiencing greater degrees of discrimination than other groups. Among the Asian heritage groups, there is diversity of experience along the lines of:

❖ *geography* – Indians reach higher levels educationally and occupationally than Pakistani and Bengali groups.

❖ *religion* – Hindus and Sikhs tend to reach higher levels than Muslims.

❖ *urban/rural areas* – Those whose ancestry is from urban areas tend to do better than those from rural areas.

I ris Blandford, a cleaner in her mid-fifties, came to Britain in 1964 from Jamaica. Here she talks about her late husband's and her own experience of work in the UK:

'We came to work. And work was what we did. We didn't do nothing but work. It killed my husband. ... My husband worked in just about everything. He worked in an ice-cream factory, he was a waiter in a hotel, but the money was better on building, so he worked as a labourer. Oh, he worked. He went off at six-thirty when it was dark and he came home when it was dark. ... I worked cleaning. I got up at half past five to go to the City. I clean one place till nine o'clock, then I come home and make the meal for the children, do shopping and clean the home, and then at five I go back to the City and work from six till eight, and then when I come home it's ten o'clock or ten-thirty. I'm getting £60 a week.' (Interviewed 1993)

Source: adapted from Blackwell and Seabrook (1996, pp. 177–8)

❖ Activity 27 ❖

What does the *In Focus* above tell you about the experience of migrant workers?

What stereotypes about migrant workers are challenged by Mrs. Blandford's experiences?

Castles and Kosack (1973) offer a Marxist analysis of the migratory labour patterns of immigrant ethnic workers. They see their situation in class rather than cultural terms, so immigrant workers face similar circumstances regardless of ethnicity or skin colour. Neo-Weberian critics such as Rex and Tomlinson (1979) disagree and point to the historical and cultural factors such as slavery and imperialism that affect black people in Britain. They face discrimination and prejudice and in Britain black people particularly are concentrated in the lower-skilled and low-paid sectors.

However, in the 1990s there is some evidence of younger black people entering higher education in greater numbers, thereby following the route to more professional occupations. As with the general population, it seems to be females more than males who are taking up such opportunities in greater numbers.

There are some reasons to be optimistic as more young British-born people of ethnic minority ancestry achieve qualifications, enter the professions and follow careers. Recent trends show that the achievements of some groups, notably Indians and black women, are high compared with previous generations.

Age

Child labour

Young people under 18 are now all but excluded from the labour market. Those who work are often in insecure, low-paid, part-time employment, such as shop work and catering. It is difficult to combine this type of employment with pursuing further qualifications. There are very few apprenticeships available to young people now compared with previous generations.

Attention in recent years has focused on the amount of child labour that is used throughout the world. The most high-profile cases have usually been in Third World countries with children as young as 6 being employed in 'sweatshop' industries such as clothing and carpet factories (see *In Focus* below). Following media publicity, the British company Marks and Spencer among others have employed inspectors to ensure that their products do not involve child labour.

While attention has focused on child labour in some developing countries, the

'Each day, from early morning until 10 p.m., Mohammed Salahuddin, a little boy with a huge smile, sews fake pearls and sequins onto black georgette. Although he is only about 11, Salahuddin has mastered complicated embroidery. The cloth will go to a high-society seamstress in South Delhi, where it will become an elaborate jacket, to be sold in America.

For his efforts, Salahuddin earns 50 rupees (about £1). He has been coached to say that he is of legal working age (16), and receives a relatively princely sum of 1, 500 rupees (£30) a month.

Salahuddin is one of an army of child workers in Osmanpur, a growing slum of 500, 000 people. Soniya Aharma, aged 9, was put out to work two or three years ago along with her five sisters and two brothers. In the mornings she crushes betel nuts, in the afternoon she goes to school. "I want to be able to study or play like other children," she said. "But if I don't work, how will I eat?"

Although child labour is illegal, and the constitution prescribes free and compulsory education to the age of 14, by the government's count there are 20 million child labourers in India – two million in hazardous industries such as mining. Activists put the figure at 55 million.'

Source: adapted from The Guardian,
30 September 1995

situation elsewhere is not necessarily much better. There are laws in Britain concerning work for those under 16, such as milk and paper rounds, but monitoring is difficult. There have been cases of young children employed in family restaurants and takeaways and as homeworkers assembling goods like toys to help parents who are on low incomes themselves.

Ageism

It seems that job prospects for older workers (usually defined as workers over the age of 45) have worsened in the 1980s and 1990s. The decline in job prospects for older employees has occurred despite a recent upturn in the economy and the creation of more jobs. Explanations for age discrimination include the fact that employers are often reluctant to recruit older staff because they are more expensive to employ (they have more experience and have climbed further up the careers' ladder). Employers may also worry that older workers will have more time off due to poor health, or that they will have family commitments (e.g. children) that mean they are less flexible about working long hours. The reality is that the over-45s are often more committed to their work and less prone to absenteeism (see *In Focus* below).

One in four men aged over 55 – and virtually half of men aged over 60 – is no longer in work. Redundancy and forced early retirement are cutting men off early from the world of work. Companies and the public lose expertise; those affected receive heavily reduced pensions; and individuals face twenty years or more of healthy life with no work.

Employers are discriminating against older men, with work shifting to younger people and from men to women. Part-time women workers are often preferred to full-time men. Older workers have been targeted for redundancy, partly because redundancy packages are easier to arrange, but also in the mistaken belief that older workers are hard to retrain and less flexible.

Physical disability

People with disabilities also encounter discrimination in the workplace. Despite government legislation to avoid this (for instance, larger companies are required by law to employ a certain percentage of disabled workers and provide adequate access facilities), many businesses still discriminate in favour of able-bodied people.

Organizations

The growth of bureaucracy

A feature of workplaces in the twentieth century has been the increase in their scale and size. Associated with this is increased impersonality and detachment. Until about 100 years ago, most people worked for small companies. The mill, the factory, the mine, the office were places where everyone would be likely to know everyone else working there. This would be reinforced by the workers living close to each other in the immediate neighbourhood, so neighbours were also workmates. At work the employer and owner would walk around and talk to everyone. Annual holidays and outings to the surrounding countryside would be organized through work. Work was an all-embracing aspect of people's lives and how they lived together.

Max Weber (1948) was one of the earliest sociologists to point to the development of large-scale bureaucratic organizations as societies industrialized. This was associated with his concept of rationality which he applied to developing organizational structures (see Chapter 7, *Theory and methods*). He saw bureaucracy as being an efficient and machine-like process, which could be linked to the efficiency associated with the division of labour in manufacturing industry. The following characteristics are often associated with bureaucratic organizations:

❖ impersonality – hierarchy of officials

❖ subordination and superordination – everyone knows their place

❖ rules and regulations to be followed strictly – no flexibility

❖ everything recorded and written down as instructions to be followed exactly.

Thus, Weber saw bureaucracy as a way of organizing administrative work and companies where everyone knew the rules and regulations, and operated them without question. He recognized the negative dimensions of this faceless type of official and inflexible organization. As bureaucracies became the dominant types of organization, Weber became somewhat gloomy over the future of society in what he referred to as 'the iron cage of bureaucracy'. Later critics have taken issue with his assumption about bureaucracy being the most efficient form of administration and organization. Today, the term 'bureaucracy' has become derogatory, being associated with inefficiency and red-tape officialdom.

Dysfunctions of bureaucracy

Sociologists such as Merton (1968) have described the 'dysfunctional' aspects of bureaucracies which have highlighted the inefficiency that can arise from size and scale. Many of us have experienced delays and frustration when dealing with large organizations. A number of other American sociologists have said that Weber simplified his model of bureaucracy into one 'ideal type' which did not cover all the possibilities and circumstances in which organizations operate.

Burns and Stalker (1961) used the typology of mechanistic and organic organizations:

❖ *mechanistic* – Similar to Weber's ideal type, this describes organizations run along clearly defined lines, following inflexible rules and regulations, with a hierarchy of officials each with a clear role.

❖ *organic* – This describes organizations operating in a more unpredictable climate or unusual circumstances compared with formal bureaucracies. Mechanistic rules and regulations are too inflexible for unpredictable circumstances. Such organizations operate by involving everyone in responsibility and control. Creative and specialist knowledge is recognized and valued.

Sociologists such as Merton, and Blau (1955), have stressed the importance of the informal or hidden dimensions of behaviour in organizations. Even 'extreme' organizations such as prisons or mental hospitals (see *In Focus* below) cannot control every member's behaviour. Corners are cut to speed up work, there are characters and rebels who subvert authority, and a host of informal dimensions go to make up the way organizations operate. This leads to questions about how rigid any bureaucracy really is in practice.

Total institutions

As well as variations in type, ranging from the more rigid mechanistic organizations to the more flexible organic ones, Goffman (1968) highlighted a particular type of organization where people live for 24 hours a day, eating, sleeping and working in the same place. He referred to this as a 'total institution'. These include organizations ranging from boarding schools, to monasteries, military camps, prisons, mental hospitals and ships at sea. Goffman obtained a post as a recreation assistant in a large American mental hospital and carried out a covert participant observation study from an interactionist perspective. He found that the hospital had a strong 'them-and-us' relationship between staff and inmates who interacted with each other on the basis of stereotypes and appropriate role distance between each other. Staff and inmates could be easily identified by uniforms. This clear and separate identification associated with role-appropriate behaviour was considered necessary for the smooth running of the organization.

Goffman generalized from the mental hospital to other total institutions where similar issues of staff–inmate roles and appropriate, expected behaviours are evident.

❖ Activity 28 ❖

Which of the following organizations are:
- mechanistic bureaucracies
- organic organizations
- total institutions?

A school, a university, the civil service, a hospital, the army, an advertising agency, a coal mine, a drugs rehabilitation centre?

Explain your reasons. Are there any you find difficult to place? If so, why?

In Focus

◆

Behaviour in a total institution

What happens when things go wrong in a total institution is portrayed in the film and novel *One Flew Over the Cuckoo's Nest*. The central character, McMurphy, disrupts the efficient running of the mental hospital ward by his rebellious and unpredictable behaviour. The authorities, in the person of the charge nurse Ratchett, eventually realize the disruptive potential and threat posed by McMurphy to the ward and his ability to change formerly compliant patients, so he has to be overcome. This is eventually done by a brain operation which reduces him to a vegetative state.

Unemployment

Think of your own circle of family and friends. The chances are that several of them are unemployed or have been unemployed at some point in their career. What were the circumstances? Was it redundancy? Ill health? Early retirement? We live in an age where euphemisms such as 'downsizing' and 'rightsizing' are applied to large-scale redundancies where workers at all levels, including senior management, lose their jobs. However, it is not the case that unemployment affects all workers equally. It is still mainly manual occupations that are the most insecure, despite frequent publicity about executive or managerial redundancies. The costs of unemployment can be great at a number of levels. The most important is at the individual level where the stress of unemployment can affect personal and family relationships, an example of this being the higher divorce rates among the unemployed. In economic and political terms, there are implications for public expenditure when large numbers are claiming unemployment benefits. One explanation of the failure of the Conservative government's policies to curb public expenditure through the 1980s and 1990s was the high levels of unemployed.

The causes of unemployment

The escalation of unemployment in Britain from the period of comparatively full employment in the 1950s and 1960s has been explained in a number of ways.

The challenge from overseas

One dominant view is that British industry has shed jobs because it is uncompetitive and old-fashioned. Examples of this are in the car and electronics industries which are now dominated by Asian countries, most notably Japan. In the 1960s, the British car industry was a significant part of our industrial economy. Today this is not the case.

❖ Activity 29 ❖

What nationality of car is owned by your household? Try to find out where the electronic goods you own such as CD players, TVs, Walkmans are manufactured. Can you identify any common features of the countries which manufacture the goods?

The global economy has developed in the latter part of the twentieth century. What were once referred to as 'Third World' countries have increasingly become involved in the manufacture of a wide range of goods, notably clothing, cars and electronics. A key factor is the cheaper labour costs which mean lower prices compared with European and American goods. Many such countries are now no longer seen as impoverished Third World economies but have prosperous thriving manufacturing bases. In the 1990s, the key economies are referred to as the 'Tiger' or 'Pacific Rim' economies, which include countries such as Taiwan, South Korea, Singapore, Malaysia, as well as Japan. In the next millennium it is expected that China, with approximately one-fifth of the world's total population, will make a significant impact in the production of manufactured goods. Many Japanese-style business practices are now being adopted by UK firms, but as the *In Focus* on p. 199 indicates, there is a darker side to the Japanese way of work.

One result of such trends is that once-successful manufacturing countries such as Britain are now no longer so – to the extent that fewer than 5 million workers out of a total of 24 million are now engaged in manufacturing.

Technology

Another factor in increased unemployment is the increased use of technology to replace workers. Various explanations have been

In Focus

◆

The Japanese disease?

'It could only happen in Japan – or so we tell ourselves. When Ichiro Oshima started work at an ad agency in 1990, he knew he'd never get ahead unless he worked himself to death. He then proceeded to do just that. For 17 months, he did not have one day off, or even dinner with his family. He only slept between 30 minutes and two-and-a-half hours a night. By the time he killed himself in 1991, he was working until 6.30 a.m., once every three days.

Although his family, in winning a court case last week, became the first to be awarded damages from an employer for work-induced suicide, Oshima is not an isolated case: in the first 11 months of last year, 63 deaths in Japan were attributed to overwork.

Could it happen here? According to the think-tank, Demos, we are certainly at risk ...'

Source: adapted from The Observer,
7 April 1996

offered for this, including that of Braverman discussed earlier (which focused on de-skilling in the context of a capitalist society). Employers give alternative views which cite the need to use the latest technologies to keep up with rival firms and countries in an extremely competitive business environment: workers have to be replaced by machines if the alternative is to go out of business.

Types of unemployment

Three types of unemployment have been identified: frictional, cyclical and structural.

❖ *Frictional* occurs when a manufacturing sector becomes outdated either through replacement with newer products or technology. The assumption is that after a short period of unemployment 'lag', workers will be re-employed in the newer industries. Earlier this century in the Midlands, workers in the declining bicycle industry moved into the rapidly expanding car-manufacturing firms.

❖ *Cyclical* is when unemployment is short-term or temporary. This can be where there are seasonal highs and lows, e.g. in agriculture where there is fluctuating demand for workers such as harvesters and fruit pickers. Another longer-term cycle concerns economies that go through booms and slumps with fluctuating demand for labour. A good

example of this is in Britain where the 1930s was a time of slump and high unemployment, while the 1950s was a time of boom and low unemployment.

The cyclical view used to be a dominant one in political thinking. It was thought that times of high unemployment would change to low if the economy was managed correctly. Such thinking dominated in Britain through the 1980s when unemployment rose to high levels. It was assumed that this was a short-term problem which could be alleviated by making British industry more efficient. In the 1990s, there is more pessimism about such a possibility and there has been increasing acceptance of the view that a certain level of unemployment is inevitable.

❖ *Structural explanations* accept the increased inevitability of unemployment in Western industrial economies. Some of the reasons, such as the increased use of technology and the growth of low-wage economies in other countries, have been outlined above. This is a more pessimistic view than the cyclical explanation. The real trends may be masked by schemes such as early retirement, by young people staying on in the education system until late teens and early twenties, and because significant groups of potential workers, such as mothers with young children, cannot work without adequate childcare facilities.

Measuring unemployment

'The unemployed is the number of people claiming benefit... at Unemployment Benefit Offices on the day of the monthly count, who are on that day unemployed and able and willing to do any suitable work.' (Department of Employment definition, 1987)

Statistics present problems for the sociologist in relation to accuracy and what they convey, and unemployment statistics are no exception to this. It is clearly in the interests of politicians in government to present as low statistics as possible. No government wants to preside over high unemployment, as it remains one of the greatest public concerns.

Unemployment statistics are not as straightforward as counting the numbers out of work. The government has strict categories for those to be counted as unemployed (see above). A key one is that only those claiming state benefits are counted in the statistics, which rules out many women caring for young children. Since the 1980s, critics of the Conservative government have pointed to the way the statistics have been 'massaged' to exclude groups who would formerly have been included in the figures. Examples of this are males over 60 and under 65, and those under 18 who now cannot claim benefits. This latter helps to disguise the true extent of youth unemployment, the assumption being that all young people are in training schemes or following further education. While the government was highlighting how the unemployment figures fell during the 1990s to less than 2 million, critics such as the Trade Union Congress were pointing to a 'real' total of 4 to 5 million,

once account was taken of potential workers in categories not qualifying for benefits, such as older people, mothers of young children and young people who would take jobs if they were available.

❖ Activity 30 ❖

Why might the figures in the *In Focus* below be misleading? Give two or three reasons.

Who are the unemployed?

Despite widespread publicity about non-manual redundancy among bankworkers and middle managers being 'downsized', it is still the case that unemployment is unevenly distributed among the working population. As a general rule, those who are unskilled and unqualified tend to be the highest proportion of the unemployed. Despite rising graduate unemployment from the 1980s, unemployment rates are still lower than among those without qualifications. In this sense governments are right to place an emphasis on expanding educational opportunities for all. However, critics point out that rather than expanding opportunities through education, you create a situation of over-qualification where graduates are now taking jobs formerly done by those with GCSE level qualifications. A good example of this is teaching: up to the 1970s, the equivalent of 5 GCSEs at grade C or above would gain acceptance to a teacher-training college; now, teaching is an all-graduate profession. A similar move is taking place in nursing. In industry, graduate trainees are recruited at supervisory level which required fewer qualifications in the past.

In Focus ♦ **Unemployment to dip**	'Unemployment is on course to dip below 2 million before the 1997 general election, according to official estimates. Whitehall officials reported the percentage of jobless	in August 1996 to be 7.5 per cent, its lowest for more than five years and well below the rate of 10.5 and 12.5 per cent respectively in Germany and France.'

There are variations in unemployment among the following groups:

❖ *working class* – The lower the skill level and lack of qualifications, the higher the unemployment rate. Similarly, insecure and temporary work, as in the building industry, is more likely to be experienced among the working class.

❖ *young people* – The disguised nature of youth unemployment through denial of access to benefits has been outlined above. Young people have had increasingly to accept work that is low paid, insecure, temporary and part time, often working and studying for further qualifications at the same time, as student grants have been steadily eroded.

❖ *older age groups* – Unemployment used to be seen as particularly affecting those over 60. In recent years this age has steadily decreased. An example is that in teaching and industry, workers of 50 and over are being offered early retirement packages, giving rise to the description of 'Third Age' groups who embark on a different life course from their 50s onwards.

❖ *women* – In general, women's unemployment is more disguised than that of other groups, as during their adult lives the dual role associated with home and family life and work may mean ineligibility for benefits as well as more restricted availability compared with men. Women are now about half the total workforce but they are heavily concentrated in low-paid, part-time occupations where many are probably over-qualified for what they do but have no choice because of childcare responsibilities. So jobs such as teachers and school dinner ladies which coincide with school hours and holidays are taken up. This is less likely to be a matter of choice than because family circumstances restrict women's opportunities.

In Focus

◆

'Bosses should employ men, not women' says Dame Barbara Cartland

'I n this terrible economic crisis when more and more people are being made redundant, I think the only sensible solution would be for every employer, if possible, to engage men and not women.

A man, if he is unemployed, is mentally frustrated and humiliated, while this does not apply to women.

What we have at the moment are children running wild as they do not have the security and attention when their mothers are more concerned with their careers than with their families. This is the result of Women's Lib insisting that women and men are equal. This is untrue, both physically and mentally. A man suffers more when he is unemployed than a woman does.

If it was a national order that married and unmarried women should not be engaged unless it is absolutely essential, then the man would have the chance of coming back to his rightful role as bread-winner and head of his family.'

Source: Citizen, March 1996

 ❖ Activity 31 ❖

What sort of sociological arguments could be provided to argue against the views espoused in the letter in the *In Focus*?

A controversial debate concerning women's choices was featured in the *British Journal of Sociology* in 1995. Catherine Hakim, a Research Officer at the London School of Economics and a well-known feminist academic, carried out a statistical analysis of women's employment since the Second World War (Hakim 1995).

She pointed out that although the number of women workers had certainly increased, a large proportion of them were in part-time employment. The result of this is that the total hours worked by women in any year since then has hardly changed, despite the large increase in numbers of women in jobs. Hakim then develops the very controversial view that this lower involvement in work on the part of many women is a reflection of their choice to take up low-paid work because that best fits their family responsibilities. She points out that through the expansion of educational provision, women's opportunities are greater now than they have ever been. A number of pressure groups have publicized women's opportunities in all walks of life, but women are not taking up these opportunities in a large-scale way. Unsurprisingly, there was a flood of responses to Hakim's conclusions, most in strong disagreement. The theoretical backdrop to such a debate is not new. In effect it is another version of a structuralist versus action approach, with Hakim taking the latter view focusing on women as conscious actors making real choices about careers and family responsibilities. Her critics highlight the structural constraints of women's lives reflected in patriarchal ideology and the discourse of what it is to be a woman in a male-dominated society.

Crompton (1997) points out that there are wide variations in the number of part-time workers throughout Europe. In Denmark there are far greater numbers of full-time women workers. The differences can be explained in relation to the provision of opportunities, a key one for mothers being childcare. This negates Hakim's idea of women choosing to work less hours.

Crompton sees the arguments that there are different types of women, i.e. some less committed to work than others, as simplistic. Women's choices must be seen within structural constraints associated with patriarchy and gender inequalities. She concludes, 'Preferences may shape the employment choices of women, but they do

---

❖ Activity 32 ❖

1 Set out the arguments surrounding Hakim's views in your own words and explain in more detail what the different feminist responses involve.

2 Conduct research among older women around the topic of choice and opportunity. Organize a debate, constructing a title based on Hakim's views.

---

not, contrary to Hakim's assertions, determine them' (see Activity 32).

Ethnicity and unemployment

Unemployment affects some ethnic minorities more than others. Links can be made with educational opportunities (see pp. 149–52), so Afro-Caribbean groups tend to have higher levels of unemployment than some of the Asian groups, for example, Indians and Chinese.

One obvious explanation of ethnic unemployment being particularly high among blacks is racism and there is evidence of this in a number of studies. Firms now have equal opportunities policies and ethnic monitoring to check on this, so there has been some improvement. Nevertheless, it is still unusual for black people to reach the higher levels of the job market, with some notable exceptions in fields such as law, trade unions and university teaching.

Regional variations

Until recently, the standard picture of the geography of unemployment in Britain was of variation, with the highest rates in Northern Britain and Northern Ireland and the lowest rates in the more prosperous South East. Within regions there were further variations and even at the level of towns and cities some neighbourhoods have had lower levels than others. For example, in London the unemployment rate in areas such as the East End and Brixton is much higher than elsewhere.

In the late 1990s, there has been a levelling of regional unemployment inequalities. This has been heralded by the Conservative government as a successful outcome of their policies to attract foreign investors, notably the Japanese, to areas of traditionally high unemployment, such as South Wales and the North East. Critics point to the flaws in measurement outlined above which mask the true extent of unemployment. Rather than making philanthropic gestures, investors are attracted to such regions because of the low wage-costs and compliance of workers in such areas of traditionally high deprivation and poverty. It is also pointed out that the decline in unemployment is more a result of the growth of insecure, part-time, temporary and low-skill jobs rather than secure, full-time, permanent and high-skill employment.

The consequences and social costs of unemployment

> 'There are no good aspects about being unemployed. It's like doing time ... there's no way out of it. You've no hope for the future. You're better off dead.' (32-year-old man, unemployed for 5 years, *from* Kay 1989)

Reduced standard of living

Unemployment involves social costs to individuals and families. There is a link between unemployment of the main bread-winner and household poverty. Despite tabloid newspaper portrayals of 'dole scroungers', implying a life of luxury, the greatest majority of unemployed people have far less income and a reduced standard of living compared with those in work. Lack of money is a key source of stress in family life and relationships. This can be heightened in a consumption-based society with constant messages through

adverts encouraging purchases of more goods which the unemployed cannot afford.

Loss of esteem

This chapter has consistently highlighted the importance of occupation as a key part of our identity and sense of belonging to society. Unemployment means that this is lost and it is difficult for many people to cope with this. There have been instances where a redundant worker has set off at the same time in the morning, as though going to work, and similarly returned in the evening, actually spending the day in the public library, in order to conceal the loss of his job from his neighbours. Unfortunately, significant numbers of the unemployed lapse into ill-health and depressive illnesses leading in a few cases to suicide. There can be no greater cost than this.

Social policy and unemployment

All governments aim to reduce unemployment as far as possible but interpretations of the effectiveness of their policies can vary. Conservatives focus on policies such as tax reductions to encourage the wealth makers and the talented to create wealth which will provide jobs for others. This policy which was a significant aspect of Thatcherism through the 1980s was judged to be 'successful' in reducing unemployment from the three million 'high' of the early 1980s to current lower levels. Critics point to statistical flaws and the replacement of stable, skilled jobs in manufacturing and elsewhere with unstable, low-skill jobs in the more insecure service and distributive industries. Such opponents advocate government and state intervention to help create 'real' jobs where there are identifiable high unemployment black spots.

A current debate concerns the minimum wage, which is opposed by Conservatives. They say it will lead to increased unemployment as it is an artificial state interference in the market for labour.

Employers will be reluctant to employ unskilled workers such as young people because the minimum wage is above the economic return when training and lower productivity costs are taken into account. Critics say that a minimum wage should be a right for every citizen to prevent exploitation. The rates advocated as a minimum are still way below the national average. Conservatives similarly oppose the European 'Social Chapter', which as well as supporting the minimum wage, greatly strengthens employee rights in the workplace.

Leisure

What do you do in your leisure time? Answers can range from sport to watching TV to the somewhat vague 'socializing'. If work for many is boring and unfulfilling then leisure is seen as having a compensatory role. After our work and work-related activities, we 'choose' our leisure pursuits which occupy our 'free time'. Some suggest that there is a 'democracy of leisure' where we all have equal opportunity to participate in a wide range of options. Sociologists question such views: they examine the role of leisure in relation to the wider society.

Sociological approaches to leisure

Any sociological study of leisure involves asking such questions as:

❖ What social influences determine our choice of leisure pursuit?

❖ What is the relationship between leisure and age, social class, disability, ethnicity, gender, and sexuality?

❖ Who controls and influences the 'leisure industry'?

❖ Is there a relationship between work and leisure?

Rojek (1993) identifies three stages in the study of leisure:

❖ *social-policy influenced studies* – This is where the leisure industry developed; leisure and its availability was seen as a 'good thing' and a right for all the population in a democratic society.

❖ *politicized studies* – These originated in the 1980s when Marxists and feminists criticized conventional views concerning the increased choice and freedom that leisure provides.

❖ the debate surrounding *postmodernity* and *postmodern experiences* – This has widened the focus of leisure theory and research to include debates about the body, social identity, images and the mass media, consumer culture and change.

Functionalist sociologists see leisure as functional for society. Boring, technologized work is the price of living in a mass consumption society, but the benefits come through an almost infinite choice of leisure pursuits ranging from watching football to playing and listening to music, or going abroad for holidays in places undreamed of by previous generations. The compensatory function of leisure is stressed. Marxist sociologists see leisure as escapism from capitalist exploitation, as reinforcing class inequalities, and as a capitalist 'leisure industry'. Feminists point to the different opportunities for leisure between men and women (see Table 5.4).

Similar issues are raised with respect to age, disability, ethnicity and sexuality. More recently, postmodernists have highlighted the changing and variable nature of leisure and its relationship to identity and life style through consumption.

Stanley Parker's work–leisure relationship

Are work and leisure related or completely separate? An early sociological study of the

Table 5.4 Participation* in leisure activities away from home, by gender 1994-95

Activity	Males	Females	All persons
Visit a public house	70	68	69
Meal in a restaurant, not fast food	60	64	62
Drive for pleasure	47	47	47
Meal in a fast food restaurant	45	40	42
Library	36	43	40
Cinema	35	32	34
Short break holiday	32	28	30
Disco or night club	29	22	25
Historic building	27	24	25
Spectator sports event	31	13	22
Theatre	19	22	21

* Percentage of the population aged 16 and over participating in each activity in the three months prior to interview.

Source: Social Trends (1996)

link between work and leisure was made by Stanley Parker (1971) who studied residential childcare officers, bank clerks and workers in 'extreme' occupations such as mining and deep sea fishing. He devised a three-fold typology of work–leisure relationship:

❖ *opposition* – This is the relationship between work and leisure where the work can be physically demanding and in some cases hazardous. Leisure is used to escape from this, so heavy drinking in the macho world of pubs and clubs is a common pursuit. Leisure serves to help forget one's work. 'Extreme' occupations such as mining and deep sea fishing are examples.

❖ *extension/complementarity* – This applied to the residential childcare officers who often engaged in leisure pursuits which were indistinguishable from their work, such as sports with the children in their care. Many professions such as teaching and management involve unclear work–leisure boundaries, such as a business dinner party or round of golf or a teacher watching and recording a TV documentary for use with a class.

❖ *neutrality* – This occurred among bank clerks who were ambivalent about their work, so leisure was neither an extension or oppositional. Leisure was about 'relaxing'.

Evaluation

Parker's work was one of the first to point to a relationship between type of work and leisure activity. There are some problems with such a typology, which simplifies the wide-ranging relationship between work and leisure. In terms of methodology, critics have pointed to the smallness of the samples in Parker's study. Can a study carried out over twenty years ago still apply to the complexity of leisure in the current age, when there is much greater choice and diversity? Roberts (1986) disagrees with Parker's model closely linking work relationships to leisure activities and emphasizes the dimension of choice available in the late twentieth century. There is a vast array of relatively cheap and accessible activities, ranging from country walks, sports and dining out to foreign holidays. Roberts points to the plurality of leisure options which has brought us close to a 'democracy of leisure'.

Leisure and the family life cycle

One of the first studies to highlight age and gender differences in access to leisure was carried out by the Rapoports (1975). They focused on the relationship between the family and leisure opportunity. They argue that during the family life cycle, leisure pursuits vary according to the circumstances. A childless, young married couple may continue similar leisure activities to when they were single, such as sport. Childrearing is a key stage on which parental resources, particularly those of the mother, are concentrated and which restricts choice. Leisure pursuits, such as bicycle rides and swimming, centre around children. When children leave home, more leisurely, 'older-age' pursuits such as walking or bowling may be taken up.

Critics point out that the Rapoports focus strongly on the stereotypical nuclear family 'norm', which is now less relevant.

❖ Activity 33 ❖

Give further examples to illustrate opposition, extension and neutrality in work–leisure relationships. Make some critical points concerning the view that we have a 'democracy of leisure'. Explain further the leisure pursuits of people living outside the nuclear family 'norm'.

Social class and leisure

At the common-sense level, class differences in choice of leisure can relate to differences between manual and non-manual occupations. In the former, average pay is lower and physical labour can obviate the need for compensatory exercise or strenuous sports which are taken up by those in sedentary white-collar jobs.

It might be thought that in a mass consumption society, leisure has increasingly become 'classless' in the American sense that we can buy any leisure pursuit we can afford regardless of social position. While it may be true that some activities such as holidays abroad and the ownership of videos and CD players have become available to large numbers, there are still clear class divisions in many activities. In terms of foreign holidays, there is a vast difference between a villa in Tuscany with sightseeing trips to art galleries in Florence, and a fortnight in Benidorm where the beach and nightlife are the main activities. Going to the opera is different from attending a 'free-and-easy' night in the local pub. Playing golf is not just about ability in that sport; there are admission procedures to golf clubs which can be highly selective, often involving recommendation by authorized members.

Clarke and Critcher (1985) offer a neo-Marxist perspective which sees leisure in class-based terms. They take issue with earlier sociological work that views leisure as individual enjoyment and free choice. They highlight the social, political and economic context which is part of the structural constraints that order people's lives including their leisure. Leisure is never wholly free nor totally determined. Shifts in employment and the decline of manufacturing industry have not improved the quality of work for many people. There are still low-paid, insecure, low-skill jobs with poor working conditions. The growth of 'white-collar' occupations has not improved this situation because many are in the most exploited areas of work, such as shops and the catering trade. 'Choice' in leisure is illusory; the old inequalities remain largely intact:

'Choice has become the ideological validation of a system which in practice denies people the power to exercise control... The freedoms exercised by the market are limited in range and kind. The production of marketable goods and services remains in private hands. The myth of consumer power disguises the extent of capital's power. ' (Clarke and Critcher 1985, p. 200)

❖ Activity 34 ❖

Explain the above quote using appropriate examples. Draw up a table with two columns headed 'Middle class' and 'Working class' and list typical leisure pursuits under each. Are there any that are difficult to place? If so, why?

Gender and leisure

Women are increasingly taking up a wider range of leisure activities but they still have fewer opportunities compared with men. Women with children are more restricted and, as family and housework studies have shown, husbands and fathers have more free time than wives and mothers. As the Rapoports highlighted in their study of leisure in relation to the family life cycle, younger single women have more free time and can go out more on an almost equal basis to young men.

Some have commented on the growing equality of opportunity for young women.

❖ Activity 35 ❖

'Leisure is not necessarily an activity; doing nothing, "staring out of the window" or just sitting down, can all be construed as leisure, especially for houseworkers.' (Deem 1984)

How does this view of leisure differ from a male perspective?

They are more confident, taking part in leisure on their own terms. A Leicester University study (Williams 1995) found that women were the fastest growing spectator group at football matches. Football crowds in the 1950s were exclusively male, whereas today they include a significant number of women.

There are, however, still restrictions on girls compared with boys, some of which are taken for granted, such as the freedom to go to public parks and remote country areas. Female joggers and cyclists can be subject to harassment such as obscene shouts from men. It is more difficult for a woman to enter a traditional pub on her own than it is for a man. Women tend to take up activities such as 'keep fit', aerobics, weightwatchers and yoga. If they go to the pub without partner or husband, it is often with other women, e.g. for darts nights, so women are facing constant subtle and not so subtle curbs on their public behaviour. Feminists see such restraints as an aspect of patriarchal ideology where men have power and control over women, either directly through harassment and violence or indirectly through their low involvement in domestic activities and parenting.

Deem (1990) points to the importance of employment in providing money, status and self-confidence for increased numbers of women. Earning a wage increases women's negotiating power within households. Social policy on leisure has improved the situation for women.

Examples of social policies which encourage women to take up leisure activities are cheap admission rates to leisure centres, women-centred sport, improved design and lighting of streets, and childcare facilities. However, there is still some way to go before full gender equality. In her research Deem found a significant number of women attending leisure centres were acting as chauffeurs for their children. A key feature of adult women's leisure is its association with children. Leisure can have a dual role which includes childcare as well as the activity. Swimming and going to the pictures are good examples of this.

❖ Activity 36 ❖

Compare the activities of adult males with those of females outlined above. Write notes comparing Catherine Hakim's response and an opposite feminist response with the following: 'Women have more restrictions on their leisure than men.'

Using examples such as aerobics and weightwatchers, explain the different influences on choice of leisure between women and men. If you were of the opposite sex, would you take part in the same leisure activities as now? Explain your answer.

Ethnicity and leisure

There is a complex relationship between ethnicity and leisure. In entertainment and sport there are many Asian and black stars, which might suggest that there is greater opportunity in such fields than in conventional employment. Closer examination shows this not to be the case (see Activity 37). In 1996 many football clubs took up the campaign 'Kick Racism Out of Sport'. Black footballers have had to put up with racist chants and abuse from opposing supporters. In his biography, England and Liverpool's football star John Barnes recounted many such incidents including banana skins thrown at him and ape-like chants. In 1997 the swimming star Sharon Davies and her black husband have had threats made against them from far right political groups. The tennis player Boris Becker is now living in America rather than his native Germany because of similar threats concerning his black wife.

The experience of discrimination and all forms of racism often lead Asian and black groups to separate activities from white groups – choosing those that declare pride in identity through music and other cultural forms. While leisure centres, theme parks and city centres with their palaces of consumption may attract the affluent, many, such as the poor and ethnic groups are dispossessed and on the margins. They are the suspected shoplifters and 'troublemakers' to be moved on by the growing army of security personnel and the police.

Gilroy (1987) sees popular culture, music and entertainment as central features of ethnic identity. Hebdidge (1990) points to the importance of the black influence on white music and youth styles. In more recent work, Gilroy (1993) sees a mixing of global cultural styles, language, music and dress which reflects difference and diversity.

In sport, Cashmore (1982) has provided further examples of racism that permeates all levels from spectators to players and administrators.

Fleming (1993) conducted ethnographic research in 1988 and 1989 in a multiethnic school in London to find out more about the sports activities of young South Asians. He notes the generally negative

❖ Activity 37 ❖

Read the *In Focus* and suggest why there may be so few Asian referees. What might be done to change this situation?

In Focus
◆
Asian referees

'Soccer top brass have set themselves an ambitious new goal ... to attract more Asian referees. Currently there are only three officials from the ethnic minorities in the Blackburn area – and the Lancashire Football Association is looking to net a few more in the coming months. Jim Parker, LFA's referee application officer said: "We would love to see more Asian referees in the game. There are a lot of Asian players in the district but not enough referees. We don't know why this is ..."'

The Citizen, 23 January 1997

image about such young people as reported by Williams (1989):

> 'The Asian pupil is typically seen as physically frail, lacking in stamina and likely to underachieve in physical education, in contrast to their stereotype as quiet, hardworking and intelligent in the classroom.'

One problem in earlier studies is the assumption of homogeneity among such ethnic groups, which are in practice characterized by diversity according to country of heritage, religion and related cultural factors. Fleming found that the barriers experienced by such young people include:

❖ forms of personal racism such as verbal abuse in contact sports

❖ fears for safety particularly in activities outside school hours

❖ cultural factors such as modesty in dress and prayer requirements

❖ lack of time particularly where religious tradition is strong

❖ parental disapproval or lack of support.

Unsurprisingly, many young Asians gravitate towards separate activities, forming their own football and cricket teams, playing in their own leagues.

The conclusion is that, as with other forms of inequality such as gender and class, ethnic access to leisure is controlled by the dominant group. Acceptance can be gained by particular skills and ultimately 'stardom' but many barriers have to be overcome. An alternative response is to celebrate ethnic identity by separate leisure activities reflecting cultural origins. Some of these, such as rock and reggae music, have been taken up and adopted by young white people as well.

Age and leisure

Clearly there are physical limitations on leisure as we get older, with younger people generally taking part in the more active, strenuous leisure and sports activities. Age stratification can apply to a range of sports:

some pursuits, such as bowls, are associated with the elderly and when younger people take part they may be ridiculed because of such associations. Other activities are considered ageless, e.g. supporting your football team.

Musical tastes can reflect age as with rock and pop music. However, some of the 1960s bands continue with increasingly aged members. Mick Jagger is a grandfather!

Holidays, too, are aimed at different age groups, some companies exercising age restrictions, e.g. 18-30 holidays for younger, fun-loving people, and Saga holidays for the over-50s.

❖ Activity 38 ❖

Do you think that the age stratification of leisure pursuits is now a more determining factor than those of social class, ethnicity and gender.

Disability and leisure

Disability in relation to leisure has not particularly featured in sociological studies. It is worth noting that opportunities for disabled people to take part in leisure and sports activities have increased in recent years. Today, most entertainment, sports and leisure venues place a higher priority on access. Participation in sport has increased, culminating in the four-yearly Paralympics which takes place after the Olympics and receives an increasingly high media profile.

❖ Activity 39 ❖

Do you think that the higher profile given to the standards and commitment of disabled athletes is helping to change general attitudes to the disabled, by changing their image from that of helpless dependants and objects of charity?

Sexuality and leisure

As with disability, the link between sexuality and leisure has not tended to be the subject of sociological study. In one sense this is understandable, as most gay men and lesbians follow leisure pursuits that have nothing to do with sexuality at all. However, today there gay clubs and other social facilities in many towns and cities which offer a common social setting for gay people. The annual Mardi Gras carnival in Sydney, Australia, attracts tens of thousands of people.

In the mass media, the traditional emphasis on heterosexual norms and the image of homosexuality as deviant meant that gay people involved in entertainment and sport used to keep their sexuality secret. Even outright 'camp' cross-dressing male entertainers such as Danny La Rue were low key about their homosexuality. There was widespread publicity after the 1950s male heart-throb Rock Hudson died of AIDs. There have been some changes in recent times with sports stars, such as tennis champion Martina Navratilova and footballer Justin Fashanu, leading openly gay life styles. In show business, the outing of comedian Michael Barrymore in the mid-1990s attracted much media attention with some predicting the end of his career. However, many entertainers, such as Julian Clary are quite open about their sexuality and build their acts – even their careers – on it.

Another aspect of sexuality is how images of masculinity and femininity are reinforced through sport. A 'man's man' has to be 'hard' and 'play to win'. Losers are wimps. Injuries have to be borne with stoicism. Scraton (1992) points out that male sexual identity is inextricably linked to power and conquest. The collective experience of being 'men' relies on the subordination of other men (young men, homosexuals) and on the subjugation of women. In a significant number of sports, particularly those involving contact, an emphasis on a strong image of heterosexual masculinity leads to virulent homophobia. Connell (1987) refers to the collective identity of men, inspired by imagery, camaraderie and social experiences, as 'hegemonic masculinity'. Patriarchal ideology, which Brittan (1989) refers to as 'masculinism', involves an emphasis on male dominance and assumptions about innate male aggression which can have an outlet in sports such as boxing and rugby.

In comparison, other sports have traditionally emphasized the 'ladylike' dimension, such as the expectation in previous decades that women tennis players would wear frilly knickers displayed under short skirts. This ruling became untenable when players began to insist on 'masculine' shorts, but disapproval was still expressed in popular newspapers. Despite this, and the fact that tennis was the first sport to cope openly with lesbiansim, women players are still often commended for the delicacy and finesse of their playing strokes, while for male players, the focus is on the power and speed of their serves, and their overall strength and stamina.

❖ Activity 40 ❖

1 If you take part in any sports, are there any examples from your experience which reinforce the above examples?

2 Explain in more detail why there may be a 'problem' for gay people who become successful in sport and entertainment. What sexuality is 'expected' of female ice-skaters and male rugby players? And what about male ice-skaters and female rugby players?

Sport as a leisure industry

From the 1970s, sport has developed into a global entertainment industry with the involvement of media tycoons and wealthy business people creating huge entertainment empires linking sport with mass media. There are many examples of a number of sports developing in this way and the most high profile and popular is football. Football clubs have become multi-million-pound entertainment industries with associated sports and leisure complexes, restaurants and facilities that would have been unimaginable in the 1950s when attending a football match often meant standing in the freezing rain for almost two hours, crammed together in large crowds with few or no facilities.

❖ Activity 41 ❖

Coursework suggestion

Many student coursework projects deal with football hooliganism, so it would be an interesting change to investigate the changing football industry from sport to a mass entertainment.

Gambling

Gambling is one of the oldest leisure pursuits and now it is a multimillion-pound industry. One of the biggest developments of the mid-1990s in Britain was the National Lottery, which quickly established itself as a topic of conversation as common as the weather or soap operas. Accompanying this have been scratch lottery cards. Such developments have been subject to controversy and concern. Gamblers Anonymous and the Methodist Church have continued their campaigns against gambling and have used the Lottery to heighten this as a new dimension of easy-access instant gambling, which they see as a worrying trend. Newspaper stories have featured the increase in children's gambling activity and the development of addictive behaviour. Some politicians have dismissed such concerns as interference in a 'spot of harmless fun'. A large proportion of the population now buy lottery tickets, to the extent that in workplaces on Friday evenings a common response to 'See you on Monday' is 'Not if I win the Lottery, you won't'! (Does this tell us something about attitudes to work for many?)

❖ Activity 42 ❖

Coursework suggestion

A coursework project could be carried out on gambling. Note ethical guidelines and do not seek to interview compulsive gamblers. An investigation of the National Lottery, covering who buys tickets, why they take part, mass media accounts of lottery winners, general attitudes to scratchcards, the involvement of children, are a few examples of areas that could be explored.

Postmodernist approaches to leisure

Giddens (1990) points out that modern societies are characterized by 'disembedding' mechanisms which enable social relationships to extend over both time and space. Face-to-face communication and interaction has declined, while telephones, faxes and e-mail have enabled instant communication across vast distances. You can obtain money and pay bills at bank cash-machines anywhere in the world. Time of communication can be controlled by means of answering machines. You can control viewing time of TV programmes by means of video machines.

Postmodern studies of leisure have highlighted the shifts in leisure patterns, and identified issues around consumption, images and lifestyle (see Chapter 2, *Culture and identity*). These studies examine how the majority of people spend their free time, rather than studying the minority sporting and recreational tastes of active enthusiasts (usually white, middle-class car owners with local access to sports and leisure centres). Veal (1993) advocates that research must investigate the ways individuals and social groups construct life style and express leisure tastes. Some see postmodernism being represented by the credit card and the shopping mall which have replaced cash and the supermarket. Postmodern consumers are spoilt for choice and construct identities around consumption patterns. Supermarket shopping can be functional, as in shopping for the family, but increasingly aspects of leisure and life style encroach. We buy bread, butter and milk as we have always done, but also are confronted with choices reflecting global imagery in consumption. Curries and associated accompaniments are displayed alongside Italian pasta. Sometimes the identity gets fused, as in the takeaway which advertises halal pizzas. Postmodern consumers have to pick their way through all this confusion.

In some sports a 'fun' element has taken over. Swimming baths have become leisure pools with inflatable animals, tropical palms and slides. The simulation of a summer holiday beach is completed by a wave machine. You can ski all year round on artificial ski slopes. Such examples show that leisure is not limited by space, time or season.

Developments in computer technology mean you can have limitless experience without leaving your armchair. Virtual reality machines can simulate travel and participation in sports. You can be a champion Grand Prix driver on a machine in your local pub. You can visit major art galleries such as the Louvre without going to Paris, by means of a CD-ROM on your multimedia computer.

Urry (1990) shows how tourism has developed in an increasingly polarized and divided society. For a privileged few, there is a quest for the increasingly exotic and unusual. We seek ever new experiences and can relive history through 'living museums', 'authentic' settings of Victorian school-rooms, mines and Viking settlements, peopled by actors in appropriate costumes who interact with us to convey the 'real' experience.

Evaluation

There is much in postmodern approaches to leisure that describes current trends effec-tively and highlights the aspects of pleasures, fantasies and pastiche in what is available. However, there are continuing issues of access to many groups in society along the familiar lines of social class, gender and ethnicity as well as other forms of inequality. Scraton and Bramham (1995) point out that,

'... postmodernism neglects many people's lives which remain influenced by their experiences of poverty, gender and racism. This is political and social reality and if we are to study and understand leisure in times of change we must explore postmodern leisure but without losing sight of persistent social inequalities.' (p. 34)

❖ Activity 43 ❖

Give more examples of 'postmodern' leisure trends. Find out the costs of a visit to a local leisure complex for a family of four. What other barriers are there to 'free' choice to participate in postmodern forms of leisure?

Current trends in work and leisure

Some newer terms that are applied to current trends are:

❖ *downsizing/rightsizing* – Where companies are reorganizing, creating 'flatter' managerial structures and Japanese-style teamworking. This also includes use of IT

for information processing, planning and associated decision-making. The result is less need for worker supervision and so fewer middle managers. Sceptics see this as newer terms for old-fashioned redundancy, albeit now hitting the middle classes.

❖ *outsourcing* – The practice of larger companies to use networks of smaller companies to make some part of their overall product. This can be linked to globalization issues as such links can be international, so a larger company can seek the cheapest components in low-wage economies

❖ *downshifting* – Where some workers are voluntarily giving up high-pressure, stressful jobs, perhaps helped by early retirement or termination 'packages', to take up less stressful work living a simpler lifestyle. In America this growing trend among some high-flying executives has been referred to as 'downshifting into voluntary simplicity' – a modern version of the 1960s 'dropping out'? In Britain a large number of teachers over 50 have taken voluntary early retirement, as schools and colleges seek to save costs by employing younger cheaper staff.

❖ *Work-rich/time-poor* – This can be related to the previous 'downshifting' trend. Increased numbers of highly paid, professional couples are working longer hours for sometimes massive salaries. Gershuny (1997) referred to such groups as 'work-rich/time-poor'. Because of the pressures, some might eventually 'downshift', but many 'buy' non-work and leisure time by employing domestic workers such as cleaners and nannies. In 1997 there were media reports featuring a one-million-pound-a-year financial consultant with five children dubbed 'supermum'. Reference was made to her 'army of domestic workers'.

❖ *New Age management* – There has been increased adoption of American-style management theories such as Total Quality Management (TQM). Terms such as 'worker empowerment' and 'client/customer focus' have become fashionable in the quest to improve the efficiency of all types of work organization ranging from hospitals to schools and railways. Under this new ethos, there are no longer patients, pupils, students or passengers, but 'customers' and 'clients'. Customer charters and quality certificates are displayed in company waiting rooms. Managers attend courses, often run by American companies owned by managerial 'gurus' such as Tom Peters, where they are exhorted to improve quality in all areas of their organization in an atmosphere of evangelical zeal. This is presented as an issue of devolvement of power and responsibility to all of a company's workers in order to improve imagery and productivity. Formerly 'invisible' workers such as cleaners and caretakers are seen as key figures in the presentation of a company's image to the public. 'The most important person in the company is the

---

In Focus

◆

12 signs that tell you to downshift

1 You always get ill on holiday.
2 You can't recall the last interesting conversation you had with your partner.
3 You have started to forget family birthdays.
4 You clutter up the house with piles of half-completed work.
5 You live mainly on junk food and ready-made meals.
6 You wake up feeling anxious and tired, even at weekends.
7 You have stopped reading books.

8 You have not learned a new skill in years.
9 You are away so often that when you come home the dog thinks you are a burglar.
10 You spend a fortune on luxuries to cheer yourself up, or to bribe your family to tolerate your absences.
11 You think you are indispensable.
12 You are drinking to much and/or have started smoking.

Source: adapted from The Guardian,
7 January 1997

receptionist or whoever meets the customer first'. British companies such as Girobank have adopted TQM since the early 1990s and claim dramatic improvements in workplace moral and productivity.

Evaluation

Conflict sociologists would see such moves as a reaction to a highly competitive and recession-dominated business climate rather than being about 'empowering' workers and improving 'quality' – which cannot be clearly defined. Such developments are more about masking inequalities and business problems in a rapidly changing economic climate where many workers are under threat of redundancy and required to work harder for the same or less pay. What *is* new is that this now also applies to managers and professional groups such as teachers, doctors and social workers.

 ## The future of work and leisure

There are a number of possibilities for the future of work and leisure ranging from the optimistic to the pessimistic.

Optimistic views

Sociologically, optimism can be linked to a functionalist perspective where technology, and in particular computers, will herald a new age of freedom where boring work is eradicated. Work will become a less central part of people's lives. Trends which are already with us, such as starting work in the mid to late twenties, early retirement at 45 to 50, part-time and jobsharing occupations, have been advocated by Charles Handy as desirable options (1984). This will help to break down the work/non-work/leisure divide, gradually making our work identity less important. So, rather than being judged as a doctor, lorry driver, teacher, plumber, miner or university professor, we are judged on our qualities as a person. Such judgements will probably be more difficult to make than those based on occupation (see Activity 44).

The boundaries between work and other aspects of our lives will gradually become less clear. This will be added to by the changed physical context of work, described

In Focus
◆
What is he?

What is he?

– A man, of course.

Yes, but what does he do?

– He lives and is a man

Oh, quite! But he must work –
he must have a job of some sort.

– Why?

Extract from 'What is he?', D.H. Lawrence

❖ Activity 44 ❖

Make a list of the qualities which might be seen as part of a person rather than as part of their occupation. Compare your answers with those of other students.

in detail above. For many, work will be at home rather than the office or the factory.

Computers will add to this sense of blurred boundaries. Already computer games are available on all PCs, so when a 'work' activity palls, a game can be played. Developments such as the internet and e-mail mean that communication becomes less formal and has more of a 'fun' element, as in 'surfing the Internet' which may involve a work dimension but also involves the idea of play.

According to the optimist, there will be much more choice and flexibility over *when*, as well as *where*, to work. After the children have gone to bed, working using a laptop in the garden on a pleasant summer's evening with a glass of chilled white wine seems more desirable than starting in an office at 8.30 after an hour's commuting through traffic jams.

The wealth created by computer technology will mean that enough income will be earned for a fairer distribution of wealth, a true 'golden age' of choice and freedom for all. There may be some form of stratification through those with specialist computing expertise compared with others, but even those in conventional 'work' will be less involved.

To summarize this view, there will be more blurring of boundaries and less work in the conventional sense. More will 'do

'Look,' said Pooh. 'I've worked out how to play Pooh Sticks on the internet.'

work' at home as and when they like and our work role and identity as recognized today will eventually disappear.

❖ Activity 45 ❖

If such trends develop how might they benefit women more than men?

Pessimistic views

Pessimists would see the optimistic views outlined above as unattainably utopian and reflecting the view of the highly educated middle classes in managerial and professional occupations. There are crucial problems which are already with us concerning the matching up of an unequal class society with large-scale unemployment and a 'high technology' future. There is little indication of how a society with equal opportunity for all can develop from our existing situation. For Marxists, the 'computing revolution' will only benefit the capitalist or ruling class – as any techno-logical innovations have always done.

Globalization and the idea of democrati-zation and empowerment of the masses through 'the information revolution' and associated global networks will not work while power and control is in the hands of a few. The only 'real' revolution will be an economic not a technological one, where the ownership of the means of production is taken over by the proletariat. It is only then that the benefits of new technologies can be distributed to all, otherwise, in the hands of the capitalist system, global communica-tions will be about escapism through sport and soap opera. There will be a rich minority who through knowledge and expertise or ownership will live barricaded existences behind electric fences with security systems and a dispossessed majority surviving at poverty levels. So, the future will be more that of 'RoboCop' and 'Judge Dredd' than the utopian dreams of earlier science-fiction writers predicting a techno-logical land of milk and honey for all.

Postmodernists

Postmodernists would be neither optimistic nor pessimistic about the future. They would certainly agree with flexibility and the breaking down of traditional barriers between work and leisure that is already occurring. They would probably doubt whether this would necessarily lead to a better future. Some people in creative occupations will gain through advancements in technology which will give greater flexibility and freedom as well as a good life style. Others will lose and increasingly become 'outsiders' as conflict theorists predict. However, not all the traditionally oppressed groups will have the same experience. For example:

❖ Women are increasingly becoming the key and most desirable workers in a world of flexible work and organizational structures.

❖ Gay people's leisure and spending power (sometimes nicknamed the 'pink pound') will continue to gain in significance.

❖ Disabled groups will gain freedom via computer technology to enter fields which were previously closed to them.

❖ Activity 46 ❖

Coursework suggestion

Use this chapter and other sources to carry out some research and do a small survey on the topic of the future of work and leisure. Cover all groups such as: younger/older people, those from different social backgrounds, classes and ethnic origins, men/women, disabled. Write a report (1000 words) summarizing your findings. You could develop this into a coursework project.

In Focus

◆

Working on tomorrow

'As the 21st century opens, demographic and employment trends mean that many characteristics of the UK labour force will be different. The workforce will be older, better educated and possess more vocationally relevant qualifications, while the number of women in the labour market will continue to increase, of whom about half will work part-time.

Projections suggest that more people will work for small employers and be self-employed. While job opportunities will continue to expand at professional, technical and managerial levels, many other new jobs will be part-time, low-paid and low-status.'

Source: adapted from The Guardian,
22 June 1996

Chapter summary

This chapter has covered four broad areas of work, organization, unemployment and leisure:

❖ definitions of work, non-work and leisure

❖ the changing nature of work and occupations

❖ work in an industrial society

❖ the ownership and control of work

❖ social inequalities in the workplace

❖ attitudes to work

❖ technology and work – mechanization and automation

❖ de-skilling

❖ conflict at work: industrial unrest, its causes and the role of the trade unions

❖ the changing workplace

- ❖ the growth of bureaucratic organizations
- ❖ postmodern organizations
- ❖ unemployment and its effects
- ❖ the changing nature of leisure
- ❖ the future of work, organizations and leisure.

 Stimulus-response question

Item A

'A research consultancy, the Unemployment Unit, claims that changes in the system of benefits since 1982 have gradually concealed the true levels of unemployment by reducing the number of those eligible for benefit. In particular, married women may not be counted if they qualify neither for unemployment benefit nor income support. At the same time, businesses are rapidly reassessing the potential of married women as the recruitment market contracts. A diminishing number of school leavers in the Nineties threatens corporate expansion, especially in the service industries – a symptom of the so-called 'demographic time-bomb'. Women who want to return to work after raising a family are regarded as a largely untapped resource.'

Source: adapted from George Parker-Jervis, 'Snapshot', *The Observer*, February 1990

Item B

'Employers must recognise that women can no longer be treated as second-class workers. They will need women employees and must recognise both their career ambitions and domestic responsibilities.'

However, aspects of government policy throughout the 1980s appear to work against this. During the last decade, there has been a shift towards 'community care', meaning that people who are affected by problems of ageing, mental illness, mental handicap or physical or sensory disability need to be able to live as independently as possible in their own homes. The greater part of care for most people at most times of their lives continues to be provided by families and friends rather than by statutory bodies. The majority of such carers are women.

Source: Adapted from Rosemary Crompton, 'Women and work in the 1990s', *Social Studies Review*, 6(5)

Item C

| | Working mothers with ... | | | |
| | a child under 5 years of age (%) | | youngest child aged 10 or more (%) | |
	1983	1989	1983	1989
Full-time	5	12	25	31
Part-time	18	29	42	43
All	24	41	66	75

Note: percentages rounded to nearest whole number

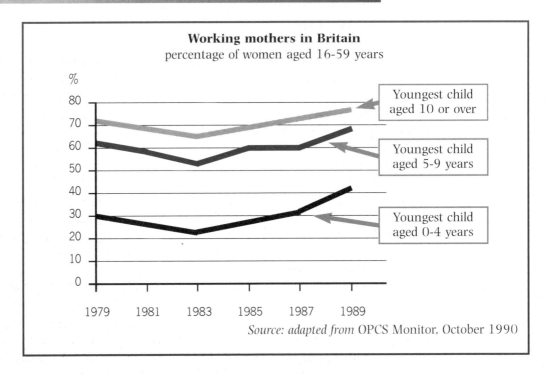

Working mothers in Britain
percentage of women aged 16-59 years

Youngest child aged 10 or over
Youngest child aged 5-9 years
Youngest child aged 0-4 years

Source: adapted from OPCS Monitor, October 1990

Questions:

1 What is meant by the 'demographic time bomb' (Item A)? *(1 mark)*

2 Between 1983 and 1989, what is the increase in the percentage of working mothers in full-time employment whose youngest child is aged 10 or over (Item C)? *(1 mark)*

3 Describe the changes in the patterns of working mothers in Britain since 1979 (Item C). *(4 marks)*

4 What are the implications of the information in the Items concerning married women for the recruitment policies of industry? Illustrate your answer with examples of what employers could do to assist female employees. *(4 marks)*

5 Using information in the Items and elsewhere, assess sociological explanations of the position of women in the work-force. *(8 marks)*

6 Evaluate the argument that 'changes in the system of benefits since 1982 have gradually concealed the true levels of unemployment' (Item A). *(7 marks)*

Essay questions

1 Examine sociological explanations of social inequalities at work.

2 Evaluate the Marxist use of alienation to describe work in a capitalist society.

3 'Industrial unrest is the outcome of a low level of job satisfaction for many workers.' Evaluate this in the light of recent trends in strikes and other forms of industrial protest.

4 'Modern organizations are more complex than Weber originally suggested.' Discuss using appropriate examples.

5 'Unemployment affects people at all levels of society.' Examine this view in the light of current sociological debates.

6 Assess the view that we live in an age where we have a 'democracy of leisure'.

Further reading

Crompton, R. (1997) *Women and Work in Modern Britain*, Oxford: Oxford University Press.

A comprehensive examination of the position of women in relation to work in the late 20th Century. Issues of changing labour markets, technology and women's and men's work are explored in detail.

Deem, R. (1986) *All Work and No Play: The Sociology of Women and Leisure*, Milton Keynes: Open University Press.

A readable and thorough account showing the restrictions on women's leisure. Relates to more 'mainstream' feminist debates surrounding patriarchy, domestic and wage labour.

Grint, K. (1991) *The Sociology of Work: An Introduction*, Cambridge: Polity Press.

A detailed coverage of most issues relating to modern developments in our sociological understanding of the world of work.

Madry, N. and Kirby, M. (1996) *Investigating Work, Unemployment and Leisure*, London: Collins Educational.

A lively and stimulating approach to the topic, full of activities and suggestions to develop understanding. Newer areas such as the impact of globalization explored in a readable and user-friendly style.

Pollert, A. (1981) *Girls, Wives, Factory Lives*, Basingstoke: Macmillan.

An ethnographic study of a tobacco factory in Bristol. Uses observation and in-depth interviews to explore women's experience of factory life and how this relates to their lives outside. Full of fascinating material and insights.

Thompson, P. and McHugh, D. (1995) *Work Organizations: A Critical Introduction* (2nd edn), London: Macmillan.

Thorough and detailed examination of a demanding area. All the most recent debates concerning bureaucracy and postmodern organizations dealt with from a critical perspective.

Chapter 6

Stratification and differentiation

❖ Preview

In this chapter we will be looking at:

- ❖ the variety of meanings of socially structured differentiation, social stratification and social class

- ❖ alternative theories of class, class position, stratification and life-chances

- ❖ competing theories of differentiation based on gender, ethnicity and age

- ❖ the problems of measuring class position, social mobility and stratification

- ❖ definitions of poverty and wealth and difficulties in studying these issues

- ❖ the development of social and sociological concepts of an underclass.

❖ Introduction

The study of social differentiation is the study of the processes that result in social inequality. Inequality is one of the most obvious and enduring aspects of social life. It can be seen everywhere: in income, in housing, in access to education, in power and in social respect. Much of this inequality appears to exist within structures, so that one aspect of inequality correlates to another or to some key factor, such as occupation. We even see inequality where we might not expect it: in health, illness and death rates, where correlations with occupation are very well established.

Until twenty or so years ago, the dominant factor established within the social structure and discussed in sociological theory was what is usually known as 'class'. The occupation of an individual or family was conventionally used as a measure of class and that kind of analysis of data became routine. Every sociologist used the concept of class from time to time and the bulk of government statistics on earnings, property, illness, births, marriages and deaths were analysed in terms of occupations. These occupations were usually grouped together by government statisticians into 'classes of occupations' and ranked in a hierarchy. Whenever statistics of any sort were analysed by occupation, they always yielded correlations of difference that were, in statistical terms, 'significant'. Because of the range of available data arranged and analysed in this way, it seemed to many sociologists that the key factor in most social analysis was class.

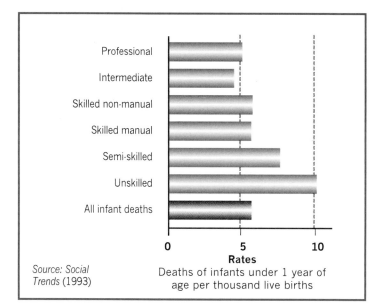

Source: Social Trends (1993)

Rates
Deaths of infants under 1 year of age per thousand live births

Figure 6.1
Infant mortality by social class of father, England and Wales 1990

Occupational class was, and remains, a key factor in the distribution of the good things of life within our society. Indeed, it is one of the key factors in the distribution of life itself, even if this is one factor that we are not always aware of. For proof of this, see Fig. 6.1.

The death of every infant is a personal tragedy and a source of great suffering for the parents but, despite an efficient National Health Service that tries to treat all equally, the distribution of deaths of children before they reach their first birthday is not evenly distributed in our society: it happens more than twice as frequently amongst children whose fathers are unskilled workers as amongst children whose fathers are in the professional occupations. There is little direct connection, surely, between what a father does at work and the health of an infant. So what are the connections? Spend a few minutes on Activity 1 now.

❖ **Activity 1** ❖

Discuss and list all the factors that might more directly have an impact on an infant: income, diet, knowledge of primary health care, access to medical services, etc.

Other factors which show statistical correlations between health and occupational class range from the earlier loss of teeth to the increase in the chance of death. In 1971, being in the unskilled occupations led to only a 15 per cent increase in chance of death (above the average chance). Fifteen years later (and older), being in the unskilled occupations led to a 53 per cent increase in the chances of death (above the average chance). These are examples of the *facts* of occupational class that we find year after year in statistical analysis. Quite simply, the facts and differentials are not going away.

❖ **Activity 2** ❖

Discuss and list the factors that you think influence and cause this differentiation in death rates.

Social stratification

The most commonly used term related to class was (and is) *social stratification*. In particular, class was seen as one system of stratification, although it was recognized that in the past many other systems had existed. The term 'stratification' was borrowed from geology, where it is used to describe a physical structure of rocks which can be divided into clear layers or bands ('strata') lying one on top of the other. In social life, the idea of layers does (or, at least, did) seem to apply, but the idea of sharp lines of division has not applied. Nevertheless, the term stratification was seen as meaningful. In the benefits that came from higher occupations, there were clearly layers and the idea of one layer sitting upon another had an instant appeal, even if the boundaries could not be made clear.

The available statistical data on individuals in British society were also kept and arranged in terms of sex and age, but these were never regarded by sociologists as key classifications of a structural sort.

The reasons for this were as follows:

❖ Men, women and children were seen primarily as being in families or family households. It was generally felt that the social class of an individual came from the family, and that the male 'head of the household' and male occupation set that level. It was also how the members of that household saw themselves and influenced the way that others perceived members of the household. The majority of married women did not work full time and very few married women earned more than their partners. Britain before 1970 was a society in which women, if married, took their status from the men they were married to and, if single, took their status as much from their father as from their own occupation. The analysis of statistics followed this social convention.

❖ Age was taken for granted as a progression which expressed very little except ageing through a class-based set of experiences. A person remained very much a member of the working classes or middle classes (or anything else) as they progressed through their life and it was felt that their *core identity* remained the same.

Government data have not been organized on the basis of ethnic background until fairly recently. So ethnic group as a source of identity was not seen as central to social analysis and descriptions of the dynamics of social change.

We have now introduced two new, key related concepts:

❖ Class is not simply a set of correlations in government acquired statistical tables – it is a *lived set of experiences*.

❖ *Self-identity* is a guiding thread running through that lived set of experiences.

We will explore these two concepts more fully to see whether class-related experiences and class-dominated identities are indeed the dominant experiences and identity sources in most people's lives.

Class: a lived experience

As a set of lived experiences, class includes feelings of being included or excluded, of being superior or inferior or just out of place, of being powerful or weak, of being respected by others or not, of self-worth or lack of self-worth. It may also include access to or exclusion from the good things in life, of deference given or experienced. The statistical differences in the distribution of health may exist and may be of 'statistical significance', but they may not be part of the daily experience of life. There are key questions about 'class' which derive from the more basic question, 'How is class experienced?' Few might want to say, 'My child died because I was a building site labourer' – that is not how most people experience life and its tragedies – but they might say, 'I couldn't get anyone in the hospital to listen to an ordinary bloke like me', if that was indeed part of their experience.

Perhaps one of the most interesting and difficult things about the study of class is that for the last sixty or seventy years, observers have been declaring that we are approaching, or have actually reached, a 'classless' society – a society in which class is *not* part of the everyday experience of the people living in that society. There must be factors which lead people to make these repeated claims to classlessness, but the long period over which they have been made should make us suspicious about their truth. If a classless society has been achieved, then why do we still need to say this? Why do we need to persuade people not to take their class into account in their everyday lives? To whom is this message addressed, if all believe it?

One aspect of class not yet discussed is that of *class identity*. We have commented already on how class is experienced, but that could be read as a rather passive mode, one of describing and responding to signals coming in from the outside. However, 'identity' is also a key to understanding the social action and the continuity of social action of a particular individual. One key example might be: 'I always vote Labour because they are more likely to look after the interests of ordinary, working-class people like me.' This is an example that has been important in the past within political debates and describes action experienced as flowing from a class position. The Labour Party was formed early in the twentieth century and that formation can be described as a *class action* – a collective action by a class of people.

Identity or identities?

There are of course many actions by individuals (or aspects of the lives of individuals) that do not express a class identity and many actions that are not structured or distributed within the society by class position. These include actions and identities determined or influenced by gender, age and ethnicity. The expression of these different types of identity is discussed in detail throughout Chapter 2, *Culture and identity*.

The complex interrelationships of these various aspects of identity with class and other social processes and power structures is well illustrated in the *In Focus* below. We can use Harriet Bradley's excellent and detailed example to consider the problems of analysis that we all face in working in the field of social differentiation.

Bradley approaches the question with a very positive attitude. She seems to believe that the young woman in question might be able to arrive at a clear identity. Other postmodernists are less optimistic and see postmodernism opening up questions that become hard to resolve. Suzanne Moore is well known for her journalism but is also

In Focus

◆

Bradley and postmodern identities

'Take, for an example, the position of a twenty-year-old Afro-Caribbean woman, whose parents were manual workers, bringing up two children on her own in inner-city Birmingham, and having to choose between low-paid work as a hospital domestic and dependency on benefits. How do we start to explain her fate? Is it because of gender that she is faced with responsibilities for childcare with no help from a man that she faces a limited range of labour market options? Or is it racism which means that the only job she can find is the stereotypical "servant" role which has been historically assigned to black women? Or is it class that led her to leave school early with limited qualifications? Of course it is all these things. And age plays a part too, as many employers have a prejudice against young workers, and prefer to employ older married women whom they see as steadier, having "settled down"...' (Bradley 1996, p. 19)

'Postmodernists argue that identity had become relatively free floating, detached from the bases of social structure which in the past were seen to contain it; we are now more able to pick and choose which of the various "yous on offer" we want to be "me": ... If we pursue our example of the young Afro-Caribbean woman, we can illustrate what the postmodernists are trying to convey. Does she identify herself primarily as a woman? Or perhaps as a single parent, in view of the state's preoccupation with the "problem" of single parenthood? Does she consider herself working class because of her parent's manual occupations, or because she herself has experienced low-paid unskilled work options? If she grew up on a council estate she may take that as a sign of being part of the working-class. But if she now lives in a more mixed area of inner-city housing, surrounded by students, perhaps she has developed loyalties to a more complex sort of community? Her ethnic origin will be very important to her. But does she think of herself as Afro-Caribbean? As Jamaican? Would she categorize herself as a "black"? As British? Or will she perhaps trace her origins further back to her African ancestry? Already we can see that she has a wealth of sources of identification open to her.' (Bradley 1996, pp. 23–4)

capable of analysing postmodern philosophy and culture in a very stimulating way. In this passage she draws on the possibilities of uncertainty:

> '"If I was your girlfriend"... so sings Prince on the hit single taken from his album *Sign of the Times*. Prince, precocious and perverse – the perfect Postmodern Man. Slithering between hetero and homosexuality, blackness and whiteness, masculinity and femininity. Simultaneously embodying a desire that in its urgency becomes disembodied, this song gives voice to an overwhelming want that pays no heed to sexual difference, until he reaches the place where men and women can really be best friends and no more. ... And it's only a song and Prince is only a pop star. And anyway he isn't my girlfriend. He isn't actually anyone's girlfriend. ... He wants to assert himself, his desire, his identity at the same time dissolving away the masculine identity that constricts him. ... Prince both recognizes the limitations of masculinity whilst clinging to them.' (Moore 1988, p.165, 166)

Our concern, then, is with a number of things. We are interested in researching, analysing and describing:

❖ the results of being in a particular *social* or *economic* classification, analysed in terms of the chances of access to the things in life usually regarded as good

❖ the *experience* and *identities* that people hold of themselves through that classification and the *social actions* they take as a result of it.

Throughout this chapter we are concerned with four types of classification and related stratifications, even though there are many more. We will focus on:

❖ class, occupation and identity

❖ gender, identity and differentiation

❖ ethnic position, identity and differentiation

❖ age differentiation.

We are also concerned with the way these four interact and the ways the patterns of interaction are changing in the modern world. To identify the direction and character of change, we have to look to the past from time to time, because the identities that most people have were formed in the past – often as a reaction to an even earlier past. However, our main concern is with the future.

The effects of stratification are evident in many different areas of society – e.g. work, education, culture. Other chapters in this book deal with these topics in some depth and we will cross-refer to specific pages throughout this chapter. Do read this additional material as it is highly relevant to the subject in hand.

Theories of class and stratification

This section concentrates on the position people hold in the economic structure and the way that is stratified into types of position that yield different economic rewards. This area of study is usually called 'class', although some emphasize the importance of property owning and some the different positions differing individuals have in a labour market. Both are aspects of class. The most influential thinker in this area over the last 150 years has been Karl Marx and he remains in that position, even though many of his predictions are discredited and many of the political ideas developed after his death are also discredited.

Karl Marx

The systematic study of social stratification and class has been dominated directly and indirectly by the writings of Karl Marx.

Marx's most influential ideas are discussed on pp. 175–7 and pp. 279–82. You are advised to read, or reread, these sections before continuing further.

In Focus

◆

Marx on the relations of production

'The general conclusion at which I arrived and which, once reached, continued to serve as the guiding thread in my studies, may be formulated as follows: In the social production which men carry on, they enter into definite relations that are indispensable and independent of their will; these relations of production correspond to a definite stage of development of the material powers of production. ... The mode of production of material life determines the general character of the social, political and spiritual processes of life. It is not the consciousness of men that determines their being, but, on the contrary, their social being determines their consciousness. At a certain stage of their development, the material forces of production in society come into conflict with the existing relations of production, or – what is but a legal expression for the same thing – with the property relations within which they had been at work before. From forms of development of the forces of production these relations turn into their fetters. Then occurs a period of social revolution. With the change of the economic foundation the immense super-structure is more or less rapidly transformed. In considering such transformations the distinction should always be made between the material transformation of the economic conditions of production which can be determined with the precision of natural science, and the legal, political, religious, aesthetic, or philosophical – in short ideological forms in which men become conscious of this conflict and fight it out. Just as one's opinion of an individual is not based on what he thinks of himself, so can we not judge of such a period of transformation by its own consciousness; on the contrary, this consciousness must rather be explained from the contradictions of material life, from the existing conflict between the social forces of production and the relations of production.'

Source: Marx (1859/1956, pp. 51–2)

The views of Marx were complex and subtle, and changed over time. Unfortunately he died before he completed his massive, four-volume work *Das Kapital* in which he tried to sum up and elaborate his ideas (Marx 1867/1970).

Marx recognized the complexities of beliefs and actions and also the complexity of the class structure which was never just two classes. In his early writing he recognized that precapitalist classes and relations existed and later on he could see the growth of the non-manual middle classes as a key change in capitalist society. Chapter 53 of the unfinished Volume 3 of *Das Kapital* is entitled 'The middle classes', but Engels (as the editor who published the work after Marx's death) closes the book with the words: 'The manuscript breaks off here.' We are left, tantalizingly, without any clear idea of whether Marx was changing his view about the progressive separation of the classes or not. Was collapse and revolution possible with a new middle class growing between the two main classes?

Karl Marx was also very aware, as a revolutionary, of the key problem or puzzle of why the workers did not always take action in their own interests. He stated the problem in his own way as: how and when does a class-in-itself become a class-*for*-itself? But he came to no clear conclusions. The working classes have, since Marx's time, only occasionally taken things into their own hands through revolutions. During his own lifetime Marx saw and experienced (at a distance) two revolutions that changed the structure of power in countries: but those revolutions failed to be socialist or communist revolutions that put the proletariat into power. These were the revolutions of 1848 in France, most German States and in Hungary, and the 1870 revolution in France. With the collapse of those few societies that said they were trying to achieve communism, the idea that the capitalist system would break down is now almost beyond belief. It would seem that the working class never quite became capable of, or interested in, acting as Marx thought they both might and should.

Chapter 7, *Theory and methods*, discusses Marx's ideas about the various ways in which the ideologies were oppressive on the lower classes in a society. When Western society seemed to be experiencing great ideological change in the 1960s and 1970s, sociologists returned to his earlier writings and looked at the structures of ideologies and how they worked.

In summary, we might say that the key questions that Marx addressed were: 'What is it about the way that people enter into in relations of production which determines that the relationships will always carry an inherent conflict or contradiction, and how is that conflict worked out?'

Max Weber

Weber accepts nearly all of Marx's views on class, but differs from Marx in a number of critical ways:

❖ Weber does not accept Marx's view of the inevitability of a simplification of the class system leading to breakdown and revolution. He thought that was quite rare and probably not to be encouraged. Weber's analytic framework led to increasing differentiation between classes rather than unification for class action.

❖ Weber saw the analysis and identification of what a class interest was at any one time as rather more problematical than Marx did. Weber emphasized that even within a class, there was little agreement as to how to act and the mechanisms for 'class action' had to be constructed, but this did not always happen. For Weber, failure to construct tools for class action showed how unclear the nature of class interest was.

❖ Weber more sharply differentiates three dimensions of power than did Marx. Weber separates *economic* power, *social*

status (or social honour as he tends to call it) and *political* power.

❖ Weber states that the relationships between the three dimensions of power are not just one-way, or all created by the economic relations of society. He assumes that any one dimension of power can influence or structure the others and that each may have aspects of its dynamic for change that are developing according to their own rules and patterns.

Weber's views on social inequalities are discussed more fully in Chapter 7, *Theory and methods* and you should read pp. 282–4 in conjunction with this section.

Although Weber accepted Marx's position on the importance of property ownership in the class formations, he also placed very much more emphasis on the 'background', status or origins of the individual:

❖ How was an individual regarded by others?

❖ What status or honour did others accord the individual?

❖ How did individuals see themselves?

In much everyday life, both in the workplace and especially away from it, the relationships that individuals have with each other are influenced by their status in respect of each other. With whom would they meet? With whom would they talk? Whom would they invite to their home? Whom would they be pleased to see their children marry? Or with whom would they have a drink in a bar or hotel? Or, indeed, in which bar?

Social status

Some of the last questions given above are not the sort of questions that Weber would have asked in his own society. We must remember that the kind of society he experienced was not the same as ours. He talked of 'social honour' whereas we would talk of 'social status': but the concepts are almost identical or very similar. Certainly we can use his ideas without difficulty. When discussions of class (or more frequently class-lessness) take place in ordinary life, we are

In Focus

◆

Weber on 'class situation'

'In our terminology, "classes" are not communities; they merely represent possible and frequent bases for communal action. We may speak of a "class" when (1) a number of people have in common a specific causal component of their life chances, in so far as (2) this component is represented exclusively by economic interests in the possession of goods and opportunities for income, and (3) is represented under the conditions of the commodity or labour markets. (These points refer to "class situation", which we may express more briefly as the typical chance for a supply of goods, external living conditions, and personal life experiences, in so far as this chance is determined by the amount and kind of power, or lack of such, to dispose of goods or skills for the sake of income in a given economic order. The term "class" refers to any group of people that is found in the same class situation.)' (Weber 1948, p. 181)

'"Property" and "lack of property" are ... the basic categories of all situations. It does not matter whether these two categories become effective in price wars or in competitive struggles.

Within these categories however, class situations are further differentiated: on the one hand, according to the kind of property that is usable for returns; and, on the other hand, according to the kinds of services that can be offered in the labour market.' (Weber 1948, p. 182)

often talking about 'social status' rather than 'class' as Marx and Weber defined it (see *In Focus* above). Society, and the individuals that comprise it, has become more and more assertive about the equality of individuals in terms of social honour or respect given in an ever wider range of situations. Weber himself was aware of great variations in tradition. He pointed out the differences between a more relaxed, more equal America and a more formal Germany (see *In Focus* below), but he never forgot that all societies have significant social distinctions.

As we turn from the twentieth to the twenty-first century, people are much less ready to 'defer', to give way voluntarily or respect the traditional social status of others. The claim to classlessness is often a claim by an individual rather than a reality.

❖ Activity 3 ❖

It is easy to think of situations in which individuals are awarded different social status and are listened to differently. Imagine a parents' meeting at a school.

• Are all parents listened to equally, irrespective of the status associated with their accent, their education or their occupation?

• What other factors might influence the way individual parents are listened to?

• Can you imagine individuals being moved to assert that they should be listened to, even though they 'ain't speaking proper'?

In Focus

◆

American 'gentlemen'

'The equality of status among the American "gentlemen", for instance, is expressed by the fact that outside the subordination determined by the different functions of business, it would be strictly repugnant if even the richest "chief", while playing billiards or cards in the evening would not treat his clerk as in every sense fully equal to his birthright. It would be repugnant if the American chief would bestow the condescending benevolence ... which the German chief can never dissever from his attitude.' (Weber 1948, p. 187)

Max Weber has said that social status groups are communities (see *In Focus* below). He says that when people speak and discuss freely with each other, and mingle in all social situations as equal, then they are a true community. They can, however, be separated from others by social distance.

When we apply some of these ideas in a broad fashion, we can see that there are many bases for status groups. Women are usually held in most societies as being of lower status than men. In more contemporary society, women, quite properly, object to this. Blacks are often held in lower status than whites in Europe, the young are of lower status than more mature people, and the elderly may have a very ambiguous status. We will look at some of these bases of differentiations later in the chapter. Crucial for Weber are the self-perceptions that people have and we must look at these in everyday life (see Activity 4).

In the arena of political power, Max Weber's ideas were less fully worked out and we are faced, as with Marx, with a

❖ Activity 4 ❖

Discuss, if possible with other sociology students, the key social status differences that you encounter in everyday life.

- Who, for you, has a lower status? When do you feel disrespected?
- When is that disrespect appropriate and when not?
- What kind of people in political power would you respect or not feel respect for?

crucial posthumous text where the editor says, 'The text breaks off here'. Nevertheless, it is clear that Weber saw political parties as the key instruments in the expression of political power. He further saw that parties could have many bases: they could be class parties or status group parties or indeed have other bases altogether. For Weber, parties did not

---

In Focus

Weber on status groups

'In contrast to classes, status groups are normally communities. They are however, often of an amorphous kind. In contrast to the purely determined "class situation", we wish to designate as "status situation" every typical component of the life-fate of men that is determined by a specific, positive or negative, social estimation of honour. This honour may be connected with any quality shared by a plurality, and, of course, it can be knit to a class situation: class distinctions are linked in the most varied ways with status distinctions. Property as such is not always recognized as a status qualification, but in the long run it is, and with extraordinary regularity.' (Weber 1948, pp. 186–7)

'In content, status honour is normally expressed by the fact that above all else a specific style of life can be expected from all those who wish to belong to the circle.

Linked with this expectation are restrictions on "social" intercourse (that is, intercourse which is not subservient to economic or any other "functional" purposes). These restrictions may confine normal marriages to within the status circle and may lead to complete endogamous closure. As soon as there is not a mere individual and socially irrelevant imitation of another style of life, but an agreed-upon communal action of this closing character, the "status" development is under way.' (Weber 1948, pp. 187–8)

'With some over-simplification, one might thus say that "classes" are stratified according to their relations to the production and acquisition of goods; whereas "status groups" are stratified according to the principles of their consumption of goods as represented by special "styles of life".' (Weber 1948, p. 193)

always fall out on neat class lines but needed detailed explanation and description.

Max Weber was an academic sociologist who was particularly interested in methodology, and his work on class and social differentiation reflects this. He was also very influenced by, and concerned with, the need for historical analysis and description. A central part of his methodology was analysing data and creating 'ideal types': that is, identifying *typical actors* and the ideas that drove them in ordinary social action. For Max Weber, the key question was always: 'What is a typical actor, and how would they act?' This often led to a very individuated approach to social action, since Weber was always analysing the data and finding more ideal types. Although Weber himself rarely used the word or concept of 'identity', his concept of the social actor is very close to that of identity, for identity has little meaning except in terms of the basis for individualized social action

This tradition has continued in modern sociology and has led to the idea of a fragmentary class structure and of fragmented identities in modern society.

Functional attitudes and approaches to class

Marx and Weber were both concerned with rapidly changing societies and societies in conflict, although the one wished to encourage rapid change and the other to seek forms of stability. In the USA in the middle of the twentieth century, the world seemed very different. There were class struggles in the USA from the 1900s through to the 1930s. Some people could still identify them after 1940, but an overwhelming majority within the country seemed to experience an immensely successful, politically and socially stable society. It was a differentiated society and one in which many groups achieved differing rewards. But it became dominated by optimism, and the feeling of an ever-expanding economy and one in which most people were becoming better off.

Some American sociologists felt that the Marxist-dominated debates on stratification, with their conflict orientation, were rather inappropriate or out of place in the kind of society that was developing in America. They tried to ask more basic questions. Central to the debates were two ideas:

❖ All known societies seemed to have some social differentiation and stratification system.

❖ It therefore seemed likely that social stratification served some overall function or purpose in making societies work.

Their key question became: how does this stratification make society *function better*?

Classic functionalism

Talcott Parsons was a sociologist and thinker whose works on sociological theory gradually came to dominate American sociology from the 1940s to the 1960s. Parsons emphasized Weber's notion of the social actor, the 'individual and his action' frame of reference. Parsons (1951, 1969) emphasized that the actor was socialized into placing values on certain types of activity in broad consensus with the rest of the population. In societies with a division of labour (i.e. all of them), that differential valuation, Parsons argued, led to a differential reward. Put another way, it is impossible to conceive of a system of values that does not also lead to social stratification. But more than that, the general value structure of the society not only creates differentiation in its valuation of differing social positions but is the *justification* for the differential reward. Parsons knew that there were many people who disagreed with the extent of differential reward, particularly those who had failed in a competitive system to achieve the better rewarded positions. He dismissed such attitudes using phrases such as 'sour grapes' but recognized that this tendency had to be kept in check.

Without the rewards, Parsons also implied, the varying positions may not be adequately fulfilled for the effective functioning of a society. This particular aspect of stratification was emphasized by Kingsley Davis and Wilbert E. Moore in an essay published in 1945. They comment that once functional differentiation exists, then, logically, there will be differential functional importance. More importantly, however, there is a differential scarcity of personnel capable of fulfilling the requirements of these positions. It is the interaction of these two features which determines the reward.

Davis and Moore's essay assumes that societies will move towards an effective and efficient functioning in attempts to ensure the survival of the society. All positions must be filled – and filled by trained, competent people who work hard and conscientiously. In order to achieve this effective functioning, there will be some positions that have to be very well rewarded to motivate people to undergo long training and to continue with the necessary diligence and effort. Other aspects of Parsons's work and functionalism are described in Chapter 7, *Theory and methods* (see pp. 285–6). Davis's, Moore's and Parsons's views may seem very sound at first, but they have been attacked in various ways.

Anti-functionalism

Melvin Tumin in 1953 published a strong criticism which looked at the logic and empirical work necessary to justify what was being claimed. He made several points:

❖ There was no way of measuring the importance of a social position other than the fact that rewards accrued to it.

❖ The model assumed a scarcity of talent that could be used or trained, while there was evidence that very little human talent was developed in most societies (as, one might add, has been demonstrated many times over by the increase in the proportion of graduates in all industrial societies since Tumin wrote).

❖ Far from being a 'sacrifice', most training was rather more pleasant than the alternatives and, in general, people had to be excluded from training and education rather than encouraged by later rewards.

❖ The more rigidly a society is stratified, the less a society finds out about the talents of those whose parents are in lowly positions: the whole edifice becomes a self-fulfilling prophecy and a rather inefficient one.

For these main reasons, and some other minor ones, Melvin Tumin was led to reject the whole functional approach to social stratification and differentiation as a rather closed system in which those who achieve the rewards create a justification for their rewards. It certainly looks like a justification for why university graduates tend to get more reward than those who do not attend college! Tumin might also have added that a great deal of reward is merely inherited and that, while it is true that families only maintain a high social position by the creation of hard-working talent, it is surprising how many indolent incompetents an established family can acquire and yet still maintain a good position for some time.

Contemporary relevance of functionalism

Is the functionalist theory still relevant? Well, people still wish to describe the social system and either criticize the outcomes (as Marx did) or justify them (as Davis and Moore did). A contemporary author and commentator in England who moves towards the justification of differential reward is Peter Saunders (1990). Saunders accepts that there can be societies that are not competitive or capitalist, but believes that state socialist societies are inefficient and collapsing. They were, at his time of writing, all being severely shaken and/or destroyed. Only a capitalist system with competition for rewards would survive, Saunders asserts, since only such a society would grow economically. Addressing the issue of equality he distinguishes three types of equality:

❖ equality of citizens *before the law*

❖ equality of *opportunity*

❖ equality of *reward*.

Saunders then goes on to discuss the last and concludes that if there is equality of outcome, then there will be no training for rare or rewarded skills and no endeavour to work hard and hold on to such positions. The weakness of this argument is that it effectively narrows the rewards to financial and economic ones, a subject to which we will return.

Saunders does tend to assume that the notion of equality before the law now exists in all societies, but seems unaware that this is something still to be achieved in detail. The Declaration of Independence and the Constitution of the United States both sought to establish equality before the law; most of the men involved in drafting it thought they had achieved it, but only because they ignored the position of women and slaves. Saunders seems rather negligent on this point, although he does concede that the principle is 'not always as rigorously applied as it might be'. Everything turns for Saunders on whether equality of opportunity exists: if it does, then society is fair, just and will function well. Although the application of the concept of equality of opportunity is not always as rigorous as it might be (and he is aware of that), Saunders is content to let his analysis stand.

Life-chances, rewards and self-images

So far in this section we have looked at the concepts of differential reward and what is seen within one society as desirable. Social differentiation seems always associated with a structure of stratification, whereby there are groups of people (or families) who come into broad classes or groups and who are rewarded differently according to those groups. The most commonly used phrase in general sociological discussion is one derived from Weber, that of *life-chances*. This concept does not refer to one specific reward, but the rewards one might expect over a lifetime (and even beyond, perhaps, to rewards that might accrue to children). What are these rewards? We have mentioned in an earlier section that these could include health and long life. We have discussed income and wealth. What we have not done is to look at the range of what may become available. Tumin (1953), briefly says that the rewards may include:

❖ sustenance and comfort

❖ humour and diversion

❖ self-respect and ego expansion.

By diversion and humour we might understand opportunities for holidays (or paid holidays), free tickets to the theatre or the horse-races, and such like. Tumin is right to include self-respect which is the mirror image of social honour: if others respect you, then you are more likely to respect yourself – and standing in the middle of that is identity. We all have images of ourselves that we more or less like, or more or less dislike. In part, these images are dependent on how others regard us and treat us. These self-images are also the basis of both our more *personal* actions and pleasures, and our more *social* actions and pleasures. The acquisition of our self-images from our interactions in the structure of society has profound effects on us.

❖ Activity 5 ❖

- List all the things that might be included in the term 'life- chances' (deriving from a social position).

- How do they affect the self-images of the participants?

- What are the key social positions that have structured what you value?

Empirical investigations and contemporary critique

There is a vast range of writings on social differentiation, class and social stratification. Many writers have long-term historical perspectives covering a millenium or more, while others are concerned to compare all societies. Many authors, however, only want to look at shorter-term changes. They are interested in what might happen in the next ten years or so, and seek the answers by looking at the past thirty years and projecting it forward. Even those with longer-term perspectives want to ask what is really happening *now* and seek the answers in empirical study that is always rooted in a 'present' for the actors (even if that 'present' has now become history for us). However, whatever we know *empirically* must be rooted in the past, even if we choose to regard it as such a recent past that it can stand as the present.

John Goldthorpe is one sociologist who has been concerned with studying changes in class, particularly in Europe, over the period 1945 until the present (and, by implication, future). He has been active in his empirical work since 1960 and has been influenced by many sociologists, especially Norbert Elias and David Lockwood with whom he has organized many empirical studies.

David Lockwood, in one of his first studies, *The Black-coated Worker* (1958), made distinctions between class situations, work situations and status situations. These distinctions are an addition to those made by Weber, but allow for social status, other influences on workers and their influence on attitude formation. Looking at clerical workers in the City of London, Lockwood noted that their class position did not distinguish them, in terms of income, very sharply from skilled manual workers. But their work situation created differing social status, differing socializing influences and differing self-images. This kind of intellectual position influences the rest of the thinking of Goldthorpe and Lockwood.

Goldthorpe has been searching for ways of mapping the changes in the occupational structures in the recent past, and with that, the changing patterns of mobility. We will refer to the mobility issues in another subsection in more detail (see pp. 254–8), but a key issue here is how people perceive themselves – indeed, whether they perceive themselves in neat, firm-edged groups at all.

Three key questions for research

Three key questions about recent changes that have political implications are asked by Goldthorpe *et al.* (1968, 1969):

1 Do the members of the manual working class see themselves as a fairly distinct group with their own class interests and orientations?

2 How can we (or how do they themselves) group the subsets of non-manual workers together so that we can say useful things about them?

3 How do movements in the occupational structure affect how people see themselves if they, as individuals, move from one group to another during their lifetime?

To consider the first question, it is worth reading some of the original works. They are published mainly under the title of *The Affluent Worker*, are interesting in themselves and also provide excellent examples of discussions of empirical research methodology.

The third question is dealt with later in this chapter, but we will look at the second question here. Goldthorpe and colleagues have made three attempts at creating a basic class system, each time modifying their position. The Registrar General used a five-class system, but this is now thought to be inadequate since it merges routine non-manual workers with skilled manual workers: a division that Goldthorpe feels is clear. For the issues under question, the idea of a ruling class represents too small a body to be researched by these techniques and so is excluded from the issues. Goldthorpe *et al.* finally focus mainly on their seven-point scale (shown in Table 6.7, p. 256).

Goldthorpe's classes still merge groups with separate educational (or 'credential') positions, separate property distinctions and separate supervision relationships. However, this is problematic both from class and status points of view and the issue varies from country to country. So Goldthorpe *et al.* modified their view for transnational studies to a different seven-class system.

Still later, Goldthorpe modified his position to an eleven-class scale that can be simplified into three broad categories. He wanted to be able to answer questions such as: how can one compare the class and status positions of small-property ownership (where, for example, someone with no credentials beyond a driving licence may own three lorries and employ two drivers) with the possession of university degrees and professional qualifications in social work (e.g. by someone who, despite these credentials, is unable, by law, to be 'self-employed' as a social worker)? Goldthorpe tried to tackle this problem by looking at the job titles his interviewees reported having and the kind of supervision they received (or the organizations they worked in). These problems of relationships are what Goldthorpe tries to tackle in his varying and developing positions. However, while giving reasons for the changes in his class systems, the reasons are poorly related to empirical data and close interviewing. Goldthorpe's views are becoming increasingly separate from the point of 'experienced identity' as discovered in interviews, and more and more concerned with his own broad-survey, data-handling problems.

Contemporary critique of Goldthorpe

Marshall *et al.* (1988) have conducted questionnaire research, directly asking respondents about political work, status and class attitudes. Although they used to analyse their data along the lines of the seven-class system of Goldthorpe, when it came to class attitudes, they found that the simple division of working class/middle class was easily used (and accepted) by people, despite the different superficial aspects of their work situation (for example, in an office, in retail, or with non-manual duties). Class identity, and the notions of class conflict are still very much more important than the later works of Goldthorpe might indicate.

To sum up, the theories viewed in this section are very much orientated towards class, class conflicts and class relationships, seen both as the main source of changing, personal class-identities and as a source of the dynamics of change in an industrial society. The theories recognize the relationship between economic and status experiences, the creation of identities and the ways in which both of these can get translated into predictable social outcomes and behaviours.

Gender differentiation and social stratification

Gender, sex and biology

The social differentiation that most of us become aware of earliest in our life is that of gender. By the time we reach the age of three, nearly all of us have a clear gender identity as boy or girl, even if, as some do, we continue to reject or object to that identity, or explore what it might be like to have a different gender identity. Chapter 2, *Culture and identity*, pp. 23–6, discusses the biological and social implications of sex, gender and cultural expectations.

Gender and class: which is the more significant?

So far in this chapter, we have looked at the classic, or traditional, positions in broad sociological theory, which assume

Table 6.1 Life tables, United Kingdom, based on 1991–93 experience

Age(x)	Males		Females	
	A	B	A	B
0 years	100 000	73.4	100 000	78.9
5 years	99 102	69.1	99 294	74.4
10 years	99 011	64.2	99 224	69.5
15 years	98 905	59.2	99 150	64.5
20 years	98 589	54.4	99 011	59.6
25 years	98 163	49.6	98 851	54.7
30 years	97 739	44.8	98 666	49.8
35 years	97 248	40.0	98 404	44.9
40 years	96 568	35.3	98 000	40.1
45 years	95 578	30.6	97 350	35.4
50 years	93 978	26.1	96 283	30.7
55 years	91 228	21.8	94 539	26.2
60 years	86 708	17.8	91 737	22.0
65 years	79 292	14.2	87 090	18.0
70 years	68 020	11.2	79 874	14.4
75 years	53 182	8.6	69 420	11.1
80 years	36 009	6.4	55 150	8.3
85 years	19 576	4.8	37 476	6.1

A = for each 100 000 born, the number expected to survive till age shown
B = average expected life in years at age shown

Source: Annual Abstract of Statistics 1996, p. 49. CSO/HMSO

that what matters is class and occupation and, above all, the position of families. They also assume that families and all individuals, particularly the old, women and children, take their class position from the head of the household, usually a male. There are still great elements of truth in this, but people are very aware now of differences within the family and between family members. Previously, these differences, such as gender differentiation, were often perceived as 'natural', probably biologically based, and not of great interest to sociology. Structured differentiation in terms of life-chances and rewards, what we call stratification, has, on the other hand, been seen as the core matter for sociology. But, how can we say what is biological, what is unimportant differentiation and what is a socially structured life-chance? Look at Table 6.1.

There are undoubtedly genetic or biological differences between men and women. Table 6.1 shows that at all ages, women are less likely to die than men, and are in that sense the healthier or stronger group. It seems initially likely that at least part of the differences shown here are biological. But how can we measure the extent of the effects of the relatively high level of separation women have from the stresses and dangers of certain types of employment? Why is that women, usually associated with a displacement from power and good life-chances, seem to be at an advantage in this respect? Is it all biological? How can it be studied sociologically?

Sociobiologists such as Wilson (1975) and Barash (1979) have taken the Darwinian evolutionary theory further than the evolution of physical types and shapes and have included the idea of evolution of *specific behaviours* – or at least a biological predisposition towards such behaviours. We do not pursue these ideas here, but only note that they exist. It is also interesting that sociobiologists, as Bleier (1984) points out, pay little attention to the huge variations amongst human societies: for example, not all cultures have 'coy' women and 'aggressive' men in sexual relationships, and Bleier names six cultures where the opposite is true. Whatever the idea of predisposition, it still needs cultural supports and mechanisms to implement it. Sociological analysis should be based on these culturally specific formations.

Gender studies and feminism

In the last three decades, there have been many studies of the differential access of men and women to power or to the good things in life, to their relative *life-chances*. Gender studies have been led by women's studies and by the particular part of the women's liberation movement that started in the mid or late 1960s (in contrast to those women's or feminist movements which started earlier).

One such movement began in the mid-nineteenth century and included many men. The goals were the achievement of social and political equality before the law in marriage and divorce rights, in property ownership and in inheritance rights. There was a steady achievement of or movement towards these goals throughout the nineteenth century. At the turn of the

century, the movement became more firmly dominated by women with the express target of achieving equal rights in the political arenas and, in particular, 'votes for women'. Once this was achieved, that particular women's movement faded away. It soon became clear that nominal political equality did not achieve a real social equality. However, a new women's movement did not start until the late 1960s, following the great success of the 'civil rights' movement amongst black Americans. That movement used a variety of non-violent and publicising means and proved a great inspiration for women to achieve their 'equal or civil rights'. It is interesting to note that the civil rights movement had extensive support from whites and made great use of that. Generally, the feminist movements of the twentieth century have not had the same sort of participation by men.

In general, the women's movement was not inspired by sociology nor did it address the world in a specifically sociological way. It contained women from a variety of political and intellectual perspectives. It has become conventional to classify the various writers and thinkers into three broad strands, or types, of feminism as it existed in the 1970s: liberal, Marxist and radical. Any such classification has to take into account the fact the distinctions are rarely clear since individual writers tend to draw on more than one perspective and develop their ideas as they work. Stacey, commenting on this description, says that the categorization 'obscures more than it reveals' (1992, p. 53).

Liberal, Marxist, and radical feminism

Central to most feminist projects are three inter-related prime activities or targets:

❖ to challenge the validity of widespread images held of women by men, and by doing this to transform the self-perceptions that women hold of themselves

❖ to discover the nature of power relationships between men and women, and to challenge and change those relationships

❖ to make the outcomes of social processes more equal between men and women in terms of the achievement of the benefits which arise from participation in society.

Liberal feminism

'Liberalism' in general may be described as starting mainly in the eighteenth century, although there are earlier roots. The political aim of liberalism was to make 'all men equal before the law' and equal in social institutions. Only quite late was it recognized that slavery and the subjugation of specific ethnic groups or of women were incompatible with liberalism. There was space for much work on equal rights for women within the frameworks of the law. *Liberal feminism* was based on the ideals of the equality of opportunity and equality of individual rights in all institutional and legal requirements. Its targets were to make unequal treatment or discrimination illegal, but above all, it was based on notions of free choice. In itself it did very little to challenge or reconstruct the gendered, cultural assumptions that underlie so many traditional cultural arrangements. Although derided by many feminists who went further in their thinking, liberal feminism should not be underestimated in its achievements.

Marxist feminism

Perhaps the most influential text in the Marxist feminist movement is that by Barrett (1980) which is summed up quite well in its title: *Women's Oppression Today: Problems of Marxist Feminist Analysis*. The orientation was to place women more clearly in the system of capitalist production and social reproduction using the generalized notions of oppression, exploitation and power. Women's role in the household was seen very much in terms of:

❖ supporting a male workforce that could work long hours

❖ providing the replacements for that workforce and preferably new recruits socialized into docility

❖ forming a reserve army of labour to help keep the wages as low as possible in order to generate great surplus values.

(Chapter 5, pp. 189–93, discusses more fully the relationships between women and work.)

Marxist feminism was essentially faced with a dilemma: should feminism try to explain the power relationships between men and women as a subset of the broader capitalist power relationships (a *single-system* model), or should it construct a separate and special theory of the power relationships of patriarchy (a *dual-system* model)?

In general, the earlier the writing, the more likely it is to adopt a single-system approach. Single-system Marxist feminists do tend to lose sight of anything specifically about women, as their concerns with overall dominance and exploitations take over. Other feminists, such as Hartman (1981), have tried to develop an account of domination of women by men through history as a system of hierarchy which is separate from, but interacting with, capitalism – a clear example of a *dual-systems approach*.

Radical feminism

Radical feminism could be described as the strand that takes patriarchy as its base. 'Patriarchy' literally means rule by *fathers*, rather than rule by men. The term was used by Max Weber to refer to types of organizational structures that were analogous to family organization in which women and young men were subjected to an authority from older males. The use feminists make of the term is more generalized: it refers to any form of male dominance in any type of relationship. Kate Millett (1971) and Shulasmith Firestone (1971) have made radical contributions and stand as two authors that illustrate this strand of feminism well. Kate Millett has suggested that all relationships between men and women are political and that men have tended to dominate by seizing control of the ideology and the production of ideas and ideology. Firestone has emphasized the relative weakness and dependency of women while bearing children. She has gone on to emphasize the ways in which men have ruthlessly applied their capacity for physical violence and rape to support their position of dominance. Taken together, these ideas seemed shocking to many: but they were meant to shock. Radical feminism insisted that there were common experiences that all women endured which were the basis of a distinct culture, sexuality and subjectivity. This strand of feminism tended to minimize the differences that arise between women because of class, ethnicity or age, and assume a communality of interests. Many men were disturbed at an apparent presentation of the whole male sex as an oppressing group, but the idea did lead to the growth of strong and effective women's organizations, e.g. battered women's refuges, women's bookshops, drama groups – all of which have had a distinctive impact on the politics and culture of their time.

Recent theorizing about women

Theorization of patriarchy

The early attempts at constructing a theory of patriarchal domination produced great excitement in the intellectual world surrounding feminism. The overall concerns of those who were disturbed by radical feminism were that sweeping generalizations were being made about all societies and cultures. Sylvia Walby (1990), while largely accepting the overall view, did offer an analysis of six main cultural areas for discussion:

❖ paid work

❖ domestic labour

❖ sexuality

❖ the state

❖ violence

❖ general cultural values and systems.

The whole drift of this type of thinking is not to see patriarchy as a single all-encompassing notion of domination in all aspects of life, but to specify with some precision how a set of power configurations in one dimension can act as a model for others. That works in two ways, of course, and opens up more clearly the possibility of change. But feminists theorists have been reluctant to abandon the notion of patriarchy altogether, since it is the main distinctive concept that feminists share. Instead, there have been attempts to modify it, and talk of patriarchal practice, ideology and discourse – and to relate these to postmodernist thought.

Feminism and postmodernism

Postmodernist thought has become very attractive because it allows for multiple sources of identity and includes the notion of discourse. Discourse is defined by Stuart Hall (1992c) as 'a group of statements which provide a language for talking about – i.e. a way of representing – a particular type of knowledge about a topic'. In general, however, the main postmodernist theorists have themselves been mainly men and have, like all liberals and most thinkers since the enlightenment, been rather gender-blind, assuming that their (male) experience was the norm – or even universal. This creates a rather odd relationship of theory:

❖ Postmodernism tends towards an individuation of personality formation and a minimization of power relationships (by stressing acceptance of the situation and images on offer from the powerful). (See Chapter 13, *Power and politics*, on the recreation of postmodern identities.)

❖ Feminism, on the other hand, usually emphasizes the power of men over women (and the limited choice available) and the communality of women's experience. Gendered identity, role-playing and gender ambiguity, together with the complexities of masculinities and femininities (especially dominant forms of masculinity) are discussed in Chapter 2, *Culture and identity*, pp. 27–8.

Interactions of gender and class

Class is always a term that brings with it a sense of hierarchy: the classes are ranked one above the other. Patriarchy is also a hierarchy, but only a two-layer system. We must now ask how the gendered identities interact in the occupational system. At the simplest of levels, we know that young men and women move through the educational system and into the occupational system in different ways. This is dealt with more fully in Chapter 4, *Education and training*.

It is clear that different jobs give different opportunities for young women to develop their feminine identities. The structure of images and expectations of others that an individual meets structures the thinking of that individual. Of course, no individual is wholly formed and determined by this process, but it may largely be so formed.

No individual can 'claim' a job – they have to apply and compete for it. The imagery and opinions of the job-givers, as relatively powerful people, are important. Take two simple examples: a young woman of 16 who wants to train as a plumber and a young man of 16 who wants to train as a secretary. Training is expensive and so those giving it will want to be sure that these career ambitions are fairly permanent and not a temporary idea. This may not be a matter of simple prejudice or stereotyping by the training awarders. They may feel that a young person crossing such gender stereotyping situations may need rather more personal determination than one working *within* gender stereotypes. This is in itself a form of institutionalized prejudice, but one that is hard to detect and hard to work against.

The result of the existing structure of the self-images of job and training applicants and those of the job and training awarders is that men and women fill different positions in the occupational structure. (See Figs 5.4 and 5.5 on p. 190 for employment tables by gender in industry and occupation.)

The outcome of this is that when women's occupations are mapped against a class-ranking system developed primarily for men, the class structure may look very 'skewed' (see Fig. 6.2). That raises the questions: 'Is the chart for men skewed?' or 'Is it that men and women exist in different but related class structures?'.

These photographs show women working out of the usual gender stereotypes, but in positions which allow them different opportunities to express their femininity in conventional ways.

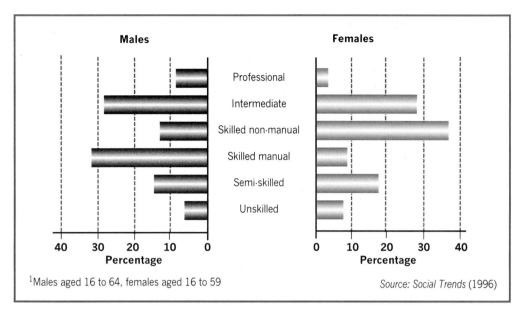

Figure 6.2
Population[1]: by
social class, Spring
1995

[1]Males aged 16 to 64, females aged 16 to 59

Source: Social Trends (1996)

Despite thirty years of very active feminism and the seeking of equality in education and at work, the situation is clear: women are still taking less-well-paid employment than men and are centred in a fairly narrow range of trades and activities – those traditionally associated with women (and perhaps traditional definitions of femininity). In the educational system there have been significant changes. Whereas in 1970 females achieved fewer qualifications than males at GCE A Level or its equivalent, they now achieve more. This change in entry behaviours and enthusiasm has not yet filtered through to occupational success.

The term 'success' implies two things: a hierarchy of reward and a desire to enter such a competition. There remains a possibility that women have not been wholly enthusiastic about entering the competitive parts of the labour market. To achieve high salaries, most people must seek a series of jobs within a hierarchy in which performance in each job relies on skills and experience developed in an earlier job. These careers usually pay rather better than a series of jobs that are not seen as being in a hierarchy. Women may prefer to work part-time or not seek careers in other ways. It is always difficult to interrupt careers and maintain the salary momentum. Taking a career-break often means starting again.

Chapter 5 discusses more fully the various theories concerning women's unequal work opportunities and the role of gender in the labour market (see pp. 189–93 and 201–2).

To answer key questions about the gender dimension within stratification systems, it is necessary to look at many sources of evidence. We need to consider the interaction of gender, ethnic identity, age, and occupation as being key dimensions in:

❖ identity formation

❖ the ways that identity opens or closes opportunities for work

❖ the ways that the expression of that identity influences other powerful decision-makers, e.g. in employment and promotion opportunities, because of existing images, stereotypes and prejudices.

❖ what the observable and measurable outcomes are.

Gender does seem to operate, in general, in slightly different ways than occupation or class. The differences in access to life-chances between men and women cannot be simply reduced to occupying different occupational positions: that difference is to a large extent what gender differentiation is about.

Ethnic background and social stratification

The issues and experiences of ethnic minority identity are complex and related to issues of economic power and cultural dominance. This is discussed more fully in Chapter 2, *Culture and identity*. As we have already seen, *power* is what creates stratification. Within a country such as the UK, we would expect to find that the various ethnic groups would have different 'life-chances' arising from their differing positions of power. Before we pursue any further discussion of this, we will need to remind ourselves of the meaning of certain key terms.

Race, ethnicity and nationality

Race

One of the commonest terms applied in issues such as those we wish to discuss is the concept of 'race'. Biologically, there is only one human race, but there are many different racial types (differentiated through skin colour, facial characteristics, etc.). Refer to Chapter 2, p. 41, for a historical analysis of how interpretations of the concept of race and racial types have become inextricably linked with racial theories and racism, i.e. notions of racial superiority and inferiority, and variations in abilities and behaviours that, in fact, have complex relationships to social factors.

Ethnicity

In contrast to 'race', ethnicity is a concept that refers to learned cultural behaviours and cultural identities that are acquired. A useful definition that the Commission for Racial Equality accepts is as follows:

> 'An ethnic minority is one whose members see themselves as sharing certain cultural characteristics, such as a common language, religion, family or social values which distinguish themselves from the majority of the population. Greek-Cypriots, Germans, Irish, Polish and Italian communities in Britain are as much ethnic minorities as Jamaicans, Pakistanis, Bangladeshis, Somalis or Nigerians.' (Frow 1996, p. 2)

One thing this definition does is to remind us of is the enormous cultural and ethnic variation within the UK at the moment. But to some extent this definition is also problematic, because it does not deal with the questions of how ethnic identity is experienced or maintained, and how it interacts with racial definitions and identities. (See Chapter 2, pp. 39–43, for discussion of ethnicity and new racism.)

The definition of ethnicity by self-awareness and assertion of cultural affinity creates many research problems, because we must first identify the self-identification of those researched. Chapter 2, p. 44, discusses the construction of ethnic identity through, for instance, the wearing of traditional clothing.

Nationality and citizenship

Nationality is a more problematic concept than it first seems. It includes ideas of national identity and nationalism, which are explored in Chapter 2, pp. 43–4. We must not confuse nationality with citizenship. Citizenship, unlike nationality, is a legal concept connected with a state and its members and says little about race, ethnic origin or nationality. Some multi-national states have tried to specify for their individual members a nationality.

Many Middle and East European states, following the traditions of the Austro-Hungarian Empire, have issued identity documents giving, in addition to a citizenship, a nationality (such as Czech, Slovak, German, Hungarian, Roman [i.e. Gypsy], etc.). Such attempts at identification prove very fragile and as likely to create rejections as acceptances within a multi-national state. For example, when the Czech Republic split from Slovakia, the

People express their identity through their clothing. The expression of an ethnic identity often takes on a particular importance in attendance at religious ceremonies (such as attendance at Friday Prayers at the mosque), at family ceremonies of all kinds (such as the Chinese wedding ceremony shown) or on particular days of importance to an ethnic group (such as the Scottish Highland Games).

question immediately arose 'do the Slovaks and Romans, living (and perhaps born) in the Czech Republic have automatic rights of citizenship to the Czech Republic?' The answer was no. Still other states, such as Germany and Israel, recognize 'national members' currently living elsewhere with other citizenship and offer a 'right to return'. In the case of Israel, this right is offered to all Jews not born in Israel but not to Palestinians who were born in the territory now called Israel.

Researching these issues in the UK

The United Kingdom does not specify nationality, race or ethnic group on its passports. Nor (at the time of writing) does it issue or require documents such as identity cards. Nor do the traditions in the UK much conform to the idea of ascribing an official nationality, ethnic group or race to someone inside its territory (although it does issue passports to some that do not 'have a right of residence'). These dimensions of identity are not part of the routine mechanisms of administration and data handling in the UK. This conforms to traditional libertarian ideals: yet it leads to all sorts of basic uncertainties about what the situation is in the UK. There is a demand for data on ethnic minorities (or race, as some persist in saying) to direct or guide social policy, but a reluctance to ascribe race or ethnic identity. Thus, in the major surveys carried out by government departments or agencies, a tradition has grown up of asking individuals to self-identify their 'ethnic origin'. However, if individuals do not respond, they tend to be allocated to 'white-European' or 'white-UK' for the purposes of data analysis. For this reason, all UK data on ethnic or racial minorities are inaccurate and tend to understate the size of the ethnic minority groups.

In the major 1991 census, individuals were asked to tick one of nine boxes describing their 'ethnic origin' or to describe themselves in words. A very large number of people used more than one box and/or wrote extra descriptions on their census form. In coding this data, some 35 categories were used but for most purposes of data analysis, these are collapsed to ten categories. This is core census data against which all other data from other surveys can be compared. Other major surveys use either the same ten categories, a further collapse to five or a selection relevant to the purpose in hand. Two major error sources are identified:

❖ For all ethnic groups, the Census process tends to undercount (or 'miss') young adults, those resident on their own and those in inner cities. With ethnic minority groups, however, the under-count is greater.

❖ It has become clear from subsequent and other studies that the three categories of 'Black-Caribbean', 'Black-African' and 'Other black' are not wholly acceptable to the current population that might, by others, be labelled 'black'. In particular, those that see themselves of mixed parentage tend to reject any simple label of black, and many people that see themselves as black, but born in Britain, will not call themselves Caribbean or African (preferring 'Black-British' as a self-descriptor).

The outcome in the census was two-fold: an expansion of 'Other black' beyond the original intentions of the survey designers and an underestimate of how many 'blacks' there might be. At the time of writing this book, the Office of National Statistics is undertaking pilot studies to see if new or other combinations of self-descriptions or categories, including 'Black-British', prove more acceptable for future surveys and censuses (including the 2001 census).

On the other hand, since the concept of ethnic origin is about self-identity of cultural affinities, whatever answer is given, it is the correct answer. But the real social system works also on other, additional bases to self-identity, i.e. on what others think of us and how they label us.

Prejudice and discrimination, and differential outcomes

Most data are gathered to inform policy formulators about social processes, but key factors in social processes are not simply *self-identities* but the *power* of the non-minority population relative to the minority. (See the *In Focus* on p. 42 for definitions of prejudice, discrimination and racism.) Prejudice and stereotyped thinking can only be researched by asking direct questions to individuals, but discrimination is about outcomes, whether those outcomes are based on prejudice or not. Discrimination is about stratification and differential access to life-chances. If we wish to know about, say, the interactions of race, ethnicity and access to housing, we can use case studies, but we cannot formulate or guide that work without basic data on outcomes, expressed in terms of life-chances. A typical research question on a social policy issue might be presented in its most simple form as, 'Who gets what kind of housing under what tenure?'.

Nor should we forget that differential outcomes can be the result of *rules* that operate against a minority, even where they are operated by non-prejudiced personnel. This is structured discrimination and it can be quite insidious and difficult to identify. Differential health outcomes, for example, may arise from differential access in health-care situations that make no allowance for non-English-speaking clients. This type of phenomenon is usually called 'institution-alized racism' (but some call it 'indirect discrimination').

Distribution of life-chances by ethnic background

By convention as much as anything, when we talk of the self-identities of individuals we tend to think in terms of ethnic minorities and majorities. These tend to be in nominal categories, i.e. they are simply different and are not in a hierarchy or stratified. However, the notion of majority does tend to imply a superiority of power relative to the minorities. When we talk of how ethnic groups are treated by others, we tend to talk of racism, since we focus on the more immediately observable or visible features of their existence. In this way we are seeing the structure of ethnic groups and their relationships very much as a system of stratification.

Britain is a very culturally rich and diverse society – one outcome of its previous imperial past. A very large number of ethnic minorities exist in Britain, each with its own history, pattern of arrival and dispersal into the wider population. In England, many of the white minorities become completely absorbed and, in the end, not differentiated in any way. Many Scots, Irish, Welsh and French lose any self-awareness of difference over a few generations, although there may be very strong cultural organizations for newcomers or those who wish to maintain a different cultural identity.

Generally, when people speak of ethnic minorities, they have in mind mainly groups that have arrived in Britain since 1945. However, the whole history of Britain is one of immigration of new groups that are now part of the cultural whole. Many think that some groups are only of recent entry to Britain. But there have been black people from Africa in Britain since 1500 (and, even further back, African Legions often made up the garrison of Hadrian's Wall). One well-known black person from the early sixteenth century was a state trumpeter, paid eight pence a day according to the records, for Kings Henry VII and VIII. He was called John Blanke (which means 'John White', so we are left in doubt as to his original or birth name). In the eighteenth century, large numbers of black people arrived in England as slaves, servants, free men and women and traders.

From 1945 onwards, the policy of British governments was to encourage the migration to England of groups from the old Empire and the developing Commonwealth to provide a new labour force for the steadily expanding economy. By the mid-1960s, most Colonies and countries in the old Empire had achieved a full independence but many individuals and families continued to wish to move to Britain. Gradually, British governments came to see the presence of ethnic minority groups as 'a problem' and passed a series of laws progressively restricting immigration from the Commonwealth. At the same time a series of race relations and equal opportunity laws were passed to improve the position of those already in the country (see *In Focus*, p. 40). The definition of migrants as 'a problem' has been common, but one that is difficult to sustain intellectually.

Migrants are always drawn from amongst the most vigorous, ambitious and successful of the populations from which they come. Some migrants are not defined as a problem. For example, since 1974, immigration from the European Union has been opened up (or allowed) in line with the treaties of Rome and Maastricht, and few see this as a problem. Defining immigration from the Commonwealth as a problem is a form of racism.

We will need a framework to help us examine the interaction of migrant groups with the economy and social structures. All migrants need first to establish a home and residence, to find work and secure themselves in the economy, and then to develop and care for their family relationships and educate their children. One of our overall purposes is to see whether race (ethnic background) or occupational position (class) provides a better explanation of differential access to 'life-chances'.

Homes and residence and ethnic minorities

Migrants have always been drawn into the largest towns of their intended country, since those tend to be the best known and offer the best chances of work. In addition, migrants often head for towns where there is already some person or relative whom they know. This leads to the development of clusters of migrant populations from particular countries or locations. Initially, migrants move into accommodation provided by the private sector or by relatives and friends. Since they lack economic power at first, the migrants tend to fill up the poorer accommodation in a town or area. They may also lack local knowledge, even language and negotiating skills. They often face direct personal prejudice and discrimination as well as institutionalized discrimination. As far as the UK is concerned, some aspects of this discrimination have been weakened by the legislation offering some protection from this. But from 1945 until 1970, when most of the migration was taking place and housing patterns were being established, discrimination in the UK was marked and obvious. In this period the Irish were often a clearly discriminated-against group as well as Caribbeans and Asians.

The arena of public housing or local authority housing is generally closed to recent migrants, and certainly was during the sixties and seventies. In this period, rules for allocations had two features that led to institutionalized racism:

❖ Most local authorities had rules that required the rehousing of existing tenants if overcrowding came about. Thus, if children of tenants married, moved a partner in, had a child, then the newly formed family would be a priority for rehousing.

❖ One factor in acquiring 'priority points' for rehousing was length of time within a given local authority or on its list for housing.

These two factors meant that until 1970 very few migrants from ethnic minorities could get into local authority housing.

We have already said that migrants tend to be drawn from fairly ambitious groups and this is shown in housing. Many migrant groups try to move into owner-occupation as soon as they can, even if this means a degree of overcrowding at first, but the particular character of the ethnic minority is a key factor in this process. In the previous two paragraphs we have emphasized their situation in terms of discrimination rather than their own particular cultural orientations. The outcome of this is shown in Fig. 6.3 and Table 6.2.

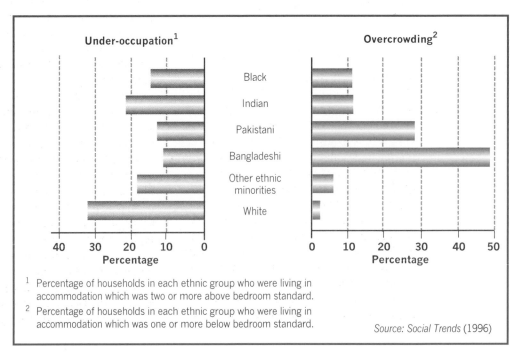

Figure 6.3
Homes: Under-occupation[1] and overcrowding[2], England, 1994–95

1 Percentage of households in each ethnic group who were living in accommodation which was two or more above bedroom standard.
2 Percentage of households in each ethnic group who were living in accommodation which was one or more below bedroom standard.

Source: Social Trends (1996)

Table 6.2 Housing tenure: England, 1994–95

	Percentages				
	Owned outright	Owned with mortgage	Rented from social sector	Rented privately	All households (thousands)
Black	8	32	48	11	369
Indian	23	60	8	9	262
Pakistani	18	50	18	14	142
Bangladeshi	8	28	59	5	63
Other ethnic minorities	10	45	21	23	229
White	26	42	22	10	18,642

Source: Social Trends (1996)

❖ Activity 6 ❖

Using these tables and statistics and any other sources you want, write an analysis of the housing situation of the ethnic minorities. State what new information or research you would wish to see.

Ethnic minorities and employment

Employment for migrants is another obvious area where the same factors which restrict access to housing will be influential: lack of local knowledge and perhaps language fluency, as well as stereotyping, prejudice and discrimination, and institutionalized racism. In addition, overseas qualifications may not be recognized. All this was true particularly between 1945 and 1970. For example, many men from Caribbean islands who had served in the British armed forces came to Britain in the 1940s and 1950s and could only enter the labour market as unskilled workers in the transport industry. They could not, like their white British counterparts from the armed forces, find employment in the police, the emergency services or the armed forces. They experienced a clear discrimination that narrowed and lowered the opportunities that they had.

The experience of the various ethnic minorities in employment in Britain has not been carefully mapped within the timespans in which the migrations took place. Now, we are talking primarily about the children of migrants, the experiences of the second generation. Little research makes any distinction between the experiences of the main migrants and their children. Research in Britain is usually conducted in terms only of self-identification. What we do know is that ethnic minorities have 'activity rates' in the economy for males that are more or less directly comparable to the white majority, but for most of the Asian groups activity rates are lower for the females. In employment terms, they are less successful than the white majority and have higher unemployment rates (see Table 6.5).

People from ethnic minorities have entered manufacturing, distribution, restaurants, and the lower grades of public service (see Table 6.3). The civil service, local authorities and other public authorities generally have felt under obligation to enhance the access of ethnic minorities to their employment, but have been only marginally successful so far. At any employment close to the controlling systems of our society, however, people from ethnic minorities remain grossly, even grotesquely, underrepresented. This applies to the higher levels of the civil service (see Table 6.4), the law, the police, parliament, banking and finance, and the judiciary. In all these areas, ethnic minorities are badly underrepresented compared with their presence in the general population.

In part this underrepresentation may be attributable to the relatively recent entry of ethnic minorities into significant careers and not to any contemporary discrimination. However, data such as those given in Table 6.4 confirm that the closer one gets to the power structures that once supported the imperialist ideals, the lower

the ethnic minority representation. The army is one of the worst arenas for this: only 1.4 per cent of the ranks come from ethnic minorities and only 1 per cent of officers (see Activity 7).

Another view is that the ethnic minorities will gradually establish more of their own businesses and create a parallel economy where a high percentage of the employees also come from ethnic minorities (see Fig. 6.4). This is certainly beginning to happen and some of the wealthiest families in Britain are headed by recent immigrants and people from ethnic minorities, and are very much in mainstream businesses. The extent to which the parallel economy will develop remains an open question.

When compared directly with the white majority, ethnic minority populations do not do very well at school until the age of 16, but each minority and gender has a different response. Clearly, for some groups,

Table 6.3 Employment[1]: by gender and industry: Great Britain, Spring 1995

	Manufacturing	Distribution, hotels and restaurants	Transport and communication	Banking, finance and insurance	Public administration, education and health	All industries[2] (= 100%) (thousands)
Males						
Black	22	18	12	10	25	130
Indian	32	22	13	14	13	178
Pakistani/Bangladeshi	31	34	–	–	–	75
Other ethnic minorities	17	29	9	13	23	108
White	31	17	9	14	15	10,702
Females						
Black	–	15	–	12	57	146
Indian	29	28	–	13	23	140
Pakistani/Bangladeshi	–	–	–	–	45	30
Other ethnic minorities	–	27	–	11	38	101
White	13	23	3	15	38	9,517

Percentages

[1] Male employees aged 16 to 64, female employees aged 16 to 59.
[2] Includes construction and other industries.

Source: Social Trends (1996)

❖ Activity 7 ❖

Using these tables and statistics and any other sources, write an analysis of the employment of people from ethnic minorities. State what new information or research you would wish to see.

Figure 6.4
Self-employment[1], Spring 1995

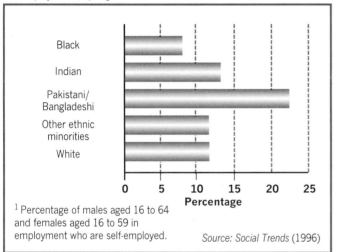

[1] Percentage of males aged 16 to 64 and females aged 16 to 59 in employment who are self-employed.

Source: Social Trends (1996)

Table 6.4 Percentage of civil service staff belonging to ethnic minorities: by grade level, Great Britain 1989 & 1995

| | *Percentages* | |
	1989	*1995*
AA	6.5	7.6
AO	5.6	6.7
EO	2.9	4.3
HEO	1.7	2.4
SEO	1.2	2.1
Grade 7	1.2	2.6
Grade 6	2.2	2.8
Grade 5	1.8	2.5
Grade 4	0.6	0.4
Grade 3	0.0	0.2
Grade 2	0.0	0.0
Grade 1	0.0	0.0
All grade levels (thousands)	**18**	**23**

Source: Social Trends (1996)

Table 6.5 Unemployment rates[1]: by level of qualification, GB, Spring 1995

Percentages	*Higher qualification*[2]	*Other qualification*[3]	*No qualification*	*All aged 16 to 59/64*[4]
Black	16	25	35	24
Indian	–	12	19	12
Pakistani/Bangladeshi	–	27	34	27
Other ethnic minorities	12	17	–	16
White	4	8	14	8

[1] Unemployment based on the ILO definition as a percentage of all economically active.
[2] Qualifications above GCE A level or equivalent.
[3] Qualifications at, or below, GCE A level or equivalent.
[4] Males aged 16 to 64, females aged 16 to 59.

Source: Social Trends (1996)

language access is poor if the language of the home and the first language of the child is not English. However, most ethnic minority groups respond to their employment possibilities at 16 and 18 by continuing in college with some determination. By the age of 25, most ethnic minority groups are directly comparable, or better, than the white majority in the number, level or range of qualifications held. At this stage the employment discrimination is revealed more clearly. When we look at the unemployment ratios of people analysed by qualification level, we can see that any explanation of ethnic minority unemployment that relies simply on the idea that they are less well qualified is inadequate. Discrimination is clear at every qualification level.

Age and social stratification

Age, like gender, is a social category that is easy to take for granted and to view as if it were an entirely natural phenomenon. All humans are born, grow up, learn, mature, pass through stages of their life and die. What could be more natural? Yet the ways in which those processes are experienced vary greatly from society to society, and age to age. They form a significant part of our everyday experiences. Many readers of this book will be experiencing great frustrations because, no matter how adult and independent they feel, they live in families that persist in treating them as children to be watched, monitored and guided. Other readers will feel some hesitation that, after years of independent working life, they are adopting the role of student with its implication of dependence and the need to seek guidance. In other words, role expectations can be confused and uncertain.

In many older and traditional societies, individuals pass through clearly structured roles, marked by rituals and ceremonies of such a clear significance that anthropologists and sociologists have given them their own special term: *'rites de passage'*. Some of these ceremonies survive, particularly within religions, into modern societies. The Christian 'Confirmation' and the Jewish 'Bar Mitzvah' can be viewed as rites of passage to an older, traditional adulthood that perhaps no longer applies as such, but still has meaning within the religions.

Our individual life course

We are all influenced by key events in our own lives and by the era in which we reach maturity. The political, economic, cultural and social events of the wider society during the period when we are 15 to 25 will have more impact on our personality and attitudes than the events of any other 10 years of our life. At the time of writing this book, it is commonplace to talk of 'Thatcher's children' or 'Thatcher's generation' to refer to young people who came to maturity when Margaret Thatcher was Prime Minister (1979 to 1990). This illustrates not only the general remarks being made here, but also the very sharp and significant changes that a single government can make. Nevertheless, we should look at such remarks with the caution of a sociologist looking for wider trends, patterns and causes.

Charles Wright Mills (1963) once defined sociology as the interaction of biography with history. All of us have an individual pattern to our lives, but these individual patterns do coalesce and general patterns can be observed. There may be sudden change, but we are also influenced by what we experience from our parents. A parent aged 50 in the year 2000 may see the years from 1965 to 1975 as their own key formative period, but will also be acutely aware of their parents' experiences of, say, 1935 to 1945. Young people reaching maturity in 2000 may also be influenced by their grandparents in a direct way. Experiences easily last three generations. In Europe in the year 2000, the influence of mass unemployment, of war and of genocide during the period 1935 to 1945 will still be strong. And so also will the influence of imperialism. In every major city of West Europe there are people who experienced the imperialism of 1935 to 1945, some as rulers and some as ruled.

We have not yet defined a 'generation' – a term that has so many uses that it may have little relevance within sociology. In a single family, its meaning is clear. In modern societies, age-categorization is less clear, with individuals passing through recognized life-stages generally in a standardized way. Those interested in behaviours in the consumer and political arenas are finding that as predictors of behaviours, life-stage categories may be as good as occupational categories (Bryman *et al.* 1987).

Figure 6.5
Possible paths through life

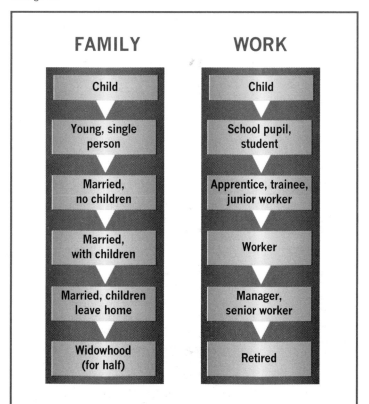

Life-stages and the life-course

The life-stage categories may be listed along two 'standardized' dimensions which may, or may not, correspond: family and work. The possible paths that a person might follow in each dimension are shown in Fig. 6.5.

We describe these as *standardized paths*, since they exist in the form of expectations or norms: there is a sense in which we are all expected to pass through these stages. There are also now smaller variations by gender expected than there were in the past.

Life-stages and citizenship

Of all these stages in the life-course, two stand out for sociological study: those of youth and old age. Youth is often seen as a period of uncertain rights and obligations, and old age as a period of withdrawal from society, its rights and obligations. A central concept that can bring the analysis of these two life-stages together was developed by T.H. Marshall in the late 1940s: the concept of 'citizenship'. In the UK, members of British society have traditionally been described as 'subjects' (of the reigning king or queen). In most European societies, the concept of citizenship has been very important since 1789 (the date of the French Revolution). In ancient societies and in feudal Europe, there were many categories of members of society, including slaves and serfs. But a *citizen* is a full member of the society, with equal rights and obligations to all other citizens and able to play a full part in the society and its political, economic and social life. The French Revolution expressed this with the slogan of 'liberty, equality and fraternity' (or brotherhood). (French society was, however, one of the last in Europe to apply this concept to include *sisterhood*.)

Having developed the concept of citizenship in the period of developing nationalism (1789 to 1945), most European societies still had a concept of foreigner or alien, of visitors or guest-workers, who might apply for citizenship but had no right to it. Indeed, while the treaties of Rome and Maastricht have greatly modified the application of 'citizenship' amongst member countries of the (now) European Union, all European societies still retain this category of 'foreigner' or 'guest-worker'.

Marshall (1954) was conscious of the great changes in social security and educational systems during the period 1940 to 1950, in Britain in particular, and saw clearly that citizenship created obligations for the wider social organizations. A political society was obliged to provide its citizens with sufficient education and, if necessary, sufficient income, housing and health-care. Sufficient, that is, for them to take an effective and dignified part in the social and political life of the community. This general concept exists in all European societies and most industrially advanced societies, although the USA stands a little aside from some aspects of this tradition.

Citizenship and youth

Since 1945, the experience of being 'a youth' has been characterized by two major changes:

❖ The period of being a 'youth' has been progressively extended and made more uncertain.

❖ With this extension, there has been a growing uncertainty about the rights and obligations of the young as citizens.

Children are not full citizens. They have rights, but those rights might be exercised by their parents, or the state, on their behalf. Certainly children have no political rights. What marks out the 'youth phase' is the progressive acquisition of rights. First of all, children acquire the right to work part-time, to leave school, to receive training, to engage in sexual activity, to vote, to receive social security income, to make contracts and so on. There is no magic single age for the acquisition of complete rights, a day when the 'rites de passage' are complete.

In general, as the age of rights tends to descend, the effective ability to participate fully in the economy as a worker has been extended. In the period 1950 to 1975, most young people who wanted to find work could easily find what was (for the time) well-paid work. During this period there developed what became known as a 'youth culture': a set of social and cultural attitudes that focused on the hedonistic enjoyment of a leisure pattern centred on music, sports, dancing and clothing. This leisure was often marked out by fairly high levels of segregation of the young from older people. These behavioural patterns were so distinct from those of adults that they were often the subject of both envy and fear by the adults (Davis 1990). Some saw them as very separate from parallel adult cultures, and relatively distinct from the class-based leisure patterns of the older citizens.

Envy and fear often co-exist and some have described 'youth culture' as a 'counter-culture': a culture in which elements are selected by the youth precisely because they oppose the cultures of the adult citizens. Hebdige (1979) has described the 'skinhead' culture as an exaggerated form of the still macho, working-class cultures that the skinheads eventually modify their behaviour into. Mike Brake (1980) has pointed out that for 'the students', their student period is a sort of moratorium from what will be expected of them in work and they can behave in ways not characteristic of their later lives. Even those who later become presidents may, for example, have sampled illegal drugs when a student!

During the period after 1975, 'youth' experienced mass unemployment and loss of income, but aspects of the youth culture have survived. Roberts *et al.* (1990) has argued that the experience of youth has become more class-orientated. Bates and Risborough (1993) have emphasized that unemployment, the Youth Training Schemes and the withdrawal of social security benefits have combined to reinforce the limitations of 'youth' to immediate income and to future high or secure income in the occupational structure. Their messages are not to take too seriously any apparent differences of youth from adults.

Age and citizenship

One experience of ageing is that of progressive withdrawal from social life and society. This is more often experienced by men than women. This is, at least, in part because of the differential commitment to their work and family identities that men and women have. Not all men have high commitments to a work-identity but previous patterns of full-time work will have taken up a good deal of time. Once work finishes, there may be a need to replace it with another activity and identity. Women in retirement from work may find it easier to occupy their time with their children and grandchildren, if they have them, than do men. Or they may find commitment to community activities easier than men.

One thing that is very clear in the late twentieth century is that older men and women find it increasingly difficult to be active in the economy as paid workers. As a result they may lack finance to participate fully in a leisure society. The age of (in effect, compulsory) retirement seems to be falling steadily – often against the wishes of the older citizens themselves. Withdrawal from the economy can be seen as a loss of citizenship, the feeling of no longer being a full member of a society.

In addition, because of the pace of change (amongst other things), the old may feel very isolated from the youth. There is often a fear and distrust of the young, who may be regarded as a mixture of vandals, graffiti artists, muggers and ramraiders. Mark Hudson, studying a community in the North East of England, found that it was 'difficult to find anyone of the older generation who had a good word to say about the young' (1994, p 45).

The old may also feel ambiguous about their own identity. As many people aged over 60 are very vigorous and healthy, they may not wish to identify with 'the elderly' who are seen as approaching decrepitude. There will be all sorts of ambiguities about experiencing a satisfactory identity as 'old' or 'elderly' in these circumstances.

We should note that, as yet, in the UK there has been little in the way of the development of a political consciousness by the old to lead to the establishment of clear and strong political organizations. In the United States, there has been a stronger, conscious development of what are known as the 'Grey Panthers', deliberately named after the earlier 'Black Panther' movements of the black civil-rights movement.

❖ Activity 8 ❖

Research what organisations exist to promote the views, concerns and rights of older people in the UK.

Why do you think that there has been less in the way of forceful political activism among older people in the UK, compared with the United States?

In looking at the economic position of the old, we have to look as much at their previous occupational and class position as at their status of being old. This draws our attention to the historical and developmental processes that apply to all sociology but also to class and stratification as processes. The old of today were once young, and formed their own occupational and class identities. A full-time factory worker aged 21 in 1938 would be 82 in 1999. Amongst her experiences might be leaving school at the age of 14. In 1938 the first legislation was passed requiring that all full-time workers should receive a one-week's paid holiday. In 1949, the first legislation for guaranteed income support was passed. She retired from full-time work in 1977, but without a full state pension in her own right and no pension from her employer and then herself drew the equivalent of the current income support. Nevertheless, she might compare her own position to that of her grandmother and see it as rather comfortable: possibly even see it as middle-class to a small degree.

Old age, occupations and incomes

The old are becoming increasingly isolated from the workforce, whether they wish to be or not. Once men reach the age of 55, if they lose employment, they rarely recover full-time work. There is more part-time work available to women and they may use part-time work as a route back into full-time work, but both men and women become increasingly reliant for their income upon their savings, their reserves and their pensions. State pensions are of declining relative value, so the earlier savings are increasingly important. The difficulty is that many of those who are now old were relatively poor or in insecure employment earlier in their lives. Even now, only just over half of those in work are in an occupational pension scheme. People in badly paid or insecure work find it hard to make provision on a private, voluntary basis. The net result is that those poor when in work, tend to stay relatively even poorer when out of work.

Very few of the current old have significant reserves and it seems unlikely that, for the foreseeable future, there will be much change. Table 6.6 does not tell us of the scale of provision being made, but it is unlikely to be great for many people. Poverty in old age and its relationship to income and the occupational structure is an important topic that we will return to in the next two sections.

Table 6.6	Membership of a current pension scheme: by gender and whether working full- or part-time, Great Britain 1993–94

	Employed			*Self-employed*	
	Occupational pension	*Personal pension*	*Any pension*	*Personal pension*	*All employed*
Males					
Full-time	60	29	89	66	85
Part-time	16	8	24	31	25
Females					
Full-time	54	22	77	46	74
Part-time	19	12	32	27	31

Source: Social Trends (1996)

Social mobility and stratification formation

Changes in occupational structures

We have already emphasized that any formation that we describe in terms of ethnic groups or occupational groups, actually comprises a large number of individuals who have their own experiences and self-identities. A classification group, such as 'Afro-Caribbean' or 'skilled-working-class' conceals many subtle and significant variations within it. However, that does not mean that the overall classification is meaningless.

Having said that, the pace of occupational change has clearly been increasing over the last 15 years and this indicates that the social structure may be moving towards fragmentation. It is not clear what this will mean for class-formation processes.

Changes are occurring in the occupational structures of advanced industrial economies, and the drift or tendency of these changes is common to that group of countries. Although there are some slight variations in the speed of change amongst the countries, the changes derive from certain common causes that would appear to be inevitable. Two important causes are changes in:

❖ consumption patterns

❖ production patterns.

In the consumption that individuals undertake, they first purchase housing, food and basic clothing. Next, they purchase manufactured consumer goods, e.g. leisure clothing. They then purchase or demand services and leisure activities. For all consumers, as they get wealthier, their *absolute* spending on the first two increases but, as a *proportion* of their total spending, it drops. This tendency has existed throughout the last 300 years and is clear. The result has been that a progressive shifting of demand from primary needs, to secondary needs (and manufacturing) and on to the tertiary or service needs.

The other major factor determining change in work practices, i.e. massive technological advances, is extensively commented on in Chapter 5, *Work, organizations, unemployment and leisure,* and both modernization and globalization are discussed in Chapter 8, *World sociology.* The main shift in employment has been from labour-intensive manufacturing and production industries to higher-skilled, more managerial, office technical and sales staff – what we might call 'intermediate', 'middle-class', 'white-collar' or 'professional' jobs. There are fewer jobs for those traditionally seen as 'skilled working-class', although the newer higher technician grade posts may

well be filled by people who entered employment some years ago as skilled craft workers.

Service and leisure industries are still generally labour-intensive, and many, but not all, jobs in the service sector can be seen as taking place in a clean environment and under situations that, years ago, would have been seen as middle-class. David Lockwood (1958) emphasized that working closely in office environments with owners and managers made the work-situation of people middle-class, even if their market-situation remained working-class.

Many of the new jobs in the services sector (in retail work, catering and public health care) do have a very precarious character. They are often part-time and, compared to full-time positions in the same industries, less secure and with fewer fringe benefits accruing to the post-holder.

Class-identity formation

What are the processes whereby people create an identity for themselves and how do they become aware of those identities as being located in a stratification system? The first part of this question is answered fully in Chapter 2, *Culture and identity.* We will look more closely here at the second part.

Initially, all individuals are influenced by their parents and the ways in which their parents express their identities and offer, consciously or unconsciously, an identity to their children. Some parents may well say to their children that they (the parents) are 'working-class' or 'professionals'. More likely, there will be a series of interactions about being ordinary people, hard-working people, not afraid 'to get our hands dirty', or 'get stuck-in'. Or remarks may be made about 'excellence', 'diligence', 'professional standards', 'a good career' and so on. When children reach the ages of 13 to 16, if they do not start to talk about exam success and targets, careers or jobs, then their parents may start to ask questions. Every young person soon gets some idea of whether what they say is highly or poorly regarded.

They will soon detect if their ambitions are seen as too high, too low or about right.

In a first employment, all people quickly gain an understanding about the available identity formations, even, or perhaps particularly, if they see that first employment as a temporary stage. For many years, over 50 per cent of people who became skilled manual workers had parents who were skilled manual workers or semi-skilled manual workers. Children of professional workers stood very good chances of becoming professional workers or managers. There was, in Britain and most of Europe, in the mid-twentieth century a tendency for the classes to reproduce themselves.

'Class', as a broad social conception of stratification, as well as a strictly Marxist concept of economic class, carried this idea of self-reproduction, with some degree of openness. 'Caste' is a term used to describe a stratification where no individual movements take place across the stratification lines. The notion of a meritocratic society emphasized the desirability of creating, through social policies, a weakening of class barriers to individual social mobility across the stratification systems.

John Major, as Conservative Prime Minister in 1990s, was by no means the first politician in Britain to claim that his policies and policy successes were weakening class divisions and making society more open. In a manner typical of politicians, he made few references to the fact that he was largely talking of status divisions and occupational mobility, and less of class and variations in the economic outcomes of an occupational hierarchy or other flows of life-chances. For him, access to promotion or mobility was the key factor. In addition, Major made very little systematic distinction between mobility between generations and mobility within a working lifetime. Generally, we have emphasized the mobility between generations rather than that within a working lifetime. Major's main emphasis was on the importance of educational opportunities as a key aspect of general social policy that affected mobility.

Social mobility studies

There have been many studies of social mobility in industrial societies: the politics of the subject make it one of perennial interest. Two large, related and very significant studies have been undertaken in Britain. The first was conducted by David Glass and his colleagues at the London School of Economics around 1949 (and published in 1954). The second is usually known as the Oxford Mobility Studies, undertaken by A.H. Halsey, John Goldthorpe and colleagues, mainly in 1972 with results published from 1979 onwards. The Glass study might be described as an attempt to create a record of the class and mobility systems as they stood at the beginning of the new, postwar era. There was a conscious feeling that new social and educational policies were to make significant changes to society and one way to measure the success of the new policies was to create a record of what they were moving from.

Glass took a national sample of individuals and acquired data on their occupational patterns and movements, and also data on the occupations of their parents when the respondents in the sample were aged 14. That last piece of data is in itself interesting. Clearly, the parents of the respondents would themselves have mobility in their working lives but the respondents might be relied on to have accurate memories of what existed when they were 14. Also, 14 was the age at which, when the sample was drawn, it was possible for the respondents to leave school and start their own working life: a key influence point in their working lives. Glass analysed the occupational changes for the respondents over time and compared it with their parents' occupations. He also organized the data into ten-year periods according to the birth dates of the individuals responding. Although Glass collected a good deal of data on women, most of the data published was on men only. Glass also used the classification systems common from the Registrar General.

We need not concern ourselves with much of Glass's data and their analysis, only that he confirmed clearly that most mobility was very short-range and that there were quite high levels of self-recruitment to all classes, but particularly with the professional classes, skilled manual workers and unskilled manual workers.

Goldthorpe, Halsey and colleagues, starting in 1970, twenty-five years after the end of the World War II, consciously wanted to replicate the work of Glass to map changes since 1945–9. They therefore adopted a very similar methodology (even keeping to the age 14). However, they had access to better computers and were able to test many more (and more sophisticated) hypotheses than Glass. In addition, thinking had moved on and they were more aware of change and an increase in the pace of change. By the time they were publishing their data, they could take more account of increasing conceptualization and new theoretical approaches to an analysis of class.

One theoretical problem always carries forward: in what way do classes become aware of their own economic interests and how do individuals come to create class-based organizations that can be seen as taking 'class action'. This is the basic Marxist problem. As Goldthorpe and Llewellyn put it:

'... mobility has to be seen, to take over Giddens's terminology, as a basic source of class "structuration": it is the rate and pattern of mobility that will determine the extent to which classes may be recognized as collectivities of individuals or families occupying similar locations within the social division of labour over time.' (Goldthorpe *et al.* 1987)

Put another way, high rates of intra- and inter-generational mobility will weaken the structuring of class formations. This makes any form of class action much harder to organize.

A second problem that they faced can be summed up as the problem of measuring the degree of openness and the degree of closure, and the recognition that these may be different phenomena. Furthermore, these two phenomena will have different impacts on structuration or class formation. Goldthorpe and Llewellyn refer to Parkin (1971) who saw clearly that class conflict could be expressed in terms of closure and exclusion: the relatively privileged groups would develop strategies to close off access to the non-privileged groups (and the children of non-privileged groups).

Finally, Halsey and Goldthorpe addressed the problems of creating a new social- or occupational-status ranking system that better reflected the realities of social life. There were anomalies in the old ranking systems. For example, many self-employed people, such as carpenters, did not enjoy a status significantly different from employed carpenters. The development of large numbers of lower managerial grades, of higher technicians and designers was not reflected in the system of classification. Finally, within the older system of the Registrar General and the Office for National Statistics, the middle 'C' category had expanded to some 50 per cent of the working population and was therefore not useful for mapping mobility. It was so large that it had to be, mathematically, 'self-recruiting' to a large degree.

Initially, Hope and Goldthorpe devised a 36-category system for classifying the data they got from their sample survey of 10,000 men from all over the country in 1972. With some caveats and hesitations Goldthorpe then aggregated his 36 categories to develop a seven-class system for mapping mobility. The seven groups could then be reduced to three for other comparisons. This system also allowed for some comparisons to be made with other systems. The classes are described in Table 6.7

Goldthorpe *et al.* described the occupations in a general status-hierarchy and also gave a statement of their relationship to systems of industrial control and direction. Their term 'service class' is one worth exploring. They take the term from Karl Renner (1953) who uses the German term *'Dienstklasse'*, a term which loses a little in the translation to 'service class'. This term

Table 6.7 Goldthorpe and colleagues' seven-point scale

❖ **Class 1 (13.6 per cent of sample)** Higher grade professionals, administrators and managers, large proprietors.	Those exercising authority and expertise on behalf of corporate bodies, plus free professionals, plus those who generally serve the system, plus medium-size, independent business people.	**SERVICE CLASS**
❖ **Class 2 (11.5 per cent)** Lower grade professionals, administrators and managers; higher grade technicians and supervisors.	The lower and middle ranges of bureau-cracies, with some degree of discretion and control. They are the subaltern and cadet levels of the 'service class'.	
❖ **Class 3 (9.2 per cent)** Routine non-manual (e.g. clerical, sales personnel), rank and file service employees.	A white-collar labour-force, functionally associated with, but marginal to, the service class.	**INTERMEDIATE CLASS**
❖ **Class 4 (9.4 per cent)** Small proprietors, self-employed artisans (non-professional workers).	A sort of 'petty bourgeoisie', with the advantages of some capital and a high degree of autonomy, in the sense of freedom from direct supervision.	
❖ **Class 5 (11.6 per cent)** Lower grade technicians, supervisors of manual workers.	A more modern 'aristocracy of labour' or a blue-collar élite, set apart from the mass of wage-labour by their functions while still marginal to the management group proper.	
❖ **Class 6 (21.2 per cent)** Skilled manual workers.	Those who have acquired a relatively high degree of skill through apprenticeship or other means of training.	**WORKING CLASS**
❖ **Class 7 (23.5 per cent)** Semi-skilled and unskilled manual workers, agricultural workers.	Those in an entirely subordinate role, subject to the authority of the employer or his agents.	

Source: adapted from Goldthorpe *et al.* (1987)

implies senior 'servants': company executives, senior civil servants, army officers and the like, rather than the fetch-and-carry type of servant. It is term quite separate from the usage of English-speaking economists when they describe a 'service sector'. It refers instead to the 'servants' of companies, the system or the state (as in the words of Othello, a General in the Venetian army according to Shakespeare: 'I have done the State some service and they know't.')

Other authors more concerned with power and control would describe such people as servants of (if not actually members of) a ruling class.

The mobility model, power and class relations

Goldthorpe and colleagues have relabelled the occupational and status groups for us in a way that helps make better sense of the hierarchy. But what we have as a result is a set of terms that are simply not part of everyday life. If they discuss these matters in everyday life, people still refer to themselves using such terms as 'working-class', 'lower-' or 'upper-middle-class', 'professional'. The terms 'upper-class' and 'ruling-class' are used by most people to describe the highest groups. Although there is no complete agreement about *how* to use this collection of terms, they *are* used, whereas Goldthorpe's terms 'service' and 'intermediate' classes are *not* much used outside the world of professional sociologists. Some sense that Goldthorpe has lost interest in the actual forms of interaction that people have, in that he does not consider the bases of interaction and power.

Nor do Goldthorpe and colleagues take much interest in analysing whether there are central sources or clusters of power, a subject that has concerned many sociologists. In a broad sense, the system works primarily in favour of the service classes, but is there another group behind that, a ruling group, that set the rules and agendas for the service classes? Whom is it that the service class serves? The Oxford Mobility group provides few answers to this.

Male mobility and class formation

The empirical precision and general value of the work of the Oxford group is not usually questioned, with one major exception. They chose, by and large, only to study and comment on the social mobility of men in their original study. This inevitably tended to treat men as 'normal' or 'typical' cases. It assumed that the class of a family (including the children) as a status grouping was determined almost exclusively by the occupation of a male 'head of household'. It tended to reproduce in theory and empirical terms what might have existed in the 1950s, but failed to confirm the social realities of the 1970s. Arguments can be made that the creation of an occupational hierarchy for women, or a hierarchy for men and women, is too difficult and that there is little agreement on such hierarchies. But that line of thought just compounds the neglect. Until

such an argument is attempted, the issue will remain unclear. In the end Goldthorpe and Payne (1987) retreated into smugness, by commenting that their feminist critics should study the subject themselves if they thought it important. They further added that their critics had chosen not even to analyse the data that Glass collected but did not use – data which remains publicly accessible in the LSE. Those interested in the debate should also look at Roberts and Woodward (1981), Stanworth (1984) and Crompton and Mann (1986).

We have already commented that young people come to their own class identity in the context of a family. There can be no doubt that most young people spend more of their time with their mother and female relatives than they do with their father and male relatives. It is therefore likely that they learn as much about their class location and identity from the females of their family as they do from the males. Furthermore, it is a reasonable hypothesis that those appearing to be upwardly (or downwardly) mobile from their father's class may simply be moving to the occupational or educational class of their mother. Basil Bernstein (1975) has done some work on considering the position of mother's educational level in the educational achievements of young people. Whatever the outcome of detailed empirical work, it would seem that if we are to understand mobility and its impact on class-identity formation, we need to look at young people of both genders and their parents. What is more, for the people who were young between 1985 and now, this might mean three or four parents and step-parents.

Conclusions of the Oxford studies

What conclusions are reached on the patterns of male mobility? One main problem is to determine which aspect to look at:

❖ the effects of parental upbringing and the ability of a favoured class to favour its own children, or

❖ the ability of an unfavoured class to penetrate the ranks of the favoured, either for themselves or for their children.

The changes in occupational structures between 1949 and 1972 and the opportunities that arose for mobility both within a working life and for those in work have set a new scene. These changes have accelerated since 1972. It is really time for a new, third survey.

In looking at the 1972 data, let us select a particular change of great interest. The numbers employed in Goldthorpe's Class 1 rose about three- or four-fold between 1949 and 1972 (although changes in definitions and the position of women make direct comparisons uncertain). This suggested that the new personnel in that class could not easily be recruited from the children of Class 1 fathers: a large number had to work their way up the labour force or be recruited via the grammar schools and universities that were expanding at the time. This is what had happened: access to Class 1 had opened up. At the same time, descent from Class 1 to other classes by the children of Class 1 fathers was reduced. In general, this pattern was repeated across the structure.

What does this actually mean? That the classes were more open or more closed? In terms of experienced relationships between the classes, we are left uncertain. All we can say is that economic demands and changes seem to be the driving force for mobility, rather than any egalitarian or purely meritocratic policies.

Income and wealth in Britain

In this section and the next, we present two examples of areas of debate that feature in both sociological and political debates, as well as in everyday discussion:

❖ the distribution of income and wealth

❖ the existence (or not) of an underclass.

Power is one dimension of the relationships and configurations between people. If life-chances are unevenly distributed, we can say that the unevenness of income distribution is a result of uneven power distribution. Nearly all people in a society would like a little more money or wealth, but many feel that the distribution is about right or is generally fair. There are organizations established to keep it that way and rectify particular errors or grievances. There are trade unions, professional associations, employers' associations, pressure groups, charities, political parties and so on. There is still debate, however, about income and wealth distribution and the effects of tax on that distribution.

A range of sociological, conceptual and empirical material exists relevant to the political and economic debates about distribution. The relevant material cannot all be covered here and may not yet even exist, but we hope to encourage you to acquire the concepts and analytical skills that you can take forward and use elsewhere.

Income and wealth

These two terms are relatively easy to define in a simple way, but there are more difficulties when we try to research them. Income can be described as a flow of money or goods and services towards an individual. Wealth can be described as a stock of goods, property, money or other assets capable of being turned into money, goods or property. When we try to define these for purposes of comparison of individuals (or their families), the problems begin. One convention is to ignore certain 'life-chance flows' because they are enjoyed in common. Defence, the fire brigades, the emergency services and hospitals are not usually seen as being a common income (although they may be). The same goes for 'national wealth' such as national picture galleries and museums, or our schools and colleges.

If we return to our problem of identifying individual income and wealth, some smaller-scale details emerge. A person owning a house, for example, can be said to have a notional income from it if they live in it – an income equivalent to what they would get if they rented it. A rich individual may lend a valuable painting to a museum for their own lifetime, or for as long as the museum wants it. Is that part of their wealth or not?

These detailed questions might strike you as trivial, but they affect the way we can research into these issues and may even become 'tax-questions'. For many years in the 1940s and 1950s, the notional income from houses was liable to tax. Wealth in pictures or houses that are accessible to the public is not currently subject to gift or inheritance taxes. Tax questions or implications certainly affect the way we can gain access to data about tax and wealth. For routine research, we tend to rely on official data from the Inland Revenue. Most people, wealthy or not, are very cautious about what they tell researchers on these questions. People can lower their guard, a little, however. For example, the Government's *General Household Survey* on expenditure is compiled from data given to them voluntarily and seems to record rather more expenditure than the Inland Revenue can detect as income!

We are concerned here with the distribution of wealth and income amongst occupational groups. There are other life-chances over and above income and wealth, but these are very hard to research and do usually correlate with income or wealth. In addition, we must recognize the concept of cultural capital (see Chapter 4, *Education and training*). A university degree or a professional qualification (or any skill) is a form of wealth, capable of being traded, through work, for income.

The benefits of work are more than the simple income, wage or salary. They may include a wide range of what are called, 'fringe benefits'. These might include:

❖ generous pay while off work for reasons of illness

❖ contributions by employers to a pension fund

❖ paid holidays beyond the legal minimum

❖ a company car

❖ childcare benefits

❖ use of facilities such as subsidized canteens or the firm's sports clubs

❖ health insurance

❖ discounts on the products of the firm.

Many of these benefits may only accrue after only two or three years' full-time service with a particular organization. We do know two things:

❖ The higher the basic salary, the greater the overall worth in percentage terms is the benefit package.

❖ These packages grew for most workers in Britain between 1960 and 1990.

More recently, the shift has been away from long-term jobs with benefits, to task-by-task contracts, without fringe benefits.

Here we are concerned with the overall patterns of distribution of wealth and income. We are particularly interested in the extremes, i.e. great wealth and privilege, and poverty and deprivation. It is not our intention to explore these in any detail, but to set a brief agenda, give some examples of statistics and then to encourage you to think about them. You should then be able to consider what else you need to know and propose research.

The wealthy

Even the most superficial glance at statistical information shows that a small minority of the population enjoys great wealth. Many people – the 'comfortably off' – have a well-furnished house, one or two cars, pension rights and some insurance. Only a very small minority hold beyond that a truly disposable wealth equivalent to one year's worth of their income. What this means is those who are 'comfortably off' are in a situation of dependency, requiring things (or employment) to stay as they are in order for them maintain their comforts.

A good half of the population may, in those sorts of terms, experience their situation as very comfortable, but probably not wealthy. Others – without the house, the cars, the pension, and with only a ten-year-old winter coat may see the comfortably-off as wealthy, but the comfortable do not experience themselves as wealthy, because they could not effectively consider turning their wealth into cash. Pensioners in the 'middle wealth' position may see their lives as particularly precarious: they do not feel able to replace their car or carpets, they see their pension declining in purchasing power and they fear they may have to sell their house to obtain domestic or health care if their health declines.

Yet great wealth does exist and is heavily concentrated. *The Sunday Times* has for many years published an annual 'Colour Supplement' which lists what they believe to be the wealthiest 1000 families in Britain. They do that because of the endless fascination of the general public with questions of wealth and who has it. Generally, our problem as sociologists is the difficulty of researching these questions. Families are hardly likely to be completely honest or regard this as a matter of proper public research and debate. *The Sunday Times* itself is inconsistent in its research, especially about whether it takes an individual or a family as its basis for research into wealth-holding. The research is based only on a mixture of public knowledge about ownership and estimates as to value. It is also uncertain as to whether it is concerned with industrial control or personal life. For example, the shares that the Leverhulme Trust own in the Lever Company are not part of the wealth of the Lever family, but, because of family influence in the trust, they are part of the Lever family's control mechanisms. Nevertheless, *The Sunday Times* supplements are useful sources from which sociologists can learn much, including the fact that the best way to ensure great wealth is to be careful in selecting one's parents! Most of the very wealthy have inherited much of their wealth. Income does not seem to be a significant question for the very wealthy. Those with great

wealth are usually able to manage their income so that, while it gives them benefits, it is not too obvious for tax purposes. It may be spread around many countries and, for research and tax purposes, may be impossible to aggregate.

Do the 1000 families constitute the 'ruling class'? Certainly the class and economic systems work in their favour. But is that number large enough to constitute a ruling class? How does wealth connect to political and ideological control (necessary elements of a ruling class notion)? The service classes are also clearly rewarded for their assistance in all this and have wealth and income well beyond what might be essential to recruit them to such positions. To investigate these questions further, look at Chapter 13, *Power and politics.*

Poverty

Within British society there is great disparity of wealth and income. But for those with very little income, wealth almost ceases to be a question. Their wealth is so small as to be almost invisible and is therefore ignored for tax and income purposes. A very large number of people in Britain are poor in the sense of having no significant amount of wealth, disposable or not.

In this chapter we will not look at all the issues surrounding the absolute or relative measurement of poverty, nor the state's role in maintaining a safety net, as these are covered extensively in Chapter 10, *Health, poverty and welfare.* We suggest you read pp. 458–68 now.

Distribution of income and wealth

On the following pages are some statistics from government sources on the overall distribution of income and wealth. These provide only a part of the picture and we would encourage you to undertake further research. Our particular recommendations are as follows:

1 Become familiar with regular series like *Social Trends, The Annual Abstract of Statistics, Labour Market Review* and *Employment Gazette.*

2 Practise your skills in reading such data in the originals and gaining an understanding of it and the ability to abstract and compare data.

3 Try to relate the theory to the tables. Ask questions such as: 'Is this material relevant to the theory? What other quantitative data do I require? Is it available?'

4 Read some main texts on poverty, wealth and distribution patterns. Ask yourself: 'What amongst these are the problems I am interested in?' and 'Where can I get more data?'

5 Ask yourself: 'What kind of small-scale qualitative studies could I design or conduct that might throw light on these data and their relationship to the main concepts and theory?'

❖ Activity 9 ❖

Tables 6.8 and 6.9 and Figs 6.6 and 6.7 below are typical of the kind of data you will be looking at in your research. Use them to begin your research in the differential distribution of income and wealth by age, gender or occupation, the percentages of population and the changing differentials over time.

Try to find similar data on distribution of wealth by ethnic background for comparison. Then apply your findings to point 5 in the list above.

Figure 6.6
Gross weekly earnings[1]: by gender and age, April 1995

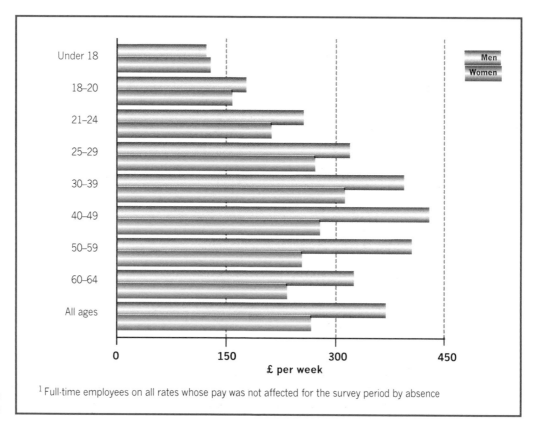

Source: Social Trends (1996)

[1] Full-time employees on all rates whose pay was not affected for the survey period by absence

Table 6.8 Real[1] gross weekly earnings[2]: by selected occupation, Great Britain

| | £ per week at April 1995 prices[1] | | | | | |
	1971	1976	1981	1986	1991	1995
Waiter/waitress	108	155	143	156	166	161
Bar staff	119	148	148	165	158	165
Cleaner	113	180	175	185	186	181
Receptionist	117	132	139	158	179	188
Caretaker	163	197	185	203	220	227
Bricklayer/mason	204	252	232	242	256	263
Carpenter/joiner	209	244	230	244	269	274
Nurse	146	194	194	223	308	329
Social worker	209	236	254	273	313	340
Primary teacher	243	295	301	312	370	401
Secondary teacher	243	327	324	333	403	435
Mechanical engineer	332	377	387	437	510	503
Solicitor	359	392	379	432	610	585
Medical practitioner	515	504	569	612	691	764

[1] Adjusted to April 1995 prices using the retail prices index.
[2] At April each year. Full-time employees on adult rates whose pay was not affected for the survey period by absence.

Source: Social Trends (1996)

Figure 6.7
Real[1] household disposable income[2], United Kingdom

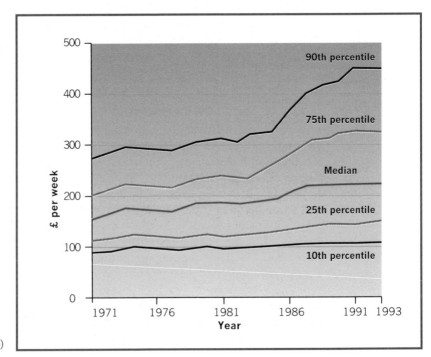

[1] Before housing costs, at January 1995 prices deflated by the retail prices index less local taxes.
[2] Equivalized disposable household income has been used for the ranking for individuals.

Source: Social Trends (1996)

Table 6.9 Distribution of wealth[1], United Kingdom

	Percentages and £ billion			
	1976	*1981*	*1986*	*1991*
Marketable wealth				
Percentage of wealth owned by[2]				
Most wealthy 1%	21	18	18	18
Most wealthy 5%	38	36	36	37
Most wealthy 10%	50	50	50	50
Most wealthy 25%	71	73	73	71
Most wealthy 50%	92	92	90	92
Total marketable wealth (*£ billion*)	280	565	955	1694
Marketable wealth less value of dwellings				
Percentage of wealth owned by[2]				
Most wealthy 1%	29	26	25	28
Most wealthy 5%	47	45	46	50
Most wealthy 10%	57	56	58	63
Most wealthy 25%	73	74	75	79
Most wealthy 50%	88	87	89	92

[1] Estimates for 1976, 1981 and 1986 are based on the estates of persons dying in those years. Estimates for 1991 are based on estates notified for probate in 1991–92. Estimates are not strictly comparable between 1991 and earlier years.

[2] Percentages and total marketable wealth are of population aged 18 and over.

Source: *Social Trends* (1994)

The underclass in Britain

We will now consider current debates about the notion of a developing 'underclass'. Poverty exists in our society. Will it always be with us? Can it be alleviated? Is there a distinction between those who are poor and those who seem to have no desire to participate in our society. Overlapping, but in some ways separate from the poor, is there a distinctive underclass?

What do we mean by the underclass? The more sociologists keep to the formal categories of classes and status groups that they have developed, the harder they find

this new concept to handle. So much so, that Dean has said, almost dismissing the concept:

'... underclass is a symbolic term with no single meaning, but a great many applications ... It represents, not a useful concept, but a potent symbol.' (Dean 1991, pp. 20–35)

But if 'the underclass' is a potent symbol, we have to ask for whom is it a potent symbol? The answer to that question is that, if the notion of potent symbol has any meaning, it must be for all of us.

What is the word 'underclass' a symbol for? What comes to your mind? For over two hundred years, West European societies have contained images which clearly relate to this idea of an underclass. Concepts such as 'underclass' are also often related to fear. In political, social and sociological discussions, there have been concepts of 'the mob', the 'undeserving poor', the 'sturdy beggars', the 'ne'er do well', the 'other side', the 'sinks', the 'underside', and so on. You will notice that we have not yet used the terms 'the poor' or 'those in poverty'. We are not talking about a social or economic situation, but a particular reaction to a concept that is to be feared.

Who expresses these fears?

❖ those who benefit from our social system

❖ those who are close to poverty

❖ those who feel responsible for social policy.

It is in the debates about social policy that 'the underclass' tend to feature. Whatever term is used to describe the group we are talking about, the term is a potent symbol for raising anxieties, uncertainties and fears. In the nineteenth century, 'the undeserving poor' was a term much used, but now the common term is 'an underclass', a term that in itself conjures up an uncertainty about its

relationship to an underworld. It is in the debates concerning social policy and social welfare provision in the United States, and in the United Kingdom during the last twenty years, that we find the particular term 'underclass' being used.

❖ Activity 10 ❖

Read the quotation from Murray (see *In Focus*) and then discuss with friends or colleagues what images come to mind relating to the underclass.

Our experience suggests that a number of other phrases will come to mind in such discussions. These usually include inner cities, unemployment, hopelessness, council estates, crime, violence and, in many cases, ethnic minorities. Is this an expression of an empirical reality or of social fear?

Such remarks are not at all unusual in discussing the phenomenon of the underclass in a general way with people who are interested in the organization, successes and problems of society. Before proceeding with discussions of these fundamentally social policy issues, we should also consider some more formal considerations of class.

In Focus

◆

Murray and the 'New Rabble'

The following quotation is from Charles Murray, a social commentator, who has been most influential in popularizing the term 'underclass'. Now, in his more recent work, he has started to use the term the 'New Rabble' – an even more emotive term.

'The New Rabble will exploit social benefit programmes imaginatively and comprehensively, and be impervious to social benefit programmes that seek to change their behaviour. They will not enter the legitimate labour force when economic times are good and will recruit more working-class young people to their way of life when times are bad. ... The new rabble will provide a large and lucrative market for violent and pornographic film, television and music. Their housing blocks will be characterized by graffiti and vandalism, their parks will be venues for drugs and prostitution ...' (Murray, 1994, p. 12)

Marx and the lumpen-proletariat

'Class' is a formal categorization of people into groups (or classes) which share certain characteristics in the market for labour, services and capital. The shared position of members of the underclass is that they are quite simply outside the market. From Karl Marx onwards, commentators have been unable to decide whether such people are in a class or are outside the class system altogether. In many of his earlier pamphlets, Karl Marx labelled this social group as 'the lumpen-proletariat'. In this he intended to include families (rather than individuals) where their means of subsistence, or their way of surviving, rarely included recourse to full-time, paid employment with a regular employer. For Marx, the lumpen-proletariat might exist on part-time work, irregular employment, irregular self-employment as hawkers or street-sellers, as well as activity which might broadly be classed as criminal, such as mugging, stealing, dealing in stolen goods, selling on, dealing in opium or other drugs or prostitution.

In describing the lumpen-proletariat, Marx is describing a style of life – one remarkably similar to the descriptions of Charles Murray. Karl Marx was also aware though of a different, but related, phenomenon that he analysed with the concept of 'the reserve army of labour'.

The reserve army of labour

Capitalism, Marx thought, generated a whole group of people who were marginalized on the edge of their societies. This group included the lumpen-proletariat, but also included a whole range of poorly skilled workers or family members not currently working. In times of economic expansion, this group might be drawn into the labour market; in poor times, however, they might be thrown out of work and back onto other resources in their family or community. This was the industrial reserve army of labour. In his later work, Marx was concerned with analysing the economic effect of this reserve army of labour on the wage levels of the poorest who continued to be in work. The effect, he concluded, was to guarantee that many of those in work would be kept on poverty wages and unable to rise out of poverty.

Marx was writing in a time before 'welfare' or 'social security' benefits could be had by individuals while still in their own home. These benefits became formalized in the UK in 1949. From then on there grew a suspicion that some chose welfare in preference to work, or took welfare benefits and worked secretly. It was feared that a culture of poverty was developing.

The 'culture of poverty'

One of the most intractable problems of society is the existence of poverty and ways of explaining it. What many casual observers notice is that the poor, as a group, tend to be recruited from the poor: their parents were poor, as were their parents' parents, and so on. Some families seem destined to stay on the margins of society for generation after generation. As individuals, some go through a life cycle of poverty: being born into a family that is very poor, rising out of poverty early in life, falling back in when children arrive, just rising out of poverty for a few years before their retirement from the active labour market which pushes them back into poverty for the rest of their life (see Fig. 10.1 on p. 467). These people seem almost destined to be poor.

'Destiny' is not a sociological concept although, since the concept is widespread, it must be described and explained. Oscar Lewis (1959) wrote a highly influential book based on a very small-scale, empirical study of a small number of families in the USA. In that book he developed the notion of 'the culture of poverty'. This refers to the probability that, where groups of families exist in poverty, they develop a set of social attitudes that makes it very difficult for any family members to escape. Parents come to take a very short-term view of life. There is only minimal planning for even medium-term expenditures, such as the purchase of clothing or shoes. An attitude develops that 'people like us' will always be poor. When money exists, it is spent quickly. Pleasures must be taken now, when available. The longer-term planning implicit in disciplined and extended education or schooling simply does not fit into the pattern. Children are not expected to plan or work hard in school and so they then find it difficult to escape a culture of poverty. In addition, there is often a casual attitude to dress, manners, behaviour and hygiene – so much so that those in this culture begin to mark themselves out from those more properly and fully participating in the labour market and in wider social patterns and interactions. Lewis and others note the way in which the leisure patterns of people in this culture rarely allow for participation in social activities with people from other groups. Their only interaction with 'the mainstreams' is through popular music or a passive watching of TV. In this way, their culture becomes separated off from the rest.

Oscar Lewis's notion of the culture of poverty finds sufficient resonance with casual observers and politicians to have become very popular. It begins to move towards an explanation that looks as if it might be sociological. In the end, it remains very descriptive and psychological. Furthermore, by focusing on individual attitudes (even if described as a culture), it can move very quickly towards blaming those in poverty for not escaping. Rutter and Madge (1976) found in a detailed study in England that:

'at least half of the children born into a disadvantaged home do not repeat the pattern of disadvantage in the next generation. Over half of all forms of disadvantage arise anew each generation.'

Quite what we can make of that against the idea of a culture of poverty is not clear. Rutter and Madge intend us to see that the culture of poverty might not be fully entrapping. If it does not entrap or get repeated, then what does that means for the whole idea of 'a culture' which, by definition, should be self-perpetuating. On the other hand, we have clear evidence, from our studies on social mobility that few other social or occupational classes recruit as many as half their members from their own ranks. So in these terms, the culture of poverty might rightly be regarded as entrapping or, if we prefer the term, self-perpetuating.

Are all the poor in the underclass?

There are other groups of the poor which remain definitely outside 'the underclass' and its attitudes, and also outside the 'culture of poverty'. Most of the elderly poor, for example, do not fit into these notions. They do not share the attitudes of the underclass or the culture of poverty. They are poor because they are outside the labour market and because, when they were in the labour market, they could not afford to buy or establish any pension rights beyond the minimum state pension. Similarly, many single-parent families, or families where members are pushed out of the labour market, are poor. Yet many of these families do not share the attitudes of the underclass or participate in a culture of poverty. After a short period (which may last as long as five or six years), they rejoin the economy, participate more fully in the labour market and are again able to broaden their social participation.

Inside or outside the system?

Those concerned with the formal categories of class (participation in the market for labour, services and capital) do have anxieties about a classification-group labelled 'outside the market'.

'Since the underclass lacks any meaningful market position, it is best conceptualized as a social category, not a class.' (Heisler 1991, p. 476)

It is clear that some social groups begin to be labelled by others as in some way outside, or on the margin of 'our' society. The social-categorization processes of society are in themselves interesting. Such categorization takes place through the interaction of the other social groups of society, with those closest to the centre of society seeing other groups as having only a marginalized claim on them. In other cases, they see some groups as having full citizenship rights. From this, we can see why the elderly poor, or those temporarily out of the labour market, may be seen as poor, but still as *full* members – citizens – of the society which should be caring for them. They are not 'the underclass' (or any other excluded group), but they are the deserving (poor). The underclass are almost by definition the 'undeserving poor' – who should at least be subject to some enquiry or suspicion, after which they may be given minimal support without actually becoming regarded fully as 'citizens'. This feeling underlies a good many debates about social policies. This is a thoroughly Weberian approach, employing the idea of social relationships between groups.

Throughout West European history, those who have seen themselves as 'good citizens' have feared those on the edge and often persecuted them. Even in societies with a strong dedication to social welfare systems, it is easy to arouse these fears and suspicions. A debate on identity cards quickly turns to the criminal tendencies of the underclass. (Identity cards make it harder for criminals and harder for social benefit fraudsters.) Whatever the truth of this, those who propose such systems rarely talk of the difficulties of those who need benefit, who may unwittingly have incorrect data on their identity files. Such people will find it almost impossible to identify any such mistakes and hard to eradicate them.

Origins of the term 'underclass'

Charles Murray stands as one example of a social commentator who has used and popularized the concept of underclass. What is particularly interesting is the way that he has progressed to the term 'the new rabble'. He is by origin and orientation a citizen of the USA, but he was invited to work with the Institute of Economic Affairs in the UK, a 'think tank' that leans towards right-wing economics. Before looking at his work, remember that, in the USA, wide sections of the underclass are African-American or Hispanic-American. Not all such Americans are in the underclass, but do often have cultural orientations that are different, in terms of taste in food, dress, music, dance and other cultural artefacts and activities. These also mark out the wider groups as different from the more dominant white Caucasian-American groups. Furthermore, less than thirty years ago, social groups with these minority origins were positively excluded from and discouraged from participating in a wide range of social activities related to the concept of full citizenship. They were discouraged from registering for voting rights, they progressed poorly in the economic, social and political hierarchies, and their education was often segregated from those of the dominant groups, as were their leisure facilities. This extended until the mid-1970s even to bizarre levels such as separatism in radio stations. It is against this background that the concept of an 'underclass' was developed in the USA.

The term 'underclass' appears to have been coined by Gunnar Myrdal, a Swedish economist who wrote extensively on the development of economic systems. As early as 1962, he was noting a tendency of industrial societies to become *postindustrial*: that is, large sections of the unskilled factory workers were about to become redundant because of technological advances and the consequent reduction in demand for unskilled workers. For Myrdal it meant that a large section of the unskilled, urban working class would become marginalized with such reduced opportunities that they might properly be labelled the underclass.

The underclass as a 'social issue'

During the years 1964–68, the Democratic Government in the USA wished to advance the civil rights of the African- and Hispanic-Americans and established a wide range of programmes to enhance the life-chances of these previously dominated social groups. Many social scientists were involved in developing these programmes. Daniel Moynihan was one such worker who actually helped to draft some speeches for the President announcing these programmes. In one of his major publications, Moynihan (1967) pointed out that

> 'the Negro community is ... dividing between a stable middle-class group that is steadily growing stronger and more successful, and an increasing disorganized and disadvantaged lower-class group.' (Moynihan 1965, pp. 5–6)

Moynihan argued that the polarization of African-American society was happening at the same time as a progressive deterioration in the very fabric of the lower-class black communities. The inner-city black ghettoes become the focus of intensive and chronic deprivation. One symptom of this was the breakdown of the lower-class family in which there was a steady and consistent rise of divorce, separation and illegitimacy, which meant that a large proportion of black families were headed by women as single parents. The origins of this deterioration in the family life of African-Americans can be located partly in the rapid migrations and urbanization of these populations from 1930 onwards. The historical experience of slavery for African-Americans positively denied and inhibited the establishment of families for several generations and this is likely to have had some long-term effects on the family experience. Moynihan was writing as a liberal who was trying to establish social patterns and structures which would support this family system and enhance the socialization and education of children. Moynihan clearly regarded himself as a 'liberal' in the areas of public policy to

which he was contributing. However, almost the same observations have now been made and transformed by Charles Murray as a right-wing contributor (a member of 'The New Right'), who clearly wishes to *reduce* social benefit and social structure policy programmes.

Is the underclass developing or shrinking?

Murray concludes that many benefit or welfare systems positively harm the social fabric. He argues that the provision of benefit for unmarried mothers creates a security for young women so that the number and ratio of never-married mothers increases. Similarly the provision of separate and generous benefits for men and for divorced or separated women encourages divorce or separation, since the total benefit paid will be greater. The provision of 'welfare' housing decreases home-ownership and all of these policies positively discourage participation in the labour market. Furthermore, the rise of single-parent households, headed by females, deprives the young male children of any adequate role models and so encourages vandalism, crime and violence. Murray paints a very despairing picture of the creation of large areas of inner-city America largely dominated by the black and Hispanic under-classes. All others migrate out of these areas, increasing the problem.

In contrast Wilson (1987) describes virtually the same phenomena in a way which gives alternative explanations and describes policy alternatives which should be able to provide stability in inner-city neighbourhoods and reinforce the mainstream pattern, norms and behaviours. Wilson describes the phenomena not as the creation of a culture of poverty but as arising out of a situation of social isolation of individuals from the dominant values and activities of the societies. He seeks policies which encourage the dominant values to penetrate these communities. Murray's policy analysis, on the other hand, has little to offer except the removal of benefit programmes. What underlies the differences between the work of Murray and Wilson is that they seem to be operating with differing concepts of citizenship.

Wilson sees the underclass as a group of citizens abandoned by the powerful social groups, as excluded by them from full citizenship. Murray sees the underclass as a group surrendering (consciously or unconsciously) its citizenship rights in exchange for a free life.

In the construction of concepts of an underclass that is composed largely of African-Americans and Hispanic-Americans, there is an interesting conception of citizenship. Underlying both positions is the assumption that the underclass is a group that can be regarded as not full American citizens. They are in some sense potential *non-citizens*. This relationship of the underclass concept to ethnic or racial origins is so strong that some commentators do not see the concept as an offshoot of class theory, but part of the sociology of ethnic differences.

Methodology of study

One of the most interesting dimensions of the social debate on notions of a culture of poverty and the long-term existence of an underclass is that the debate proceeds largely on the basis of commentary, consideration of official statistics and other secondary sources. What we lack is longitudinal studies, ethnographic studies, participant observation studies or anything which tries to map the experiences and identities of the underclass themselves in an empathetic way. It is almost as if they are so separate from the way that 'we' are, that we do not expect to comprehend them. Murray has enlivened his writings with material gained in interviews, but he has not built a systematic study of 'the new rabble' themselves, as he calls them.

❖ Activity 11 ❖

Read the *In Focus* below and then answer the following questions:

1 What are the reasons given for why Ross and Stacey are unlikely to get married?

2 What evidence is offered that young males are 'essentially barbarians'?

3 Distinguish the idea of a culture of young males from the idea of a culture of poverty

4 How can the Welfare State encourage stable and committed parenting?

5 How would you design small-scale qualitative research to take your interests further?

In Focus

◆

Why get married?

'The real scandal of the system is not what you get if you cheat, but what you get if you play it straight. ... Suppose we imagine a pristine benefit system and utterly honest clients. The story is heavily loaded against marriage. Here are the economic facts of life facing a fictitious pair of honest young people – let's call them Ross and Stacey – who are in their late teens and have been keeping company.

Stacey has discovered she is pregnant. She didn't do it on purpose – I am not appealing to the image of the young woman who gets pregnant to get a council flat. Blame it on the sexual revolution, if you wish, or nature having its way, as it has with young people throughout time. Stacey would just as soon not have an abortion, if she can afford to take care of the baby. She and Ross sit down and have a talk about marriage.

Ross has a job paying £228 a week (just below the standard for manual workers, and better than most unskilled young men just getting started).

continued on p. 270

After taking into account deductions for income tax, national insurance, rent and community charges, then adding in their family credit and all other pertinent means-tested or universal benefits, Ross and Stacey and the baby will have an after-tax net of about £152.

But suppose they don't get married. Then they will have £216 – £74 in benefit for Stacey and the baby, none of it taxed, plus Ross's after-tax income as a single unmarried person, which amounts to about £142. Their weekly premium for not marrying is £64 a week, £3,328 a year, a 'rise' of 42 per cent over their married income. Ross and Stacey would have to be soft to get married.

If Ross is unemployed, Stacey has even less incentive to marry, for the most obvious of reasons: before, at least Ross had a job and prospects for the future. Without a job, Ross has no attractions as a future provider. Even in the present, he is worth less as a husband than as a live-in lover. Adding up the income support for a couple with one infant and the family premium, they would have £94 a week, plus a council flat. But if they *don't* get married, the same benefit package will amount to £108 – a difference of £14 a week. Little as it may seem to those for whom such sums are pocket money, it amounts to a rise of 15 per cent over the income they would have if they married.

There are other advantages to claiming income support separately. The benefits of one cannot be reduced to pay off the other's debts as long as they are unmarried. This sounds especially good to Stacey, seeing that Ross is a bit irresponsible in money matters. If Stacey wants to supplement her income after the baby is born, the first £15 of her earnings will be disregarded when computing her benefit – three times the 'disregard' if she is married. All in all, Stacey has no

economic reason whatsoever to swallow her doubts about Ross and try to get him to marry her. Staying single makes sense for her. As for Ross, why not remain free? He knows very well he has a wandering eye. He's in full flood of young male adulthood. *Why get married?*

This is the first reason why the New Victorianism will not percolate down to the New Rabble. In the low-skilled working class, marriage makes no sense. *Of course*, a high proportion of young women from low-income neighbourhoods and their boyfriends do not get married now. Even higher proportions will not get married in the future, as the illegitimacy ratio in low-income neighbourhoods continues to be pushed by this persistent economic reality.

This is not the whole story, however. Lower-class culture in Britain will continue to deteriorate, even after the New Victorianism is in full bloom elsewhere, because the next generation in lower-class Britain will know no other way to live.

When I wrote about the nascent British underclass five years ago, I briefly referred to young males as 'essentially barbarians' who are civilized by marriage. That image has become all too literal in the American inner city, where male teenage behaviour is often a caricature of the barbarian male: retaliate against anyone who shows you the slightest disrespect ('disses' you). Sleep with and impregnate as many girls as possible. Regard violence as a sign of strength. To worry about tomorrow is weakness. To die young is glorious. What makes these attitudes so disturbing is not just that they describe behaviour, but that inner-city boys articulate them as *principles*. They are, explicitly, the code they live by.'

Source: Murray (1994)

Chapter summary

❖ Social stratification is concerned with the structured differentiation of varying access to the chances of the good things in life.

❖ One major cause of such differentiation lies in occupational and class structures.

❖ Other significant differentiations are created by gender, ethnic background and age.

❖ The occupational and stratification systems of all West European societies are changing and the older structures are becoming less significant.

❖ People now experience more fragmented identities than in the past.

❖ Identity is initially created in a family of origin and mobility is constrained by that origin.

❖ Income and wealth remain unevenly distributed and the differentiation appears to be growing.

❖ One aspect of the growing differentiation appears to many to be the creation of an underclass.

Coursework

A good range of the work described in this chapter consists of medium- or large-scale surveys which are not easily undertaken by students. However, regular review of the statistical sources made available by central government (see Further reading below) can constitute useful course work. This work could include updating any charts in this volume.

Small-scale ethnographic research work can be exciting and can extend your skills as observers and commentators. Some topics have been suggested in the text. Other postmodernist studies looking at and analysing the language of discourse in official literature are possible. This could be extended to arenas where 'class' has a practical importance, such as sales literature from estate agents.

An analysis of the labelling and stereotyping language used by your own social groups could also yield interesting results and create new levels of awareness.

Essay questions

1 Select one dimension of social stratification (other than class) and briefly assess its usefulness in explaining the distribution of 'life-chances'.

2 What sociological evidence can be presented to support the claim that sociological theories of social stratification have ignored the existence of women?

3 Evaluate the Marxist accounts of Class Conflict.

4 How far does sociological evidence support the idea that an 'underclass' has emerged in Britain?

5 To what extent do sociologists agree that the identities of people in Britain are fragmented by many forms of stratification?

6 How far does sociological evidence support the view that the gaps between the classes is widening.

Further reading

Bradley, H. (1996) *Fractured Identities: Changing Patterns of Inequality*, Cambridge: Polity Press.

This is by far and away the best single book to supplement this chapter.

Warde, A. and Abercrombie, N. (eds) (1994) *Stratification and Social Inequality: Studies in British Society*: Lancaster: Framework Press.

This series of ethnographic case studies will bring a sharp feel of reality to the subject.

Westergaard, J. (1995) *Who gets What? The Hardening of Class Inequality in the Late Twentieth Century*, Cambridge: Polity Press.

On income and wealth differentiation, the works of Westergaard are always useful and this is particularly good.

Scott, J. (1991) *Who Rules Britain?*, Cambridge: Polity Press.

On matters of power (not dealt with in this chapter, but see Chapter 13, Power and politics) the writings of John Scott are all relevant.

Chapman, R. and Rutherford, J. (eds) (1988) *Male Order: Unwrapping Masculinity*, London: Lawrence and Wishart.

Connell, R.W. (1995) *Masculinities*, London: Polity Press.

The above two books both look at issues of masculinity and identity in ways not considered in this chapter.

Bonner, F., Goodman, L., Allen, R., Janes, L. and King, C. (1992) *Imaging Women: Cultural Representations and Gender*, Cambridge: Polity Press.

This book provides interesting of images of women.

Two titles in the *Investigating Sociology* series from Collins Educational are relevant to this chapter: that by **Paul Taylor** entitled *Investigating Culture and Identity* and that by **Nick Madry** and **Mark Kirby** entitled *Investigating Work, Unemployment and Leisure*.

Statistical information is useful on these matters and regular statistical sources such as *Social Trends* have already been referred to in the text, with many of the tables and figures reproduced in this chapter taken from this source. In addition we recommend three particular 'one-off' volumes from the Office for National Statistics:

Social Focus on Ethnic Minorities (1996)
Social Focus on Children (1996)
Social Focus on Women (1996).

These are all available from the HMSO.

Chapter 7

Theory and methods

❖ Preview

In this chapter we shall be looking at:

- ❖ the foundations of sociology in the work of Comte, Marx, Durkheim, Weber and Freud

- ❖ how sociology has developed in the twentieth century into a number of theoretical perspectives:
  - – functionalism
  - – structural functionalism
  - – conflict theory
  - – social action theory
  - – ˙ ethnomethodology

- ❖ recent developments in social theory: feminism, poststructuralism, postmodernism

- ❖ whether we can ever have one sociology with one theoretical perspective

- ❖ sociological methods: quantitative and qualitative

- ❖ ways of collecting data for sociological analysis, both primary and secondary

- ❖ the ethics of social research

- ❖ the role that social theory and sociological methods have played in the analysis of suicide.

❖ Introduction

As we saw in Chapter 1, there are a number of theoretical perspectives in sociology each with its own way of looking at the social world. In part, this diversity of theories and methods is because what we are studying – people in society – have their own views on what social life is like. Sociologists are, in the end, both sociologists and ordinary members of society! In this chapter we will look at a range of social theories and sociological methods which give us the tools for analysing the social world.

Sociology deals with four sets of issues:

- ❖ *Theory – what* we study: the subject matter of sociology. It is here that we find the various perspectives mentioned above – functionalism, structural functionalism, structuralism, conflict theory and so on – and the wide range of sociological concepts which are discussed throughout this book – for example, social class, gender, ethnicity, bureaucracy and so on.

- ❖ *Methodology – how* we study society. This involves two sets of issues:
  - – how we find out evidence, e.g. about the extent of poverty

Figure 7.1
Theoretical Approaches in Sociology

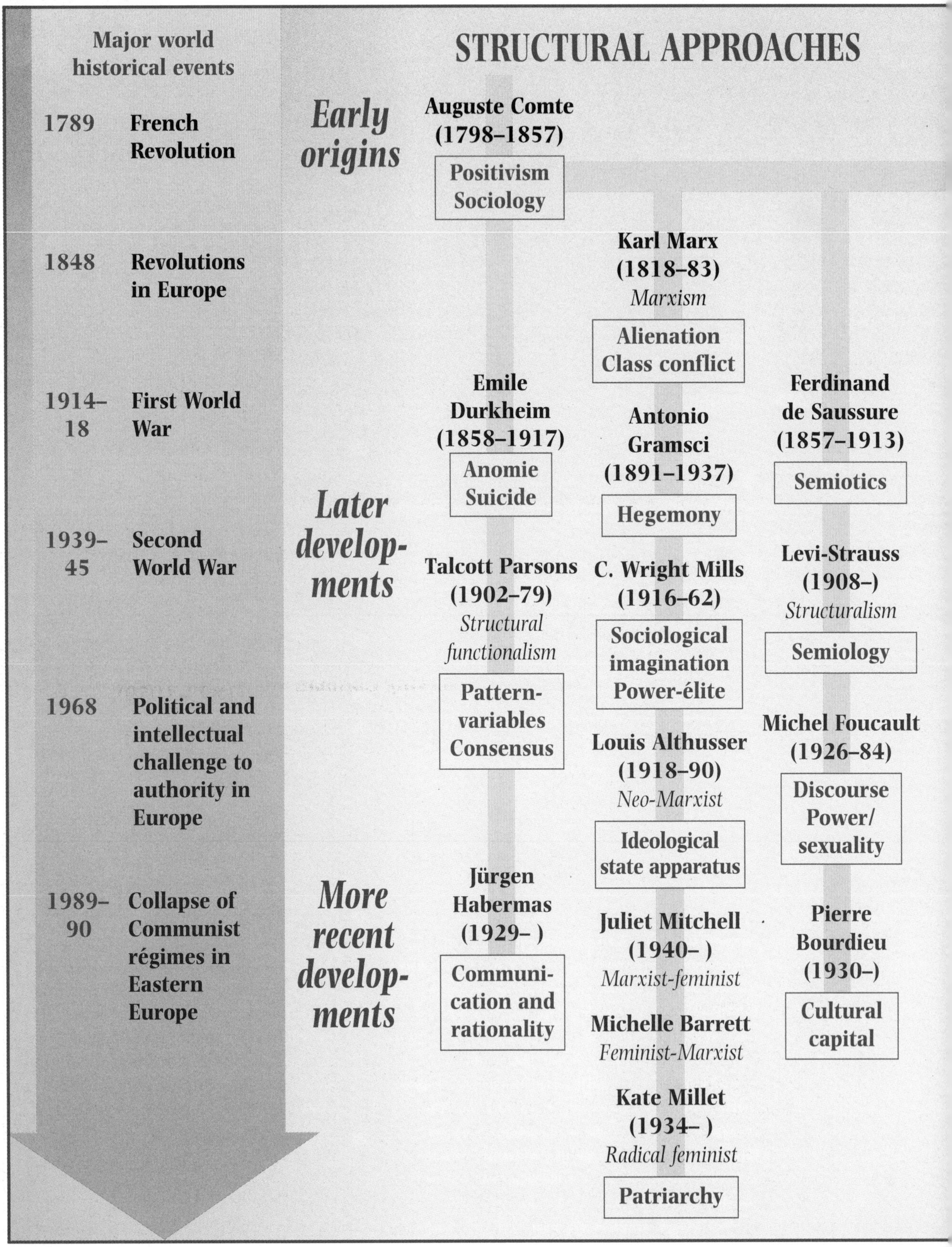

Major world historical events		STRUCTURAL APPROACHES		
1789	**French Revolution**	*Early origins* **Auguste Comte (1798–1857)** Positivism Sociology		
1848	**Revolutions in Europe**		**Karl Marx (1818–83)** *Marxism* Alienation Class conflict	
1914– 18	**First World War**	**Emile Durkheim (1858–1917)** Anomie Suicide	**Antonio Gramsci (1891–1937)** Hegemony	**Ferdinand de Saussure (1857–1913)** Semiotics
1939– 45	**Second World War**	*Later develop- ments* **Talcott Parsons (1902–79)** *Structural functionalism* Pattern- variables Consensus	**C. Wright Mills (1916–62)** Sociological imagination Power-élite	**Levi-Strauss (1908–)** *Structuralism* Semiology
1968	**Political and intellectual challenge to authority in Europe**		**Louis Althusser (1918–90)** *Neo-Marxist* Ideological state apparatus	**Michel Foucault (1926–84)** Discourse Power/ sexuality
1989– 90	**Collapse of Communist régimes in Eastern Europe**	*More recent develop- ments* **Jürgen Habermas (1929–)** Communi- cation and rationality	**Juliet Mitchell (1940–)** *Marxist-feminist* **Michelle Barrett** *Feminist-Marxist*	**Pierre Bourdieu (1930–)** Cultural capital
			Kate Millet (1934–) *Radical feminist* Patriarchy	

SOCIAL ACTION APPROACHES

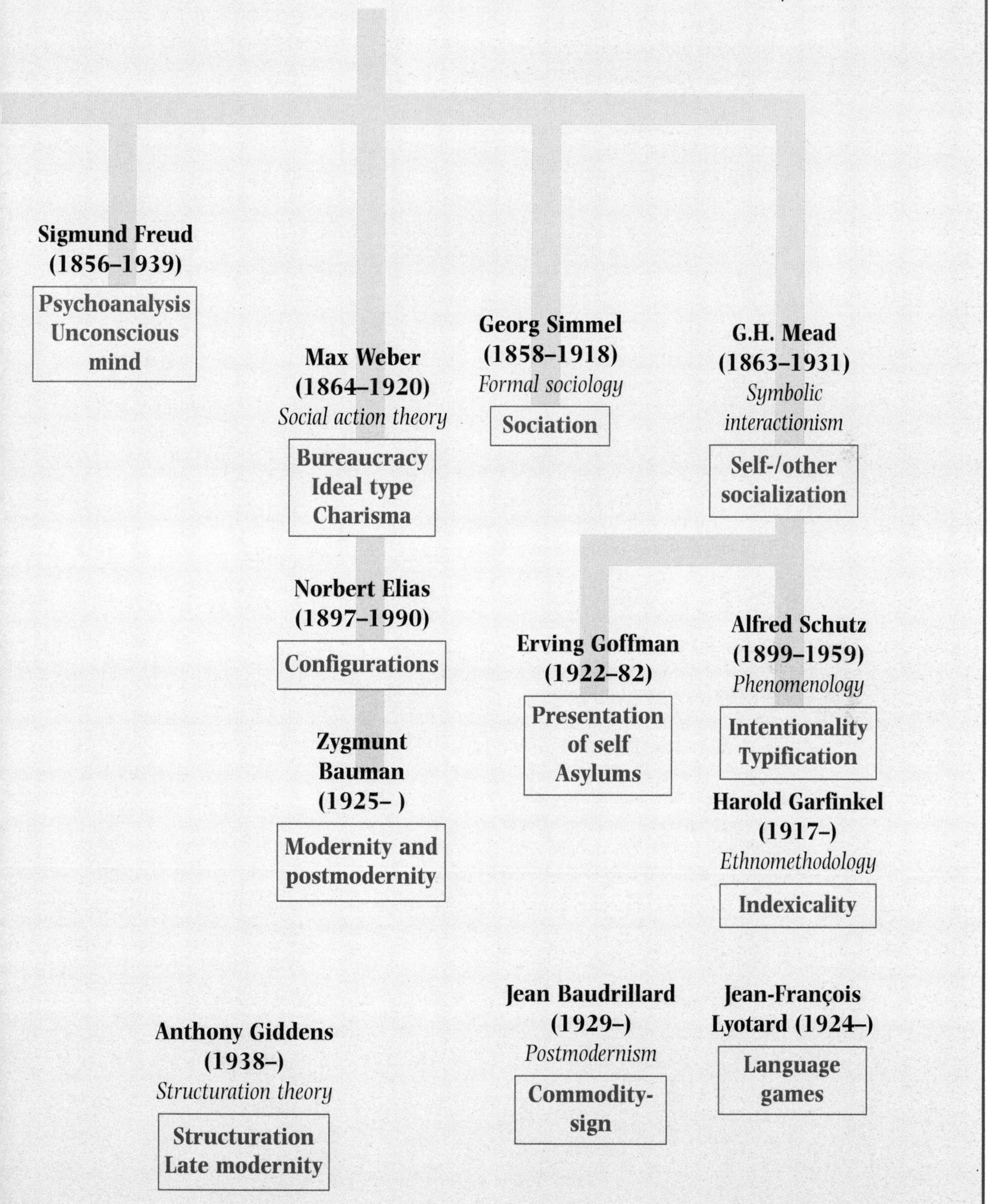

**Sigmund Freud
(1856–1939)**

| Psychoanalysis
Unconscious
mind |

**Max Weber
(1864–1920)**
Social action theory

| Bureaucracy
Ideal type
Charisma |

**Georg Simmel
(1858–1918)**
Formal sociology

| Sociation |

**G.H. Mead
(1863–1931)**
*Symbolic
interactionism*

| Self-/other
socialization |

**Norbert Elias
(1897–1990)**

| Configurations |

**Erving Goffman
(1922–82)**

| Presentation
of self
Asylums |

**Alfred Schutz
(1899–1959)**
Phenomenology

| Intentionality
Typification |

**Zygmunt
Bauman
(1925–)**

| Modernity and
postmodernity |

**Harold Garfinkel
(1917–)**
Ethnomethodology

| Indexicality |

**Anthony Giddens
(1938–)**
Structuration theory

| Structuration
Late modernity |

**Jean Baudrillard
(1929–)**
Postmodernism

| Commodity-
sign |

**Jean-François
Lyotard (1924–)**

| Language
games |

– how we analyse and present that evidence.

❖ *Practical issues* – *what we do with* the studies that we carry out. As governments and industry frequently sponsor research and set the agenda for what is being investigated, this area can become quite political.

❖ *Value issues* – *why* we study certain aspects of society and *whether* we should study them. It is important to be aware of the ethics of research. If, for example, we are doing observation studies of drug-taking, we must be aware of the ethical and legal issues.

 ## Social theories: a brief introduction

As already suggested, diverse social theories have been developed to explain the modern world. In order to try and make sense of this diversity, we can classify social theory into two types:

❖ *Structuralist theories* – These stress the way that society and social rules constrain and control what we do. These include theories which argue:

– that social *consensus* is normal

– that social *conflict* is normal.

Sociologists influenced by Durkheim usually see structure and consensus as central; those influenced by Marx usually emphasize structure and conflict.

❖ *Social action theories* – These emphasize the role that individuals and groups play in making society and social rules. They include a whole range of theorists influenced by Weber and Mead and include *symbolic interactionism* and *ethnomethodology* theories.

Look at the 'timeline' diagram in Fig. 7.1 on pp. 274–5. This gives a list of the most important sociologists with their dates, along with the major theories and concepts associated with each sociologist. The historical events are also important.

You will see that some of these people wrote a long time before their ideas became really important. For example, Marx's ideas became important to sociologists only in the 1960s and 1970s, eighty years after his death. So, just because some sociologists are dead does not mean their ideas cease to be important.

Sociology: early origins and historical background

Sociology developed in the late eighteenth and nineteenth centuries, a period of profound change involving:

❖ large-scale movements of people from rural areas to cities

❖ political upheavals and revolutions

❖ huge increases in economic productivity

❖ the development of empires, including the British empire

❖ the development of new political systems, including democracy.

This was the period when the modern world in which we now live developed. A lot of what sociologists do, therefore, is the study of *modernity*.

The founders of sociology

As suggested in the introduction, the founders of sociology were interested in what the modern world was like and what it was like to live in that world. As we shall see, they all had worries about modernity – Marx's concern with how workers were exploited, Durkheim's worries over excessive individualism, Weber's concerns about the effects on our daily lives of materialism and bureaucracy. Their work was trying to understand and explain the modern world.

There is debate about who the founders were. Sociologists generally agree that they include Comte, Marx, Durkheim and Weber. However, there were other people who had a great influence on the development of sociology who were not, in any sense, sociologists – these include philosophers (e.g. Hume) and psychologists (e.g. Freud). Many important writers – women and black people – are not included in the list of founders.

Auguste Comte (1798–1857)

Comte wanted to establish a scientific study of society which could be used as a basis for changing society. For him, sociology could contribute to the wellbeing of society because sociologists would be scientists using a scientific method. Scientific method was only possible in his times; previous societies had, for whatever reasons, been unable to develop a scientific approach and had, for example, been dominated by religious thinking.

The emphasis on science here is important. Comte believed that a scientific approach:

❖ would allow social change to be planned in a rational fashion

❖ was the best way of studying society – better, for example, than a religious or philosophical approach

❖ was possible, even though people would know they were being studies, unlike the things that natural scientists study, such as atoms and bacteria.

Comte advocated something called *positivism*, which is a way of characterizing the methods of the natural sciences. Positivism involves three very important ideas:

❖ The world we live in is made up of things that are causally related to each other, e.g. we might say that unemployment causes poverty.

❖ There *are* things which exist independently of our awareness of them, e.g. there are social classes even though many people deny this.

❖ The existence of things and how they are related causally can be demonstrated by *empirical* means, i.e. by *collecting evidence*.

So, for Comte, a good sociologist will:

1 develop a hypothesis, e.g. 'unemployment causes poverty'

2 test this hypothesis by data collection

3 find the hypothesis either verified or refuted.

Many subsequent sociologists, such as Durkheim, have tried to apply this model. However, others, such as Weber, have claimed that there is something about human beings and human societies that makes positivism an inappropriate method of study. In addition, some authors looking at how scientists work – e.g. Karl Popper (1959) and Thomas Kuhn (1962) – argue that this is not what scientists *really* do.

Emile Durkheim (1858–1917)

Durkheim wanted to establish sociology as a scientific enterprise and, in this sense, comes closest to using positivism as the way sociologists should do their work. Like Comte, Durkheim was concerned about how orderly modern societies were. In particular, he was concerned that the

There is considerable debate about what scientists actually do, that is, how scientific they are. Popper argues that when scientists develop hypotheses, they often do this on the basis of some hunch or guess, rather than by some rational process. Kuhn goes further. At any one time science will be dominated by a *paradigm* – a pattern or model. For example, the view that the universe was created in a big bang is accepted by most scientists and drives what they study. They will rarely study something outside that paradigm and will build their careers on such studies. The acceptance of a paradigm will mean that they may not even recognize that there is anything wrong with it; they may ignore data and research which challenges the paradigm. Finally, Kuhn argues that changes in scientific paradigms – scientific revolutions – are more to do with the workings of the scientific community than with evidence and research.

individualism of the modern world would make social order difficult to maintain and that the solutions to this problem suggested by socialism would not work (see below for a discussion of Marx). In addition, Durkheim argued that a scientific study of society included the idea that people do not, in fact, choose what they do. On the contrary what he called *social facts* – the family, social class, religion – constrain what we do and exist even if we do not recognize that they exist.

In fact, Durkheim's sociology stresses both *social structure* and something called *function*. We can look at one of Durkheim's early works to illustrate this double concern. In *The Division of Labour in Society* (1893/1947), Durkheim identified two types of social structure:

❖ One was found in premodern societies and he called this *mechanical solidarity*.

❖ The other is found in modern societies and he called it *organic solidarity*.

Emile Durkheim

Mechanical solidarity

In the first, the division of labour is simple, with little specialization in what people actually do – there are no teachers, footballers, musicians. What keeps such societies together – the basis of social order – is a combination of a simple religious belief system, repressive laws and powerful community rituals.

Studying things that people are not aware of is a common feature of sciences; they often study things that *underlie* what we normally see. Durkheim's argument that social facts are there, even if people are not aware of them, is very like a physicist arguing that most of what we perceive as a solid table is empty space! For the sociologists, there are structures underlying what people do and believe, in the same way that for physicists, there is a structure underlying the world we live in.

The point here is that it is the social structure which makes people follow the rules and provides a mechanism for dealing with deviants. Religion and law have the important function of maintaining what Durkheim calls social solidarity. In addition, crime might look as though it is a form of disorder but, in fact, contributes to social solidarity. This raises two questions:

❖ Can a society without religion or crime be orderly?

❖ Can there by social institutions which do not contribute to social order, i.e. are what we might call *dysfunctional*?

❖ Activity 1 ❖

Identify any social institution or behaviour which does not seem to contribute to social order. Is that institution or behaviour dysfunctional?

Organic solidarity

For Durkheim, there are distinct problems with organic solidarity with its complex division of labour and people being very specialized. The authors of this book do the writing, someone else produces the paper to print it on, someone else sells it and so on. Durkheim says this complex division of labour makes us *interdependent* – as authors, we have to rely on publishers to get what we write published, who have to rely on printers to produce the pages for the book. However, this is not a very secure basis for solidarity, particularly because the common belief systems of mechanical solidarity no longer exist. For Durkheim, in the modern world people are likely to be *anomic*, i.e. lacking in social or moral standards, because there are no clear guidelines for what they should do. The modern world is, therefore, likely to be disorderly and unstable. Durkheim wanted his sociology to form a securer basis on which social order in a society with organic solidarity could be established.

❖ Activity 2 ❖

Using this chapter and other parts of the book, answer the following in no more than three sentences each :

1 What does Durkheim mean by anomie?
2 What, in the modern world, leads to anomie?
3 How can anomie be reduced?

Most of Durkheim's writings are about issues of social structure and problems of modernity.

❖ In *Suicide* (Durkheim 1897/1952), as well as demonstrating that sociology can be scientific, Durkheim indicated that it is the social structure and the particular problems in modern societies which lead to individual acts of suicide.

❖ In *The Elementary Forms of Religious Life* (Durkheim 1912/1961), Durkheim identifies the basic functions of religion – to link people together into communities as well as analysing what happens to religion in modern societies, in particular, its decline.

❖ In *Education and Sociology* (Durkheim 1903/1956), he describes how education is central in maintaining social rules and getting people to accept those rules.

Karl Marx (1818–83)

Marx was concerned to show the importance of the social structure and to analyse and explain it in a scientific way. However, whereas Durkheim was a basically conservative thinker, seeing the importance and benefits of consensus, Marx was concerned with the contradictions within society – for example, poverty existing alongside huge wealth – and how these contradictions could be resolved. He felt that revolutionary change was the way to resolve these contradictions, which made his views much more political than Durkheim's.

Marx emphasized the importance of :

❖ the economic system

❖ social class (Marx 1867/1970)

❖ something he called 'ideology', explained below (Marx 1845/1970).

The economic system

Marx was mainly interested in how the particular type of society he called *capitalist* developed. To explain this, he used a model of the historical development of societies which gave the economic system a crucial role.

Modern capitalist societies did not just appear. They developed out of other societies and Marx's view of historical development suggests that the sequence goes from simple tribal societies to ones in which social class becomes important. For us as sociologists, the crucial move is from feudal to capitalist societies.

In a capitalist society, it is the economic system which produces the goods and services which satisfy wants and needs. Increasingly, for Marx, these wants and needs are *socially* defined. The economic system consists of the *means of production* (the technology available) and the *social relations of production* (the way that technology is socially organized to get things produced) – see *In Focus* below.

Together, the means of production and the social relations of production make up the *economic base* of society. The other aspects of society – beliefs, laws, the state – are related to that economic base and serve to support it.

Social class

Social class was as crucial to Marx's theory as was the economic system. Societies that produce surpluses are also societies that have social-class divisions – in feudal societies these were between nobility and serfs; in capitalist societies the division is between capitalists and workers. In both cases, the former – nobles and capitalists – own the means of production and determine what the social relations of production are going to be (see *In Focus* at the top of the next page for an example of this in practice).

❖ Activity 3 ❖

Write short notes – no more than half a side of paper – on what Marx meant by 'exploitation' and 'alienation'. Give an example of each, using information from this chapter and other parts of the book.

In Focus

◆

Means of production

All societies have technology which provides a means to produce goods and services. Societies can be distinguished, however, in terms of the extent to which that technology allows the production of surpluses; in simpler societies, surpluses may be small, whereas in modern societies surpluses are produced which can then be sold, stored for future sale and so on. The way that surpluses are produced and distributed will vary: in our society, surpluses are produced, for example, in enormous factories using complex computer technology. These surpluses are consumed by people who have the money or credit with which to consume them.

In Focus

◆

A Marxist view of a car plant

The modern car plant is an example of how important social class is for Marx. First, capitalists own factories and the raw materials that factories use. However, without workers the factories and raw materials would lie idle. Workers are needed to make the factories productive; this is what Marx called the *labour theory of value* because it is the value of what the worker does that produces commodities, makes them valuable and leads to profit. However, the capitalist does not pay the worker the full value of what he produces. Imagine a worker producing one Volkswagen Polo per day selling at £11,500. He is not paid anything like that amount for his day's work. The factory owner justifies this in terms of the risk in producing cars and in terms of required levels of profit. However, for Marx, the risk is exaggerated and the profit comes solely from what the worker is not paid. This difference between the value produced and the pay received is a measure of how the worker is *exploited*. In addition, the workers are not in control of the system and their relationships with each other become difficult; this is what Marx terms *alienation*. The workers and capitalists are interdependent but in conflict: the worker wishes to maximize wages and the capitalist to maximize profit. In the long term both cannot occur. This is why, for Marx, capitalism has to end.

The conflict between workers and capitalists always exists even when neither are aware of it – it is part of the capitalist *system*. In sociological terms, it is *structural*. Marx wrote extensively about how the existence of conflict would become clear to workers and how, when that occurred, they could challenge the capitalist system itself and organize for a different – and better – system. This organization of the working class would include trade unions and political parties which would seek to enhance workers' awareness of their exploitation. This awareness is what Marx called *class consciousness*. The alternative to capitalism is what Marx termed *communism* which would involve the end of social-class divisions (Marx and Engels 1848/1967). He thought communism could do this because of the enormous productive capacity of the capitalist means of production. Under capitalism, that productive capacity was wasteful as it aimed to satisfy many false needs, e.g. for numerous types of cat food and washing-up powder!

A Marxist future under communism posed two problems:

❖ If we look at societies such as the former Soviet Union, we have to ask whether they were really like Marx's predictions of the communist future. The reality of the USSR in the 1930s – labour camps, forced collectivization of agriculture – looked very different from Marx's predictions, but it is difficult to know whether the fate of the USSR was a result of its isolation by the big capitalist economies.

❖ Although he argues that social-class divisions will disappear with communism, Marx says little about gender and ethnicity and whether those divisions will remain.

Ideology

Marx is clear about what he thinks of the capitalist system and what it does to the mass of the working population who are unaware of the real situation. In part, for Marx, this is a result of powerful ideologies which serve the capitalists. For Marx, the idea of democracy is an ideology which suggests that society is run in the interests of everyone when, in reality, it is run in the interests of capitalists. The education system can be one system through which this ideology is reproduced, painting a false picture of a society in which everyone is benefiting.

According to Marx, it is not just ideology which keeps the masses unaware of, and therefore accepting of, the capitalist system; it is the need to work in order to live.

We could look at this in the context of the unemployment and housing benefits system. The debate about the need for benefits and their level has crucial importance here. One argument for keeping benefits low and for insisting that people prove they need them, is because benefits are costly. At another level, however, the benefits system must not discourage people from work, because it is hard work that keeps people from thinking about the unfairness of the system itself.

Max Weber (1864–1920)

Max Weber

Like Durkheim and Marx, Weber was interested in the development of the modern. He was concerned about modernity and in particular about the effect of materialism and large-scale bureaucracies on social life. He described the nature of the modern world by looking at both social action *and* social structures (Weber 1978).

Social action

Human beings are unique for Weber because they decide to do things in order to achieve certain ends. The attempt to understand what people do and the meaning that has for them gives rise to Weber's particular way of approaching sociology, which he calls 'verstehen', literally translated as 'understanding'.

There are four ways we can act:

❖ We can do things because we have always done them – what Weber calls *traditional action*.

❖ We can do things because we are driven by some ultimate value, such as the building of god's kingdom of earth – *value-oriented action*.

❖ We can do things because we want to achieve some particular goal, e.g. the efficient running of a school – *goal-oriented* or *purposive rational action*.

❖ We can do things because we are driven by powerful emotions and cannot, because of this, do anything else – *affective action*.

Social structure

There are two aspects of social structure which flow from these types of action.

❖ *Social inequalities*

For Weber, inequality is associated with both:

– social class: this includes a whole series of life chances (e.g. property ownership, possession of skills) which carry varied power in the market place

– social status: relating to life styles which can link to social class.

Both class and status can give power and social advantage. This is a more complex view of inequality than that proposed by Marx.

Power is not a separate dimension of inequality for Weber. Rather it is something that you can have on the basis of your class position, your status position or a combination of both (see also *In Focus* on the following page).

The relationship between power and social class and status is shown in the histories of political parties in the UK. The Labour Party was born as a social-class party supporting equality. The Conservative Party was always the party for those with economic power, but regularly campaigned as a life-style party, that is, one which claims to represent the British way of life. The recent history of the Labour Party suggests that it is concerned to appeal to more people and has done this with a life-style message, e.g. rather than aligning itself with trade unions, New Labour emphasizes common values associated with the British way of life.

❖ *Type of domination*

Recognizing the importance of social action and of the structures of inequality that develop in different societies, Weber was also concerned with how groups come to dominate in society and how they claim to have a *legitimate right* to dominate. For him, three types of domination play a central role in all the types of social action:

– *Traditional domination:* Obedience should be given because it has always been given in the past. In such a system, the right to dominate is likely to be passed down within families, e.g. a monarchy.

– *Charismatic domination:* Obedience is given to someone who proclaims a new message which promises to transform people's lives. Chapter 14 explores the importance of charisma in the sociological understanding of religion.

– *Legal rational domination:* Someone demands obedience on the basis of a *legal right* to dominate, as well as the formal qualifications to do so.

The types of action, forms of social inequality and types of domination are what Weber calls *ideal types*. That is, they are abstractions from real societies which allow sociologists to study things without being affected by the immense complexity of real societies. Using abstractions and models is, in fact, something which all sciences do and is not, therefore, a particular weakness of sociology.

The modern world, bureaucracy and materialism

According to Weber, the modern world tends to be characterized by rational action, social-class inequality and legal-rational domination. Other types of action, inequality and domination are present, but are subordinate. The modern world has a dominant form of organization which Weber terms *bureaucracy* and a dominant approach to social life which is materialistic. These give the modern world its distinctive character. As Weber puts it:

'Material goods have gained an increasing and finally an inexorable power over the lives of men ... In the field of its highest development, the United States, the pursuit of wealth [is] stripped of its religious and ethical meaning ... No one knows who will live in this cage in the future ...' (Weber 1904/1974, pp. 181–2)

'[Bureaucracy will produce] a polar night of icy darkness and hardness ...' (Weber 1919/1970, p. 128)

Bureaucracies are large-scale, hierarchically organized structures in which, at least formally, people are qualified to do what they do. Social life in a world of bureaucracy becomes more predictable, calculable, controlled and rational. There are clear lines of communication and responsibility, and everything that happens is recorded and filed so that there can be consistent decision-making over time. This is what the modern world needs. Weber had a more complex and less optimistic view than this. He thought that bureaucracies were less

In Focus

◆

Bureaucracy and the individual

If you think about your contacts with bureaucracy, you can perhaps see Weber's point. More or less every contact – say, getting a passport – requires the filling in of forms, having photographs authenticated, and so on.

For the bureaucracy this is *rational* – it allows files to be made, records to be kept and so on. However, for the individual, the bureaucracy may seem impersonal and incapable of responding to individual need.

able to respond to the needs of unique individuals and produced a world in which magical, mystical and emotional activities became more and more impossible (see *In Focus* above).

❖ Activity 4 ❖

Is your school, college or university a bureaucracy? If you think it is, what features of it make it a good example of a bureaucratic organization?

We have already seen that most sociologists either stress the importance of social structure in constraining people or emphasize that social action has an important role to play in making social structures. This is the essential distinction between structuralist and action theorists. Weber, in fact, does not sit happily in either of these camps. In a paper written in 1922 (Weber 1978) he shows how religious sects arise because of structures of underprivilege – poverty, lack of food and so on. In that sense, structures of inequality produce and determine support for religious sects – a *structuralist* approach. However there is a somewhat different view in Weber's work on the role religion played in the development of capitalism (Weber 1904/1974).

Weber became interested in the extent to which capitalism had not only first developed in the West, but in those areas of the West that were Protestant. The interesting thing here is what sort of explanation Weber was offering. There are three possibilities:

1 He was offering a *causal* explanation, that is, being a positivist; in this case,

Protestantism would be seen as the cause of capitalism.

2 He was offering a *multicausal* explanation and still being a positivist; in this case, Protestantism would be seen as one of several causes of capitalism.

3 He was not offering a causal explanation at all.

Sociologists are not agreed on what Weber was suggesting. On balance, he was not offering a single-cause explanation: there was a lot more to the development of capitalism than religion, for example, a financial economy, cities and bureaucracies.

The real choice is between a multicausal explanation (in which religion is one of many causal factors in the development of capitalism in Western Europe) and an explanation which rejects causes completely, in favour of some idea of an *affinity* between religion and capitalism. The answer is not in Weber's work and, unfortunately, later sociologists disagree on an explanation of this issue.

Sigmund Freud (1856–1939)

Freud was not a sociologist, but his work has had a great influence on the development of social theory. Freud wrote about what makes social order possible, about the effect of early life experiences on adulthood and about the significance of sexuality. In addition, he established a therapy – *psychoanalysis* – which sets out to help people come to terms with how they live their lives, lives often full of unhappiness and confusion.

The themes of social order, early life and sexuality are closely related. For Freud, sexuality is important from earliest infancy.

Sigmund Freud

As children develop, they learn the sexual rules of the society in which they live, particularly through their relationships with their mother and father (1905/1977). In most societies those rules emphasize heterosexuality. Something much more deep-rooted happens to sexuality. For Freud it is *repressed* because social order rests on controlling sexual feelings. That repression allows the energies that would be used in sexual activity to be *sublimated* into other activities, such as work and artistic creativity (1930/1985). Another way of looking at this is to say that, although sexuality is repressed, the feelings to do with it do not go away; being repressed, they become *unconscious*. They therefore continue to affect our day-to-day conscious lives. Unconscious feelings are, for Freud, revealed in dreams, forgetting things, slips of the tongue and so on, as well as in more serious symptoms of mental illness. What Freud is arguing here is that what we commonly take to be distinctions between the normal and the pathological, and between health and illness are misleading.

What makes Freud particularly interesting is how he differs from theorists like Marx and Durkheim. In particular, he opposes their idea that that societies progress and get better. Freud does not believe that social change can make people happier with their lives – at best we come to terms with unhappiness. In fact, the founders of sociology divide into those who see progress as very likely (Marx and Durkheim), those who are sceptical about social progress (Freud), and those who are more ambiguous in their views of progress (Weber).

❖ Activity 5 ❖

Do you think that British society has progressed and improved during your lifetime ? If you do, what precisely has improved?

Developers of social theory

In the twentieth century, sociologists – many of them working in universities – have developed the ideas of the founders, just discussed. They have tended to emphasize the importance either of *social structure* or of *social action*.

The focus on social structure

Structure and consensus

Perhaps the most important development of ideas about social structure came from the American sociologist Talcott Parsons (1902–79), who tried to links ideas about social structures to the functions that those structures perform. Society, for Parsons (1951), is a social system with certain basic problems which social institutions have to solve. All societies must have systems to make them work (see Table 7.1). All societies must socialize people, control them, have leaders and so on. They are *functional prerequisites*. In this sense, society is like a human being. Every part of the human body has a function to perform and all those functions together keep the structure going. When things go wrong, the body corrects itself – when we get a virus, the body's immune system tries to get rid of it. Similarly, when things go wrong in society – e.g. a rise in crime – the legal system comes into operation and tries to reduce it. Society therefore is a self-equilibrating system: order is always maintained without major changes in society. In the end, the system *functions*.

Table 7.1 Parsons' analysis of social systems and the problems they solve

Problem	Institution
How to adapt to and use the environment ('adaptation')	Economic system
How to set the goals that people pursue ('goal attainment')	Political system
How to coordinate what people do ('integration')	Legal system
How to set and maintain basic values ('pattern maintenance')	Cultural system

❖ Activity 6 ❖

To what extent is the society you live in orderly?

- If you think it is orderly, how is that social order maintained?
- If you think it is disorderly give three examples of disorder and then explain why you think that social disorder occurs.

Robert Merton (1957), building on Durkheim's work, extends this idea of function by making a distinction between *manifest* and *latent* function. The manifest function of going to a football match is to see the team you support and see it win. There are, however, latent functions of that social activity; for example, forming a group of people with similar views into a community with a powerful set of beliefs.

The analogy that compares society and crime to the body and illness shows up some of the problems of the Parsonian approach:

❖ Most obviously, neither the body nor society works perfectly: the immune system often does not eradicate illness and society cannot abolish crime.

❖ Parsons *assumes* the existence of social order and consensus about values. He fails to explain *how* they occur and does not address the issue that many people feel that there is a lack of consensus.

❖ He says very little about how people coerce others to do what they want; the idea of domination, so important for Marx and Weber, is absent. Order seems to come about peacefully and to be guaranteed by the way the social system works.

❖ There is no account of social change in Parsons. If the social system works, then there does not seem to be any need for change.

There is another philosophical objection to Parsons' work and that of many other functionalists. Their explanations are *teleological*, that is, they describe things in terms of their ultimate purpose. Take the example of the family. For functionalists, the family performs necessary and universal functions, e.g. producing functioning human beings. These universal functions have to be performed – for Parsons, integration is essential and any institution which performs this functions can be called a 'family'. Following this logic, the family is functionally necessary and, therefore, universal. We need to be aware of the circular nature of this argument.

One of the major problems with Parsons' view is the assumption that everything in society has a function, even things which look totally dysfunctional: child abuse, crime, war, etc.. Take the example of social inequality. At the structural level, inequality may be functional; it exists in the majority of societies yet social order *is* maintained. However, it could be *dysfunctional*. If I am paid badly and see other people being paid well, may that not discourage me from working hard and therefore harm society?

Debates about how much top people should be paid illustrate this problem. Many low-paid workers feel aggrieved about very high pay for directors of large companies and say it is unfair and is a disincentive to work hard. Those receiving high pay say they deserve it because of their qualifications, experiences, stress and so on. People with low pay say, 'Hold on, if nurses didn't do what they do, you could well die following a car accident, so who is more important and deserves the higher pay?' The point is that functionalist answers cannot deal with the power struggles which, in the end, determine who gets paid which salary.

Structure and conflict

The example of pay differentials indicates that there is an alternative approach to structure and function that is much more interested in social conflict and sees any consensus as, at best, temporary. This approach has developed out of Marx's works and has produced two varieties of conflict theory: one which emphasizes the power of structures to impose consensus and the other which gives people a powerful role in challenging those structures. This distinction is between what sociologists usually call *structural* Marxism and *humanist* Marxism. A key representative of the former view is the French philosopher Louis Althusser (1918–90). Humanist Marxism includes the work of Herbert Marcuse (1898–1979) and Antonio Gramsci (1891–1937).

Structuralist and humanist Marxism developed in response to two related problems:

- ❖ The socialist revolution that Marx predicted did not seem to be happening.

- ❖ Communism in the Soviet Union did not look much like the communist future that Marx had predicted.

For both Gramsci and Marcuse, the lack of revolutionary change was the result of the power of ideology, but not simply an ideology forced on people. Gramsci (1971) used the term 'hegemony' to describe what he thought was happening – that the ruling class does not rule by political force alone, but engineers consent by establishing alliances with other groups. For example, it may forge an alliance with teachers, even though those teachers are not part of the ruling class. An ideology which does come

to dominate is the result of debates and battles between powerful and less powerful groups.

What Marcuse (1964) adds to this is the idea that the workers are often excluded from this construction of consensus and have, as a result, great difficulty in seeing any alternative to the existing order of society. The thinking of the mass of the population has become *one-dimensional* when it should be *critical*. Marcuse says that intellectuals have a important role to play in developing this critical perspective.

Althusser's view (1969) is a more structural one because, even when he considers the role of the state (or what he calls '*repressive state apparatuses*') and of education and the mass media ('*ideological state apparatuses*') he still argues that their primary role is to maintain the existing structure of society by making opposition very difficult. In addition, he takes the view that social change cannot occur until the structural conditions are right. No amount of political opposition to the ruling class will become revolutionary if the times are not right. However, Althusser does not spell out clearly or in detail the conditions needed for revolutionary social change.

The focus on social action

We will now turn to some writers who see social action – what individuals *do* – as far more important and interesting than social structures. This view of the social world takes a number of forms:

- ❖ *Phenomenology* – which developed out of the work of the Austrian philosopher Alfred Schutz (1899–1959)

- ❖ *Symbolic interactionism* – developed by the American George Herbert Mead (1863–1931)

- ❖ *Ethnomethodology* – as in the work of the American sociologist Harold Garfinkel (1917–).

Schutz and phenomenology

Schutz (1932/1972) does not talk about society but about *lifeworlds*. For him the lifeworld is a stock of shared meanings available to a social group, such as 'democracy' or 'fairness'. This set of meanings is taken for granted and is a form of common-sense knowledge. This common-sense knowledge is what society is and it is precarious. There are two points here that are important for sociologists:

❖ We think the social world is constraining and given, whereas it is, in fact, produced by us as social actors. Hence, Durkheim got it wrong.

❖ Part of the work of sociologists is to expose the extent to which what we do is taken for granted and common-sensical.

As we will see, these ideas become important in considering ethnomethodology.

Mead and symbolic interactionism

Mead (1934) has his own distinct view on the nature of the social world. *Symbolic interactionism* is exactly what the name implies – it is interested in how individuals interact through the use of *symbols* and how this relates to the development of the *self*. Part of Mead's work is about the socialization of children. Initially, children learn by imitating the actions of others, but they soon come to learn to play different roles. This role playing involves taking the role of another person – for example, the mother – and trying it out. This leads the child to develop a sense of its self, of its differences from others. Eventually, the child learns to take the role of what Mead calls the 'generalized other' – to move from identifying with one particular person to people in general.

This view of socialization becomes part of a much wider view, that interaction between all human beings is symbolic and involves the exchange of symbols which have meanings generated in social contexts. Not only is this a very different view of sociology from those who emphasize the role of social structure but it also leads to

particular sociological methods – called *qualitative* or *ethnographic* – which look at how people interact and at the meanings they give to those interactions.

Together, the insights of phenomenologists and symbolic interactionists have produced a way of looking at the social world which stresses the role of social actors, often in small scale, face-to-face situations. This is shown in Goffman's work on the self and in Garfinkel's development of ethnomethodology.

Goffman and the social self

Goffman (1969) is concerned with how we present ourselves to others as competent social actors. In addition, his studies of institutions suggests that, although they may look very different – public schools, asylums, prisons, the army – they work in similar ways as far as individuals are concerned.

The self, for Goffman, is a role-player very like an actor in a play. If you play a part in a play, there are lines and stage directions to follow, but there is the possibility of being innovative. However, the important point is who the real person is. In taking on a social role we are, in some ways, making people believe that we are who we seem to be and that we really are committed to this role. This is not necessarily the case.

If we take the example of a school, then when a teacher is in the classroom, he or she performs the expected role; in the 'offstage' situation of the staff room, the teacher may admit to feeling the class went badly, to not being a good teacher and to regarding the students as lazy and stupid. For Goffman, the difficulty is in deciding which is the real teacher. Indeed, it is doubtful if, for Goffman, there is a real person underlying all the roles that people play. Now try Activity 7 on the next page.

Garfinkel and the rules of social life

Garfinkel (1984) was the first to use the term *ethnomethodology* to describe what he was doing. This involves two related ideas:

❖ Activity 7 ❖

You are either pupils in a school, or students in a college or university.

- What does the social role of pupil or student involve?
- How do you play that role?
- Do your teachers and lecturers know the real 'you'?

❖ As Schutz indicates, social life is inherently precarious – anything could happen in social interaction.

❖ People do not realize it is precarious because they have, without being aware of it, strategies to make it seem secure.

Ethnomethodologists spend a lot of time looking at *microsociology*, i.e. small-scale and small-group activities.

Garfinkel, for example, is interested in three things:

❖ how people *construct* their social world

❖ how they *account for* that social world

❖ how that world comes to be *meaningful* for them.

A whole range of underlying and unstated cultural assumptions, which we make when we interact with people, stop the world being meaningless and precarious. In that sense, ethnomethodology is a sociology of everyday life.

Think about using a telephone. There are rules about using it which we hardly think about. We cannot see the person we are talking to and so do not, for example, remain completely silent. Instead, while you are listening to the other person you will says things like 'yes', 'um', 'uhuh' and expect them to do the same thing when you are talking. These rules are not written down, like legal rules. There are similarly unstated rules when you meet someone – many people say things like 'Are you all right?' or 'How are you?'. These are not really questions which require an answer and people know you are not asking them

about their health. They are, in this case, ways of interacting.

You can see how taken-for-granted some of these 'rules' are and how potentially precarious social life is by breaking them. Indeed, Garfinkel encouraged his students to engage in ethmetholodogical experiments. You might try, the next time someone phones you, being totally silent. The person on the other end of the phone is likely to get disturbed and say things like 'Are you there...?'. In the context of telephone usage, the rules may go some way to explain why people do not like answerphones – they do not interact with you because they are not social. You could also try playing chess using the rules of draughts. Again confusion and anger are likely to result because you are not playing the game of social life, as well as not playing the game of chess!

These 'experiments' are not just a matter of playing or being silly, although they may have ethical implications, in that you must be careful which types of social interaction you disrupt. They show several things:

❖ how far our interactions with other people are governed by rules

❖ how rules develop as part of the social interaction

❖ how rules are usually unstated and not written down.

Contemporary social theory

Few of these ideas have disappeared. However, social theorists of the last quarter of the twentieth century have begun to develop them in new and interesting directions. These include the development of feminist theory, poststructuralism and postmodernism.

Feminist theories

Feminist theories allow us to explain the often oppressed position of women in both modern and premodern societies. This explanation includes the idea that many societies – premodern, modern *and* postmodern – are *patriarchal*, that is, organized around male dominance. We have also seen how feminist theories have led to the development of a politics of gender through which women seek to challenge their oppression. Later in this chapter, we will look at some of the arguments which feminist theorists have put forward concerning the way that sociological theories and methods have profound implications for women sociologists.

Poststructuralism

Poststructuralism developed out of the work of a French linguist, Ferdinand de Saussure (1857–1913), who argued that it is the structure of language (grammar and so on) that allows it to work and gives it meaning. These ideas were developed by a number of people. Claude Levi-Strauss (1968), for example, applied them to small-scale societies, particularly their myths and belief systems. Roland Barthes (1972) applied them to aspects of the culture of modern societies including national flags, photography and the human body.

One of the thinkers influenced by poststructuralism who is particularly attractive to sociologists is the French philosopher Michel Foucault (1926–84). Like many poststructuralists and related thinkers, his work can often seem difficult

and off-putting, but he is saying things of great importance for sociologists. A summary of his views and their relevance to sociology is given below.

❖ Foucault studied some of the things that *sociologists study* – prisons, hospitals, professions, politics (1971).

❖ He was particularly interested in *modernity* and what happened to things like power, sexuality and social control in the modern world (1976).

❖ He was interested in the relationship between *power, knowledge* (e.g. medical knowledge – see *In Focus* below) and what he called '*discourse*', i.e. ways of thinking and writing about social life.

❖ Foucault is interested in *how power works*. In the modern world there is considerable stress on self-discipline and self-policing. We discipline ourselves by constantly reflecting on what we do. This does not mean that external controls disappear – indeed, if we look at the many video cameras in shops, we see how often we are under surveillance. (Now try Activity 8.) However, video surveillance affects us even if we do not know the cameras are switched on! Foucault argues that this does not mean that there is more social order. For him, we live in a discipl*inary* but not necessarily a discipl*ined*, world (Foucault 1979).

In Focus

◆

Foucault's view of power

Foucault's view of power is very different from Marx's. According to Marx, one social class – the ruling class – has power and everyone else lacks power, unless they can seize it from the ruling class. For Foucault, because power is part of every social interaction, we all have it – in particular the power to resist someone's attempt to control us. Exercising power is not just about saying no; it is about having the freedom to make decisions and to talk constantly about what we are not allowed to do. Foucault looked at how the Victorians seemed to repress people's sexuality, and how this occurred at the same time as people – experts – were writing an enormous number of discourses on sexuality (medical books, popular books and so on) which, in particular, said what was normal and what was pathological. In other words, nineteenth-century experts were providing the rules of sexuality and the knowledge they produced had political consequences. Knowledge and power can be two sides of the same coin.

❖ Activity 8 ❖

Identify four examples of technologies of surveillance which influence your day-to-day lives.

❖ Foucault is interested in *identities* and how they constrain and limit what we do. He is opposed to the positive postmodern view which says that we can choose identities and change them as we wish. Foucault says that all identities constrain what we can do. Some identities – that of a criminal or gay person – are restricting, because what is called the 'normal' world sees criminals and gay people only in terms of their criminality and their sexual orientation. It is as if they do not have normal family lives and friends, and support the football teams that other people support.

❖ As a thinker, Foucault is *close to Freud* in that he is convinced that societies develop and change. In studies of the history of punishment and of mental hospitals, he argues that the way in which we deal with criminals and the insane has changed over time, but that modern methods of treatment are not superior – they are just different.

Postmodernism

Postmodernism is discussed in various places throughout this book. Outlined here are the basic ideas of those sociologists and philosophers who have argued that we now live in a postmodern world. There are two views on the nature of postmodernity:

❖ One view, developed by Fredric Jameson (1991) and others, is that we live in a world of global capitalism and that it is the various aspects of culture that are postmodern about that world. We have capitalist structure and postmodern culture.

❖ The second view, developed by writers like Jean Baudrillard (1988), is that the social structure itself has become postmodern, particularly as a result of changes in the way that technology – including technologies of communication – now operates. Both social structure *and* culture are postmodern in this view.

The contrast between modernity and postmodernity is summarized in Table 7.2. The emergence of postmodernity includes:

❖ *Structural* aspects – more global capitalism, faster communication

❖ *Political* aspects – new social movements, identity politics

❖ *Cultural* aspects – mass produced images become more important

Table 7.2 The contrast between modernity and postmodernity

Modernity	*Postmodernity*
Local and regional capitalism	Global capitalism
Social class as major social division	A diversity of social identities
Politics based on social class	Politics of new social movements
Belief in social progress	Rejection of idea of progress
Stress on life chances	Stress on life styles and consumption
Limited global communication	Instant global communication shrinking time and space
Emergence of super-powers	Collapse of super-powers emergence of nationalism

❖ Aspects influencing *identity* – consumption as a way of changing identities.

What seems to be clear is that these changes do not affect everyone. People without jobs and housing are, for example, unlikely to benefit from advances in technologies of communication and to change their identity by buying new clothes.

One sociology or many?

The emphasis in this chapter has been on the diversity of social theories and this has significant implications for answering an important question: can we ever develop *one* sociology which combines the insights of the founders and those who have developed the subject? One reason why sociologists might want to answer this question is to do with the political power of sociology. If we can provide one agreed approach to the social world, people might listen more to what sociologists have to say.

There is no simple answer to this question. We have already seen that one group emphasizes the importance of social structure, while another sees social action as being more significant. There are two ways of responding to this difference:

1 We can simply say that they are two ways of looking at things. We can go further and say, for example, that the basic views of Durkheim and Weber on how society works are totally different. This would imply that you cannot build one sociology by mixing together Durkheimian and Weberian sociologies.

2 We can say that you *can* combine sociologies which emphasize structure and those which emphasize social action into one theory. This is one of the aims,

for example, of Anthony Giddens who, in the 1990s, developed what he terms 'structuration theory'. Giddens wants us to abandon the argument between structuralists and action theorists. Giddens defines structuration theory in the following way:

'I introduced the idea of structuration because I wanted to get at the mutual relationships between individuals and larger social settings. It seemed to me that a great deal of sociology was based on the idea that you could explain our activities by references to larger social structures, but in that approach we don't really appear as we are – knowledgeable people who know quite a lot about why we act as we do. The point of structuration was to capture that active interplay between the individual and the social; and I use the term structuration rather than structure, because structure sounds more of a static term. I think you have to see that the social world is made and remade through what we do in our everyday activities.' (Chignell and Abbott 1995)

The idea that the world is made and remade by us is, of course, the central insight of people like Mead. Giddens goes on to develop an approach to the self in which people constantly work on making themselves and changing themselves.

Giddens' work is an important attempt to develop a single approach to sociology, linking the more structural views with those emphasizing social action. Sociologists are divided about whether this is possible, with some arguing against the idea that there can be one, agreed approach to sociology. The authors of this book do not take a view for or against Giddens.

Sociological methods

The theories discussed above tell us what society is like and indicate the concepts with which to describe and analyse

societies. As well as theories and concepts, sociologists use a huge range of methods to gather and interpret data about society.

Obtaining data

We can summarize the available methods in tabular form (see Table 7.3).

The distinction between *primary* and *secondary* sources is important:

❖ Primary sources of data involve the sociologist in finding things out first-hand.

❖ Secondary sources use existing data that may not have been collected by sociologists.

Also, some methods are particularly associated with positivism (see p. 277), e.g. experiments and questionnaires. Others are associated with social action theory (see p. 282), e.g. participant observation.

We will look at each of these methods in turn and indicate their various strengths and weaknesses.

Methods producing primary data

Methods for producing primary data include experiments, surveys and questionnaires, and observation. We will look at each in turn.

Experiments

Physicists and chemists use experiments. These involve testing some idea –

a hypothesis – in laboratory-controlled conditions. In that sense, the researcher produces an artificial situation.

It is doubtful if we can do similar experiments in sociology. If people know they are being experimented on, they are likely to change their behaviour. If they are experimented on covertly and do not know they are part of an experiment, that raises ethical issues. It is also difficult to set up experiments involving large numbers of people, although sociologists often want to study large groups.

Surveys: interviews and questionnaires

Sociologists do a lot of surveys. They are also used by companies to assess the demand for and success of products and by political parties to assess their support. Surveys usually involve relatively large numbers of people, particularly if they are questionnaire-based surveys. Questionnaires that use interviews tend to involve fewer people and produce qualitative, rather than quantitative, data.

There are many different survey methods. People can be interviewed face to face, either in their own homes, places of work, on the street or somewhere else. The interview can be unstructured, semi-structured or structured:

Table 7.3 Methods of obtaining data

	Type of data	Method	Theoretical perspective
Primary	Quantitative	Experiments	Positivism
	Qualitative	Observation	Action theory
	Quantitative	Surveys: questionnaires	Positivism
	Qualitative	Surveys: interviews	Action theory
Secondary	Quantitative	Official statistics	Positivism
	Qualitative	Mass media, diaries	Action theory

❖ *Unstructured* interviews are non-directive, giving the interviewee lots of opportunities to say what he or she wants to say. Interviewees are asked to talk generally about an issue – for example, 'Tell me what you think about abortion'.

❖ *Structured* interviews are much more directive and give the interviewee less leeway. Interviewees may be asked specific questions, such as 'Are you in favour of abortion, or against it?'.

❖ *Semistructured* interviews may contain elements of the other two.

Unstructured interviews produce large amounts of qualitative data about what people feel, think, do and believe. In practice, most interviews contain all types of questions.

❖ Activity 9 ❖

Design a short, five-question interview to assess the extent of racial discrimination in Britain. Try the interview out on one other person.

Did the interview allow you to find out the extent of racial discrimination?

Interviews do not have to be done whilst the interviewee is with the interviewer. It is now common to interview people using the telephone. For example, banks will ring customers to interview them about how they feel about the services offered. In addition, focus groups are increasingly being used where groups of people discuss issues either with or without the presence of an interviewer.

Many interviewers who interview in face-to-face situations will record the interview, making sure that they get the interviewee's permission and assuring them of confidentiality. Unfortunately, transcribing the recording is time-consuming and expensive, but it does mean that there is a record of everything that was said.

If an interview is not recorded, then ways of writing down the essential things that people say must be developed. It is often difficult to do this in practice and hard to decide, at the time of the interview, what is essential and what is less relevant.

There is a fine line between an interview and a questionnaire. Some interviews will start with a short questionnaire in order to identify a person's age, gender, religious affiliation, education and so on, and will usually have simple tick-boxes for the answers. An enormous number of questionnaires are delivered and filled in every day. Most come by post, but some are administered, like an interview, in a person's home, e.g. the Census which occurs every ten years.

Where the questionnaire is sent by post, it is important to include guidelines to help the recipient fill it in. It is also important to avoid confusing questions or questions that assume the person understands the issues, but also to get answers that will *mean* something to you. An example of a poorly constructed question would be to ask people to answer the question, 'What do you think of the government's policy on the single currency?', by ticking boxes 'in favour', 'against' 'don't know'. The answers will not mean much if you get a lot of 'don't knows'. This question also relates to the second problem: if a lot of people say 'don't know', is that because they are not interested, have not yet reached a conclusion or simply do not know the policy? This indicates a general disadvantage with posted questionnaires. If you are interviewing someone face to face, you can at least check responses.

❖ Activity 10 ❖

Design a ten-question questionnaire to assess the way that other pupils or students would vote in a general election and why they would vote that way.

Think about asking the right questions and bear in mind any problems you found with the racial discrimination interview (from Activity 9). See *In Focus* on p. 295 for questionnaire guidelines.

Whether you decide to send out questionnaires with open-ended or very specific questions, follow the guidelines given below:

1 *Avoid ambiguous and imprecise questions.*

Suppose you ask students how much time they spend reading and give them the choice between: 'a great deal', 'an average amount', and 'very little'. The answers require the student to have some idea what the alternatives mean. When you look at the answers, one person ticking the 'a great deal box' may mean something very different from another.

2 *Remember that people forget things.*

If you ask people of 35 what they did as children, they might have forgotten.

3 *Ask questions that people can answer immediately.*

This means you should avoid asking questions that require people to find things out.

4 *Avoid hypothetical questions.*

If you ask people 'What would you do if you won the National Lottery?', they may see that as so unlikely that they either do not answer or give an ill-considered answer.

5 *Avoid leading questions.*

Asking 'Don't you agree that abortion is wrong?' may predispose people to agree with the question.

6 *Avoid offensive questions.*

Many issues that sociologists look at are sensitive. If you are studying sexual orientation, then people who are gay may object to the question 'Are you homosexual?'

7 *Think about the interviewee.*

Think about the appropriateness of the interviewer. If you are studying violence by men against women, a male interviewer might not be appropriate.

8 *Think about the order of questions.*

It is important that questions follow on from each other. Sometimes, if someone answers 'no' to a question, they may not need to answer subsequent questions. You need to make that clear. If there are sensitive questions, leave them to the end and put the questions that are easy to answer at the beginning. This gives the respondent confidence.

See *In Focus* above for a list of guidelines to bear in mind when formulating a questionnaire.

For both questionnaires and interviews, there is the issue of *who* you involve in the survey. Sampling is very important and this makes well-sampled studies more accurate than ones which, for example, just stop every fifth person in the street. Researchers will often start with a *sampling frame*. A commonly used frame is the electoral register, which includes the names and addresses of all people over the age of 18. An alternative frame could be a doctor's patient lists, although unlike the electoral register, these will be subject to strict confidentiality rules and not freely available.

Once a sampling frame is decided, it is necessary to decide who will be sent a questionnaire. Several alternatives are available: random sampling, quota sampling, snowball sampling and stratified random sampling. All are ways of trying to get a representative group of people to be in your survey and to reduce bias.

❖ *Random sampling* tries to ensure that each person has an equal chance of being selected to receive the questionnaire or to be interviewed.

❖ However, there is more to it than this. If we are studying the views of men and women on religion, we need to ensure that the sample is representative of the total population. Because the population is made up equally of men and women, we do not want twice as many men to receive the questionnaire as women and so we *stratify* the sample to ensure equal representation.

❖ *Quota sampling* involves deciding what proportions of each group should be interviewed and then getting interviewers to meet those quotas. Surveys of shopping carried out in shopping malls will often involve more women than men on the assumption that women are more likely to do the shopping.

❖ *Snowball sampling* aims to counter the difficulty of getting sampling frames for specific groups, e.g. drug users, by starting with a few people who then identify further people, and so on.

Once you have designed your question-naire or your interview schedule, it is best to try it out on a small group of people. This is called a *pilot study* and allows you to find out if the questions work in practice. If they do not, then you have the opportunity to change them before involving the whole sample. Where the questionnaire is to be sent to people, it is necessary to send guide-lines for filling it in and, probably, a stamped, addressed envelope for its return. The questionnaire should be typed or wordprocessed and enough space should be left for people to write their answers – especially if the questions are open-ended.

Observation

A third source of primary data involves observing what is going on. There are many ways of doing this. Imagine you want to study club culture in Manchester and decide that questionnaires and interviews are inappropriate. You have several alternatives:

❖ Go to clubs and openly identify yourself as a researcher, but still become part of the social situation of the club.

❖ Go to clubs as an observer but do this covertly, e.g. by working behind the bar.

❖ Go to clubs and play the role of clubber, not saying you are a researcher, and see how club culture works.

By each of these methods, researchers try to avoid imposing their views of what is happening and claim that observation provides the most reliable picture of the social life of the group being observed. The differences between the three options described concern two sets of issues:

❖ how far the observer affects what is going on

❖ the ethics of covert observation.

Participant observation was the method favoured by those social anthropologists who studied small-scale, non-industrial societies, particularly during this century. They went to societies that had often never seen outsiders before, not knowing the language and customs, and were strict about non-intervention. They would not, for example, provide advanced medical care for sick people. The anthropologist is an outsider in that sense, but still lives with the people and tries to build up a picture of what their society is like. The problem, of course, is how far the presence of the researcher influences what happens in the group that is being observed. There is obviously some effect, but good observation – often called *ethnography* – is as unobtrusive as possible.

Unobtrusive observation is less likely to affect other people's behaviour – the researcher being the club barman will have little effect – but there are ethical issues involved in cases where observation is of deviant activity. If you decide on unobtrusive observation then you need to consider whether what you are doing is ethical and how far you go in participating – if you are a participant observer in a criminal gang, do you participate in criminal activity, for example?

There are advantages to observation, in particular the insight you can get of how groups actually work. However, observation does have disadvantages, in that you cannot study very large numbers of people and cannot replicate what you do, in order

Table 7.4 Primary research methods in sociology

Method	What happens	Advantages	Disadvantages
Experiments	Create conditions. Compare results.	Scientifically rigorous.	Very difficult in sociology.
Questionnaires Open-ended questions	Respondent writes something.	Respondent can explore and develop answers.	More difficult to analyse.
Closed questions	Respondent ticks boxes.	Can control answers and limit waffle; easy to code and analyse answers.	Get little idea of respondent's feelings and attitudes.
Interviews Unstructured/ Semistructured	Interviewee is encouraged to talk. Interviewer may tape-record interview.	Respondent is able to say almost anything and may raise issues the sociologist has not thought of.	Difficult to test reliability of results. Cost of recording and transcribing audio tapes.
Participant observation	Sociologist becomes a part of the group being studied.	Sociologist can get to know the group and see how it works close at hand.	Danger of too close identification with the group.
Respondent diaries	Respondent is asked to keep a diary on a topic over a period of time.	Gives respondent control of the process and allows them to write openly and freely.	Respondents may not do the diaries regularly and may make things up. Difficult to analyse.

to test if what you have found is reliable. As we will see later, many studies use a combination of methods, something which sociologists call *triangulation*, to have the benefits of both surveys and observation.

Table 7.4 summarizes the advantages and disadvantages of different methods.

Methods using secondary data

Many sociologists use data that already exist. This is not a form of laziness but involves a recognition that official statistics can tell sociologists a lot about society.

Official statistics

Many sources of official data will be available where you are studying. A lot of official data are available from the Office for National Statistics, previously called the Central Statistical Office (see Table 7.5).

Many of these official sources of data are invaluable because they contain huge amounts of information on very large numbers of people. As long as you know who has collected them and for what reason, you can use them very effectively.

Official statistics rarely tell us *everything* that we want to know. It is clear, for example, with crime statistics that they do

Table 7.5 Data available from the Office for National Statistics

Title	Book/pamphlet	CD-ROM	Floppy
Annual Abstract of Statistics	yes	no	no
1991 Census	yes	no	no
Economic Trends	yes	no	no
General Household Survey	yes	no	no
Monthly Digest of Statistics	yes	no	no
Population Trends	yes	no	no
Regional Trends	yes	yes	no
Social Focus	yes	no	yes
Social Trends	yes	yes	yes

The census has many sets of data published separately, for example:

Title	Book/pamphlet	CD-ROM	Floppy
Ethnicity in the 1991 census (in 4 volumes)	yes	no	no

Other sources include:

Title	Book/pamphlet	CD-ROM	Floppy
Criminal Statistics, England and Wales (*Source*: Home Office)	yes	no	no
Eurostat (social and other data on Europe) (*Source*: The Office of Official Publications of the European Community, Luxembourg)	yes	no	no
UK Christian Handbook (*Source*: Christian Research Association, London)	yes	no	no
The ESRC Data Archive (*Source*: Economic and Social Research Council, Essex University)	no	yes	no
The European: The European Directory of Non-Official Statistical Sources (*Source*: Euromonitor, London)	yes	no	no

Finally, note that the Office for National Statistics has its own website: http://www.ons.gov.uk/welcome.htm

❖ Activity 11 ❖

Look at the statistics from *Social Trends* on participation in sports, games and physical activities (see Table 7.6).

1 What are the main differences in participation between people in professional, skilled manual and unskilled manual jobs?

2 How would a sociologist account for these differences?

3 What are the leisure pursuits of your teachers/lecturers? Do they fit the pattern identified in these statistics?

Table 7.6 Participation[1] in sports, games and physical activities: by socio-economic group[2], Great Britain 1993–94

	Professional	Employers & managers	Intermediate & junior non-manual	Skilled manual & own account non-professional	Semiskilled manual & personal service	Unskilled manual	All socio-economic groups[3]
				Percentages			
Walking	57	46	42	39	36	31	41
Swimming	27	19	18	10	11	8	15
Snooker/pool/billiards	11	12	8	17	10	9	12
Keep fit/yoga	13	12	18	6	9	8	12
Cycling	14	9	9	10	8	9	10
Darts	6	5	4	8	6	6	6
Weights/training	7	5	5	6	4	3	5
Golf	9	10	5	6	2	2	5
Running/jogging	11	6	4	3	2	2	5
Soccer	6	3	3	6	3	3	4

[1] Percentage participating in the four weeks before interview.
[2] Socio-economic group is based on the person's current or most recent job.
[3] Includes full-time students, members of the armed forces, those who have never worked and those whose job was inadequately described.

Source: Social Trends 26 (1996, p. 224)

not tell us at least two very important things:

❖ They do not tell us what real crime rates are, as not all crime is reported.

❖ They tell us nothing about the social processes involved in being discovered committing a crime, being charged, tried, found guilty and sentenced.

Historical sources

Historical materials are particularly useful for sociologists who are interested in looking at how things change over time. For example, a lot of Foucault's work on changes in how we treat the mentally ill (1971) used documents from the eighteenth and nineteenth centuries. These included acts of parliament and casebooks of hospitals. Laslett's studies of changing family structures used parish records going back several centuries (Laslett 1979).

It is important to recognize that a lot of data about the past are *not* available. If you go to the Public Records Office in Kew near London and ask for documents about the working of the Home Office in the nineteenth century, you will find that some documents are missing, perhaps destroyed by fire or thrown away in error. As for modern data, you will find that some government documents only become available after thirty years.

You need to ask a number of questions about historical documents in order to see if they are useful and reliable. Imagine you are researching the issue of immigration control and are looking at documents about the 1905 and 1914 Alien's Acts which restricted some forms of immigration into Britain. You will needs to ask all sorts of questions:

❖ Is the document genuine?

❖ Who wrote the document?

❖ When was it written?

❖ Where was it written?

❖ Why was it written?

❖ How close was the author to the real events?

❖ Does this document agree with others, contradict them or add something totally new?

In the end you will have to realize that using historical data is a *matter of interpretation* and you need to make your interpretation as convincing as possible. This may require the additional skills of a trained historian.

Personal sources: diaries, autobiographies and letters

A whole range of personal documents is available, some of them also being historical documents. They include:

❖ documents that researchers have asked people to prepare. For example, you might be studying how students survive in higher education and ask them to write diaries of their day-to-day experiences. You might also ask them to write short autobiographies. These produce enormous amounts of information and you have the decide what is relevant.

❖ existing diaries and autobiographies which sociologists can use – A good example of how sociologists can use such materials is provided by Foucault's *I, Pierre Rivière, Having Killed My Mother, My Sister and My Brother* (1973). In this study Foucault compiles all the documents relating to this case,

including diaries, autobiographical sketches, as well as medical and legal materials, to provide what is nearly a complete picture of this particular case. The *In Focus* on the next page shows another short example of an autobiography.

❖ Activity 12 ❖

Read the piece by Gail Lewis (see *In Focus* on p. 301). What does it tell us about:

• why people migrated from Jamaica to Britain?

• what problems they faced when they arrived in Britain?

There are, of course, limitations to biographies. Most obviously, they are one person's perception of what is happening. In the case of Gail Lewis's autobiography, you would need to supplement it with other sociological work on migration and what happens when people do migrate.

Letters can also be a useful source of information. In Burgess's study of a comprehensive school (1983), they had three roles:

❖ to fill in the details of past events before Burgess started his research

❖ to complement his observations in the school

❖ to shed extra light on the social relationships in the school.

Mass media reports, novels and other cultural artefacts

Finally, the full range of cultural artefacts should not be ignored: novels, newspapers, paintings, comics and so on. Almost any aspect of culture can be a source of information for sociologists – they will quite often study newspapers, for example, to gain insights into society.

The front pages from the *Sunday Mirror* and the *Observer* (see p. 302) show that

In Focus

◆

**Gail Lewis,
*From
Deepest
Kilburn***

'I was born on the 19 July 1951 in a "Mother and Baby Home" – the euphemism for an unmarried mothers' home. And, like Billie Holiday, when Mum and Dad got married I was three. I was sent to my (maternal) grandmother for that occasion, so I missed the whole thing, which I'm sure was a real shame, since all of the parties my parents and their friends had – and there seemed to be one nearly every weekend – were fun for us kids too, with endless supplies of bun, crisps, R Whites and ginger beer (home-made of course).

That was also when I was first exposed to what I now know as the "contradiction between race and gender", but then it was just the trouble between Mum and Dad.

The first home I remember was a basement flat at 61 Granville Road, Kilburn. We lived there until 1960 and so my memories of the 1950s are split between that house and that of my Mum's mum who lived in Harrow on a late-twenties council estate, one of those new estates which was to provide a lot of working-class people in the London suburbs with their first decent housing.

The Granville Road flat was completely different. The whole house, a big late-Victorian terrace, was let as a tenement, in a combination of bedsits and two-room flats, to black people, mostly Jamaicans. ... My Dad had lived there since his arrival in this country in 1950. ... It was, of course, a lonely and tremendously brave thing to do, just to "dig up" (as they say in Ja) and try your chances in the "mother country" especially for a young man of 18 with no knowledge of what to expect. It was an act based on complete trust in the propaganda being dished out by the British government and by various British firms and public corporations, and on the need to find employment and a better career than underdeveloped Jamaica could offer. ... In some respects I suppose you could say that the decision to uproot paid off – he has a house and a skilled job and lives relatively comfortably. But it's not been without its costs: the obstacles to racially mixed marriages, the continual adjustment to the effects of racism on black people's lives and the disappointment that has been woven into the lives of many black people of that generation. They came looking for the rainbow and got abuse, subjugation and disillusionment instead.

My Mum was the only white person who lived in the whole house, a point not unnoticed by me since I often asked her how come she lived there with us when everyone else was black – or brown as I would have said then. As she would later remind me, children can say very painful things.'

Source: Heron (1995)

newspapers can provide an insight into British society. However, newspapers provide a *variety* of views and you need to analyse them as carefully as you would novels or biographies.

❖ Activity 13 ❖

What do the newspaper front pages on p. 302 tell us about British society?

Why is it that the basic news items in the two newspapers are different?

Presenting data

This book contains many examples of the ways in which sociologists can present data: charts, tables, histograms, graphs and so on. It is often more informative to present data in one of these forms as well as using long sentences and paragraphs in which conclusions are summarized. Some examples of different forms of presentation are listed on p. 303. Look at the examples listed, what they illustrate and how they are used in this book to support arguments:

Examples of front pages from national Sunday newspapers: *The Observer* (a broadsheet) and *The Sunday Mirror* (a tabloid)

- tables – see Table 7.6 on p. 299
- histograms – see Fig. 9.5 on p. 372
- graphs – see Fig. 9.1 on p. 361
- pie charts – see Fig. 3.4 on p. 80
- maps – see Fig. 9.10 on p. 388
- charts – see Fig. 7.1 on pp. 274–5.

Interpreting data

We need to consider two important issues in the interpretation of data:

- causes and correlations
- reliability of qualitative data.

Causes and correlations

Sociologists are like natural scientists in that they assume that the social world is orderly: nothing in society happens at random – there is always a cause, e.g. 'Unemployment causes crime'.

The search for causal relationships is both important and difficult in sociology. We cannot say that *one thing* – e.g. unemployment – causes crime; there may be a number of *variables* that influence crime rates – e.g. the opportunity to commit crime, the absence of a police presence and so on. This raises two further points about causal explanation in sociology.

- Such explanation is often *multicausal* – sociologists can rarely identify single causes.

- There are two elements to a causal explanation: an *independent variable* – in this case, unemployment – and a *dependent variable* – in this case, the crime rate. Here, causality operates from the independent to the dependent variable and not the other way around – crime does not cause unemployment. What is an independent variable in one investigation might be a dependent one in another, e.g. rising costs of labour cause unemployment.

There are two other important points to note here about causal relationships:

- We have looked at how people being studied have their own views of what is happening, which may influence a researcher's findings, i.e. people's awareness of the situation being studied may itself be a causal factor. This effect can be minimized by doing covert observation.

- There is often a *correlation* between variables – for example, between someone's football team losing a match on a Saturday and absenteeism from work on a Monday morning. A correlation means that there is a regular relationship between them; it does not necessarily, or even *usually*, tell us that there is a causal relationship. A sociologist is unlikely to claim that football teams losing matches *cause* absenteeism, but they may say that there is a strong or weak correlation between defeat and absenteeism.

The strength of the link is measured by something which is called the *correlation coefficient*. Where the coefficient is 0, there is no link at all. A coefficient of 1 indicates a complete link. Where the link is −1, there is an inverse relationship. Sociologists are happy to take 0.6 and above as indicating a strong link between variables.

The identification of causes is a powerful political weapon. The ongoing debate about smoking and its relationships with lung cancer indicates that there is a lot at stake for both smokers and the tobacco industry if causes and strong correlations can be established. One of the most important elements here is the possibility of compensation if smoking is strongly correlated with cancer and the consequent claims on insurance companies.

The reliability of qualitative data

Strong correlations give data reliability and are often important in convincing people that sociologists have something of relevance to say. Such strong correlations are most likely to result from quantitative studies. This suggests that smaller-scale qualitative studies are less powerful, in that they often cannot establish correlations.

Qualitative studies are *different from* quantitative studies, rather than being *inferior to* them. They allow detailed study of what goes on, for example, in a classroom. It is possible to interview people about their experiences of the classroom, to set up focus group discussions and so on. People who fund research may want studies which demonstrate strong correlations, but that does not make qualitative studies less valuable.

It is possible to increase the reliability and predictive value of qualitative studies by using a variety of methods to study the same thing – this is called *triangulation* and will be briefly discussed later. There are also longitudinal studies which focus on a group of people over a long period, allowing sociologists to look, for example, at how attitudes change over time.

Note that there are computer packages that aid the interpretation of both quantitative and qualitative data:

❖ SPSS, MINITAB, and PARADOX are useful for analysing quantitative data.

❖ ETHNOGRAPH, KWALITA and QUALPRO are useful for analysing qualitative materials.

Issues in sociological methods

There are three issues that should be given particular attention:

❖ triangulation

❖ ethics

❖ the debate about feminist research.

Triangulation

Sociologists recognize the advantages and disadvantages of the different methods of data collection they have available. They also recognize which methods are appropriate to which issues. Those wanting in-depth data on the self-esteem of disabled people are likely to choose a qualitative method, using in-depth interviews. If they wanted to look at relationships between voting behaviour and social class, a large-scale quantitative survey would be more appropriate.

However, many researchers will triangulate, i.e. use different methods within the same piece of research. This allows them to develop different types of data and to check one body of data against another. The large-scale study of voting behaviour and social class may also include smaller-scale interviews to discover why people from one social class are more likely to vote for the Conservative party and why, for example,

young people are less likely to vote than older people, regardless of their social class position.

❖ Activity 14 ❖

Design a study of attitudes to vegetarianism to illustrate the advantages of using a variety of methods of analysis. What advantages does triangulation have over using just one method?

The ethics of research

Research is not a neutral activity. There are some obvious ethical issues about *what* sociologists study, *who* is doing the studying and *what happens* to the research findings.

The decision not to study a certain issue might not be because the sociologists lack the methods, but because the study would be highly inappropriate. In addition, much research funded by governments and business is for specific purposes, with which the sociologist might not agree (see *In Focus* on the next page).

In this particular case, a sociologist was studying the effects of professional working

In Focus

◆

Uproar at BBC over working mothers evidence

'The BBC is embroiled in a bitter internal battle over last week's *Panorama* programme as fresh research emerges flatly contradicting its conclusion that working mothers jeopardize their children's education.

Some BBC managers believe the programme was "unnecessarily alarmist".

Last night John Ermisch, professor of economics at Essex University, said the most recent statistics indicated that children with two working parents did better at school. His claim is based on the largest study of working mothers in the nineties and contrasts with the *Panorama* assertion that "women who juggle a full-time job with motherhood may jeopardize their children's future". Prof. Ermisch accused Panorama of "gross irresponsibility".

Internal BBC criticism came at Wednesday's regular programme review board, chaired by Alan Yentob, the director of programmes. Lorraine Heggessey, editor of QED and a working mother, lambasted the programme for "scaremongering". Mark Thompson, a former editor of *Panorama* and now controller of BBC2, queried if it might have looked at wider research.

It was agreed the programme raised important issues but that it had flaws. There was particular concern about the title *Missing Mum* which, according to one executive, "crucially summed up its line right at the start". Mark Damazar, head of BBC weekly programmes and in overall charge of Panorama, defended the edition.

Prof. Ermisch has examined the effect of family background on educational attainment by matching parents and teenagers over five years, using a nationwide sample of 5,500 households and 1,565 pupils.

"There is no evidence that having a mother in employment when the child was aged 14 reduces educational attainment, and it may indeed increase the odds that the child obtains qualifications of A-level or higher. Having a mother in a managerial job when a boy was aged 14 significantly increases his educational attainment," he concludes.

Panorama made its claim on the basis of a University of North London study of families in the London borough of Barking and Dagenham. Its author, Professor Margaret O'Brien, in an interview in today's *Observer*, says she would not generalize from her work: "One would expect educational achievement to be different in different areas."

It emerged yesterday that Panorama staff asked Essex University last year for assistance in making the programme. A source said: "Some work was done for them, but it wasn't what they wanted."

Sarah Powell, who presented the programme, agreed she had been in contact with the university. "They did some initial work and we discussed paying for a researcher to do some further analysis but they thought it would take too long. No mention was ever made to us of Prof Ermisch's work."

Prof Ermisch works at the ESRC Research Centre on Micro-Social Change at Essex – the centre approached by Panorama. "I didn't speak directly to Sarah Powell but I am surprised she didn't pick up on the work we were doing. The programme made me very angry. It made claims on the back of the most meagre evidence," he said.

Ceridwen Roberts, director of the Family Policy Studies Centre, who appeared on the programme, said: "I have a lot of experience of television and radio but never have I felt under so much pressure to say what the interviewer wanted me to say. She was not interested in any conflicting view. Panorama is the flagship of current affairs and has an obligation to be impartial."'

Source: *The Observer*, 9 February 1997

couples on their children's success in school. Most of the newspapers focused on the negative outcomes of the report, i.e. that working had an adverse effect on performance in school. The claim made by the university was that the findings of the report did not fit the *Panorama* agenda. The claim that the researcher makes – backed by other researchers – is that the findings *Panorama* reported were inaccurate. The point for sociologists is that when research enters the public sphere, it may be misinterpreted and used for a variety of purposes over which the original researcher has little control.

There is another problem, in that some studies may be unpopular with some people, e.g. a study of the extent of poverty may not come up with results that, say, the government would want. This has led Howard Becker (1967, 1976) to ask what sociology is for and to come up with the idea that sociologists have to takes sides – in the case of poverty, for the poor and against governments. For him, a good sociological study makes some people annoyed because it challenges common-sense assumptions about society. This, of course, raises issues about who pays for sociological investigations and the extent to which, if it is governments and research councils, they should be pleased.

The debate about feminist research

Most of the founders and developers of sociology were men; feminists have referred to this as 'malestream sociology'. Some feminists argue that there is a need for theories and methods in sociology which are developed by women and will be distinct from those developed by men. Abbott and Wallace (1996) put it this way in summing up the debate about feminist methods:

> 'Research methods are not just "tools of the trade": what gives meaning to the research is the underlying theory and epistemology [theory of knowledge] used. The methods at the more quantified 'positivistic' end of the spectrum claim to be more scientific and neutral and for this reason feminists have attacked them, arguing that they in fact represent a malestream view of the world under the guise of science. Feminists have tended to espouse qualitative methods as the better means of carrying out feminist research because they imply more equality between researcher and researched.' (p. 301)

If we accept this, then a women's sociology would use particular methods and study some areas that are not often studied by male sociologists, e.g. why women are paid less than men for the same work or why there are so few women head teachers of secondary schools (Abbott and Wallace 1996) (see also *In Focus* below).

Theory and methods in action: the case of suicide

The study of suicide presents an extremely useful insight into the role of social theories and methods in studying a major social issue. The first major sociological study of suicide was carried out in the late nineteenth century by Emile Durkheim. He used official statistics available from a number of European countries to develop an explanation of four types of suicide.

In Focus

◆

Non-sexist approaches

The concern with feminist theories and methods has led to the development of non-sexist ways of researching and writing. Eichler (1988) suggests that there are non-sexist ways of doing research and the British Sociological Association – the professional organization of sociologists – recommends ways of writing that avoid both sexism and racism. These include the more obvious use of 'he/she' rather than simply 'he'; and the less obvious avoidance of using the term 'coloured' in favour of 'minority ethnic'.

Durkheim called suicide a *social fact* which could, and should, be explained by reference to other social facts, including marital status and religious affiliation. He was attempting to demonstrate the effectiveness of sociological explanations and reject non-sociological approaches.

Durkheim chose to study suicide for a number of reasons:

❖ *Personal* – A close friend of Durkheim's committed suicide when they were students at university and this event encouraged Durkheim to look into the subject more deeply.

❖ *Academic* – Durkheim was writing about individual and psychological reasons for suicide. It is still the case today that coroner's inquests will say that someone has committed suicide because 'the balance of the mind was disturbed'. For Durkheim, the interesting question was whether social factors might influence a person's state of mind. In this sense, Durkheim was interested in the social context of suicide.

❖ *Accessibility* – Because most European countries had statistics of suicides, Durkheim was able to develop a comparative approach in order to see how and where suicide rates varied between societies. This use of comparison was something which Durkheim saw as being as close as sociologists could get to laboratory experiments. In *The Rules of Sociological Method* (1895/1938), he argued that it is a central part of all sociological analysis.

Durkheim's approach to suicide is *positivist*. He developed hypotheses, used statistics and provided general causal explanations of suicide rates. As we will see below, other sociologists (Atkinson, for example), have been highly critical of such a positivist approach to suicide.

On the basis of studying statistics on suicide rates, Durkheim identified a number of variables which affect rates of suicide:

❖ religious affiliation

❖ degree of urbanization

❖ age

❖ marital status

❖ children

❖ level of education.

❖ Activity 15 ❖

Look at the six variables that Durkheim identified and explain in a sentence how each variable might affect an individual's sense of belonging to the wider society.

Durkheim believed that suicide rates were dependent upon the degree of social integration experienced by individuals and the degree to which society regulated individual behaviour. Too little or too much of these would predispose people to suicide. This led Durkheim to propose that there were four types of suicide related to degrees of integration and regulation, summarized in Fig. 7.2.

❖ *Altruistic suicide* occurs where there is excessive integration within a social group resulting in a strong sense of duty and loyalty. There are many examples of this ranging from the suicide bomber who lays down his life for a political cause, to a soldier who smothers a grenade to save his platoon. In general, altruistic suicide occurs where there is little emphasis on the individual and is more common in premodern than in modern societies.

Figure 7.2
Types of suicide

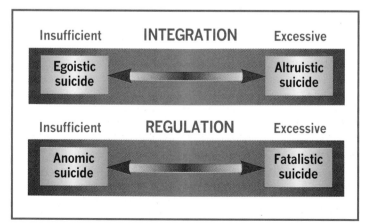

❖ *Egoistic suicide* occurs in societies where there is insufficient integration and a stress on individualism. An important element in egoistic suicide for Durkheim is the nature of religious affiliation. Affiliation to those religions which emphasize the role of the individual and underplay that of the group or community, e.g. Protestantism, are likely to result in high levels of egoistic suicide. Those which emphasize community and family, e.g. Roman Catholicism and Judaism, inhibit such suicides. In the modern context, the well-publicized suicides of young rock artists such as Kurt Cobain in the early 1990s could also be seen as examples of egoistic suicide, where self-interested pursuit of destruction is sought without regard for others left behind.

❖ *Anomic suicide* is a feature of those societies undergoing rapid social change where there is confusion over norms and values. It is connected to times of rapid increase in economic prosperity and economic decline. In both cases, expectations are rapidly changed but social rules are slow to adjust to these economic changes. The dramatic rise of drug abuse in increasingly affluent societies such as America and Britain could be another feature of anomic society. Both egoistic and anomic suicide are likely to be most common in modern societies with their emphasis on individual choice and economic prosperity.

❖ *Fatalistic suicide* occurs in societies where there is excessive regulation. People in slave societies and concentration camps are subject to near total control, so it is not surprising that they do not care whether they live or die and that some take their own lives.

Evaluating Durkheim's approach

There is much to agree with in Durkheim's explanation of suicide rates in different groups and societies. His views on the key importance of social integration and the right levels of regulation can be seen as almost common-sensical in today's terms. Charitable organizations such as The Samaritans recognize the importance to people of a sense of purpose and belonging (social integration). People who have to deal with suicides in prisons can recognize the ill effects of an overly regulated society (regulation).

A number of studies from the 1930s to the 1960s supported Durkheim's explanation of suicide. They pointed to some weaknesses in the use and analysis of statistics and the need for more scientific rigour but, on the whole, accepted the positivistic direction as correct. Following his approach, Sainsbury (1955) found that suicide rates in London boroughs were highest where levels of 'social disorganization' – for example levels of divorce and illegitimacy – were also highest. Some who supported Durkheim's general approach were, however, critical of the vagueness of Durkheim's usage of terms like social integration, hence Sainsbury's use of key indicators of integration like divorce and illegitimacy. Similarly, variables such as family and religion were never clearly explained in terms of how their effects on individuals could be isolated as distinct influences.

Some pointed to statistical weaknesses in the official data and began to argue that in societies where suicide was strongly rejected on religious grounds, reporting of suicide might not occur regularly. This developed into a general criticism of Durkheim's positivism and a social action approach to suicide was taken up by a number of researchers in this field, notably Jack D. Douglas in America and J. Maxwell Atkinson in Britain.

Jack D. Douglas

Jack D. Douglas (1967) pointed out that as well as the physical act of suicide, there are different meanings that people give to what they do, including:

❖ *Transforming the self* – This is where a person commits suicide in the belief that their present existence will change to a

Fire from the Sun

Swiss investigators unable to trace messianic leader or confirm whether tragedy was collective suicide or mass execution

'Swiss police were questioning several people about the mass deaths of 52 members of a doomsday cult yesterday as two more dead bodies were found in a farmhouse in Quebec. ... Members of the cult found dead in a farmhouse at Cheiry in western Switzerland were injected with a "powerful substance" before they died, police revealed yesterday. But it remained a mystery whether the 52 cultists who died in the two villages in Switzerland and a third site in Canada were the victims of a suicide pact or mass execution.

"In all the bodies examined so far we have found signs of an unidentified powerful substance," Mr Piller said. "It could have been a laxative or a sedative, a lethal substance or just a tranquillizer. We don't know for the moment." ...

Serge Thierrin, volunteer fireman, said: "To see 22 or 23 people lying dead like that, at first it was like a film. It was horrible. As far as we could tell, it was collective suicide. I don't know, however, if it was voluntary for everyone."'

Source: The Guardian, 7 October 1994

---

better one. A number of religious sects have encouraged members' suicides to enable them to ascend to heaven (see *In Focus* above).

❖ *Transforming the self for others* – There is a famous historical example of this type of suicide. The Antarctic explorer Scott's ill-fated expedition to be the first to reach the South Pole in 1912 ended with all those involved perishing. At a later date their diaries were found, one giving an account of how one of the party, Titus Oates, who felt his illness was holding back the others announced that he was going out and 'would not be back for some time'. He never returned and apparently froze to death. Thus a sick man's act of suicide was transformed into a selfless act of heroism and he became a national hero.

❖ *Achieving fellow feeling* – The aim is to elicit sympathy, with the person often hoping to be discovered before death. In 1995 a man attempting suicide was found dead in his car. Because of the location he had chosen, a spot popular with walkers, it was judged that he was hoping to be found and this intention was foiled because thick fog descended soon after he became unconscious.

❖ *Gaining revenge* – This is where someone aims to get back at others; for example, a victim of bullying may leave a note exposing his or her assailants' activities.

For Douglas, what is missing from Durkheim's account are the meanings which people give to suicide. Even if there are statistical patterns, with some societies having high rates and others low rates, these patterns do not tell us about *why* people commit suicide and the *meaning* which people give it.

J.M. Atkinson

J.M. Atkinson (1978) argues that coroners play a crucial role as definers of suicide. Whereas Douglas focuses on the individual and the variety of meanings that may be attached to their acts, Atkinson, through ethnomethodological study, examines the role of coroners who have to pass verdicts at inquests into the range of suspicious deaths.

Suicides are unusual in that, by their nature, there is rarely a direct witness to the act. So, in this sense, it is the role of the coroner to decide whether death was deliberate, an accident or caused by others. Coroners therefore have a key role to play in the construction of suicide statistics, in particular because they look for a variety of clues in deciding whether a death is a suicide. These include:

❖ *Suicide notes* – Some coroners told Atkinson that if there is no suicide note, they would rarely pass a suicide verdict unless evidence from other sources was overwhelming. It is estimated that around 30 per cent of suicide victims leave notes. It is quite likely that a number are destroyed by grieving relatives, particularly if the relatives are cited as a factor in the death. This, of course, links with Douglas' category of suicide as a means to gain revenge.

❖ *Method of death* – How the death occurred is important, with certain methods being more strongly associated with suicide than others. Hanging and overdoses are seen as typical suicides, whereas drowning is less so. Even with drowning there are clues for the coroner: if the victim was fully clothed they might have slipped into the water by accident; if they are naked with clothes neatly folded on the canal bank then this shows planning and intent, and may well indicate suicide.

❖ *Location and circumstances* – Coroners assume that serious suicide attempts occur in hidden and secret places. Suicides that take place where discovery prior to death is likely are assumed not to be serious attempts. They are seen as cries for help and often called attempted suicides or 'parasuicides'. Steve Taylor (1988) doubts whether this distinction can always be made. He likens the frame of mind of someone in a prospective suicide situation as akin to someone playing Russian Roulette.

❖ *Life history and mental condition* – The coroner can call expert witnesses such as family doctors and psychiatrists. Any indication of depressive and mental illness is taken as a likely sign of suicide. Financial problems and emotional states, such as in the aftermath of divorce, are also seen as suicide-inducing circumstances.

The above indicates the framework within which coroners operate; suicide verdicts are only passed in the light of this framework. Deaths which do not fit into this pattern may not be recorded as suicides. Therefore, to develop a causal theory of suicide based on statistics which are arrived at as a result of such assumptions and inquest procedures is a pointless venture. Atkinson carried out further research using comparisons between the verdicts of Danish and English coroners. He gave each group the same real case studies of suspicious deaths and asked what verdict they would reach on the evidence given. He found that Danish coroners gave more suicide verdicts than English ones. The Danish suicide rate at the time was much greater than the English one, so this study provided powerful evidence to support Atkinson's case that statistics are *socially constructed* rather than objective indicators of events such as suicide.

Atkinson and other ethnomethodologists working in other fields than suicide discredit the usefulness of sociological theories based on official statistics. They suggest that such statistics are only a reflection of the common-sense assumptions and decisions of officials working in the organizations which produce such statistics. These do not reflect the truth or reality of such events. For sociologists, the proper study of suicide must involve an examination of the work on the part of officials in arriving at definitions of what is or is not a suicide. The operation of officials is also important, for example, in analysing levels of criminal behaviour.

Studies inspired by the views of Atkinson and other ethnomethodologists can involve qualitative research using in-depth interviews, observation, conversation analysis of court transcripts and similar techniques designed to explore the micro-world of everyday social life.

Very different assumptions lie behind this approach to sociology, than those of more structuralist theories where official statistics are seen as valid reflections of social life and a key to explaining aspects of society such as crime and deviance.

Recent developments in the debate

Until the 1980s, the debate about suicide was polarized between those who supported Durkheim within a positivist framework and social action theorists who not only challenged Durkheim's work but raised more general criticisms concerning the emphasis on social structures.

However, recently, those approaches favoured by Atkinson and others have been criticized, and writers like Steve Taylor have claimed that Durkheim was a realist rather than a positivist. Barry Hindess (1973) developed a critique of those who emphasize the importance of the common-sense views, for example, of coroners. He argued that not only do coroners have common-sense views but so do those ethnomethodologists who have criticized Durkheim. For him, sociologists should be aware of how far their common-sense views affect how they operate.

Taylor's argument (1988) is that Durkheim was fully aware of the social construction of suicide statistics but still insisted that discovering and analysing broad statistical patterns was an important thing for sociologists to do. In this sense, Durkheim was a *realist*. Taylor devises two categories of suicide which he sees as a way of including the meaning of suicide into a Durkheimian perspective.

❖ *Ectopic suicide* – These are inner-directed suicides, and include two types. In *submissive suicide* the person has decided their life is over and they have nothing to live for – perhaps their spouse has died. *Thanative suicide* is where a person is insecure about themselves and puts themselves in dangerous, life-threatening situations – they might drive dangerously.

❖ *Symphysic suicide* – These are other-directed and there are two types. *Sacrifice* is where someone feels that others have made their life unbearable and commits suicide as a form of revenge where the people responsible are publicly exposed; *appeal* is where the person concerned is uncertain how others around them feel about them and use suicide or an attempt to display this dramatically.

As Fig. 7.3 indicates, the suicide rate in Denmark is about 7 times greater than that of Greece. From Atkinson's perspective this could demonstrate the role of Danish coroners as compared to those in Greece, who may be more reluctant to pass suicide verdicts for a variety of reasons. Realists

Figure 7.3
Suicides in
EU countries

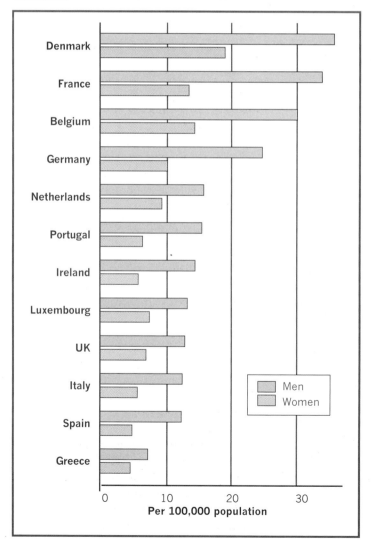

❖ **Activity 16** ❖

Take each of Taylor's four types and in two to three sentences give a case study as an illustration. Are there any famous suicides that you could fit into one of these types?

would partially accept this but would point out that such a dramatic difference cannot entirely be explained in this way. This then leads to a comparison of Danish and Greek society. Durkheimian indicators of anomie may be sought by comparing rates of divorce and family breakdown between the two societies. In fact, Denmark has one of the highest divorce rates in Europe and Greece one of the lowest; such indicators can be linked to an explanation of suicide rates.

The comparison of Danish statistics with those from other European countries indicates that the different approaches have different things to offer and may not be as contradictory as they at first appear to be

We have looked at sociological approaches to suicide in some detail here to illustrate what the study of an important social issue tells us about social theories and the methods that sociologists use.

Chapter summary

❖ The founders of sociology were Comte, Marx, Durkheim, Weber and Freud.

❖ The main interest of the founders was in the development of modernity and what modern societies were like.

❖ Sociology has developed since its original foundations were established; the developers of sociological thought have either emphasized the importance of social structure or social action.

❖ There is now considerable interest in sociology in three areas: feminist theories and methods, poststructuralism and postmodernism.

❖ Sociological methods collect and use both quantitative and qualitative data. Some methods – e.g. surveys – are particularly good at providing quantitative data; other methods – e.g. interviews and participant observation – provide qualitative data.

❖ As well as collecting new data, sociologists also use existing data – official statistics and historical documents, for example.

❖ Quantitative data can be analysed using statistical packages and techniques. Generally, such analysis does not identify causes but does identify correlations.

❖ Most sociologists would not use one method of analysis but would triangulate.

❖ Doing sociological analysis involves theoretical, practical and ethical issues.

Stimulus-response questions

1 Everyone goes to school between the ages of 4 and 16. Increasing numbers continue their education beyond the age of 16. How would this be explained by:

(a) a functionalist

(b) a conflict theorist

(c) a social action theorist?

2 There are many social theories which sociologists use to understand the social world.

(a) What are the main differences between theories which emphasize social structure and those which emphasize social action?

(b) What does Giddens mean by 'structuration theory'?

3 You have decided to study the extent of name-calling against girls/women in a school/college/university. Which sociological methods would you use? Give reasons why you would use the methods you have chosen.

Further reading

Many of the texts written on social theory and sociological method can be hard-going, but the following are worth looking at:

Bell, J. (1993) *Doing Your Research Project: A Guide for First-Time Researchers in Education and Social Science*, Buckingham: Open University Press.

Gilbert, N. (1993) *Researching Social Life*, London, Sage.

Jones, P. (1993) *Studying Society: Sociological Theory and Research Practice*, London, Collins Educational.

Layder, D. (1994) *Understanding Social Theory*, London, Sage.

Chapter 8

World Sociology

❖ Preview

In this chapter we will look at:

❖ how sociologists have explained social change

❖ how these explanations can be applied to recent and current changes in world society

❖ concepts and theories of world development

❖ concepts and theories of globalization

❖ demographic, industrial, and urban changes and their impact in a world context

❖ health, education and gender as aspects of development.

❖ Introduction

It is a commonplace to say that we live in a society where social change is a continuous and rapid process. Indeed, it was the fact of rapid social change that prompted nineteenth-century sociologists such as Comte, Durkheim, Marx and Weber to develop their early theories. The pace of change has accelerated during this century, not only for individual societies and nation-states (which were the focus of interest of the early sociologists), but also for the world as a whole. One of the major changes of the latter half of the twentieth century has been the greater interdependence of nation-states, both economically and culturally, to the point where some contemporary sociologists write about a 'world society' and take the concept of 'globalization' as the main focus of their work. Giddens, for example, has argued that 'the world has become in

❖ Activity 1 ❖

'The King Kong Chinese Smörgåsbord 3Restaurant' Restaurant sign in Australia.

'I am at an altitude of 33,000 feet over Austria, flying from London to Delhi in an American-made aeroplane owned by a British company, sitting next to a Gurkha soldier, watching an Indian film, drinking German beer and Welsh spa water, writing in English with a Japanese ballpoint pen, eating a meal which includes Danish butter, US Carnation milk, Indian pickle, Greek yoghurt and chicken donatello, served by an Australian stewardess. I wonder where my clothes were made.'

Before reading this chapter, consider these two quotes. What do they tell you about world society and the world economy in the late twentieth century? Write down your ideas in five short phrases or sentences.

important respects a *single social system* as a result of growing ties of interdependence which now affect virtually everyone' (Giddens 1989, p. 519).

In this chapter, we will discuss social change in the twentieth century and how it is affecting individual nation-states, the relationships between them, and world society as a whole.

'Development': terminology

The term 'development' came into common usage towards the end of the 1940s. It was used to describe the process whereby the poorer countries of the world were changing and, in the optimistic mood of the times, could be expected to become richer through the processes of industrialization and modernization of their economies. For the next forty years or so, many different terms were used to distinguish between the countries of the world. Each one had its adherents and each one meant something different from the others:

❖ *Rich and poor* – These terms are usually understood in terms of the Gross National Product (GNP) of a country and the income per head of its population. The GNP of a society is the value of all the goods and services produced in that country each year. GNP per head of population is the measure often used to compare wealth differentials between countries.

❖ *Industrialized, newly industrializing and pre-industrial/agricultural* – These terms refer to the dominant method of production in the society. They are particularly favoured by economists.

❖ *North and South* – Broadly, the North includes the USA, Canada, Europe and the UK, the former Soviet Union, Japan, Australia and New Zealand, while the South includes Latin America, most of Africa and Asia. This term was used in a major report published in 1980, *The Brandt Report*, which proposed a new model for trading relationships between North and South.

❖ *First, Second and Third World* – The First World is North America, Western Europe and the UK, Japan, Australia and New Zealand. The Second World referred to the former Soviet Union and Eastern Europe. The Third World refers, broadly, to Latin America, most of Africa and Asia. Clearly, this way of classifying the countries of the world has been less useful since the collapse of the former Soviet Union and the emergence of many newly independent nation-states.

❖ *Developed and developing* – Broadly speaking, these two terms group countries into the same groups as North/South above. It is an optimistic model, which suggests that poorer countries could all be on the road to economic development

❖ *Developed and underdeveloped* – Again, this places countries into the same groups but suggests the more pessimistic explanation that the poverty of many countries is because they are being actively exploited by the richer countries of the world.

The term 'development' has, then, become increasingly controversial. As Waters (1995) has stated:

'There has always been a problem in describing countries with differing positions in any developmental ascent. In the 1960s there were "developed" and "underdeveloped" countries; in the 1970s there was the "first world" and the "third world", the state-socialist societies poised awkwardly between them; in the 1980s we spoke of "more developed" and "less developed" countries; and today of "industrializing nations".' (p. 20)

However, the terms involving the idea of 'development' are probably still the most popular in everyday use, though 'North/South' is still used and 'Third World' is often used to refer to the poorer countries, often without much idea of who or what make up the 'First' or 'Second' worlds.

It is important to recognize that these categories conceal a tremendous amount of variety, especially in the Third World. The rich/industrialized/North/First/developed countries certainly enjoy a higher GNP, higher incomes per head, a higher standard of living, better standards of health and literacy, lower death rates and longer life expectancy than the countries of the Third World, but the problems in the First World of pollution, the loss of community, rising crime rates and the diseases associated with stress provide some counterbalance to these.

The poorer/South/Third/underdeveloped countries tend to have higher child death-rates, high levels of illiteracy and lower incomes. They depend on producing cash crops or single commodities for export and have high levels of debt. However, they include not only desperately poor countries such as Ethiopia, Bangladesh and Nepal, but also the newly industrializing countries (NICs) such as the 'four tigers' of Asia (Hong Kong, Singapore, Taiwan, South Korea) and the relatively poor (such as many countries in South America). There is also variety *within* many Third World countries, with some individuals and families enjoying extreme wealth (as in the First World), while others starve. And where in this scheme would you place China and India?

It is for these reasons that a single, generally acceptable set of terms is unlikely to emerge. The situation is simply too complex. In addition, the terms 'developing' and 'underdeveloped' are used to refer to a wider range of changes than they referred to twenty years ago. For example, Foster-Carter (1992) argues that we should be aware of and sensitive to a number of aspects of the term 'development':

❖ anthropology, which provides us with the concept of culture and the detailed study of small groups

❖ geography, which provides us with the concept of place and the importance of spatial aspects of social relations

❖ a comparative historical dimension, which gives us comparisons over time and place

❖ globalization, with its implications of a world system.

By taking account of these dimensions, sociology in the twenty-first century will be set in international and world terms. As Foster-Carter has said:

'A sociology which is attuned to and builds in the global and international dimension of every phenomenon will serve us much better for both the inter-pretative and practical challenges which lie ahead, than any attempt to defend the boundaries of an allegedly distinct enterprise called "development sociology".'

Therefore, in order to take account of more recent thinking on these issues, we also will go 'beyond development' and refer in this chapter to world sociology.

Given that we need a reasonably familiar shorthand when discussing these matters, we have to choose one of the above sets of terms. This chapter will normally use the terms 'developed' and 'Third World' for the sake of simplicity, but you should be aware of just how much variety is encompassed within these terms.

Theories of social change and development

In this section, we will initially compare two sociological perspectives on social change. We will then link these to some theories of development and underdevelopment. The two perspectives are:

❖ the *evolutionary* theories derived from the work of Comte, Durkheim and Parsons

❖ the *revolutionary* theories derived mainly from the work of Marx.

You should bear in mind from the Introduction to this chapter that, whereas the early sociologists tended to focus on individual nation-states, more recent theories of development take a global view and emphasize the interdependence of nation-states – economically, politically and culturally.

Evolutionary theories of social change

Evolutionary theories of social change start from the assumption that human societies, as they modernize, move from a relatively simple structure towards increased complexity. Industrial societies are, therefore, more complex than any preceding types.

This theory was, like much early functionalist theory (see Chapter 7, pp. 285–7), greatly influenced by Darwin's biological theory of evolution. In Darwin's theory, the development from a single-cell organism, such as an amoeba, to a more complex, higher animal species is explained in terms of adaptation to the environment. For evolutionary theorists in sociology, there are direct parallels between biological development and the development of human societies. If a society does not adapt, it does not develop, or even survive. In adapting, it inevitably becomes more complex.

The view that societies have evolved towards greater complexity is associated with the work of several 'founding fathers', particularly Durkheim. His model proposes an increasing differentiation of social structure as societies move from being based on mechanical to organic solidarity (see Chapter 7, pp. 278–9). This model in turn influenced Tonnies' work on the move from 'Gemeinschaft' to 'Gesellschaft' (see Chapter 9, p. 366).

Another important evolutionary theory is that of Talcott Parsons. Parsons claims that societies evolve from the simple to the more complex – for example, Australian aboriginal society to 'Archaic' (Ancient Egypt) to 'Historic' (China, India) to 'Modern' (USA). This, he argues, can be analysed as a process of the progressive differentiation of social institutions. As societies evolve, their economic and political systems become separated from one another as well as from family, legal, cultural and other systems. All these subsystems, however, are interrelated and together form a complex whole. According to Parsons, industrial societies are at the highest stage of evolution (Parsons 1951).

Modernization and development theories

This evolutionary model of social change is the basis for some of what are usually referred to as 'modernization' theories of development. According to Webster (1984), development depends on 'traditional' values being displaced by modern ones. He argues that in a 'traditional' or pre-industrial society, three crucial features are apparent:

1 The value of traditionalism itself is dominant. That is, people are oriented to the past and they lack the cultural ability to adjust to new circumstances.

2 The kinship system is the decisive reference point for all social practices, being the primary means through which economic, political and legal relationships are controlled. One's position in the kinship system and, hence in the society, is ascribed, not achieved. That is, it is a reflection of the status or standing of the family, clan or tribe into which one is born; one's position only changes as one moves up the family hierarchy.

3 Members of the traditional society have an emotional, superstitious and fatalistic approach to the world: 'what will be, will be', 'things have always been this way'.

In comparison, 'modern' society has contrasting characteristics:

1 People may still have traditions but they are not slaves to them and will challenge any that seem unnecessary or get in the way of continued cultural progress. They are not dominated by 'traditionalism'.

2 Kinship has a very much less important role in all areas of society (even within the family) because of the need for geographical and social mobility which weakens family ties. Moreover, one's position in the economy, polity, etc., is earned through hard work, high achievement and motivation and not determined by kinship.

3 Members of the modern society are not 'fatalistic' but forward-looking and innovative, ready to overcome the

obstacles they find in their way, particularly in business affairs, reflecting a strong entrepreneurial spirit and rational, scientific approach to the world.

Rostow's theory of economic growth

Whereas the theories above focus mainly on changing values and culture, Walt Rostow's model emphasizes economic factors and, more specifically, the role of technology in the process of development. Rostow's model identifies five stages of economic development (Rostow 1960):

1 traditional society

2 preconditions for take-off

3 take-off

4 drive to maturity

5 age of high mass consumption.

In this model, 'take-off' from traditional society requires the emergence of a political élite as well as the availability of capital and technology. The emergence of science and technology are central to the stage of take-off into development. The 'drive to maturity' is characterized by a high percentage of national income being reinvested, leading to the creation of a sound economic infrastructure and, finally, to a shift towards consumer goods and services. This, then, leads to a society where higher personal income and greater leisure time stimulate mass consumption.

Evaluation

The work of Parsons and Rostow provides a framework within which to understand, in cultural and economic terms, how certain countries develop a 'modern' economy.

❖ Activity 2 ❖

Read carefully the summary of Kerr's convergence theory below and then do the following tasks:

1 Summarize in your own words what is meant by 'convergence'.

2 Discuss how the theory may apply in the 1990s compared to when it was originally put forward in the late 1950s.

3 Outline the changes that have taken place in the 1990s which suggest that convergence theory might be revived.

In Focus

◆

Kerr and convergence theory

An even more highly developed version of modernization theory, founded on functionalist analysis, is based on the work of Clark Kerr and is known as 'convergence theory'. Kerr argued that all societies which reached the stage of industrialization would, whatever their political systems, ultimately converge towards a single type (Kerr *et al.* 1962). Industrialism, he argued, represents a specific kind of social system whose 'needs' must eventually be met, in any society, by similar 'solutions' in terms of social structure. For example, once a society has made a commitment to the science and technology of industrial production, the need arises for an educated, mobile and diversified labour force. Universal systems of education, with selection for advanced training in specialist skills, are required. At work, managerial hierarchies are needed to co-ordinate a complex division of labour.

At the time Kerr was writing, this was an important prediction about the future of the two great superpowers, the capitalist USA and the communist USSR. Today, his theory and predictions should be reappraised. As Poland, Hungary, Czechoslovakia, Romania and the former USSR begin their programmes of liberalizing economics and political reforms, convergence theory may enjoy renewed popularity.

Source: adapted from Jary and Jary (1991)

Nevertheless, a number of criticisms can be made:

❖ One of the strongest criticisms of modernization theory is that it entirely ignores the impact of colonialism and imperialism on Third World countries. It fails to acknowledge that economic growth is as much about the power to control resources as it is about the *desire* or *ambition* to do so.

❖ Another major criticism of the theory is its ethnocentrism. It assumes that 'modern', Western values are needed by Third World countries, attaching little value to their own cultures and traditions. It is more likely that these countries would want to balance modernization with aspects of their traditional culture

❖ It overstates the move from 'traditional' to 'modern' values in industrialized countries. Family ties, traditional and spiritual values, and community spirit are not as extinct as the theory would suggest.

Marxists and modernization theory

Modernization theory has been criticized by some Marxists. Nevertheless, writers such as Nigel Harris in the 1980s, who adopted a classical Marxist perspective, produced an analysis which has some consistency with modernization theory. However, where classical Marxist theory emphasizes *revolutionary* change, modernization stresses *evolutionary* change. Harris also points to abrupt change being imposed on Third World countries from outside. Nevertheless, he regards the development of capitalism in the Third World in an optimistic and positive way in the sense that it is progress towards an eventual socialist society.

Harris (1987) argued that we now have a single, interdependent, interacting, global manufacturing system. He also argued that the nation-state is becoming increasingly irrelevant and that transnational corporations attempt to identify the cheapest location to site their particular productive activities. According to Harris, the growing interaction of nation-states is the main uniting factor, and nationalism will decline in importance. Thus for Harris, the globalization of manufacturing and trade and the growing independence of nations is a hopeful sign for the Third World.

Underdevelopment or 'dependency theory'

Underdevelopment theory, sometimes called 'dependency theory' first emerged in the early 1950s, though it did not attract much attention from sociologists until after the decline of functionalism in the late 1960s. It derives from a neo-Marxist perspective and particularly from Lenin's writings about the concept of imperialism.

Imperialism is the political and economic domination of one country or countries by another, and leads from alien rule imposed by force, to economic domination and exploitation. Lenin, who was influenced by Marx, emphasizes the economic dimension (Christman 1987). For Lenin, imperialism is primarily the result of the capitalist system attempting to resolve its crisis of profitability. This crisis could be resolved through advanced economies expanding overseas. This would allow for a control over a global market, access to cheap foreign labour and a cheap supply of raw materials.

Thus, imperialism – 'the drive to conquer and subjugate other peoples' (Giddens 1993) – of which colonialism was one expression, assisted the Western economies' development but, at the same time, impoverished industrializing nations because resources predominantly went to the nations that were already industrialized.

Dependency theory, following this lead, argues that the countries of the Third World have been consistently exploited by Western powers, with the result that they have been prevented from developing and have, in fact, been actively *under*developed. Historically, many Third World countries were once economically wealthy with their own traditions, values and beliefs. Many had already achieved impressive levels of cultural and economic development. They were, however, less developed in military technology and less ruthless in warfare. They were also highly vulnerable to European diseases. Many of these nations were not 'underdeveloped' prior to their contact with the West.

Contact with European countries, particularly since the sixteenth century, and latterly with the USA, has exploited, distorted and impoverished these societies. In fact, the wealth and 'development' of the North has been built on the exploitation of the South. The development of the North is based on the underdevelopment of the South, without which it could not have happened. The countries of the Third World now depend on the industrial nations for their economic survival. Economic, and hence political, world power rests with the USA and Europe (and formerly the USSR).

Dependency theory therefore challenges the main assumption of modernization theory, which is that societies everywhere are engaged in economic and social progress which reaches its highest form in Western societies. Instead, it argues that

societies are in conflict and exploitative relations with each other, with the countries of the Third World being economically dependent on, and hence dominated by, the wealthy countries. This is the latest stage in a historical process outlined in Table 8.1 on the next page. This table gives a brief history of the relationship between First and Third World countries, conceptualized in three phases: *merchant capitalism, colonialism* and *neo-colonialism.*

Figure 8.1 shows how Europe, West Africa and the Caribbean were connected in a commercial network which was advantageous for Europe but disadvantageous for many countries in Africa.

Frank's theory of underdevelopment

André Gunder Frank (1981), a German-born economist writing in the 1960s, is regarded as the first major proponent of dependency theory. He argued that the persistent poverty of the Third World is a reflection of its 'dependency' and that this dependency, produced by the workings of world capitalism, has created under-

Figure 8.1
A map of 'triangular trade'
Source: Davidson (1984)

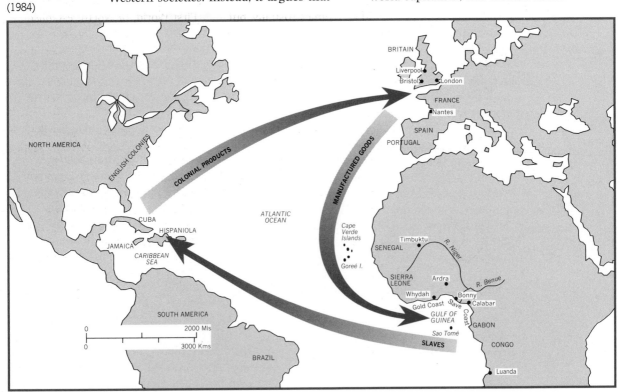

Table 8.1 Periods of underdevelopment

Merchant capitalism

Merchant capitalism refers to the accumulation of capital in Europe through trade and plunder, mainly during the early period of capitalist expansion. This began in the 16th century and continued to the late 18th century. One of the most profitable forms of merchant capitalism was the slave trade (see Fig. 8.1).

This trade had damaging consequences for the African countries affected:

❖ It is likely that the trade had a serious impact on the growth of the African population.

❖ European traders had a particularly harmful affect on the existing political and economic pattern of African culture.

European greed and the African share-out: a cartoon view from America

Colonialism

In the stage following merchant capitalism, European countries acquired overseas territories as colonies – the main period of expansion being 1850 to 1900.

Merchant capitalism established the basic pattern of production in the Third World countries, namely their economies were geared towards the provision of a narrow range of raw materials for export to the developing industries of Europe. More and more land was cultivated for one or two cash crops with less and less being available for the indigenous populations on which to grow their staple food. If the demand for these cash crops on the world market fluctuated, they had major consequences for the Third World economies (usually, but not always, for the worse).

It could be argued that the influence of Western imperial powers was not entirely negative. The various European countries transferred capital, technology (including health technology), methods of production, and democratic political and legal structures to the Third World.

Neo-colonialism

Neo-colonialism means a new form of colonialism, a form of socio-economic domination that does not rely on direct political control. This period of exploitation for underdevelopment theorists has continued in the period since 1945 when many of the colonized countries have achieved independence.

Such theorists, such as André Gunder Frank and Immanuel Wallerstein, argue that the neo-colonial relationships are nowadays played out in the context of a global capitalist economic system. (Their ideas will be developed later in the chapter.)

The major form of this global domination is through the activities of transnational corporations (TNCs). TNCs, based in the First World, or North, establish subsidiaries in the countries of the Third World, particularly in those offering cheap labour. However, and this is the crucial point, the wealth that is created by these subsidiaries is then transferred back to the wealthy country where the TNC is based.

Thus, from this view, the growth of the TNCs since 1945 is the principal feature of neo-colonialism, as corporations increase their economic grip on the raw materials and labour power of Third World nations.

❖ Activity 3 ❖

1 Figure 8.1 illustrates the triangular trade between Europe, Africa and the Caribbean. Describe the trade links between the three continents.

2 Table 8.1 gives a brief outline of the phases of underdevelopment. What are the key features of this underdevelopment from merchant capitalism to neo-colonialism?

3 From the eighteenth century, Europeans' conceptions of black African people changed from seeing them as different but equal, to different but inferior. This occurred particularly during colonialism. What factors do you think led to this conception of African people by Europeans at that time?

development in the Third World. Frank further argued that the periods of merchant capitalism and colonialism forced Third World countries to specialize in the production of goods that were mainly for export and orientated to the food and raw material needs of the imperial powers.

Frank argues that there is a 'chain of dependence' from the highly advanced countries of the world to the under-developed countries. He describes this as a hierarchy of 'metropolises' with their subordinate 'satellites', creating a chain through which the economic surplus is passed upwards from the poor to the wealthy within a nation, and then from the poorer nations to the wealthier ones. For example, the USA is a metropolis, with the cities of Latin America as its satellites, though they are themselves metropolises with their own satellite rural areas.

Evaluation

The work of Lenin and Frank provides an explanation of the dependency or under-development of Third World economies. However, a number of criticisms have been made of Frank's work.

❖ Frank's description of the character of Third World underdevelopment appears to argue that Third World countries are static and can never develop at all. As the surplus is taken out of these countries, no indigenous development is possible. This has simply not been the case, however. Many Third World countries since the 1970s have had economic growth, including Argentina, Mexico, Brazil and some East Asian countries. Therefore, some academics who support underdevelopment theory, such as Cardoso, and indeed Frank himself, have had to rethink their theoretical position in the light of real historical events.

❖ The second criticism is that Frank emphasizes underdevelopment in terms of the exchange and transfer of the surplus from satellites to metropolises, at the expense of the way in which surplus is extracted through the system of production that prevails in Third World societies. Laclau agrees with Frank that there is one world-capitalist system, but differs in that he argues different modes of production occur within this world system, and that Frank's theory oversimplifies this.

❖ Warren (1981) is also critical of Frank for only partially analysing production relations. Warren does not believe that the underdevelopment of the Third World will persist indefinitely. He argues that what are thought of as aspects of underdevelopment or 'dependency' are in fact the features typical of any society which is going through the socio-economic transition to capitalism. Clearly, Third World countries do rely on advanced industrial economies for support in economic growth, especially through the sharing or purchase of advanced technology. However, Warren claims that industrializing countries generate their own capacity for growth and will, over time, become less dependent as Western capitalist imperialism declines.

Globalization

❖ Activity 4 ❖

- Visit your local supermarket and identify the country of origin of a range of products.
- Do you find that the products come from particular parts of the world? Are there any reasons why certain products may be produced in particular parts of the world?

Globalization is a relatively new concept in sociology. However, economists and others who work in and write about the transnational corporations and international business have been using it for some time. Giddens describes globalization as follows:

'The world has become in important respects, a single social system, as a result of growing ties of inter-dependence which now affect virtually everyone. The global system is not just an environment within which particular societies like Britain develop and change. The social, political and economic connections which cross-cut borders between countries decisively condition the fate of those living within each of them. The general term for the increasing interdependence of world society is *globalization*.' (Giddens 1989, p. 520)

A more recent definition reinforces this sense of the interdependency of nations. It says that globalization is:

'a social process in which the constraints of geography on social and cultural arrangements recede and in which people become increasingly aware that they are receding.' (Waters 1995)

A central feature of globalization is that many contemporary economic, political, social and environmental problems cannot be fully understood if study is limited to the level of the single nation-state. More recent writers have argued that these problems need to be seen in terms of global processes, going beyond the level of the nation-state. Global processes increasingly influence people's lives and have begun to supersede the influence of the nation-state.

There are positive and negative aspects to increased globalization. For example, the growing cosmopolitanism of cultural life may be seen as a positive force. We can now holiday in America, eat Indian food or listen to music from around the world. This widens our experience and may result in a greater understanding of, and respect for, the culture and traditions of other people.

On the negative side, the power of transnational companies can be regarded as dangerous in that they are not democratically accountable to the peoples of the nation-states in which they operate.

Three factors in globalization have become particularly significant in the last few decades:

❖ the growth of TNCs

❖ the new international division of labour

❖ transformation in the global scope of the mass media

First, we will look at the growth of TNCs.

The growth of TNCs

Historically, the growth of large business organizations falls roughly into three stages:

1 *Family capitalism* (nineteenth century and early twentieth century) – Large firms in the UK, USA and Europe were predominantly run by individual entrepreneurs and then passed on to their descendants.

2 *Managerial capitalism* (early to mid-twentieth century) – By this stage, professional managers began to have more influence as the family structures and skills were unable to manage the growing complexity of national and international business.

3 *Institutional capitalism* (mid-twentieth century onwards) – This is made up of a network of businesses and their leaders who are concerned with decision-making not just in a single firm, but through a network of international organizations. Within this period one sees the growth of TNCs which operate across national boundaries. These organizations are worth studying because of their size and potential influence.

According to Sklair (1993):

'The largest TNCs have assets and annual sales far in excess of the Gross National Products of most of the countries in the world. In 1990, about 60 countries (excluding Eastern Europe and all countries with under one million people) had GNPs of less than 10 billion US dollars.

Fortune magazine's "Global 500 Industrial Corporations" (July 1992) shows 135 TNCs with annual sales in 1990–91 in excess of $110 billion. Thus, such well-known companies as Ford, General Motors, Shell, Toyota, Volkswagen, Nestlé, Sony, PepsiCo, Coca Cola, Kodak, Xerox, have more economic power at their disposal than the majority of the countries in the world.'

In 1992, the 600 largest TNCs accounted for more than one-fifth of the total industrial and agricultural production in the global economy. Clearly these companies which operate internationally with offices and plants in other countries provide both benefits and problems to the host countries in which they operate. These are summarized in Table 8.2.

Table 8.2 Hosting TNCs: benefits and problems

Benefits to the host country	*Problems for the host country*
Capital for growth and development	Increased dependence
Technology for modernization	Decreased sovereignty
Access to foreign markets	Increased exploitation
Positive contribution to balance of trade	Inappropriate technology
Provision of employment	Displacement of local firms
Provision of foreign exchange	Possible relocation
Increase in output and efficiency	Transfer pricing
Domestic expenditure	
Generates prosperity	

In Focus

◆

Going global

'Transnationals' or 'multinationals'?

The two terms are used inter-changeably. 'Transnationals' (TNCs) is more precise, but 'multinationals' is more common usage. The United Nations defines these companies as 'associations which possess and control means of production or services outside the country in which they were established'. Although they may operate in dozens of countries, hiring workers and managers of all nationalities, most are firmly controlled in their nation-state.

Item A: Going global – the big players

❖ The combined sales of the world's largest 350 multinationals total nearly one third of the combined gross national products of all industrialized countries and exceed the individual gross national product of all Third World countries.

❖ More than 90 per cent of all multinationals are headquartered in the industrial world. France, Germany, Japan the UK and the US account for 70 per cent of all foreign investment by multinationals and about half their total number (see Table 8.3).

❖ The largest multinationals operate in dozens of countries and employ thousands of employees. PepsiCo, the world's biggest beverage company, has more than 500 plants and 335,000 workers in over 100 countries. Nestlé, the giant Swiss food manufacturer, operates in 126 countries with more than 200,000 employees.

Item B: More players, fewer winners

❖ There are now 35,000 multinationals with some 150,000 foreign affiliates. The largest manufacturing and service companies accounted for $3.1 trillion of world assets in 1990; about $1.2 trillion of that was outside the multinationals' home countries.

❖ Multinationals control 70 per cent of world trade, i.e. between branches owned by the same parent firm.

❖ Although the total number of multinationals is increasing, a small number of companies dominate the most major areas. Across a range of industries, the top five companies in each sector typically account for 35 to 70 per cent of total sales in that sector (see Fig. 8.3 on next page).

Item C: Third World bargains

❖ Western corporations have expanded investment in the Third World over the last few years as poor countries relaxed foreign investment restrictions. In 1991 nearly 30 countries made it easier for multinationals to invest, and corporate investment jumped from 19 per cent in 1990 to 30 per cent in 1992 (see Fig. 8.2 below).

❖ As part of 'structural adjustment' programmes, Third World nations have been forced by the International Monetary Fund and World Bank to sell off state-owned enterprises at bargain-basement prices. In 1990 more than 70 countries had privatization programmes in place and sold state firms worth $185 billion.

Figure 8.2
Investment by multinational corporations in developing nations (1985-91)

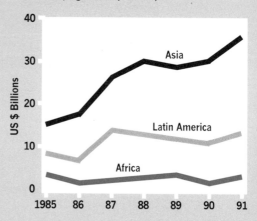

Table 8.3 Biggest companies in the world ranked by industry (1991)

Industry	Company	Country	Sales ($bil)
Aerospace	Boeing	US	29.3
Beverages	PepsiCo	US	19.7
Building materials	Saint-Gobain	France	13.3
Chemicals	El du Pont	US	38.0
Clothing	Levi Strauss	US	4.9
Computers, office equipment	IBM	US	65.3
Electronics	General Electric	US	60.2
Food	Philip Morris	US	48.1
Forest products	International Paper	US	12.7
Industrial/farm equipment	Asea Brown Boveri	Switzerland	28.8
Mining/crude oil	Ruhrkohle	Germany	14.9
Motor vehicles/ parts	General Motors	US	123.7
Petroleum refining	Royal Dutch/Shell	UK/Netherlands	103.8
Pharmaceuticals	Johnson & Johnson	US	12.4
Publishing/printing	Bertelsmann	Germany	9.1
Rubber/plastic goods	Bridgestone	Japan	13.2
Scientific/photo equipment	Eastman Kodak	US	19.6
Soaps/cosmetics	Procter & Gamble	US	27.4
Tobacco	RJR Nabisco	US	14.9
Toys/sporting goods	Yamaha	Japan	3.6

Figure 8.3
Top five multinationals as percentage of worldwide sales by sector, 1992

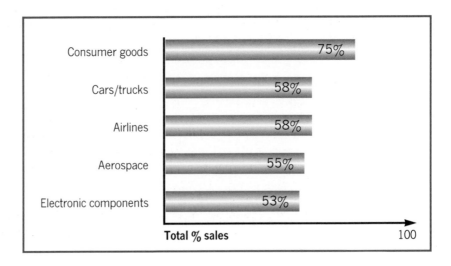

Consumer goods 75%
Cars/trucks 58%
Airlines 58%
Aerospace 55%
Electronic components 53%

Total % sales   100

❖ Activity 5 ❖

1 What do Items A and B (see *In Focus*, pp. 12–13) tell us about transnational and multinational corporations? Why do you think it is important that we study them?

2 According to Item C, what are the implications for transnational companies operating in Third World countries? Use the information contained in the text to help you to answer this, particularly Table 8.3 summarizing benefits and problems for host countries.

The new international division of labour

One version of the globalization thesis focuses on the effects of transnational corporations on international employment patterns. This work is associated with Froebel *et al.* (1980). The central theme of this thesis is that the old division of labour (where colonies produced raw materials which were then processed in the colonial power's industrial centres) is breaking down and being replaced by a new division of labour, whereby firms in the developed countries have begun to move labour-intensive production to the Third World countries to save money because labour costs are cheap. This has cut the costs of manufacturing for the developed countries, but resulted in job losses in manufacturing in the developed world.

Evidence for the new international division of labour thesis

❖ The fastest-growing economies in the world are to be found in East Asia, particularly Hong Kong, South Korea, Singapore and Malaysia. Economic growth in East Asia averaged 7.5 per cent between 1974 and 1993, while the equivalent figure for the developed world was 2.9 per cent.

❖ In 1960, the core of the industrial world in Europe and North America produced 71 per cent of the world's products and 78 per cent of manufacturing output. By 1981 the figures had fallen to 60 per cent and 59 per cent respectively (Harris 1987).

❖ The World Bank estimates that the share of world output taken by developing countries will reach 60 per cent by 2020, with the developed world's share down to 35 per cent.

❖ After the Industrial Revolution took hold in about 1780, Britain took 58 years to double output. From 1839, the USA took 47 years. From 1885, Japan took 35 years and from 1966, South Korea took just 11 years.

Paul Kennedy, Director of International Security Studies at Yale University, has argued that globalization could have detrimental affects on low-paid workers in the European Union and the USA (Kennedy 1996). These workers will be challenged in the production of manufactured goods by workers in Hong Kong, Japan, Korea, Malaysia, Singapore and Taiwan.

He suggests a world conference to identify a process for establishing policies to deal with the challenges from what he sees as the increasing pace of modernization and globalization.

The global mass media

The tendency towards globalization can also be seen at a cultural level, with the advances in communications technology meaning that the ownership, images and messages of the mass media are becoming more and more uniform across the globe. Television and associated media like newspapers, magazines and book publishing, films, etc., are concentrated in relatively few large TNCs. We will now look at the globalization of culture and social problems with a global dimension, such as AIDS, drugs and environmental problems (see also Chapter 12, *Mass media*).

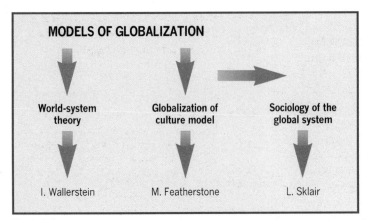

MODELS OF GLOBALIZATION

World-system theory	Globalization of culture model	Sociology of the global system
I. Wallerstein	M. Featherstone	L. Sklair

Figure 8.4
Models of globalization

Models of globalization

Sklair has identified three different competing models of Globalization theory and research (see Fig. 8.4).

We will start by looking at Wallerstein's model, which concentrates on the emergence and evolution of the European world-system and in which a differentiation between three types of state is made.

World systems theory

Wallerstein's is one of the most influential sociological arguments for considering the world as a single economic system. According to this theory, countries are continually being drawn into the developing capitalist world economy. To understand Wallerstein's view, first we need to look at Waters's three possible types of world system (Waters 1995, p. 23):

1 *World-empires* – A multiplicity of cultures are unified under the domination of a single government; there have been many instances of world-empires, e.g. Ancient Egypt, Ancient Rome, Ancient China, Moghul India, Feudal Russia, Ottoman Turkey.

2 *World-economies* – A multiplicity of political states, each typically focusing on a single culture (nation-states), are integrated by a common economic system; there has been only one stable instance of a world-economy, the modern world-system, integrated by a single capitalist economy (which includes state socialist societies).

3 *World-socialism* – Both the nation-state and capitalism disappear in favour of a single, unified political and economic system which integrates a multiplicity of cultures; there is no instance of world-socialism and it remains a utopian construct.

Wallerstein concentrates on the emergence of the European world-system and traces it from the sixteenth century to the present day. This corresponds to Waters' *world-economy* model.

Within the capitalist world-economy, an international division of labour has developed in which different countries find themselves in on of three possible states, namely *core, semi-periphery* or *periphery*.

❖ *Core states* – These states are developed, rich and dominant within the system and are made up of the most industrialized countries in the late twentieth century (e.g. Western Europe, USA and Japan).

❖ *Semi-periphery* – These states are closely linked to core countries by various kinds of dependent trading relationships. These state could be emerging from the periphery or possibly were core states which are now in decline.

❖ *Periphery* – These are poorer states and therefore somewhat economically dependent on the core states.

Central to Wallerstein's argument is that you can map out the development of the world economy and see clearly that the core states have established a position where they can exploit the resources of the countries in the peripheral areas.

The problem with Wallerstein's model, however, is that it is based mainly on economic and political factors, without considering cultural factors. Wallerstein (1995) has attempted to reconcile this in his more recent paper 'Culture as the Ideological Battleground of the Modern World System', but most sociologists remain unconvinced that the world-system model can deal with cultural issues adequately.

Globalization of culture model

This model of globalization derives from research on the 'globalization of culture' – an area of research associated with the journal *Theory, Culture and Society*, edited by Mike Featherstone, who has made his own contribution in the area of consumerism. Other writers on the globalization of culture debate include Roland Robertson on culture in general, Bryan S. Turner on modernity and postmodernity, and J. Urry on tourism.

These writers have certain common themes running through their writings on the globalization of culture:

❖ They are all interested in the question of how individual and national identity can survive in a 'global culture'.

❖ They tend to emphasize the cultural over the political and/or the economic.

Some writers have talked of a global culture being eclectic, universal, timeless and technical and this is why it poses real problems in terms of individual and national identity. The concept of identity is not used here to describe a common pattern of life, but the more subjective feelings and valuations of any population which possesses common experiences and one or more shared cultural characteristics – whether they be customs, language or religion. According to Anthony D. Smith (1995b), these feelings and values refer to three components of their shared experiences:

❖ a sense of continuity between the experiences of succeeding generations of the unit of population

❖ shared memories of specific events and personages which have been turning-points of a collective history

❖ a sense of common destiny on the part of those collectively sharing the experiences.

A collective cultural identity can be linked to nationhood and has some link with the past, whereas a global culture is essentially memory-less. Thus, there is a difficulty in attempting to construct a global cultural identity, because at any point in time, it will be historically specific, being based on shared memories and a sense of continuity between generations (see also Chapter 2, *Culture and identity*).

Sociology of the global system

Leslie Sklair (1991) attempts to lay the foundations of a sociology of the global system. He aims to move away from simply analysing the global system from the position of the nation-state. While not ignoring the nation-state, the model he proposes offers in addition a conception of the global system based on transnational practices. Transnational practices are practices that originate with non-state actions and their cross-state borders. Sklair's analysis places them in three spheres: the economic, the political and the cultural/ideological.

❖ TNCs are the most important institutions for economic transnational practices.

❖ The transnational capitalist class (TCC) is the most important institution for political transnational practices.

❖ The culture/ideology of consumerism is the most important institution for transnational cultural ideological practices.

With this model, Sklair directs attention away from the nation-state and towards transnational capitalists. According to Sklair:

'The research agenda of the global system model is concerned with how TNCs, transnational capitalist classes and the culture/ideology of consumerism operate systematically to transform the world in terms of the global capitalist project. The transnational capitalist class includes the following groups of people:

❖ TNC executives and their local affiliates

❖ globalizing state bureaucrats

❖ capitalist-inspired politicians and professionals

❖ consumer élites (merchants, media).

This class sees its mission as organizing the conditions under which its interests and the interest of the system (which usually, but not always coincide) can be furthered within the context of particular countries and regions.'

Sklair tends to emphasize a single, dominant global system – namely the capitalist one. This dominance, he believes, derives not simply from economic, political and military strength, but also from the appeal of 'the ideology of consumerism'. This is reflected in advertising and Western-made consumer items throughout the world. One example of this is what Ritzer calls the process of 'MacDonaldization', 'the process by which the principles of the fast-food restaurant are coming to dominate more and more sectors of American society, as well as the rest of the world'.

The principles of such a process are as follows:

❖ *Efficiency* – MacDonaldization compresses the time-span and the effort expended between a want and its satisfaction.

❖ *Calculability* – It encourages calculations of costs of money, time and effort as the key principles of value on the part of the consumer, displacing estimations of quality.

❖ *Predictability* – It standardizes products so that consumers are encouraged not to seek alternatives.

❖ *Control* of human beings by the use of material technology – This involves not only de-skilling of workers, but control of consumers.

In summary, therefore, MacDonaldization represents, according to Waters, 'a reordering of consumption as well as production; a rationalization of previously informal and domestic practices, that pushes the world in the direction of greater conformity' (Waters 1995, p. 144).

❖ Activity 6 ❖

1   Compare and contrast the three models of globalization reflected in the work of Wallerstein, Featherstone and Sklair.

2   Select a variety of pictures from newspapers and magazines which you think best reflect global culture. These pictures may well involve popular consumer products in the West found in a different social context.

3   Using Wallerstein's world-system theory, identify countries that might be found in the core, semi-periphery and periphery of his model. Do you think it is feasible that South Korea could soon be one of the core countries and Britain one of the semi-periphery countries?

◆ Demographic trends and industrialization

Demography is the study of human populations. There are few issues which have caused more controversy – politically or socially – than the question of population. There has been much concern about the growing world population and its impact on the environment and the consequences for future generations.

Before we can study the sociology of demography, we must first define some key terms:

❖ *Birth rate* or *crude birth rate* – the number of live births per thousand of the population in a given year

❖ *Fertility rate* – the number of live births in any one year per thousand fertile women in the population between the ages of 15 and 44 years; although used less often, fertility rate is a more accurate reflection of the level of child-bearing than the birth rate and can be more usefully used for comparative purposes

❖ *Death rate* – the number of deaths per thousand of the population in a given year

❖ *Migration* – the movement of people from one area to another

❖ *Emigration* – the movement of people *out of* one country on a permanent basis

❖ *Immigration* – the movement of people *into* a country on a permanent basis

❖ *Net migration* – the difference between the number of immigrants and the number of emigrants; this may be expressed as a loss (emigrants) or as a gain in population (immigrants)

❖ *Population structure* – changes in either birth or death rate or migration affect not just the size of the population but also its structure in terms of its age, sex and ethnic composition.

Figure 8.5
The march of the billions

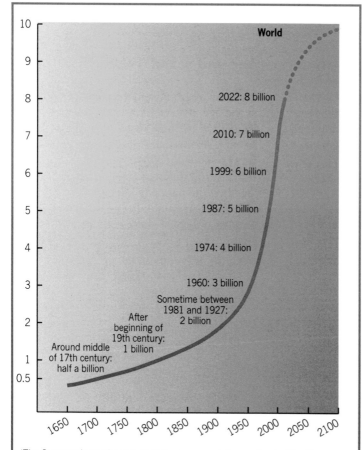

'The S-curve shows the growth in human population, estimated for the period 1650–1980. Between 1825 and 1925 a second billion was added to the first. The third billion came in the next thirty-five years, the fourth billion during the fifteen years following. The United Nations expects a population of perhaps 8 billion by 2025 on certain assumptions of fertility and mortality.'

Source: Independent Commission on Population and Quality of Life (1996)

World population

In this section we will analyse world population changes and attempt to explain why the world population has changed so dramatically in the last 200 years.

According to the organization Population Concern, the world population was more than 5.5 billion in mid-1994. If you look at the graph below, you will see that most of the increase has occurred in the last 100 years. You can also see how steep the increase in population has been since the 1950s.

The global population growth rate was at its highest between 1965 and 1970, but has now slowed to around 1.8 per cent a year with the expectation that it will continue to slow down. However, despite this decrease in the rate of growth, the population is expanding from a wider base, so the annual increase in *absolute numbers* is still growing. For example, in 1992 over 93 million extra people were added to the population (after deaths had been taken away from the overall total). By 2000, the annual figure for additional people is likely to rise to 98 million.

The tremendous increase in the population over the last 150 years is due more to the decline in mortality, rather than an increase in fertility. Basically, more people are now expected to survive into adulthood, have children, and live to a relatively old age.

As can be seen in Table 8.4, a high proportion of the world's population live in newly industrialized and Third World countries. Of these, over half are in Asia. Overall, Asia has a population density of 95 persons per square kilometre, which is close to Europe's density figure. But in other continents, namely Africa and Latin America, the densities in both cases are less than 20 persons per square kilometre. Clearly, density figures need to be interpreted with care. Since these figures are averages, they do not reveal national and regional variations. You should also be aware that density figures in themselves do not reveal the crucial factor, namely *the rate of growth* (see Table 8.4).

Table 8.4 Geographical spread of world population

Region	Population 1993 (millions)	Rate of natural increase (%)	Population 2020 (millions)	Life expectancy at birth (years)
World	5,056	1.6	8,525	65
Europe	513	0.2	516	75
N. America	287	0.8	371	76
CIS	285	0.6	320	70
Oceania	28	1.2	39	73
China	1,178	1.2	1,546	70
Asia (exc. China)	2,079	2.1	2,778	61
Latin America	460	1.9	589	68
Africa	677	2.9	1,552	54

Source: 1993 World Population Data Sheet, PRB and Population Concern

'The view that population growth occurs only in developing countries is inaccurate. Four industrialized nations, namely the United States, Canada, Australia and New Zealand are also projected to continue growing. Much of the growth will derive from immigration (people moving into these countries) and higher fertility amongst recent immigrants. Future demographic growth in these and other industrialized countries will depend, also, on their immigration policies.' (Independent Commission on Population and Quality of Life 1996)

Figure 8.6
Typical age–sex pyramids

Age and sex of a population

One way of graphically representing changes in the age and sex of a population is with a population pyramid (sometimes also called an 'age–sex pyramid'), which uses horizontal bars to represent the proportion of people of either sex in different age groups. Put together, the bars often form a diagram that looks like a pyramid, hence the name. A number of typical shapes can be identified in Figure 8.6.

❖ Figure 8.6a represents an expanding population, where both birth rates and

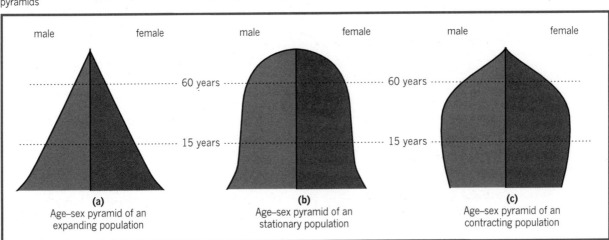

(a) Age–sex pyramid of an expanding population

(b) Age–sex pyramid of an stationary population

(c) Age–sex pyramid of an contracting population

death rates would be high. The shape tells us that the population has many young people, but few elderly people, and it is typical of many developing countries.

❖ Figure 8.6b shows a fairly stationary population with fewer children. Most of the population is between 15 and 60 years.

❖ Figure 8.6c represents a contracting population: the birth rate is steadily dropping year by year and there are many elderly people. Figures 8.6b and 8.6c are more usual shapes for developed countries.

Population pyramids tell us something about the population structure and are an

aid to planning. For example a 'baby boom' can be identified and planned for accordingly by government policy (e.g. increasing the funding for nursery education). In some developed and developing countries, the challenge of the next century lies in coping with ageing populations, since the capacity of these countries' social security systems are already at full stretch and are unlikely to be able to meet the needs of all.

Figure 8.7 shows how an age–sex profile of the population of the UK in 1989 and projections for 2025. Table 8.5 gives a breakdown in numerical terms.

Figure 8.7
Population pyramid – sex and age profiles of the population

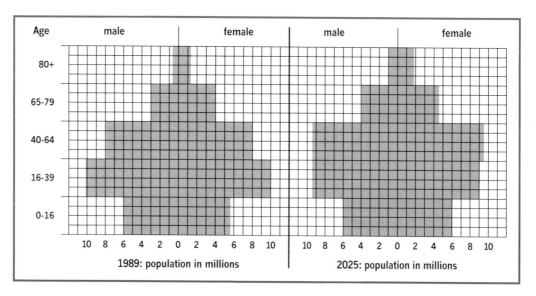

Table 8.5 UK population: numerical breakdown of the age–sex profile

1989 (population in millions)

	0–15	16–39	40–64	65–79	80+	All ages
All	11.5	20.4	16.3	6.9	2.1	57.2
Males	5.9	10.3	8.1	3.0	0.6	27.9
Females	5.6	10.1	8.2	3.9	1.4	29.3

2025 Projections

	0–15	16–39	40–64	65–79	80+	All ages
All	12.1	18.6	19.0	8.5	2.9	61.1
Males	6.2	9.5	9.5	3.9	1.1	30.2
Females	5.9	9.1	9.5	4.6	1.8	30.9

❖ Activity 7 ❖

Study Figs. 8.6 and 8.7 and then answer the following questions:

1   What do the pyramids assume about the ratio of males and females in the population? Why is this less likely to be the case in reality, particularly for the over-60 age group?

2   Using Fig. 8.7 and Table 8.5, contrast the male and female population in 1989 and projected in 2025 for the following age groups:

   •   0–16
   •   16–39
   •   80+

What trends can you detect?

Demographic transition

Demographers refer to changes in the ratio of births to deaths in Western Europe from the nineteenth century onwards as the 'demographic transition'. During this period there has been a change in the population sizes and structures of these societies. The demographic transition has been described as a three-stage process where at each stage, one type of population stability is replaced by another.

1   *Stage One* refers to conditions in which both birth and death rates are high. In this situation the population hardly grows as the high number of births is counterbalanced by the level of deaths. This condition is characterized by traditional societies.

2   *Stage Two* occurs when the death rates fall while fertility rates remain high. In this situation there is a population growth. This began in Europe and the USA in the early part of the nineteenth century.

3   *Stage Three* is the third and current stage when birth rates start to fall near to death rate levels. At this stage the population is again reasonably stable.

Using the stages of demographic transition, many Third World countries are well into the second stage: whereas death rates have begun to fall, birth rates are still high in comparison with the birth rates in First World societies.

Population policies in newly industrialized countries

It is interesting to speculate whether demographic transition will repeat itself in the two countries which have two-fifths of the world's population: China and India. Both countries have attempted to introduce policies to control their population growth. India was one of the first countries in the world whose government actively supported family planning: there were policies of compulsory vasectomy and sterilization in the 1970s. However, progress in reducing population size has been slow, because death rates are also declining as people live longer as a result of factors such as better medical treatment. In China, with a more centralized government, control reductions have been more dramatic. In the 1970s the Chinese government introduced the 'one-child per family' policy. A range of incentives were introduced to promote the policy, including better housing, free health-care and education. In a country where male offspring are valued above females, this policy has led to widespread infanticide of female babies. In the long term, the imbalance of the ratio of males to females in the overall population could cause problems. Such population policies are highly controversial – as we pointed out at the start of this section, few issues have aroused more political, social and moral division than the question of demography.

Industrialization and urbanization

Industrial production processes and urbanization have been regarded as two of the key factors which have brought about the transition to economically advanced societies. Together, they make up what is usually meant when people refer to 'industrialization' or 'industrial society'. Countries wishing to emulate the economic success of the First World have therefore sought to bring about changes in their own economies through similar processes, in order to develop into modern industrial societies. However, these processes cannot necessarily be replicated and, indeed, have not always come about in exactly the same way – even in the developed world.

At this point, it is useful to introduce the term 'newly industrialized countries' (NICs) to refer to those countries which have attempted or are attempting, successfully or not, to become industrialized. This section will look at the development strategies adopted by NICs and at the consequences of industrialization and urbanization.

> '*Industrialization*: the general process by which economies and societies in which agriculture and the production of handicrafts predominate become transformed into economies and societies where manufacturing and related extractive industries are central.' (Jary and Jary 1991, p. 305)

The criteria used to decide whether a country is industrial*ized* or industrial*izing* vary, but indicators include:

❖ the percentage of the labour force employed in manufacturing and service sectors as compared to primary production

❖ manufacturing output as a proportion of GNP.

It is worth remembering, however, that in many industrialized and industrializing countries, small-scale artisans and intermediate handicrafts production co-exist with larger-scale industrial production.

Development strategies

In looking at the varied approaches of NICs to industrialization, we can identify two broad types of development strategy:

❖ import-substituting industrialization (ISI)

❖ export-oriented industrialization (EOI).

Import-substituting industrialization (ISI)

The aim of ISI is to produce manufactured goods locally for the home market, which is expected to expand, and thereby to reduce imports from other countries. It was assumed that this would save scarce foreign exchange and allow further investment, mainly in light industries. The production of 'heavy' manufacturing and goods for export would come later. Thus, rather than development towards the *outside*, development would occur towards the *inside*.

But, according to Barnett (1988), import substitution ran into a number of difficulties.

❖ The Latin American economists who advocated this strategy believed that their industries needed protection from foreign competition and therefore needed tariff barriers, import quotas and subsidies in order to shelter the new infant industries. Critics have argued that this was inefficient and that, in the absence of competition, there is no way of choosing rationally which branches of production you should specialize in.

❖ To set up industries, you need capital goods which initially would have to be imported. These would have to be paid for with foreign currency. To earn this would require increasing exports of primary products. TNCs (transnational corporations) could provide the physical and educational resources to make this possible but, all too often in practice, they come to monopolize these infant markets and therefore undermine them.

❖ There is the problem of the level of demand for the goods produced. Apart from a small élite, few of the mass population of NICs could afford to buy luxury goods, cars, televisions, etc.

Therefore the ISI strategy, which had been intended to create less dependency, all too often ended up creating new forms of dependency in which countries become trapped.

Export-oriented industrialization (EOI)

EOI strategies were developed in the late 1960s and 1970s in parts of Latin America and East Asia to produce manufactured goods for export. Rather than relying heavily on the traditional primary products of agriculture, mining and quarrying, several NICs have diversified into such areas as electronics, steel and shipbuilding. These strategies since the 1960s appear to be very successful, particularly for the East Asian 'four tigers' – Taiwan, Singapore, Hong Kong and South Korea.

These successful economies have encouraged other NICs to devise their own export-oriented strategies, such as establishing export-processing zones (EPZs), special areas set aside for the production of light industrial goods for export. Foreign investors are invited to provide the infrastructure and to employ cheap local labour in producing these light industrial goods for export, in order to repeat the experience and success of countries such as Taiwan and Singapore.

Values

The argument for establishing EPZs tends to assume that economic strategies learned from other countries are the causal factors of the NICs' success. However, an important internal consideration regarding the East Asian NICs is that they have a strong cultural link, namely the Confucian ethic, as the basis for their economic success, emphasizing such values as respect for authority, social cohesion and education. This prompts a comparison with Weber's 'Protestant Ethic' thesis as a causal factor in the growth of capitalism in Western economies (see Chapter 7, p. 284).

Critics question whether NICs nowadays can really emulate the 'four tigers of Asia'. Many NICs, particularly Taiwan, developed in the 1960s with massive inputs of foreign aid. Today, few countries can realistically hope to receive that volume of aid.

Despite the apparent signs of success of EOI in certain countries, some critics argue that most NICs have only succeeded because their typically authoritative political regimes have kept wages low by suppressing trade union opposition to management and democracy.

A strong value base: workers in a Japanese factory attend the singing of the company song and recitation of the company creed

The consequences of industrialization in NICs

Clearly there has been a price to pay, in economic, social and ecological terms, for the rapid industrialization experienced by NICs. In economic terms, the cost of industrialization involves investment programmes which affect present consumption patterns in a society. These countries have had to defer immediate gratification in favour of long-term goals. In the long term, industrialization is a strategy that will improve the living standard of a population. Unfortunately, this can mean that present generations have to suffer in order to improve the standard of living for subsequent generations. In social and cultural terms, there is the problem of attempting to preserve 'cultural traditions' in terms of religion, language, lifestyle, etc., against the need to produce a 'modern' economy which can compete in world markets.

Finally, there are the ecological costs of industrialization which concern us all, including such issues as the depletion of the ozone layer, global warming, acid rain and industrial toxic wastes. An area of future concern is the rapid industrialization of China and India whose combined population is a high proportion of the world's population. At the present time, the richer Northern hemisphere consumes a very high proportion of the world's energy resources. The USA, with just over 4 per cent of the world's population, uses 24 per cent of all energy produced. By contrast, India with 16 per cent of the global population, uses only 2 per cent of total energy. However, the potential for increased consumption, and therefore pollution, in the Southern hemisphere is now one of the biggest threats facing the global environment. The problems of further pollution of the earth by increased industrial output is a real one. Further ecological problems include the reduction in non-renewable energy supplies such as oil and coal, and the increased use of fertilizers, toxic herbicides and pesticides in increasing world food-production. The term 'agri-business' is used to describe the way in which food production has become increasingly mechanized.

All these factors need to be considered if industrialization is to increase. However, despite this increase in food production, many people in Third World countries still go hungry while continuing to supply food to the West.

Urbanization related to development

Throughout the world, the number of urban dwellers is rapidly increasing. If we define 'urbanization' as a growth in the proportion of the country's population living in cities and towns, then as a percentage of the total population, the proportion of urban dwellers stands at 45 per cent and will soon become a majority. Such rapid urbanization is particularly associated with new industrialized nations, where the urban population is growing several times as fast as the rural population. This is happening as a result of migration and urban growth (increases in the size of towns and cities).

It is estimated that by the year 2010, there will be 26 'mega-cities' in the world and, according to the UN, 21 of these cities will be in developing countries – 14 in Asia alone. To give an example, Tokyo is now the world's largest city with over 25 million people, followed by Brazil's São Paolo, which could have a population close to 20 million (*Population Concern* Spring/Summer 1995)

Urban growth in the developing world

Urban growth in the developing world is most commonly attributed to migration of peoples from rural areas into the cities. While this is to some extent the explanation, surveys suggest that the growth is mainly due to high fertility and low mortality.

Developing countries might appear to be following the pattern of industrial nations, where the growth rate of towns and cities has meant over 70 per cent of the population is concentrated in urban areas.

However, the pattern of urbanization in the developing world is different in many respects. During the Industrial Revolution, the cities of Europe attracted people from the countryside to work in the factories, but in developing countries today, only a fraction of their workers would obtain a job in industry. While the expansion of European cities was often accompanied by a fall in the rural population, in the developing world *both* rural and urban populations are now rising simultaneously, placing pressure on resources and services, such as clean water, housing and health care.

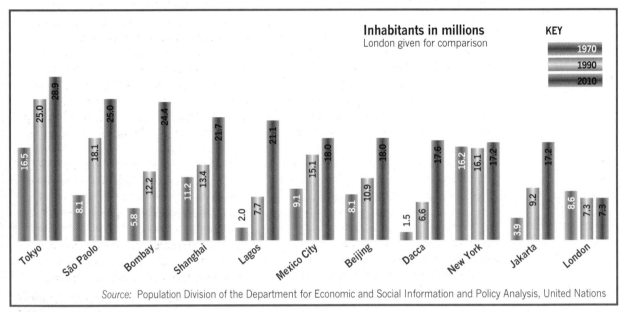

Inhabitants in millions
London given for comparison

KEY
1970
1990
2010

Tokyo: 16.5, 25.0, 28.9
São Paolo: 8.1, 18.1, 25.0
Bombay: 5.8, 12.2, 24.4
Shanghai: 11.2, 13.4, 21.7
Lagos: 2.0, 7.7, 21.1
Mexico City: 9.1, 15.1, 18.0
Beijing: 8.1, 10.9, 18.0
Dacca: 1.5, 6.6, 17.6
New York: 16.2, 16.1, 17.2
Jakarta: 3.9, 9.2, 17.2
London: 8.6, 7.3, 7.3

Source: Population Division of the Department for Economic and Social Information and Policy Analysis, United Nations

Figure 8.8
The world's most populous cities: past, present and future

❖ Activity 8 ❖

Study Figure 8.8.

1 Place each city in order of population size in 1970. Which were the three largest cities in 1970 and how many people lived in each?

2 Which were the three largest and three smallest cities in 1990 and how many people lived in them?

3 Which two cities are predicted to be the largest in the year 2010 and how many people will live in them?

4 Which parts of the world experienced the highest rates of urbanization between 1970 and 1990?

5 What explanations can you provide for the above trends?

❖ Activity 9 ❖

Read about the Indonesian Transmigration Programme (see *In Focus* on p. 339) and then answer the following questions:

1 What is meant by the term 'transmigration' in this passage?

2 Demographers often refer to 'push' and 'pull' factors when discussing the movement of a population. Can you identify the 'push' and 'pull' factors in this case? Could you add any other reasons for the population movement?

3 Why did the programme have only limited success? Can you think of any reasons why the programme in its present form is not being continued by the Indonesian government?

In Focus

◆

Development policy in practice: transmigration in Indonesia

Transmigration is the term given to Indonesia's massive government programme to move people from the fertile but overcrowded islands of Java, Bali, Madura and Lombok to the less densely populated outer islands (see Fig. 8.9).

Java accounts for about two-thirds of Indonesia's population but only 7 per cent of its land area. It has an average population density of 801 per square kilometre (km^2); in irrigated areas this rises to 2,000 people per km^2. Java has fertile volcanic soils which allow intensive agriculture without heavy application of fertilizer, but the other islands generally have poor tropical soils. As a result of the continuous use of land and its population growth, by 1980 productivity and incomes in parts of Java had declined.

The Transmigration Programme, which had international recognition and financial support from the World Bank via loans, was established in order to move families to less crowded islands. Between 1979 and 1984 an average of just over 60,000 families moved each year, but this has declined in recent years.

In total, some 730,000 families have transmigrated – just over three million people.

Assessment of the programme

Many transmigrants have had a struggle to survive and between 15 and 20 per cent have returned home to Java. A number of problems arose which led to heavy crop losses. Added to this, many transmigration areas were isolated, making it difficult and expensive for settlers to buy and sell their produce.

It now appears that this programme has only been a limited success and basically failed in its chief aim of limiting the growth of population on the heavily populated islands.

The total cost of the programme has been high – over $7 billion, about 10 per cent of which has been met by foreign aid. Government thinking on the programme is now changing – it now wants to promote rural development in the outer islands, so that people will migrate without government support.

Source: adapted from Population Concern,
Spring/Summer 1995

Figure 8.9
The islands of Indonesia in SE Asia

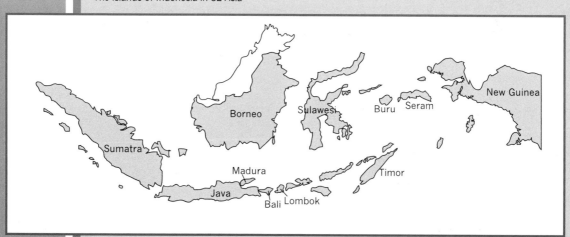

Health and world sociology

In Chapter 10 of this book, we discuss the difficulties involved in measuring the levels of health and illness in a population. Despite these problems, it is still possible to show that there is a broad correlation between a country's *per capita* income and its levels of health, measured in terms of life-expectancy, infant mortality and overall death-rates, as well as in terms of the incidence of particular diseases.

Looking at these indicators in broad terms, there is no denying that, over the past thirty years or so, there has been steady progress in standards of health all over the world. There are local variations and fluctuations but, overall, death rates, including infant mortality rates, have been falling and life expectancy rising. However, there are wide variations between North and South and between regions.

Patterns of disease and ill health

In the North, the two major causes of death are cancer and heart disease. These conditions are associated with particular life-styles, including rich and fatty diets, smoking and stress. They are conditions which become more likely to occur the longer a person lives.

Such diseases do also exist in the Third World, but there the biggest killers are communicable diseases which, along with malnutrition, produce high infant-mortality rates and shorter life expectancy.

Communicable diseases include diarrhoea (a major killer, especially of young children), and bacterial or viral diseases, which include polio, cholera, hepatitis and typhoid. There are also air-borne diseases, such as tuberculosis, pneumonia, whooping cough, diphtheria, meningitis and influenza. All these diseases are still found in the North, but there they can be effectively treated and are rarely fatal, whereas in the Third World they account for a third of all deaths.

Another category of diseases, more specific to hotter climates, involves insects. The best known is malaria, transmitted by mosquitoes. Other diseases in this category include bilharzia, carried by a water snail,

Figure 8.10
Distribution of HIV-infected adults alive as of mid-1995

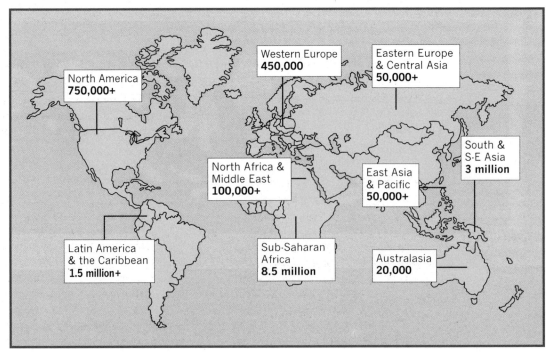

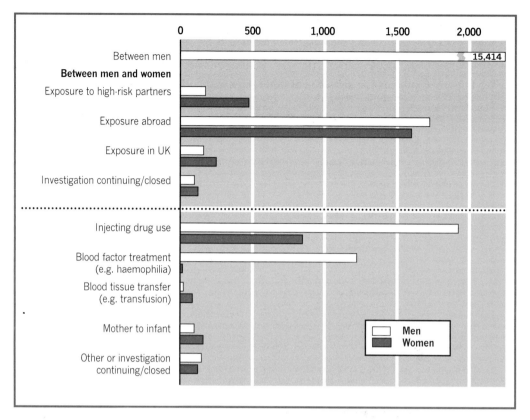

Figure 8.11
Number of cases
of HIV-infection
in UK to end
September 1995

trypanosomiasis (sleeping sickness), elephantiasis and river blindness. All these diseases affect and kill millions of people in the Third World.

A third category of disease involves physical contact, including leprosy, yaws, VD and, more recently, Aids. According to Foster-Carter (1984), the global incidence of syphilis and gonorrhoea in the late 1960s was over 50 million and 160 million respectively.

Social factors associated with health

Many of the diseases mentioned above were commonly found in the UK and Europe in the 19th century. Their control is the result of improvements in living standards, including safe drinking water and improved sanitation, improved nutrition and better literacy levels. McKeown (1976) has shown that these improvements, which essentially prevent disease, account for more of the improvement in health than does the

In Focus

◆

Aids in the South

'Aids has now reached most countries and is spreading at the rate of at least one million infections a year – 80 per cent of these through heterosexual intercourse. The majority of sufferers are in the South. In some communities in Central Africa, one person in five is thought to carry the virus. It is difficult to predict what effect Aids might have on population growth rates, but because the death rate from Aids is highest among children and young adults, it could have a serious effect on future developments in certain countries.'

Source: Myers (1994, p. 181)

progress of curative medicine or even the extent of vaccination and immunization.

Immunization policies in the South have certainly controlled diseases such as malaria, smallpox and polio, but other diseases including diarrhoea and various respiratory infections are unlikely to be eradicated without improvements in living standards such as access to clean water, adequate sanitary and waste disposal systems and an adequate diet. Third World countries can also benefit from the introduction of primary health-care systems alongside Western-influenced urban, hospital-based systems.

Gender and world sociology

Gender has been a theme in every chapter of this book. Most analysis of gender issues has focused on women and sociologists have only recently given attention to men in industrialized societies. This section will focus more on women, because of the substantial inequalities that still exist between men and women in many Third World nations.

According to Foster-Carter (1984):

'Women form 50 per cent of the world's population ... It is estimated that this half of us work two-thirds of all work hours in the world and are responsible for 50 per cent of world food production. Yet they receive only 10 per cent of world income and own a derisory 1 per cent of world property. They have other obligations too: one third of all families are headed by women.'

There are exceptions to this. In parts of Africa, women traditionally have had more power and status than in South or East Asia, or even in Europe. They had, and still have, important socio-economic roles, as farmers, producers of craft goods and traders. Examples of this today are to be found in the market-women of several West African societies.

Women and development

The status of women varies from one part of the world to another. The world's poorest women live on the edge of subsistence. They are economically dependent and vulnerable, and often politically and legally powerless. As wives and mothers, they are caught in a life-cycle which begins with early marriage and may end in death from childbirth.

Worldwide, women grow about half the world's food, but most own no land. They work long hours and are concentrated in the lowest-paid occupations. Three almost universal and strenuous tasks – fetching water, gathering firewood and grinding corn – are in may cultures almost invariably performed by women.

Increasingly in the 1980s and 1990s young women, notably in South or East Asia and Latin America, are working not in agriculture, as mentioned in the last paragraph, but in factories, producing goods ranging from textiles to electronics for export to world markets. Young female labour is cheaper to recruit, more pliable and more docile.

❖ Activity 10 ❖

Read the extract on the next page about women in India and attempt to answer the following questions:

1. What do you think Bumiller means when she says in the passage, 'Women have been displaced from traditional labour and medical advances have ensured that discrimination against them can now begin at birth'?

2. In what ways do you think the lives of Indian women are different from those of women in Britain?

3. Bumiller concludes that Indian women's lives are how most women in the world spend their lives, and that it is societies like America which are unusual. What does she mean by this?

'I have come to the conclusion that if I did not work among the poor, I have at least told their stories and unveiled a part of their lives. This book was my mission – to inform, to enlighten and to prove that the women of India are more like us than they are not. This does not change the fact that the majority of women in India continue to live deplorable lives and are still held back by the overpowering forces of poverty, history, tradition, religion and caste. The country has not solved its most basic problem, overpopulation, which burdens women most heavily and makes all of the other problems worse. Men still control the power structure, and modernity has been a mixed blessing. Women have been displaced from traditional labour, and medical advances have ensured that discrimination against them can now begin before birth. And yet, in the four decades since India's independence, there has been a marked improvement in some women's lives.

... But slowly I realized that the way Indian women live is the way the majority of women in the world spend their lives. It is Americans who are peculiar. Ultimately I realized my journey to India was a privilege.'

Source: Bumiller (1991)

 ## Education and world sociology

Every society has arrangements for educating its younger members in order to pass on certain skills, knowledge and values from one generation to the next. In pre-industrial nations this process is usually carried out informally within family and kinship networks. Complex industrial societies have also developed a more formal educational system with specialized places to learn, formal curricula and teachers. The system is usually geared towards a particular age-group of pupils.

Formal education has often been regarded as integral to the development process, with governments taking measures (often supported by foreign aid) to expand the quantity and improve the quality of schooling in their countries. However, there is no simple cause–effect relationship between education and development.

In this section we will look at this relationship from different sociological perspectives.

Education, modernization and underdevelopment

Modernization theory sees a formal education process as a good thing and a necessary element in the modernization of any society. The education system is seen as having a number of functions: economic, political and cultural. From this perspective, investment in education will lead to higher standards of living and more secure economic futures. Establishing schools and raising literacy levels has been an issue of great concern to governments and to the peoples of industrializing nations.

Dependency theory is more critical of formal education, particularly in the form it has taken in many Third World countries. In economic terms, the criticism is that too much is spent on secondary and tertiary education for a small élite, at the expense of a basic mass education. The result is an educated élite, who cannot find white-collar or professional jobs, plus an illiterate or undereducated majority. Given the lower level of industrial development in these countries, most of the better-paid jobs are in government, and there are not enough such positions to go round.

In terms of the political and cultural function of education, this perspective sees the creation of an isolated and rootless élite, over-identifying with the value systems of the capitalist North, especially the value of individualism. Thus, where modernization theory sees a Northern-style formal education as beneficial, dependency theory is more critical and sees such education as creating further dependency on the wealthy countries of the world.

Global patterns of education

Participation and enrolments in education have increased globally in the last thirty years. Over a billion young people – one-fifth of the world's population – are enrolled in formal education today, compared with around 300 million or one-tenth of the world's population in 1953, the earliest year for which UNESCO has global estimates of enrolment.

There is an imbalance between girls and boys enrolling. According to the figures in the World Education Report 1995, in the age-group 6–11 years old, nearly a quarter (24.5 per cent) of the world's girls are estimated to be out of school (85 million) compared with around one-sixth (16.4 per cent) of the world's boys (60 million).

Largely as a consequence of this imbalance in participation in formal education, the literacy rate of the world's women (71.2 per cent) is significantly lower than that of men (83.6 per cent), although the gap is slowly closing (see Table 8.6).

Nearly two-thirds of the world's illiterate adults are women (565 million), most of them living in the developing regions of Africa, Asia and Latin America (see Table 8.7 on the next page).

Table 8.6 Estimated adult literacy rates[1], by region, 1980 and 1995

	1980			1995		
	MF	M	F	MF	M	F
World	**69.5**	**77.2**	**61.9**	**77.4**	**83.6**	**71.2**
Developing countries	58.0	68.9	46.8	70.4	78.9	61.7
of which:						
Sub-Saharan Africa	40.2	51.8	29.2	56.8	66.6	47.3
Arab States	40.8	55.0	26.2	56.6	68.4	44.2
Latin America/Caribbean	79.7	82.1	77.5	86.6	87.7	85.5
Eastern Asia/Oceania	69.3	80.4	58.0	83.6	90.6	76.3
of which: China	66.0	78.6	52.7	81.5	89.9	72.7
Southern Asia	39.1	52.8	25.4	50.2	62.9	36.6
of which: India	40.8	55.3	25.3	52.0	65.5	37.7
Least developed countries	36.5	48.3	24.9	48.8	59.5	38.1
Developed countries	96.6	98.0	95.4	98.7	98.9	98.4

[1] Percentage of literate adults in the population aged 15 years and over.

Source: World Education Report 1995 (UNESCO)

Table 8.6 Estimated illiterate population (millions) aged 15 and over, 1980–2000

	1980			1995			2000		
	MF	*F*	*%F*	*MF*	*F*	*%F*	*MF*	*F*	*%F*
World total	**877.4**	**551.4**	**62.8**	**884.7**	**564.7**	**63.8**	**880.8**	**564.6**	**64.1**
Developing countries *of which:*	848.4	530.6	62.5	871.8	556.7	63.9	870.0	558.1	64.2
Sub-Saharan Africa	125.9	76.2	60.5	140.5	87.1	62.0	143.4	89.3	62.3
Arab States	55.8	34.5	61.8	65.5	41.2	62.9	67.9	42.9	63.3
Latin America/ Caribbean	44.1	24.7	56.1	42.9	23.4	54.7	42.1	22.7	54.0
Eastern Asia/ Oceania	276.1	186.3	67.5	209.9	149.5	71.2	182.4	132.3	72.6
of which: China	218.8	147.9	67.6	166.2	119.5	71.9	143.5	105.7	73.7
Southern Asia	345.9	207.2	59.9	415.5	256.1	61.6	437.7	271.8	62.1
of which: India	250.6	152.7	60.09	290.0	182.7	62.8	300.8	190.5	63.3
Least developed countries	135.4	81.2	59.9	166.0	101.0	60.8	178.0	109.0	61.2
Developed countries	29.0	20.9	72.0	12.9	7.9	61.6	10.7	6.5	60.5

Source: World Education Report, 1995 (UNESCO)

As can be seen from Table 8.7, there are estimated still to be some 885 million people who cannot read and write. Countries such as Cuba have reduced illiteracy rates amongst adults by heavy mass-literacy campaigns. India has promoted self-help education by which communities draw upon their own resources in ways which do not involve high expenditure. Those who can read and write and have specific skills are encouraged to support others whom they coach in their spare time. The self-help scheme discussed above comes close to the ideas developed by Ivan Illich in his criticisms of formal education.

❖ Activity 11 ❖

1 Analyse the figures given in Table 8.7. In particular, compare the totals given for the world's illiterate population with the overall population figures shown in Fig. 8.5 on p. 331. Can you see grounds for optimism in the illiteracy trends?

2 Why do you think there is such a markedly higher proportion of illiteracy among women?

What ways can you think of of tackling the specific problem of illiteracy among women?

In Focus
◆
Education in China and Hong Kong

Table 8.8 compares China with Hong Kong, returned to China in 1997 after 150 years of British colonial rule. China is now an industrializing country, whereas Hong Kong is already highly industrialized.

Table 8.8 A comparison of the educational system of the People's Republic of China (PRC) and Hong Kong

	PRC	*Hong Kong*
Pupil population	220 million	1 million
Educational goals	Explicitly political – education is to serve proletarian politics, to produce faithful supporters of the Chinese road of socialism and modernization	Apolitical – all-round development of pupils and to fulfil manpower needs
Structure of school system	Predominantly 6 + 6 + 4	6 + 5 + 2 + 3
Ideological orientation	Socialist and paternalistic	Colonial – capitalist and individualistic
Span of universal compulsory education	9-year, partially implemented	9-year, fully implemented
Curriculum control	Highly centralized	Highly centralized
Curriculum development	State-monopolized and controlled, dominated by academics	Government-led, but with greater degree of partici-pation by principals and teachers
Curriculum arrangement	Highly academic and compartmentalized; lacking in diversity	Academically-oriented, but recently vocationalized and diversified
Medium of instruction	Chinese or Han-Chinese	90 per cent English (in policy, but less in practice)

Source: adapted from Postiglione (1991)

❖ Activity 12 ❖

1 What problems does China have in formally educating such a large school population?

2 Compare and contrast the two education systems described in Table 8.8 and state how you think this is linked to their particular political philosophies.

Foreign aid, loans and debt

Foreign aid

There are several different types of aid or help which richer states in the world can give to poorer nation-states. Official government aid is distributed through overseas development agencies (ODA). Non-governmental organizations (NGOs) also provide aid and assistance. NGOs range from large aid-agencies through to small charities, such as Oxfam and Christian Aid.

In 1994 the total amount of aid given by ODAs was some $59 billion. According to some estimates, less than a quarter of this reached the poor themselves. Much of the money is used for 'mega-projects' or tied to purchases from donor countries or paid in 'debt reliefs' straight to banks. Nevertheless, the aid given by Western countries and Japan is much higher than that provided by non-governmental or charitable agencies (at about $5 billion, the latter accounts for less than 10 per cent of aid given by ODAs).

Since 1969, members of the Development Assistance Committee (DAC) of the Organization for Economic Cooperation and Development (OECD), to which all major aid donors belong, were set a goal by the UN whereby the richer nations of the world would contribute 0.7 per cent of their GNP in aid to poorer countries. However, in 1994 the average aid given by DAC members stood at 0.3 per cent. Only the Netherlands, Norway, Sweden and Denmark have ever reached the 0.7 per cent target. Japan is now by far the world's largest donor.

Advantages and disadvantages of aid

It was at the Bretton Woods Conference in 1944 that the world's leading politicians set an agenda to reorganize the world economy. For the first time in human history, *universal* institutions – the International Monetary Fund (IMF), the World Bank and the General Agreements on Tariffs and Trade (GATT) – were established to tackle global economic problems. A dominant view at the Conference was that the depression of the 1930s and the rise of Fascism could be traced to the collapse of international trade and isolationist economic policies.

Since the 1980s, the emphasis amongst major donor countries has been to re-emphasize the principles of a global or world economy. Borders between countries were to be as porous as possible to goods and capital from anywhere in the world. The IMF and World Bank were to be key institutions in this process. GATT set the rules for open economies and free trade.

However, much of the official aid tends to go towards funding large, expensive projects, even though critics argue that smaller-scale projects would be more advantageous to poorer countries, in that they may better serve the local population and meet immediate needs. Some major projects (such as building dams and creating artificial reservoirs) may actually be economically disadvantageous to some groups and may have grave ecological consequences for a geographical area. The ecological consequences of official aid will be discussed later in this section.

Another major change since the 1980s has been the more stringent requirements set by donor countries.

Tied aid is advantageous to the donor country since it is given on condition that the recipient country buys specified goods and services from the donor country. One final problem with aid is that Western governments may use it for political reasons.

In Focus

◆

Official aid

- ❖ *Bilateral aid* – grants negotiated directly between one national government and another.
- ❖ *Multi-lateral aid* – grants provided by international organizations such as UN agencies and the World Bank.
- ❖ *Tied aid* – grants given on condition that they are spent on the purchase of goods from the donor.

Loans and the debt crisis

By the end of the 1980s a debt crisis affected many countries in the Southern hemisphere. Total debt from these countries actually shot up from $751 billion in 1981 to $1,355 billion in 1990. The debtor countries as a group began the 1990s a full 61 per cent more in debt than they were in 1982. Sub-Saharan Africa's debt increased by 113 per cent during this period.

In 1982 a major financial crisis hit Mexico, which then threatened to default on its repayments. A major plan was therefore negotiated between the US and Mexican governments to prevent a global financial collapse. The solution was 'structural adjustment programmes' or SAPs. According to David Ransom:

> 'SAPs require privatization, cuts in public expenditure, increases in exports and absolute adherence to the principals of free trade. These principals are indifferent to the eradication of poverty: they are largely responsible for its creation'. (*New Internationalist*, November 1996)

Thus SAPs restructured the debt and avoided the debt crisis.

The debt boomerang

According to Susan George (1993), the debt crisis among recipient countries also affects the donor countries. She has called this the 'debt boomerang'. The idea that policies from donor countries towards recipients can have consequences for themselves is summarized briefly below:

❖ *Environment* – Debt-induced poverty causes Third World people to exploit natural resources in the most profitable and least sustainable way, which causes an increase in global warming and a depletion of genetic bio-diversity. This ultimately harms the North too.

❖ *Drugs* – The illegal drugs trade is a major earner for heavily indebted countries like Peru, Bolivia and Colombia. The social and economic costs of the drug-consuming boom in the North is phenomenal – $60 billion a year in the US alone.

❖ *Taxes* – Governments in the North have used their taxpayers' money to give banks concessions so that they can write off so-called 'bad debts' from Third World countries. But in most cases this has not reduced the actual debts of poor countries. By 1991 UK banks had gained from tax credits for more than half their exposure. The eventual total relief will amount to $8.5 billion.

❖ *Unemployment* – Exports from rich countries to the Third World would be much higher if those countries were not strapped by debt, and this would stimulate manufacturing and employment in the North. The loss of jobs due to 'lost exports' is estimated to account for one-fifth of total US unemployment.

❖ *Immigration* – The International Labour Organization estimates that there are now about 100 million illegal immigrants and refugees in the world today. Many go to the richer countries of the North to flee poverty and the effects of IMF-imposed economic policies.

❖ *Conflict* – Debt creates social unrest and war. Iraq invaded Kuwait in 1990 largely in retaliation for the latter's insistence that Saddam Hussein's regime in Iraq repay a $12 billion loan.

The notion of a 'social boomerang effect' is discussed in Ullrich Beck's book, *Risk Society* (1992). Beck argues that we live in a new era of modernity which he calls 'reflexive modernity'. Beck argues that there are increased risks associated with modern industrial production. These risks have consequences for everyone on the planet (see Chapter 13, *Power and politics*, pp. 599–600).

Rwanda (largely because of the genocidal civil war) and Mozambique received more aid in 1994 than their total income from all other sources. Rwanda's aid was equivalent to about 125 per cent of the country's GNP; Mozambique's was equivalent to 100 per cent. Other countries, such as Guinea Bissau (75 per cent) and Nicaragua (40 per cent), receive so much foreign aid as a proportion of their income that they are 'dependent' – i.e. without it their economies would collapse.

In absolute terms, China is the largest single recipient of foreign aid (over $3 billion in 1993), followed by Egypt ($2.3 billion), Indonesia ($2 billion) and India ($1.5 billion). Israel, too, is a major recipient ($1.2 billion). Rich donors have major strategic interests in all of these countries, which either have large populations (like China, India and Indonesia), or (like Israel) are wealthy, so that aid is a much less significant part of their total income.

New world order

In the 1980s and 1990s there have been social, political and technological changes on a scale much greater than ever before. Some sociologists have argued that postmodernism provides the best analysis for understanding global issues (see Chapter 13, *Power and politics*), while others argue that a Marxist explanation makes sense of the contradictions and problems we face.

Whichever theory is adopted, uncertainty and pessimism nowadays prevail, in clear contrast to the more optimistic emphasis of the 1950s and 1960s. This uncertainty derives, in part, from the various wars and serious environmental disasters that have taken place over the past decade. Combined with this has been the collapse of the USSR and the Communist system in Eastern Europe that began with the removal of the Berlin Wall in 1989. Although this collapse has ended what was known as the 'Cold War' between East and West, it has also changed the balance of world economic and political power and led to greater uncertainty. Changes in the balance of political power have had implications for Third World countries. Foster-Carter (1992) recognized the impact of communism in the Third World, not least because, in addition to Russia, countries such as China, Mongolia, Cuba, Vietnam, Ethiopia and Mozambique adopted a communist economic and political framework based on Marxist principles.

Many former Communist countries have now adopted a market economy and moved away from planned and interventionist policies. Singapore, Hong Kong, Taiwan and South Korea have developed into the most rapidly growing economies based on planned intervention and an adherence to the free market.

Implications for the Third World

The consequence of the political and economic changes in the last decade has meant that the USA has emerged as *the* major superpower. As a result, Third World countries have had to adjust to the global market, with the assumption by donor countries that only free markets can reduce poverty. According to Foster-Carter (1992):

> 'On the one hand, there is little now to prevent the US intervening in any place at any time should it so desire. On the other hand, the West may now become less paranoid, or simply be indifferent to either hunger or anger at least in poorer and strategically unimportant parts of the Third World, since there is no USSR to take advantage of it.'

It is true that there is uncertainty about the future, but perhaps there are also some grounds for optimism, that is, if the United Nations has a more effective voice in global society. The rise of non-governmental organizations is also a hopeful sign. Organizations such as the Red Cross, Amnesty International, Oxfam, and Greenpeace increasingly provide a voice on a range of issues relating to the Third World. Although these organizations lack political and military power, they exert a moral authority which cannot easily be ignored. More importantly, they can transcend national boundaries, prejudices and politics, and through worldwide mass communication, draw our attention to global issues.

Chapter summary

❖ The founders of social change and development include Comte, Durkheim and Marx.

❖ A major interest of the founders of sociology was modernity.

❖ Evolutionary theories of development assume that societies become more complex as a result of technological and economic development.

❖ These theories have been criticized by other sociologists, who argue that the growth of capitalism has led to the 'dependency' of the Third World.

❖ There is now much interest in theories of globalization and how nation-states have become interdependent. The growth of transnational corporations (TNCs) is also analysed to see how they operate from one country to another.

❖ A study of world sociology includes an analysis of demographic trends, industrialization and urbanization. Development strategies have been adopted by some newly industrialized nations (NICs) in order to compete in world markets.

❖ Issues such as health, gender and education are seen as important aspects of development.

❖ The dependence of nation-states in the world today is an important focus when analysing aid and debt, as are the possible ways in which present social, political and technological changes could lead to a new world order.

Essay questions

World Sociology is a new AEB topic, so these questions come from the proposed AEB 1998 specimen paper.

1 'Third world countries are the helpless victims of the world capitalist system.' Assess the view expressed in this statement.

2 'Explain and evaluate the contributions of modernization and dependency theories to an understanding of health inequalities.'

Past examination questions on development:

1 Evaluate the view that there has been a process of globalization in which societies operate within an integrated, worldwide system. (AEB 1995)

2 Critically discuss the view that economic growth is only one aspect of development. (AEB 1996)

Further reading

Many of the books written on world sociology and development are quite challenging for A-level readers, but the following are worth studying:

Waters, M. (1995) *Globalization*, London: Routledge.

This gives an excellent and up-to-date overview of the issues discussed in this chapter.

Foster-Carter, A. (1984) *The Sociology of Development*, London: Macmillan.

This provides a good introduction to development issues.

Hulme, D. and Turner, M. (1990) *Sociology and Development. Theories, Policies and Practices*, London: Harvester-Wheatsheaf.

Yearley, S. (1996) *Sociology, Environmentalism and Globalisation*, London: Sage.

Chapter 9

Community and localities

❖ Preview

In this chapter we shall be looking at:

- ❖ the debate surrounding the definition of the word 'community'
- ❖ the distinction between urban and rural communities, and the changes that have taken place in urban places and villages
- ❖ the processes which encourage urban growth (*urbanization*) and those which encourage loss of population from cities to the countryside (*counter-urbanization*)
- ❖ the social consequences of urbanization and counter-urbanization
- ❖ sociological arguments surrounding the impact of industrialization and urbanization, particularly with regard to community

- ❖ the evidence for and against the 'loss of community' thesis
- ❖ the reasons why different social groups, particularly ethnic groups, can be found in different parts of the city
- ❖ the sociological arguments concerning power and conflict in urban and rural areas
- ❖ the particular problems of the inner city and sociological explanations of them
- ❖ the debate about the future of the city and community.

❖ Introduction

Where are you from? Where do you live? It is taken for granted that asking such questions can help us piece together an image of the kind of person we are talking to. When people say they are from 'England', 'Manchester', 'Orkney' or wherever, they give clues to their social identity. The place a person lives in is not just a matter of geography, but has social significance. Being part of a place or community involves contact with neighbours and friends. It may include sharing work and leisure time with other people in that area. The idea that

community is focused on places can be seen in television programmes like *EastEnders*, *Emmerdale*, *Neighbours* and *Coronation Street*.

The early sociology of community

Sociologists have long been concerned with the importance of *place* on social life. The classical theorists of the nineteenth century were primarily interested in the effects of rapid industrialization and urbanization. Most were pessimistic and believed that the destruction of traditional village life could pose a threat to social order. This belief that community life was better in the past remains today. Those associating with the political Right hark back to the 'good old days' of cohesion and order when everyone knew their place, whilst those on the Left mourn the loss of sharing, cooperation and being supportive of each other in times of trouble. This means we hear the word 'community' from all political parties used in a variety of ways.

In the first half of the twentieth century, sociologists continued with the 'loss of community' debate and the view that there was a distinction between the ways of life to be found in rural and urban areas. 'Community Studies' involved the detailed research of real urban and rural communities. Much attention was given to the *city*, particularly its inner zone. The Chicago School (see p. 383) aimed to explain why different social groups lived in distinct parts of the city.

During the 1960s the study of community became regarded as old-fashioned. Its strong association with functionalism (covered later in this chapter), with its inability to provide insight into the obvious conflicts found within communities, made it unpopular. Moreover, research tended to be on rather marginal places, such as mining towns, from which generalizations about society as a whole could not be made.

Many early theorists assumed that modernization destroyed community, so there was little to be achieved from studying something that was seen as largely irrelevant in the modern world.

More recent developments

From the 1970s a more radical analysis became dominant. Neo-Marxists and Neo-Weberians, being mainly concerned with power, conflict and the inequalities between places, argued that places could not be studied in isolation, but needed to be regarded as part of wider social and economic processes. The problems of the inner city, urban decay, unemployment, racial conflict and disorder, became of crucial concern. Riots in areas such as Brixton in London and Moss Side in Manchester in the early 1980s gave such issues urgency amongst British social scientists.

Many of these themes have continued in the work of more modern writers. Detailed research has been carried out on the local effects of the massive changes that have taken place in the global economy. There remains a concern with conflict, but this has been extended beyond those conflicts caused by economic factors. For example, we can now see a growing sociological interest in environmental issues and the campaigns centred around them. Postmodernism has been an important influence in recent years. The focus is on the cultural, the ways individuals and groups construct and reconstruct 'community' as a source of social identity in an ever-changing society.

The above is a brief review of the development of the sociology of localities and its key themes. Geography and History students may feel they are on familiar ground; of all topics, localities benefits from a multi-disciplinary approach and you should be aware of the insights other subjects may give.

Defining community

Like many words used by sociologists, 'community' has a common everyday use.

❖ Activity 1 ❖

1 Write down as many phrases as you can think of which include the word 'community', e.g. community spirit, European Community. If possible, do this activity in pairs.

2 (a) Write a dictionary definition of 'community'. This should include what you regard as its most essential characteristic.

   (b) Table 9.1 is a summary of 94 definitions of community. Compare these with the definitions you came up with.

   (c) Discuss why having so many different definitions may cause difficulties for sociologists examining community.

Table 9.1 Analysis of 94 definitions of community

- 69 agree that community includes: social interaction, area, some ties or bonds in common.

- 14 definitions include some common characteristic, other than area.

- 15 defined community using a rural area.

Source: Bell and Newby (1976)

After Activity 1 you will realize that the word 'community' is used in many different contexts and has a wide variety of meanings. This lack of precision does indeed cause difficulties. For example, when debating central issues like 'loss of community' different sociologists could be talking about different things. Moreover, in practical research, how can 'community' be measured if we are not sure what it is we are actually measuring? The many meanings of community have the effect of making analysis difficult. However, the common uses of the word community can be broken down into three broad categories: places, social relationships and shared identity.

Places

Community is often linked to geographic areas, villages, towns – even schools. Community exists as a product of people interacting together as a result of the place in which they are located. In this sense, community can operate on a number of scales. For example, on the international level, 'the European Community' (now the European Union) was defined by the boundaries marked on a map of the countries which comprised it.

Social relationships

Sociologists tend to avoid definitions of community which imply that geography is the major determinant of social life since this ignores the ability of humans to overcome the constraints of their environment. Just because people live on the same housing estate does not necessarily mean that they 'feel' part of a community. Most sociologists accept that the most important feature of community is that it contains a set of social relationships that are usually focused on a particular place. For example, *Coronation Street* is merely bricks and mortar. It is the intriguing goings on between the characters which make it a 'community'. The view that community is primarily concerned with relationships also suggests the existence of obligations and responsibilities. This idea that communities should be warm and caring is found in the writings of many sociologists as well as generally within society. Thus the term 'community care' assumes such relationships do exist and that provision is made for the needs of vulnerable groups in a given area, such as the elderly (see p. 455).

Community is about social relationships, exemplified in the long-running and enormously popular Granada Television programme, *Coronation Street*

Shared identity

In some cases the term 'community' is used to refer to groups of people who are unlikely to live in the same place or have social contact. 'Community' can be applied to groups who feel they are bound together by common experience or identity. We talk of the 'gay community' in this way. Often those who belong to a particular religious faith are regarded as a community. Particular events may bind people together, even if this is only transitory. For example, celebrations like those for VE Day or the Millenium may serve to create feelings of being part of a community which may extend beyond local or even national frontiers.

It seems that 'community' has different meanings depending upon the context in which it is used. The difficulties in clarifying it has led to some sociologists suggesting that 'community' should be replaced with a different term.

In search of a new word for community

Philip Cooke (1989) is particularly critical of the use of 'community' by sociologists. He sees it as a 'catch-all' phrase and offers three main reasons why it is not acceptable:

❖ It is *not precise enough geographically*. If sociologists need to focus on the social activity of particular places then the fact that 'community' is sometimes used as an expression of identity without reference to a specific place makes the term too broad.

❖ The word 'community' carries with it an image of being in some way *closed to outside forces*. Cooke emphasizes that the social life of particular places must be looked at as part of wider social and economic processes. For example, the decision of the Ministry of Defence to relocate its administration from Bath to Bristol in 1996 has fundamental implications for the well-being of the people of the two cities.

❖ Cooke further argues that 'community' incorporates the idea of *stability*. This hides the fact that conflict is an inevitable feature of community life and this in itself can bring about change.

Replacing the term community?

In response to the ambiguities of the term 'community', attempts have been made to develop a term which is narrower in scope. Giddens (1984) offers the word 'locale':

'Locales refer to the use of space to provide the 'settings' of interaction, the settings of interaction in turn being essential to specifying its contextuality... Locales may range from a room in a house, a street corner, the shop floor of a factory, towns and cities, to the territorially demarcated areas occupied by nation states.' (Giddens 1984)

Although the term 'locale' clearly emphasizes the importance of the place in which social activity occurs, problems remain:

❖ Giddens has failed to narrow the geographic boundaries sufficiently. A 'room' to a 'nation state' just about covers every eventuality without precisely defining the 'places' with which the sociology of localities should be concerned.

❖ Locales appear to be backdrops to social interaction. Cooke sees this as much too passive. People have interests in particular places and fight to promote and defend them. For example, different groups compete for their share of lottery money in order to develop projects which will enhance their area. Bitterness has arisen as a result of the areas outside the South East of England perceiving that they have not been given a fair share of the cake. Places involve power and innovation. Thus, Glastonbury has become the home of the 'New Age' and the Greenpeace festival because individuals and organizations put their ideas into practice even when other groups resisted. The character of a place is not just the result of its natural and economic attributes but of the actions of people who live there.

Since Cooke sees both 'locales' and 'community' as inadequate, he suggests the term 'locality' instead:

'A locality is the space within which the larger part of most citizens' daily working and consuming lives is lived.' (Cooke 1989)

According to Cooke, places provide a base for individuals or groups to fight to extend or defend their rights. This could be a dispute concerning noisy neighbours, the siting of a new superstore or any other issue generating conflict. The idea of communities being active entities influenced by outside economic and social forces is clearly seen in the work of sociologists interested in the effects of economic 'restructuring', discussed on page 378. These studies appear to justify the rejection of the term 'community' in favour of 'localities' since they reveal that people who share a particular geographic space may have very little else in common.

Why 'community' should not be abandoned

Not all sociologists are happy with the term 'localities'. Day (1995) sees it as a term produced *by* sociologists *for* sociologists which may have very little meaning in the lives of the people they are describing. What is more likely to be of real importance are the social groups which can be found within localities. Some sociologists have questioned the extent to which boundaries drawn by researchers around localities actually coincide with those in the minds of ordinary people. It seems that too much attention has been given to the *economic* aspects of community at the expense of those concerning local *culture* and *identity.*

Cohen (1985) argues that 'community exists in the minds of its members, and should not be confused with geographic or sociographic assertions of fact.' In this he is emphasizing the *subjective* nature of community: people *think* themselves into a place. They create ideas of being special and distinctive from others. Once they have decided what makes them unique, they can present this identity to others by showing how they are different or similar by using symbols. These symbols may include dress, accent, forms of slang, taking part in events and other features of style. For example, Rap artists use all these ways to indicate their distinctiveness and, like others who adopt the same symbols of identity, they connect themselves to a particular place, the 'ghetto'. 'Community' in this sense is a symbolic boundary.

Day and Murdock (1993) believe we should be concerned with the way people see themselves and their location in society, their understanding of space and their relationships to particular places. Community then can be seen as an emotional bond which exists in the minds of its members and as such remains worth investigating. Bauman (1992) argues that the concept of community has enjoyed a recent popular revival. We can see this in such terms as 'community care' and 'community action'. This makes the study of community a highly relevant contemporary issue.

It may seem that the argument about how 'community' should be defined and whether we should use the term at all seems rather trivial when 'real' communities and issues could be discussed. Nevertheless, it is

Glastonbury festival

important for the purposes of analysis to clarify the complex meanings of key words. As you read this chapter, look out for the various ways sociologists use terms such as 'community' and 'locality', and try to identify the ideological bias that these words may incorporate.

Urban and rural life

When we think of life in the city and life in the countryside, we tend to emphasize contrasts. Sociologists, too, have long been concerned to examine apparent differences in rural and urban living. Often, city life is described relatively unfavourably compared to village life. In particular, the city is perceived as lacking the community networks found in small settlements. However, some sociologists have questioned this view of rural life as harmonious and orderly. They argue that there is evidence to the contrary, historical as well as contemporary. Further, there is evidence of stable community life within urban areas. Detailed sociological research has shown that social life in different places is highly varied and is difficult to classify simply into urban and rural patterns. The following section examines these issues in more detail.

Images of rural and urban life

❖ Activity 4 ❖

1   In two columns, list the images you have of the differences between urban and rural life.

2   When you have finished your list, read carefully the information on rural and urban life given in Table 9.2 which summarizes the distinction between urban and rural life given in Ferdinand Tonnies' *Community and Society* (Tonnies 1957).

    Discuss the ways the views given are similar or different to your own.

3   What other examples can you think of to indicate the difference between 'Gemeinschaft' and 'Gesellschaft' forms of society?

Table 9.2 Distinction between urban and rural life

	Rural life	*Urban life*
Term used	'Gemeinschaft'	'Gesellschaft'
Meaning of term	Community	Association
Nature of social interaction	Face-to-face contact. Individuals know each other personally and in many different social roles. Social interaction involves depth and is on many levels.	The individual has many fleeting, superficial interactions. People relate to each other in an impersonal way, often on a professional or business level. People deal with each other in specific roles and for practical purposes.
Place of the individual	The individual is locked into a web of family and friendships.	The individual is largely isolated from others.
Example	The village Postmistress or -master is likely to know many customers by name, occupation and interests. They may meet each other in the local pub and at other social events. A visit to the village Post Office is likely to involve a chat about themselves and other mutual acquaintances.	The atmosphere in a large city Post Office is one of bureaucracy. The customer is dealt with formally. People queue with other strangers and have little inclination to speak to them. The purpose of the visit is purely to complete a transaction, and customers and server wish to get it over with as quickly as possible.

Continued on next page

Table 9.2 *continued*

	Rural life	*Urban life*
Forms of social control	*Informal:* gossip, ridicule, peer and family pressures.	*Formal:* public legislation, public opinion.
Status	*Ascribed:* status is determined by birth. If you're born a peasant, you'll stay a peasant in the eyes of others!	*Achieved:* status is determined by hard work and individual talents. You are judged by 'what you are', not your family background.
Overall view of relationships	Complete, full – 'holistic'.	Partial and segmented.

Source: Tonnies (1957)

❖ Activity 5 ❖

1 Read the information about Georg Simmel and the Urban Personality (see *In Focus* below). Then complete the right-hand column of Table 9.3, summarizing Simmel's views of the impact of urban life on an individual's personality.

2 In what ways do you think the city can be 'potentially liberating'?

3 Then read through the information about Wirth (see *In Focus* on p. 360). In your own words, what does Wirth mean by his definition of the city as a 'relatively large dense and permanent settlement of sociologically heterogeneous individuals'?

4 As a short essay and incorporating precise information from the sources, identify the differences between urban and rural life.

In Focus

◆

Georg Simmel and the Urban Personality

Simmel applied Tonnies' ideas specifically to the urban environment and argued in his most famous essay ('The metropolis and mental life', Simmel 1950) that city life creates a unique type of personality, a particular sort of mentality geared to the rush, complexity and calculation of urban life. In the market economy of the city, money, self-interest and rational calculation form the basis of relationships. There is no time for sentiment, the pace of life is too fast for habits to form and so to cope the individual becomes blasé – reserved and withdrawn. He treats other people as objects rather than individuals – as a means to an end. In this 'urban jungle', some thrive (the urban 'cowboy', the city 'slicker'), while some drop out or even die (the tramp, the homeless, the suicide). However, Simmel also saw the urban environment as potentially liberating, allowing individuals to escape traditional controls and the pettiness of small town life and to express their own individuality and creativity. He also recognized its dangers – of the individual feeling lost and being merely a cog in an enormous organization of things with no one to turn to.

Source: Slattery (1990), p. 241

Table 9.3 A summary of Simmel's view of rural and urban living

Rural	*Urban*
People do things because it's traditional – it's always been done that way.	
Interaction involves deep involvement and warmth.	
People are bound to many others. They respect each other and 'know their place'.	
Pace of life is slow and stable.	
The individual is subordinate to the community.	

Wirth proposed a minimum sociological definition of the City as a 'relatively large, dense and permanent settlement of sociologically heterogeneous individuals'. It was these characteristics that distinguished city life from life in the country. The very size, density and heterogeneity of the city create social segregation, impersonality and both social and geographical mobility. The individual no longer has a set place; relationships (at work, in shops, on the street) are highly rational, superficial and transitory. Amid the city crowds it is easy to feel lost. In the urban 'Rat Race' only the fittest thrive. Amid the multitude of such daily physical encounters, there is little social meaning. City dwellers tend to be nervous, irritable, even a little schizoid, and can all too easily feel lost, alienated and powerless. To find some sort of security, some sense of belonging, city dwellers join a wide variety of associations or move into areas of like-minded people. But Wirth was not totally pessimistic. He saw the possibility of cities settling down and establishing some sense of permanence and character. Moreover, he regarded urbanism not only as the way of life of the city but of modern society.

Source: Slattery (1990), p. 244

Many sociologists have accepted that different ways of life can be found in rural and urban areas. The culture of the city is referred to as 'urbanism'. Often the world of the 'city slicker' is contrasted unfavourably with that of the 'country bumpkin'. Life in cities may be seen as isolated and lonely, whilst that of rural areas as being blessed by a sense of belonging and integration. In other words, urbanism is seen as having less community in the social relationship and identity sense.

The move to urban living

The process whereby an increasing proportion of a country's population live in built-up areas is termed 'urbanization'. It is a global phenomenon, although its timing, pace and causes vary from country to country. The urbanization of economically developing countries is discussed more thoroughly in Chapter 8, *World sociology*. Here, the aim is to examine the urbanization of the economically developed world, which is strongly associated with the rise of industrial capitalism during the nineteenth century. The migration from the countryside into towns can be explained in terms of 'Push' and 'Pull' factors. 'Push' factors are those which force people to leave a place, whilst 'Pull' factors are a destination's perceived attractions. Urbanization in nineteenth-century Britain was a combination of these.

Push factors: the Agricultural Revolution

❖ The mechanization and modernization of farming, particularly during the eighteenth and nineteenth centuries, reduced the demand for labour and forced people to leave the land.

❖ During this time 'enclosure' led to rights to land being taken away from the peasantry, again forcing people to leave. One of the most extreme examples is the clearance of the crofters from the Highlands of Scotland.

❖ Rural poverty and squalor were exacerbated by weakening feudal bonds. The Agricultural Revolution reduced the need for the aristocracy to seek the cooperation of the peasantry by providing them with support, as they had previously done.

Pull factors: the Industrial Revolution

❖ The growth of industrial capitalism involved mass production in factories located in specifically advantaged places such as the coal fields. These provided the energy source for the 'new' steam technology. Factory production required concentrated labour and the displaced rural workers readily moved to find work. Once established, a spiral of growth was set in motion. The supply of labour and the establishment of communications and support industries attracted even more factories and even more hopeful migrants.

❖ The expanding towns also promised a more modern lifestyle, free from the restrictions of feudalism. Unfortunately, as we shall see, the developing capitalist cities held their own problems for the emerging urban working class.

Cities like Manchester and Birmingham grew as a result of enormous economic changes which radically reshaped the social system. We can only imagine what it was like to live through an age when society transformed in a lifetime from rural agricultural to industrial urban. It is perhaps not surprising that at that time great thinkers like Marx and Durkheim were so concerned with such issues as the process of social change and the establishment of social order.

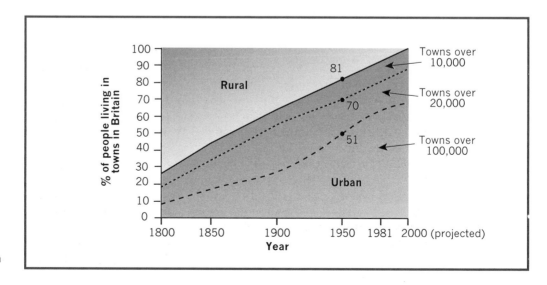

Figure 9.1
The growth of urban population

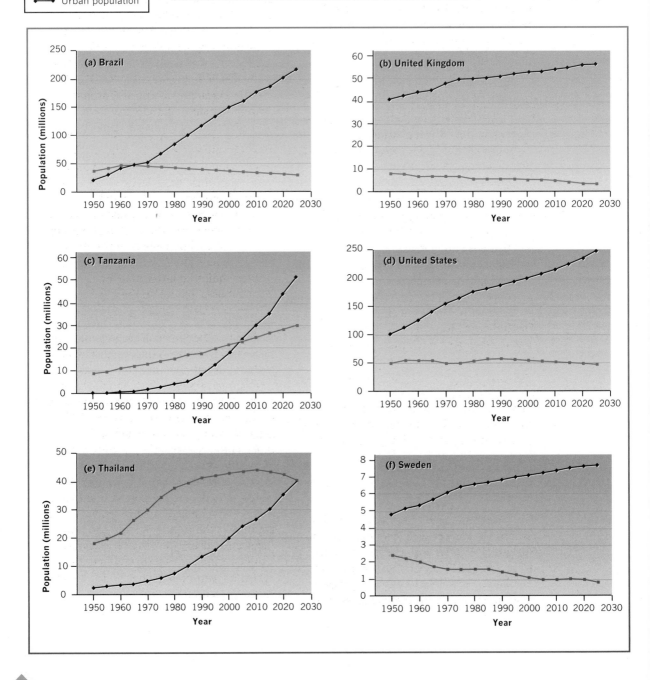

❖ Activity 6 ❖

1 (a) Accurately describe the trends shown in the graph in Fig. 9.1.

(b) What do you consider to be the main causes of the trends shown by the graph?

2 (a) Describe the main differences between the urbanization patterns and predictions for selected economically developed and less developed countries shown in graphs in Fig. 9.2.

(b) Suggest reasons for these differences.

Figure 9.2
Urbanization patterns for six different countries

Rural population
Urban population

(a) Brazil

(b) United Kingdom

(c) Tanzania

(d) United States

(e) Thailand

(f) Sweden

Consequences of urbanization

Increases in size

By the end of the eighteenth century, there were few large cities in Britain. London, with a population in 1811 of 800,000, was by far the biggest, while the majority of the others were relatively small market and administrative centres in a rural economy. The rapid urbanization of the following century was a product of the Industrial Revolution. By 1901, only 10 per cent of the British population were employed in agriculture and the population of London had reached four million. New industrial centres like Manchester merged into the surrounding expanding towns to form giant conurbations. In the twentieth century, these conurbations joined together to form vast 'super cities', given the name 'megalopolis' (Gottman 1961). For example, along the Eastern seaboard of the USA, 'Bosnywash' (Boston, New York, Washington, etc.) stretches over 450 square miles and has a population of forty million. It is not surprising that Wirth and others saw this growing vastness as having consequences for ways of living.

Changes in function

The Industrial Revolution brought about a new technological base and a new class structure. Power was wrested from the rural aristocracy and became housed in the central areas of cities, in what is now known as the central business district (CBD). Cities and towns became increasingly manufacturing and trading centres serving the needs of capitalism.

Residential segregation

The cities came to house the new classes required by the changed economic system. This involved a rearrangement of the use of urban space. The rapidly growing urban population became sorted into segregated areas according to their social class. The working class collected around their workplaces whereas previously they had been dispersed. Distinctive immigrant neighbourhoods emerged. The larger British cities each had their 'little Ireland' and their American counterparts had their own 'little Sicily', 'little Chinatown' and so on. The higher social classes took advantage of improved transportation and their ability to buy property in more favourable areas to ensure their own exclusion. They could afford to isolate themselves from the deprivations of the hastily-thrown-up working-class slums. Probably the best known description of early spatial segregation was written in the early 1840s by Engels in *The Condition of the Working Class in England*. The central business district was surrounded by:

> '... unmixed working people's quarters stretching like a girdle averaging a mile and a half in breadth ... outside, beyond, this girdle, lives the upper and middle bourgeoisie, the middle bourgeoisie in regularly laid out streets in the vicinity of the working quarters ... in free, wholesome country air, in fine comfortable homes, passed once every half or quarter hour by omnibuses going into the city.'
> (Engels 1844, p. 8c)

Engels' observations of segregation were supported by his contemporary, Faucher, and both are represented in Fig. 9.3.

However, there is considerable debate as to the degree of segregation actually present in the Victorian city. David Ward (1980) suggests that prior to the end of the nineteenth century only the polar extremes of society were living in completely separated areas. The rest of the city was characterized by social mixing and frequent residential mobility. In Leeds only 13 to 20 per cent of the population were recorded at the same address after ten years. Thus, although some spatial segregation was evident, it was perhaps not to the extent found in modern cities.

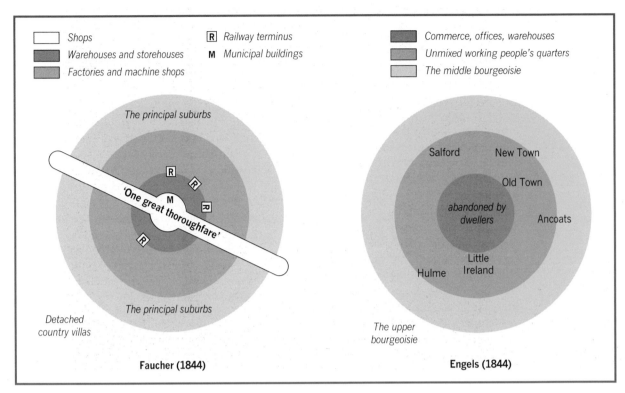

Figure 9.3
Models of
Manchester
Source:
Knox (1992)

Urban working class deprivation

Whatever the case regarding the impact of rapid industrialization and urbanization on residential areas, most accept that one consequence was the deplorable conditions in which the new working class were forced to live. Dillon's survey of 222 lodging-houses in the Irish quarters of Leeds in 1851 showed that 536 rooms were occupied by 2429 people, almost five to a room. As a result of poor sanitation and water supply, infectious diseases like cholera were common. It is argued that the hardships and prospects, illustrated by Table 9.4 below and the picture on p. 365, made the slums of the new industrial cities havens of crime, vice and social unrest.

Table 9.4 Mortality in the Victorian city

Class	Average age at death	
	Manchester	*Rural England*
Professional persons and gentry; and their families	38	52
Tradesmen and their families	20	41*
Mechanics and labourers and their families	17	38

*including farmers and graziers

Source: Report on the Sanitary Conditions of the Labouring Population of Great Britain (1842)

The rear of terraced houses in London, engraving by Gustave Doré 1872

 ## The loss of community?

The 'destruction' of community is the consequence of urbanization with which sociologists have been most concerned. The classical theorists tended to view the processes of industrialization and urbanization through which they were living with some trepidation. They too distinguished between rural and urban ways of living. They generally agreed that the move to the cities severely disrupted the community basis of rural existence. In their work you can identify a rather romantic notion of community.

The consensus view: functionalism

Functionalism regards society as being like a biological organism. It is a system of inter-related parts bound together by core values which everyone shares. Society is characterized by cooperation, balance and harmony. Functionalists regard social stability as normal and therefore have difficulty in adequately explaining the complexities of social change. Generally, societies are regarded as 'evolving' from simple to more complex forms.

Durkheim (1893/1947) sees pre-industrial societies being held together by 'mechanical solidarity'. This form of society is typified by many of the attributes associated with rural living. Value consensus, i.e. agreement on what is worthwhile and important in social life, is strong. Everyone knows each other. They do a similar limited range of things, have common interests and outlooks. Relationships are close, face to face, personal and clearly demarcated by tradition. Industrialization and urbanization threw up a different social system. A central feature of modern industrial society is its extensive division of labour. Each individual is reliant on numerous other unseen individuals for their daily needs. Durkheim argued that this inter-dependence would eventually provide 'organic solidarity', a new basis for social order. In such a system, relationships would be more rational, impersonal and individualized. However, Durkheim did foresee a number of teething problems before the adjustment from 'mechanical solidarity' was achieved. Initially he feared that the pace of social and economic change in the nineteenth century would break down traditional social controls. The new urban dweller would be isolated beyond control, in a state of 'anomie' (normlessness). Thus, Durkheim's argument regards the impact of modernization both negatively and positively. He welcomes the potential of economic advance and the establishment of organic solidarity. However, he mourns the passing of traditional community life which he sees as being destroyed by urbanization.

The work of Ferdinand Tonnies and George Simmel, examined previously, is also in the functionalist tradition (see Table 9.2 and *In Focus* on p.359). The ideal types of *'Gemeinschaft'* and *'Gesellschaft'* forms of society are in many ways parallel terms to Durkheim's mechanical and organic solidarity. Both Tonnies and Simmel tend to emphasize the destructive consequences of urbanization on individuals and community life.

Although functionalism has been heavily criticized (see below), it did stimulate considerable theoretical debate about, and empirical research into, the consequences of urbanization, not least the influential Chicago School.

The conflict view

Karl Marx and Friedrich Engels

The Marxist view of the impact of the development of industrial capitalism on urban and community life operates within a very different theoretical framework. The notion of a harmonious social system is replaced with an emphasis on class conflict, exploitation and oppression. Nevertheless,

like Durkheim, Marx and Engels held ambiguous opinions about the emergence of the industrial city. On the one hand, it represented a step closer in historical development to the ultimate socialist society. The new working class were massed together in the workers' districts of large cities. They shared common experiences of exploitation and therefore the seeds of class consciousness and revolution were more likely to flourish. On the other hand, the squalor in parts of the Victorian city were appalling and led to Engels arguing in a similar vein to Durkheim:

'The very turmoil of the streets has something repulsive, something against which human nature rebels ... The brutal indifference, the unfeeling isolation of each in his private interest becomes the more repellent and offensive, the more these individuals are crowded together within a limited space.' (Engels 1844, pp. 57–8)

Although Marxists regard the true basis of 'community' as being social class rather than place, this quote does suggest Engels believed that rapid urban growth did destroy social relationships.

In truth, Marx and Engels said relatively little about the city as such. It has been more modern writers who have drawn upon Marxist concepts to discuss the vital issues of power and conflict within the city and to place community life within the wider working of the capitalist economic system.

Max Weber

Although Weber wrote specifically about the medieval city, he made some mention of modern industrial ones. However, whereas he regarded the former as the 'cradle of modern society', his remarks concerning the Victorian city were as negative as those of the theorists above. Like Engels, he deplored the horrendous conditions of the working class. Weber argued that the independent medieval cities had fostered rationality, administrative systems, democracy and a merchant class which encouraged progress.

Rapid industrialization and urbanization destroyed this innovation and cities became mere reflections of capitalism itself. Again, it is more contemporary neo-Weberians who have had a greater impact on urban sociology than Weber himself. Like Marxists they emphasize that society is based on conflict but suggest that this conflict is broader than social class.

To summarize, the classical theorists of the nineteenth century saw industrialization and urbanization as destroying communities. However, empirical research during the twentieth century has shown that:

❖ people have the capacity to rebuild communities

❖ rural life, past and present, does not match the romanticism connected with it.

Evidence for and against the 'loss of community' thesis

Community in the city: the discovery of urban villages

Detailed studies of urban areas have revealed the capacity of human beings to create communities even in the most difficult of environments. Gans (1962)

Urban living in the 1990s

Crispin Hughes/Photofusion

found in his study of the inner parts of Boston and New York that people were far from socially isolated and could rely on informal groups of friends and family to provide support. Suburban life is thought to be particularly privatized, yet Gans revealed a considerable degree of cohesion and neighbourliness even if this was not comparable to the Italian quarter of his inner area research.

The best known discovery of urban working-class communities in Britain was in Bethnal Green in the East End of London in the 1950s. Young and Willmott's classic study *Family and Kinship in East London* (1957) describes an integrated web of relationships focused on the bond between mother and daughter. Life was seen as open and social with children playing in the streets, back doors ajar, gossip on the doorstep, men in the pubs and women at the launderette, corner shop or bingo. Thus, the studies showed that territorially based communities existed in urban areas in reality, just as they do in the soap worlds of *Coronation Street*, *Brookside* and *EastEnders*.

A number of factors were identified as encouraging urban community formation:

❖ a stable, long-established population

❖ shared experience arising from a narrow occupational structure (the docks, the mine or textile factory, etc.)

❖ mutual need in times of adversity.

However, we must be wary of replacing the rural idealism of Durkheim, Tonnies and Wirth with an exaggerated view of the virtues of urban villages. Living on top of each other, people prying into your personal affairs and worries over money are just as likely to cause friction as harmony. Thus Knox points out:

> 'The mutuality of the urban village is underlain by stresses and tensions which follow from social intimacy and economic insecurity, and several studies of working class neighbourhoods have described as much conflict and disorder as cohesion and community.' (Knox 1992)

Urban communities: an update

The studies described above were part of the community tradition of the 1950s and are now outdated. The conditions which established traditional working-class communities have long been undermined. Inner-city populations are now transient, moving either by choice or because of redevelopment. Furthermore, inner-city industries have collapsed, destroying the old occupational identity. Young and Willmott (1986) found in a later study of Greenleigh, an outer-city estate to which many East Enders had moved, less community with families being more home-centred and isolated. Holme (1985) found similar trends in Bethnal Green itself. Goldthorpe, Lockwood and colleagues (1968, 1969) in their study of Luton discovered a more privatized life style than was associated with the old working-class community.

It would seem that urban communities had been found and lost. However, these findings have in turn been reassessed. Returning to Greenleigh, Young and Willmott (1986) suggest that the social networks established were extensive and did provide support. Although Devine's (1992) study of Luton is based on a small sample of 62 interviewees, she claims that the privatized worker is somewhat of a myth. Many of the relatives and friends of the people who migrated to take up jobs in Luton's car industries followed them. This meant that the old sociability persisted and people maintained a web of contacts outside the home. The *In Focus* below describes an update of Willmott's (1963) study of Barking and Dagenham using a survey of 600 young people, the 1991 census and qualitative interviews.

It seems that the destruction of traditional working-class communities has not been as radical as was first believed. However, inner cities remain associated with community breakdown. High crime rates, illegitimacy and riots are all cited as evidence of disorder. The issues of the inner city will be discussed more fully below, but the idea that their problems are a result of lack of community is contested. Just as drug-taking, prostitution and violence may be seen as indices of breakdown, so the self-help schemes initiated to tackle them may be viewed as signs of community vitality. One example of this community activity is

In Focus

◆

Updating Willmott's study

The updated study and Census data show that kin contact and association do not appear to have changed significantly since Willmott's study of the borough in the 1950s: 72 per cent of the households had a relative visit their home within the last week; about half the sample had kin living nearby with 20 per cent of these having a local kin network of over 10 relatives; and 51 per cent had daily or weekly contact with their maternal grandmother. In some ways the community has stayed static through the period. However, the types of families and households created by Barking and Dagenham inhabitants is changing. There is a clear pluralization of life styles – for instance more dual-earner households and one-parent households than the 1950s.

Number of kin in neighbourhood (%)

1–4 relatives	63
5–9 relatives	21
10–19 relatives	11
20–29 relatives	4
30+ relatives	5

(N = 276, excluding those with no kin in neighbourhood (n = 271) and missing values cases)

Barking and Dagenham have witnessed an increase in marital breakdown, but the pace of change appears slower than in other inner East London boroughs.

Source: adapted from O'Brien and Jones (1996)

KWAD (Knowle West Against Drugs) set up by local mothers to fight against this Bristol's estate's serious hard-drug problem.

In short, the discovery of urban communities suggests that the proponents of the 'loss of community' theses were wrong to see urbanization as automatically destructive. Second, the fact that the characteristics of community associated with rural areas could also be found in cities undermined the notion of two completely opposed life styles. Above all, the notion that where you lived determined how you lived was refuted.

Conflict in the old village

Those supporting the loss of community thesis have a highly romantic view of village life in the past. However, far from being harmonious and cohesive, radical theorists have highlighted that pre-industrial villages were riven with the divides of any class-based social system. Raymond Williams in *The Country and the City* (1973) revealed the true nature of 'Merrie England'. Life for the peasantry was one of oppression, poverty, squalor and control by the landed ruling class. They were tied to the land by an ideology of tradition. Fear was also a means of control, with rights to land and home being governed by their submission to labouring for the land owners. Williams believes that the apparent order of village life was imposed, a 'mutuality of the oppressed'. They were bound together by need rather than underlying consensus. The fragility of such 'communities' is reflected in the rioting that took place throughout the eighteenth century. Newby (1980b) also sees *Gemeinschaft* as a mythical concept. The fact that villagers shared a common occupational experience and knew each other as workers, neighbours, friends and relatives, inevitably produced a strong sense of identity. Nevertheless, he concludes:

'... that the distance in wealth, income lifestyle and, most importantly, authority decisively marked off the occupational community of the agricultural workers from the more geographically widespread network of local farmers and landowners, creating the kind of "oppositional" subculture and social imagery characteristic of similar urban working class communities, with a nascent class conflict never far from the surface of day-to-day relationships.' (Newby 1980b, pp. 57–8)

Village society had a recognised social order. The squire, his family and the vicar were the most important people locally. Farm labourers and others were expected to show respect for their social 'superiors', who were usually also their masters.

❖ Activity 7 ❖

Look at the picture on the left and read through the description of village life (see *In Focus*, p. 370)

1 In what ways are these views of pre-industrial rural communities similar to those of Durkheim and Tonnies?

2 Explain why such positive views of traditional rural life must be treated with caution.

3 Why do sociologists have to be careful when relying on historical sources?

In Focus
◆
Village life

England had been a land of villages where people lived their whole lives, for few travelled more than a few miles. The local squire was normally a humane father figure to whom all turned for advice – after all, his family had occupied the manor for generations and he had the habit of forgetting that his tenants owed him rent if the harvest was bad. His wife and daughter would lead the social life of the area and visit the sick, perhaps teach in the Sunday School.

There was a clear social division between the few wealthy families and the poor, but they all lived close to each other; rarely would one find a village where the poor all lived in one part. The village was a community in a very real sense, and its very smallness gave it its special character – a character that remained throughout Victorian England, despite the Great Changes (i.e. industrialization and urbanization).

Source: Jones (1971)

The move to the country

Whereas nineteenth-century Britain was characterized by urbanization, so the later part of the twentieth is associated with a relative increase in the proportion of people living in the countryside. This process is variously termed 'counter-urbanization', 'de-urbanization', 'urban dispersal' and 'urban–rural shift'. It is a feature of all western industrial societies. Just as early industrialization involved the growth of major conurbations, so its later development has seen their population decline. Figure 9.4 on p. 371 summarizes the causes of counter-urbanization.

Now do Activity 8 which asks you to analyse the information in Table 9.5.

Note: The rates in Table 9.5 are calculated from official mid-year estimates (provisional estimates for 1991), adjusted for boundary changes. Shift refers to the difference in growth rate between 1971–81 and 1981–91. The district classification is a modified version of the OPCS district typology: 'metropolitan' includes the central Clydeside conurbation area.

Source: Champion (1993)

Table 9.5 Population in Great Britain, by type of district (Champion 1993)

Type of district	1981 (thousands)	Change 1981–91 (thousands)	Shift (%)	1971–81 (%)	Shift (% point)
Great Britain	54,814.5	1,240.3	2.3	0.8	+1.5
All metropolitan Britain	19,831.6	−359.7	−1.8	−6.7	+4.9
London	6,805.6	−2.5	0.0	−9.6	+9.6
Inner	2,550.1	16.2	0.6	−16.7	+17.3
Outer	4,255.4	−18.7	−0.4	−4.8	+4.4
Metropolitan districts	13,026.0	−357.2	−2.7	−5.1	+2.4
Principal cities	4,324.3	−235.1	−5.4	−11.6	+6.2
Other districts	8,701.7	−122.1	−1.4	−5.8	+4.4
Non–metropolitan Britain	34,982.9	1,600.0	4.6	5.6	−1.0
Large cities	3,674.7	−44.0	−1.2	−4.2	+3.0
Small cities	1,922.9	35.3	1.8	−0.6	+2.4
Industrial areas	7,440.3	124.6	1.7	3.2	−1.5
New towns	2,548.9	188.3	7.4	15.1	−7.7
Resort, port and retirement	3,367.9	266.0	7.9	5.8	+2.1
Urban and mixed urban/rural	9,840.3	560.5	5.7	7.5	−1.8
Remoter, mainly rural	6,188.0	469.2	7.6	10.2	−2.6

The ECONOMIC factor

Modern industry is largely 'footloose' – it is free from traditional locational constraints. New high tech and tertiary industries seek greenfield sites with good motorway access, away from the high rents, congestion and other central city problems. For example, one of the few areas to show 'real' economic growth in Britain is along the M4 corridor. As employment decentralizes, so does the workforce. Today, we can shop in a hypermarket, work on an industrial estate and spend our leisure in multiplex cinemas and drive-in fast-food outlets, all in out-of-town locations.

The CULTURAL factor

Post-war relative affluence has allowed many people to make their dreams of a 'country cottage with roses around the door' come true. On the other hand, the negative image of the city, compounded by fears of rising crime and rising house prices, have served as an additional 'push'. Many people have moved to villages within commuting distance of urban areas, whilst others have retired or bought second homes in more remote areas, like the South West of England.

THE CAUSES OF COUNTER-URBANIZATION

The TRANSPORT factor

Developments in transport technology have effectively made geographical space shrink. Rail and the private car have allowed widespread commuting. For example, rail electrification in the Eastern counties has drawn them into London's commuter belt.

The GOVERNMENT factor

Post-war government policy regarding cities served to encourage decentralization:

1 large council estates developed on the edges of cities to house the overspill population from inner-city redevelopment
2 the development of New Towns, such as Stevenage, Milton Keynes and Skelmersdale
3 strict controls on urban development.

Fig. 9.4
The causes of counter-urbanization

❖ Activity 8 ❖

1 Using the information in Table 9.5, draw a graph to represent percentage population change for 1981–91 using the same scale as the graph in Fig. 9.5 on p. 372.

2 Give reasons for the patterns shown in the graph.

3 Identify the trends between 1971 and 1991 by comparing the graph in Fig. 9.5 with the graph drawn in question 1.

4 Suggest reasons for any changes in the patterns of change.

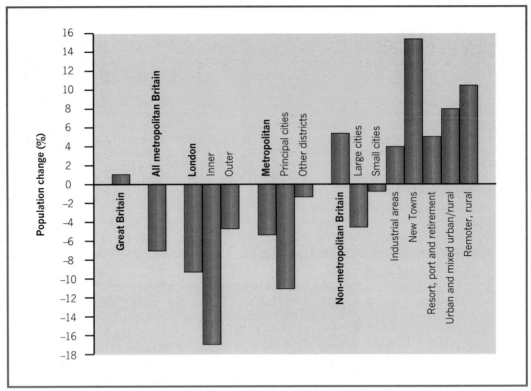

Fig. 9.5
Population change in Great Britain between 1971 and 1981

We have already seen that the romanticized view of village life in the past held by the nineteenth-century theorists could not stand up to closer examination. Likewise, the movement of urban dwellers into the countryside during the 1960s and 1970s represented a further challenge to two key assumptions made in the loss of community thesis. These assumptions are:

1 that rural life is characterized by consensus, cohesion and stability – in other words it more closely fits our notion of 'community'

2 that there is a clear difference between urban and rural life styles.

The village: a place of conflict and change

One of the consequences of relatively affluent, middle-class people moving into a village is the disruption of the traditional rural class system. Whereas, the rural working class, farmers and landowners can

be distinguished by their economic ties to the land, the newcomers are divorced from this relationship. They add a new dimension to the social mix of the village, providing new opportunities for social conflict and cleavage. Thus, D. Thomas, in a study of eleven villages within the commuter belt of Nottingham, concluded that for those who worked on the farm:

'The village is the centre of their lives. They are often born within a few miles of where they now live. They are restricted in outlook and their involvement outside the village area. But for the middle classes, their sphere of association and contacts is wider than the village community which is seen largely as a dormitory and a place to spend the weekends.' (Thomas, quoted in Knox 1992)

Newby's studies of East Anglia also revealed a polarization of villages into 'them and us' on the basis of insider/outsider rather than social class. He argues that this can only be fully understood by seeing

Weekenders!
© Posy Simmons

counter-urbanization as one of a web of changes in rural life. These changes include:

❖ The mechanization of agriculture – This reduced the demand for labour enormously so that a worker has to be a 'jack of all trades' rather than a skilled specialist.

❖ Changes in land organization – Tenancies have declined and land ownership by independent farmers and major institutions has increased.

❖ 'Agri-business' – Agriculture increasingly works fully to the principles of the market with its economies of scale and factory farms.

According to Newby (1980b), these changes have had a profound effect on traditional class relationships. He believes that the old oppositional, rural, working-class subculture is in retreat and, although a differential relationship between farm workers and employers remains, the gap in identity between them has lessened. He argues that the bond between farm workers and land owners can be strengthened in the face of an 'invasion' of people with the wealth and power to challenge traditional interests and authority structures:

'The former occupational community then tends to retreat in upon itself and become what might be called as "encapsulated community", since the locals now form a community within a community – a separate and dense network encapsulated within a total social system.' (Newby 1980b

The East Anglia studies and others have shown that contemporary rural life is far from unchanging and cohesive. Moreover, the close proximity of groups with widely differing economic and social interests brings inevitable conflicts. Housing is one issue which can be a source of bitter contention. The demand for rural properties 'with character' can serve to force prices beyond the reach of low-paid rural workers. At the same time, it is in the newcomers' interests to preserve the rural charm for which they have paid so dearly by resisting any developments of cheap housing or industry. Such actions fuel resentment, particularly since they exacerbate depopulation by the young. In Wales, the 'take-over' of houses by outsiders is a major force behind nationalist fervour to the extent that there have been incidents of properties owned by English people being fire-bombed. Furthermore, the change in the social characteristics of the villagers also leads to a change in the kinds of services required. The more mobile newcomers can make use of the shopping facilities of the city. Village shops close or convert into delicatessens, the local pub becomes a glorified restaurant, and local people's needs and old centres of community life are undermined. The Fearnbeg study (see *In Focus* on p. 374) indicates that rural conflicts can be more than just about resources.

Conflicts of interests are also likely to arise between the urban 'refugees' and landowners. To maximize profits, modern farming often requires changes in the environment such as the removal of hedgerows and the drainage of land.

In Focus

◆

The Fearnbeg study

The following quotes were taken from [one] week's fieldnotes:

'I am a local because I've lived here all my life.'

'If you live and work in [Fearnbeg], even if you are an incomer, and if you have a family here, then surely you are a local.'

'I wouldn't think of them as real locals though. Maybe they are, but I don't think of them as locals.'

'The only people who can call themselves local are the ones who were born here and brought up here.'

(Payne 1994)

However, the conflict has deeper roots than this. In a recent study of the Scottish village of Fearnbeg, we found this same concern about incomers and locals. Yet there was enough housing to go round, there were no commuters, unemployment was virtually nil, the school was expanding and there was a general sense of optimism. Most incomers were Scottish with rural backgrounds and the same age and social class as many locals. So why did the local/incomer distinction loom so large?

The point is not that locals are literally born and bred in Fearnbeg, because relatively few actually were. Rather, the somewhat flexible 'rules' can be adapted to exclude those whom locals wish to define as outsiders. 'Born and bred' is a symbolic way of marking a boundary between those with whom locals feel they belong and others. To be 'on the inside' is to gain a sense of identity and solidarity.

Part of that identity comes from being able to attach oneself to other traditional values. The local can be a Scot rather than British, a Celt or Highlander rather than a Scot, a Fearnbegger rather than a 'down country' person. Each identity has its own sets of symbols and meanings. Crucially, it is when one culture contacts another, as when Fearnbeg meets the wider society or it representatives ('incomers', or 'bonglies' – i.e. tourists), that self-awareness arises, and boundaries become marked in this symbolic way. Being 'local' is something that makes one feel superior; membership of this 'exclusive club' is something special to hold on to.

Source: adapted from Payne (1994)

❖ Activity 9 ❖

1 What is regarded as the source of conflict in Fearnbeg?

2 Suggest how 'locals' may separate themselves from 'incomers' in a symbolic way.

3 How are the researchers defining community in this extract?

Farmers may wish to diversify by establishing tourist facilities, golf courses or even sell land for development. Again, the newcomers, allied with wider conservation interests, are likely to fight to ensure that such changes do not take place. Local people may accuse outsiders with 'their city ideas' of interfering in the affairs of country folk which they do not truly understand.

Hunting epitomizes the old rural class system. The controversy surrounding it can partly be understood in rural–urban terms. Whereas urbanites may see it as barbaric, for locals it may be seen as part of a traditional way of life, a necessity and much-needed employer.

It could be argued then that counter-urbanization has helped to destroy the integrated community which was one of the original appeals of country living. However, although harkening back to the 'good old days' is common amongst locals, we have to be wary of accepting this subjective perception of community decline at face value. Certainly Newby (1980a) believes

class system may have changed but it is certainly not dead and remains an important source of oppression and conflict. The 'Diary of a rural worker' (see *In Focus* below) indicates that rural poverty is as much a feature of rural areas as it is inner urban ones. Thus, the value of Newby's study is that he recognized that just as issues of power and conflict illuminate city processes (see p. 394) so they could give insight into rural ones.

A further breakdown of the rural–urban divide?

According to Carter (1990) the effects of counter-urbanization mean we have to ask:

'Is it possible or meaningful to make any distinction between what is urban and what is rural. It would seem that the two are so intertwined in the composite regional system that separation ... makes little sense.'

Pahl's (1968) study of commuter settlements within a fifty-mile radius of London reached a similar conclusion. The villages are merely extensions of suburbia and can best be described as a 'dispersed city'. In an earlier work, *Urbs in Rure* (1965), Pahl substantiates Newby's insider/outsider divide. He suggests that a village may have a variety of contrasting

that social ties were more likely to be closely intertwined when everyone worked on the land, but at the same time the gross inequalities and poverty of traditional rural life should not be ignored. Even if greater unity did exist in the past, this may have been a product of mutual need rather than genuine harmony. Further, the old rural

---

In Focus

◆

Diary of a rural worker

Green and peasant land

John Abbot is given a Third World shock when he opens his pay packet.

'North Shropshire is undoubtedly a beautiful part of the English countryside, with numerous quaint farmhouses and patches of ancient woodland dotted about among green rolling hills. Yet for the jobless and impoverished, this rural idyll offers little by way of employment opportunities, since just about the only local industries still in existence are those directly connected with agriculture. As a result, the area is characterized by a low-wage economy, with an annual earned income of £4,500 regarded by many employers as excellent pay and often advertized as such in local newspapers.'

Source: The Guardian,
15 May 1996

communities with little in common and which rarely mix and so are in this way similar to urban areas. Given the speed of development since electronic communications, it is not difficult to envisage the age of the 'fax cottage'. It is already possible to be functionally part of the city but physically separate. Community can exist on a global scale. Figure 9.6 opposite illustrates Jewson's vision of the future city in which rural settlements are absorbed. He describes this Megalopolis as:

'an open, polycentric lattice-work of small- to medium-sized settlements, linked together by fast roads and high-tech electronic communication systems. There are green wedges in the spaces between built-up areas, but in a vast carpet of linked neighbour-hoods, the distinctive boundaries of town and country disappear.'

Thus although the nature of a locality, be it village or city, may to some extent influence life styles and relationships, this is minor when compared to wider social processes (see Fig. 9.6).

In Focus

◆

A rural–urban continuum

ost rural geographers and sociologists agree that it is more realistic to think not of sharp contrasts between rural and urban areas, but of a whole range from strongly urban to strongly rural. This rural-urban continuum model is supported by research by Frankenberg and Pahl, although Pahl has suggested that it is not just separate settlements which fit along this continuum but that a single 'village' or rural area may have a variety of contrasting communities within it. The rural village that has an executive housing estate built at its edge (e.g. Hilderstone in Staffordshire) may exemplify this. The contrasting communities may have little in common and mix rarely, and there may even be animosity between them.

A final approach to understanding 'rural' and 'urban' extends from this model, and tries to quantify it to help clarify ideas. This involves working out an Index of Rurality from social and economic statistics for each area. One such calculation was undertaken by Paul Cloke, and calculated an index based on:

1 number of females aged 15–45
2 proportion of population working in primary, secondary and service sectors
3 population change in the last 10 year census period
4 commuting-out pattern
5 distance from a town of 50,000 population
6 proportion of the population aged over 65
7 household amenities, e.g. the proportion of the population with an 'inside wc'
8 population density
9 in-migration over the last 5 years.

The score for each area was calculated, and four categories were then identified: extreme rural areas, intermediate rural areas, intermediate non-rural areas, and extreme non-rural areas. Extreme rural areas tended to be found in the remoter parts of England and Wales, with Newcastle Emlyn in west Wales being the most extreme rural area. The extreme non-rural areas tended to be closer to the large cities, with many of the 'villages' of Surrey, Hertfordshire and Essex falling into this group.

Adapted from Foskett and Foskett (1992)

Figure 9.6
The development
of cities
*Source: adapted
from* Jewson
(1991)

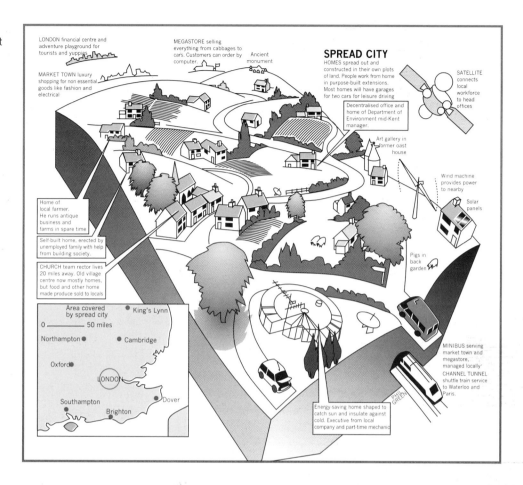

Community in modern society

Communitarianism

Evidence suggests that the state of community in modern society is debatable both in rural and urban areas. Whatever the reality, people do seem to believe that community has declined and that something valuable has been lost. In the USA this has led to the development of a powerful movement called 'communitarianism', the significance of which can partly be seen in the rise of alternative communities generally associated with right-wing Christian fundamentalist organizations.

Communitarians believe that the loss of community has produced a decline in moral standards and greater social instability. Like functionalists, they are concerned with consensus and conformity. Communitarians

see themselves as resisting dangerous liberal tendencies and excessive individuality. Etzioni suggests that the rebuilding of communities could be encouraged in several ways:

❖ Locally based institutions, such as schools, neighbourhood and voluntary groups, should be strengthened: 'Communities congeal around local institutions' (Etzioni 1995). Examples of such organizations would be neighbourhood watch schemes.

❖ The use of space needs to be planned to allow people to look out for each other. People should be able to watch over each other's children and property. They should be able to monitor and exert pressure on those who are failing to conform to the community's standards. Thus, some of the lack of community on

1960s high-rise estates can be blamed on architects and planners.

❖ Communitarians tend to associate the breakdown of community with the breakdown of the traditional nuclear family. They advocate a return to marriage and traditional gender roles. This will ensure good parenting and the effective socialization of the young.

An evaluation of communitarianism

Day (1995) gives a number of problems with communitarianism:

❖ 'The content of his [Etzioni's] discussion is very weak. A mixture of simple anecdotes and recommendations which are so general and bland as to be hard to criticize.'

❖ It is a very conservative and reactionary view. It assumes that 'normal' communities and families were those of the past. Even if these existed in this romanticized form, communitarians fail to recognize that to return to this would advantage some rather than others. For example, men would gain at the expense of women if traditional patriarchal relationships were to be reinstated.

❖ Etzioni recognizes that modern society is characterized by a plurality of social groups which can be hostile to each other. For example, the East End of London is often perceived as an identifiable community but is divided, sometimes violently, on racial grounds. The East End also illustrates how community can be used in a negative way with racist political movements drawing upon ideas that the 'community' is under threat from outsiders. Etzioni believes that a more tolerant society is possible yet provides few practical ways of achieving this. Communitarianism fails to give adequate attention to issues of power, inequality and conflicts of interest. Such divisions will not be solved by appealing to 'shared values' as Etzioni suggests. Moreover, the values which communitarians take as self evidently 'core' are those of the middle class.

❖ Pahl (1995) has a more positive view than communitarians of people in modern society. He argues that traditional communities may have changed radically but this does not mean that people have become completely individualistic. He suggests that:

'They are generally warm and friendly people trying to come to terms with themselves and their relationships ... There is no need to fall for a phoney communitarianism: what is needed is an acceptance that most people are struggling on as best they can with the help of their friends.'

Pahl criticizes those who fail to appreciate how people behave in their everyday lives. He believes people can build a diverse and tolerant society without being controlled by a forever watchful community.

Locality studies: the effects of economic restructuring

Earlier community studies tended to be inward looking, concentrating on the inner workings of a community. Locality studies hoped to combine detailed localized research with an awareness of the effects of wider social and economic changes. They were particularly interested in how different places experienced restructuring. This refers to the transformation of the old traditional industrial system to a modern high tech one. The localities researchers recognize that although restructuring is a global process, it has different consequences for different places.

Many studies of localities suggest that restructuring has a destructive effect. Beynon et al. (1989) argue that the collapse of traditional industries, such as shipbuilding and iron and steel on Teesside, caused the fragmentation and polarization of the community. Waddington et al. (1991) concluded that the unity of the traditional communities on the Yorkshire coalfields had been shattered by the power of the social and economic changes which had overwhelmed them.

Life is the pits in dead-end crescent

A street named desire – for jobs and a community at work.
Twenty-three households cope with the death of an industry.

> 66 We were 50 and they just booted us out. It's the young men round here I feel sorry for. There's work about, but nobody wants to pay for it. 99
> **Derek Chilcott, former miner, No. 1**

> 66 You can't replace 5,000 miners' jobs in this part of South Yorkshire with 3,000 jobs at Meadow Hall shopping centre. I don't want to sound sexist, but they're part-time jobs for women. 99
> **Mike Mellard, former colliery clerk, No. 3**

> 66 It was a shock when the pit shut. I was upset for my dad. He's had it very hard since. 99
> **Diane McCormack, miner's daughter, No. 11**

> 66 The miners always used to go around together, whether they were going to work or going for a drink. Everybody was very friendly. It's different now. 99
> **Ivy Hill, widow of a former pit deputy, No. 22**

> 66 Scargill was right. He might have been wrong in his tactics, but he was spot on about what was happening. 99
> **Peter Perry, former miner, No. 4**

> 66 If Labour gets in next time, they should make the Tories dig out the pits with their bare hands. 99
> **Harry Scholfield, former miner, No. 8**

Source:
The Observer,
2 July 1995

A report by Sheffield University, *Confronting Industrial Demise,* reveals that almost half of the country's former miners are still without permanent work, despite promised retraining.

A second report, by Sheffield Hallam University, focused on Thurcroft, which is six miles from Rotherham, as a microcosm of the impact of all pit closures. Its key findings included:

❖ Half Thurcroft's ex-miners are unemployed and a third have had no job since the pit closed.

❖ Replacement jobs are mainly in the service sector, low-paid and low-skilled, involving substantial overtime.

❖ Family incomes have fallen significantly, with more than half living on less than £150 a week.

❖ Most former miners underwent some form of retraining, usually British Coal's Jobs and Career Change Scheme, although there is little evidence that it increased their chances of finding a permanent job.

❖ Activity 10 ❖

The extracts above and on p. 380 (see *In Focus*) concern the effects of restructuring on the declining Yorkshire coalfield and the high-tech growth town of Swindon. Describe the effects of restructuring on these two places.

In Focus
◆
Case study: Swindon

As at the economic level, in social and cultural terms the town has become increasingly fragmented and complex. Working-class solidarity, collectivism and community ties have given way to home-centred individualism and social fragmentation. In a sense this reflects the growing homogeneity of local and regional culture and ways of life. The locality has become more like other growth centres in the outer south-east. But this internal fragmentation is all the more marked because of the contrast with patterns of life associated in the past with rail engineering, the scale of expansion and in-migration and the pace of economic transformation. Once everybody, it seemed, was 'inside'. Economic and social change, however, has turned the town inside out.

Source: Basset *et al.* (1995)

Managing change

Most localities theorists suggest that it is impossible to fight off the changes caused by restructuring but they do recognize that local communities and their leaders can mobilize and organize to manage such changes. Some localities seem to be able to do this more effectively than others. Cowen (1990) found that in Cheltenham, local government officials and conservationists helped to revitalize the town by promoting its regency past and its closeness to London, to make it an attractive site for office relocation. Although earlier localities studies tended to overemphasize economic issues, later studies did recognize the ability of places to reinvent themselves. For example, Glasgow has successfully marketed itself as a city of 'culture', partly overcoming its previously grim image. Thus, although the restructuring process is global, its effects will be different in different places. Moreover, the different resources, including human, found in a locality ensure that responses to change will vary and different localities can develop in unique ways.

Community and modernity

Postmodernists and those who share similar ideas about the modern world believe that the nature of contemporary society has had important implications for individuals and community today. Some of these changes include:

❖ *The shrinking of time and space* – Technological advance means that in terms of time-distance, places are actually in the same place. You may find this a rather difficult idea to grasp at first. Consider the Internet and your ability to 'surf' the global network from your own PC. We can watch major events like the Olympics 'live' because they can be transmitted simultaneously by satellite. This means that any one place can be affected by the events and activities of other distant places. Moreover, the source of any change might not even be known. It is in this sense that we refer to the 'Global Village'.

❖ *Fluidity and movement* – Lash and Urry (1994) see the modern world as very fluid. It is made up of rapid and constant flows of people, money, information, ideas, goods, images, etc. Nothing seems to be fixed or stable any more.

❖ *Diversity and complexity* – For post-modernists, the modern world is fragmented, fragile, disjointed and always changing. It is increasingly diverse and complex.

What then are the consequences of these aspects of the modern world for individuals and community? Many sociologists, including Lash and Urry, argue that it leads to feelings of insecurity and 'placelessness'. People have problems of self-identity, of knowing who they are and where they belong. Giddens (1990 and 1991) believes that the communities as described in the studies of the 1950s and 1960s have disappeared. They have been 'disembedded' or separated from their local environment. This means people no longer have 'real' communities to make them feel secure about themselves. One way of dealing with this is for individuals to 'use' the idea of community in a subjective way to create their own identity and sense of belonging to those who are seen as similar. Thus Bauman (1992) argues:

> 'Postmodernity, the age of contingency, is for the thinking person also the age of community, of the lust for community, search for community, invention of community, imagining community.'

This view is like the belief that community is a 'symbolic boundary', discussed on p. 356 and illustrated by the Fearnbeg study (see *In Focus*, p. 374).

In sum, just as objective communities are said to have become less significant as a result of global trends, the 'idea' of community has become more important. The issues surrounding the social construction of identity are discussed more thoroughly in Chapter 2.

Evaluation

The rave culture: a proto-community in action?

This approach is said to offer a new direction in the study of people and their relationship to space. However, Massey (1991) suggests that there is little empirical evidence to substantiate the claim that

people are now suffering a sense of placelessness and insecurity. Just because people have an awareness of their place in the global scheme of things does not mean this discounts the possibility of a strong sense of belonging to a more localized community. Further, shared interests in new space-shrinking technologies does not necessarily lead to sad, lonely individuals whose only contact with others is through the screen of the computer. It can also produce locally based clubs and associations which may strengthen community life.

Proto-communities

The view that people construct a sense of shared identity can be seen in the work of Paul Willis (1990). Proto-communities are those whose members share a common life style and show this to outsiders by presenting themselves in a symbolic way. For example, you can tell someone who is part of the 'rave culture' or the 'surf scene' by their style of dress, taste in music, way of speaking and the places and events they go to.

Proto-communities are different from 'traditional' communities in the following ways:

❖ 'Life style' is something individuals create or adapt for themselves, whereas traditional communities are pre-existing structures into which someone is born. Proto-communities allow individuals freedom of choice and they may decide to reinvent themselves many times. Traditional communities are fairly restrictive and fixed.

❖ Traditional communities are concerned with the production of goods and services, whereas proto-communities are concerned with consumption. Adoption of a life style generally means you have to show it by buying the image that goes with it.

❖ Traditional communities are rooted in a particular place, but proto-communities do not have to be.

❖ Traditional communities are real, whereas proto-communities exist as a result of people using their imagination.

In Focus

◆

'Underworld' – true postmodernists feeding off the madness of the modern world

Underworld are in every sense an odd group. Rick Smith and Karl Hyde had been at it for years in a musical history well documented and were approaching a brick wall when they, like countless others, discovered acid house and met with Darren Emerson who injected a solid direction through the groove of the four to the floor. Mixing Smith and Hyde's knowledge of the business and love of dance music with Emerson's knowledge of club culture they have built a monstrous sound, a new pop music based on both chaos and stability, where the whole rule book is gradually being rewritten. The Underworld sound has diverse sources of inspiration distilled into a seamless whole. Check it for jungle, blues, acid, Phillip Glass and twanging guitars both aimed at the dance floor but also for chilling out.

Underworld's live performances are built primarily on their intricate musical montage but they are much more than merely a live rendition of their records. Apparently they never rehearse and have no set lists, an anarchic approach which sees songs mutate and run off in tangents from their original forms; each set is exclusive to that show. The trio pored over banks of Electronic sound using the mixing desk as an instrument in its own right. Karl barks out his fragments of thought, implying the spirit of what he is trying to put over rather than a linear account of the subjects he is singing about. Behind them, projected cut up type and half lyrics flash across the screen disorientating the audience with its supposed meaning-lessness. The key to Underworld's music is complete artistic freedom which allows them the spontaneity that hundreds of bands can only dream of. They don't really behave like a band at all. True postmodernists feeding off the madness of the modern world, off multi-media and the lawlessness that results from it. Truly original.

Source: The Essential 96 Official Music Festival Programme

❖ Activity 11 ❖

1 Identify the features which make the group Underworld 'true postmodernists'.

2 In what ways can Underground be seen as part of a proto-community?

3 To what extent do you believe that proto-communities are true communities?

4 Reflecting on your answer to question 3, in what way are you defining community? Has this definition changed from your answer to the first activity in this chapter?

Community and values

Community in modern society remains a highly controversial issue. We can see that sociologists still have very different views of what communities are and what they should ideally be like. Communitarians see the traditional view of community with its binding social ties and obligations as highly desirable. Others see this as limiting an individual's freedom and welcome the possibilities of choice and creativity offered by a postmodern society. However, Keith and Pile (1993) see dangers in this. Symbolic communities exist because people imagine they, and those like them, are different from others. It involves the exclusion of those who are not like them and reduces toleration of diversity. In this argument, community is not regarded as something for the good of the individual or society, but a possible evil.

Patterns in the city: the Chicago School

The Chicago School has been highly influential both in sociology and geography. It developed in the early part of this century and is associated with the work of R.E. Park, R D. McKenzie, E. Burgess and L. Wirth. A mere village of three hundred and fifty people in 1830, Chicago had grown to over a million by 1900. It represented a true 'melting pot' of immigrants from Europe and other parts of the USA. The Chicago theorists were greatly influenced by functionalism and similarly shared a concern with how order could be established out of chaos. Indeed, the social problems generated by rapid urbanization were a prime motivation behind their analysis.

Further similarities with functionalism can be seen in the Chicago School's use of biological analogies. R.E. Park developed an ecological approach, applying the terms of invasion, competition, dominance and succession to why different groups became located in different parts of the city. Initially, first generation migrants head for the inner city where cheap accommodation and employment can be found. As they become established, they 'invade' into more desirable surrounding areas and compete against and succeed the previous residents who move elsewhere. Meanwhile, their place in the inner zones is taken by a new migrant group and the process begins again. Over time the relative attractiveness of areas changes and further competition occurs before a new city equilibrium is achieved. As each group becomes established in an enclave it responds to the new urban environment surrounding it by producing a new way of life. Park, therefore, believes that the city is divided into a 'mosaic of little worlds which touch but which do not interpenetrate' (Park 1950).

Ernest Burgess made these ideas famous in the model of the city as a series of concentric zones (see Figs 9.7 and 9.8).

Figure 9.7
Urban areas of Chicago (after Burgess)

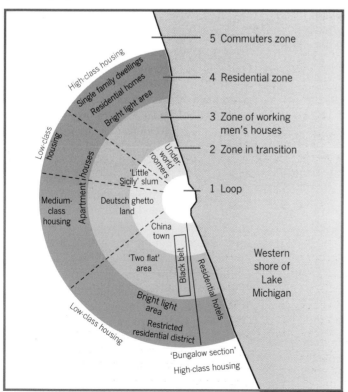

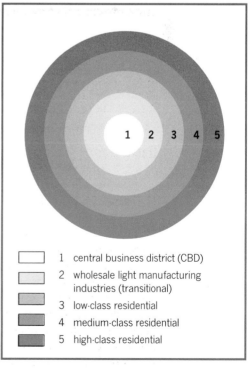

Figure 9.8
The Burgess concentric model of an urban area

The five zones can be described as follows (Waugh 1990):

1   The central business district contains the major shops and offices and is the centre for commerce, entertainment and the focus for transport routes.

2   The transition or twilight zone is where the oldest housing is either deteriorating into slum property or being 'invaded' by light industry. The inhabitants tend to be of poorer social groups and first generation immigrants.

3   Areas of low-class housing are occupied by those who have 'escaped' from zone 2, or by second generation immigrants who work in nearby factories. They are compelled to live near to their place of work to reduce travelling costs and rent. In modern Britain these zones are equated with the inner cities.

4   Medium-class housing of higher quality which, in present-day Britain, would include interwar, private, semi-detached and council estates.

5   High-class housing occupied by people who can afford the expensive properties and the high cost of commuting. This zone also includes the commuter or suburbanized villages beyond the city boundary – though there were few commuters when Burgess produced his model in 1924.

In sum, the Chicago theorists believe:

❖ The built environment does generate distinctive ways of life.

❖ The city is divided into separate social areas based on ethnicity and class.

❖ These social patterns are largely the product of external, almost natural processes.

The Chicago School: an evaluation

The Chicago School provided the framework for much subsequent urban sociology during the interwar period. Many detailed studies emerged into the ways of life of the 'natural areas', particularly the zone of transition. However, a number of problems have been identified, outlined below.

The model and real cities

The zoning of real cities was compared to the Burgess model and from this research it became apparent that it was rare to find clearly segregated areas and a neat pattern of concentric circles. Cities are far more complex phenomena than this simplistic model implies. However, Park and colleagues never claimed that their analysis of Chicago was universal or comprehensive.

The model as deterministic

Stronger criticisms concern the ecological concepts employed by these theorists.

> 'At times the Chicago School seems to have been unduly dazzled by the brilliance of their biological analogies and to have ignored the substance with which they worked.'
> (Timms 1976)

It was too environmentally deterministic, assuming that the behaviour of people was determined by their surroundings and failing to consider sufficiently people as actively making decisions and choices within the constraints of income and opportunities. In some cases people may make a choice to move into the inner city even though they have the means to live in the outer rings (see gentrification, p. 386). Areas can have a symbolic value which makes them highly desirable wherever their location. For example, Clifton in Bristol lies within a mile of the city centre yet is one of the most sought after residential districts. Likewise, decision making on the part of planners in British cities dramatically changed the Burgess configuration of zones. The development of large outer-city estates of public housing produced large concentrations of the working class in this zone. Moreover, the notion that the urban environment generates distinctive life styles is also deterministic. Wirth, for example, sees the size and density of cities as generating psychological stress, yet cities like Hong Kong and Singapore score low on indices of social disorder. However, Park did explicitly recognize the significance of cultural variables and the debate really concerns how much weight should be given to these compared to ecological factors.

Wider social and economic processes

Marxists believe that any analysis which side-steps fundamental questions concerning the nature of capitalism is inevitably flawed. Harvey in *Social Justice in the City* (1973) argues that far from being natural phenomena, cities are the product of the economic and social relations of capitalism. Social patterning is literally the 'concrete' representation of the inequalities of capitalism and the ability of some groups to shape space in their own interests. The city therefore cannot be understood by divorcing it from the economic system in which it is set. Castells (1977) accuses the Chicago School of being ideologically conservative, even a smoke screen hiding the reality of city processes. However, Smith (1989) believes this to be unfair:

'In identifying the modern city as the immediate enemy of democracy, the Chicagoans were not ignorant of capitalism's contribution to the danger. But the market, however distorted, was as it still is, sacred in American society. Attack it and you lost all practical influence over affairs. The Chicagoans were above all, practical.'

It is up to you to consider the ideological and practical implications of these two perspectives, i.e. those of the Chicago School and the radical theorists.

❖ Activity 12 ❖

1 (a) With reference to a map of a city with which you are familiar, to what extent would you agree that the Burgess model applies?

   (b) What factors could account for any variations from the model?

2 Read the assessment of the Chicago School (see *In Focus* below) and identify how practical and ideological considerations influenced the School.

In Focus

◆

Evaluating the Chicago School

Despite the strong liberal conscience which enlivened the Chicago School, direct attacks upon capitalism as a system were almost non-existent. There were three reasons for this. First, the Chicagoans were genuine believers in the values of individualism and freedom. Second, attacks upon specific business practices were liable to lead to dismissal since businesspeople dominated the governing bodies of universities (as Veblen pointed out in *The Higher Learning in America* (1918) which was largely based upon the University of Chicago). And third, Chicago sociologists such as Park and Wirth hoped that professionals could educate public opinion to curb the excesses of big business. Thorstein Veblen, who taught at Chicago between 1892 and 1906, criticized the social sciences for being, so he thought, weak-kneed in the face of power and prejudices of big business. C. Wright Mills and Alvin Gouldner later produced similar criticisms of the Chicagoans.

Source: Smith (1989)

Contemporary migration into the city

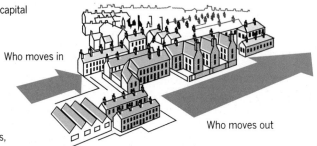

Elderly living on low incomes, no longer with a family, and wishing cheaper housing near to the CBD and other services (shops, library, hospital)

Newly wedded couples with little capital and no family – first-time buyers

Poor families with limited resources

Who moves in

Immigrants from overseas especially those with limited money, education and skills

Young, middle-class professionals, or those seeking desirable enclaves of Victorian and Edwardian houses

Inner city areas

Who moves out

Those with higher incomes now capable of buying their own homes in suburbia

Those with higher skills and qualifications – especially moving to new towns

Parents with a young family wishing for gardens, open space and larger houses

Figure 9.9
Movement in inner-city areas

Although it has been emphasized that the dominant flow of population is outwards from the Western conurbations, this does not exclude some inward movements. In fact, population loss from the major cities has slowed remarkably in the 1990s, with London in 1994 even seeing a slight growth. One noticeable flow into specific inner city areas like Islington in London is by affluent middle-class people. Ironically, the motivation seems to be a backlash against country living. Younger sections of the middle class appear to be attracted to the idea of old-style, terraced communities with a nostalgia for Victorian and Edwardian architecture. These exclusive high-status areas are said to be undergoing 'gentrification'. Their existence indicates that we cannot treat inner-city dwellers as homogenous.

In reality, the city is a dynamic system reflecting the varied choices of people who live within it. The choice to live in the town or country partly reflects a person's position in the life cycle. The safety and tranquillity of the country may be more appealing to the retired or people with families than to the younger generation who are attracted by the thrills associated with city life. However, choices are always constrained by access to resources.

Another group of people who have generally moved into Britain's inner cities due to constraints rather than choice is postwar new-Commonwealth immigrants. Although the following concentrates on their particular experience, two provisos should be kept in mind:

❖ Most immigrants entering Britain are white, from the European Union and old Commonwealth. This includes Australia, Canada and New Zealand.

❖ In most years, more people leave Britain than migrate into the country.

The settlement patterns of 'new Commonwealth' immigrants

The 1991 census was the first to contain a question on ethnic origins. It allowed people to allocate themselves to seven categories – white, Indian, Pakistani, Bangladeshi, Chinese, Black Caribbean and Black African. Even though such categorization is sensitive and subjective, it did allow researchers to examine settlement patterns on a large scale when previously they had relied upon surveys with limited samples. The scale and legal enforcement of the census adds enormously to its reliability. However, the categories from which respondents could select have been criticized:

❖ A mixture of choices based on skin colour and ex-nationality were given. Thus, would a person with a Ugandan Asian background be classified as Indian or a Black African?

❖ The categories are argued to be too broad, which meant a rather large number of people opted for 'other', for example 'White' would include people of Irish extraction and from any other country for that matter.

❖ Some categories hid significant cultural differences. 'Indian' included Sikhs, Muslims and Hindus.

❖ Activity 13 ❖

The reasons why each ethnic group came to Britain can be explained in terms of the 'Push' and 'Pull' factors described earlier. The forces behind post-war migration are well documented. They are of interest to sociologists, historians and geographers alike. Your aim should be to utilize cross-disciplinary sources to discover the factors behind new-Commonwealth migration.

1 Divide your class so that each group can research the history of migration for a different ethnic group.

2 Design a summary sheet of 'Push' and 'Pull' factors.

3 Display or present your findings to the group.

In Focus

The geography of ethnic minorities (Robinson 1994)

The 1991 data demonstrate how the spatial distribution of all the groups is still heavily dependent upon the geography of opportunity which existed when their migration to Britain was at its peak. A substantial literature shows that Black and Asian workers acted as replacement labour, initially filling those jobs and economic niches vacated by whites. In the late 1950s when Afro-Caribbean immigration was at its peak, there were the low-paid service jobs in the overheated southeast and the manufacturing jobs in the expanding car plants and engineering works of the southeast and West Midlands. The Afro-Caribbeans therefore did not have to move far from their port of entry to find work. When the Indians were arriving in the 1960s, they were able to avail themselves of some of the same employment opportunities in the same regions, but they also had to search further afield for work, whether it be in the clothing and footwear industry of the East Midlands, the foundries of Yorkshire or the transport undertakings and textile mills of the larger northern cities. By the time the Pakistani population arrived they were forced to look even further afield for employment, in particular to the struggling textile mills of the north-west and Yorkshire which were fighting to drive down costs in the face of strengthening world competition. Finally, by the time the Bangladeshis arrived in the late 1970s and early 1980s, the recessions of 1973 and 1979–81 had laid waste too much of manufacturing industry in the regions, to the extent that there were few vacant niches left to fill. The Bangladeshis thus had to push even further towards the periphery of the UK to take up those few opportunities which did still exist, but they also retreated to the southeast, where small businesses and services stood a better chance of success. Once these patterns were established, chain migration, fertility, the attractions of ethnic clustering, the concentration of some groups in council housing and racial exclusionism have generally succeeded in perpetuating them, although this now seems to be less true for the Indian population.

Figure 9.10
Change in population
numbers between
1987 and 1991

(a) Afro-Caribbeans
(b) Indians
(c) Pakistanis
(d) Bangladeshis

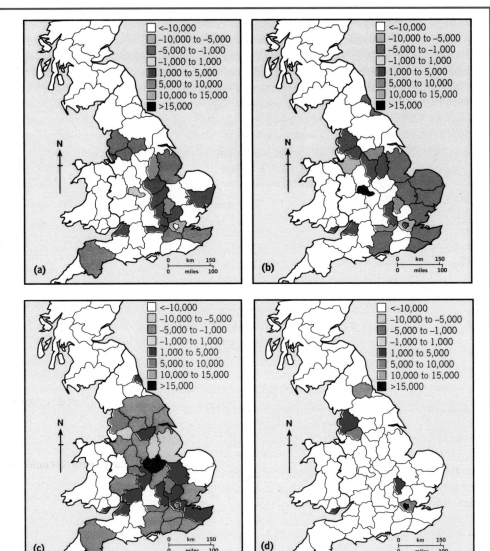

❖ Activity 14 ❖

Study the *In Focus* on the previous page and
Fig. 9.10 above.

1 Describe the distribution of settlement for
each ethnic group.

2 From the information in the *In Focus*, draw
a time line of migration into Britain,
summarizing the reasons for the variation
in the pattern of settlement.

3 The article identifies five factors for the
continued concentration of ethnic minorities:

(a) chain migration

(b) fertility

(c) the attractions of ethnic clustering

(d) the concentration of some groups in
council houses

(e) racial exclusionalism.

Explain the meaning of each factor and how it
reinforces concentration.

Urban settlement patterns

Not only are ethnic groups concentrated regionally, but there is also a clear urban bias in their distribution. The 1991 census revealed that no ethnic group had less than two thirds of its population resident in the conurbations compared to one third of the total white population. Furthermore, ethnic minorities are concentrated disproportionately in inner city areas. These areas were initially attractive to immigrants providing cheap rented accommodation and easy access to jobs. Later, the established community offered security and support. Within cities, further segregation in ethnic settlement can be identified. In Greater London, Jamaicans are associated with Brixton, Anguillons in Slough, Sikhs in Southall and Bengalis in East London. Again, we must be wary of treating ethnic minorities in an undifferentiated way.

Changes in settlement patterns

❖ Activity 15 ❖

1 Read the article on the next page (see *In Focus*) and identify the changes that have occurred in the location of different ethnic groups.

2 Why are the terms 'Jewish Future' and 'Irish Future' used to describe the prospects of Asians and Afro-Caribbeans?

3 Give reasons for the differences emerging in the locations of Afro-Caribbeans and other ethnic groups.

Although the article suggests significant change in the settlement patterns of ethnic minorities, Vaughan Robinson (1994) argues that 'perhaps the most significant finding from this analysis of the 1991 Census is the relative absence of geographical changes'. In other words the settlement pattern established when people first came to Britain largely remains today. Some movement is identifiable and Robinson relates this to the relative affluence, relative arrival time and housing tenure of different ethnic groups. The Indian population is more likely to be mobile, moving southeast and to the suburbs. This is linked to their higher representation in the middle class which gives them more chance of being owner occupiers and the resources to move. In contrast, forty per cent of Afro-Caribbeans are council tenants and this group are disproportionately working class, restricting their freedom to be mobile. Nevertheless, decentralization is evident for Afro-Caribbeans in London. Whether this is simply a 'spill over' from neighbouring inner-city areas or a genuine expansion of the Afro-Caribbean middle class remains to be seen.

Thus, the Indian pattern of migration does to some extent support the pattern of invasion and succession proposed by the Chicago School. However, the relative stability of most ethnic groups in the least desirable locations does not. It seems that early theorists failed to recognize the barriers to social and geographical mobility that discrimination and prejudice imposed. It is to the issue of differences in access to scarce resources that we now turn.

Access to housing

There is a link between the least desirable places to live and the distribution of ethnic minorities. In fact, the percentage of ethnic minorities in the population of an area is sometimes used as an index of deprivation! It is understandable that early migrants took advantage of the cheapness and centrality of the inner cities, but why have they tended to remain relatively concentrated there? Why have they generally remained on the bottom rungs of the housing ladder?

'Blacks move towards suburbs'

*Census findings reveal growth of 'ethnic villages' in search for
a better qualty of life*

The black population is now mostly British-born and does not live in African-American style ghettos but instead has moved from the inner cities to 'ethnic villages' in the suburbs, according to the latest academic study of the official census.

The study, published yesterday by the Office for National Statistics, also suggests that Britain's 500,00 black Caribbeans face an 'Irish future', while the 1.5 million Asians face a 'Jewish future'.

'This means the black Caribbean population is working class, waged labour, state educated and council housed, while the Asian population will become self-employed, owner-occupiers and white-collar workers with professional qualifications', said the study's author, Ceri Peach of Oxford University.

'The Jewish future seems to be coming about for the Indian population and to an extent for the Pakistani population, although not for the Bangladeshis.' There was evidence among black Caribbeans of a 'gender divide between the white-collar, female, socio-economic structure and the male manual structure. Certainly the model of the African-American ghetto has not come about.'

The 1991 census, which asked people about their ethnic identity for the first time, revealed Britain's ethnic minorities mostly consist of postwar immigrants and their children. Their numbers are small – around 3.5 million or 5.5 per cent of the population – but rapidly growing with in some cases a majority of children born in Britain.

The move to the suburbs is most evident among the black Caribbeans, with a significant flight during the 1980s from London's inner-city areas such as Lambeth, Tottenham and North Kensington to London suburbs such as Brent and Croydon.

The highest concentration of black Caribbeans is in Brent, North London, rather than the more traditional areas of Brixton or Paddington. Over the last 30 years families have generally moved out of privately rented flats into council housing. Nearly half own their homes.

The black Caribbean population is far more integrated than in the United States. The Pakistani and Bangladeshi communities do, however, live in high concentration 'ethnic villages', particularly in West Yorkshire, the West Midlands and East London.

There is a high level of mixed black Caribbean and white households, accounting for up to a third of black households. Single mothers account for 37 per cent of the households. There is also increasing evidence of the emergence of black British identity, with more than 70,000 people describing themselves this way in the census. Professor Peach says the black population is hard working but disadvantaged with unemployment rates more than double the white average.

The study says the key social differences between the ethnic groups lie in their patterns of family life: 'The Indians, Pakistanis, Bangladeshis and Chinese show traditional family patterns. Single person households are rare. There are few ethnically (mixed) and single parent households, while extended families are signficant. Self-employment is above average.

'The black groups have a more open and assimilated social structure. Single parent households with dependent children are common. Ethnically mixed households are frequent and multi-family households are rare.'

Source: The Guardian, 12 June 1996

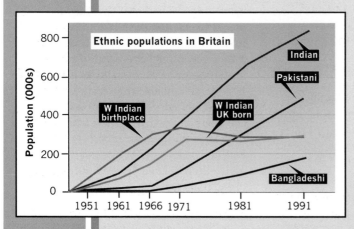

A Neo-Weberian approach

In 1967 the publication of Rex and Moore's *Race, Community and Conflict* caused quite a stir. In part, it was a reaction against the ecological approach and sought to explain housing inequalities by reference to social rather than 'natural' processes. In achieving their aim of analysing the poor housing situation of low-income new-Commonwealth migrants, Rex and Moore were heavily influenced by Max Weber. First they analysed conflicts, differences in power and status between social groups competing in the housing market. They believed that people can share significant common opportunities on other bases than the Marxist concept of social class. Table 9.6 shows the seven 'housing classes' identified from their study of Birmingham. A housing class represents a group's ability to be successful in the private and public (council) house markets. This is obviously linked to income, but not purely so.

Table 9.6 Rex and Moore's seven housing classes

Class	Characteristics
1	The outright owners of large houses in desirable areas
2	Mortgage payers who 'own' whole houses in desirable areas
3	Local authority tenants in houses built by the local authority
4	Local authority tenants in slum houses awaiting demolition
5	Tenants of private landlords
6	House owners who must take lodgers to meet repayments
7	Lodgers in rooms

Source: Rex and Moore (1967)

Like Weber, Rex and Moore emphasized the importance of the 'social actor' (see p. 282), particularly those who have the power to control and define others. With respect to housing this means it is necessary to analyse the operation of the 'gate keepers' to the housing supply. These important 'managers' are banks and building societies, estate agents, vendors, public housing officials and such like.

Disadvantage in the private sector

Ethnic minorities generally have a lower proportion of owner occupiers than other groups. Their concentration in low-paid, unstable occupations means it is difficult for them to satisfy the conditions banks and building societies require for a mortgage, including the raising of a deposit. Thus, the rules of house buying are indirectly discriminatory to people with a low income. Furthermore, the decisions of key gatekeepers, like building society managers who decide on the suitability of an applicant for a mortgage, may involve informal racism. Moreover, Knox (1992) argues that the covert practice of 'Redlining' inner-city districts caused further difficulties. The areas within the red line are disqualified from normal finance and this meant that many Asian people resorted to pooling resources, multiple occupancy and expensive loans.

Disadvantage in the public sector

Rex and Moore further argue that the formal and informal practices of local authority housing departments are also discriminatory. For example, early immigrants could not get a council property because they failed the length of residency requirement. Moreover, allocation is dependent upon a housing officer's report which may be subject to conscious or unconscious racism. Henderson and Karn's 1987 study of Birmingham substantiated Rex and Moore's claims that ethnic minorities were denied equal access to local authority housing. Some of their findings were:

❖ Asians tended to receive older houses than white people.

❖ West Indians with children were more likely to receive a flat than white families with a similar number of children.

❖ West Indians were given their area preference much less than white applicants. A black person applying for a 'white' estate was much less likely to obtain it than a white person or a black person applying for a 'black' estate.

Henderson and Karn (1987) suggest that a range of perceptions on the part of housing officers resulted in ethnic minorities being disadvantaged. West Indians suffered inequality because priority was given to married rather than cohabiting couples and living together was more common amongst this group. Another assumption was that white people who were offered inner-city property would reject it, whereas black people would not. The study claims that housing officers tended to bow to pressures from white residents not to give tenancies to ethnic minorities on majority white estates. Not surprisingly, ethnic minorities were least satisfied with their council accommodation.

The biased allocation of local authority housing further reinforces the residential segregation produced by unequal competition in the private market. The selling off of council properties has further disadvantaged working-class ethnic minorities since they are least likely, for the reasons discussed above, to be in a position to buy. Those council properties remaining tend to be the least desirable and in increasingly short supply. This means that their choice becomes more restricted and there is a greater need to use the private rented sector.

To sum up, Rex and Moore revealed that ethnic minorities are disproportionately represented in the lowest housing classes. This was a result of:

❖ the poor position of ethnic minorities in the labour market.

❖ the discriminatory practices of housing institutions.

Evaluation

The study by Rex and Moore of ethnic minorities' access to housing in Birmingham was a major contribution to understanding the inequalities they faced. It triggered further interest and debate in this crucial area. Nevertheless, a number of criticisms have been made:

❖ It is suggested that the areas used in the study were not typical inner-city areas and the housing classes devised are not generally applicable. However, these criticisms are somewhat unfair. Rex and Moore recognized that Sparkbrook had an unusually high percentage of multiple occupation. They did not claim that the housing classes for Birmingham were carved in stone, but that they were useful for understanding the differences in housing opportunities in this particular city.

❖ Marxists prefer to emphasize the significance of social class above all else. From this perspective, ethnic minorities are the most oppressed portion of the working class and are not separate from it. Their housing situation can be fully explained by analysing their class position and their role as a 'reserve army of labour' without introducing the complication of housing classes. Rex himself came to recognize that the theory of the 'underclass' was more useful than that of housing classes (see p. 263).

❖ A further problem of Rex and Moore's work is that it fails to give sufficient attention to the fact that people can alter their housing-class position. After all, most people experience the lower housing classes at some point in their lives, as students know only too well! Also, some groups may remain in a particular location even when they have the means to improve housing class. For example, the Indian community has been upwardly mobile yet remains relatively concentrated, partly because of the cultural, protective and entrepreneurial benefits of established communities.

In Focus

◆

Labour migration from the Caribbean

Over the next 20 years the situation changed considerably. The Caribbean population gained increased access to the council sector while their presence declined in the private rental sector and, to a lesser extent, the owner-occupied sector. Two factors were particularly important in making this entry to the council sector possible. First, some of the urban locations of the migrant populations were declared slum areas and demolished. Home-owners among the affected households were offered accommodation in council houses. Second, over time, the migrants had acquired a greater understanding of the state housing system and increasing numbers of private tenants were being housed through council waiting lists.

Some changes have also occurred within the owner-occupied sector as a limited number of migrant households have gained access to better quality housing. Discrimination by vendors and estate agents, which initially excluded Caribbean and other postwar migrants from the more desirable housing of the host cities, has decreased, and some migrants have moved into good quality housing. In other cases, vast improvements have been made to original purchases.

Finally, over the past two decades, the state has adopted a policy of selling public housing to tenants. This has proved a mixed blessing for Caribbean tenants. Research has shown that a disproportionate number of Caribbean households have been allocated the least desirable categories of council housing (Parker and Dugmore, 1977/78). This has taken the form of accommodation on estates of high-rise flats in inner urban areas, and older properties on suburban estates which lack many of the amenities of new housing. Meanwhile, in general, households exercising the 'right to buy' have opted for houses in preference to flats and the newer, suburban estates have been the most popular areas. Caribbean households who occupy this more attractive housing category and are financially able to apply for purchase have grasped the opportunity to become owner occupiers. However, for the majority, purchase is financially impossible or undesirable due to the type and location of their housing. For households in poor locations, the option of transferring to better council housing in other areas is reduced as such property is sold off.

Source: Byron (1994)

Figure 9.11
Tenure categories of the Caribbean population
Source: Byron (1994)

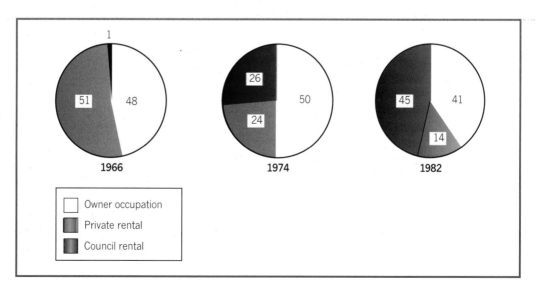

❖ Activity 16 ❖

1 Describe the changes that have occurred in the housing tenure of Afro-Caribbeans.

2 What factors may account for the improved housing position of Afro-Caribbeans?

3 With reference to the article and New Right housing policy (see p. 396), how will contemporary housing policy effect Afro-Caribbeans?

4 To what extent does Fig. 9.11 support the argument of Rex and Moore?

❖ Activity 17 ❖

Test yourself by answering the following essay question:

Examine sociological explanations of the disadvantages experienced by ethnic minorities in housing.

Aim to write about three to four sides of A4.

Power and conflict in the city

Urban sociology in the 1970s moved away from the established 'ecological' and 'community' frameworks to evolve a far more radical analysis. Neo-Weberian and Neo-Marxist approaches revealed that:

❖ Both urban and rural communities contained conflicts of interest between groups with unequal amounts of power.

❖ Such inequalities and conflicts can only truly be understood by examining the broader workings of the socio-economic system. Capitalism is held responsible for the physical form of the city and the ways of life found in both rural and urban places.

These points have been an essential part of the critique of the arguments presented above. It is now intended to examine these highly influential approaches with particular reference to conflict in the city.

The battle for urban resources

Newspapers often have reports on area-based groups campaigning to prevent an individual or organization implementing or ending a project in their locality. A whole host of issues appear to spur people into action, including the location of supermarkets,

the building of roads, or the closure of hospitals and schools. What is at stake is the spatial distribution of urban resources which can have significant implications for the quality of life in a given area.

Different land uses, such as factories, roads, health centres, shopping complexes, sports grounds and sewerage works, have attached costs and benefits. For example, a factory creates jobs but will also bring increased traffic noise pollution and absorb valued open space. These effects, termed externalities, generate conflict as communities seek to force activities with negative consequences to go elsewhere whilst maximizing positive ones. This inevitably leads to conflict with those wishing to develop the site as well as with other communities. Moreover, locational issues are just as likely to divide communities as to unite them. For example, the building of a leisure complex will be seen as an asset by people interested in sport, but an unnecessary nuisance by those who are not. Often the conflict concerns the relative closeness of a development. Figure 9.12 shows how the zones of tolerance for particular activities vary. Often the argument is that a development is necessary but 'not in my backyard' (Nimby).

Figure 9.12
Preferred residential distance from different public facilities
Source: Knox (1992)

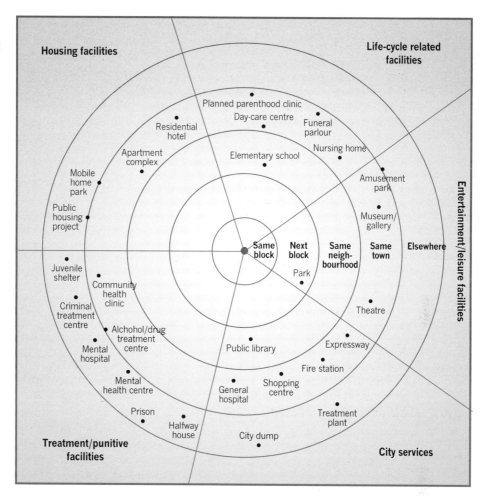

An unequal battle

Significantly, conflicts concerning the location of urban resources do not take place between groups on an equal footing. The general rule is that those with more wealth, power and knowledge have the greater ability to protect and promote the interests of their area. After all, the motivation to resist threats to the value of your property or quality of environment tends to be more when you already have something worth fighting for. We have already seen that the territory of the city is roughly divided on the basis of social class. Localized conflicts can, to a limited extent, be viewed as an extension of class conflicts. For example, the middle classes in England have often been successful in resisting threats to the 'Greenbelt' whilst in the USA many areas surrounding the more affluent

suburbs are zoned so that any further residential development has to be low-density. Both actions seem to ensure that cheap working-class housing is not built in these areas.

However, it would be misleading to suggest that locational conflicts are purely on class lines and that the middle class always win. A study of 16 services in 12 West German cities revealed a more complex pattern. Secondary schools, public open space and nursery facilities were found to be more highly concentrated in middle-class districts. Leisure, sports, entertainment centres and sheltered housing were evenly distributed. Working-class areas had relatively more day-care centres, elderly provision and play groups. Goschel *et al.* (1982) also found that certain working-class inner-city and peripheral districts were very poorly serviced in relation to most facilities.

The role of the bureaucrats

It is clear that the people who have the power to give the go-ahead to a project are key players in the conflicts of the city. It is these officials whom local pressure groups hope to influence. We have already seen the importance neo-Weberians give to public and private sector 'gate-keepers' in relation to housing. This emphasis on urban managers as the mediators of access to scarce urban resources is known as the 'managerial thesis'.

However, how accountable are such people to the communities they apparently serve? Weber talks of the 'dictatorship of the official' and others accuse planners of becoming an 'urban ruling class' pursuing their own ideological dreams of the cityscape with little reference to the people they are planning for. Certainly, some of the high-rise estates of the 1960s bear testament to such claims. Today, it is argued, greater consultation does take place. However, this often involves communities showing preference for a particular choice from a set of plans that have already been devised.

The issue of how responsive urban power holders are to the community falls within the realms of political sociology.

The Neo-Marxist approach

Marxist urban sociology emphasizes above all the importance of class conflict at the societal level as well as how it is played out within the urban arena. It is the argument by theorists like David Harvey (1973) and Manuel Castells (1977) that this conflict surmounts all other social divisions which distinguishes them from Neo-Weberians. Moreover, they are less concerned with the middle levels of the power structure than the dominance of the economic elite which sets the boundaries within which managers manage.

From a Marxist perspective, the city can be viewed as part of the superstructure which reproduces the capitalist economic system. The capitalist city developed in response to the economic need to have a concentrated labour supply. Its physical form, inequalities and conflicts are determined by the relations of production of capitalism.

The local and national state can ensure the city serves the interests of capitalism in the following ways:

❖ *Economic efficiency*

The planned provision of urban infrastructure, roads, communications and other essential services subsidizes capital and increases efficiency.

❖ *Demand orchestration*

The state can orchestrate demand through public works like road building. Major building projects stimulate the construction industry and those with which it is associated.

❖ *Social class reproduction*

The state provides services like council houses, schools, hospitals and theatres. For Marxists, the provision of these services is one of the ways the labour force and the culture of capitalism are reproduced. We have already seen that occupational class largely determines where someone lives in the city. Governments can encourage the reproduction of blue-collar workers in blue-collar neighbourhoods and white-collar in white-collar neighbourhoods by the way in which they distribute urban resources. As Goschel's study indicated, middle-class areas tended to have relatively more schools whereas working-class districts had more services which compensated for their problems. In this way, the most exploited sector of the labour force is maintained and convinced that welfare capitalism is caring and legitimate. Further, the concentration of social groups into territories encourages class-based subcultures which, through socialization, reinforce the divides within the working class and limits the development of full class consciousness.

Even though urban policy may help to reduce conflicts, the contradictions of capitalism mean that they can never be fully buried. Recent economic restructuring has led to the collapse of industry in the cities of the North and the inner cities in particular. Further conflicts arise as residential areas and open space are swallowed by speculative developments. The construction industry builds for those who can afford to buy, but not for those who have the most desperate need. Big capital comes into conflict with small capital. For example, some of the strongest opponents of hypermarkets are small shopkeepers. Most of this conflict is institutionalized within the framework of local government but it can also spawn oppositional community action. For example, one campaign against the building of a superstore on green land in a suburb of Bristol led to a demonstration by 2,000 people.

Collective consumption and social movements

Manuel Castells (1977) believes that modern urban conflicts are primarily about collective consumption rather than production. By the goods and services of collective consumption he means schools, hospitals, leisure facilities, etc., which are consumed by us all. For Castells, class conflict is no longer primarily concerned with workplace issues like wages and conditions, but the relative distribution of these urban resources. Conflicts generated by collective consumption have the power to forge new broad alliances between the working class and middle class in opposition to capitalist values. For example, the closure of a hospital is likely to be detrimental to the interests of both classes. An action group which persists for some time in such conflicts is termed an urban social movement. Castells believed that such movements had the potential seriously to challenge the capitalist economic system. A spectre haunts the world: will the urban crisis become an urban revolution?

The rise of urban protests and violence during the late 1960s and beyond seemed to support Castells' argument. Such turbulence was a result of a deepening economic crisis resulting in increased unemployment and demand for welfare provision, particularly in the inner city. At the same time, cities saw a slump in their revenue as the more affluent sector of the tax base moved outwards. In some cases this fiscal crisis was so severe that cities like Liverpool and New York were threatened with bankruptcy. Thus, just as issues of collective consumption became more acute, both for the inner city dweller and the suburbanites who still demanded the use of the facilities of the central city (even though they no longer paid for them!), the authorities could least afford them. With cutbacks, rather than expansion of service provision, the tensions of the city deepened.

Evaluation

❖ The revolution which Castells predicted never happened. He failed adequately to explain where and why urban dwellers would become a conscious revolutionary force. In *The City and the Grass Roots* (1983) he admitted that such movements were extremely rare and recognized that the concept of collective consumption was far too narrow to explain all the conflicts of the city.

❖ Castells could not have predicted the extent to which collective consumption has been privatized. Private health, education, housing and the sell-off of public utilities like water and gas have been the bedrock of New Right policy. Those who can afford to buy shares, join private health schemes and buy their children's education are likely to have very different interests from people looking to the state to provide such items of collective consumption. People providing for themselves privately may be more interested in tax and spending cuts than the retention and expansion of public services. Rather than uniting city people, issues of collective consumption are just as likely to divide.

❖ Saunders (1983) believes Castells under-estimated the conservative nature of most urban social movements. We have already seen how middle-class property owners tend to be more successful in protecting the interests of their area, even if this is detrimental to the less privileged. He argues that privatization adds to this conservativeness.

❖ Castells can also be criticized on theoretical grounds. Some Marxists believe that he has betrayed the legacy of Marx and Engels by giving too much significance to conflicts of consumption rather than production. Furthermore, there is an overconcern with capitalism determining human action and an underplaying of the importance of humans as independent social actors.

Neo-Marxism has been highly influential in breaking the mould defining how urban issues should be analysed. Notwithstanding ideological considerations, the concern with urban conflict and inequality has produced enormous insight and extensive research. The setting of rural/urban processes within a wider socio-economic framework has moved the sociology of localities beyond localized studies.

Environmentalism and New Social Movements

Paul Bagguley (1993) believes that the conflicts in urban areas are far more complex and varied than can be explained by the Marxist concerns of production and consumption. He argues that some of the most important contemporary urban and rural conflicts are concerned with environmental issues and these fall outside Castells' analysis. Campaigns, such as those against the building of the Batheaston by-pass and the tearing up of Twyford Down have persisted for a long time and forged new alliances between dreadlocked 'road warriors', middle-class professionals and small and large property owners. Crook *et al.* (1992) see great significance in these movements and believe they represent a major change in the way political protest in rural and urban areas takes place. Sociologists use the term 'new social movements' to differentiate them from the old social movements of the past (see Chapter 13, *Power and politics*).

Differences between old and new social movements

Table 9.7 summarizes some of the major Differences between old and new social movements.

An environmentalist perspective on a campaign against the building of a new road

❖ Activity 18 ❖

Study the illustration on this page, the photograph on p. 399 and the articles on p. 400.

Then discuss to what extent the movement described has the characteristics of a new social movement.

Table 9.7 Differences between old and new social movements

	Old	**New**
	Ideal types of social movements	
Issues	*Material*, economic, such as wage rises and conditions of work.	*Non-material*, social or environmental, such as gay rights, feminism, conservation groups.
Values	Belief that people's lives will improve with continued *economic growth*.	Belief in an individual's right to be *free* and *autonomous*.
Structural 'root'	The inequalities resulting from capitalism – *the social class system*.	Concerned with social institutions 'outside' the state and economy – 'civil society'. The aim may be to protect or change such institutions as the family.
Social 'base'	*The working class*	Some sociologists argue that the social base of *new* social movements is the *new middle class* – public sector professionals like teachers and social workers. Others believe they *cut across class* divides.
Internal organization	*Centralized*, bureaucratic. People elect representatives.	Lack of central organization, rather loosely linked groups. This organization is called *'polycephalous'* meaning *'many-headed'*. People actively *participate*.
Forms of action	*Corporatist* – representatives negotiate with employers or governments, *election* campaigning.	*Direct action, protest*, adoption of *'life style'* like New Age travellers.
Rationality	Aim to achieve measurable goals such as wage rises and election results.	Aim to achieve long-term, ultimate ideal.
Incentives	To gain economic and material benefits.	Satisfaction from defending what a person sees as morally right and the fun gained from being involved.
	e.g. Trade unions	e.g. Green Movement.

On the road to Carmageddon

Car rage is the new focus of rebellion – and it's challenging the very way we live. Urban and rural guerilla groups are trying to undermine car culture and defy a government committed more in word than deed to changing it.

A typical urban car snarl-up
Photo: Julia Martin/Photofusion

In Focus

◆

'Pieces of
the action'

Pieces of the action

Underground Britain is going public by producing the first directory of 'disorganisation'. Alex Bellos reports

'They like to be known as "disorganisations", campaign groups with undefined structure and mixed aims, but they are suddenly showing all the signs of organisation. Britain's fragmented counterculture, politicized by the Criminal Justice Bill, has – as the bill has become an act – grown into a sophisticated, almost formal network whose wider aims now transcend the concerns of the legislation.

It is often said that the Criminal Justice Bill was the Government's biggest gift to alternative Britain. Certainly, the opposition to its draconian clauses on hunt saboteurs, ravers, travellers and squatters has brought together these groups (perhaps because they were all mentioned by name) in a way no single issue has in recent years.

With the publication this month of The Book, the first "directory of active groups", the diverse network of campaigners and activists is given the stamp of a kind of officialdom. Within its 86 pages, 200 groups are listed – with their aims, their resources and the alliances they have forged with each other. The DIY culture has at last built its own house.

The picture The Book paints of "underground" Britain is vibrant, with thousands of young people taking a new interest in a politics that does not fit along traditional lines. The overriding themes that can be picked out are anarchy, green values and libertarianism.

The network embraces technology. About half are on the Internet, there are bulletin boards and web sites, and several distribute their information on e-mail. In fact, their structure resembles the Internet in that there is no central power and members pool together resources.'

Source: The Guardian, 29 July 1995

In Focus

◆

from
Letters to
the Editor,
*The
Guardian*,
8 August
1995

Head-on crash at Newbury

'Yesterday, it was Twyford Down, tomorrow the beautiful countryside around Newbury. The spectre of the bulldozer has come to haunt dozens of communities up and down the land but, everywhere, people are fighting back.

Anti-road campaigning is a popular pursuit these days. We begin our campaigns as ordinary people leading ordinary lives: students, grandmas, councillors or 30-something housewives like me. Before we know it, we're attending rallies, lobbying politicians and declaring that we will fight these roads to the bitter end. We do not do this because we relish the thought of a few black eyes from Group 4, or because we fancy a short spell in Holloway or Wormwood Scrubs. We do it because, in this instance, the Government has not kept its part of the bargain between citizen and state. It has stopped listening. We are left to protect our children's heritage, health and future quality of life because the Government has no interest in doing so.

There are some politicians who like to caricature us as, at best, a tiresome partnership between the great unwashed and middle-class busybodies, or, at worst, as a group of sinister troublemakers out to subvert democracy. They don't seem to have grasped the fact that opposition to road-building now goes much further than nimbyism to a genuine concern about the long-term social, health and environmental consequences of unbridled traffic growth.'

Name and address of writer withheld

Explaining the rise in environmentalism

Beck (1992) offers a number of reasons why concern for the environment has grown in modern society:

❖ He suggests that many of the old issues of survival in western societies have largely been solved. Most people have adequate incomes, diets and housing so can turn their attention to non-economic issues.

❖ The rise of environmentalism can also be seen as a result of the Earth being perceived as increasingly at risk. In the past, nature was regarded as something which human beings could exploit and master. For centuries it had sustained economic growth. Today, people are beginning to question whether economic growth can continue when resources like coal, oil and gas are running out. Moreover, environmental problems like global warming and the hole in the ozone layer are seen as the consequence of economic development. Beck claims that the old certainties have gone and one of the main anxieties that people face in contemporary societies is the feeling of impending environmental disaster. This feeling of insecurity is global. Mass communication means we all know about the threat to humanity. It affects all social groups which is why organizations like Greenpeace and Friends of the Earth have so much middle-class support.

❖ Beck suggests that this feeling of insecurity has increased because people no longer have faith in science to provide all the answers and all the solutions. Indeed, some claim that science has actually contributed to the environmental crisis.

❖ Nature can no longer be separated from society. Human intervention has been so widespread that there is some doubt that any 'real' nature free from human influence can be found at all. Even our own nature is being taken over by such things as in vitro fertilization and genetics. Beck claims that the human species has 'socialized' nature. Now the fear is that nature will have its revenge, that it is 'pay back' time.

Thus environmentalism is a result of deep individual insecurity resulting from the above processes. Peter Dickens (1993) suggests that:

'Now in the risk society, the main set of problems concerns the highly problematic outcomes of tech-cum-economic development. Even if the old issues are not wholly solved they are becoming overshadowed by the distribution of risk.'

In Focus

◆

Criticisms of Beck and the 'risk society'

But are even these newer sociological perspectives adequate? Do they provide sufficient understandings of 'risk' and the relationships between the human and the natural worlds? Have they, in their attack on science, its vulnerability and contemporary critique, gone completely overboard in rejecting what science has to say about people and their environment? Furthermore, are literally all risks on the apocalyptic global scale which Beck and Giddens refer to? Surely many risks still operate at a fairly small scale. What, anyway, is the true nature of these 'risks'? Can they be adequately understood without the kinds of detailed understanding offered by, say, physicists or natural scientists? Notions of 'risk society' surely themselves run a risk; that of severely fetishizing 'risk' and, in the end, not offering sufficient insight into what it consists of and who it is really affecting. Perhaps most fundamentally, are they recognizing the implications of their own arguments? If it is now impossible to understand nature outside society, and vice-versa, then presumably this has important implications for sociology itself. The study of society must somehow incorporate an understanding of nature.

Source: adapted from Dickens (1993)

1 Identify the key criticisms that Dickens makes of the idea of 'risk society'.

2 Discuss to what extent you agree with this critique.

The inner city

The plight of the inner city illustrates many of the arguments which have emphasized conflict and the need to examine patterns of structural inequality. Geographically, the inner city is identified as the area which developed in the nineteenth century and is sandwiched between the central Business District and the suburbs. To this effect it broadly corresponds to the zone of transition of the Burgess model (see Fig. 9.8, p. 383). However, it is seldom a continuous area nor exclusively central. Broadbent (1985) suggests that some of the most deprived urban localities are in fact out-of-city estates built to rehouse decentralized inner-city inhabitants. Indeed, Janet Foster's study of two hard-to-let council estates verifies this, with the Broadwater Farm Estate in London having a number of advantages compared to a more isolated estate on the outskirts of Hull. Peter Hall (1981) emphasizes that the term inner city implies much more than location and he outlines three features which distinguish it:

❖ *Decline* – The inner city is an area of absolute and relative loss of both population and employment opportunities. Moreover, the movement is socially selective. Those who can afford to move out do so, leaving a concentration of the elderly, single parents, unskilled and other disadvantaged groups. This loss undermines the local tax base of the area just as public demand for services increases.

❖ *Deprivation* – Within the inner city there are areas in poor environmental condition, with large numbers of rundown houses, high rates of overcrowding, acute unemployment and many other characteristics of social disadvantage.

❖ *Common perception of collective despair* – Hall argues that the two factors above combine to produce a feeling of helplessness – that nothing can be changed. This statement that individual and community action is not a feature of inner-city life is debatable.

Paul Harrison (1983), in a detailed study of the London borough of Hackney, drew similar conclusions to Hall. This was further supported by the *Faith in the City* reports commissioned by the Church of England (1985 and 1995). Thus, most urban areas do contain concentrated zones of multiple deprivation, frequently in the inner city but not always so. Moreover, Harrison agrees with Hall that one of the consequences of inner-city decline is further community break down. He sees a very different picture from the 'urban villages' discussed earlier:

'In Hackney there are many conflicts: Young against old, rate payers against squatters, tax payers against claimants, dog owners against non-dog owners, black against white, not to mention moral, religious, sexual or class cleavages. The collapse of social control is seen in the high crime rates. There is precious little community to start with, but crime dissolves it even further.' (Harrison 1983, pp. 736)

The economic and social problems of the inner city can be explained by referring to the processes which led to counter-urbanization. (see Fig. 9.4, p. 371). Indeed, the rise and fall of the inner city can only be understood in relation to the wider operation of global capitalism. Economic restructuring has led to the decline of the

Tower blocks such as these were built in the 1960s to solve inner-city housing problems.

the physical environment or the culture of poverty apparently found in these areas, fundamentally the problems of the inner city are largely the result of lack of investment. Once economic decline has set in, further circles of deprivation are difficult to avoid.

The government response

The severity of these problems has led to considerable government intervention. There is a general political consensus that action is necessary, although funding and the appropriate means is a matter of great contention. The 1960s and 1970s were marked by wholesale clearance and redevelopment reflecting the belief that changing the environment could also bring wider social benefits. The resulting architects' dreams of high-rise and deck-access living became recognized as social and environmental nightmares. In recent

traditional industries which initially led to urban development in the nineteenth century. The inner city no longer provides the least-cost location for a high-tech, service-based economy. Although there have been explanations which have blamed

'Britain's cities may be dysfunctional planning disasters. But is that any reason to live in the country?'

'Meanwhile, back in the discredited inner cities, a different kind of cycle rules. It starts with economic decline as industries and trades become obsolescent. This leads to unemployment which, when combined with immigration, gives rise to concentrated poverty, which in turn leads to a steady decline in services: public transport, health, education, garbage collection, and care and maintenance of the local environment. If you want to see how stark the run-down of services can be in a declining area then consider this comparison of Bracknell with the Easterhouse district of Glasgow. Both have a population of around 50,000, but Bracknell has six times more shopping floor-space, 23 post offices to Easterhouse's five, 15 banks compared with one, and eight public libraries to Easterhouse's two.

The vicious spiral continues with the rapid decay of the housing stock because

owners are too poor to undertake repairs and rents are too low to encourage landlords to do so either. Upper floors fall empty, shops and cafes go downmarket and then out of business. Crime, in the form of vandalism, mugging, drug-dealing and arson, increases and the area becomes another one of Britain's urban blackspots. Littered streets of boarded-up, fly-posted, shuttered or wire-meshed shops, grotty launderettes, tiny "supermarkets" and derelict sites in which (to quote the Henley report again) the main actors are a "growing band of people who gain no benefit from the regeneration of city centres and whose fortunes are generally declining ...". The coexistence of increasing prosperity and expanding poverty clearly raises important questions about social coherence. This polarization creates the potential for the spread of no-go areas.'

Source: The Observer, 7 August 1994

years there has been a change of direction. Now it is hoped that in partnership with private industry, the economy of inner cities can be rebuilt.

However, the motivation to provide assistance was not purely economic or humanitarian. The riots of the 1980s made it politically expedient. The volatility of the inner city has continued into the 1990s with riots in Newcastle, Salford, Luton and Bradford. Although often classed as race riots, most reports, including official ones like the Scarman Report, have recognized that specific incidents are merely the fuse igniting the powder keg of anger and frustration caused by long-term disadvantage. It is to one particular government response to the inner-city problem that we now turn.

In Focus

◆

Case study: London's Docklands

The Dockland area of London developed largely in the nineteenth century with industrial and colonial expansion. However, twentieth century changes in shipping and trading patterns have made [the docks] obsolescent and the area one of the most deprived in Britain (see photo left).

The fight against mass unemployment, poverty, dereliction and poor housing has been part of urban policy since the end of World War II. Here the more contemporary activities of the LDDC (London Docklands Development Corporation), established in 1981, will be used to illustrate how redevelopment can intensify social conflicts. According to a brochure in 1985, the LDDC promised that the Docklands would be:

'rare among new developments in postwar Britain for having industry and commerce, housing and leisure facilities, coexisting instead of being kept apart. In consequence, people will be able to live, work and play in the same area. The sterility of so many developments elsewhere will have no place in the Docklands.'

Rejuvenation was to be achieved in partnership with private investors. The belief was in demand-led planning whereby the resources of the LDDC are used to facilitate the objectives of private developers. The emphasis was on economic and national interests rather than localized social problems, but with the intention that benefits, such as more jobs for local people, would eventually 'trickle down'. The most famous project is that of Canary Wharf, 'the Manhattan of the Thames' (see photo below). This was built by a Canadian company to satisfy the expanding international financial markets which could no longer be

squeezed into the City. Thus, the nature of the development was a product of London's position as one of three great world financial centres, alongside New York and Tokyo.

Canary Wharf promised 120,000 jobs alone. In addition to prestige office developments, high-tech and media industries were also attracted. Badly needed communications, housing, leisure and tourist facilities were rapidly put into place. The speed of the development was partly due to the centralized power of the LDDC which freed it from normal planning controls and allowed it to override other bodies, even locally elected ones. The visual change in the Docklands is dramatic, but it is argued that the manner in which development was carried out did not coincide with the needs of the people who live there.

A number of criticisms have been made:

1 Housing

80% of the new housing constructed has been for private sale and at a price beyond what local people can afford, even though two-thirds of the land given to the LDDC had initially been allocated for local authority housing. According to Naughton (1994), places like Canary Wharf do not regenerate their locality but destroy it and create instead the kind of space, where, in due course, people will be questioned by security guards simply because they are walking the streets.

2 Social polarization

Most of the development is in stark contrast to the council estates and the indigenous working-class culture of the area. The prestigious housing developments are filled with young professionals (YUPPIES) and the resulting resentment has caused friction between newcomers and locals.

3 Employment

Most of the jobs created require qualified and skilled labour which the local workforce cannot provide. Only 13% of new jobs are filled by established residents with most employees simply transferring into the new premises from elsewhere. Meanwhile, traditional industries continue to decline and unemployment rates are higher than before redevelopment (see Fig. 9.13)

Big money is moving in

Massive luxury riverside development – public housing cut to nil.

Large enterprises moving in (bringing their own workforce) get incentives while small local firms are squeezed out – few new jobs will be created.

Don't let it push out local people!

Local action groups are unhappy about the ways in which Docklands is being developed. The campaign slogan reproduced here was used on a community poster in Wapping entitled 'The Changing Picture of Docklands'.

4 Lack of community consultation

The LDDC was not required to examine the views of the local community. Melanie Phillips argues that it was:

'a quango responsible to central government, unaccountable to local people who felt that they simply could not influence it to address their own interests. The new jobs it brought were not for them. Its opulence became an affront, the winking triangular obelisk of Canary Wharf a grievous provocation.'
(*The Guardian*, 6. March 1994)

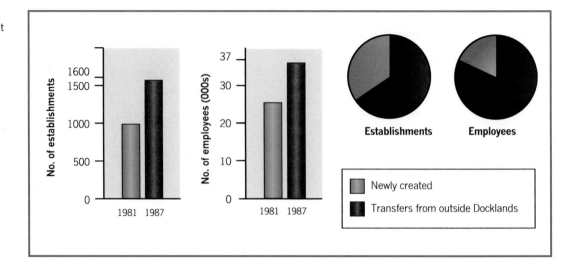

Figure 9.13
Employment
change in
Docklands
1981–87
Source:
Matthews
(1991)

In Focus

◆

**Case study:
London's
Docklands
(ctd)**

Phillips suggests that the alienation felt by the people of the Isle of Dogs has contributed to the success of the British National Party in this area. In circumstances where no one else appears to care, the politics of race will find ears to listen and further split the community.

Thus, a report commissioned by the Department of the Environment to assess the impact of urban policy in 1994 concluded that:

'The assumption that any general improvement in local circumstances, whether or not it is of immediate benefit to the poor, will eventually work its way through, appears not to be working.' (Robson *et al.* 1994)

In response to such criticism the LDDC, developers and local authorities have negotiated a deal whereby 1500 'social homes' will be built, 2000 jobs guaranteed, and a £2.5m trust established for training for people in the local area. However, the fortunes of the whole of the development have been at times questioned. The recession in international finance led to fears that Canary Wharf would become something of a white elephant. In 1994 a third of its office space was vacant. To some extent circumstances have improved but it will always be vulnerable to economic recession while the dominance of the 'city' remains. MacGregor and Pimlott (1991) do not believe that such 'flagship' projects can greatly affect essentially social problems. They propose a radical policy requiring major public expenditure. However, in a context where urban policy is seeing cuts in funding and the market rules supreme, any significant change in inner city policy seems unlikely.

The changes in the Isle of Dogs illustrate how overwhelming outside economic and political forces can be. Nevertheless, this is not to say that people who live in inner cities accept change passively nor that local campaigns are always fruitless. The extract on p. 408 (see *In Focus*) indicates that community can exist in inner-city areas and that it can be a powerful force in determining its nature.

❖ Activity 20 ❖

1. Explain how the role of the LDDC reflects the philosophy of the New Right.

2. Study diagrams in Fig. 9.14. Compare the People's Plan with that of the LDDC.

   (a) Discuss the view that national consider-ations must always override local considerations.

   (b) Discuss to what extent you regard the People's Plan as viable or merely nostalgic.

3. To what extent does the case of the Docklands illustrate the view that the nature of the city is a product of power and conflict?

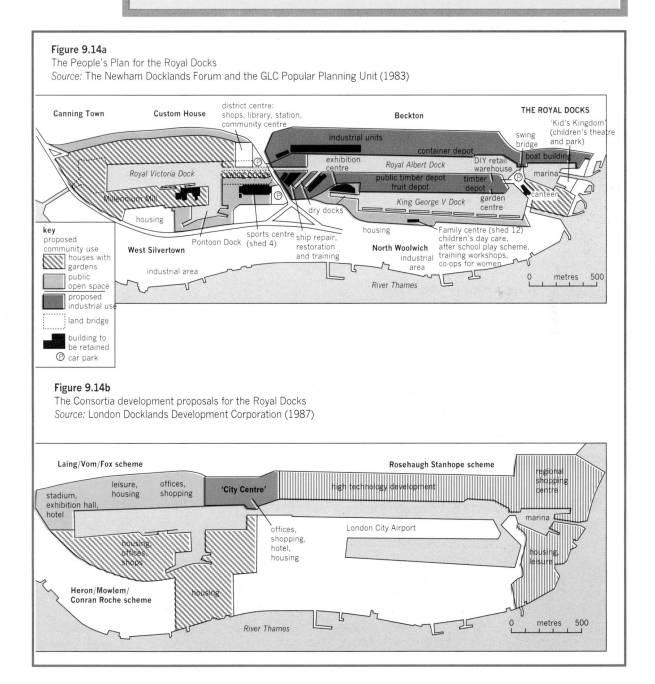

Figure 9.14a
The People's Plan for the Royal Docks
Source: The Newham Docklands Forum and the GLC Popular Planning Unit (1983)

Figure 9.14b
The Consortia development proposals for the Royal Docks
Source: London Docklands Development Corporation (1987)

In Focus

◆

**Waterloo
sunrise**

Waterloo sunrise

**Community spirit has triumphed over big business at London's
Coin Street riverside development. David Spittles reports.**

Locals call it the battle of Waterloo –
a fight for community housing that
started 2 years ago when property
developers announced a massive office
complex, including Europe's tallest
skyscraper, for a neglected 13-acre site on
London's South Bank.

The victory will be celebrated later this
month when Environment Secretary John
Gummer cuts the ribbon at the latest
housing scheme to be developed by Coin
Street Community Builders, the grass-
roots organization that sprouted up to
oppose the plan proposed by a consortium
led by the Vestey Group.

Gummer's presence will add a touch of
irony to the proceedings. The DoE was
branded by community activists as a
friend of big business at the time of the
first public inquiry in 1979, which cleared
the way for a scaled-down version of the
office scheme. This plan hit the rails in
1980 when Labour gained control of the
Greater London Council, which owned
half the land. There was another year-
long public inquiry, and again the

Government gave the go-ahead for a
revised office scheme.

The community group fought on,
forming alliances with the local
authorities, Southwark and Lambeth, and
exploiting the planning process.
Eventually, the office developers pulled out
and sold their land holding to the GLC.
One of the last acts of Ken Livingstone's
administration was to sell the freehold of
the entire Coin Street site to the non-profit
community group for £1 million. Since
then, the group has gone on to provide
more than 1,000 homes, a craft market,
open green space, landscaped gardens, a
river walkway and is now masterminding
perhaps the most exciting factory
refurbishment in London.

It is a success story that contrasts
strikingly with the anonymous yuppie
enclaves further down river in Docklands.
Coin Street Community Builders won
where Olympia & York lost.

Source: adapted from The Observer,
5 February 1995, p. 13

Chapter summary

❖ The term 'community' is interpreted
in many different ways. It has been
suggested that 'community' should be
abandoned and replaced with 'locales'
or 'localities'. However, these are also
controversial. We must examine closely
how sociologists use such terms and the
values this incorporates.

❖ Large-scale urbanization in Western
societies began in the nineteenth century
with the development of industrial
capitalism. Marxists have argued that the

city continues to reflect and satisfy
the needs of the economic system.

❖ Many theorists have argued that
modernization has led to a 'loss of
community'. However the discovery
of 'urban villages' revealed that
communities can exist, even in the
face of rapid economic transformation.
Conflicts were also found in both rural
and urban places.

❖ Wirth argued that cities developed a
distinctive way of life. However, the

evidence above and the effects of counter-urbanization suggest the separation of rural and urban life styles is too simplistic. Moreover, both rural and urban places need to be understood in the wider context of the socio-economic system. This now needs to be considered on the global scale.

❖ Different social groups are segregated into different areas of cities. The Chicago School used an ecological framework to explain this. Neo-Weberians have shown the importance of urban managers in controlling access to housing and devised the idea of 'housing classes'. Marxists have rejected this and believe that residential segregation can be explained by referring to the inequalities generated by capitalism. The concept of the 'underclass' is also used to explain the housing position of ethnic minorities.

❖ Both Neo-Marxists and Neo-Weberians have focused upon the conflicts found in urban and rural communities. Manuel Castells emphasized the importance of social movements involving collective consumption. However, it is now recognized that urban and rural conflicts are far more varied. Sociologists are now increasingly concerned with environmentalism and new social movements.

❖ Sociologists are interested in how large-scale social and economic changes affect different places. Locality studies revealed that economic restructuring is experienced and responded to in unique ways. Restructuring has caused particular problems for inner cities and this has led to controversial government intervention.

❖ The importance of community in contemporary society is debatable. Communitarians call for a return to 'traditional' community life. Postmodernists suggest that 'real' communities have declined, but modern society provides the possibility for individuals to use the idea of community in an imaginative way in the creation of identity. However, community can be seen as restricting individual freedom and generating conflict since it requires the exclusion of those deemed to be different. However, there still appears to be a widespread desire for community in contemporary life.

Coursework

Communities and localities offer many possibilities for coursework since just by living in a place you have ease of access to a wealth of material. For students of geography it also provides titles that could be appropriate in this subject as well as sociology.

The census provides information on the social characteristics of particular places. Since it is longitudinal you can examine changes that have occurred and support this with more qualitative research on how people perceive change in their area. For example, you could investigate the experiences of 'newcomers' and 'locals' in a village that has undergone counter-urbanization.

Another possibility is to examine the significance of a localized conflict, perhaps concerning a development project or environmental issue. You could seek to apply the ideas of new social movements or community as a symbolic boundary to these particular circumstances. This could involve a wide range of methods, including participating in meetings or protests, although you will need to be aware of the legality of such activities. It may also lend itself to the contents analysis of local media reports, survey and informal interviews.

There are many other suitable topics. However, always ensure you check the feasibility of your project with you course tutor.

Essay questions

1 Critically examine the view that de-urbanization has blurred the distinctions between rural and urban life. (AEB 1996)

2 Assess sociological explanations of both social problems and social conflict in cities. (AEB 1996)

3 To what extent have sociological studies supported the popular stereotype of the countryside as an idyllic alternative to the stresses and strains of living in cities? (AEB 1995)

4 Evaluate the usefulness of the concept of housing classes in explaining why ethnic minorities are generally over represented in inner-city areas. (AEB1995)

5 'Because the concept of community is defined in so many different ways, it is of little use to an understanding of rural and urban life in modern society'. Critically discuss this statement with reference to relevant sociological studies. (AEB 1994)

6 Compare and contrast Weberian and Marxist approaches to urban sociology. (AEB 1993)

7 Assess the different ways in which sociologists have attempted to explain the apparent loss of community in modern society. (AEB1992)

 Further reading

Books which cover most of the material necessary in this topic in a general way include:

Knox, P. (1992) *Urban Social Geography: An Introduction*, London: Longman.

Slattery, M. (1990) 'Urban Sociology', in *New Directions, Themes and Perspectives in Sociology*, Ormskirk: Causeway Press.

Mellor, R. (1992) *Change in Urban Life, Issues in Sociology*, London: Nelson.

Savage, M. and Warde, A. (1993) *Urban Sociology, Capitalism and Modernity*, London: Macmillan.

More specific articles focusing on contemporary debates include:

Day, G. (1995) 'Community, locality and social identity', in *Developments in Sociology*, 12, Ormskirk: Causeway Press.

Payne, G. (1994) 'Community and Community Studies', *Sociology Review*, 4(1).

Bagguley, P. (1993) *Urban Sociology, Developments in Sociology*, 9, Ormskirk: Causeway Press.

Chapter 10

Health, poverty and welfare

❖ Preview

This chapter covers several large and important topics: health, poverty and welfare. Although the AEB syllabus treats health as separate from poverty and welfare, there are significant overlaps and links between the topics, and we have therefore included them all in this chapter.

❖ The topic of *health* is covered between pages 411 and 457.

❖ *Poverty* and *welfare* are covered on pages 458 to 473.

In this chapter we shall look at:

❖ health and illness as social constructs

❖ variations in health, illness and health care by class, gender, age, ethnicity and region

❖ sociological explanations of the social variations in health

❖ the development of public and private health care

❖ mental health

❖ the different ways poverty has been defined and measured

❖ the different sociological explanations given for poverty and the evaluations of them

❖ the role of the welfare state and an assessment of its success in reducing and eliminating poverty.

❖ Health: Introduction

'How are you? Are you well?' These are familiar greetings which we know are only making a vague reference to physical and other aspects of our well-being. As sociologists we are interested in breaking down more precisely what individuals in different social groups and cultures mean by 'health' and 'illness'. Whereas health in a simple sense can be regarded as the absence of disease, illness refers to the subjective feelings of an individual. When analysing the idea of health and illness as social

constructs, sociologists recognise the enormous variety of definitions both culturally and historically. They are interested in explaining why a person's chances of living a long and healthy life are just as much determined by social characteristics as they are by biological ones. The pattern and distribution of health and illness across society shows great inequalities and this has aroused both political and sociological concern. This means another important area that we need to investigate is government policy and the significance of both the NHS and the private health-care systems. The medical profession and health issues are of great public interest. If we look at the TV listings for any one week, we find numerous medical dramas and documen- taries. Your study of the sociology of health will give you greater insight into this funda- mental aspect of everyday life and allow you to challenge some of the common assumptions made about health and the medical profession.

 ## The social construction of health and illness

If you are a keep-fit enthusiast, you may see health as being equated with physical fitness. The body builder may equate it with the strength and definition of muscle tone, the swimmer with the ability to do a certain number of lengths of the pool. For others, health may be associated not with physical activities, but with the ability to relax and switch off from life's pressures. For those with disabilities, it may be about the ability to cope with job or family expectations.

❖ Activity 1 ❖

Read through the following list of statements about health and tick those which seem to you to be important aspects of health. Tick as many as you like.

For me, 'being healthy' means:

1 Following my doctor's orders ☐
2 Being able to cope with the pressures of life ☐
3 Enjoying a satisfactory sexual relationship ☐
4 Feeling in harmony with nature and the universe ☐
5 Being able to cope with changes in my life, such as bereavement ☐
6 Being objective and seeing things in perspective ☐
7 Accepting myself and the different sides of my personality ☐
8 Taking regular exercise ☐
9 Having access to medical treatment when I need it ☐
10 Rarely getting colds, and then only getting mild symptoms ☐
11 Being the ideal weight for my height ☐

12 Living until I am in my eighties ☐
13 Being free of physical pain ☐
14 Never having a major illness or accident ☐
15 Being open and able to trust people ☐
16 Getting on well with my parents and family ☐
17 Being able to do what is expected of me, at home and at work ☐
18 Going to the doctor or dentist for routine check-ups ☐
19 Being able to relax and enjoy my hobbies ☐
20 Not having any bad habits, such as smoking or taking drugs ☐
21 Being able to recognize and express my feelings ☐
22 Eating a balanced diet ☐

Now add statements about any other aspects of health which you think are important.

On your completed table write the letters P, M or S to indicate whether you consider each statement to be mainly concerned with physical (P), mental (M) or social (S) health.

Referring to your completed chart, assess whether you tend to see health as mainly physical, mainly mental or mainly social?

Compare your views of health with others.

It is clear that there are many different approaches and definitions of health and therefore a corresponding variety of explanations of ill health. Leslie (1980) has developed a threefold classification to simplify the complexity of health models.

1 *Mechanistic* – where the body is regarded as a machine and illness is seen as functional breakdown

2 *Naturalistic* – theories which emphasize holism and balances of forces which are thought to control physical and mental well-being

3 *Ethical* – theories which see illness as divine or supernatural retribution, and health as a reward for living in a correct manner.

The biomedical approach

This approach is dominant in Western societies and is a *mechanistic* definition of health. According to Engel (1977) this view includes: 'the notion of the body as machine, disease as the consequence of breakdown of the machine, and the doctor's task as repair of the machine...' Disease or genetic factors are seen as the cause of ill-health. If you consider your last visit to the doctor you will have been asked to describe your symptoms. If you said you had a sore throat then you would expect the doctor to examine it in order to diagnose the problem and give you a prescription that specifically dealt with sore throats. In this way health is seen as an objective fact with identifiable biological causes – medicine's concerns are treating symptoms in a neutral, rational, scientific way. Here, health is regarded as the absence of disease.

❖ **Activity 2** ❖

1 Think about the last time you visited the doctor and the kind of questions you were asked. Was the focus on one particular aspect of your health, or was there concern for your general well-being?

2 Were you given a general examination or was it restricted to the particular area of complaint?

3 To what extent does your own experience confirm the description of biomedicine outlined above?

4 Two positive definitions of health are illustrated below.

  (a) Compare these definitions with that of Biomedicine.

  (b) Which definition is closest to your own understanding of health?

In Focus

◆

The WHO view of health

The World Health Organisation (WHO) 1984 proposed a concept of health as:

'the extent to which an individual or group is able, on the one hand, to realize aspirations and satisfy needs; and on the other hand to change or cope with the environment. Health is, therefore, seen as a resource for everyday life, not the objective of living; it is a positive concept emphasizing social and personal resources, as well as physical capacities.'

Source: WHO/EURO (1984)

Wellness is Fun, Romantic and Hip, Sexy and Free

Holistic Health T Shirt

The response of biomedicine

The BMA (British Medical Association) has responded to some of the criticisms levelled against biomedicine. In 1986 a BMA report claimed that alternative practices were a fad which could be ignored but by 1993 they were recommending that such 'discrete therapies' as chiropractic, herbalism, homeopathy and acupuncture should be registered. The need to treat people as a whole is increasingly recognized, e.g. stress caused by social and environmental conditions is seen as having physical effects and the need to have a less clinical approach in relation to terminal illness and childbirth is now taken as good practice.

Since 1991 British GPs have been able to delegate patients to be treated by therapists on the NHS (as long as the doctor remains clinically accountable) and to send their patients for treatment at one of the five NHS homeopathic hospitals. By 1992 1,700 GPs were employing alternative practitioners and many are themselves now training in acupuncture and other therapies.

This shift has not just been taking place in the UK; Fischer and Warde (1994) comment on the almost complete integration of osteopathy with conventional practices in the USA. In France 80 per cent of homeopathic medicine is on prescription. Although biomedicine remains the dominant definition of health, the increased acceptability of alternative models has led to them being called 'complementary' in recognition of their role alongside conventional treatments.

Alternative, cultural and traditional models of health

The biomedical approach has been strongly criticized for assuming that health and illness can be defined objectively.

> 'The fact of health is a cultural fact in the broadest sense of the term, which is to say at once political, economic, and social. Which is to say it's bound up with a certain state of the individual and collective consciousness. Each period has its own notion of normality.' (Foucault 1983, p. 175)

It can even be claimed that where a symptom is common it will be defined as 'normal' rather than as an illness. For example, tiredness in Western societies is generally seen as the result of a busy life style and something that should be tolerated. Different cultures can interpret the symptoms of disease in different ways. Evans-Pritchard (1980) shows that among the Azande people, illness was defined as a matter of a person being inflicted with a spell. The ill person is diagnosed by a Shaman who, after much consultation regarding the victim's likely enemies, reads the entrails of a chicken in order to identify the witch. Accusations can then be made and the spell lifted. Although such beliefs may appear irrational from our own cultural perspective, Evans-Pritchard emphasizes that they make perfect sense to the Azande. Many examples illustrating the cross-cultural variation in perceptions of health can be found in *Culture Health and Illness* by C.G. Helman (1990).

Traditional models of health are based upon very different premises to biomedicine. For example, prior to the dominance of the scientific approach, much of Western medicine was influenced by the Greek legacy that the human body comprised four humours, blood, phlegm, yellow bile and black bile (see Fig. 10.1 opposite and the cartoon on the left).

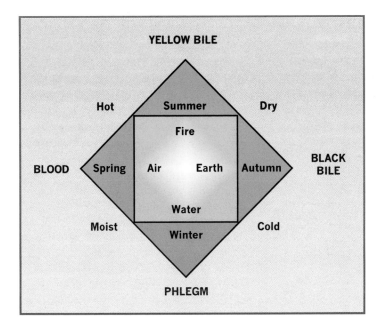

YELLOW BILE

Hot · Summer · Dry

Fire

BLOOD · Spring · Air · Earth · Autumn · BLACK BILE

Water

Moist · Winter · Cold

PHLEGM

Figure 10.1
The Greek theory of the four humours

and illness mean that it is impossible to take health as something which is self-evidently biological. Health must be viewed as a social construct.

❖ Activity 3 ❖

Look at Fig. 10.1, the cartoon on p. 414 and the *In Focus* below. How would you classify each: as mechanistic, naturalistic or ethical?

In essay style, explain with examples why historical and cross-cultural evidence can be used to justify the sociological argument that health is a social construct. Your work should be no more than two sides of A4 paper.

If all the humours were in balance, then the person would enjoy good health. If they were not, the role of the physician was to restore balance by means such as purges and blood-letting, combined with herbal remedies. Similar notions are found in Chinese and Indian models of health which also emphasize the need to consider the emotional and spiritual aspects of the person and not just the physical symptoms. In Chinese medicine a person's well-being is determined by the balance of Yin and Yang energy. Yang represents the forces of heat, fire and light and so any excess will be shown by fever. Yin, on the other hand, represents cold, damp and dark forces, and too much Yin may produce colds and chills. These examples of cross-cultural and tradi-tional variations in understanding health

Variations in perceptions of health within societies

The socially constructed nature of health and illness can also be shown by the fact that even within one society different understandings are used by different groups of people and any individual may use any number of health explanations depending upon their circumstances. Many of us will accept the principles of biomedicine but also use such ideas 'as wrap up warm or you will catch a cold'. We are well aware that colds are transmitted by germs but this does not mean that other models of health are excluded. Individual perceptions of health and illness, rather than the professional view, have become an increasing focus of sociological research.

In Focus
◆
Bangkok, Thailand: 3-year-old faith healer

'Police used roadblocks at the week-end to stop a 3-year-old faith healer using 'magic' tree bark to draw thousands of peasants to his village.

Aided by lavish media attention, he drew crowds to pay 20 baht (50p) for a bowl with candles, incense and the bark. Some came in chartered buses from as far away as Bangkok, 150 miles to the south-west.

His parents, interviewed in the Ban Muang daily, said that the boy could heal because a divine doctor had possessed him. Belief in spirits is widely prevalent in Thailand. A senior ministry official warned the public that their illness might worsen if they chose supernatural over proper treatment.'

Source: The Guardian, 11 August 1986

A study by Blaxter and Patterson (1982) found a functional definition of health amongst Aberdeen working-class women. The women reported they were ill only when they could not perform their usual activities, paid work, housework, childcare, etc. The quote below indicates that many women reported their health as satisfactory despite disability and discomfort.

'After I was sterilized, I had a lot of cystitis, and backache, because of my fibroids. Then when I had the hysterectomy, I had bother wi' my water works because my bladder had a life of its own and I had to have a repair ... Healthwise I would say I was OK. I did hurt my shoulder – I mean this is nothing to do with health but I actually now have a disability, I get a gratuity payment every six months ... I wear a collar and take valium ... then just the headaches – but I'm not really off work a lot with it.' (Blaxter and Patterson 1982, p. 29)

The study referred to above shows that the working-class women had very low expectations of health and believed the cause of their illness lay outside their control. However, D'Houtaud and Field (1984) found that the French middle class had a more positive, holistic perception of health which included the belief that the individual could intervene and take responsibility for their own well-being.

❖ Activity 4 ❖

Coursework suggestion

The aim of your research is to find out how non-professional people view health. You could either:

1 Ask people their views on the causes of some common complaints (for example, headaches, colds, spots, stiff joints, etc.) and what they consider to be appropriate treatment strategies.

2 Ask people what they mean by being in 'good' health.

You could extend this in a comparative way by doing the tasks described below.

3 Ask similar questions to professional health promoters, such as nurses, health workers, doctors, pharmacists, health education workers and showing the difference in responses.

You will need to prepare carefully for this research and should refer to Chapter 7 on research methods before you start.

You need to consider the following questions:

• What will your *sample* size and type be? You may wish to concentrate on differences by age, gender, social class or ethnicity.

• What *methods* will you use? Questionnaires? Interviews? Diaries?

• How will you *implement* these methods? Face to face? Group? Tape recording? Postal?

• What *ethical issues* does your project raise?

• How will you *present* your results? As a graph, text, or as a written or oral presentation to a group?

You should discuss these issues fully and provide a written justification for your chosen approach.

Finally, you should evaluate the success of your research and identify how it could have been improved or developed.

Alternative or complementary medicines

Alternative models of health and illness have always co-existed with the biomedical view. Interest in traditional and alternative approaches has grown rapidly (particularly in those of Eastern origin) with sales of alternative medicines in the UK increasing from £20.7 million in 1988 to £32.5 million in 1992. Sharma (1992) gives survey evidence that half the French population and a quarter to a third of the British have used non-biomedical treatments. In Britain there are well over 100 alternative medical treatments with over 90,000 practitioners. The most popular are acupuncture, homeopathy, osteopathy, and herbalism. Others, such as aromatherapy, reflexology, shiatsu, crystal healing and colour therapy, are also attracting more followers. They tend to focus on the patient as a whole person, with many claiming to work by utilising the body's own healing power and/or by using natural herbal remedies. Again, this plurality of perspectives indicate that health is as much a social construction as biological fact.

Alternative medicine: just marginal, or a challenge to biomedicine?

Sharma investigated this issue by interviewing 30 people from the Stoke-on-Trent area who had used one form of alternative medicine in the past 12 months. Her sample was obtained by inviting readers of a local newspaper to volunteer their experiences. Sharma found five main reasons why people turned to alternative medicine:

❖ Some thought that biomedicine emphasised the treatment of symptoms and failed to get at the root cause of an illness or failed to be preventative. The respondents appreciated the healer tackling the problem at what they considered to be a fundamental level.

❖ Some were afraid that conventional drugs could be addictive and disliked the prospect or experience of side effects.

Others felt that the drugs available, e.g. antibiotics, were too powerful for their current need which meant that if they really needed them in the future they would be less effective. One of the appeals of alternative treatments was their perceived lack of side effects.

❖ Some felt that treatment offered by their doctor was too radical or invasive.

❖ Some thought that conventional medicine had failed to fully respect their experience of illness and its social effects. The healers were thought to be more aware of their patients' distress and respondents appreciated the lengthy consultations that were given.

❖ Many respondents were dissatisfied with the usual doctor/patient relationship present in biomedicine. They felt alternative medicines gave a more active role to the patient.

Sharma found that if someone experienced success with one alternative therapy they were likely to turn to other forms of alternative treatment, however, they rarely gave up biomedicine entirely, particularly where serious illness was concerned. Rather, they operated with different models of health in different combinations in different contexts with the main reason given for using alternative treatments as dissatisfaction with conventional medicine. Sharma concludes that the use of alternative therapies is not a minor issue and that many of those who have not used alternative practitioners have similar dissatisfactions with the nature of the dominant biomedical approach.

❖ Activity 5 ❖

Explain why the way Sharma obtained her sample could lead to questions concerning the reliability of her findings.

With reference to Chapter 7, suggest and justify an alternative way of selecting a sample suitable for this project.

In Focus

◆

**Perspectives
on comple-
mentary
therapies**

'Anyone can set up as a complementary practitioner or therapist. Doctors, nurses and certain state-registered professionals (e.g. dentists and physiotherapists) must by law have a certain minimum training before they can practise. But there are no government requirements for training in complementary medicine.

Some complementary practitioners choose to join registering bodies which require certain levels of training. But there may be several bodies for any one therapy, all of them claiming to register practitioners. For many therapies there is no agreement on the training required to be a competent practitioner. And some practitioners are not registered with any organization.

How does this affect you? If a practitioner isn't properly trained his or her treatment could injure you. Alternatively, he or she may not spot a problem which should be seen by a doctor.'

Source: Which? Way to Health?

'Some doctors are sceptical about the benefits of complementary medicine, even though many people say that they have been helped by it. The problem is that few rigorous trials have been used to text the effects. Why? There are genuine difficulties testing some therapies – though not as many as some people make out. But in the end, the standard of proof that some doctors demand before they will accept a complementary treatment works is more than many conventional procedures have undergone.

Most evidence on the benefits of complementary medicine is anecdotal – individual examples which don't always add up to firm scientific proof.'

Source: 'Alternative Medicine on Trial', *Which? Way to Health?* 1992

Ouch! £3 billion a year:
That's what the alternative bad back doctors could save the NHS

'Bad backs cost Britain £3 billion a year – and 67 million lost days annually. Osteopaths claim they can save the country all that pain, lost time, and cash with the kind of treatment which just doesn't exist on the NHS. Herbalists believe that alternative therapies could wipe millions of Britain's drug bill.

Yet just 15 years ago, according to Graham Mason, chairman of the General Council and Register of Osteopaths, a GP who referred a patient to an osteopath could be struck off. And other alternative therapists are considered to be witch doctors by some conventional doctors.

Source: Glasgow Evening Times, 1993

❖ Activity 6 ❖

Sociology requires you to develop skills of evaluation. Using the extracts given in the *In Focus* on p. 418, the text, and your own knowledge and research, discuss the arguments for and against alternative medicines. You may wish to consider the effectiveness of different treatments in different circumstances.

A postmodernist view

Can biomedicine really be the only complete explanation of health and illness? Postmodernists view contemporary society as highly fragmented and changeable. It is made up of a many different groups of people with great variations in experience and outlook. Baudrillard (1988) argues that in this fluidity science is becoming increasingly mistrusted in its ability to offer full explanations of phenomena. People in an age of mass communications have access to a huge variety of models of health from which they can choose. Biomedicine is no longer the only legitimate model of health and may be 'bought into' or 'out of' depending on individual choice and circumstance.

One of the interests of postmodernists is how the various models of health attract different levels of esteem and importance. The *In Focus* below outlines the postmodernist view of how this has happened.

Thus, postmodernists see biomedicine as socially created knowledge like any other. In contemporary society the dominance it has achieved is being resisted. In addition to the use of alternative medicines, other examples of resistance are discussed below.

The power of the profession

Members of the British Medical Association (BMA) and The Royal College have privileges as a result of being in the medical

In Focus

◆

Discourse

'Power is of crucial concern to postmodernists. Power is not necessarily tied to the economic controllers (capitalists) – it is more subtle ... Knowledge about the body becomes power – those who have the knowledge must ensure that others believe it to be a form of knowledge that is superior to their own.

The possessors of this knowledge can then exercise control over others: doctors can claim that their knowledge of the body is superior to their patients ...

Paul Bellaby analysed the way people in a pottery factory took time off for illness. Medical discourse (a doctor's way of understanding the body and phrasing explanations about the body) tends to carry status for many people. In Bellaby's study, doctors were shown to "medicalize" problems occasionally in order to allow women to have paid time off work. Morning sickness during pregnancy became "hyperemisis" and stress caused by looking after people at home was called "anxiety state". These examples may be viewed as positive (to workers).

However, medical discourse has also medicalized human conditions such as being overweight (obesity), being sad (depression) and being worried (anxiety). We might ask what effect the medicalization of these conditions has on individuals who view themselves as obese, anxious or depressed? In addition, Oakley, in *Women, Medicine and Health* (1993), claims that the medical "profession" has medicalized childbirth, making it a "medical" problem rather than a natural process. Women are encouraged to give birth to their children in hospital rather than at home. We might ask whose interests are being best served by requiring that women give birth in hospital?'

Source: Senior (1996)

profession that other occupations envy. Doctors can expect a high salary, prestige, and freedom to carry out their work with relatively little outside interference. Their professional organization (the BMA) ensures that recruitment is controlled so that over-supply never threatens pay or status and in times of trouble it insulates the individual from criticism and accountability since it is largely self-policing. In effect, the power of individual doctors results from the position of medicine as a social institution which has achieved its rights and authority by being granted legal recognition by govern-ments. It can be argued that the reason biomedicine is the dominant definition of health is due to its political rather than medical superiority, which allows it to define other approaches as having less value. If it is accepted that the medical profession has power then we need to ask how this power has been achieved and in whose interests it works. In answering these questions we will draw on a number of contrasting theoretical perspectives which emphasize the role of medicine as a form of social and ideological control.

Pfeffer (1987) gives a contemporary example of professional power. She suggests that the definition of infertility as an illness resulting in desperation on the part of the childless is more useful to the professional than it is to the patients who are generally perfectly healthy. Pfeffer claims:

'We know that these doctors and scientists want to be able to continue *in vitro* fertilization and embryo transfer. These professionals have claimed that the new methods of assisting reproduction are indispensable in their endeavours to help their infertile patients ... What we do not know is if this same desire is shared by the majority of men and women who are infertile, most of whom will not undergo *in vitro* fertilization and embryo transfer.'

It is cynical to assume that all the professionals involved in IVF are purely motivated by status and funding for their high-tech and expensive treatments. However, it does raise the issue that the professionals' power to define infertility as a desperate condition does effectively stigmatize those involved and fails to consider the complexity of people's responses and even the positive benefits to be had from being childless.

❖ Activity 7 ❖

Discuss the view that the definition of infertility as an illness and its medicalization is more to the advantage of professionals than it is to the 'patients'.

Conflict approaches to health and illness

Ivan Illich

Illich (1976) argues that the power of medicine in industrial societies is under-mining the freedom and ability of the individual to take responsibility for themselves. He suggests that modern medicine is literally a 'sickening' force which actually creates illness.

'A vast amount of clinical care is incidental to the curing of disease, but the damage done by medicine to the health of individuals and populations is very significant. These facts are obvious, well documented and well repressed.'

Illich identifies three kinds of 'iatrogenesis', i.e. illness caused by health care in industrial societies:

❖ *Clinical* – resulting from harmful medical intervention, e.g. poor surgery, side effects and addiction to drugs. Well-known examples include the thalidomide scandal of the 1960s where the drug caused severe deformities.

❖ *Social* – including the medicalization of fertility and pregnancy. It means social problems, such as abortion and surrogacy, become medical and technical problems to be dealt with by doctors rather than society at large.

❖ *Cultural* – involving individuals giving up their independence and allowing experts to control their lives, which means they lose the capacity to deal with human weakness and vulnerability in a personal way.

Illich (1976) discounts the grand claims of biomedicine as ideological. In support of this notion, McKeown (1976) has shown that the fall in the death rate in the last two centuries has more to do with improvements in nutrition, public health and improvements in people's general living conditions and environment.

❖ Activity 8 ❖

Think of examples from your own experience and knowledge that would support or refute the views of Illich.

Neo-Marxism

Neo-Marxist theorists like Vincente Navarro (1978) agree with the criticisms of biomedicine offered by Illich. However, they emphasize that this definition of health and the institutions for health care in capitalist society have an important role in preserving the interests of the dominant class, e.g:

❖ The medical profession serves as a gatekeeper, a means to define those who are officially sick and so unable to work. Part of their role is to control the workforce.

❖ The medical profession serves the needs of capitalism by maintaining a healthy workforce which increases productivity and profit.

❖ The medical profession is a major consumer of the products of capitalism. High-tech medicine requires a massive industry in terms of drugs and equipment and these need constant updating. O'Rourke (1994) points out that one of the ways to save one and a half million children's lives would be to provide rehydration salts for victims of diarrhoea at a cost of $500,000. However given the rationality of capitalism there is not much profit to be had in selling 20-cent packets of salts to the world's poor.

❖ Biomedicine defines illness as a result of individual misfortune or failure to follow a healthy life style. The values of biomedicine are very close to those of capitalism itself. No consideration is given to the wider social context which has generated most illnesses. Thus, a depressed patient is drugged or counselled so that they can cope with the social system which has made them ill. Valium is another means to combat revolution.

❖ Another aspect of ideological control is the cultivation of the belief that medical science can provide the answers and solutions to what are really problems generated by the inequalities of capitalism.

❖ The existence of a state health service further legitimates 'caring capitalism'. Doctors are an essential tool in supporting the health-damaging capitalist system. They are part of the public relations system of the ruling class and in return for their services they are rewarded with high status, high income and protection from criticism.

Feminism

One of the weaknesses of the perspectives described above is that they have failed to consider the particular experiences of women and biomedicine, the rise of which in the mid-nineteenth century meant that for the first time professional health care was dominated by men. Childbirth and pregnancy became defined as a medical complaint with women as maternity cases in the hands of expert male practitioners and midwives having to be supervised by doctors. Feminists argue that the biomedical model, with its concerns for functions, turned women into reproductive machines. Just as biomedicine serves to control the productive power of the working class, so too it controls the reproductive power of women. However, we must be wary of viewing women as passive in this process of medicalization and of denying its benefits in reducing risk during childbirth.

Like neo-Marxists, radical feminists see biomedicine as legitimating inequality. The example of 'hysteria' described on p. 452 shows how the medical profession could be useful in protecting patriarchy by defining women who tried to defy cultural views of femininity as abnormal. A further

ideological role of biomedicine is that it can create a smoke-screen to hide the social reasons lying behind ailments which particularly affect women.

❖ Activity 9 ❖

To what extent would you agree that the different women shown in the photos below are victims of patriarchal imagery? Write a paragraph outlining your views.

In Focus

◆

Eating disorders: the search for the perfect body?

Ninety per cent of cases of anorexia and bulimia affect women between 13 and 18 years old. The majority are above average intelligence. Feminists see significance in the incidence of the disease being related to adolescence when pressures to conform to cultural definitions of femininity become most acute. They argue that the high value placed on physical beauty can generate illness. Self-esteem is linked to how people perceive themselves and how they would ideally like to be. The ideal self is partly constructed from the cultural values concerning physical appearance. In modern societies the mass media is very important in conveying the image of the beautiful body. Where there is a wide gap between an individual's perception of real self and ideal self then anxiety and possibly eating disorders can occur.

Radical feminists argue that what is beautiful is defined by men and is a means by which women are controlled. This is rather a conspiratorial approach, yet the coincidence of a 360 per cent rise in

anorexia between 1985 and 1995 in the USA and the emphasis on thinness illustrated by 'superwaifs' like Kate Moss lend support to the feminist argument that eating disorders are an exaggerated response to the cultural demand that women should be thin. Similarly the willingness of women to undergo cosmetic surgery in order to achieve what is perceived as physical perfection shows how much women feel they are judged by how they look.

Orbach (1989), whilst recognizing that media imagery is significant, believes that eating disorders are a way of controlling life and fighting for independence: they should not be seen as slimming diseases but a means of surviving in a patriarchal social system.

Supermodel, Kate Moss

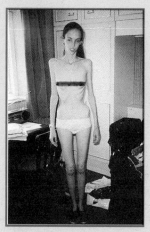

An anorexic woman

In Focus

◆

What every woman knows

Half the women on the pill in Britain were warned this week that the brands they use may be harmful...

'There has never been more emphasis on drug safety than today and public expectations of medicine have never been so high. But there is no such thing as an absolutely safe drug or medicine. With the pill, it is a question of balancing the small risk associated with it against the side-effects and risks associated with alternative contraceptives and with pregnancy should birth-control fail.

So, how risky are the seven 'third generation' pills singled out by the Government's drug safety committee? A lot depends on age, weight and family history of potentially dangerous blood-clotting.

What about smoking, long blamed for fatal complications in pill users? Smokers are not more likely to suffer from venous blood clotting which occurs in the leg and then causes a fatal blockage in the lung. However, they should not be lulled into a sense of false security. A heavy smoker on the pill has a 20-fold increase in risk of having a heart attack.

How many deaths are linked to the pill? It is estimated that 18 women a year die as a result of it, but there are more than three million users. And often forgotten are important non-contraceptive benefits. Top of the list must be protection against cancer of the ovary, which kills 4,000 women a year, and cancer of the womb lining, which kills about 2,000 a year.'

Source: The Guardian, 'Outlook', 21 October 1995

Figure 10.2
Comparing risks

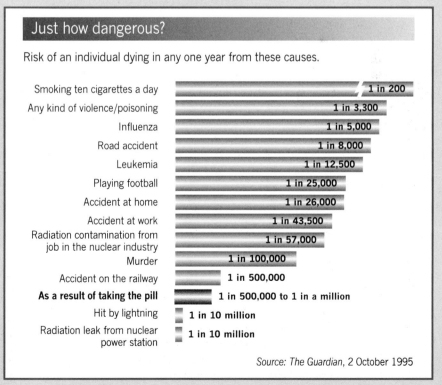

Just how dangerous?

Risk of an individual dying in any one year from these causes.

Smoking ten cigarettes a day	1 in 200
Any kind of violence/poisoning	1 in 3,300
Influenza	1 in 5,000
Road accident	1 in 8,000
Leukemia	1 in 12,500
Playing football	1 in 25,000
Accident at home	1 in 26,000
Accident at work	1 in 43,500
Radiation contamination from job in the nuclear industry	1 in 57,000
Murder	1 in 100,000
Accident on the railway	1 in 500,000
As a result of taking the pill	1 in 500,000 to 1 in a million
Hit by lightning	1 in 10 million
Radiation leak from nuclear power station	1 in 10 million

Source: The Guardian, 2 October 1995

❖ Activity 10 ❖

Looking at the *In Focus* on p. 423 and Fig. 10.2, discuss to what extent the case of the contraceptive pill supports the conflict approaches discussed above.

Take time to interpret the sources and apply the theoretical arguments. You should produce a short essay approximately one to two sides of A4.

Becoming sick

The biological causes of sickness are not the concern of sociology but we have much to learn by investigating the social processes involved in becoming ill. Sickness and bodily examinations are times when we feel vulnerable and we hope to be treated with care and sensitivity. One of the things that we all look for in a doctor is a good bedside manner. This means that the relationship between the professionals and their patients is an important sociological issue.

The sick role: A functionalist view

We have already seen that Marxists and postmodernists, among others, have commented on the power of doctors to identify who is genuinely ill and to officially exempt people from work. Although taking a very different theoretical position, Talcott Parsons (1951) also recognizes the importance of the professionals in allowing people to drop out of their normal life for a while and take on the new role of being sick.

❖ Activity 11 ❖

Reflect on the last time you had flu.

- How did others respond to you – parents, friends, teachers, employers, colleagues?
- What things were you allowed to do because you were ill that would be less approved of if you were well?
- What things did you no longer have to do because you were ill?

It is likely that your answers to the questions in Activity 11 show that having flu is not always that bad! You may well be able to lie in bed all day, not have to go to work or school and be pampered by a sympathetic carer. For Parsons, taking the sick role allows people temporarily to suspend their normal roles and responsibilities in a socially acceptable way, thereby minimizing social disruption. However, being sick does entail obligations. The patient must wish to get better and take steps to hasten their recovery. Once a certain amount of time has passed, the patience of others is likely to wear thin and the person who is sick will be expected to seek professional help and go along with their advice. Patients who fail in these obligations may then be considered malingerers and the legitimacy of the sick role withdrawn.

Parsons also identifies two further characteristics of the sick role:

- ❖ The patient is in a vulnerable position and must put themselves in the hands of medical experts. In Parsons' view of the doctor–patient relationship the patient is compliant, passive and powerless.

- ❖ The sick are also deviant because they are no longer satisfying normal responsibilities. Just as in the neo-Marxist analysis above, an important function of health professionals is to sort out the work shy from 'real' cases of sickness. In this way Parsons agrees that the doctor is an important agent of social control, but this is socially beneficial rather than operating in the particular interests of a dominant social group.

Evaluation of Parsons' views

Parsons' work was one of the first to recognize the significance of the social expectations surrounding becoming sick. He showed that a biological analysis alone is inadequate and his concept of a sick role has been usefully employed in later micro-scale research. However a number of criticisms have been made:

❖ *Not every one accepts there is a sick role.*

Parsons' work can be accused of being deterministic as it implies that once sick, everyone slips into the sick role. This fails to recognize that people can refuse to see themselves as ill and carry on regardless. In cases where people are suffering from diseases which carry social disapproval, such as AIDS, people are likely to make a determined effort to avoid being labelled sick. Similarly, disabled people may refuse the sick role and demand the right to work and live independently. In sum, Parsons fails to give sufficient attention to individual choice and free will.

❖ *The legitimacy of the sick role does not apply in all cases.*

There are some illnesses which are seen as an individual's own fault. For example, AIDS has been associated with intravenous drug use and so sufferers do not deserve the sick role because they have engaged in socially disreputable lifestyles. Where such attitudes exist and the sick role is not legitimated, rights to care may also be withdrawn, e.g. there have been cases where smokers have been denied heart surgery.

❖ *The Doctor is not always God.*

Parsons is criticized for his view of the all-powerful doctor and the meekly subservient patient. Interactionists have emphasized that the relationship between doctor and patient is a negotiated one with both participants having active roles. There are also instances where patients have refused to accept doctors' diagnoses and have challenged the professionals. However, the accusation against Parsons that he sees the patient as powerless is somewhat unfair. He does recognize that there can be significant variations in patient influence, ranging from high doctor-control through equality of input to considerable patient control.

❖ *The sick role is only beneficial in some cases.*

Parsons' view of the sick role is more appropriate where the illness is curable. For example, many groups representing the disabled have campaigned against the level of dependency required by the sick role. For most people with an incurable illness or a disability, it is important to maintain as much normal functioning as possible, thereby avoiding the damaging effects of the learned helplessness of sick role.

Many of these criticisms of Parsons come from the interactionist perspective. We can see this in their concern for negotiated roles, individual choice, the effects of stigmatized labelling and the ability of people to develop strategies and variations in response to similar situations. These ideas can be seen in the theme of mental illness, as we shall see later.

We must be wary of assuming people's understanding of health purely by knowing their social background. Van Dalen *et al.* (1994) did not find clear class differences and believe that some of the earlier studies did not consider sufficiently the different abilities of social groups to understand the questions asked of the them, or the variations in their abilities to express complex abstract ideas to a middle-class interviewer. Recent research has adopted a more qualitative, ethnographic approach than the structured or semistructured interviews of previous work in order to gain insight into the way non-professionals' views of health are changeable depending upon the context. Stainton-Rogers (1991) recognizes the capacity of people to switch from one model of health to another. For example, finding a small wart on a child's hand may lead an individual to try the 'old wives' tale' of rubbing it with steak and burying the meat under a busy footpath. The wart may be left alone in the belief that it will do no harm and will drop off in its own good time. If it begins to look red and angry then a more biomedical approach is likely to be taken, mixed with 'praying to god' that it's not a melanoma (skin cancer). In this way health can be viewed as a relative concept with often contradictory models operating at different times and in different situations.

The social constructionist view of health: a cautionary note

The social constructionist approach has certainly moved the study of health beyond the physiological, and most people recognize the importance of social factors. However, Sheeran (1995) argues that perhaps the argument has been taken to extremes. She asks the question, 'Is illness only a social construction?', and summarizes key themes in the social constructionist view as follows:

❖ Concepts of health and illness vary, both cross-culturally and historically.

❖ The medical profession has the power to impose its 'biomedical', 'scientific' definitions of illness

❖ Illness can be compared with deviance, especially in relation to the defining of deviant behaviour as mental illness.

❖ Official statistics reflect social processes rather than 'real' rates of health and illness.

❖ Social and economic conditions, such as poverty, help create illness.

The first three of these themes relate to the material in this section of the chapter, whilst the last two are covered in the next section of this chapter.

Sheeran is highly critical of those who argue that biomedicine is no more valid than other models of health. While we are all likely at some time to have been dissatisfied with our medical treatment, these incidences should not blind us to the great health advancements achieved by scientific medicine generally and to the personal benefits we may receive from the cures and preventative knowledge derived from biomedicine. The strengths of biomedicine should not be ignored for the sake of ideological argument. Sheeran states that because biomedicine is based on rigorous scientific procedures then it can claim special status. Thus, although social constructionist approaches have offered a new dimension to the study of health they are in the process of revision, with a greater emphasis on realism.

❖ Activity 12 ❖

'Health and Illness must be viewed as social constructs rather than biological facts.' Assess the evidence for this view.

Before attempting this essay, look back at pp. 13–15 in Chapter 1. Follow the essay advice carefully. Aim to keep within four sides of A4 paper, so be clear about exactly what *evidence* you are going to present and evaluate.

Inequalities in health and illness

It will probably be of no great surprise for you to discover that the chance of a long and healthy life is dependent upon an individual's social characteristics. These characteristics include social class, ethnicity, gender, age and where you live. In the discussion below these are treated largely as independent variables although in reality they interact in very complex ways. Much of the research into health inequalities has been motivated by a sense of social injustice, with equal access to physical and mental well-being being regarded as a basic human right.

Two research landmarks into health inequalities in the UK were the *Black Report* (Department of Health and Social Security 1980) and the *Health Divide* (Whitehead

1987). Both were controversial since they identified the failure of the NHS to seriously address differences in health opportunities and claimed that the best explanations for such differences lay in the structure and unequal nature of British society. A 1993 Department of Health Report showed a greater willingness to accept the significance of social factors, highlighting that:

'In the last twenty years an extensive research literature ... has shown continuing, and in some cases increasing, differentials in mortality and morbidity rates between socio-economic groups, men and women, regions of the country and ethnic groups.' (DHSS 1993)

Measuring health inequalities

We have already seen that definitions of health and illness are socially variable. When something is difficult to define then problems of measurement arise because researchers can not agree exactly what should be measured. Apart from surveys which ask people whether they *feel* healthy there are few positive measures of health. Most researchers have concentrated on larger-scale health patterns and so there has been a tendency to rely on easily accessible official statistics.

Mortality and morbidity are both indicators of poor health. Mortality concerns death whereas morbidity concerns the social distribution of particular diseases. Mortality figures can be regarded as relatively reliable if very crude measures of health. They tell us about life expectancy but give little indication as to the quality of someone's health experiences whilst alive. Morbidity rates indicate the likelihood of social groups contracting particular ailments.

Like many official statistics, the figures are socially constructed and so cannot be taken at face value. The problems of these sources of data are discussed below.

Patterns of health by social class

It may be taken as self-evident that where there is poverty there will also be disease. We are all familiar with the distressing media images of people affected by malnutrition in less economically developed countries. We may also recognise that this was a common experience in Britain in Victorian times. We might expect that the high living-standards of twentieth century industrial societies and the existence of modern health-care systems would go some way to eradicate health differentials. Evidence suggests that this is not the case – see Table 10.1 and the *In Focus* overleaf.

Table 10.1 Deterioration in self-assessed health over 7 years

Percentage of Health and Lifestyle Survey respondents who said that their health was good in 1984/86, whose opinion had deteriorated to 'fair/poor' in 1991/92.

| | Age in 1991/2 | | | |
| | 25-45 | | 46-66 | |
	%	(N)	%	(N)
Men				
Non-manual social classes	11	(312)	11	(331)
Manual social classes	14	(359)	25	(321)
Women				
Non-manual social classes	10	(453)	13	(453)
Manual social classes	14	(485)	20	(364)

Source: Blaxter (1990)

In Focus

◆

Health fact file by social class

❖ Currently in the UK, life expectancy for men in professional and managerial occupations is 7 years more than for those who are unskilled.

❖ Infant mortality in social class 1 is half that of social class V.

❖ According to a report for the King Edwards Hospital Fund 'we estimate that the annual excess of avoidable deaths in the manual working class in men and women aged 16–74 between 1979 and 1983 was 42,000 people' (Jacobson *et al.* 1991).

❖ In 65 out of 78 categories of disease males in higher social classes were least likely to suffer the condition. For women this is the case for 62 out of 82 disease categories. Only skin cancer shows some reversal of this pattern.

❖ Young men, aged 25 to 44 in unskilled occupations have four times the risk of dying from lung cancer, stomach cancer and heart disease than professional workers.

❖ Power *et al.* (1991), when comparing social-class differences in health in the early years, found that, 'in childhood an overall relative risk of three for accidents and violence conceals differences of tenfold or more for deaths from falls, fires and drowning.'

Figure 10.3
Consumption of alcohol above sensible* levels: by gender and age, 1992

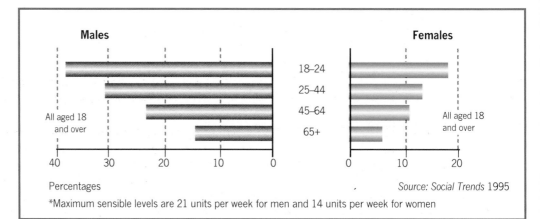

Source: Social Trends 1995

Percentages

*Maximum sensible levels are 21 units per week for men and 14 units per week for women

Figure 10.4
Death rates for people aged under 65: by gender and selected cause of death

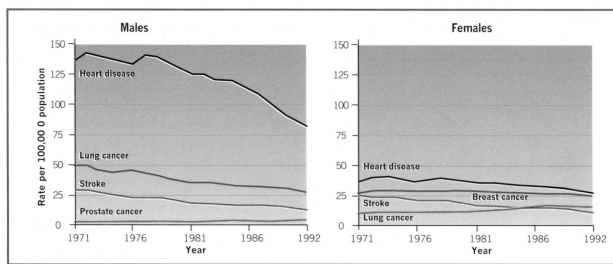

The latest Office of Population, Censuses and Surveys (OPCS) survey was one of four studies of psychiatric morbidity commissioned by the Government and carried out between April 1993 and August 1994. It found that the most prevalent neurotic disorder in the week before interview was mixed anxiety and depressive disorder, affecting 71 adults in every 1,000, followed by generalised anxiety disorder, affecting 30 per 1,000. All neurotic disorders were more common among women than men. Psychosis, mostly schizophrenia and manic depressive disorder, affected four people in every 1,000.

The overall rates of alcohol and drug dependence were 47 per 1,000 and 22 per 1,000 respectively. Men were three times more likely than women to be alcohol dependent and twice as likely to be drug dependent.

The survey also found that alcohol and drug dependence were most common among young adults, particularly men aged 16-24.

The survey covered a sample of 10,000 adults living in private households, plus a supplementary sample of 350 adults with psychosis living in private households.

Source: The Guardian, 15 December 1994

Table 10.2   Expectation of life: by gender and age

	1901	*1931*	*1961*	*1991*	*1992*	*1996*	*2001*	*2021*
Males								
At birth	45.5	57.7	67.8	73.2	73.6	74.4	75.4	77.6
At age								
1 year	54.6	62.4	69.5	73.8	74.1	74.8	75.7	77.9
10 years	60.4	65.2	69.9	73.9	74.3	75.0	75.9	78.0
20 years	61.7	66.3	70.3	74.2	74.5	75.3	76.1	78.2
40 years	66.1	69.3	71.4	75.1	75.4	76.3	77.2	79.3
60 years	73.3	74.3	74.9	77.7	77.9	78.6	79.5	81.4
80 years	84.9	84.7	85.2	86.4	86.5	86.8	87.2	88.2
Females								
At birth	49.0	61.6	73.6	78.7	79.0	79.7	80.6	82.6
At age								
1 year	56.8	65.3	75.1	79.2	79.5	80.1	80-9	82.8
10 years	62.7	67.9	75.4	79.4	79.6	80.3	81.1	83.0
20 years	64.1	69.0	75.6	79.5	79.8	80.4	81.2	83.1
40 years	68.3	71.9	76.3	80.0	80.2	80.9	81.7	83.5
60 years	74.6	76.1	78.8	81.9	82.1	82.6	83.3	84.9
80 years	85.3	85.4	86.3	88.3	88.5	88.8	89.1	90.0

[1] Total number of years which a person might expect to live.

Source: Social Trends (1995)

Table 10.3 Prevalence of cigarette smoking by sex and socio-economic group (%)

| | | Socio-economic group | | | | | | All over |
		A	B	C1	C2	D	E	16
Men	1972	33	44	45	57	57	64	52
	1984	17	29	30	40	45	49	36
	1990	16	24	25	36	39	48	31
Women	1972	33	38	38	47	42	42	42
	1984	15	29	28	37	37	36	32
	1990	16	23	27	32	36	36	29

Source: Social Trends (1993)

❖ Activity 13 ❖

Read the two *In Focus* panels on pp. 429 and 430, and study carefully Tables 10.1 to 10.3 and Figs 10.3 and 10.4.

1 Make a bullet-point list of variations in health by social class and gender.

2 For each point, try to explain why this variation has arisen.

Alternatively you could do this as a group activity:

1 Divide your group into two teams.

2 Spend 15 minutes analysing the source items to identify variations in health by social class and gender.

3 Spend another 15 minutes making up questions based on your findings. The questions must allow the opposition to identify a statistical pattern and give an adequate explanation for it, i.e. you must know the answers to your questions!

4 Ask someone to run a quiz in which the questions given to each team should be those made up by the opposing one.

Marks should be decided upon by the quiz leader, e.g. 1 mark for identifying the statistical pattern correctly, up to 4 marks for quality and fullness of explanation. Bonus marks to be given for added points of value.

Explaining the patterns

The chances of a long and healthy life appear to be strongly mitigated by the factor of social class. Sociologists have offered various explanations for these patterns, which can be broadly grouped as:

❖ those which question the validity of the statistics

❖ those which argue that health determines social status rather than the other way around

❖ those which emphasize the life styles of individuals and groups

❖ those which emphasize social and economic inequalities that fundamentally affect a person's life experience.

❖ those which highlight differences in access to health care.

We will look at each explanation in turn.

Questioning the statistics

This explanation is sometimes referred to as the 'artefact explanation' since it suggests that any apparent inequalities in health by social class are not so much a result of real differences but have been produced by the way statistics have been compiled. Most statistical sources have used the Registrar General's categorization of occupational class (discussed in Chapter 6, *Stratification and differentiation*). It is argued that this makes the health gap appear worse than it is since the shrinking social class V has a disproportionate number of older members when compared with the expanding, and so more youthful, middle classes. By comparing social class V with other classes, what is being revealed is health differences by age and not by social class. However, Marmot *et al.*'s longitudinal study of civil servants which began in 1967 suggests official statistics underestimate the link between social class factors and mortality. Twenty years on, civil servants of various grades were asked to assess their own health. The survey found that the gap in self-reported health had in fact widened even though the differences in income between the grades had lessened. Ferrie *et al.* (1995) argue that there was more stress and insecurity, particularly amongst the lower grades, as a result of the restructuring of the civil service into the private sector and this produced a deterioration in physical and mental health. Even though most sociologists now recognize that the classification of social class is a problem they still accept that the differences in health are real.

The social selection explanation

In this view poor health is seen as the selector of social class. If you are frail and weak then you are less likely to be able to hold down a good job and are more likely to be unemployed. Blane *et al.* (1994) found that between the ages of 10 and 14, health differences by social class disappeared and only re-emerged between ages 15 to 29 as people acquired their own occupational class. Rahkonen *et al.* (1995), in a comparative study of Britain and Finland, confirmed that it was the young person's own class and not that of their parents which was most important in explaining their level of health. In the National Child Development Study, Power found that young people who were downwardly mobile compared with the occupational class of their parents were more likely to have poor self-rated health than those who were upwardly mobile (Power *et al.* 1991). However, Power and colleagues did not believe that health was the main determinant of mobility or that the correlation between health and social class was a simple one. They found that many factors could contribute to the health of a person at age 23. These included inheritance at birth, socio-economic circumstances in the early years, health and education throughout childhood and the individual behaviours of the young adults. In short, the social selection explanation can only account for a small proportion of the health differentials between the social classes.

Cultural-behavioural explanation

This explanation suggests that if individuals in social class V looked after themselves properly then the differences in health would be reduced. Essentially, lower social groups need to change their attitudes to food, exercise, alcohol and smoking. The message is less chips, white bread, puddings, lager, cigarettes and watching TV and more of the healthier lifestyle of the middle classes. Health education is seen as the answer so that the socialization cycle which leads people into unhealthy lifestyles can be broken.

However, research suggests that although behaviours like smoking are important they can only explain inequalities in health to a limited extent. Woodward *et al.*'s (1990) study of Scotland found that men and women in social class V had a risk of coronary heart disease 3.26 and 4.72 times that of men and women in social class I. After taking into account a great many behavioural and physiological risk factors, including smoking and alcohol consumption, the excess was still 2.44 and 2.15 times. Blaxter (1990) supports this view and suggests that when it comes to people working and living in the most difficult and stressful circumstances then behavioural factors are a secondary issue. A middle-class smoker still has better health prospects than a working-class smoker.

The cultural-behavioural approach is criticized for blaming the victims of ill health for their own difficulties rather than focusing attention on structural inequalities. However, it could be said that whatever the material circumstances, it costs nothing to go for a walk, very little to go swimming and costs a lot more to smoke and drink. Increasingly, sociologists have been interested in the complex ways the lifestyles of social groups living in particular places are connected with social, economic and biological factors. Although we can say that behaviours like smoking are individual choices, in reality people's preferences are limited by the traditions and circumstances of their life.

The structural materialist explanation

This explanation was the one favoured by the Black Report and the main reason why it was politically unpopular. By identifying the source of health inequalities as being the nature of the social structure, then the solution proposed was a redistribution of wealth and income and major social engineering. According to this argument there are many material factors which have a causal relationship with health and the experience of them is largely determined by a person's social class. Inadequate income leads to inadequate diets, poor quality housing, lack of space for children to play and other material disadvantages which effect health. Lower-class jobs are likely to have greater risk of accidents and pollution. They are also likely to be more insecure and boring which increases stress and behaviours like smoking and drinking to reduce it. Evidence to support the materialist view can be seen in the fact that as the gap between rich and poor in Britain has widened so too have health inequalities. In a comparative study of developed societies Wilkinson (1993) found that countries with the highest life expectancy were not necessarily the wealthiest, but the ones which were most equal. He suggests that:

> 'If Britain was to adopt an income distribution more like the most egalitarian countries in Europe ... it would add about two years to average life expectancy.' (p. 18)

Moreover, countries like Japan and Italy with narrowing income inequality have also experienced the fastest increases in life expectancy.

The case for the materialist view is strong but it has been recognized as inadequate on its own. Sweeting and West (1994, 1995), in their longitudinal study of the health of young people in Glasgow, found that material factors for this group were less important for health and job prospects than the quality of family life. They examined three aspects of the family – structure, conflict and culture – for direct and indirect effects on health and well-being. The most important variable seemed to be family conflict rather than single parenthood, class background or poverty.

Increasingly, sociological discussion is moving beyond linking health too closely to material factors. Greater attention has been given to a wider range of psychological variables which are connected to health – stress, perception of being in control of one's life, satisfaction with self, depression and hostility. These undoubtedly are linked to the distribution of resources, but they do not only result from absolute poverty. Relative deprivation – feeling you are not living the life regarded as normal by others – erodes self-satisfaction and a sense of control and is experienced as humiliating – which is equally damaging to health. These feelings of being disadvantaged can not only lower self-esteem and increase stress but also lead to behaviours which may affect health. A person may skimp on basic necessities so they can buy the things which they feel make them like others. In this way they may be satisfying psychological needs but affecting physical ones. This may explain, for example, why some very poor families take large loans to buy the toys they believe their children need and want for Christmas, even though it means spending the rest of the year scraping together sufficient money to pay off the debt.

Inequality in access to health care

According to Dr J. Tudor-Hart (1971) 'the availability of good medical care tends to vary inversely with the need for it in the population served'. The 'inverse care law' means that the more medical care a social group needs the less it is likely to get. It is argued that middle-class people are more knowledgeable about the services available and more assertive in demanding they receive the best possible treatment, particularly of a preventative kind. Cartwright and O'Brien (1976) also found that the health professionals treated people differently according to their social class.

Table 10.4 GP consultations with middle and working-class patients aged 65 and over

	Middle-class	Working-class
Average length of consultation (minutes)	6.2	4.7
Average number of questions asked by patient	3.7	3.0
Average number of problems discussed with doctor	4.1	2.8
Average number of symptoms mentioned to interviewer prior to consultation	2.2	3.0

Source: Patrick and Scramble (1986)

❖ Activity 14 ❖

Describe the patterns shown by Table 10.4 and offer suggestions for them.

Tuckett and Kaufert (1978) argue that middle-class patients have greater input into the decisions regarding their health care because they generally have better language skills and greater self-assurance.

In principle if not in practice, the NHS is freely available to all. However, access to private health care obviously depends upon the ability to pay. The professional classes are more likely to be able to afford to have medical insurance and to be offered schemes as part of their employment package. Women and the lower social classes are less likely to be in this situation. It is argued that the expansion of private health has served to widen the health gap between social groups. It is claimed that the private system is being used to 'leap-frog' patients who can only rely on the NHS.

In sum, access to health care appears to favour the middle class because:

❖ they are more effective in negotiating with medical practitioners

❖ they have better knowledge which enables them to make better use of health services

❖ they are more able to afford private care.

Differential access to care cannot explain completely the differences in health by social class. Moreover, from a conflict perspective, the NHS was never intended to eradicate health differences. Certainly it was hoped to improve the condition and efficiency of the labour force, but it also served to legitimate the capitalist system which actually produced inequalities in health.

All the explanations above offer some insight into the inequalities in health by social class. During the 1980s they tended to be regarded as exclusive, with people taking up entrenched positions in different camps. Macintyre (1996) has identified a different mood amongst researchers. Now there is a move to look at the links between the different explanations – which promises the development of a more sophisticated analysis of the ways inequalities in health are produced.

In Focus

◆

Poor diet for families on income support

'Families on income support cannot afford to give their children the same level of diet which was available to children living in workhouses 90 years ago, says NCH.

The charity ... released a study claiming that more than 1.5 million families on income support cannot afford decent food.

An 1876 workhouse diet would at today's prices cost £5.46 per week, according to the Food Commission in its report for the charity. But it estimates current income support levels allow £4.15 a week for a child's food.'

Source: Community Care, 3 February 1994

In Focus

◆

For richer, for poorer

'Age for age, death rates are four times as high in the poorest areas of Britain as in the richest and three times as high amongst the most junior as among the most senior civil servants working in your own government departments ... This is not primarily because of smoking and misguided dietary choices.

More important are the various stressful effects of low socio-economic status and subordinate institutional positions. In particular, the lack of control over events both at home and at work, the effects of insecurity and socio-economic stress on family life and lack of social support from friends and the community more widely, tend to increase the proportion of the population living with chronic stress. This is now known to lead to rapid ageing as well as increased susceptibility to infections and degenerative diseases including heart problems.

Overall there is a remarkably strong relationship between a society's average death rates and the amount of inequality. Nine different research groups have shown that more equal societies are healthier.'

Source: Richard Wilkinson,
The Guardian, 11 November 1996

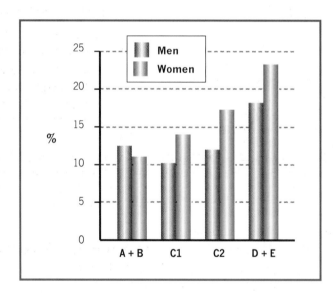

Figure 10.5
Clinical obesity
by social class

In Focus

◆

£9 million campaign launched to change 'couch potato' culture

'A three-year, £9 million government health education campaign was launched yesterday aimed at changing "couch potato" Britain by encouraging everyone to take at least 30 minutes' moderate exercise five times a week.

The campaign, Active for Life, has been launched after a survey for the Health Education Authority found that seven out of 10 women and six out of 10 men are not active enough to benefit their health.

The initiative is stressing that people do not need to take vigorous or formal exercise such as squash, running or aerobics. Instead, walking to work, taking the stairs instead of the lift, cycling, dancing or gardening can have significant benefits.'

Source: The Guardian, 20 March 1996

❖ Activity 15 ❖

1 With reference to Fig. 10.5 and the second *In Focus* on p. 434, outline the main points of the cultural behaviourist explanation for health inequalities.

   What criticisms can be made of the cultural behaviourist approach?

2 Give examples in your own words of the 'various stressful effects of low socio-economic status' which can damage health, discussed in the second paragraph of the *In Focus* at the top of p. 434.

3 Explain how social disintegration, social inequality and health are connected.

4 In what ways will the policies recommended by the HEA (see *In Focus* at the bottom of p. 434) be different from those suggested by the writers of the previous two *In Focuses* (p. 433 and top of p. 434)?

5 Using evidence from the three *In Focuses* on pp. 433–434, Fig. 10.5 and elsewhere, evaluate the explanation given by the materialist structuralist approach for health differences between social classes.

Gender and health

Patterns of health

A weakness of much research on the inequalities of health by social class is that the particular health experiences of women are either ignored or assumed to be identical to those of men. Feminist research has gone some way to complete the picture. Official statistics can be used to identify differences in the mortality and morbidity of men and women in Britain.

Mortality

❖ Life expectancy at birth in 1994 was 78 years for women and 72 for men.

❖ Male babies are more likely to die before birth or in the first year of life. In 1993 the infant mortality rate was 7.8 for boys and 6.2 for girls.

❖ Heart disease is the major killer of both men and women, although the rates are significantly higher for males. For women, the gender-specific cancers of the reproductive organs and breasts are significant causes of death.

Morbidity

❖ Chronic illness (that which is long standing and limiting) is higher for women than men.

❖ Two thirds of disabled people are women.

❖ On average women see their doctor six times and men four times per year.

❖ Women form 57 per cent of admissions to mental hospitals and are more likely to be diagnosed as suffering from depression, dementia, neurotic and psychotic illnesses.

It is unexpected to find that although women live longer than men, they can expect to suffer worse health, both physically and mentally.

Explaining differences in health by gender

❖ Activity 16 ❖

Discuss the reasons for differences in mortality and morbidity by gender. Think particularly about the relative importance of cultural and behavioural explanations, compared with biological ones.

Statistics and gender

Again, we must not take the official health statistics at face value since the manner and processes by which they are constructed may lead to distortion. Below are some of the reasons suggested why the statistics relating to gender and health need to be treated cautiously:

❖ The health of women may appear to be worse than that of men because their longer life-expectancy increases the risk of chronic illness, senile dementia and therefore the regular use of medical services. However, the statistics do indicate that women suffer more chronic disorders in all age categories.

❖ Looking at the gender variable alone can give an inaccurate picture and may need to be combined with social class and ethnicity if a more honest view is to be achieved. For example, 45- to 64-year-old men in social class V suffer more chronic illness than equivalent women. Women in class V have worse mortality than men in class I. The issue of class and gender is particularly difficult to research since women's social class is often taken to be based on that of her husband. The concentration of women in certain occupations may also be more significant than gender itself. Thus, changing the variables being measured can lead to changes in the patterns revealed by the statistics.

❖ Macfarlane questions whether the greater use of medical services by women really indicates worse health. She argues that once consultations for contraception, pregnancy, childbirth and genito-urinary disorders (male and female) are excluded the health gap by gender virtually disappears.

❖ Other reasons for statistics being unreliable are linked to the cultural behavioural argument. For example, men may feel they need to 'soldier on' rather than show weakness in the face of ill health by visiting the doctor. On the other hand admitting frailty, particularly emotional problems, is more compatible with femininity and this could explain women's more frequent medical consultations. Likewise, professionals may be more willing to assign the sick

role to women than men. Women may go to the doctors on their children's behalf and so have more opportunity to discuss their own problems. In this way the health statistics may reveal more about interaction processes than real differences in health.

Biological explanations

There are obviously differences in the health experiences of men and women that can be attributed to biology, particularly those concerned with reproduction. Hormonal differences can account for some variation in the occurrence of particular illnesses e.g. the higher rate of heart disease amongst men before the age of 50 can partly be accounted for by the lack of protection provided by the hormone oestrogen. However, sociologists believe that such biological explanations can only provide very limited answers regarding gender inequalities and health. In the majority of cases, differences resulting from biology can be overridden by social, economic and environmental factors.

Cultural and behavioural explanations

It is argued that gender socialization and society's role expectations of males and females lead to differences in behaviours which produce inequalities in health. Men are more likely to take part in risk activities, like driving too fast, to drink alcohol and smoke more, and to have greater involvement in violence. It is interesting that as cultural expectations change and the smoking, drinking and working patterns of men and women become more alike so do patterns of health. The way females are conditioned to be passive and helpless may make it more difficult for them to cope with stress and more willing to accept definitions of themselves as depressed. However, this is contested since the higher rate of male suicide could be a result of men having less opportunity than women to off-load their personal difficulties because our culture encourages men to keep their problems to themselves. Expectations relating to gender may also influence the type of treatment received. Clark (1994) argues that because heart disease is seen as a man's illness, women who visit the doctor with similar symptoms are likely to receive slower diagnoses, later referral, fewer tests and so have a reduced chance of recovery. These behavioural differences are recognized as being of considerable significance, particularly when they are combined with the materialist argument below.

Materialist and structuralist explanations

In these explanations, gender differences in health are accounted for by inequalities in the resources which make for good health and the different social positions men and women occupy. The dangers of some traditionally male occupations can be used to explain higher male mortality particularly in younger age groups. Moreover, many of these traditional heavy industries have undergone decline while employment opportunities for women have increased. This has exposed more men to the stresses of unemployment which can be especially acute given the importance attached to 'the man being the breadwinner' in our society.

Women are more likely to be in poverty as result of their concentration in low-paid employment and they are more often reliant on state benefits as a result of old age or single parenthood. This means they are more prone to illnesses resulting from poor housing, inadequate diets and stress produced by insecurity. Certain female occupations involve their own health risks, e.g. airborne fibres in textiles have been linked to respiratory complaints and repetitive strain injury (RSI) has, after a struggle, been recognized as a debilitating problem associated with the use of computer keyboards.

However, radical feminists emphasize that it is the housewife–mother role which literally makes women sick. It involves mundane, tedious work with little satisfaction, reward or status. Childcare and the care of the infirm of the family involves great responsibility and frequently social isolation. The mother figure is also expected to be the emotional sponge for other family members. Graham (1994) argues that the social position of women can be linked to health-risking behaviours. Not surprisingly, the more poverty and caring responsibilities women face, the higher the levels of smoking. Ironically, this can be viewed as a rational and health-saving response in the face of stress. Formal employment can also increase stress since, as Chapter 5 has shown, women often take the 'dual burden' of both house and outside work. Thus the differences in the structural and material circumstances of men and women can account for health differences.

❖ Activity 17 ❖

Critically evaluate sociological explanations for differences in mortality and morbidity by gender and social class.

This is a demanding essay because you need to deal with many themes if you are to satisfy the question. Look back to Chapter 1 for essay guidance and aim to write your answer within four sides of A4 paper.

If you divide your essay into two parts, one on social class and the other on gender, you are likely to be too superficial. Instead, structure your essay around the concepts and explanations, such as behavioural and cultural views, and illustrate these with reference to both class and gender. Make sure you also refer to mortality and morbidity and build in evaluative points throughout.

Ethnicity and health

Patterns of inequality

The Black Report can be criticized for giving little attention to ethnicity as a dimension of health and illness, because other statistical sources indicate that there *are* differences in mortality and morbidity rates by ethnic group. Some of these differences in the UK are outlined below:

❖ If age is standardized, people from minority ethnic groups have a higher mortality rate when compared with the white population.

❖ Some diseases are strongly associated with ethnicity:

– The blood disease *sickle cell anaemia* mainly affects people of African and Caribbean descent.

– *Thalassaemia* affects haemoglobin in red blood cells and occurs largely in communities originating from Cypress, the Middle East, Pakistan and India.

– *Cystic fibrosis* is a genetic illness concentrated in the white population.

However, we must be aware that all these diseases can be found in all ethnic groups and that the most common causes of death for everyone regardless of race are heart attacks, strokes and cancer.

❖ Table 10.5 indicates that there are ethnic differences in the pattern of causes of death.

❖ Skellington and Morris (1992) confirmed statistical differences in diagnosed mental ill health. People of African and Caribbean descent are more likely to be admitted to psychiatric institutions, particularly as compulsory admissions, and are more likely to be given such treatments as electro-convulsive therapy (ECT).

❖ Children born to mothers from the New Commonwealth have a higher risk of dying before birth or in the first year of life. Babies born to mothers originating from the Caribbean are at the greatest risk, while those of Pakistani and Bangladeshi mothers are more likely to be born with disabilities and congenital illness.

Table 10.5 Ethnic differences in the pattern of causes of death

African	*higher rates*	strokes, high blood pressure, violence/accidents, maternal deaths, TB
	lower rates	bronchitis
Indian Sub-Continent	*higher rates*	heart disease, diabetes, violence/accidents, TB
	lower rates	bronchitis, certain cancers
Caribbean	*higher rates*	strokes, high blood pressure, violence/accidents, diabetes, maternal deaths
	lower rates	bronchitis

Source: Sociology Review (1993, 3(1))

Table 10.6 Ethnicity and infant mortality

Mother's country of origin	Still births (rate per 1000 total births)	Neonatal[1] deaths (rate per 1000 live births)	Postnatal[2] deaths (rate per 1000 births)
United Kingdom	4.4	4.3	3.2
Irish Republic	5.1	3.7	3.4
Bangladesh	8.6	3.9	1.6
India	5.3	5.1	2.2
Pakistan	9.1	7.8	6.4
East Africa	6.9	5.6	2.0
Caribbean	5.7	8.4	4.2

[1] Neonatal deaths: deaths at ages before 28 days after live birth

[2] Postnatal death: deaths at ages 28 days and over, but under one year of live births

Source: Sociology Review (1993, 3(1))

❖ Activity 18 ❖

1 Use a suitable technique to graph the data in Table 10.6.

2 The data is given as rates. What does this mean and why is it more useful than raw totals?

3 Describe the differences in infant mortality by ethnicity and suggest reasons for these.

Statistics and ethnicity

The patterns discussed above are generally accepted but, as is the case with all official health statistics, those concerning ethnicity do need to be treated cautiously. There are particular difficulties with the way ethnicity is recorded and categorized which can add to the problems of data interpretation.

❖ Before the 1991 census, researchers largely relied on birth and death certificates, which do record a person's country of birth. This meant that information was limited to people born outside the UK and ignored the British-born black population. It was also impossible to separate white people born in countries like India and Kenya from other ethnic groups.

❖ McKenzie and Crowfoot (1994) suggest that relying on country of origin is particularly inadequate since it can obscure significant variations in the health of different groups from the same country. For example, Punjabis, Gujaratis, Muslims, Hindus and all the other groups originating in India may have as many differences in their patterns of health as they do similarities.

❖ The 1991 census and more recent NHS information did partly overcome these problems by specifically asking questions on ethnic origin. However, the categories provided were a rather confusing mix of race, nationality, religion and culture. Furthermore, it is up to individuals to allocate themselves to a particular group and this can vary between people. For example, a Ugandan Asian may have to decide if they see themselves as African, Indian or Black. Also different questionnaires use different categories even within the NHS and this makes comparative studies difficult.

❖ The reliability of the census as a source of information for the differences in health by ethnicity is also questioned by Raleigh and Balarajan (1994). There seems to have been a significant under-return from the lower classes generally and ethnic minorities form a larger proportion of this group.

In sum, these issues have made it difficult to calculate reliable rates and ratios regarding ethnicity and health. This in turn has caused problems in establishing the factors which underlie apparent disparities. Nevertheless, explanations have been attempted similar to those offered for the inequalities in health by social class.

Explaining differences in health by ethnicity

Biological explanations

Although certain diseases do have particular ethnic associations (as described above), sociologists largely reject genetic explanations in preference for those which emphasize social and economic factors. Sheldon and Parker (1992) believe that an over-concern with specific illnesses and ethnic health differentials revealed by statistics can be misinterpreted as indicating that ethnicity is the cause of health differences, when in fact the explanations are far more complicated. They suggest more attention should be given to material circumstances and the cross-cutting social variables of class and gender. It may be that genetics have *some* bearing on the higher rates of heart disease and high blood pressure found amongst people born in the Caribbean and the Indian sub-continent but this is assumed to be relatively minor and difficult to disentangle from the stresses caused by living in a society where many are economically disadvantaged and face additional pressures of racism.

Cultural and behavioural explanations

As with social class, this explanation identifies inadequacies in the lifestyles of ethnic minorities as causing health disadvantages. Thus in the 1980s the relatively higher levels of rickets found amongst 'Asians' was seen as resulting from their vegetarian diet lacking sufficient vitamin D. This failed to consider that only 25 per cent of 'Asians' in Britain are predominantly vegetarian, that vegetarian food does not necessarily lack vitamin D and that, ironically, government guidelines to eat more vegetables, fibre and less meat would bring Western diets more closely in line with Eastern ones! Likewise, the higher heart disease rates of Indians, Pakistanis and Bangladeshis in Britain has been blamed on the excessive use of ghee, a cooking fat, even though those living in the country of origin actually have significantly lower rates. The failure of Asian and Afro-Caribbean women to use Western medical services adequately has also been blamed for the higher risks their babies face during pregnancy and in the first year.

These explanations have undergone heavy criticism and from reading the problems of cultural explanations in relation to health inequalities by social class you may well be able to predict what some of these are. Hunt (1995) identifies three difficulties:

❖ Ffar too many generalizations have been made about 'Asian' and 'Caribbean' cultures with insufficient recognition given to the diversity that can be found amongst them. Not only do such generalizations obscure great cultural and religious differences but they also fail to see the importance of variations by social class, gender and region.

❖ The cultures of ethnic minorities tend to be described as if they are exotic and inferior, and as though a change in deficient life style is necessary to solve any health inequalities they experience. This 'blame the victim' approach detracts attention from wider structural inequalities and the inadequacies of the health service in providing for the needs of multicultural Britain.

❖ Cultural and behavioural approaches also tend to see cultures as unchanging, when, in reality, ethnic groups will adapt their life styles in response to their experience of living in a new country – just as the host culture may itself be modified. For example, a visit to the supermarket suggests that 'British' food is truly international. It would seem likely that over time, patterns of health and illness by ethnicity will become similar, with any significant differences being more successfully justified by the explanations below than by reference to differences in cultural practices.

Materialist and structural explanations

As we have seen, these are the explanation most preferred by the authors of the Black Report and they can be usefully applied to the differences in health by ethnicity. The relative concentration of people originating from the Caribbean or the Indian sub-continent in low-paid manual occupations (see Chapter 6) means they are more likely to lack the material conditions linked to good health, such as job security, good working conditions, decent housing and a risk-free environment in which to live. Chapter 3 has shown how Asian and Afro-Caribbeans suffer disadvantage in access to housing, and reports by the Departments of Health and Environment have verified that poor housing conditions directly effect physical and psychological health. This argument is suggesting that social-class position within a capitalist economic system also provides the best explanation for the inequalities by ethnic group. Not only does the relative concentration of Afro-Caribbeans, Pakistanis and Bangladeshis in the lower social classes explain their health disadvantages, but also the relative health advantages of groups like Asians of East African origin can be explained by their superior social-class position and the material advantages this brings.

Although the materialist argument is more successful than either the genetic or cultural approaches in explaining health

In Focus

◆

Race, inequality and health

'The health of ethnic minorities involves a complex interplay between health needs on the one hand and access to health care on the other. This relationship takes place within a broader framework of social, political, economic and other forces which shape the lives of black people in Britain. We have identified four different sets of factors which are relevant to an understanding of health inequalities. Not all are of equal importance. Genetic factors have a limited impact on overall health trends. There is little concrete evidence at the present time that cultural/behavioural patterns have a significant impact on inequalities in the health of ethnic groups. In any event, such lifestyle factors must be seen in the context of the material environment in which people live and work and must be placed in the social and political context of a racist society. Evidence suggests that as a result of racism, both direct and indirect, black and ethnic minority people have poorer access to health resources such as employment, good housing, education and transport facilities than other social groups and that racial differences in health reflect these differences in general social and economic environments of black and white groups.

The health needs of Britain's black population are similar to those of the poorer sections of the white population, but they encounter additional problems of lack of knowledge, insensitivity and personal and institutional racism in their interaction with the NHS.'

Source: Sociology Review (1993, 3(1))

differences between ethnic groups it still fails to adequately explain why they should be so particularly disadvantaged. For example, when comparing black and white people sharing the same social-class position black people are more vulnerable to unemployment. Racism in the private and public housing markets has also been shown to compound inequalities generated by social class. Racism, therefore, is a further constraint on access to the conditions of life that are more conducive to good health. Furthermore, racially inspired physical abuse may be one reason why the category of death by violence/accidents is bigger for ethnic minority groups than for white people.

❖ Activity 19 ❖

1   What four factors does the *In Focus* on p. 441 identify as relevant to understanding health inequalities?

2   Which factors are seen as of less significance? Explain why this is so.

3   In your own words identify and outline the explanation preferred by the writers of this *In Focus*.

4   Suggest examples of the criticisms the article makes of the NHS.

◆ Health and old age

Common sense tells us that mortality and morbidity will increase with age. For example, much of the age inequality in mental illness can be attributed to senile dementia. Even the differences by social class lessen. The ticking of the biological clock obviously explains much of the differences by generation, but sociologists also have views on this subject.

must be wary of individualizing the problem. Again we must ask questions about our cultural values which do not associate being 'sporty' or actively fit with old age. The labelling of old people as helpless may mean they come to see themselves as such. This is not to deny that many old people ignore negative stereotyping and live with the motto, 'You're as old as you feel!'

Culture and lifestyle

One argument is that if old people improved the way they live then they would also improve their health. The Allied Dunbar National Fitness Survey (1992) found that 40 per cent of men and women aged 65 to 74 did not take part in any moderate or vigorous activity. Thirty per cent of men and fifty per cent of women did not have sufficient strength in the muscles around the thigh to rise easily from a low chair. Amongst women aged over 55 only 50 per cent had sufficient leg power to climb stairs easily and unaided. Lack of exercise is also connected to heart disease, obesity, osteoporosis and other diseases. However, we

Material and structural explanations

This approach claims that health is directly related to a person's economic and social circumstances, such as the quality of their home and the diets they can afford. Since the elderly constitute a disproportionate number of the poor it is not surprising that their health situation reflects this. The elderly have particular difficulties with housing in that they are more likely to be living in ageing properties requiring repair and lacking in amenities. Cost and physical disability may prevent an old person from maintaining their home adequately. However, Arber and Ginn (1991, 1993) stress the importance of looking at an old person's social position *before* retirement if we are to understand their current circumstances. If you've been a middle-class professional with the ability to save and purchase additional pension cover then your financial situation on retirement is likely to be very different from some someone in social class V. They also argue that the health problems of elderly women cannot be explained just by longer life expectancy. Women are less likely to have the income provided by an occupational pension and are more likely to out-live their partners and need institutional care.

Ageism and the health service

A very controversial explanation for the inequalities in health is that old people do not have equal access to the health service. Although the number of elderly is increasing, a survey by community Health councils in 1990 found that 77 per cent of health authorities had reduced the number of long-term care beds and were not replacing them with private contracts. There have been concerns that old people have been denied access to the care they need and have been forced to sell their homes to buy it in the private sector. In 1992 The National Association of Health Authorities and Trusts stated that nursing-home care should not be a function of the NHS, even though an earlier circular from the Department of Health had said that no patient was to be transferred into private care against their wishes or those of their relatives. It seems that access to an NHS bed could also depend upon your knowledge of your rights. One of the arguments why such low priority is given to the health care of the elderly is the dominance of the biomedical model of health. Geriatric care does not provide the same opportunities for cure, indeed the concern may well be with a dignified death, and this sits uneasily with the goals of biomedicine.

❖ Activity 20 ❖

1 Read the *In Focus* on the next page and think about the ways in which the elderly are denied equality of access to health care.

2 What long-term problem do the elderly represent for the NHS?

3 Role play: A meeting is being held to discuss elderly care provision in the local Sprogwell Health Authority. A number of people with different interests are present

   – Sprogwell Health Authority
   – Sprogwell NHS Trust
   – medical staff
   – old people's groups
   – children of old people who are full-time carers
   – community groups representing general community interests.

Situation: Sprogwell has seen no increase in central government funding this year. The area's elderly population will grow by 15 per cent in the next ten years. How will the area distribute and/or increase resources for health-care provision?

Task: Hold a meeting with different people adopting the roles above and discussing the options they favour. Take a vote on the proposals that have been made.

In Focus
◆
Physicians slate 'ageist' health bias

'Elderly people are suffering discrimination at the hands of the health service, in breach of medical ethics, and possibly wasting resources, the Royal College of Physicians said yesterday.

Discrimination is sometimes explicit – some units have age limits for certain treatments – but in most cases it is unspoken, based on an assumption that the elderly should be at the back of the queue because they have less time to live.

The report follows a row last month over the case of two pensioners in north London and Brighton denied treatment because of their age.

The college also highlights growing worries about long-stay nursing beds for the elderly. Health authorities and social services are starting to argue over who should pay for these, and some old people are being forced to spend their savings or sell their homes if they need such care.

The report points out that of a population of some 58 million there are more than 10.5 million aged 65 or over. It says admissions of elderly people to hospital are increasing by 4 per cent a year, and over the next 35 years the proportion of the population over 65 will rise by 30 per cent, with a 66 per cent increase in those over 85. Almost half of all public spending on health and social services goes on those over 65.

... Elderly people are being denied access to coronary care units and to "clot-busting" drugs after heart attacks. There has been an assumption that older people can't benefit from treatment or have greater side effects, but there have been no scientific trials.

Professor Leslie Turnberg, president of the college, said a public debate should be held if health care was to be rationed for the elderly. "When a scarcity of resources is driving the way we practice, people are making unconscious choices on the basis of life expectancy."

The college's report states: "The guiding principle upon which the provision of acute medical care to elderly people is based must be that there is to be no direct distinction or negative discrimination on grounds of age."'

Source: Chris Mihill, *The Guardian*, May 1994

Spatial inequalities in health

The area you live in can also influence health. In Britain levels of health tend to decline as you move up from the South to the North of England and Scotland. Another gradient is between urban industrial areas and rural ones. This is common in most economically developed countries although generally reversed in less economically developed ones. We do need to recognize the importance of geographical scale since using national or regional data can hide important local differences. For example, Pyle (1990) has examined regional or spatial variation in infant mortality in North Carolina and found that the areas of highest infant mortality were in poor, isolated rural areas and in deprived metropolitan ones. Townsend *et al.* (1988) also found health differences at the electoral ward level in their study of the North of England. This research used a deprivation index which combined statistics on car ownership, housing tenure, unemployment, and overcrowding to establish a geographical correlation between mortality and social conditions.

The problem for sociologists is to work out if the differences are a result of the place or simply a reflection of the people who live there. It seems likely that since social groups are distributed unevenly that the explanations already discussed are likely to be relevant. For example, the fact that inner cities have high concentrations of the lower classes, ethnic minorities and the elderly must have some bearing on the poor health profile of these areas. However, Duncan *et al.* (1993) suggest that people with similar individual risk factors may have differing health experiences depending upon where they live. Phillimore and Morris (1991) compared areas of Sunderland and Middlesborough, two areas which were similarly socially and economically deprived but found that Middlesborough had a higher mortality. One possible explanation could be differences in the physical environment, especially air pollution resulting from the petrochemical industry around Middlesborough. Of increasing concern is the widening health gap between places. Bryce *et al.* (1994) for England and McLoone and Boddy (1994) for Scotland found that improvements in rates of coronary heart disease mortality were less in deprived areas than affluent ones. Thus, although environmental conditions alone can not account for spatial differences they could be contributory factors.

Inequality in the spatial distribution of health care

Where you live is also important in relation to the level and quality of health care available to you. In terms of hospital beds and the provision of specialist services, the south is more fully provided for than the poorer north, although all political parties have sought to decentralize and there has been some improvement in regional allocation of resources. On the other hand, the trend to larger hospitals in urban areas has been to the detriment of people in the countryside. Research into the care of cancer patients has shown that the quality of care is a major influence on survival, and the provision of such care varies considerably between hospitals. Indeed, one of the justifications for introducing the principles of the market to the NHS is that successful specialist centres should be encouraged to flourish by attracting more resources from health authorities outside the immediate area and from fund-holding GPs. Arguably one effect of this could be that the chances of getting the best treatment for a particular condition could become increasingly dependent upon where you live.

Table 10.7 Mortality of men and women in different regions of Britain 1979–80 plus 1982–3 (direct standardized death rate per 1000)

Region	Men 20–64	Single women 20–59	Married women 20–59
Britain	5.57	1.43	2.23
England and Wales	5.43	1.41	2.17
Scotland	6.92	1.62	2.89
South West	4.82	1.32	1.93
South East	4.88	1.29	1.97
Wales	5.86	1.43	2.34
North West	6.37	1.69	2.52
North	6.43	1.53	2.50
Strathclyde	7.14	1.66	3.06
Central Clydeside	7.86	1.78	3.23

Source: Townsend *et al.* (1988)

445

'Death rates among men are almost twice as high on inner-city estates as in well-off districts, according to an OPCS analysis. The study is one of the first to look at health differences at the level of electoral wards.

The average standardized death rate in 1990-2 was 96 per cent higher among men and 73 per cent higher among women, on estates in inner cities than among those in 'prosperous' wards.'

Source: The Guardian, 20 March 1996

Table 10.8 Heavy consumption and problem drinking by Regional Health Authority (RHA), 1993

| RHA | Men | | Women | |
	Heavy consumption %	*Problem drinking %*	*Heavy consumption %*	*Problem drinking %*
Northern	38	11	16	6
Yorkshire	35	10	15	5
North Western	34	10	14	5
Mersey	33	11	15	7
Trent	30	8	11	4
West Midlands	32	10	13	5
East Anglian	25	6	12	5
Oxford	28	7	12	5
NW Thames	26	8	10	6
NE Thames	22	9	9	5
SE Thames	28	12	16	4
SW Thames	24	7	15	4
Wessex	28	7	13	3
South Western	25	8	14	6

Source: OPCS (1995)

❖ Activity 21 ❖

1 With reference to Tables 10.7 and 10.8 and the *In Focus* above, make a list of bullet points identifying some of the main patterns in the regional distribution of health.

2 What characteristics of the environment in particular areas may lead to differences in health?

3 We have already examined a number of sociological explanations for variations in health. Using the material provided here, discuss why spatial differences in health arise. It is important to draw upon the social class material discussed earlier in this chapter.

Providing health care

Our experience of being ill can be improved by the people around us who look after us. The people in the front line of this care are often family, particularly women. We call this 'informal care' (see Chapter 3, *Families and households*). Later in this chapter we will discuss the policy of community care, which also relies heavily on the family. In most cultures taking care of the sick is seen as a societal duty not just a familial one. In the USA, health care is mainly funded through private insurance with the state providing a minimum safety net for those who cannot afford their own provision. In Britain the majority of formal care is by the NHS, funded through general taxation and national insurance contributions made by employers and employees. The NHS was established in 1948 as a cornerstone of the welfare state and incorporates the principle of health care as a citizen's right, whatever their economic and social circumstances. In practice we have seen that access to care is not equal and varies according to social factors such as where you live, social class, age, ethnicity and gender. The NHS coexists with a small but rapidly growing private sector. Another source of formal support comes from voluntary and charity organizations. Often people can access a range of care, e.g. a cancer patient may need biomedical treatment, community and family care with additional support from charitable organizations such as Macmillan nurses. The following section of this chapter concentrates on recent changes in the NHS and the controversy that surrounds them.

The New Right: Is the NHS safe in their hands?

When the NHS was established, it was hoped that the running costs would decline as the population became healthier. However, this did not happen and by the 1980s, costs were perceived by the Thatcher government to be spiralling out of control. Costs grew as a result of:

- ❖ an ageing population
- ❖ increasing cost of drugs and medical technology
- ❖ the development of new treatments leading to increased demand.

In 1991 major changes were put into effect, aimed at increasing the capacity of the NHS to treat patients without putting an undue burden on the state:

- ❖ District Health Authorities (DHAs) became 'purchasers' of health care for their resident populations, buying services from hospitals and doctors.

- ❖ General practitioners (GPs) could choose to manage their own budgets, buying services in the interests of their patients independently from the DHA. This is known as 'fundholding'. All GPs have to be financially accountable and must operate within budget targets such as ceilings on prescription drugs.

- ❖ Hospitals could opt to become self-governing 'trusts', selling services to fundholding GPs, DHAs, private patients and other hospitals. They would be given resources by the NHS but would be able to determine their own policies and salary scales.

- ❖ Management had to be effective at all levels and all medical staff, including the most senior, were to be accountable to management for lack of efficiency. Health services were to be audited and inspected. They were expected to achieve set performance targets, such as minimum waiting times for appointments.

The main drive behind the policy was to introduce the principles of the free market into the NHS by creating an 'internal market', a divide between providers (Trust and non-Trust hospitals, GPs and the private sector) and purchasers of health care (DHA, fundholding GPs, private patients). Services such as cleaning and catering could also be contracted out to private companies. The competition between providers would encourage greater efficiency.

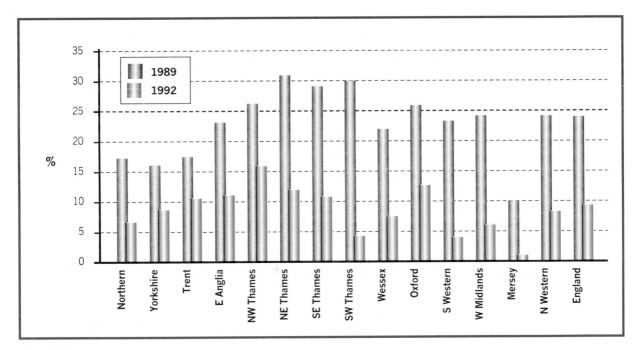

Figure 10.6
Percentage of patients waiting more than twelve months for operations in England

Continuing controversies

The changes to the NHS outlined above have caused a great deal of political and public debate. Efficiency, productivity and output did improve. Lengths-of-stay were cut; costs per acute case fell. Two-year waiting lists have nearly all been abolished. The number of patients treated in hospitals rose by more than 20 per cent in 10 years, far higher than was expected. The NHS is now more self-critical, accountable and self-aware. However, many criticisms of the changes have arisen.

Has it just been about cost cutting?

Is all the discussion about efficiency really a way of avoiding funding the NHS adequately? According to the National Association Of Health Authorities the shortfall in funding between 1980 and 1990 was £4.4 billion. However, the NHS did receive a greater percentage of public spending, 14 per cent in 1991 compared with 11 per cent in 1981, when other sectors of the welfare state saw decline. The Right claimed that the NHS saw an increase in spending of 20 per cent in real terms between 1980-1990. However this

growth may be less significant than at first glance. The actual costs of medical care have increased far more sharply than average prices and so in reality the level of funding has been inadequate to satisfy demand and there have been many stories of bed shortages and underuse of highly expensive facilities. It is likely that cutbacks were limited by the strength of public support for the NHS and the power of groups such as the BMA and the Royal Colleges.

Is it privatization by stealth?

The New Right are accused of lacking commitment to the principle of free health care embodied in the establishment of the NHS, yet they know it would be political suicide to establish a fully private system. Nevertheless, the changes have encouraged the private sector. The fear generated by the rhetoric that we can 'no longer afford the NHS' has led to a rapid uptake of private health insurance aided by tax relief. It is argued that the growth of the private sector has increased inequality of access to health care, and Fig. 10.7 shows a strong link with age and social class. Regional inequality has also been reinforced with a concentration of

Figure 10.7
Social-class differences in private health insurance cover in Britain

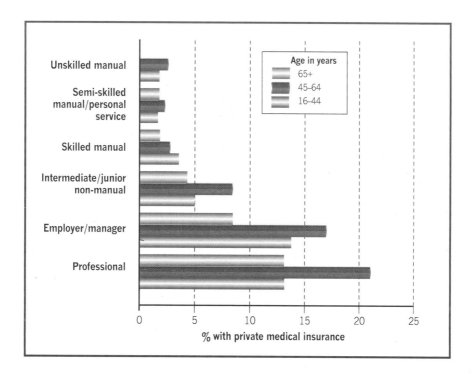

private beds around London and the South East. Mohan (1988) has commented on the perverse effect of allowing the independent sector to develop in a way which is contrary to that required by public policy. The private sector deals overwhelmingly with quality-of-life procedures which tend to have the longest NHS waiting lists. However, even the privately insured population use NHS facilities for over half of their hospital stays. The private sector is also encouraged by fundholding GPs buying their services and NHS hospitals raising income by increasing the number of private beds.

Do we have a two-tier system?

It is argued that fundholding means that inequality in access to health care is being built into the system. Patients with fundholding GPs can 'queue-jump' and get the best available treatment because their doctors can shop around rather than being tied to the hospital with which they are contracted. Hospitals are said to be prioritizing patients from fundholding doctors to ensure the continued purchase of their services. Many have suggested that fundholding practices have been over generously

resourced compared with the money made available to the DHA to buy the same services for the patients of non-fundholders. Also the availability of a particular service depends on what is purchased by the DHA e.g. IVF sterilization and some expensive drug therapies are available on the NHS in some areas but not in others.

More conflict and less efficiency?

It is argued that the reforms have demoralized the employees of the NHS and divided medical staff and management. The shift in power towards managers has been actively resisted. It has been difficult to reconcile managerial values of cost-effectiveness and loyalty to the organization and the medical priority of quality in patient care. For example, doctors may prefer to prescribe expensive drugs that are efficient, rather than cheaper ones that are less efficient. As the need for more control and more managers has increased then the cost of administration has expanded. The indicators used to measure efficiency have also been questioned. The number of patients seen in a given time tells us nothing about the quality of their experience. The survival rates of particular operations may tell us more about unwillingness to operate on high-risk patients than the skills of particular surgical departments. The pressure to reduce waiting lists could have led to some patients being given priority over those who were in most urgent need simply because the former were nearer to the time limit.

Day and Klein (1991) question how much real competition there is in the internal market of the NHS. DHAs generally continue to buy services from the hospitals that have always provided for the local people. They suggest that although the current NHS is unstable there is in fact more continuity than at first may be apparent. As yet it is too soon to fully assess the effects of the changes that have been implemented. Whatever the outcome, there remain unresolved questions concerning the future funding of the NHS, its organization and relationship with the private sector.

Understanding mental illness

Of all health problems, mental illness is probably the one surrounded by the most fear and misunderstanding. It is important to make a distinction between mental illness and mental or learning disability, and to recognise that mental illness is not related to intelligence. In 1994 a survey in the UK of 10,000 adults, an additional 1,100 homeless and 1,500 people who had been in psychiatric care, found that one in seven adults experienced depression, anxiety or some other kind of psychological problem. Severe mental illness, such as schizophrenia and manic depression, affects four people in every thousand. The severity of various conditions can be viewed as being on a continuum as in Fig. 10.8. Most of us slide up and down this scale to varying extents during our lifecourse and there are many famous people who have achieved outstanding success despite suffering recurring mental illness, e.g. Winston Churchill, Virginia Woolf, Spike Milligan.

Figure 10.8
The continuum of severity of mental illness

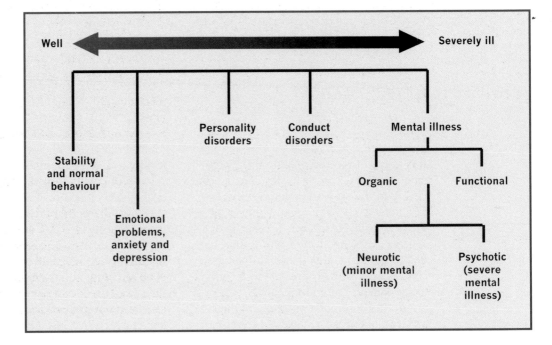

Mental illness as social construct

What may be regarded as abnormal or 'mad' in one society may be seen as perfectly normal in another and so mental illness provides a good example of how health, illness and deviance are socially defined and how these definitions constantly change (see also Chapter 11). For example, being an unmarried mother or having sex outside of marriage is seen as relatively normal in contemporary society. Earlier this century, either state was enough to put a woman into a psychiatric hospital.

Michael Foucault offers a historical perspective which shows that mental illness and the 'treatment' given depend as much upon social factors as they do biological ones. Using a range of primary sources, he attempted to 'reassemble' changing cultural attitudes in Europe. He argues that up to the mid-eighteenth century, mental illness was regarded as a result of possession by 'dark forces' or a disturbance in the four elements or passions of the brain. In the early medieval period he claims that sanity and madness intermingled, with both being seen as opposing aspects of being human. He argues that madness was associated with holiness, wisdom and genius and so the court jester, through his madness, was allowed to ridicule the establishment in a way that was denied to the sane. Likewise, religious madness was given respect and often sainthood. However, Porter (1986) sees this as hopelessly romanticized. He suggests there is little evidence that the 'normal' and the 'mad' were integrated. Rather the insane were rejected and frequently locked away in outhouses or cellars. For example, it is almost certain that Jane Austen had a mentally handicapped brother who was removed from the family and lodged elsewhere at an early age. Lower-class 'lunatics' faired even worse. In some cases they were persecuted as beggars and pushed from one parish to another. In others they were chained by the family and treated in a similar way to domestic animals.

According to Foucault incarcerating people in the 'mad house' was relatively rare until well into the eighteenth century. Attitudes to insanity hardened then, with its causes being seen as a product of moral weakness or over-indulgence. Treatments included physical restraint, purging and blood letting. Later the Victorians took a more humanitarian view, although the institution was still seen as the only safe place for the mad. It became viewed as a retreat for those who could not cope with the outside world. In the twentieth century mental illness became defined as being caused by a physical malfunction or psychological disturbance often in early childhood. Mental illness became medicalized and treatable, according to the biomedical model, through drugs, surgery, ECT (electro-convulsive therapy) and psychotherapy. Today there are many psychiatric schools of thought and not just one model of mental illness. Recently we have seen radical shifts in attitudes to the institution as the primary source of care. The emphasis now is on care in the community, as discussed below.

❖ Activity 22 ❖

Draw a time line beginning with the medieval period and ending with the present day. At appropriate stages along this line, make notes to show how the understanding of mental illness has changed over time.

Mental illness as social control

Read the two *In Focus* panels on p. 452. They both illustrate the power of the dominant to define the behaviour of those with less power as abnormal and as demonstrating mental illness. They also illustrate how definitions can be changed as a result of the resistance of those defined by them.

Hysteria takes its name from the Greek word for womb. It was a female mental disorder which was increasingly diagnosed during the period 1870 to the beginning of World War I – which coincided with the rise of the women's movement and the campaigns for greater independence, political rights, employment and educational opportunities. Feminists writers such as Showalter (1991) believe that hysteria illustrates how cultural ideas of 'proper' feminine behaviour shape the definition and treatment of female insanity. For example, according to Darwinian psychiatry, hysteria was the result of family heredity exacerbated by the stress of puberty and sexual frustration. Hysterics' wish for privacy and independence, and their assertive and rebellious actions were regarded as unnatural. Indeed, the supposed psychological and physical dangers of female rebellion were seen to justify the committal of radical women. 'Over-education' and opposition to marriage were also identified as causes.

Showalter argues that hysteria can be seen as a form of protest in circumstances where women have few other means of expression. The role of the psychiatrist is to reconcile women to their socially defined role so some would believe that if it is natural for women to be dependent and passive, then women who are not must be abnormal and require help to regain normality.

This example illustrates how definitions of mental illness can be used to legitimate dominant values and to censure those social groups with less power. In 1952 The American Psychiatric Association (APA) produced its first official list of mental disorders which included homosexuality as a 'Sociopathic Personality Disturbance'. In 1968 it was recategorized as a 'sexual deviation', along with paedophilia, sadism, fetishism and others. For many years the gay community largely accepted this definition of sickness in preference to the labels of criminal or sinful which were also used. However, by the late 1960s the definition of homosexuality as abnormal became increasingly challenged and a campaign similar to the black civil rights movement was fought against the APA. The campaigners were able to draw on more contemporary social and psychological research to promote their case and eventually, in 1973, homosexuality was removed from the APA's lists.

FEELING HOT UNDER THE COLLAR AND INTOLERANT? YOU'VE CAUGHT A SEVERE DOSE OF HOMOPHOBIA!

Challenging the existence of mental illness

Szasz (1974) rejects the biomedical model of mental illness altogether. He argues that people call others 'mad' when they do not like them or when they disagree with their behaviour. It is a convenient means of controlling those who are perceived as socially disruptive. In this way there is no objective normality or abnormality. If staying indoors was regarded as normal, there would be no such illness as agoraphobia. If slavery wasn't seen as the normal condition for black people in the Southern states of America in the early nineteenth century, there would not have been a mental illness called 'drapetomania', seen as affecting slaves who ran away. However, although we may accept Szasz's analysis in some instances, he can be criticized for ignoring the real personal suffering that mental illness causes and the relief that can be given by psychiatric treatment.

❖ Activity 23 ❖

In essay style , and including examples, discuss the view that mental illness is not an objective fact but a product of political struggle.

Inside the asylum: an interactionist view

Just as sociologists have challenged conventional ideas about mental illness, they have criticized the traditional view that the institution is the best place to treat the mentally ill. Erving Goffman (1968) claims that the psychiatric hospital creates its own subculture – its own adjustment mechanisms which allow both staff and patients to survive but at the expense of any therapeutic goals. Using an interactionist perspective he claims that the mentally ill do not get cured in hospital, rather they learn to act mad and this reduces any chance of returning to the outside world. Goffman argues that once a person has been labelled as sick they go through a series of phases:

❖ the process of mortification

❖ learning a new role

❖ responding to the label 'mentally ill'.

The process of mortification

In this phase the patients identity is stripped away, including powers of self-determination. The attack on a person's dignity may include the removal of personal clothing and possessions, the control of even the most basic things such as going to bed, visiting the bathroom or smoking. There will be a lack of privacy and their inferiority will be reinforced by having to call the staff by their professional titles.

Learning a new role

This phase involves the rebuilding of the person's identity in accordance with the expectations of the institution. Those who comply will be given rewards and privileges whilst those that don't will be 'punished' with such things as isolation, physical restraint, drugs, ECT and even surgery.

Responding to the label 'mentally ill'

Goffman recognizes that people can interpret their experience in different ways and this leads to differences in their reactions to the hospital situation. He identifies five variations of response:

❖ *Withdrawal* – People become extremely introverted and this is seen as confirmation of their mental illness.

❖ *Rebellion* – People actively resist the label and the attempt by the institution to remould them. Again this can be interpreted by the professionals as the person needing further and more intensive treatment.

❖ *Institutionalization* – The patient comes to accept themselves as mentally ill and believes that the hospital is the best and safest place for them. They become frightened of the outside world and they do what they can to remain inside.

❖ *Conversion* – The person comes to accept their new role and tries to become the perfect patient, acting as a 'creep' towards the staff.

❖ *Playing it cool* – This is the most common response and one of the ways to limit damage to the self by the institution. People keep their heads down, keep out of trouble and use a mixture of the responses outlined above in a flexible way.

Overall, Goffman suggests that the interaction processes in the hospital can lead to behaviour which reduces the chance of being released and being able to cope in society at large. He suggests that similar processes occur in other areas of social life.

Evaluation

This and other research did lead to a reassessment of the effects of institutionalization because it gave more in-depth insight from the patient's point of view. It has resulted in more sensitive hospital regimes and encouraged the move towards alternative care in the community. However, Goffman's ground-breaking work is not without its critics. Like many studies of the interactionist school, it is accused of being too small-scale and lacking in rigour. It relies heavily on Goffman's *interpretations* of the patients' experiences and these might not accurately reflect the actual feelings of those concerned. Indeed, Goffman was aware that his sympathies for the patients and his negative view of psychiatry may well have influenced his work. He also gives little attention to wider social processes outside the hospital which could be an important influence on individuals' understanding of their experience. Strauss *et al.* (1978) further suggest that Goffman was unduly pessimistic about the patients' situation as Strauss's own research gave evidence that it *was* possible for them to negotiate changes in their treatment and their release. Moreover, Goffman only dealt with the response of individuals whilst Strauss recognized the importance of group behaviour. Lastly, although Goffman's pessimistic findings may apply in many cases, many people *do* receive successful treatment and overcome their mental illness to rebuild their lives.

Inside the asylum: an ethno-methodological experiment

Rosenhan (1975) was interested in how people came to be defined as insane and developed an experiment to see how the staff of mental hospitals made sense of 'patients' who behaved normally. Research volunteers sought medical help, claiming they were hearing voices – a common symptom of schizophrenia. They were admitted to twelve hospitals where they ceased to simulate any symptoms but despite their normal behaviour, none of the volunteers were recognized as fakes. All were eventually diagnosed as schizophrenic and all discharged with the illness being in 'remission'. Then Rosenham reversed the experiment by telling hospital staff to expect people to try to gain admittance by faking illness. In the next three months, 41 out of 193 cases were identified by staff as being suspicious, even though all were genuinely seeking help. Rosenham is scathing of psychiatrist's belief that they can define mental illness objectively and with accuracy. He argues that 'any diagnostic process that lends itself so readily to massive errors of this sort cannot be very reliable'. Notwithstanding the ethical considerations of the experiment, this research is a serious challenge to the superiority claimed by biomedicine in the area of mental illness.

The community care debate

You will probably be aware that attitudes to the treatment of people with mental illness have changed significantly in recent years. We have seen the closure of institutions, a reduction in the number of hospital beds and the development of care provision within the community. The idea is that people can be supported to live much more successfully in their own homes than they can by shutting them in the artificial world of the hospital. Many people associate the 'care programme' approach with Conservative Government policy of the 1990s, although, in fact, the run-down of the institutions began 35 years ago. However, legislation passed in 1991 and 1993 created the impetus which has resulted in the return of thousands of patients to the communities from which they originally came. Each person being discharged is provided with a care plan, a professional 'key worker' and/or access to medical and/or social work teams. The idea is that these professionals give the support which allows the patient to live in either their own home or with their families, as well as monitoring the need for possible further hospitalization. The principles of community care have enormous support both medically and across the political spectrum, however, the actual practical implementation of the policy has come under a great deal of criticism.

Arguments for community care

❖ It is a far more humane treatment of the mentally ill. Very few patients represent any risk to the public and they should be entitled to as fulfilled a life as possible.

❖ It avoids the institutionalization which made it difficult for people to return and function in the outside world. The main-tenance of existing social relationships makes normalization more likely.

❖ It is far cheaper and the savings made and the funds raised from sale of the assets of the old institutions can be redirected into more effective health care generally.

❖ Given the development of drugs which can be injected and which are long-acting, community care is now practical.

Arguments against community care

❖ In some areas institutions were run-down too quickly, without the framework for community care being adequately put into place. The ad hoc mix of care agencies has led to problems in communication. Vulnerable people have slipped through the care net.

❖ Too many psychiatric beds were lost. Patients now face the 'revolving door' problem. The hospitals are under so much pressure for bed that people undergoing treatment are returned too soon to the outside world and so are then quickly readmitted.

❖ In some cases people have been released who are dangerous and whose problems are so severe that they cannot adequately survive in society. This has led to suicides, and a few cases of members of the public being killed by ex-patients whose level of psychosis was not recognized.

❖ The professional carers are often poorly trained as well as low paid.

❖ 'Community care' is a laughable term. Many ex-patients are socially isolated or placed in the care of families who struggle to meet the person's needs. In many cases, 'communities' have campaigned against the location of the mentally ill in their area.

❖ Ex-patients can find themselves living in poor housing conditions. There has been an increase in the number of private care homes and although many provide good service the fact that they are unregulated and can be established by people with no experience in mental health has led to cases of abuse and neglect. Also, since there is a heavy reliance on local authority housing, large numbers of people with mental-health problems have found themselves in the least desirable housing in the least desirable areas.

❖ The move to community care is about cost-cutting rather than about really improving the lot of one of the most vulnerable sections of the population.

This brief study of mental illness has illustrated that if we are to understand this condition then we must use sociological as well as psychological analysis. The way mental illness is understood and treated remains a controversial medical and social issue.

❖ Activity 24 ❖

Produce a written argument or hold a class debate on the success or failure of the community care policy. The material provided here, as well as your own library and media investigations, should be used as evidence in your assignment.

In Focus

◆

Care in the community?

'The brain-damaged ex-boxer has no home and no prospect of getting on. His nose dribbles constantly and his eyes are dull. He was found, hungry and incontinent, in Acton, four miles east of the hospital, by a Roman Catholic Priest. Community care has done nothing for him.

He says he lives in a council flat, but Annette — a support worker at a day centre run by Acton Homeless Concern said: "He'll say different things to different people. The truth is he's been on the streets for five years."

Four years ago, the centre saw 11 homeless people a day and seldom encountered a psychiatric patient. Now, 200 people pass through each day. Half have psychiatric disorders. At least two have committed suicide since 1990.

The recent Tomlinson Report on the future of hospitals in London confirmed the impression that the run-down in psychiatric beds has given thousands of mentally ill people squalor and destitution rather than the happy, independent lives that supporters of community care promised.

About half of the 60,000 homeless people either sleeping rough or in bed-and-breakfast accommodation in the capital had "significant psychiatric problems", the inquiry found.'

Source: Independent, January 1993

With care and support, ex-patients can lead dignified and fulfilled lives in the community

In Focus

◆

**'Careless-
ness'
in the
community?**

'Mental health groups have called for major investment in community services after a highly critical inquiry report on Christopher Clunis found a "catalogue of failure and missed opportunity".

Clunis, a schizophrenic released from a psychiatric hospital, stabbed Jonathan Zito to death in a London tube station.

Last week's independent report points to a catastrophic breakdown in communications between social services, police, the health service, and housing, as well as a failure by several workers to recognise the gravity of Clunis's condition. It says every psychiatric service should establish a specialist team with earmarked funding to support them.

Even though Clunis committed 20 assaults, seven involving weapons, most agencies appear to have concluded he was harmless. Among the inquiry's recommendations are an urgent need for more psychiatric and medium secure unit beds in London, more crisis centres, and more investment in approved social workers.

Health Secretary Virginia Bottomley responded to the report by announcing a further £10 million for London mental health services, far less than many agencies believe is needed.

Bottomley accused Haringey social services of having "made some of the most serious mistakes". The report says Haringey's frontline advice and assessment team was "considerably understaffed". But Haringey council leader Toby Harris dismissed her comments as a "desperate attempt to deflect criticism from the government's appalling policies". The advice team was now fully staffed, he added.

Inquiry team member Richard Linghain, Scilly Isles social services director, said the case showed quick and professional action was essential. "Advice and guidance from approved social workers is absolutely crucial," he said.

Mental health charity MIND immediately called on the government to plough an additional £300 million into community services.

MIND director Judi Clements said she doubted whether practitioners "working under so much pressure" should be criticised. But Jayne Zito, whose husband was killed, said staff were partly to blame. "They failed in their professional role and their statutory duty."'

Source: Community Care, 3 October 1994

Cartoon © Fran, *Community Care*, 7 July 1994

❖ Poverty and welfare: Introduction

What it means to be poor is an important question for sociologists to investigate. On one level we can watch the grinding poverty of many people living in economically developing countries beamed to us in the comfort of our living rooms. However, when we voice our own feelings of not always being able to afford the things we would like, this is poverty of another kind. The idea that poverty can mean different things is an important issue for sociologists, since how it is perceived influences how it is measured, how much is discovered and what solutions or welfare policies are required to tackle it. In addition to these themes, this section is also concerned with the sociological explanations given for the

existence and perpetuation of poverty in economically developed countries. (Chapter 8, *World sociology*, discusses poverty on the global scale.) The explanations range from those emphasizing that poverty is the fault of the individual or their cultural environment to those which see it as a structural feature of society and the inadequacies of measures to deal with it. Poverty has long been recognized as a social problem requiring official action. Some regard poverty as a threat to social order whilst others construct the problem of poverty as a question of social justice. The nature of welfare provision and its relative success in Britain forms the theme of the last part of this chapter.

Poverty: definition, measurement and extent

❖ Activity 25 ❖

Write your own 'dictionary definition' of what you see as poverty. Compare your version with that of others in your group and discuss the similarities and differences.

Absolute poverty

Absolute poverty can be defined as the minimum required to sustain life. People are in absolute poverty when they no longer have sufficient resources for actual physical survival. This definition can be extended to include a wider range of 'basic human needs' such as access to safe drinking water, sanitation and education.

Relative poverty

In modern Britain we could say poverty is a thing of the past. Using an absolute definition this may well be justified but commonsense and our own observations tell us that poverty does still exist if we regard it in a relative way. Relative poverty is measured

by members of a particular society, according to the conventions of the day, making a judgement of what is considered a reasonable and acceptable standard of living and style of life

Individuals, families and groups in the population can be said to be in poverty when they lack the resources to obtain the types of diets, participate in the activities and have living conditions and amenities which are customary, or at least widely encouraged and approved, in the societies to which they belong (Townsend 1979).

Townsend sees resources as both income and assets such as housing, company benefits, education, health and other social services. In a rapidly changing society, definitions of poverty based on relative standards will be constantly changing as luxuries become so common that they are

seen as necessities. For example, elderly relatives may talk of the first time they saw television, yet today we expect to see at least one in every home.

❖ Activity 26 ❖

Look at the photo on the left (of Bombay in India) and the one on p. 367, taken in London. To what extent do you agree that both photographs show scenes of absolute or relative poverty? Give reasons for your answer.

In Focus

◆

Sen vs Townsend

t looks as if the long debate between the absolutists and the relativists has been, to some extent at least, a case of shadow-boxing. The battle lines in this debate have been drawn most sharply between Amartya Sen and Peter Townsend. Taking issues with the relativist position, Sen has argued that:

> "Poverty is not just a matter of being 'relatively' *poorer than others* in the society, but of not having some basic opportunities of well-being – the failure to have certain minimum 'capabilities'. The criteria of minimum capabilities are 'absolute' not in the sense that they must not vary from society to society ... or over time ..., but people's deprivation is judged absolutely, and not simply *in comparison with* the deprivation of others in that society." (Sen 1985, p. 655) [our italics]

In other words, we cannot call someone 'poor' just because he or she has less than other people without regard to what that person possesses and what the others possess. Or, as Sen put it, "It would be absurd to call someone poor just because he had the means to buy only one Cadillac a day when others in that community could buy two of these cars each day" (Sen 1985). Moreover, Sen argues that there is an "irreducible absolutist core in the idea of poverty". Townsend's main objection to Sen's argument is as follows:

> "The problem about this reiteration of the virtues of an 'absolutist core' to the meaning of poverty is the underestimation of the importance of needs other than for food (and perhaps other 'physical' goods and facilities) in the countries of the Third World like India and Pakistan and not just the rich countries of the First World like Britain." (Townsend 1985, p.655)

But on closer inspection of the arguments between Sen and Townsend and among many other of the protagonists, we discover that the real difference between contemporary approaches to poverty is not actually between relative versus absolute concepts. Virtually everyone agrees that poverty is a relative phenomenon but the differences lie in the degree of generosity or parsimony built into the definition. In other words both the meaning of human needs and the extent to which they must be satisfied if an individual is to be classified as "poor" are still questions open to research and discussion in the social sciences.'

Source: Walker and Walker (1995)

❖ Activity 27 ❖

In your own words summarize the reasons given for the retention of the idea of absolute poverty in the *In Focus* on the previous page.

In essay style and making reference to the *In Focus*, discuss the usefulness of relative and absolute definitions of poverty.

Subjective poverty

People defined as poor by other people's standards might not actually regard themselves as poor. Poverty may include aspects of life other than the material or those considered significant by the sociologist. For example, the Balinese may see themselves as culturally rich compared with the Western tourists they see, but obviously are materially disadvantaged when the price of an air ticket is more than the average Indonesian annual salary.

Evaluation

Absolute definitions are too simplistic and inflexible. What are defined as minimum needs are variable within societies and between societies. A coat and a flush toilet may well be a minimum requirement for a person in a British city but the same could not be said for some one living in the Amazon rainforest. A person's 'needs' are not simply subsistence requirements but are determined by the social context in which they live. For example, British parents may well sacrifice their own needs to ensure that their children have the Christmas presents that others have. This behaviour is not about physical survival but about the wish to fit in with what is regarded as customary. The absolute definition is accused of proposing a style of life for the poor which is significantly different from those in the rest of society. Although the idea of relative poverty has gained widespread acceptance, there is considerable controversy over how it can be

accurately measured. Since what is regarded as a normal life style changes between and within countries and over time, comparative studies are particularly difficult. It is argued that one of the problems of relative definitions is that poverty can never be eradicated since the poorest section of society will never be able to afford the lifestyle generally considered to be normal. However, Townsend does believe that raising benefit levels, targeting unemployment and limiting the wealth of the super rich can make inroads into relative poverty. He does not believe that poverty can be dealt with in the short term, but that long-term measures to redistribute wealth and income could be effective.

Measurement and extent

'Measuring poverty is an exercise in demarcation – lines have to be drawn where none may be visible and they have to be made bold. Where one draws the line is itself a battlefield.' (Desai 1986)

Since poverty is a contested concept there is little agreement on how to measure it. The use of an absolute or relative definition will determine:

❖ the tools or 'yardstick' used to measure poverty

❖ at what level the poverty line is drawn

❖ how much poverty is seen to exist.

Seebohm Rowntree

As a philanthropic nineteenth-century entrepreneur, Rowntree was concerned about the extent of poverty in Britain. With Charles Booth he attempted to find out the minimum amount of food, fuel, clothing and shelter necessary for a healthy life as defined by experts. These goods could then be priced and those with an income below that needed to cover the cost of them could be said to be the poor. In the first study by the Rowntree foundation, in York in 1899, 33 per cent of the population were found to be in poverty. In two subsequent studies, in

1936 and 1950, the figures fell to 18 per cent and 1.5 per cent, even though these studies did include additional goods like newspapers and tobacco in their poverty yardstick. Using Rowntree's almost absolute measure, poverty could be seen as a residual problem concentrated in specific groups of people like the elderly who could be targeted by the welfare state.

However, the way Rowntree measured poverty is said to have underestimated its extent. People are not likely to have expert knowledge of the best ways to spend their income. More importantly, diets and lifestyles are set by social convention and these are rarely the most efficient ways of using resources. In sum, the measurement tool was too crude and the numbers of people classified as poor too few because of the failure to fully recognize the relative nature of poverty.

Official measures

Another way of measuring the extent of poverty is to use the criteria set down by the state. In the USA the official index is taken as the minimum cost of an adequate diet multiplied by three. Britain has no official poverty line, but the level of benefits provided by the welfare state can be seen to be the minimum deemed necessary for an acceptable quality of life.

However, official measures are criticized for failing to take into account the relativity of poverty and for being closer to absolute measures. Indeed the benefit levels in Britain were initially based on the measurements used by Rowntree. These indices are equally unreliable because many people entitled to claim benefits do not do so and, since the benefit levels and who has the right to claim them fluctuates with political whim, it is difficult to use the statistics for comparative purposes. More generous benefits can actually create more people officially recognized as poor.

Another way the British government has defined poverty has been an income less than 50 per cent of the average (see Table 10.9). This has the advantage of not being tied to benefit levels and allowing comparisons between countries and over time. However, this measure tells us more about income inequality than poverty itself.

Peter Townsend

Townsend is a major critic of how poverty has been officially measured and of the social policies developed in Britain to deal with it. In 1968–69 he surveyed 2052 households using a 'deprivation index' designed to measure poverty in a relative way. The index included twelve items Townsend believed could be seen as normal aspects of life for most British people (see Table 10.10). Each household was given a score depending on the number of the twelve items absent and this was then related to income, the numbers of people within the household and the number of dependants. He claimed that he had objectively calculated that below an income of 150 per cent of basic supplementary benefit levels, the amount of deprivation rapidly increased. In his influential research, Townsend found that 22.9 per cent of the population lived in poverty; the official figure was 6.1 per cent.

Table 10.9 **Numbers and proportions of individuals living below 50 per cent of average income before and after housing costs**

Year	Before housing costs:		After housing costs:	
	millions	%	millions	%
1979	4.4	8	5.0	9
1981	4.7	9	6.2	11
1987	8.7	16	10.5	19
1988/89	10.4	19	12.0	22
1991/92	11.7	21	13.9	25
1992/93	11.4	20	14.1	25

Source: Oppenheim and Harker (1996, p. 39)

Table 10.10 Townsend's deprivation index

1 Has not had a week's holiday away from home in the last 12 months.

2 *Adults only.* Has not had a relative or friend to the home for a meal or a snack in the last four weeks.

3 *Adults only.* Has not been out in the last four weeks to a relative or friend for a meal or a snack.

4 *Children only (under 15).* Has not had a friend to play or to tea in the last four weeks.

5 *Children only.* Did not have a party on last birthday.

6 Has not had an afternoon or evening out for entertainment in the last two weeks.

7 Does not have fresh meat (including meals out) as many as four days a week.

8 Has gone through one or more days in the past fortnight without a cooked meal.

9 Has not had a cooked breakfast most days of the week.

10 Household does not have a refrigerator.

11 Household does not usually have a Sunday joint (3 in 4 times)

12 Household does not have sole use of four amenities (flush WC; sink or washbasin and cold-water tap; fixed bath or shower; gas or electric cooker).

Source: Townsend (1979)

However, Piachaud (1981), whilst recognizing the importance of measuring poverty in a relative way, is critical of Townsend's deprivation index. He argues that some of the components of the index have more to do with taste than poverty. People may choose not have cooked breakfasts or roast dinners rather than going without them because of necessity. It is not clear what some of the indices have to do with poverty or why some of them were selected in preference to other aspects of life. Townsend is accused of being arbitrary, with the index reflecting his own personal opinions. Further, the index focuses on private aspects of behaviour. He does not include more public aspects such as deprivation at work, of environment or of public services.

In his more recent work Townsend has tried to overcome some of these criticisms. In a survey of 2703 Londoners in 1985–6, he asked people a long list of questions about their diet, clothing, housing, facilities, environment, location, employment and many aspects of social life. He made some allowance for variations in taste. Alongside this objective measure, Townsend attempted to measure poverty subjectively. He asked people their opinions on the meaning of poverty and how much money they thought was needed to stay out of poverty. Townsend comments on the closeness of the subjective and objective measures, with both indicating that the rates of minimum benefit levels fall short of need by over 50 per cent.

Joanna Mack and Stewart Lansey

The research by Mack and Lansey in 1983 and 1990 also aimed to discover the extent of relative poverty. In the first study they surveyed 1174 people, asking them what they regarded as necessities or desirable for a normal life in modern Britain. They discovered that people shared similar ideas on what were necessities and if 50 per cent of the respondents agreed then that item was included in the poverty index (see Table 10.11). When surveying households for the absence of these 22 necessities Mack and Lansey asked to see if this was to do with choice or because of lack of resources. Those who were in poverty were those who had an enforced lack of three of those things defined as a necessity. In 1983 Mack and Lansey found 5 million adults and 2.5 million children were in poverty (13.8 per cent of the population). By 1990 the public perceptions of necessities had changed and the number of items on the index increased to 32. Some of the new things considered to be necessities included a telephone and a reasonable standard of home decoration. In 1990 the researchers found that the numbers of people lacking 3 or more necessities had increased to 11 million. Moreover, two thirds of the poor were on state benefits.

Table 10.11 Index for Mack and Lansey: Proportion of respondents deeming items to be necessary

Items	1990 %	1983 %
A damp-free home	98	96
An inside toilet (not shared with another household)	97	96
Heating to warm living areas of the house if it's cold	97	97
Beds for everyone in the household	95	94
Bath, not shared with another household	95	94
A decent state of decoration in the home	92	*
Fridge	92	77
Warm waterproof coat	91	87
Three meals a day for children**	90	82
Two meals a day (for adults)	90	64
Insurance	88	*
Fresh fruit	88	*
Toys for children**	84	71
Separate bedrooms for every child over 10 of different sex**	82	77
Carpets in living rooms and bedrooms in the home	78	70
Meat or fish or vegetarian equivalent every other day	77	63
Celebrations on special occasions like Christmas	74	69
Two pairs of all-weather shoes	74	78
Washing machine	73	67
Presents for friends or family once a year	69	63
Out of school activities**	69	*
Regular savings of £10 a month	68	*
Hobby or leisure activity	67	64
New, not secondhand, clothes	65	64
A roast joint, or its vegetarian equivalent once a week	64	67
Leisure equipment for children**	61	57
Television	58	51
Telephone	56	43
An annual week's holiday away, not with relatives	54	63
A 'best' outfit for special occasions	54	48
An outing for children once a week**	53	40
Children's friends round for tea/snack fortnightly**	52	37

* Not included in the 1983 survey
** Asked of families with children only.

Source: Frayman 1991, p. 4

The studies by Mack and Lansey try to overcome the accusations made against previous studies of relative poverty of being arbitrary in their approach. However, as in all surveys, this cannot be completely overcome. Inevitably the sociologist must initially decide upon the range of choices from which people can select, whereas the respondents could well have had ideas about necessities that Mack and Lansey had not even thought to include. Closed questions mean that it is impossible for people to discuss their feelings in depth or to qualify their views, e.g. someone may have all the items on the index but of such inferior quality that they can be regarded as being poor. The decision that poverty occurs when three items are lacking is another arbitrary decision imposed by the sociologist. Why this number and not any other? We also have to be cautious in accepting the evidence that poverty has increased, (although other studies, including official figures like those in Table 10.9 do substantiate this), since the larger index means there is a greater possibility of a household having an enforced absence of three necessities.

❖ Activity 28 ❖

Coursework suggestion

Update Mack and Lansey's index by using a survey. Ask people what they consider are necessities. Surveys need careful construction and you should refer to Chapter 7, *Theory and methods*.

Are there any new items to be added to the list? How do your findings compare with the earlier studies and what implications might this have for the level of poverty? Evaluate the success of your survey technique.

Who are the poor?

Table 10.12 Official figures and unofficial poverty

Key facts in 1990/91

- adults in poverty — 9.6 million
- children in poverty — 3.9 million
- proportion of adults in poverty — 1 in 4
- proportion of children in poverty — 1 in 3

Poverty lines = half national average income £ weekly 1993 prices)

- half average income (per capita) — £112
- single adult — £45
- couple with no children — £82
- couple with three children — £137

Groups likely to be poor

- unemployed — 7 in 10
- lone parents — 6 in 10
- single pensioners — 4.5 in 10

Large groups among the poor

- couples with children — 4.9 million
- pensioners — 3.5 million
- unemployed — 2.1 million
- couples with a full-time worker — 1.5 million

Source: Independence Educational Publishers (1993)

Figure 10.9
The risk of poverty[1] by economic status in 1992/93

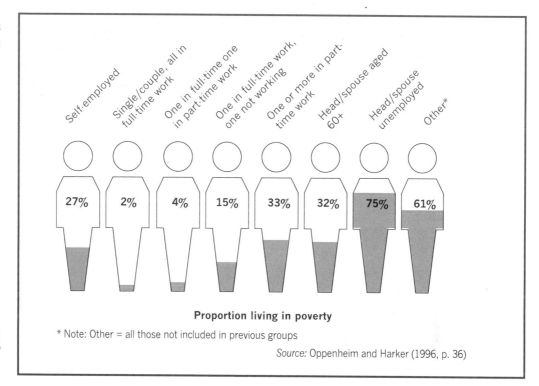

Proportion living in poverty

* Note: Other = all those not included in previous groups

Source: Oppenheim and Harker (1996, p. 36)

[1] Poverty is defined as living below 50% of average income after housing costs

Figure 10.10
The risk of poverty by family status in 1992/93

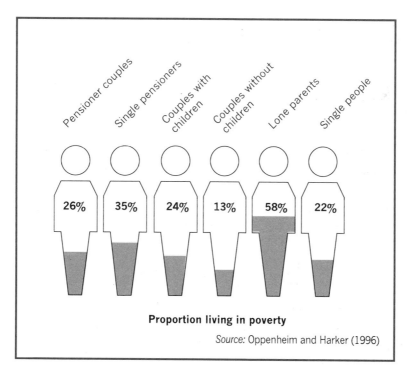

Proportion living in poverty

Source: Oppenheim and Harker (1996)

Table 10.13 Percentage of social security claimants by sex: Britain, 1993/94

Benefit	Men	Women
Industrial injury disablement benefit	86	14
Invalidity benefit	73	27
Maternity benefit	nil	100
Non-contributory retirement pension	20	80
Retirement pension	35	65
Sickness benefit	58	42
Unemployment benefit	76	24
Widow's benefit	nil	100
Reduced earnings allowance	81	19
Attendance allowance	29	71
Child benefit	3	97
One-parent benefit	9	91
Invalid care allowance	31	69
Mobility allowance	52	48
Severe disablement allowance	38	62
Family credit *	43	57
Income support	48	52
Disability living allowance	52	48
Disability working allowance	60	40

* Figures are based on sex of main earner.

Source: House of Commons, *Hansard*, 25 May 1995, cols 695-7

Table 10.14 Weekly earnings for men and women in London by race, 1986

White men	£195.00
Black men	£165.00
White women	£133.00
Black women	£109.00

Source: Child Poverty Action Group (1992)

❖ Activity 29 ❖

Using Tables 10.12 to 10.14, the *In Focus* below and Figs 10.9 and 10.10, identify and illustrate with statistics the social groups most at risk of poverty.

Suggest reasons for the variation in the concentration of poverty by gender, age, social class and ethnicity. You should make reference to Chapter 6, *Stratification and differentiation*. You will also find the first reference in Further reading at the end of this chapter useful, as well as the *In Focus* on p. 474. You should give at least three reasons for each group and explain them clearly.

In Focus
◆
Women and poverty

Women ... are less likely than men to be receiving the superior contributory benefits and more likely to be receiving the inferior non-contributory equivalents. Many women are entitled to neither (leaving aside benefits for children) and are therefore reliant on means-tested income support or on a man for economic support.

Explaining poverty

To understand why poverty exists you will need to look at the sociological explanations for the existence of inequality in society as a whole. This means it is important that you refer to Chapter 6, *Stratification and differentiation*. Particular attention needs to be paid to the debate concerning the underclass. After reading the relevant section, ask yourself whether the poor *do* constitute a separate social class. In this section we will examine and assess sociological arguments that focus specifically on the causes of poverty.

Individualistic approaches

This is a non-sociological explanation and places the blame for poverty on a person's own short-comings. They may be lazy, wasteful, have minimal capabilities and lack initiative. Often a distinction is made between the 'deserving' and 'undeserving' poor. Those worthy of assistance include the elderly, children and the sick – people who have fallen on hard times through no fault of their own. These views were strongly held in Victorian Britain and led to punitive welfare provision in the form of the workhouse.

Such ideas remain common and have seen a political resurgence with the New Right. The *In Focus* on p. 471 outlines David Marsland's argument that too 'soft' welfare measures can make people poor by trapping them into a culture of dependency.

Most sociologists do not accept that individuals are to blame for their own poverty. They recognize that the distribution of societal resources is beyond individual control. The arguments of the New Right have been strongly criticized. Bill Jordan in the *In Focus* on p. 471 outlines the case for a more generous welfare system, viewing its current meanness as a cause of poverty since benefits are so low that they do not raise people above the poverty line.

The culture of poverty

This approach does not directly blame the individual for their situation, but does agree with the New Right that the way of life of the poor is a cause of poverty. This culture includes attitudes such as fatalism– nothing can be done to improve one's circum-stances, present-centredness – living for today rather than for tomorrow, apathy, family instability and little political involvement. These attitudes, and therefore poverty, are passed by socialization from one generation to another.

Oscar Lewis (1961), who first identified these traits, believed that the 'culture of poverty' thesis was most applicable to the poor of economically developing countries. However, Harrington (1992) argues that similar values are found amongst the disadvantaged of wealthy nations. This approach does tend to give a very passive view of the poor and ignores the vitality of many impoverished communities and the range of self-help schemes they develop. There is also little evidence to support the view that poverty is always inter-generational because people slip in and out of poverty at different points in the life cycle (see Fig. 10.11).

Figure 10.11
Poverty during the life cycle

Childhood	Youth	Married with children	Middle-aged, children leaving home	Old age

Poverty line

Poverty

❖ Activity 30 ❖

Explain why the life cycle is important in relation to the social distribution of poverty.

How can this idea be used to counter the individualistic approaches?

Poverty as situational

From this perspective, poverty should not be blamed on individuals or the culture they belong to but can be seen as a product of the economic and social position of specific social groups such as the low paid, unemployed, sick and the elderly. It is argued that the poor share mainstream values but their difficult circumstances mean they are unlikely to achieve them – so values such as fatalism can be viewed as realistic and rational. This view parallels the social democratic approach discussed below. If the economic circumstances of the poor were improved by effective welfare measures then they would adopt mainstream behaviour. Ulf Hannerz (1969) believes that situational constraint and the culture of poverty ideas should be combined, suggesting that the values of the poor do arise out economic circumstances. However, once established, the culture of poverty can limit progress even if opportunities improve.

Radical approaches

Marxist and other conflict theorists criticize the explanations above for concentrating too much on individuals and specific social groups and failing to fully recognize that poverty is a structural feature of a capitalist economic system. Marxists see the existence and perpetuation of poverty as serving the interests of the ruling class. For example, low pay serves as a base level from which all workers compete, and fear of poverty and unemployment ensures that wage demands are driven downwards. However, the Marxist analysis does not fully explain why such groups as women and ethnic minorities are concentrated amongst the poor, nor why poverty evidently continues in countries which have undergone socialist revolution

Townsend agrees that poverty is strongly linked to social class but adopts a Weberian conflict approach. The majority of the poor are unskilled and semi-skilled and as such have a weak position in the labour market. Women, minority ethnic groups and the disabled have the additional problem of discrimination. The difficulty for these groups in competing successfully in the labour market means that they are concentrated in low-paid, insecure jobs, supplemented by inadequate benefits. Townsend believes that the state can address the problem of inequality in society and create a more equitable distribution of resources.

Tackling poverty in Britain

The way social policies develop to deal with poverty will reflect the way its causes are perceived. Thus, if you believe that it is a result of individual failings then you would be unlikely to give any assistance at all! In this section we are going to examine the role of the 'modern' welfare state in Britain and its success in reducing or eliminating poverty.

The origin of the welfare state

There is a common misconception that the welfare state began in the 1945–51 period of the post-war Labour government. In fact its history is much longer. However the structure of the modern welfare state and many of the principles operating today were established then. The mood for social reform arose out of war time experience.

Many felt they had earned a fairer society by virtue of their efforts and deprivation. Politicians recognized the new climate of opinion and a variety of government reports were carried out during the war into a number of social issues. The most important was the Beveridge Report (1942) which identified the five giant evils which it was believed to be the duty of the state to tackle and eliminate. They were:

❖ *Idleness* (unemployment) – the government was to take active measures to create jobs

❖ *Want* (poverty) – to be solved by a universal National Insurance Scheme and a system of benefits

❖ *Squalor* (poor housing) – to be defeated by extensive state housing, the development of New Towns and effective planning

❖ *Disease* (poor health) – to be challenged by the NHS established in 1946

❖ *Ignorance* (lack of education) – to be defeated by free secondary education for all following the 1944 Education Act.

During the Second World War and in the years immediately following, legislation was passed to establish the institutions of the modern welfare system. There was a general acceptance of the social democratic ideal that the state should intervene in the workings of the free market to cushion people from the inevitable problems of capitalism, including unemployment and poverty. It was recognized that some social groups did not represent a source of profit and would not be catered for by the private sector. The state needed to take steps in the interests of social justice and to avoid the conflicts a grossly divided society would contain. In the early days, many believed that the welfare state was the ultimate in achieving a citizen's rights, with caring capitalism seeing them through 'from cradle to grave'. However, the statutory sector has never been the only, and some would argue, the most important provider of welfare in Britain. Other sources of provision include the voluntary, private and informal sectors. The informal sector consists of the support

provided by friends and family particularly women (see also Chapter 3, *Families and households*). The range of welfare-providers has led to the use of the term 'welfare pluralism' to describe the situation in Britain.

Recent trends in welfare policy

Since 1979 there have been marked changes in welfare provision in Britain – the nature of the welfare state and its future development have been subject to heated political debate. The policies of the New Right have reflected their overall philosophy and wish to curtail the spiralling cost of the state system which is seen as stifling economic growth. The free market is regarded as capable of providing wealth and happiness for all by ensuring that prices and wages find the correct level thereby creating full employment and a match between supply and demand. As the economy expands so the benefits of growth filter to all levels of society. The emphasis is placed on self reliance, personal initiative and individual responsibility. However, although the New Right have criticized the welfare state for being a financial burden and for creating a culture of dependency, they have not suggested abolition but rather a radical overhaul. The changes to welfare provision generally incorporate many of the themes we have already discussed in relation to recent changes in the NHS and also in education.

Streamlining the system

Recent welfare policies have seen more *selective* and *residual* provision, the argument being that scarce resources should be targeted at the most needy. This contrasts with the approach of *universalism*, which views the provision of welfare as a citizen's right, as in the case of child benefit. Part of the paring down of welfare availability is the desire to discourage the culture of dependency. Thus, whereas in the past people could obtain one-off grants for important

Cartoon © Fran, Community Care, 18 May 1996

items such as a cooker, now people have to apply for a discretionary loan from the social fund which must be paid back. The unemployed must produce evidence that they are actively seeking work and they cannot refuse employment without penalties to their benefits. The long-term unemployed are also expected to work for their benefits in community projects.

Encouraging greater pluralism

Policies have directly and indirectly encouraged the provision of welfare by the private, voluntary and informal sectors. We have seen how family members have been affected by the move to care in the community. Likewise, the raising of the age of entitlement to income support from 16 to 18 in 1988 certainly reduced young people's financial dependence on the state, but increased dependence on the family. The New Right also believe that the voluntary sector could expand to take on more statutory duties currently provided by social services, particularly in areas such as childcare. It is argued that independent welfare agencies are cheaper to run, more innovative and responsive to specific needs of groups of people. However, others argue

that it is difficult to see how an under-funded voluntary network could have the resources, expertise and organizational structures to cope.

Some would argue, controversially, that the welfare state is being privatized, pointing out the following trends:

❖ The private sector is being encouraged to provide services, for example the rapid growth of old people's homes.

❖ The state is reducing its subsidies to service users, e.g. the introduction of charges for dental and eye tests and the rapid rise in the cost of prescriptions.

❖ State housing has been sold whilst limits have been put on new council house building encouraging people to look for homes in the private sector.

Has the welfare state been successful?

The way we answer this question partly depends on what we believe the intention of the welfare state is and whether we define poverty in a relative or absolute sense. If we see the purpose of the welfare state to be a modern day 'Robin Hood', redistributing resources from the rich to the poor and fighting inequality, then the answer is that the system has been unsuccessful. The relative ineffectiveness of the NHS and state education to close social divides in health and opportunity are discussed earlier in this chapter and in Chapter 4, while Chapter 6 examines how variations in income and wealth have remained virtually unchanged throughout this century. However, the welfare state can be viewed as a safety net for society's most vulnerable groups and as such, it does blunt the edges of inequality. Absolute poverty has mostly been abolished in Britain, but whether this is the result of welfare provision or economic growth is debatable. The studies by Townsend, and Mack and Lansey have shown that relative poverty continues to exist and grow. The *In Focus* on the next page points to negative and positive evaluations of the welfare state from different sociological perspectives.

In Focus

◆

For and against universal welfare provision

'Universal welfare provision creates a dependent population'

Arguments for the proposition:

❖ Universal welfare provision (UWP) increases public expenditure and means that there is less money to invest elsewhere in the economy, which in turn would increase the general standard of living.

❖ The creation of huge centralized bureaucracies to administer UWP weakens the strength of 'natural' sources of welfare and support – the family, the local community and voluntary organizations.

❖ Often the most needy do not get the help they need because the do not know how to 'work the system' for all their entitlements.

❖ UWP takes away people's sense of personal responsibility and encourages welfare dependency.

❖ It makes staying unemployed a viable option for many people.

❖ It facilitates the growth of single-parent families.

Source: adapted from Marsland (1989)

Arguments against the proposition:

❖ UWP brings everyone's standard of living up to an acceptable level.

❖ It frees people from dependence: countries which rely on selective systems (like the USA) create large underclasses of disadvantaged people with no legal route out of poverty.

❖ If people lack the opportunities UWP provides for earning and saving, they will turn to stealing and cheating, thus creating a violent and unsafe society for us all.

❖ The selective welfare system is more likely to encourage dependency than UWP. If an unemployed person is entitled to free education, health and benefits, but a person in paid employment must pay for schools, health, food, etc., out of their wages, then many low-paid or unskilled people will not be able to afford to work. People will lose their incentive to work and save.

Source: adapted from Jordan (1989)

❖ Activity 31 ❖

1 Do the arguments for and against the proposition have any points in common? If so, what are they?

2 Hold a class debate on this issue. Before doing this you may wish to do further research by referring to newspaper sources.

3 In essay style evaluate the view that the welfare state has created more poverty than it has solved. You should write at least two sides of A4 and draw upon theoretical and empirical material.

Here we are concerned with examining the the evidence regarding the redistributive effects of taxation and which social groups are advantaged by welfare provision.

Taxation

Direct taxation includes income tax and this does take a larger percentage of the income of the rich. Indirect taxation includes VAT and duties on goods like cigarettes and petrol. These 'spending taxes' are not related to income and take a disproportionate amount of the income of the poor. Recent policy has been to reduce income tax and raise revenue indirectly. In a study examining the effects of tax changes between 1985 and 1995, Giles and Johnson found that the poorest tenth of the population has lost on average £3 per week or 2.9 per cent of their income, whilst the richest tenth gained £31.30 or 5.5 per cent of their income. Moreover, the wealthy are more likely to have sources of income, including government-supported saving schemes like TESSAs (Tax Exempt Special Savings Accounts) and PEPs (Personal Equity Plans), and fringe benefits such as free medical insurance which are tax exempted. This has led to claims that, relatively, the poor are now worse off than before particularly in the light of benefit cuts.

Who is most advantaged by welfare provision?

It seems common sense that the most disadvantaged will make the greatest use of the welfare state and so gain most from its benefits. Certainly, those claiming benefits such as the Job Seekers Allowance obtain something that those in work do not. Such benefits do represent a safety net which you are not allowed to go through, in principle if not in practice. However, Le Grand takes a closer look at who gains most from the welfare state.

Education

Le Grand (1982) found that the most wealthy did receive slightly less benefit in the early stages of education, but when higher education like university is taken into account then the state system could be viewed as a subsidy to the middle class. This is because the higher social classes are much more likely to stay longer in education, and higher education is the most expensive sector of the system. Indeed, the capitation formula for schools gives more money per head for 16-18 year olds than it does for those of compulsory school age.

Nevertheless, the expansion of higher education and the provision of student grants has allowed increasing numbers from lower social groups to receive education at degree level. The recent reduction in the state contribution to student grants, tougher means testing, the fall in value of the grants and private loan schemes may deter those

most disadvantaged from entering higher education, as well as being a burden on the middle classes. The introduction of an internal market is also criticized for concentrating resources in already advantaged schools in middle-class areas.

Housing

Le Grand concluded that the richest households received nearly twice as much state subsidy to housing than the poorest households – because higher-income households gain significantly from indirect benefits such as tax relief on mortgages and being exempt from capital gains tax as property increases in value. However, in terms of *direct* expenditure on housing benefits and council house maintenance and management, the poor do gain most. But, under New Right policy, there has been a cutback in direct subsidy, by the sale of state housing, increasing rents and tightening the criteria for benefits and housing.

Transport

Le Grand argues that on balance the higher social classes benefit most from state policies on transport. The lowest social groups are less likely to benefit from expenditure on road building and possile subsidies to rail and bus companies because they travel less extensively. One of the largest subsidies is to the commuters in the Southeast, who are disproportionately middle-class.

Health

There is considerable evidence to support the view that there is an 'inverse care law' whereby those with most need have access to the fewest medical resources. Various reasons have been offered for this and you should refer back to the section 'Inequalities in health and illness' (see p. 426).

Evaluation

The welfare state does not automatically advantage the poorest groups in society. It has not been a means to reduce social inequalities, although it has provided a minimum level below which it has been recognized that people should not be allowed to fall. The welfare state has done more to address absolute rather than relative poverty. It is argued that the more selective and residual policies of the New Right have lowered the safety net, increasing poverty in both senses and thus widened the gap between rich and poor.

Radical views of the welfare state

Marxism

The main elements of the Marxist view of the welfare state are:

❖ The welfare state was created to pacify the working class by giving them a stake in society and, through the discipline imposed by the education system, making them obedient to their employers. It is an agent of ideological control, making people believe in 'caring capitalism'.

❖ The welfare state benefits capitalists by giving them a healthy, well housed, well educated workforce. The state also supports the unemployed – the reserve army of labour – ready for capitalists to use during economic expansion.

❖ The costs of the welfare state are not borne by capitalists but by the state with money raised through the taxation of the working class.

❖ As Le Grand has shown above, the wealthy can gain direct advantages from the system.

However not all Marxists have such a negative view or merely see the system as functioning to satisfy the needs of capitalism. Gough (1979) sees the introduction of the welfare state and the growth of social expenditure in the 1960s and 1970s as a direct result of working class pressure. It can be seen as a working class achievement, a concession wrested from capitalism. However, the recent cuts and changes in welfare policy indicate that the victory was short lived. For Marxists the welfare state can never eradicate poverty. This will only be achieved when the structural inequalities built into the capitalist system are dismantled.

Feminism

Feminists see the welfare system as incorporating the patriarchal ideology found in the rest of society. It is a means by which women's subordinate social position is maintained and reinforced. For example:

❖ Until recently married women's income tax affairs had to be handled by their husbands so a women was legally obliged to disclose all her financial information to husband, but not vice versa.

❖ Prior to a European court ruling, married women could not claim an Attendance Allowance for looking after an infirm relative, although married men or single women could.

In spite of the modernization of benefits it is argued that welfare provision still assumes that a women's role is to be married, dependent and in the home, with the man as breadwinner. Feminists influenced by Marxism see this as directly supporting the nuclear family needed to maintain and reproduce the labour force for capitalism. The belief that the primary role for women is in the home means that when they do work in *paid* employment, low wages can be justified since they are merely supplementing the income of their husbands. Radical feminists identify men in general rather than capitalists in particular as responsible for women's oppression. They suggest a female withdrawal from and opposition to patriarchal society and its welfare institutions. They suggest that women's self-help groups, women-only hospitals, clinics and co-operatives offer the best chance of escaping from their situation. For liberal feminists, reform is possible and women can implement changes by getting into positions of power or pressure group activity. Sexist welfare policies can be repealed and modified, as in the case of the two examples above.

❖ Activity 32 ❖

Official measures like Table 10.9 on p. 461 and the studies discussed earlier suggest that poverty and inequality have increased in recent years. The Rowntree Report described in the *In Focus* below reached this conclusion in 1995. Read the article carefully and complete the questions below.

1 From the extract and elsewhere describe the evidence that poverty has increased.

2 Identify the reasons the article gives for the growth of poverty and express them in your own words.

3 In what ways may recent changes in welfare and taxation systems have contributed to rising poverty?

4 Explain why the trends identified may lead to problems of social cohesion.

5 The article suggests a number of strategies for dealing with the problem of growing poverty. To what extent do you believe that Social democrats, the New Right, and the various radical approaches would accept these as viable? Explain your answer.

In Focus
◆
Growing inequality means the poor keep getting poorer

'The gap between rich and poor is now so wide that it is damaging the cohesiveness of society without bringing any attendant economic benefits, says the Joseph Rowntree Foundation Inquiry into Income and Wealth. And there are no signs that the adverse trends are easing up....

The poorest 20 to 30 per cent of the population has failed to share in economic growth since 1979, with the experience of poverty and exclusion much higher in the non-white population, the report says.

Income inequality in Britain has grown faster in recent years than any other comparable industrial country. Since 1977 the proportion of the population with less than half the average income has more than trebled.

There is no single reason for the rise in inequality, but among explanations on offer the report identifies the most important as rising unemployment and growing economic inactivity, so more people are living off income support, which has grown progressively less valuable; the rise in single parents; and the way in which wage growth has differed for poor, middle income and richer groups in society.

There is also a growing polarity between "work rich" and "work poor" households. Between 1975 and 1993 the number of two-adult household where both adults worked has jumped from 51 to 60 per cent, while the proportion with no earner has increased from 3 to 11 per cent. ...

Whereas only 18 per cent of the white population was in the poorest fifth of the population, more than a third of the non-white population was in the poorest fifth with the brunt being borne by West Indians, over 40 per cent of whom are in the bottom group, and Pakistani/Bangladeshis, with 50 per cent in the bottom group. Indians, by contrast, are disproportionately represented in the middle and second highest income groups.

... The position of children in low income groups is of particular concern, with the inquiry worried that they are locked into neighbourhoods where most families are poor ...

Whilst the group agreed that the incomes of low paid workers need boosting, there was dispute over how this should be done. Some members favoured a minimum wage; others an extension of in-work benefits; and still others a combination of the two.'

Source: adapted from Will Hutton, *The Guardian*, 10 February 1996

Chapter summary

Health

❖ Sociologists have argued that health is a social construction. How health is understood varies historically and cross culturally. Even within modern complex societies a range of models of health exist, even though biomedicine remains the dominant, if not unchallenged, means by which health is understood. Sheeran has rejected a pure social constructionist view.

❖ Sociologists have recognized the importance of power in the study of health. Radical theorists suggest that some illnesses, like anorexia, are a product of inequality and exploitation. They also perceive medical professionals as agents of social control. The dominance of biomedicine is a result of its ability to impose its superiority on others. Weberians, Marxists, feminists, postmodernists and non-Marxist conflict theorists like Ivan Illich all have something to say on this issue.

❖ Being sick can be viewed as a social role that individuals can adopt. Parsons has emphasized the beneficial functions this can have for the individual and society. He is criticized for having a deterministic view of the doctor–patient relationship. Interactionists use the idea of the sick role in a more active and flexible way. This can be seen in Goffman's study of a mental asylum.

❖ The social distribution of health and illness is also socially constructed. Social factors such as ethnicity, gender, age, region and social class have an interlocking role to play in an individual's prospects of a long and healthy life. Sociologists have questioned the validity of official health statistics. The explanations offered for the social patterning of health include biological factors, cultural/behavioural, structural/materialist and differential access to health care. Generally it is accepted that the structural/materialist argument is the strongest, with cultural values also having significance.

❖ Health care can be provided formally and informally. Often the burden of informal care falls on women. The main source of formal care in Britain is the NHS, founded in 1948. It is a universal right but not everyone benefits equally. The introduction of an internal market and other changes have led to heated debate. The significance of the private sector has been increasing in Britain, although only 12 per cent of the population have health-care insurance.

❖ The study of mental illness illustrates how ill health and deviance are socially defined. Throughout history there have been many ideas about the causes of mental illness and its treatment. Often the people who are defined as abnormal are those who challenge the dominant value system. The examples of hysteria and homosexuality illustrate this. Community care (not just for the mentally ill) is the current controversial policy regarding mental ill health.

Poverty

❖ Poverty can be seen as absolute or relative. Absolute refers to having less than is needed for physical survival but is often extended to include other basic needs. Relative poverty is defined in relation to the style of life regarded as normal in a particular culture and is the most widely accepted definition used by sociologists.

❖ The influential studies of poverty by Rowntree, using an essentially absolute definition, and the relative studies of Townsend and Mack and Lansey have reached different conclusions regarding the extent and growth of poverty. There is a considerable controversy about the ways these studies measured poverty.

❖ Poverty has been explained as a result of individual inadequacies. Some sociological approaches have explained it in terms of the cultural values of the poor. The New Right identify the welfare state as creating a culture of dependency, whilst other see the meanness of provision as trapping people into poverty. Radical theorists see poverty as a structural feature of society and believe it can only be solved by social transformation or major social engineering.

❖ The welfare state, established in the post-war period in Britain, has not abolished poverty in a relative sense and has not reduced social inequality. Although it provides a safety net for the most disadvantaged, Le Grand has shown that in many areas, welfare provision advantages the middle class and that taxation is not redistributive. Changes to the welfare state, influenced by New Right philosophy, have been seen as a cause of widening inequality.

Essay questions

Health

1 Evaluate the contribution of social factors to the distribution of different types of illness in society. (AEB 1992)

2 Outline and assess different sociological explanations of the continuation of social-class inequalities in health and health care. (AEB 1993)

3 'The medical profession exercises a monopoly of power over health care and does so largely in its own interests.' Assess this view. (AEB AS 1993)

4 'Health and illness must be seen as conditions which are both socially caused and socially defined' Examine the evidence for this view. (AEB AS 1994)

5 'Health care is more effectively provided by the private sector than the public sector.' Evaluate the sociological arguments for and against this point of view. (AEB 1994)

6 'The culture of poverty thesis attempts to explain the poorer health of less advantaged groups in terms of their values and lifestyle.' Assess the evidence for and against this view. (AEB 1995)

7 Assess the contribution of sociologists to an understanding of mental illness. (AEB AS 1995)

Poverty

1 'The welfare state has blunted the extremes of poverty, but has failed to achieve its goal of eliminating it.' Explain and assess this view. (AEB June 1993)

2 'Despite many sociological studies on poverty, it is still not possible to define a 'poverty-line' which will be supported by all.' Critically examine the argument for and against this view. (AEB June 1994)

3 Assess the view that different definitions and explanations of poverty reflect different ideologies. (AEB June 1995)

4 'Some have argued that the major reasons for the continuation of poverty are the behaviour and attitudes of the poor.' Critically discuss the sociological arguments and evidence in support of this view. (AEB June 1996)

Coursework ideas

Health

There are a large number of possibilities for social research in the topic of health, and some ideas have been included earlier in this chapter. Whatever topic you decide upon, you must be aware that the ins and outs of a person's illness are a private matter and beyond the bounds of enquiry for a sociology student.

Two potentially very interesting and contemporary issues are alternative medicines and eating disorders:

❖ You could survey the extent to which people have experimented with alternative models of health. You could include questions on their attitudes towards biomedicine and the alternatives. You may follow up with more in-depth interviews with relevant professionals and those who have raised interesting issues from your survey.

❖ Since eating disorders largely affect women, you could survey some women on what they consider to be the perfect body, how much they worry about weight and their attitudes to media imagery.

There are many other suitable topics. However, always check the feasibility of your project with your course tutor first.

Poverty

Poverty can be an humiliating experience so you should be cautious of direct research into the feelings of those who you regard as poor. However, people's views of the causes of poverty or the role of the welfare state could be interesting areas to investigate. It is probably best to narrow your focus. For example, you could look at how people perceive the problem of homelessness, its causes and the role of the welfare state in dealing with it.

Further reading

The following titles provide useful further reading on *health* issues:

Trowler, P. (1996) *Investigating Health Welfare And Poverty*, London: Collins Educational.

Curtis, S. and Taket, A. (1996) *Health and Societies: Changing Perspectives*, London: Arnold.

Davey, B. and Gray, A. and Seale, C. (ed.) (1995) *Health and Disease: A Reader*, Milton Keynes: Open University Press.

Graham, H. (1992) *Issues in Sociology: Health and Welfare*, London: Nelson.

Blaxter, M. (1996) 'The social patterning of health', in *Developments in Sociology*, Vol. 12, Ch. 2, Ormskirk: Causeway Press.

Senior, M. (1996) 'Health, illness and postmodernism', *Sociology Review*, 6(1).

Sheeran, Y. (1995) 'Sociology, biology and health', *Sociology Review*, 4(4).

Note that *Sociology Review* has various articles on the patterning of health by race, gender, and social class.

The following titles look specifically at the issues of *poverty*:

Oppenheim, C. and Harker, L. (1996) *Poverty the Facts*, London: Child Poverty Action Group.

Walker, C. and Walker, A. (1995) *Poverty and the Poor, Developments in Sociology*, Vol. 10, Lancaster: Causeway Press.

Scott, J. (1994) *Poverty and Wealth: Citizenship, Deprivation and Privilege*, London: Longman Group UK Ltd.

Alcott, P. (1993) *Understanding Poverty*, London: The Macmillan Press Ltd.

Chapter 11

Deviance, crime and social control

❖ Preview

In this chapter we shall be looking at:

❖ how sociologists have defined deviance and how useful these definitions are

❖ the relationship between deviance, crime and social control

❖ non-sociological explanations of deviance and crime, including common-sense, biological and psychological explanations

❖ sociological approaches to deviance and crime, including functionalist and Marxist, interpretive theories

❖ the issue of whether crime and deviance is a social construction or a fact

❖ feminist approaches to the subject and women as criminals and victims

❖ contemporary debates about deviance and crime in relation to social class, gender, ethnicity, age, sexuality and related themes

❖ the study of the victims of crime and deviance – victimology

❖ official statistics of crime and what they represent

❖ new directions in thinking about crime and deviance, in particular the postmodernist contribution.

❖ Introduction

This chapter focuses on a topic that is in the forefront of the popular imagination. News-stories about crime and deviance feature regularly in the media. Fictional crime, detective and police series consistently top the programme ratings. Bestselling crime writers such as Ruth Rendell and Colin Dexter become millionaires. Our fascination with the subject is reflected in our everyday conversations where accounts of crime and deviance often evoke fear and concern as well as outrage. The more horrific the crime or deviant act, the more it attracts and interests people.

❖ Activity 1 ❖

Collect up to ten popular news-stories featuring crime and deviance and summarize their dominant themes and concerns in the form of a table.

Conduct a small survey asking people to define deviance. Ask them how much time they spend daily thinking/reading/talking about crime. Make two to three pages of notes summarizing the key themes which emerge.

Horror films displaying brutality and violence are watched by many. There is a widespread view that we live in extremely violent and crime-ridden times.

Theoretical perspectives: an overview

There are many sociological perspectives on crime and deviance, reflecting the theoretical diversity which features throughout this book. Traditional approaches to the subject tended to take an *absolute* position, emphasizing the *differences* between deviants and others. More recent approaches have stressed the *relative* dimension, emphasizing the *similarity* between those who are judged deviant and others. Each of the following perspectives will be examined in greater depth later in this chapter.

Functionalism

Functionalists see deviance in terms of an aspect of society that is not working, so crime is a product of an *anomic* (see p. 489) society with unclear guidelines on right and wrong behaviour. Some functionalists also point out that in several senses deviance is a necessary part of society: it gives us a yardstick by which to judge our own behaviour and it provides work for people such as the police who have to deal with its outcomes.

Subcultural theories

Subcultural theories highlight marginal groups within society, such as young working-class males living in urban areas. They explain deviance and criminality in terms of gangs and peer group influences, masculinity and a sense of rejection by the wider society, one outcome being educational failure.

Marxism

From a conflict perspective, Marxist-influenced approaches point out that crime and deviance are an outcome of a capitalist society which is based on wide-ranging inequalities. The powerful or ruling class dictate what constitutes crime and deviance through their control of the legislative process. The crimes of the powerful are not dealt with as severely as those of the most deprived and exploited groups, such as the unemployed. The state, the police and law-enforcement agencies act on the behalf of the ruling class to protect their privileged position.

The 'New Criminology': Left realism and the New Right

Some of the problems of the traditional Marxist perspective (such as the predominant focus on crimes against property and the 'Robin Hood' analysis which sees the working-class criminal as hitting back at the injustices of capitalism), were taken up by the 'new criminology' of the 1970s. There are two types of realist approach:

❖ *Left realist* critics of traditional Marxist approaches have pointed out that it is not the powerful who lose most from crime. On the contrary, crime *is* a problem for the more vulnerable groups in society, such as black and Asian people, and women living in the deprived areas of towns and cities.

❖ Opposing interpretations are provided by *New Right* (or *right realist*) approaches. As with left realism, these highlight crime as a growing social problem but differ in their explanations of causes, emphasizing individual responsibility for criminal acts and the decline of moral values in society, resulting from factors such as the breakdown of the family, lack of discipline in schools and the decline in religion. Their answer is to strengthen key institutions such as marriage and family life and to reintroduce harsher forms of punishment as a deterrent.

This was summarised in the 'Prison Works' penal policy of the Conservative Home Secretary in the late 1990s. The result of this has been a massive expansion in prison building with an increase of 1000 prisoners a month in early 1997.

Interpretive models

Another dimension is provided by interpretive approaches, notably *labelling theory* with its emphasis on the *relative* nature of deviance. Behaviour such as illegal drug use may not be particularly harmful or threatening to other people, but certain groups, for example New Age travellers, attract attention and are stereotyped for behaviour which is different from what the majority of people judge to be normal. Another aspect of interpretive approaches is that of ethnomethodology. *Ethnomethodology* looks at how *definitions* of deviance are arrived at as a result of the decision-making of officials in organizations such as courts.

Feminism

Feminist approaches show how women criminals are seen in terms not just of the nature of the crime they have committed, but as women who have gone against dominant patriarchal ideas of womanhood. The dimension of women as victims – particularly of male violence and sexual crimes – is also highlighted. Similar themes emerge when ethnicity is considered.

Recent theories

The final section of the chapter will examine some of the more recent themes raised by such areas as postmodernism, and the patterns and trends that are emerging at the end of the twentieth century. Questions about the increasing fragmentation of society and less clear boundaries around right and wrong behaviour will be examined. Will the future be increasingly lawless and violent with a breakdown in morality? Or, will things continue much as they always have done, with crime and deviant acts being an inherent part of any society?

The relationship between crime and deviance

Defining deviance

Consider the following definitions of deviance offered by sociologists:

❖ 'Deviance may be considered as banned or controlled behaviour which is likely to attract punishment or disapproval.' (Downes and Rock 1988)

❖ 'Deviance is behaviour that violates the standards of conduct or expectations of a group or society.' (Wickman 1991)

Crime can be simply defined as the breaking of the law or legal rules, as opposed to deviance, which refers to the breaking of social rules.

❖ Activity 2 ❖

- Read the *In Focus* on p. 481 and decide whether Howard Hughes' behaviour falls into the category of deviance as defined?

- Reflect on your first impression of the description of the man, before you knew who was being described. Does this further

information alter your view? Are terms like 'eccentric' or 'odd' now more appropriate than 'deviant'. If so, why?

- How does the case of Hughes compare with the definitions of deviance that are given above?

Picture a man living alone in a dark room with curtains permanently drawn, spending his final years lying naked in an armchair watching old films on TV. He has few personal contacts as he has an intense fear of germs – to the extreme that he places tissue paper on the floor to step on as he walks. The man described is Howard Hughes, who was a multimillionaire American businessman and one of the world's richest men.

In May 1982, Colonel 'H' (Herbert) Jones died a hero, leading his parachute regiment into the Falklands Battle of Goose Green. He was awarded a posthumous Victoria Cross for his 'devastating display of courage'.

In his book, *Not Mentioned in Despatches*, Spencer Fitz-Gibbon (1996) raises questions about the nature of Colonel Jones's heroic act. His fellow soldiers admitted that he was an impatient, impulsive man who had suddenly left his post and charged alone towards a heavily armed Argentinian position. The Argentinian soldier who shot and killed him said he could not believe anyone would do such a foolish thing.

How do we now see Colonel Jones? A straightforward 'comic book' hero with outstanding courage and valour, or a deviant who lost his life in a vain attempt against impossible odds? A closer examination of many of our historical heroes might cause us to make similar revisions of their actions. These two case studies show the complexity of how we arrive at definitions of heroism and deviance.

❖ An act can be *criminal and deviant*, i.e. breaking both social and legal rules. For example, most people would agree that battering an old lady to death is both criminal and deviant and deserves a punishment such as imprisonment. Other acts of killing may be more complex: what happens, for instance, if the killing occurs in wartime? The 'killer', who in other contexts would be condemned as a murderer, might be applauded and called a hero.

❖ An act can be *deviant but not criminal*, i.e. breaking social, but not legal, rules. Examples of this include acts that are seen as deviant when they occur in a certain context, such as a male manager wearing a dress to the office or someone talking loudly in the middle of a concert performance. Close examination of such instances show how delicately balanced our social world can be. Minor transgressions of behaviour which may be acceptable in our own private realm become very different when occurring in public. They can elicit a range of responses from hilarity, to embarrassment, disgust and outright condemnation.

❖ Acts can be *criminal but not deviant*. You might think that all crimes are deviant, but is this always the case? Take the example of speeding: breaking the speed limit is a criminal offence, but the majority of drivers do it at some time or other. The question arises as to how it is seen by others. If someone is found guilty of a minor speeding offence and fined, are they subject to social disapproval? Similar examples include tax evasion and fiddling expenses.

❖ Activity 3 ❖

1 Give three further examples of each of the three categories described above.

2 Write a short essay of around 500 words addressing the issue of why the relationship between crime and deviance is not straightforward.

As hinted at above, whether an action is seen to be criminal or deviant can depend on the *time*, *place* and *social situation* in which it occurs.

1 *Time* – *when* the act takes place, e.g. drinking alcohol at nine in the morning compared with nine in the evening

2 *Place* – *where* the act takes place, e.g. an adult running naked across a nudist beach as compared with a school playground

3 *Social situation* – the *context* in which the act takes place, e.g. chanting and flag-waving in a museum as compared with the same behaviour on a football terrace.

There are situations where all the above can apply simultaneously, e.g. a man in swimming trunks opening a can of beer in a bus queue at 8.15 a.m. in mid-winter!

Someone with a problem of time, place *and* context...

The problem of order

Most definitions of deviance contain some idea of social rules. What social rules are, why some people obey them and others do not, has interested sociologists, philosophers and theologians for centuries. This has been referred to as *the problem of order*. Some religions apply the idea of 'original sin' to babies and young children, i.e. we are born evil but by practising our faith and living a moral life and doing good to others, we can gain redemption. Materialist philosophies such as Marxism disagree with such views and see evil or badness as rooted in the way capitalist society is organized and structured. Marxists argue that by replacing capitalism with socialism and by ending exploitation and inequality, evil will be defeated.

Emile Durkheim was one of the first sociologists to raise issues connected with the problem of order. He is often associated with the functionalist perspective which emphasizes stability and equilibrium. Order is maintained through the interconnectedness of our main social institutions, such as the family, education and religion, which create a sense of group and societal solidarity. Durkheim used his study of religion to highlight the way religion acts as a form of social cement. So, an act of worship gives the people taking part a feeling of group identity, thus helping to maintain order in society. His idea of the *collective conscience* in the context of a small-scale society can be used to explain how social identity as opposed to individualism develops.

Consider the example of gossip. Gossip is a feature of most human societies and often has negative connotations. However, from a Durkheimian perspective gossip has a vital role to play in fostering the collective conscience. For instance, what is happening when people engage in supposedly malicious talk about a man engaging in an extra-marital affair? The collective conscience 'theme' is adultery. Adultery is seen as a potential threat to the orderly world of marriage and family life. Gossiping to others about such matters helps to clarify ideas on the collectively approved social codes, such as fidelity in marriage and family responsibility.

Deviance as boundary maintenance

In the twentieth century, the American sociologist Talcott Parsons addressed the problem of order from a functionalist perspective, stressing that deviance acts to set the boundaries around approved of behaviour. He referred to this as the *normative order* and believed that deviance is sociologically significant because an understanding of why some people break social rules helps us gain a better understanding of why most people supposedly obey them.

Developments in the sociology of deviance

The earliest origins of sociological approaches to deviance were in *criminology*, the study of crime and criminals. A key assumption behind early approaches was that the criminal or deviant was different from the rest of the population. Early work was focused on anatomical, physiological and biological differences. Later on, psychological explanations were offered. In the twentieth century, the sociological approach developed through the functionalist

perspective. All this early work stressed the different nature of the deviant. There was also the assumption that there could an agreed definition of a deviant act. In other words, the 'social rules' could be explained and ideas of right and wrong behaviour were clear to the majority. Deviance and crime were *absolute*, i.e. social facts which could be objectively measured and explained through such indicators as crime statistics.

More recent work in the field of the sociology of deviance such as labelling theory, Marxist and feminist approaches, has raised doubts about such assumptions. Here, the *relative* nature of deviance and criminal activity is stressed – deviance, not beauty, is in the eye of the beholder.

More recently, attention has been paid to issues of power and social control to illustrate the unequal treatment and labelling of different social groups by gender, ethnicity and social class. Issues of law enforcement are a feature of such debates.

Figure 11.1 The changing nature of criminology and the sociology of deviance

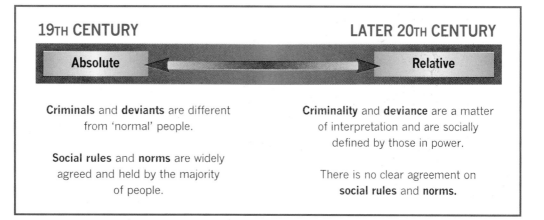

Deviance and social control

Social control can be seen in terms of the agencies which curtail and limit our behaviour. Take the example of being without money. An obvious answer to this problem may be to steal some, but we do not do so, because of a number of influences.

If we think it is morally wrong to steal, we may have acquired this belief from our parents, our religion or our education. Here the family, religion and education act as agencies of social control. Alternatively, we may not steal because of fear of being caught and punished. Here the law and associated institutions such as the police act as agencies of social control.

Sociological perspectives on social control range from the *positive* (whereby social control is seen as maintaining order, stability and social harmony), to the *negative* (whereby social control is seen as an instrument of oppression used by the powerful few to keep the powerless majority in their place). The positive or functionalist view can be described as *voluntary*, we obey the 'social rules' because we believe it is right to do so. The negative or conflict perspective sees social control as *coercive*, i.e. it keeps us in our place through various forms of oppression ranging from punishment to ideological domination.

Table 11.1 Agencies of social control

❖ The family

The family is seen as the prime agency of socialization and social control. (See also Chapter 3, *Families and households*.)

❖ The school

Probably the next most important agency after the family is the school. Teachers, like parents, inculcate ideas of right and wrong in children. There are countering theoretical and philosophical debates as to how this works to the benefit or detriment of children. (See also Chapter 4, *Education and training*.)

❖ Work

Work can be an agent of social control: we subject ourselves to the discipline of work requirements in order to earn a living and, if we are lucky, to gain a sense of personal and creative satisfaction. In the workplace, managers and supervisors control employees. (See also Chapter 5, *Work, organizations, unemployment and leisure*.)

❖ Religion

Religious belief can have a powerful effect on a person's behaviour. Fear or love of a god or gods can be a guiding principle in ideas of right or wrong and moral codes. As religion comes to play a less central role in the lives of many people (secularization), so it becomes less powerful as an instrument of social control. (See also Chapter 14, *Religion*.)

❖ The mass media

In Westernized societies, children spend more time watching television than they do at school: television has become a 'surrogate childminder'. Are children presented with an atomized and fragmented view of the world through television? Is advertising an agency of social control emphasizing the owning of material possessions as the only route to personal happiness? (See also Chapter 12, *Mass media*.)

❖ The law and the courts

In a large complex society it is impossible to have social control by means of personal contact, so impersonal and supposedly impartial rules and codes are laid down through legislation. The underpinning of the British legal system can be linked to our Judaeo-Christian religious tradition. The ideology of the law is that it affects all members of society equally, as summed up in the idea of 'blind justice'. Many sociologists representing a range of theoretical perspectives would question this.

❖ The police

The police are probably the most visible manifestation of social control in public. They wear distinctive uniforms, patrol the streets and are a clear reminder of consequences of wrongdoing.

As with the law, there are contradictory views of the police's role in society, some seeing them as oppressors representing the establishment, others as guardians and protectors in an increasingly crime-ridden world. The police themselves recognize their contradictory functions in a complex society with varying degrees of involvement in community and social policing, antiracist policies, high-tech crime-fighting, antifraud work and the control of illegal drug abuse. The role of the police in relation to crime and deviance is covered later in this chapter.

Agencies of social control

Table 11.1 summarizes some of the most influential agencies of control that operate in society.

Deviance, social problems and sociological problems

The study of deviance might be seen as the study of social problems such as crime. However, what is or is not a social 'problem' is a matter of judgement. Many people agree that unemployment, poverty and crime are social problems but will disagree about the causes. Social problems are subject to a range of interpretations. What then is the difference between social and sociological problems? Crime might be seen as a social problem – crime is clearly 'bad' for society. The sociological problem is how to explain the concept of crime and how to examine the various explanations for it.

Non-sociological explanations of crime and deviance

The common-sense view: deviants are different

The *common-sense* view is that deviants are in some way *different* from the rest of us normal, rule-following types. Of course, a 'normal' person may commit an isolated deviant act, but the real deviant is one who consistently proves to be different from the rest of us. According to this view, deviants are those who are inherently bad or mad or both – serial killers such as Fred and Rosemary West are insane and deserve severe punishment.

Perceptions of deviance permeate our everyday world and judgements of others – so, if we are thin, we may see fat people as deviant, and vice versa. We may like to think that such perceptions are more prevalent in childhood, but much of our daily world as adults is full of such examples of intolerant stances often couched in language such as 'He's a nutcase'. Clearly, the behaviour and language of the school playground is not necessarily outgrown when we become adults.

Biological explanations of deviance

Cesare Lombroso (1836–1909) is commonly regarded as the founding father of criminology. He was an Italian army doctor who developed an interest in criminality and engaged in anatomical and physiological research into the differences between criminals and 'normal', law-abiding citizens. He purported to find clear physical differences in criminals, relating to a variety of biological characteristics such as prehensile toes, large skull girth and

Lombroso's views on deviance are aptly summed up in the following quote:

'This was not merely an idea, but a flash of inspiration. At the sight of that skull, I seemed to see all of a sudden, lighted up as a vast plain under a flaming sky, the problem of the nature of the criminal – an atavistic being who reproduces in his person the ferocious instincts of primitive humanity and the inferior animals.

Thus were explained anatomically the enormous jaws, high cheek bones, prominent superciliary arches, solitary lines in the palms, extreme size of the orbits, handle shaped or sessile ears found in criminals, savages and apes, insensibility of pain, extremely acute sight, tattooing, excessive idleness, love of orgies, and the irresistible craving for evil for its own sake, the desire not only to extinguish life in the victim, but to mutilate the corpse, tear its flesh and drink its blood.'

Source: Lombroso (1897)

extra nipples. He saw criminals as atavistic throwbacks to earlier primitive humans whose behaviour was barbaric and savage (see *In Focus* above).

We may now see the views of Lombroso and other nineteenth-century criminological researchers as outdated and unscientific but Lombroso's biological tradition has continued to the present. In the 1960s American researchers linked criminality in aggressive male offenders to their possession of an extra Y-chromosome. This discovery was seen as a breakthrough in identifying a genetic basis for violence. But it also caused scientific controversy, with critics pointing to the methodological weaknesses. The extra Y-chromosome males were from a small sample of convicted violent offenders. Critics pointed out that many violent men were not in prison. Genetic research is still being carried out with a continued quest for the elusive 'criminal gene' which could identify a potential criminal before birth. The moral and ethical issues this raises are obvious and have attracted widespread protests about the perceived possibilities of genetically engineering to eradicate humans with such defective genes, thus eventually creating a 'perfect' human society. Leading geneticists have now pointed to the implausibility of a 'criminal' gene. In the early 1990s there were similar controversies over

the supposed discovery of a gene for homosexuality, which became referred to as the 'gay gene'. Such controversies are very much part of the sociological debate about deviance and its social context.

❖ Activity 6 ❖

Briefly summarize the biological explanations of deviance. What do you consider to be the ethical issues raised by these approaches?

Explore further the implications of a genetic link with deviance. If a genetic link *were* found, what sorts of preventive measures might be advocated and what sorts of ethical issues might be raised?

Such attempts to differentiate criminals and deviants from the rest of us on the basis of physical differences are controversial. More worrying are the political links with far-right views such as fascism. Adolf Hitler thought it was possible to breed a 'super race' at the same time as he was exterminating 'deviants' such as Jews, homosexuals, gypsies and those with dissident political views. The translation of such views into the context of modern genetic and biological research has raised obvious concerns. Despite such issues, the everyday world is full of examples of people using a biological explanation of deviance: 'I don't like the look of him, he's got shifty eyes' or 'I knew he was a wrong'un the moment I set eyes on him.'

These everyday statements indicate that the ghost of Lombroso still haunts the popular imagination!

Psychological explanations of deviance

Psychological explanations, like biological explanations, still emphasize the differences between 'normal' people and those who are deviant. Rather than focusing on physical differences, psychologists emphasize the different mental characteristics of deviants. These differences can be in intelligence; deviants have low or qualitatively different forms of intelligence such as cunning. Their personalities may be defective in some way, with terms such as 'psychotic' and 'psychopathic' being used to categorize those committing the worst types of deviant acts:

❖ *Psychotics* are those who commit serious crimes such as murder without an awareness that their act is wrong, using explanations such as 'God commanded me to kill'.

❖ *Psychopaths* are deemed to be more dangerous and harder to catch as, although they are aware that what they do is wrong, they have no conscience about it and are willing to lie and/or blame others to avoid capture.

Related psychological explanations are those describing the deviant as an 'emotional cripple', which may be a result of a damaged childhood, abusive parents and so on.

Getting inside the criminal mind is a popular interest, as demonstrated by the popularity of mass-media forensic-psychology TV programmes such as *Cracker* and films such as *The Silence of the Lambs*.

In common-sense or everyday terms, people often characterize those they judge to be deviant with pejorative psychological terms such as 'nutter' or 'headcase', showing that despite the possible short-comings of such explanations, they are still strong in the popular imagination.

Although there is a level of plausibility to psychological explanations of deviance and crime, there are a number of problems with this type of approach. As with earlier approaches, there is still an emphasis on the individual and their difference from others who are supposedly 'normal'. There is no social context or structural level of explanation which locates deviance and crime within society.

The impact of biological and psychological theories

Biological and psychological theories may have been criticized for focusing on the individual, but they have nonetheless been influential in the creation of *social policies* aimed at crime prevention. Biological theories have resulted in what Jock Young (1988) has described as the 'medicalization' of crime prevention. One example of this is the widespread use of tranquillizing drugs in British prisons to help 'quieten down' aggressive or troublesome offenders. This sort of treatment has been described as the use of a 'chemical straitjacket'.

Psychological approaches as described above have resulted in similar attempts to 'treat' the criminal at the individual level; examples are psychological counselling to correct bad behaviour and educational programmes to change the offender to a more law-abiding citizen. Young links the development of such policies to the change in criminology from explanations of crime as a product of deprivation and poverty.

◆ Sociological explanations of crime and deviance

Sociological explanations of deviance tend to concentrate on the social aspects of deviance, whereas the common-sense, biological and psychological explanations tend to concentrate on the individual person. However, just as most psychologists accept that individuals exist in a social world that influences their behaviour, so most sociologists recognize that we are not solely socially determined and that individuals in similar social circumstances behave in different ways. Take the common example of the correlation between unemployment and crime. A high number of convicted criminals may have been unemployed, but this does not necessarily mean that all unemployed people become criminals. Social circumstances such as unemployment can be strong predictors of the probability of committing crime, but there are many unemployed people who do not commit crime. This may be where an individual or psychological level of explanation may be required. In this sense there is complementarity between the individual and social levels.

According to Young (1988):

'Theories of society do not come into being out of the blue. They arise out of the hunches and intuitions of people trying to make sense of the world around them: they arise out of real problems facing people in the social world which confronts them.'

Young points out that this general point about theory is applicable to explanations of theoretical trends in postwar criminology. The assumptions about the causation of crime have strongly influenced theorizing. Most sociologists see deviance as an integral part of all societies, so a society without any form of deviance is impossible. As well as this aspect, some theories see deviance as a positive feature of society,

helping to reinforce ideas of right and wrong. Others point to the negative dimensions where deviance and crime are a reflection of an unequal and exploitative society.

Functionalist approaches to deviance

You should by now be familiar with the basic assumptions behind the functionalist approach. With regard to deviance, there are two main dimensions:

❖ Deviance acts in a positive way to reinforce ideas of right and wrong in society.

❖ Deviance provides work.

Deviance as a necessary reinforcement of right and wrong

We measure our own behaviour against that of others by our social contacts who reinforce the boundaries of acceptable and unacceptable behaviour. The earlier example on gossip illustrated how this works in practice. Courtrooms and prisons can be settings where public examples are made of wrongdoers, further reinforcing collective norms and values.

Making an example of wrongdoers...

Emile Durkheim particularly highlighted this dimension of deviance as a sort of measuring stick of approved behaviour by suggesting that all societies have deviance in them. For Durkheim, a certain level of deviance is inevitable in all societies, but problems can arise if there is too great an amount as this can threaten social stability. He used the concept of *anomie* to explain how societies undergoing rapid social change can experience confusion over right and wrong behaviour. This sort of analysis can be applied to modern affluent societies undergoing rapid change where there is confusion over common values. The successful businesswoman might be admired until it is discovered that some of her business dealings are fraudulent. How do we react to this? Does 'success' in business mean we excuse fraudulent practice as a legitimate means to such ends? Or do we see all fraud as wrong and worthy of punishment? Such confusions fit Durkheim's idea of anomie which means that society has lost clear general guidelines on what is right or wrong. More recently, the New Right have picked up on such views and expressed their concern at the 'breakdown' in morality indicated by the rise in illegitimacy and broken families. The New Right relate such moral breakdown to uncertainty and relativism.

Durkheim also saw problems in societies where there are low levels of crime and deviance. These societies remain static and injustices may remain unchallenged. A certain level of deviance from accepted norms is a way societies can evolve and change, possibly for the better. History is full of examples of such figures ranging from Mahatma Gandhi to the Suffragettes. In the modern context, Nelson Mandela and his struggle against the South African apartheid regime is an example of a 'deviant' who at one time was referred to as a terrorist. His battles have resulted in social changes for the better for the majority of South Africans; he has become the honoured President of his country and a revered world statesman.

❖ Activity 7 ❖

'Today's terrorist is tomorrow's freedom fighter.'

Discuss with appropriate examples in the light of the arguments presented above.

Deviance as a provider of work

Another dimension of deviance highlighted by some American sociologists is that deviance provides work for people. Crime prevention is a multimillion pound industry which employs large numbers of people, such as the police, solicitors and probation officers. Large amounts of money are spent on research and the technology of crime prevention – for example, modern cars positively hum with antitheft mechanisms.

❖ Activity 8 ❖

1 Besides car security, what other businesses have arisen as a result of crime?

It could be argued that such businesses have a vested interested in arousing fear of crime among potential customers. How does this influence the way they present crime, e.g. in advertisements?

2 'If the police won the fight against crime they would put themselves out of a job.'

In what ways will we always have crime and deviance regardless of how successful the police and authorities might be?

Connect this to Durkheim's views.

In Focus

◆

Marx on gainful employment?

'The criminal produces not only crimes but criminal law, and with this also the professor who gives lectures on criminal law and in addition to this the inevitable compendium in which this same professor throws his lectures onto the general market as "commodities". This brings with it augmentation of national wealth ...
The criminal moreover produces the whole of the police and of criminal justice, constables, judges, hangmen, juries, etc.; and all these different lines of business, which form equally many categories of the social division of labour, develop different categories of the human spirit, create new needs and new ways of satisfying them. Torture alone has given rise to the most ingenious mechanical inventions, and employed many honourable craftsmen in the production of its instruments ... Would locks have reached their present state of excellence had there been no thieves?' (Marx 1867)

Marx died in 1883, but the above extract seems remarkably modern. Some have suggested that this passage indicates agreement with a functionalist approach, but it needs to be noted that here Marx is using a somewhat ironic tone.

Does all crime serve a function?

The above discussion raises issues which are familiar to functionalism, such as: 'Is *all* deviance functional?' Surely there are many examples of deviant/criminal acts which are socially destructive and could not be seen as reinforcing 'collective sentiments'. To take a particularly distressing example, how can the act of the gunman in the killing of sixteen young children and their teacher in Dunblane, Scotland in March 1996 be interpreted as serving some sort of purpose or function? The Labour Leader, Tony Blair, told the House of Commons that every parent in the land would clutch their children more tightly in the light of such an outrage, but is it the function of such a level of atrocity to make people appreciate life and their loved ones more?

Some critics, such as Erikson (1966), have pointed out that Durkheim's functionalist emphasis on deviance as a way of boundary setting and maintenance around the collective conscience implies that all are affected equally. Erikson highlights the differences in *power* between groups, so some are controlled more directly than others. An example of such power differences is the public confessions of adultery by Prince Charles and Princess Diana, which has not significantly altered their position in society. Compare their situation with that of a working-class woman confessing adultery to a violent husband.

Robert K. Merton and strain theory

The American functionalist sociologist Robert Merton (1968) took Durkheim's concept of anomie and developed what became known as the *strain theory*. He took the USA in the 1930s as an example of a society where a dominant value was to 'get rich quick' (also known as the 'American Dream'). A problem is that it is not possible for everyone in society to attain this goal – common sense tells us that not everyone can become a millionaire in any society. Merton addressed the issue of how the majority cope with the impossibility of everyone becoming rich. A more recent example of Merton's theory is Britain in the 1980s. The 1980s are described as the decade of Thatcherism when the 'get-rich-quick' philosophy highlighted by Merton in relation to 1930s America re-emerged. This was the decade of the 'yuppie': the self-seeking individual who made a fortune on the money markets while living an extravagant lifestyle. Such images were reinforced by pictures of lunchtime champagne-drinking in Stock Exchange bars.

Merton's argument was that the burning desire to achieve success, actively promoted deviant behaviour. If the legitimate path to success was blocked, people would be tempted to achieve it through devious means. Merton went on to explain that people choose different patterns of deviance. His five-point scale of responses to the goals of success are listed in Table 11.2.

Evaluating Merton's contribution

Merton's theory provides us with reasons why people commit deviant acts. However, his critics say that he fails to address sociological issues of power and social class – as summarized in the following quote from Taylor (1971):

'It is as though individuals in society are playing a gigantic fruit machine, but the machine is rigged and only some players are consistently rewarded. The deprived ones either resort to using foreign coins or magnets to increase their chances of winning (innovation), or play on mindlessly (ritualism), give up the game (retreatism), or propose a new game altogether (rebellion). But in the analysis nobody appeared to ask who put the game there in the first place and who takes the profits.'

Another criticism levelled at Merton is that he gives no explanation of why a particular person chooses one form of deviance as compared to another. However, he does emphasize the role of socialization and differences between the social classes.

Table 11.2 Merton's five-point scale of responses

1 *Conformity*	This is the response of the majority, the stereotypical 'law-abiding citizen' who uses conventional means, such as a job, to pursue the approved of goals of success which may never be reached.
2 *Innovation*	Socially acceptable means, such as a job, are rejected, but the goals of success are still pursued. So a person might resort to crime to become rich, as in the case of gangsters such as Al Capone. Another 'innovation' could be gambling or trying your luck in the National Lottery.
3 *Ritualism*	This is where the means to the goals are accepted and conformed to, but the person loses sight of the goals. The person, therefore, goes through the motions but has no real interest in the outcome. For example, the student who lavishes attention on the presentation of an essay, but doesn't answer the question that has been set.
4 *Retreatism*	This response involves giving up or losing sight of both means and goals, by opting out or dropping of conventional society, e.g. a 'down-and-out' living a life of oblivion through drink or drug abuse. Such behaviour could occur in any social class, possibly giving rise to the 'tramp-who-was-once-a-duke' stereotype.
5 *Rebellion*	As in retreatism, both goals and means are rejected, but *alternatives* are constructed. An example would be the political revolutionary who rejects conventional society and strives to create a new society by means of a violent revolution.

The working class are less rigid in their adherence to conventional norms and values, so it is easier for them to engage in 'deviant' acts such as gambling.

A final criticism of Merton's theory, as with most functionalist analysis, is the assumption it makes that there are dominant norms and values, and that there is widespread agreement of what these are. Other views described in this chapter disagree. The functionalist view is furthest from the relativist position – which is a feature of most recent sociological analyses of deviance.

❖ **Activity 9** ❖

Conduct a small survey to find out if there is common agreement on right or wrong behaviour. Construct a scale of deviance indicating behaviour where there is common agreement, e.g. rape, to that where there are differing views, e.g. gambling. Relate this to such sociological categories as age, social class, gender, ethnicity, religion, culture. What do your findings tell you concerning absolutist (functionalist) views compared with relativist views on deviance?

Subcultural theories

Subcultures are usually defined as those groups which are in some senses antagonistic to mainstream values but which do not provide head-on opposition. The best examples occur among young people, who might rebel against their parents' values for a temporary period by becoming a 'Mod', 'Skinhead', 'Punk', 'Raver' or whatever suits the era and fashion of the time. Eventually they 'grow up', become adults and – sadly perhaps – tend to become very much like their parents (see Activity 10).

Some groups of people are antagonistic to the wider society and want to overthrow it or change it by revolutionary and/or violent means. Such groups are referred to as *contracultures*.

❖ **Activity 10** ❖

Which of Merton's five responses do you think best fits the young people described in the first paragraph about subcultures?

Groups which reject mainstream society but create their own separate alternative are called *countercultures*. An example from the 1960s is the hippie movement. Some hippies joined communes and tried to develop simple, self-sufficient, agricultural lifestyles, which indicated their rejection of modern society's consumerism and competitive 'rat-race' values. The hippies are now seen as the countercultural forebears of the 1990s New Age travellers.

When there are clashes of values between mainstream society and a counterculture, the counterculture can *evolve into* a contraculture. In the early 1990s this has been demonstrated by civil disobedience and protest against such things as the spread of roads and motorways, the export of live animals to the continent and the restrictions placed on rights of access to the countryside. The 1994 Criminal Justice Act brought such issues to the fore and changed coexistence to confrontation between various countercultures and the authorities (see Chapter 9).

The origins of subcultural theory are associated with the Chicago School of Sociology in the early part of the twentieth century. A number of key figures in the establishment of the *interactionist* approach worked together to examine sociologically the dramatic social changes brought about by successive waves of immigration on a city like Chicago. They were among the first to identify a *zoning* process whereby groups of similar cultural background and country of origin occupied the same neighbourhoods, creating what later urban social scientists have identified as *urban villages* (see Chapter 9). In the context of city neighbourhoods, the cultural identity of Italian, Greek or Chinese can lead to the formation of rival subcultural gangs, particularly among young males (as featured in the classic film *West Side Story*).

Albert Cohen on subcultures

Cohen (1955, 1966) was an American sociologist who was one of the first to address the issue of subcultures and gangs among young working-class males. He challenged certain aspects of earlier socio-logical work on deviance including Merton's. He pointed out that deviance among young working-class males in gang subcultures was not necessarily related to economic or financial ends. Cohen explained such deviant activities as vandalism and robbery in terms of the *status deprivation* and frustration experi-enced by many young working-class males. He cited the example of their educational experiences which invariably result in them being classed as outsiders and failures by middle-class teachers. They are placed in the lower streams and gain very little from their time at school. They do not accept the middle-class goals of academic success and attainment and create their own sense of status among their peers. They leave school without qualifications and end up unemployed or in dead-end jobs. They live in inner-city areas with endemic poverty and deprivation. In this context, and in particular as a reaction to the *'middle-class measuring stick'*, belonging to a subcultural group such as a delinquent gang provides a sense of belonging and status. Gangs reinforce an oppositional identity where 'having a laugh', 'mucking around' and horseplay are the milder forms of deviance, and fighting, vandalism and inter-gang violence are the more serious forms.

Evaluating Cohen's views

A number of more recent British ethnographic studies have provided support for Cohen's views, including:

❖ James Patrick's *A Glasgow Gang Observed* (1973)

❖ David Hargreave *et al.*'s *Deviance in the Classroom* (1975)

❖ Paul Willis' *Learning to Labour* (1977)

❖ Stephen Ball's *Beachside Comprehensive* (1981)

In addition, Cohen's status-frustration explanation of juvenile deviance can be supported at the common-sense and experi-ential level: we can all recognize from our own school experience examples of the youths that Cohen describes.

However, there are still assumptions in this approach of some sort of *dominant value system* that is rejected by delinquent youth. More relativistic theories, such as those within an interpretive framework, question such views and deny a commonality of values which we all aspire to or reject.

In Focus

◆

Gang culture

Mixing myth with menace as street youths ape their fierce Triad elders

Around the back streets of King's Cross station, the names Triad or Wo-Sing-Wo (WSW) are well known to many of the loitering youngsters, often playing truant from school.

Like Learco Chindamo [jailed for murdering school headmaster Philip Lawrence] some of them are members of the WSW, which has acquired a ferocious reputation in the area, some of it rooted in reality and some of it based on urban myths of gangsters, guns and violence.

The question is whether the youth gangs are simply made up of boys trying to emulate Triad heroes, or whether senior Triads have attempted to recruit children. Police are quick to reject suggestions of organised Triad recruitment in schools, although last year, officers in London started an inquiry into such claims.

Other young gangs known to be operating in the area of north London include the Black Dragons and the Latino Lions.

Source: The Guardian. 18 October 1996

Another criticism that has been made of earlier subcultural theories is that they deal only with males as members of subcultural groups, females are largely ignored. Feminist theories from the 1970s pointed out such omissions in so-called 'male-stream' sociology (Abbott and Wallace 1996).

❖ Activity 11 ❖

Suggest some explanations for why Cohen's and similar studies do not deal with females. What assumptions do they make about women and their role? Think about issues such as the visibility of subcultural groups and that the sociologists in this case are male.

Cloward and Ohlin

Cloward and Ohlin (1961) addressed similar issues to Cohen and developed aspects of subcultural theory linking his work to Merton's concept of anomie. They looked at different forms of deviance and identified three levels:

❖ *Criminal subculture* – This occurs in areas with an already established criminal underworld where in effect young men are 'apprentice criminals' from an early age. They learn the craft of robbery and other types of stealing from older men. A good example of this is Jimmy Boyle, a now reformed hardened criminal, whose father was killed in a Glasgow gangland shooting. Boyle was brought up in a particularly deprived area of Glasgow where criminality was common amongst men.

❖ *Conflict subculture* – This is where there is no clearly identifiable criminal underworld to socialize young men into a life of crime. Here, young men turn to gangs and territorial boundaries for their identity. James Patrick, a teacher in a Scottish remand centre, carried out an ethnographic participant observation study of such gangs in Glasgow and found clear territorial demarcation which formed the basis for arranged gang fights with weapons on a regular basis. The life of the gang often revolved around such issues. More recently, the topic of football hooliganism has been analysed in this way by John Williams of the Leicester University Centre for Football Research. He points out that the break up of traditional working-class neighbourhoods in the postwar period meant that territorial identities based on streets and neighbourhoods changed to football clubs and their grounds. So, a large successful club such as Manchester United can attract a minority of hooligan followers from a widespread national and international area.

❖ *Retreatist subculture* – This applies to those who, in Cloward and Ohlin's terms, are 'double failures'. They are neither able to become proper criminals as in the first level or members of violent gangs as in the second. Instead, they resort to drug abuse financed by petty crime such as burglary, shoplifting and, occasionally, male prostitution.

The previous section raised the issue of the invisibility of females in gang studies; a similar point can be made concerning ethnicity. British studies up to the 1980s featured mainly white working-class males. This was less so in American studies: *Tally's Corner* by Elliot Liebow looks at a black subculture and *Street Corner Society* by William Foote Whyte examines an Italian community in Boston. However, ethnic identity was not a central focus in such studies. An early subcultural study in Britain which placed ethnic identity more centrally was *Endless Pressure* by Ken Pryce. He studied the Afro-Caribbean community in the St. Paul's district of Bristol and was able to use participant observation more effectively as he was himself of Afro-Caribbean origin.

In the 1990s, the issue of ethnicity and youth subcultures has featured in the mass media with reports of ethnic dimensions to gang warfare between Muslim, Hindu, Sikh

'Julia', member of a gang in San Antonio, Texas. The gang members' fingers spell out a sign for their gang and the gun Julia points is loaded.

Such theoretical criticisms of earlier theories of deviance can be linked to general sociological themes concerning structural and action approaches (see Chapter 7, *Theory and methods*). Matza's work in the field of deviance addresses the shortcoming of the structuralist approach. In his study of juvenile delinquency in America, he questions the seemingly double standards of the young men. The men condemn similar acts of crime to their own in much the same way as any law-abiding member of the public. Matza explains this by pointing out that there are surface common values that most people adhere to, for instance the value of fidelity in marriage. However, on occasion these can be replaced by opposite values (called *subterranean values* by Matza) so a previously faithful husband on a business trip commits adultery. (In Freudian terms the 'monsters of the id' occasionally surface in us all.)

Another concept introduced by Matza is *techniques of neutralization* which applies to how people explain their seemingly untypical behaviour. In the case of young delinquents, an excuse such as 'I was drunk at the time' may be used to underplay the harm of a deviant act. 'They can afford it' or 'The insurance will pay for their loss', or 'Everyone else does it' are common examples of neutralization techniques.

and Afro-Caribbean groups in a number of British inner-city areas. A number of cities have experienced outbreaks of violence and riots that have centred around ethnic differences. Similar issues to some of the earlier studies cited, such as territoriality and the high status of fighting and violent activity, have been noted. A more disturbing trend has been the growth in use of weapons such as knives and guns which have resulted in some widely publicized deaths.

Matza's approach

The theories covered so far are *structuralist* in that they see deviance as an aspect of the social structure of society. Critics point out that such structuralist approaches are *deterministic*, in that they see deviants as a product of their position in the social structure. For example, Cohen sees lower working-class males' delinquency as a reflection of structural forces that are in a sense beyond their control. To put it another way, such delinquents lack free will or choice; they seem to be programmed like robots to live out their lives of criminality. A related issue to this is that such approaches highlight the distinctiveness of delinquents, whereas much research indicates the very ordinary nature of many of the young men concerned.

❖ Activity 12 ❖

Try to think of two further examples where deviant behaviour has been explained in similar ways to those above.

Another aspect of Matza's work concerns the frame of mind of a young person committing the deviant act. Unlike previous approaches which imply that delinquents deliberately plan and organize their crimes beforehand ('Let's steal a car tonight'), he suggests that they just drift into such activities ('We were just out for a laugh when

Joey suddenly breaks this car window and we all jump in and went for a drive'). In other words there may be a lot of spontaneity and impulsiveness in deviant actions. Such a state of drift applies particularly to young working-class males in deprived inner-city areas who are marginalized and spend a lot of time hanging around, 'waiting for some action' in a world of deprivation and unemployment.

Evaluating Matza's work

Matza's work is of theoretical importance because he has addressed the shortcomings of the structuralist approach and its tendency to see things in deterministic terms. Matza's theories bring in elements of the action approach which focuses on the way behaviour is adaptable and flexible and involves dimensions of choice and free will. However, he still recognizes the structural constraints on behaviour. Our position in the social structure along class, ethnic and gender lines is a determining factor in our choice and life options, so this explains why young, urban, working-class males are involved in delinquency. However, within these structural constraints there are options as to how such males behave, which helps to explain why not all such males resort to delinquency and the variety of forms that such delinquency can take.

Critics of Matza have pointed to the difficulty of precisely pinning down the concept of drift for research purposes. If young men in surveys say, 'It just happened', in explanation of an act of vandalism, it may be a reflection of the context of the research. In other words, the respondents are providing responses or excuses which 'let them off the hook' in the eyes of the authorities. When relating details of their behaviour to their peers, explanations, generally full of bravado, are very different.

Such issues highlight some more general methodological problems in sociological research. These have been raised by qualitative researchers who argue that quantitative survey style research does not produce valid or truthful data because often respondents give 'approved of' accounts. This phenomenon can be particularly heightened in deviancy research when, for obvious reasons, deviants may not wish to disclose the true reasons for their actions.

Conflict theories of deviance

So far we have seen that traditional subcultural theories have followed on from the functionalist assumption that there is consensus over a common core of norms and values. Deviants and juvenile delinquents may reject particular values and create alternatives, but they are still aware of conventional norms. Evidence for this can be seen in the use of such phrases as 'Going straight' or 'Settling down' to describe someone who has given up delinquent activity. The next set of theories we will examine disagree with this assumption of consensus and instead revolve around *conflict*. Conflict theorists point to the different, and sometimes antagonistic, values of those engaged in crime.

Marxist approaches to deviance and crime

There are few direct references in Marx's work to crime and deviance. However, his views are not difficult to ascertain if you are familiar with his work.

Marxist theories of deviance did not really develop in Britain until the 1960s, when groups such as the National Deviancy Symposium based at York University started to use Marxism as a theoretical tool for the study of deviance. Marxist approaches are both *structuralist* (they focus on the structural forces that create deviance) and *relative* (they acknowledge that the boundaries between right and wrong are not clear-cut).

For Marxists, the question of *who defines* crime and deviance is as central as *who is defined* as criminal and/or deviant.

Marxist approaches to deviance have been through three main stages:

❖ traditional Marxism

❖ neo-Marxism and 'new' criminology

❖ 'new' left realism.

Traditional Marxism

Traditional Marxist approaches to crime and deviance see such issues in the context of the critique of capitalist society. A key dimension in the explanation is that of conflicting class relations. Definitions of crime and deviance raise questions of who defines and who makes the laws. The ruling or capitalist class have the power to oppress and exploit the proletariat or working class. Power at the economic or 'base' level permeates the whole of society at other cultural, ideological or 'superstructural' levels.

Effectively, the law is capitalist law which favours the capitalist system. For example, the state may support capitalist interests by giving businesses development grants, interest-free loans or access to state-owned land for factory building. In addition, the state may be reluctant to pass strong antipollution laws or health and safety legislation which might restrict the growth and development of capitalist enterprises (see *In Focus* below).

In addition to examining the way the law supports capitalist interests, another dimension of the traditional Marxist approach is to examine how the law is not even-handed in its treatment of different social class groups.

The Marxists claim that the punishment for a crime may vary according to the social class of its perpetrator. So killing a person as a result of the pursuit of profit is treated more leniently than killing a person during an armed robbery. Armed robbery, a predominantly 'working-class' crime, receives jail sentences of up to thirty years, whereas business fraud, a predominantly 'middle-class' crime receives much lighter sentences.

❖ Activity 13 ❖

1 Collect news articles and reports of crimes and compare the sentences given for business crimes and for crimes such as bank robbery. Do they support the Marxist case?

2 'One rule for the rich and another for the poor'. Show how either the Union Carbide or Guinness cases (see *In Focus* overleaf) supports the Marxist view of crime in a capitalist society.

In Focus

◆

The dangers of unrestricted capitalism – Bhopal, India 1984

The events surrounding the tragedy at Bhopal provide a good case study of how capitalist enterprises can be supported by the state on a global scale. Union Carbide, an American-owned, multinational company, set up a pesticide plant in Bhopal. In 1984 the plant accidentally leaked deadly gas fumes into the surrounding atmosphere. The leakage resulted in over 2,000 deaths and numerous poisoning-related illnesses including blindness. Investigations since have revealed that the company set up this particular plant because pollution controls in India were less rigid than in America. In Snider's terms (1993), the Indian state supported such capitalist development in the interests of allowing profits to be made. Marxists would point out that there have been no criminal charges despite the high death and injury toll. They would see the company owners as the true criminals in such a scenario.

This case involved fraudulent leaks to the financial markets by Guinness directors which artificially boosted the price of Guinness shares. The directors concerned made sizeable profits for the company directly and indirectly for themselves. One of the convicted offenders, Gerald Ronson (one of Britain's 100 richest people), received a one year sentence in Ford Open Prison and was released on parole after serving about six months. During his time in prison he had access to a telephone and his wife continued to run the group of companies he owned. Since his release he has continued to be a successful businessman. Another of the convicted offenders, Ernest Saunders, received a five-year sentence and was released after about eighteen months as a result of being diagnosed as suffering from Alzheimer's disease. Since then it has proved to be a misdiagnosis and Ernest Saunders is now a successful business consultant!

Definitions of business crime from a Marxist perspective

From a Marxist perspective, crime can be defined as:

❖ *Corporate crime* (or *business crime*): This term is usually applied to businessmen and women holding positions of power within companies who engage in fraudulent activities on behalf of their companies to raise profits for shareholders. Often, as in the Guinness affair, such people are major shareholders themselves and so stand to gain personally.

❖ *White-collar crime*: This is a more generic term for a range of crime in business and office-type environments which can range from fiddling expenses through to a wages clerk fraudulently claiming salaries for fictitious employees, and on to large-scale financial swindles.

❖ *Organized crime*: The best-known examples of organized crime are the Mafia and the gangsterland world of figures such as Al Capone in the USA in the early part of the twentieth century. Italian society is a good example of the way organized crime can result in a complex web of politics, the law and big business all being intertwined in a world of corruption and violence.

Traditional Marxist explanations for working-class crime

The crimes of the working class are mainly the theft of property. As such, traditional Marxism interprets them as an understandable response to a situation of poverty where stealing is the only way to support a family. This is the 'Robin Hood' view, with the poor stealing from the rich to redistribute wealth among the poor. It is such a stance that has been a particular target for attack from the more recent neo-Marxist approaches such as left realism. Another interpretation is that crime is a way of hitting back at the exploitative system, a form of 'proletarian revenge'. In this analysis, traditional Marxism views attacks on property and acts of industrial sabotage as one way in which oppressed working-class people can hit back at the system. Another view is that crime is an outcome of an exploitative society offering demeaning work and little sense of creativity and involvement. The Marxist concept of *alienation* can be applied here. In the Marxist sense, alienation does not simply mean lack of fulfilment at work; alienation at work produces alienation from life itself and may result in a worker seeking escape through drink or drugs or may lead to him/her committing acts of violence.

❖ Activity 14 ❖

Consider the case of a drunken factory worker who beats his wife. Is the Marxist explanation for his behaviour in terms of alienation a satisfactory one?

Include the moral dimension and ask yourself whether traditional Marxist approaches make structural excuses for bad behaviour.

Criticisms of traditional Marxist explanations of deviance

Critics of traditional Marxism see its explanations as overly deterministic. In particular, they argue that Marxist approaches deny people choice in how they behave. Critics also argue that traditional Marxism grossly oversimplifies matters: if the root cause of crime is capitalism, then the establishment of a socialist society should mean an end to crime. Such views were propounded in the context of the Soviet Union in the 1950s when no official figures of crime were ever made public. Indeed, the USSR implied that crime was a capitalist problem. It was not until the greater openness of the Gorbachev era in the 1980s that it was admitted that crime was a huge problem for the Soviet Union.

Neo-Marxist approaches: the new criminology

The publication of *The New Criminology* by Taylor *et al.* (1973) marked a turning point in radical approaches to an understanding of crime, which until then had been rooted in the Marxist tradition. The authors recognized some of the problems with a straightforward Marxist account which explained all crime as a product of conflictual class relations in a capitalist society. They combined Marxist structural explanations with insights from more interpretive traditions, such as labelling theory, to develop a more holistic approach which recognized individual choices and actions, societal responses, and the reactions of criminals and those who deal with them in the context of structural constraints.

In the final chapter of *The New Criminology*, Taylor *et al.* set out the key issues that the study of crime should address:

❖ *The wider origins of the deviant act* – These are the structural level explanations which can be linked to traditional Marxism, such as the unequal and exploitative nature of a capitalist society.

❖ *The immediate origins of the deviant act* – Why does the person act in a deviant way, e.g. is theft for financial gain or simply fun?

❖ *The act itself* – If poverty is the motivation, why do some people rob banks, others burgle houses and others shoplift?

❖ *The immediate origins of social reaction* – Why are there different responses from different people to the deviance? Why do family members respond differently from the police?

❖ *The wider origins of reactions to deviance* – What is the wider background to reactions such as law creation and mass media responses?

❖ *The outcome of the social reaction on deviants' further action* – Here insights from labelling theory are used to show how those labelled as deviant respond to their label.

❖ *The nature of the deviant process as a whole* – This combines all the previous issues and synthesizes them into a complex total explanation which will be a more satisfactory account than the more simplistic, one-dimensional accounts such as are provided by Marxism.

Stuart Hall's *Policing the Crisis*

Hall focused on the issue of mugging in the 1970s to illustrate dimensions of the influential new criminology of that time (Hall *et al.* 1979). The early 1970s were a time of considerable political unrest in Britain. The newspapers were dominated by strikes, inner-city unrest and escalating violence in Northern Ireland. Such images contrasted sharply with those of earlier postwar years where there was an impression of a more harmonious and peaceful society. According to Hall, this background of unrest caused an apparent lack of control and influence on the part of the government. The media and politicians seized on the issue of mugging as an issue which reflected a growing outcry from the public about crime in general. The police provided information to the press of violent street robberies of a particular kind and this resulted in lurid media images of badly beaten elderly white ladies who had been attacked and robbed in the streets. There were often thinly disguised references to the culprits' ethnicity which highlighted the 'black' dimension of the crimes. All the features of a media-fuelled moral panic were in place and this diverted attention away from the government's problems in terms of managing the economy. There were increased calls for extended police powers, which had the effect of oppressing the black young male community in inner cities. Black youths were frequently subjected to 'stop and search' procedures in the street and this resulted in the general alienation of a significant proportion of the black community.

Hall and his colleagues looked at the reporting of street crime over a significant period of time. They found that the rate of increase in violent crime had been higher in previous decades, but had not been publicized at the time. They argued that, in the early 1970s, by concentrating on street crime rather than the economic crisis of the day, the media had acted to support the establishment. In this sense, their approach was Neo-Marxist: crime was a structural phenomenon.

❖ Activity 15 ❖

Go back to the summary list on p. 499. Identify and explain those points which apply to Hall's study.

Left realism – Jock Young's attack on left idealism

In the 1980s, one of the co-authors of the *New Criminology* developed a view that was dramatically different from original neo-Marxist influenced work. A number of surveys of the victims of crime, including the Islington Survey (Jones *et al.* 1986), had revealed the extent of regional, class, gender and ethnic variations. The highest proportion of victims were inner-city dwellers, lower working-class, female and of black and Asian backgrounds. This survey questioned some versions of earlier Marxist approaches which presented two images of the criminal: the criminal as a Robin Hood figure, robbing the rich to give to the poor, and the criminal as the victim of a deprived social position, forced into crime by such factors as unemployment and school failure. Young's critical attack on this position is nicely summed up in the following quote (Lea and Young 1984):

> 'There was a belief that property offences are directed solely against the bourgeoisie and that violence against the person is carried out by amateur Robin Hoods in the course of their righteous attempts to redistribute wealth. All of this is, alas, untrue.'

In 1988, Young referred to such Marxist-influenced structuralist approaches as *left idealism* and criticized their under-playing of crime and its victims, as well as their over-emphasis on capitalism as the only causal factor. He points out that crime is endemic in all types of societies and in many, including Britain, has risen dramatically despite increasing affluence. This latter statement challenges conventional postwar criminological orthodoxy that crime is caused by poverty and unemployment. Left realists emphasize that *relative deprivation* (see Chapter 10, *Health, poverty and welfare*) is the key to understanding rising crime in an affluent society. A stroll down any high street shows that we live in a consumer society surrounded by material goods which we are encouraged to possess. In Marx's phrase, late-capitalist industrialism encourages 'commodity fetishism' where possession of objects becomes an end in itself. For those people not in secure employment with rising standards of living, the message of consumption can be a source of frustration, so it is not surprising that some resort to crime. Their victims are more likely to be those who are vulnerable and are an easy target for theft.

Young's work raises theoretical issues with his criticisms of an over-deterministic emphasis on the economic and social structure of a capitalist society. On this point he refers to Japan, which is a highly developed capitalist society with a low crime rate. He offers a more interpretive perspective, presenting the criminal as an active agent making real choices about committing crime, rather than as a victim of 'the system'.

Young also attacks the political dimension of Neo-Marxist perspectives which obscures or glosses over important aspects of crime which need to be addressed. He questions their assumption that the overthrow of capitalism will lead to a crime-free socialist society. In all known communist and socialist societies there are identifiable problems of crime. Young's approach is referred to as left realism because he accepts that the structural dimension of capitalism is a causal factor of crime, even though not the only one. Realism asserts that crime rates are a product of four interacting factors:

- ❖ the police and other agencies of social control
- ❖ the public
- ❖ the offender
- ❖ the victim.

Administrative or managerial criminology

As part of his left-realist perspective, Young also cites the failure of Home Office-inspired administrative criminology. Here there is an emphasis on the management of crime through preventive technological developments such as surveillance cameras, security and efficient locking mechanisms for cars, homes and related property and possessions. Other measures proposed by the Conservative government of the early 1990s included an expanded prison-building programme and minimum sentencing of a more punitive nature for persistent offenders. The debate about gun ownership following the Dunblane massacre raised the question of how to manage crime prevention in one area (see *In Focus* below).

In Focus

◆

In Focus – Guns and violent crime

The Dunblane massacre in March 1996 raised the issue of the control of guns in Britain. In the USA there has been a constant struggle between those who wish to abolish or severely limit the ability to own guns and those who see gun ownership as a right.

Violent deaths and injuries by guns are clearly a factor in America's phenomenally high murder rate and there is a clear argument for prohibition. However, pro-gun-ownership advocates argue that it is a constitutional right of all Americans to own a gun. Some see the ownership of guns as a deterrent to crime essential for protection of one's property and against street crime such as mugging and rape. With regard to the latter, there is a feminist view that women need guns as protection against more physically strong male assailants.

In the UK, the pro-gun lobby tends to focus on the sporting and hunting usage of guns, using the argument that it is deranged or exceptionally deviant people who kill, not the guns. In 1995 in the North East of England, a killer entered a school armed with knives and killed a teenage girl and injured several others.

Official statistics and realist criminology

As well as criticizing left idealists for their political assumptions about the causes of crime, realist criminologists of the left and the right engage in a debate about official figures of crime. Traditional approaches tended to raise questions about what such statistics actually represented. Neo-Marxists saw crime figures as a reflection of the inequitable attention of the law and the police on groups such as ethnic minorities and the working class.

Interpretive approaches raise questions about the way statistics are socially constructed through organizations such as courts and the police. Aaron V. Cicourel (1976) examined the work of the juvenile justice system in California in the 1970s and showed how the police and the juvenile courts processed accused offenders. This occurred in different ways depending on the background of the accused. For a similar offence, a black working-class offender was more likely to receive a custodial sentence than a white middle-class youth. At first this might be seen as clear support for a Marxist view but Cicourel interpreted his findings in a different way. He points out that juvenile courts, unlike adult courts, operate from a welfare perspective, i.e. they take into account the longer-term welfare of the offender when they determine sentences. The issue they address is: 'What will be in the best interests of the young person concerned to prevent them reoffending?' In terms of the offender from a stereotypically deprived background (poor, single-parent family, low educational attainment, other criminals in family, etc.), removal from such potentially crime-producing home and neighbourhood influences is beneficial, so a custodial sentence is likely. In the case of a juvenile from a stable home background (professional parents, 'good' neighbourhood, etc.), it is seen that a non-custodial sentence, where the parents and family can exert influence to prevent further wrongdoing, is in that young person's best interests.

In what ways is this different to a Marxist perspective? Such an approach raises serious questions about what statistics of juvenile delinquency represent. In ethnomethodological terms, the statistics are a reflection of the everyday decision-making activities of officials who operate on the basis of common-sense understanding of events (as illustrated by Cicourel's research). The logic of this argument is that statistics do not really represent the reality of crime and other forms of deviance such as suicide, so to build explanations on such figures is futile. An important theoretical difference emerges here: interpretivists influenced by ethnomethodology, such as Cicourel and Atkinson, study the decision-making of officials in organizational settings such as courts, while the traditional positivistic approach seeks to offer an explanation of deviance using crime statistics as an accurate representation of criminal activity.

Another issue raised is the qualitative change in the nature of crimes, where escalating violence and the use of knives and guns as weapons has become an everyday occurrence. There are now American-style security guards in British schools, colleges and universities, and in 1996 the police were empowered to enter schools to search pupils who may be in possession of knives or drugs. Realists doubt that such issues are solely the creation of a media-influenced 'moral panic' (see Chapter 12, *Mass media*).

The response from 'the old guard': left idealists

In an article responding to Jock Young's dismissive attacks on left idealism, Phil Scraton (1991) defends neo-Marxist influences. He sees that there is an issue about the victims of crime being the more vulnerable members of society and suggests *critical criminology* does recognize such concerns:

'Clearly there is an acceptance that there exists a whole range of behaviours, some defined as crimes – others not, which cannot and should not be tolerated. Critical analysis has questioned how certain acts become defined as priorities for regulation, selective law enforcement and longer sentencing and why specific individuals or identifiable groups are more heavily and differentially policed. Put another way, critical criminology has recognized the importance of distinguishing between acts defined as crime but also has drawn attention to the process of criminalization and the politics of criminal justice.'

❖ **Activity 16** ❖

1 Referring to the quote from Scraton, give examples of 'crimes which cannot and should not be tolerated'.

2 Who are the 'specific individuals' and 'identifiable groups' who are 'more heavily and differentially policed'?

3 Explain 'the process of criminalization' and the 'politics of criminal justice' from a Marxist perspective.

Scraton places emphasis on the structural determinants of crime and deviance in the context of a class-based capitalist society, which links his work with neo-Marxism. He is also keen to highlight inequalities with regard to ethnicity, gender and other oppressed groups. Such an approach sees the answer to crime as lying in the political and economic realm. Failure to recognize the political economy of crime and its genesis leads to 'tinkering' with the existing system. This will fail because the root causes have not been addressed. In this context, all previous prescriptions and social policies to reduce or eradicate crime are bound to fail, including Jock Young's advocacy of a 'multiagency approach'. The following passage by Young refers to this, as well as his view of approaches such as Scraton's, as being part of a 'far and distant utopia':

'For the left idealists nothing can be achieved outside of dramatic, political change. This prospect of waiting for a far and distant utopia is hardly consoling in terms of the real problems which vulnerable sections of the population now face. Left realism argues that gains are possible but they must be part of a co-ordinated strategy involving a multiagency approach. To tackle crime, interventions have to be made on the level of family support, employment, youth facilities, design change, changes in police patrol methods, target hardening, victim support, etc., involving the agencies of local authorities, the police, voluntary groups, education authorities, etc.' (Young 1988)

❖ **Activity 17** ❖

Compare and contrast the Scraton and Young extracts above, putting their views in tabular form. Use categories such as 'definition of crime', 'interpretation of criminal statistics', 'root causes of crime', 'criminals', 'victims', 'answers to crime'.

The New Right approaches to criminology

Another form of realist criminology has different origins from the left realism rooted in Marxism. 'Right realism' has connections with the New Right approaches dealt with elsewhere in this book. Such approaches place less emphasis on the political and social dimensions of behaviour and focus on individuals and their responsibility for their actions. In criminology, a particularly influential figure is J.Q. Wilson (1977) who became an advisor on penal policy to President

Ronald Reagan. Like their counterparts on the left, right realists point out that conventional assumptions about the relationship between poverty and crime are questionable. Postwar America and Britain has seen rising affluence and standards of living accompanied by dramatic increases in crime rates. So the link between social deprivation and crime does not seem to exist. Further historical evidence of this lies in the oft-cited example of the 1930s in Britain and the USA, where during the Depression unemployment and poverty were high, but crime rates were very low in comparison to today.

Right realism has intellectual links with functionalism and early sociologists such as Durkheim. There is an emphasis on the *cultural* dimension of declining morals and good behaviour, particularly among young people, which connects with concepts such as anomie. Criminologists on the right see social order as under threat in the context of a growing climate of greed (see Merton's work on p. 490).

Under target by the New Right are 'trendy' progressive teaching in schools, the pro-abortion lobby, and the more libertarian attitude towards homosexual relationships and cohabitation (as opposed to monogamous, heterosexual marriage). The New Right argue that more libertarian attitudes have led to a generation of confused young people who have no clear ideas on morals and right and wrong. It claims that such confusion has led to a dramatic rise in escapist illegal drug use and, for some, increased propensity to commit crimes and associated deviant acts.

Right realist social policies

Right realist social policies operate on two main fronts:

❖ introducing more effective deterrents through better detection mechanisms and tougher punishment for offenders.

❖ addressing the decline of morality through the strengthening of marriage and responsible parenthood, and a greater emphasis on discipline in schools and on morality as part of religious instruction.

Evaluating New Right approaches

There is a certain common-sense appeal to some aspects of right-realist analyses and policies on crime, but questions need to be raised about whether they are perhaps simplistic and unworkable, given the current state of society. Is it possible to return to a 'Golden Age' when families were stable, schools offered orderly and disciplined environments, and religion was influential in moral guidance?

Regarding the feasibility of right-realist policies, the evidence on the effects of control, deterrence and stronger punishment do not seem to substantiate their views. In Britain in the mid-1990s, crimes against property (e.g. cars) and bank robberies did decline somewhat, which might be seen as vindication of preventative measures (e.g. effective car locks and alarms). However, in the same period, crimes against the person rose, so rather than crime reducing, there may be a channelling effect from property crime to other forms such as racial attacks.

Interpretive (phenomenological) approaches

Phenomenology is a philosophical view that emphasizes the subjective and introspective nature of our experience. It has had some influence in sociology notably through the work of Alfred Schutz and has led to developments in theory such as symbolic interactionism and ethnomethodology. A general way of referring to such approaches is *inter-*

pretivism, which applies to the full range of theories and research strategies. In the field of deviance and crime, interpretive approaches are strongly relativistic and see the deviant or criminal as no different from other people. Two quotations will help to illustrate this perspective:

'Deviant behaviour is behaviour that people so label.' (Becker 1963)

'Sometimes I ain't so sho who's got ere a right to say when a man is crazy and when he ain't. Sometimes I think it ain't none of us pure crazy and ain't none of us pure sane until the balance of us talks him that-a-way. It's like it ain't so much what a fellow does, but it's the way the majority of folks is looking at him when he does it.' (Faulkner 1930)

Labelling theory

Interactionist approaches to deviance have been developed into *labelling theory*. Its founding figure is Howard S. Becker, whose work in the 1960s focused attention on what became the labelling approach to deviance. At its most basic, labelling theory involves a number of fairly simple ideas:

❖ Deviance (and crime) have to be witnessed by others.

❖ Certain perceptions of the act have to be made.

❖ It has to be labelled or defined as deviant by others.

❖ The person committing the act has eventually to recognize and accept that both the act and they themselves are deviant.

❖ The people witnessing and perceiving the act see the person committing it as deviant.

❖ Activity 18 ❖

To illustrate the processes involved in labelling, consider a young person breaking a window. Give three interpretations of this act, including those that see the act as deviant and those that do not.

In a well-known article, 'On becoming a marijuana user', Becker (1963) illustrates the labelling approach to the process of becoming deviant. Using marijuana does not only involve the physiological effects of the drug, it also involves social processes: the new user learns or is socialized into appropriate behavioural responses to the drug. This can involve body posture, clothing and, importantly, the language in which the experience of the drug is described (see *In Focus* below).

Those who can remember first smoking a cigarette or drinking alcohol will be able to recall similar social processes, even to the extent that the desire to cough, be sick or a dislike of the taste is suppressed in order to maintain 'cool' in front of peers.

In the case of marijuana use (an illegal activity), further dimensions than peer group expectations are involved. The activity must be secret and hidden from the outside 'conventional' world. Users are marginal and reinforce their identity strongly with each other, to the extent that their activity is 'normal' and morally justified. A deviant 'career' is followed where lifestyle, occupation and social roles come to revolve around the deviant activity.

In Focus

◆

Acquiring the habit

'I came on like I had turned on [smoked marijuana] many times before, you know. I didn't want to seem like a punk to this cat. See, like I didn't know the first thing about it – how to smoke it, or what was going to happen, or what.

I just watched him like a hawk – I didn't take my eyes off him for a second, because I wanted to do everything just as he did it. I watched how he held it, how he smoked it, and everything. Then when he gave it to me I just came on cool, as though I knew exactly what the score was. I held it like he did and took a poke just the way he did.'

Source: Becker (1963)

This might carry on until caught by law-enforcement authorities. A fine or imprisonment results in a different awareness of the drug-taking act. The public display of disapproval through the courts and prison cells with locks and bars brings home to the actor the significance of their act as deviant. After punishment, this awareness of the implications of their deviance can drive them further into the illegal drug-taking world. For example, they may lose their job and eventually 'drop out' of mainstream society, further reinforcing deviant identity and themselves as 'outsiders'.

Edwin M. Lemert (1972) referred to the early stages, when the act is engaged in among peers with little awareness of society's attitude, as *primary deviance*. After apprehension and punishment by the authorities, if the deviance is continued this added dimension of awareness of the implications is *secondary deviance*.

Evaluating labelling theory

Labelling theory has offered a useful insight into the processes of becoming deviant through an action approach. This can be contrasted with more structural approaches which look at large-scale cultural, political and economic forces which create deviance.

There is some attraction to the labelling approach with its emphasis on people as active agents in their social worlds, rather than helpless puppets or robots subject to a grand-scale social force such as capitalism which is beyond their control. The descriptions of labelling processes have plausibility and a certain common-sense appeal. However, critics have pointed to the weaknesses of labelling theory in a number of areas. Labelling theory implies that we are all potentially deviant, but does not adequately explain why some engage in deviant acts and others do not. In other words, what *motivates* people to commit deviant acts? Using Becker's study of marijuana users, there is a sound analysis of the process of becoming deviant, but no explanation of why some are in that position to be labelled in the first place. In

essence, it is the lack of a *structural* context such as social class and youth that means there is a missing dimension to labelling theory's explanations. Closely connected to this is the failure to recognize the power of some groups to apply labels to others. Such themes were illustrated in a study of illegal drug users in Notting Hill, London carried out by Jock Young (1971). The hippy drug-takers were seen as the deviants by the police who represented the establishment. The power dimension is involved as the police have powers of arrest and prosecution which results in the deviant label being more successfully applied to the hippies.

❖ Activity 19 ❖

Why have antimotorway protesters caused some difficulties in terms of conventional labelling processes?

Ken Plummer's defence of labelling theory

Ken Plummer (1979) takes issue with labelling theory's critics for failing to recognize the real nature of its task. This was to examine the social processes governing the nature, emergence, application and consequences of labels. In this sense, labelling theory is a partial theory within the interactionist tradition, which sees society as constructed through an exchange of gestures (body postures, closeness and touch), symbolic communication (clothes and talk) and negotiated meanings between people.

The importance of issues of power and inequality at the structural level are not ignored or underplayed, rather they are not part of labelling theory's analysis, but such issues can be *accommodated within* the labelling framework. Becker himself does not claim that labels themselves are the root cause of deviant behaviour. The transition from primary to secondary deviance is a complex process full of contingencies, so labels can be provisional, negotiable or rejected.

Becker (1963) recognizes the power and political dimension in the labelling process when he says:

'In addition to recognizing that deviance is created by the responses of people to particular kinds of behaviour, by the labelling of that behaviour as deviant, we must also keep in mind that the rules created and maintained by such labelling are not universally agreed to. Instead, they are the object of conflict and disagreement, part of the political process of society.' (Becker 1963)

Another criticism is that of dealing with areas of social life that in some senses celebrate deviance. Deviants themselves are portrayed as larger than life, exotic and colourful in contrast to the more boring, straight, conforming majority. Certainly a glance at some of the studies of male gays (Laud Humphreys), hustlers and beats (Polsky), professional criminals (Laurie Taylor) and drug-users (Becker, Young) confirms this impression of a form of vicarious fascination with and anthropological voyeurism of an interesting and colourful social world. Criminals and gangsters become larger than life 'folk heroes' who are in some senses hitting back at the oppressive nature of conventional society.

In this context, Alvin Gouldner (1971) contemptuously described the work of Becker and others as 'Underdog Sociology'

which had failed to deal with core issues of power and inequality. Large areas of deviance, such as violence against women and robbery, are not dealt with. However, labelling theory never set out to offer a *universal* explanation for every known form of crime. The task was to examine areas of social life where the processes of labelling were most applicable. In the study of the mass media, labelling theory has made a very useful contribution to the analysis of 'moral panics' through the approach known as *deviance amplification* (see Chapter 12, *Mass media*).

Ethnomethodology

As indicated in a previous section, ethnomethodologists approach deviance in a different way to traditional positivist approaches. Unlike positivists, they are not concerned to explain the causes of deviance as reflected by statistics or social surveys or to develop an understanding of *why* deviance occurs. Rather they are concerned to examine *how* actions or acts come to be defined as deviant and/or criminal, or, non-deviant and/or non-criminal. The processing of the deviant through such agencies as the police and courts is seen as the appropriate area for study. So ethnomethodologists have looked at juvenile justice in America (Cicourel 1976), how juries arrive at their verdicts and the role of coroners at inquests into possible suicide cases (Atkinson 1978).

Women and crime

Up to the 1970s, it could be argued that the sociological study of females and crime was almost non-existent. Carol Smart, a British sociologist, was one of the first to place deviance and crime within a feminist perspective, in 1976. She pointed to the predominance of male criminologists and sociologists of deviance explaining crime

and criminals as a male phenomenon. Smart and other feminist criminologists developed such themes into a general feminist critique of male-dominated (they call this 'malestream') sociology, as well as highlighting the distortion that male accounts give to theories and studies of crime and deviance.

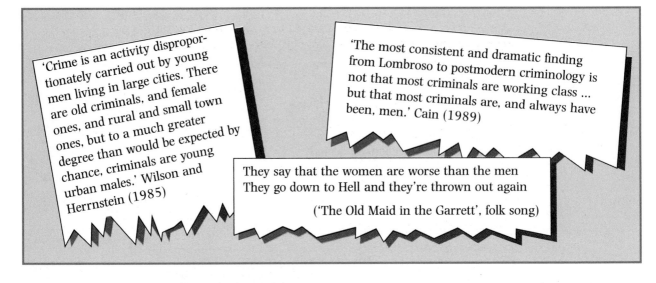

'Crime is an activity dispropor-tionately carried out by young men living in large cities. There are old criminals, and female ones, and rural and small town ones, but to a much greater degree than would be expected by chance, criminals are young urban males.' Wilson and Herrnstein (1985)

'The most consistent and dramatic finding from Lombroso to postmodern criminology is not that most criminals are working class ... but that most criminals are, and always have been, men.' Cain (1989)

They say that the women are worse than the men
They go down to Hell and they're thrown out again

('The Old Maid in the Garrett', folk song)

❖ Activity 20 ❖

1 In what ways do popular and mass media images reflect the misogynist view of deviant females indicated by the folk song quoted above?

2 Conduct a small survey of press stories concerning women criminals such as Rosemary West and Myra Hindley.
   - What images are presented?
   - What explanations are offered for their behaviour?

An indication of female-to-male crime rates is given by the numbers of people in prison:

❖ For every one woman prisoner, there are 24 men.

❖ In 1995 there were 55,000 men and under 2,000 women in prisons.

Feminist approaches to crime and deviance focus on a number of issues which we will examine here in turn.

❖ A comparison of male and female crime *rates* clearly shows far higher rates for men than women.

❖ There are clear differences between the *types* of crime committed by men as compared with women, as the statistics in Table 11.3 indicate.

❖ There are different *punishments* given to men as compared with women. A common-sense view is that women are treated more leniently by the police and the courts.

❖ There are different explanations of *why* men *become* criminal as compared with women, including biological, psychological and sociological.

❖ There are differences in the types of *victims* of crime between men and women.

The 'chivalry' factor

Some sociologists have pointed to a 'chivalry factor' in the interaction between female offenders and the police and within courts. Arrest rates for police officers show a higher rate of arrest of women by women. Mott's early-1980s study of cautioning (1983), showed female offenders were more likely to receive a caution in comparison with males, who would be treated more severely for a similar offence. So is it true that women can 'get away with murder'? Feminist criminologists have responded by suggesting the reverse, that women are treated more harshly than men (see below). For example, they receive

Table 11.3   Offenders found guilty of, or cautioned for, indictable offences: by gender, age and type of offence: England and Wales, 1994

	Males by age					Females by age				
	10–13	*14–17*	*18–20*	*21+*	*All (10+)*	*10–13*	*14–17*	*18–20*	*21+*	*All (10+)*
Theft and handling stolen goods	60	47	36	37	40	85	72	62	61	66
Other indictable offences	2	6	15	21	16	1	4	14	18	12
Drug offences	1	10	22	16	15	1	4	11	9	7
Violence against the person	10	13	10	13	12	8	14	9	9	10
Burglary	18	17	13	8	11	3	3	2	1	2
Criminal damage	6	4	3	3	3	1	2	1	1	1
Sexual offences	1	1	1	2	2	0	0	0	0	0
Robbery	2	2	1	1	1	1	1	0	0	–
All indictable offences (thousands [= 100%])	22.8	80.6	75.3	248.1	426.8	9.4	23.0	12.3	51.0	95.7

Percentages

Source: Social Trends (1996)

❖ Activity 21 ❖

Summarize the trends in male and female crime indicated in Table 11.3. Are there any 'typically male' or 'typically female' types of crime? If so, how would explain these trends?

unsympathetic treatment when victims of domestic or sexual violence. Women criminals are often seen as 'unwomanly' and there is often a focus on their sexuality (e.g. Rosemary West's apparent bisexuality was put forward as evidence of her deviance). Other women are described as 'butch' or unfeminine. The evidence on sentencing seems to be mixed. Women who commit crimes, but who also fulfil stereotypical female roles as wives and mothers, seem to receive lighter sentences. Women who do not are treated harshly.

Francis Heidensohn (1985) gives the following reasons for the inattention paid to women by sociologists and criminologists:

❖ *Vicarious identification* – This is where crime and deviance is celebrated or glamorized by male criminologists; the deviant is a subject of academic fascination. The impression given in many such studies of deviants is of secret admiration of these rebellious ones who, for some Marxist-inspired researchers, are in the vanguard of the struggle against mainstream bourgeois society's repressive institutions.

❖ *Male dominance of sociology* – As males predominate in the profession of sociology, it might not be surprising that males are the chosen field of study in an area such as crime.

❖ *Lower recorded levels of female crime* – The statistically low levels of female crime and criminals (see above) makes study either unnecessary or trivial. As the introductory quote to this section suggests, crime is an overwhelmingly male phenomenon, so why the need to study female crime which is comparatively insignificant? A social policy point can be made here, in that much research funding is chanelled into the clearly identified social problem of crime among young males, effectively sidelining the 'minor' area of female crime.

❖ *Malestream theories of deviance and research* – According to Heidensohn, most theories and research are based on stereotyped views about women. The invisibility of women in sociological studies is a reflection of assumptions about their place in the home, rather than out on the streets where crime and deviance supposedly predominate. Consider how many of the theories and studies cited in this chapter focus on males. For example, Cohen's status frustration theory focuses on young working-class men, but why could it not also apply to young working-class women? Matza's concept of 'drift' (1964) applies to male delinquency and Marxist-influenced theories similarly focus on males in their explanations of deviance.

The stereotyped view: 'women's place is in the home, rather than out on the streets where crime and deviance supposedly predominate...'

Pat Carlen's study of female criminality

Pat Carlen and colleagues carried out a study of female prisoners in 1985 to see if their criminality could be directly compared to that of males. Her sample of 39 women aged 15 to 46 was predominantly working-class. The women had committed a range of offences including theft or handling stolen goods, fraud, burglary, arson and violence, so in terms of social class and types of offence they were similar to male offenders. Carlen's study points to the following 'myths which permeate both the criminal justice system and the prisons':

❖ Rather than being serious and intentional criminals, the women involved in crime are simply deviants from what are *supposed* to be their natural, biologically determined roles.

❖ In the courts, judicial misogyny results in divorced women, single women and women with children in care being more likely to receive custodial sentences than other female offenders.

According to Carlen *et al.* (1985):

'the essential criminal woman does not exist. Women who break the law come from all kinds of backgrounds, though, as with male lawbreakers, those women who land up in prison are much more likely to come from the lower socio-groups than the higher ones'.

Differences occur in obvious categories – for example, women are convicted in far greater proportions for prostitution-related crime, men for sexual offences. (Surprisingly shoplifting, often considered a female crime, is carried out equally between men and women.) Although, when the opportunity is there, women will engage in the same kind of criminal behaviour as men, Carlen does identify gender differences in the reasons and motivations behind some criminal activity (see also *In Focus* on the next page). Women are proportionately more involved in property crime and theft which can be linked to poverty. If the 'feminization of poverty' view is accepted, i.e. that the effects of relationship and marriage breakdown drive more women into poverty than men, then it would appear that women's crime is about putting food on the table for their children, rather than personal gain – as is the case with men.

In Focus

◆

Girl gangs

There is growing evidence from Britain and America of increasing numbers of girls and young women becoming involved in delinquent gangs – a pattern of behaviour previously dominated by males. Earlier studies, such as those by McRobbie and Garber (1976), focused on differing socialization patterns between boys and girls. Girls are more isolated in the private sphere of the home, theirs is a 'bedroom culture' where much time is spent listening to music, making up, doing hair alone or with one or two best friends. Going out usually is associated with meeting or being near boys, so when there is involvement in delinquency it as an accomplice (the old idea of the 'gangster's moll'), for example carrying an offensive weapon for their boyfriend. Such views may have applied to young women in the 1970s but they could be less applicable today. News reports indicate that there are violent girl gangs who engage in similar activities to boy gangs, such as fighting and mugging. The criminal statistics do not reflect a major increase in violent crime among young women, but there may be some underrecording. The chivalry factor mentioned above could apply when male police officers have to deal with violent girl gangs, whose offences may be judged as less 'serious' than those of males. Few sociological studies of girl gangs have been carried out, but Campbell's research into New York female gangs and her self-report studies show that such activity is comparable to that of male gangs.

Sources: Campbell (1984, 1986)

Explanations of women's criminality

Lombroso, the nineteenth-century criminologist, suggested that women were evolutionarily arrested in comparison with men (Lombroso and Ferrero 1895), i.e. closer to savages, children and animals. Women who became criminals were seen as doubly deviant: they were deemed to be evolutionary 'throwbacks' and an 'anathema' to their sex. In other words, female criminals were judged to be 'worse' than male criminals. Despite the sexism and lack of credibility of such views, popular and mass media conceptions of female criminals still include judgements that women who commit serious offences are doubly deviant because they are going against conventional ideas about femininity.

Biological and physiological approaches

Biological approaches to explanations of female criminals still continue and have recently been described as *essentialist*, i.e. there are essential differences between men and women and these can be linked to biological differences. A modern illustration of this would be female deviant behaviour being explained in terms of female hormones. There have been a number of court cases in Britain and America where defending counsel for accused women have emphasized that a criminal act has been committed as a result of premenstrual syndrome (PMS). Critics of feminism claim that such cases undermine the feminist view that women are equal to men, but then they have always used biological differences as a way of justifying women's inferior social position and lack of opportunity (summed up in the phrase 'biology is destiny'). More recent feminist work notably by Michelle Stanworth, has suggested that there has been an over-concentration on inequality in terms of social differences between men and women. There *are* physical differences and these can legitimately be taken into account. So, explanations of women who commit crime as a result of PMS are acceptable and do not echo earlier, sexist biological determinism.

❖ Activity 22 ❖

1   What are your views on the biological
    explanations given above? Can you
    think of any circumstances in which
    similar explanations could be given for
    male deviant behaviour?

2   If hormonal differences are accepted
    in the context of crime, does this raise
    problems in other contexts, e.g. as a
    justification for denying women
    positions of responsibility at work
    because at certain times of the month
    they might act 'irrationally'?

Dr. Katharina Dalton has published
articles on the effects of PMS on women's
behaviour in relation to criminality in
medical journals since the 1960s. In 1991
she gave evidence as an expert witness in
court: 'I get girls sent to me all the time
who think it's a nice easy defence, usually
by solicitors who haven't got the faintest
clue what it is.'

Evaluating biological explanations of female deviance

The dangers of accepting biological explanations are that they support ideas of differences between men and women which
could be used to justify inequality in the
field of work opportunities, particularly
when the 'irrational' dimensions of PMS are
emphasized. The problem with studies such
as those of Dalton (1961) are those of retrospective methodology and the possibility of a
form of 'self-fulfilling prophecy' with respect
to behaviour during the menstrual cycle.
In other words, asking about behavioural
cycles linked to menstruation can shape
women's responses toward ideas of
irrationality and untypical behaviour at
certain times of the month. So in this sense
PMS can be 'socially constructed'. Parlee
(1982) tested this by asking a sample of
women to fill in questionnaires daily for
three months. She made no reference to
menstrual cycles. Few fluctuations of mood
were reported. However, when asked retrospective questions about the effects on their
moods of the cycle most said they experienced anxiety, irritability, depression and
tension in the premenstrual phase.

Psychological explanations of female deviance

The psychologist H.J. Eysenck (1970) drew
up a scale of *introversion* (inner-
directed/withdrawn) and *extroversion* (other-
directed/outgoing) in relation to criminal
personality types. He found that extroverts
were more likely to become criminals. He
examined groups of married and unmarried
mothers, finding the latter more likely to
be promiscuous and therefore deviant.
They were extroverts with higher degrees
of emotionality and neuroticism in
comparison with married mothers. Such
a theory links the views of Eysenck with
those of the New Right in relation to single
parenthood and the breakdown of the traditional family which is linked to rising crime.
Are such views of two broad personality
types satisfactory? Consider the introvert
personality which seems to correspond
more closely to the most deviant of
criminals such as mass murderers (the
'lone' gunman) and serial killers. What
social explanations in relation to poverty,
powerlessness and inequality are missing
from such individualistic explanations?

Gender socialization

This explanation focuses on the different
ways girls and boys are socialized as
reflected in the nursery rhyme:

'What are little girls made of?
Sugar and spice and all things nice ...

What are little boys made of?
Slugs and snails and puppy dogs' tails ...'

Socialization within the family can
involve preparing girls for marriage,
domestic life and childrearing. This may not
be conscious on the part of mothers and
fathers, but the influences within and

outside the family are widespread. For evidence on this, examine toys that are aimed at girls. There is still a huge market for gender-role toys such as dolls, toy domestic appliances even ironing boards, surely the most boring domestic activity of all! Boys' toys rarely involve domestic or family associations, but often involve aspects of war (guns), space (rockets), sport (bats, balls) and transport (cars). Outside the family, secondary agencies of socialization such as school may be offering a less gendered and more equal opportunities curriculum, but 'hidden curriculum' dimensions of appropriate female behaviour still abound. Girls' misbehaviour is often corrected by references to femininity as in: 'That's not what I would expect of a young lady.'

Another significant influence in the socialization process is the peer group. This is particularly strong in adolescence when the potential for deviant activity is greatest. Girls have to tread a delicate line between rebelliousness and going against stereotypical ideas of femininity. An example of this is in sexual behaviour where for girls to have many sexual partners is judged to be deviant and attracts names such as 'slag' and 'slapper'. Compare this with the way boys who have a number of sexual partners are regarded.

Some evidence of changes and challenges to conventional ideas of femininity during young adulthood could perhaps be seen in the emergence of girl gangs (see above) and so-called 'girlies' or 'ladettes', the equivalent of the 'lads' (but note the childish-sounding names that are used, a possible example of the continuing practice of 'putting women in their place').

Social control

There is overlap between social control and socialization. Social control could be seen as the most overt or visible means of affecting behaviour. Frances Heidensohn (1985) identifies three main areas where social control of women is in evidence:

❖ *In the home* (the private sphere) – The demands of housework and childcare

mean that a woman's chance to be freely 'out and about' and potentially breaking the law are severely restricted compared to men. Patriarchal relations within the family mean a man can limit his wife's movements to acceptable social areas which are either domestic-related (shops, children's school) or 'approved of' social activities such as keep-fit classes.

❖ *In public* (the public sphere) – On the streets, women who are not accompanied by men can often be subject to a variety of forms of control ranging from embarrassment (catcalls, wolf whistles) to harassment (touching, pinching) to danger (sexual assault, rape). The 1986 Islington Crime Survey found that 54 per cent of women compared with 14 per cent of men often or always avoided going out after dark because of fear of crime. Lurid news-stories featuring women victims of such crimes add to the climate of fear experienced by women.

❖ *At work* – Many workplaces are still dominated or controlled by men. Where there are mainly female workers, it is still likely that a man will be in charge. Women who assert themselves are seen as 'bossy', ambitious women are 'pushy'.

Opportunity

Socialization and social control as described above combine to mean that women's opportunities to commit crime if they wished to are severely limited compared with men. As an example, imagine a burglar whose cover for entering houses was as a window cleaner carrying a bucket and ladder. If the person was male, the bogus window cleaner would scarcely be noticed. But what if the person was female?

Women's liberation

One explanation of why women's crime may have increased is the liberation of women. This challenges some dimensions of the previous explanations of the restrictions on women and suggests that equal opportunities and the influence of feminism have led to rising confidence and assertiveness among women. Freda Adler (1975) emphasizes such social changes in women's position and links these to a rise in female crime, notably in previously male-dominated areas such as robbery and juvenile delinquency. However, there is some evidence that juvenile delinquency is less likely to continue into criminal behaviour for adult women, whereas in recent years it has increasingly become so for young men. This returns us to previous ideas concerning opportunity and social control. Such young women are probably likely to be trapped in the private sphere of home and childrearing.

Studying the victims of crime (victimology)

'We normally think of a victim of mugging as being someone elderly, usually female, who has been attacked in the course of being robbed. We think of a burglary as either constituting the ransacking of an empty house during the day or an act of premeditated stealth during the night. We think of the victim of rape as being female, usually young, who fought "within an inch of her life" to resist her attacker (who was a stranger and attacked in a public place).' (Walklate 1994)

Until the 1980s the sociology of deviance and criminology concentrated on crime, its measurement and causation, and criminals. This perhaps echoed the popular consciousness that unless the victims were particularly shockable then little attention was paid to them.

❖ Activity 23 ❖

What do the statistics tell us about the victims of crime?

Crime statistics indicate a complex picture concerning the victims of crime. Analysis needs to be carried out concerning particular types of crime in relation to its most vulnerable victims. Sometimes the boundaries around the criminal and the victim are clear cut, such as in the case of rape which is legally defined in Britain as the forceable penetration of a vagina by a penis. Therefore the victim of rape is always female and the perpetrator of rape is always male. Similarly, the victim of child abuse is a child and the perpetrator is an adult. Some groups may wish to change this, as in the case of men's groups who are pressurizing for the widening of the definition of rape to include anal penetration in order to include men as victims. Other areas of statistical representation of victims challenge conventional assumptions. For example, it is widely assumed that the most common victims of violent assault are women, particularly elderly women as victims of mugging. The statistics in Table 11.4 disprove this.

However, as with all statistics there are potential misrepresentations and distortions. For example, crimes of violence appear to be dominated by those on the streets where the offender is unknown to the victim. This gives a picture of victims who are predominantly young and male. So a lone young male walking home late at night who is set upon by a knife-wielding gang resulting in severe injuries is seen as a statistically typical victim.

In reality, however, evidence of domestic violence points to the underrepresentation of victims of violence in the home who are predominantly women and children. A combination of fear, emotional blackmail ('Don't tell your mum, she'll be upset') and possibly loyalty to the perpetrator (an indication of the power of familial ideology) results in non-reportage of such crimes. In this sense, domestic violence that is recorded in the statistics is clearly only the 'tip of the iceberg'.

Table 11.4   Victims of violence: by gender and age, 1993

Percentage in each age group who had been a victim once or more

England & Wales	Males by age			Females by age		
	16–29	30–59	60+	16–29	30–59	60+
Domestic	1.1	0.6	0.1	3.6	1.5	0.1
Mugging	1.9	0.5	0.2	0.7	0.6	0.3
Other	12.1	3.4	0.4	4.5	1.6	0.3
All victims of violence	14.5	4.4	0.7	8.3	3.5	0.8

Source: Social Trends (1996)

Table 11.5   Victims of crime: by ethnic group, 1993

Percentage in each ethnic group who had been a victim once or more

England & Wales	White	Afro-Caribbean	Asian	All ethnic groups
Household offences				
Home vandalism	4.3	3.9	4.8	4.3
Burglary	6.3	12.9	8.0	6.5
Vehicle crime (owners)				
Vandalism	8.1	12.1	9.8	8.2
Theft	19.6	25.7	23.0	19.7
Other	10.2	9.5	8.9	10.1
All household offences	32.6	36.2	34.3	32.6
Personal offences				
Assaults	3.8	6.6	3.1	3.8
Threats	3.5	4.0	3.2	3.4
Robbery/theft from person	1.7	2.7	3.4	1.8
Other personal theft	3.7	5.2	3.2	3.7
All personal offences (excluding sexual offences)	8.5	13.2	9.3	8.6

Source: Social Trends (1996)

This is Michael's story.

'It would start with a smack. But then there was no stopping him. It was as if he forgot who I was.

But he'd usually remember to hit me where it wouldn't show. When he didn't I'd be kept off school. Once he broke my arm. My mum told the hospital I'd had an accident.

If a teacher asked me about a cut or bruise, I'd just lie.

Finally a neighbour saw the mess my face was in and reported it.

I'll always be grateful to my counsellor. He said I wasn't to blame. He helped me to feel better about myself. He was the father I never had.'

There are thousands of cases like this each year, from every level of society. But there are thousands more victims of less obvious forms of cruelty.

Some people wouldn't even think of them as abuse. But imagine being constantly shouted at. Or ignored. Or criticised for everything you do.

The emotional effects can be just as painful as those caused by more obvious forms of abuse, including low self-worth, humiliation and loneliness.

Some children have even been driven to kill themselves.

Because of all this, the NSPCC is launching a campaign called 'A Cry For Children.' It's a cry to everyone to

stop and think about the way they behave towards children.

To recognise the impact that any form of cruelty can have on a child. And to realise that the way children are treated affects their whole lives.

Please answer the cry.

If you, or someone you know is suffering abuse, call the NSPCC Child Protection Helpline on 0800 800 500.

Or if, after reading this, you would find more information helpful, please call us on 071 825 2775.

NSPCC
A cry for children.

Voluntary organisations, such as the NSPCC, campaign to highlight the private suffering of many victims

It could be suggested that official statistics largely represent those victims of crime and deviant acts *in public places* where witnesses are present. The victims of *private* deviant and criminal acts go largely unnoticed.

Sandra Walklate (1995) identifies two approaches to the study of victims, that of *positivist victimology* which originated in the 1980s when criminal victimization studies were started, and the more recent *realist victimology* which has links with realist criminology. Walker points out that to claim the legitimate status of victim, innocence must be shown. So acts carried out by strangers on perceived vulnerable people such as women (rape and sexual attacks), the elderly (robbery and mugging), children (physical and sexual abuse) and ethnic groups (racist attacks) involve a clear idea of an innocent victim.

Now try Activity 24 below. This activity could be developed into a research project which involves devising a social survey to examine public perceptions of victimhood. You could use mass media resources, CD-ROM, etc., to gain a wider picture. Theoretical background could be from such areas as labelling theory and similar approaches. Contact your local police and victim support groups for background information (the Citizens' Advice Bureau should be a useful source). You should not attempt to identify or interview victims themselves, particularly in sensitive areas such as abuse. This would be counter to the ethical guidelines given for a project of this nature.

❖ Activity 24 ❖

Indicate which of the following are 'clear victims' and which not, giving reasons.

Do you think it is possible or acceptable to divide 'victims' up in this way at all?

1 a 45-year-old male homosexual beaten up by a young man who thinks he is being propositioned in a public lavatory

2 an 80-year-old lady savagely attacked and raped in her home by two 16-year old males

3 a school bully beaten up by a group who had been his victims

4 a man who is regularly beaten by his wife

5 a woman who is regularly beaten by her husband

6 a sexually abused daughter who stabs her abusing father to death

7 a man who dies after a sado-masochistic hanging activity goes wrong

8 a 22-year-old child molester who was sexually abused by his father and uncle from when he was 2 years old

9 an 80-year-old man who shoots and kills a teenage burglar

10 a woman who is very drunk and goes with a man to his room and is raped.

Positivist victimology

This approach originated in America and was developed through the 1980s by a number of studies, notably the Home Office British Crime Surveys (BCS). The first BCS (1982) controversially stated that a 'statistically average' person aged 16 or over can expect:

❖ an assault resulting in injury (even if slight) once every century

❖ the family car to be stolen or taken by joyriders once every 60 years

❖ a burglary in the home once every 40 years.

The message from such studies was that the risk of crime was not so great as feared and this eventually developed into the view that it is not crime itself that is the problem but the 'fear of crime'. This became incorporated into Home Office social policy and police conventional wisdom. Widespread publicity campaigns to highlight such themes were mounted. Various agencies, notably the popular press, were identified as heightening a sense of moral panic about crime which was not justified by the victimization surveys. There is some support for such views. Statistics indicate that crimes involving sex and violence are around six per cent of the total amount of indictable offences, but approximately forty per cent of the content of the popular press is devoted to such incidents.

❖ Compared with other life chances, such as premature death from smoking or alcohol abuse, the risk of being a victim of crime is small.

❖ Those risks which do exist are evenly distributed amongst the general population.

❖ Those most likely to be victims of assault are male, under 30 years old, single, go out to pubs and clubs regularly, drink frequently and may assault others.

Realist victimology

Walklate suggests three differences between realist and positivist victimology. Realist victimology:

❖ focuses on 'problems as people experience them' Young (1988)

❖ is committed to examining the age, gender, ethnic and class dimensions of the processes of criminal victimization

❖ uses local, geographically focused, criminal victimization surveys as a way of developing a picture of the nature and extent of criminal victimization

Additionally, the difference between the empirical findings of the national victim-ization surveys and the local surveys provide an insight into the political debate between 'positivist' and 'realist' victimology.

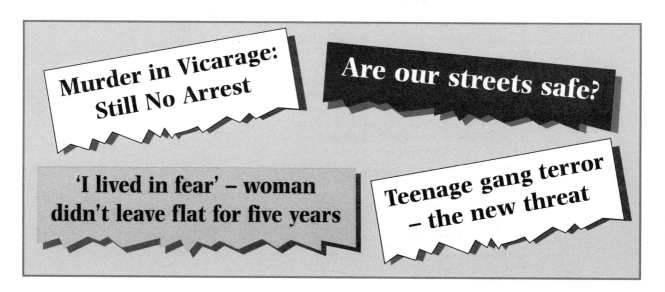

Murder in Vicarage: Still No Arrest

Are our streets safe?

'I lived in fear' – woman didn't leave flat for five years

Teenage gang terror – the new threat

The findings from the locally based surveys offer a clear challenge to the view that crime is a rare occurrence. For many people the fear of crime is a real experience. One survey in Islington in 1986 found a street where more than half the residents had experienced theft from or of their cars. In addition, in the borough in 1985, there had been 1,200 incidents of sexual assault, 2,569 incidents of domestic assault, and 870 racial assaults. In 1990, a follow-up survey found the burglary rate to be twice the national average and that eight per cent of women had reported an incident of sexual assault in the previous 12 months. Similar high levels were found in surveys on Merseyside and in Edinburgh. The author of one commented:

> 'There can be no doubt that both in terms of quantity and the impact of crimes examined, the poor suffer more than the wealthy. The problems appear critical for the 20 per cent of the Merseyside population living in the poorest council estates...' (Kinsey 1985)

As well as the poor being disproportionately affected, women are vulnerable:

> ' ... the cycle of violence and fear confronted by women limits their participation in public to the extent of virtual curfew.' (Crawford *et al.* 1990)

Evaluating the positivist and realist approaches

There are clear differences between the two approaches to the study of victims. Large-scale British Crime Surveys indicate that the risk of crime is not great and that the 'problem' is the fear of crime not crime itself. The fault lies with a crime-obsessed mass media which creates moral panics and amplifies deviance out of all proportion to its actual occurrence. The realist response is to point to the political convenience of this for a 'law and order' government. They show that crime is actually rising and has done dramatically since the advent of Thatcherism in 1979. Vulnerable groups such as the poor, women and ethnic minorities living in deprived inner-city neighbourhoods are greatly affected by crime. As a recent car advert stated 'there is no such thing as an average person' in response to the stress placed on this in the British Crime Surveys. Crime affects people unequally and far greater proportions of victims are to be found among the more vulnerable sections of the population.

❖ Activity 25 ❖

1 What ways are available to the middle and upper classes to protect themselves from the effects of crime which are not available to the poor and deprived?

2 Analyse whether the risk of being a victim of crime been over-exaggerated, or whether crime is a real problem for vulnerable groups in society such as the poor, women and ethnic minorities.

Official statistics of crime

Crime rates are often represented in a sensational manner in the news, particularly emphasizing that things are becoming much worse. Main news-stories commonly highlight rises in violent crime. What is the sociological reality behind such figures? It has already been noted that, generally, crime rates are rising. From a few hundred thousand recorded crimes per year in the 1950s and 1960s to approaching 6 million in the 1990s is certainly a dramatic rise, but as always, we need to look more closely and make a number of qualifications.

Table 11.6 Notifiable offences recorded by the police: by type of offence, 1981 and 1994

	England & Wales		Scotland		N.Ireland	
Thousands						
	1981	1994	1981	1994	1981	1994
Theft and handling stolen goods,	1,603	2,561	201	235	25	33
of which: theft of vehicles	333	534	33	42	5	9
theft from vehicles	380	844	–	80	7	7
Burglary	718	1,261	96	88	20	17
Fraud and forgery	107	146	21	24	3	5
Violence against the person	100	220	8	14	3	5
Criminal damage[1]	387	930	62	89	5	3
Robbery	20	60	4	5	3	2
Sexual offences, 19	32	2	4	–	1	
of which: rape	1	5	–	1	–	–
Drug trafficking –	18	2	6	–	–	
Other notifiable offences[2]	9	25	12	62	3	2
All notifiable offences	2,964	5,258	408	527	62	68

[1]In Northern Ireland excludes criminal damage valued at £200 or less.
[2]In Northern Ireland excludes 'possession of controlled drugs' and 'offences against the state'.

Source: Social Trends (1996)

One of the clearest indicators of crimes of violence is the homicide or murder rate. Murder victims' dead bodies are almost always discovered and the police are usually successful in detection. Historically, the increase in the annual number of murders is not that dramatic, particularly in the case of murder by strangers. Some of the most shocking murders are those involving children as victims. Year on year, however, the average number of children killed by strangers is only seven, and this has not changed this century. Even more shocking than the killing of children by adults is when such killing is carried out by children themselves. The rarity of this must be noted. When two boys aged 10 were convicted for killing James Bulger, a 2-year-old, in Liverpool in 1993, shock and outrage were expressed in the mass media. It should be noted that the two boys concerned were the first of their age this century to be convicted of murder. Experts have commented that it is impossible to extrapolate from such a tiny sample to theories concerning the increased violence of children.

Other factors which qualify the crime statistics are:

❖ *The increase in population* – Particularly in the younger age group (see Table 11.3) who are the most involved in crime of any age group. In Britain, as this age group has fallen in the 1990s so correspondingly have certain categories of crime such as street robbery and violence.

❖ *More laws to be broken* – This can be noted with the increase in cars: now there are laws on seatbelts, tyre safety, windscreen washers and so on, which did not exist in the 1950s.

❖ *More police with increased technological support* – An increase in numbers of police will result in an increase in arrests and convictions. Despite the complexity of the police role, ranging from controlling public disorder to helping people in distress, their key responsibility is still held to be catching criminals, and they are accountable to and judged by the public mainly on this. However, the police themselves admit that they probably only deal with about 10 per cent of the total crimes committed, so is the increase in crime a real increase, or are the police becoming able to deal with more of the unrecorded acts? Here the iceberg analogy is used.

Interpretivists argue that statistics are of little use in revealing the true amount of crime and have advocated the study of decision-making in legal settings such as courts as a more fruitful task. To build causal theories of crime based on statistics is seen to be a mistaken endeavour. Realists disagree: while recognizing the flaws in the collection of statistics, they say that the increase in crime statistics has been so great that it is a 'real' increase and this is what needs explaining through theorizing and research.

❖ Activity 26 ❖

Look at Figs 11.2 and 11.3, as well as Table 11.7. Describe in your own words the point of the iceberg analogy in relation to crime figures. A similar explanation can be applied to sexual offences against women. Rather than increased police numbers, what explanations could be offered for an increase in convictions for such offences?

Figure 11.2
Reasons for not reporting crime, England & Wales, 1993
Source: Social Trends (1996)

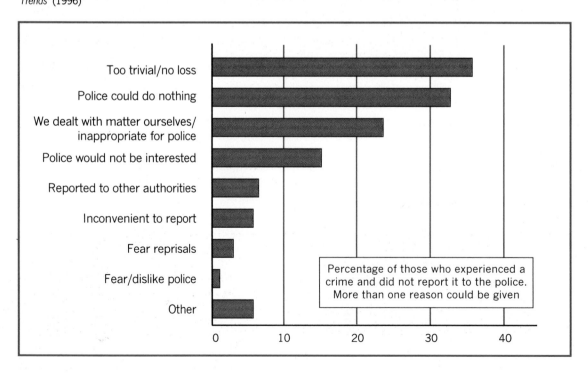

Too trivial/no loss
Police could do nothing
We dealt with matter ourselves/ inappropriate for police
Police would not be interested
Reported to other authorities
Inconvenient to report
Fear reprisals
Fear/dislike police
Other

0   10   20   30   40

Percentage of those who experienced a crime and did not report it to the police. More than one reason could be given

Table 11.7   Clear-up rates for notifiable offences: by type of offence, 1981 and 1994

	England & Wales		Scotland		N.Ireland	
Percentages						
	1981	*1994*	*1981*	*1994*	*1981*	*1994*
Sexual offences,	73	76	65	80	71	89
of which: rape	68	74	74	79	45	69
Drug trafficking[1]	–	102	99	100	100	87
Violence against the person	75	77	83	77	47	67
Fraud and forgery	70	52	78	79	66	65
Theft and handling stolen goods,	38	24	28	26	27	31
of which: theft of vehicles	28	19	26	24	14	19
theft from vehicles	23	13	–	14	12	8
Criminal damage[2]	27	17	22	20	17	36
Burglary	30	21	20	17	22	20
Robbery	25	22	26	29	15	20
Other notifiable offences[3]	91	94	90	98	33	88
All notifiable offences	38	26	31	37	27	36

[1] In England and Wales offences cleared up in 1994 may have been initially recorded in an earlier year.

[2] In Northern Ireland excludes criminal damage valued at £200 or less.

[3] In Northern Ireland excludes 'possession of controlled drugs' and 'offences against the state'.

Source: Social Trends (1996)

Figure 11.3
Recorded and unrecorded crime: the iceberg analogy

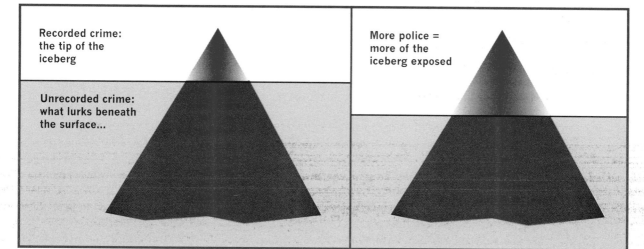

Recorded crime: the tip of the iceberg	More police = more of the iceberg exposed
Unrecorded crime: what lurks beneath the surface...	

New directions: the influence of postmodernist thinking

A key theme in this chapter is that the study of deviance and crime in sociology has evolved from an *absolute* view (where deviants and criminals are seen as different from normal conforming people) to a more *relative* view (where deviance and criminality are seen as part of a wide spectrum of behavioural options available in our lives). Theoretically, there has been a shift from *positivism* to *interpretivism* and more recently, to *realism* in approaches. Your reading of this chapter should have shown that this has not been straightforward. There are still theories around that see crime in an absolute way, not as something exaggerated by popular perception, the mass media or moral panics. There have also been criticisms of the relativist stance of the interpretivist tradition.

Behind the shift towards relativism in sociology, has been a wider moral and political move towards acceptance of diversity and the creation of a climate of tolerance.

There have been criticisms of ethnocentrism where one's own social group or society is seen as superior to others. The recognition of equal rights for women, the growth of multicultural, multi-ethnic and diverse societies has brought such issues to the fore. Whereas once, single-parent families were classed as deviant, today they are increasingly accepted as another 'lifestyle choice'.

Sociology's link to such issues can be partly connected to its leftist and critical traditions which have exposed unequal power and social inequality. The powerful and dominant have often been associated with the identifying of deviant groups who are invariably the relatively powerless groups in society. Shifting attitudes to homosexuality are a good example of such trends. Tim Davies (1995) points out that sociologists have tended to ignore homosexuality as a subject of study, but many of the theories of deviance could be applied to it.

Davies highlights the contribution of Foucault and his use of discourse. The

❖ Activity 27 ❖

Select two or three of the main theories in this Chapter and apply their approach to homosexuality. Which are absolute and which are relative?

discourse surrounding homosexuality may have changed from that involving ideas of perversion to that of acceptance, but Davies doubts how far this has gone. Certainly, many more high-profile figures are open about their homosexuality than before (including entertainers such as Elton John or actor Sir Ian MacKellen, and including politicians and religious leaders) and this may indicate increased acceptance and tolerance of diverse sexuality. However, for every such example that makes headlines, there still large numbers who live secret lives, afraid that exposure of their sexuality may ruin them. There have also been furious debates in the USA and Britain concerning whether gay people should be allowed in the armed forces, whereas in countries such as Holland gay people are openly accepted.

The example of homosexuality helps to show how sociology can contribute to explaining changes through time in how deviance is defined and reacted to. It is clear that assumptions about increased tolerance of diversity need qualifying. Single parenthood might be acceptable in royal circles but single mothers in lower socio-economic positions still find themselves the subject of deviant labels and attacks from New Right thinkers.

Evaluation of postmodernist approaches

Postmodernist approaches feature the idea of diversity which can be linked to acceptance and tolerance; reactions to deviance are less predictable. Critical theorists respond to this by pointing to the degree of intolerance that still persists. Gay people are still being beaten up and murdered, politicians are still advocating harsher punishments for criminals, single mothers are still being seen as scroungers, ethnic groups and women are still being subjected to violence. In this sense, the study of deviance and crime has not changed as dramatically as postmodern views might hold. Having said that, newer aspects such as the focus on feminist issues, victims and realist explanations, have moved us on from the earlier emphases on deviance and crime which concentrated on young working-class males living in urban areas.

Chapter summary

- ❖ The topic of deviance, social control and crime has been a central one for sociologists for many years. The explanation of why people become deviants or criminals and how they are judged by society helps us to understand the nature of social order and control. Examining how and why people become, or are defined as, deviants helps us to address issues of why people conform. This is a key sociological task.

- ❖ There is no doubting public fascination and interest in particular areas of deviance such as crime – newspaper and TV coverage confirm this, as does the amount of daily conversation devoted to such topics.

- ❖ The sociology of deviance and criminology covers a bewildering array of theories, concepts and competing explanations which all need careful and systematic study.

- ❖ Marxist-influenced approaches highlight issues of power and inequality which are likely to remain relevant, even as new approaches are developed.

- ❖ Newer areas of the topic, such as feminist approaches and victimology, point to the need for further research and explanation concerning women's and ethnic minorities position in society. The probable next developments are for groups such as homosexuals and the disabled to be considered in similar ways.

- ❖ The insights from the 'micro' perspectives of interactionism and ethnomethodology will make their contribution to our fuller understanding of a topic that is of interest to us all.

- ❖ More general theoretical and methodological issues are raised when debates concerning official statistics are examined, as in the section on crime figures.

- ❖ However complete our understanding may eventually be, it is certain that, as Durkheim suggested over 100 years ago, human societies will always contain those who are 'deviant' in one form or another.

Stimulus–response question

Using the information from this chapter and the items below, answer the following questions:

1 Give two brief explanations for the rise in crime indicated in Item A. *(2 marks)*

2 Give three reasons *for* and three *against* accepting such statistics at face value. *(6 marks)*

3 Why is Young critical of Marxist approaches to crime? *(4 marks)*

4 What is Scraton's response? *(4 marks)*

5 Evaluate the usefulness of official statistics of crime to the sociologist. *(9 marks)*

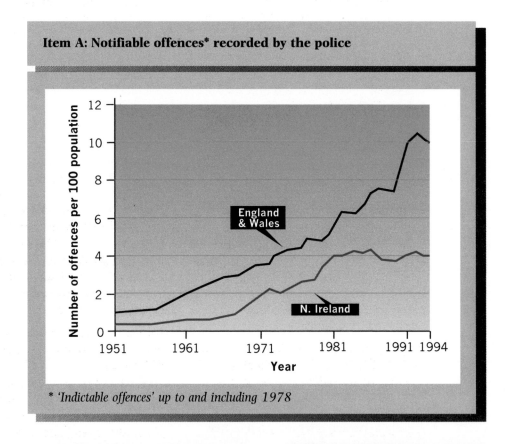

Item A: Notifiable offences* recorded by the police

* *'Indictable offences' up to and including 1978*

Item B

'For the left idealists nothing can be achieved outside of dramatic political change. This prospect of waiting for a far and distant utopia is hardly consoling in terms of the real problems which vulnerable sections of the population now face.' (Young 1988)

Item C

'"Realism", of whatever political persuasion, is irretrievably locked into the established order, definitions, priorities, and practices of social democracy.' (Scraton 1991)

Essay questions

1 Examine the contribution made by functionalism to our understanding of crime and deviance.

2 Critically examine the relationship between deviance and power. (AEB 1996)

3 'The usefulness of crime statistics in sociological research depends on the theoretical approach adopted by the sociologist.' Critically explain this view. (AEB 1996)

4 'Lower status groups have higher crime rates because they are denied access to the legitimate means of achieving success enjoyed by more privileged groups.' Assess this view. (AEB 1996)

5 Outline gender differences in patterns of crime and examine sociological explanations of these patterns. (AEB 1996)

6 'It is as important to consider the victims of crime as it is the criminal to gain as full a sociological understanding of crime as possible.' Discuss.

7 'Left realism has highlighted the failure of traditional Marxist-influenced approaches to explaining crime and deviance.' Discuss.

Further reading

Campbell, A. (1984) *The Girls in the Gang*, Oxford: Basil Blackwell.

An interesting empirical study set in New York which looks at what is traditionally seen as a male phenomenon from a new angle. It considers within a comparative feminist framework the growth of and reasons for female gangs.

Maguire, M., Morgan, R. and Reiner, R. (eds) (1994) *The Oxford Handbook of Criminology*, Oxford: Clarendon Press.

A comprehensive reference book comprising an encyclopaedic collection of essays covering most topics in an accessible manner.

Pearson, G. (1983) *Hooligan: A History of Respectable Fears*, London: Macmillan.

A fascinating historical study which effectively demolishes utopian views that there has ever been a crime-free peaceful society. Problems with youth are as old as time itself!

Tierney, J. (1996) *Criminology: Theory and Context*, Hemel Hempstead: Prentice Hall/Harvester Wheatsheaf.

A good, detailed overview of developments in criminology which is very thorough, tracing historical origins and covering most recent debates in an accessible manner.

Walklate, S. (1995) *Gender and Crime*, Hemel Hempstead: Prentice Hall/Harvester Wheatsheaf.

A well-written and clear introduction to this topic. Most aspects of gender and crime are covered including victimology, sexual violence, police work, women and the law and social policy. An important contribution to feminist approaches to crime.

Young, J. and Matthews, R. (eds) (1992) *Rethinking Criminology: The Realist Debate*, London: Sage.

A good collection of articles from a realist position which also covers a critical stance and looks at the successes and failures of social policy on crime in the USA and Britain.

Chapter 12

Mass media

❖ Preview

In this chapter we shall be looking at:

❖ definitions of the mass media

❖ a history of the development of mass media

❖ explaining the media – early psychological approaches, the hypodermic syringe model

❖ Marxist approaches – manipulative and hegemonic models: the media as capitalist media

❖ pluralist approaches – the market decides: 'we get the media we deserve'

❖ newer social issues in relation to the media – gender (feminist approaches), ethnicity, age, social class

❖ interpretive approaches – media-audience interaction is a two-way process

❖ methodological criticisms of media research

❖ postmodernism and the media – globalized media, choice and diversity, self-identity and consumption: the possible end of the mass media.

❖ Introduction

This chapter examines the mass media and their relationship to society, starting with a look at issues of defining the mass media. Most definitions cover communication, the role of technology and a large or mass audience. (Note that in this book, 'media' is taken to be a plural noun ('the media are...'), but you may come across it used elsewhere as a singular noun.)

Sociologists have stressed the *power* of the media to control and influence such audiences. Non-sociologists, such as politicians and religious leaders, have expressed concerns about the *influence* of the mass

media on children and young people, particularly highlighting the media's portrayal of sex and violence. A short history of the media charts the development of a mass media from its early beginnings to national newspapers and television.

We will examine explanations of the mass media, starting with early accounts developed from psychology. These tended to focus on the way the media affect individual or small group behaviour. A key assumption was that the media act like a hypodermic syringe 'injecting' their recipients with powerful, drug-like messages.

Does this cause bad behaviour? The evil doll Chucky from the film *Child's Play* was cited in the trial of the two boys who murdered toddler James Bulger, as a possible negative influence (see p. 535)

Such recipients are like sponges soaking up and absorbing the information conveyed. The popular imagination still carries this image, particularly with reference to violent crime and juvenile delinquency. Video nasties and violent horror films are seen as causing young people in particular to imitate and take part in similar activity.

Sociological explanations have revealed the complex nature of the relationship between behaviour and the mass media. It is too simple to see ourselves as sponges soaking up messages or as agents made to behave in certain ways because of what we read, see or hear. Nevertheless, the media undoubtedly have some influence because of the millions of pounds spent annually on advertising.

Structural sociological approaches such as Marxism and feminism emphasize the power of the media to influence and control our behaviour. Some see the media as an *ideological* tool which is used by more powerful members of society to support the status quo. Marxists see the media as *capitalist*; feminists highlight the *patriarchal* nature of the media and other conflict sociologists raise similar issues with relation to ethnicity, sexuality, disability and other disadvantaged groups. All such approaches stress the way the media shape our view of the world to accept and condone inequalities and the way society is run.

The *pluralist* approach differs from this. Here the view is that we 'get the media we deserve'. Market mechanisms mean that there is a vast array of choices available to the consumer, whose purchasing power determines which media are successful. The argument goes that in a liberal, democratic society – within limits that exclude extreme violence or pornography – anyone is at liberty to publish or broadcast whatever views they wish. Their success or failure depends on people buying their newspaper or watching or listening to their programme.

Structural approaches would see this as naive. We might have a vast range of 'choice', but this is channelled along lines of diversion, triviality and escapism and the established power structures in society are rarely challenged.

A vast range of choice for the consumer: do we get the media we deserve?

❖ Activity 1 ❖

Make a list of media influences that do not affect your behaviour, for example particular adverts or programmes. Now consider where you have been influenced to act in some way by such media sources. Compare and discuss your findings with a partner.

Photo © Sally Lancaster/Photofusion

❖ Activity 2 ❖

Do you agree with the last statement? Think of recent examples, such as the debate about the monarchy, and present the opposing pluralist and conflict positions.

We will examine the role of the media in relation to social differentiation and stratification focusing on gender, ethnicity, age groups and social class.

A more recent major theoretical development has been that of *interpretive* approaches to the study of the media. These stress the more interactive dimensions of the relationship between the media and individuals and groups. There is a clear challenge to the view that we are media-sponges; rather we are active participants in disseminating and attributing meaning to the abundance of media messages in our daily lives. The media can be influential but the way this works is often complex and unpredictable. There are differing views on the way people interpret media images. An example in the late 1990s is the all-female pop group 'The Spice Girls'. Some interpreted their success as a good image for young women or strong women getting on in the world on a par with men. Others saw this as another teenybop phenomenon used by business and the capitalist system to make profits from manufactured rebelliousness which would be rejected when sales fell. Others see it all as a bit of fun and a harmless part of growing up for young adolescents.

From the 1980s on, there has been a range of developments in studies of the media. Sociologists have been influenced by work from a number of inter-disciplinary fields such as cultural and media studies, linguistics, art and literary criticism, and semiotic studies of signs and images. Postmodernism in relation to the media is a key aspect of current debates. This is tied in with developments in computer technology such as CD-ROM, and interactive and multimedia programmes. Such developments, along with cable, satellite and digital broadcasting, have opened possibilities of choice and diversity unimagined in the early media age. Consumers of the media can 'pick and mix' and construct identities from a vast array of sources. The media cease to be *mass* media which provide a common experience for all; instead they become a source of information and entertainment tailored to individual needs.

The twenty-first century should see the spread of such forms of the media; in the future, discussing what was on telly last night will become as outdated as going to the music hall.

What do we mean by the mass media?

By now you will be familiar with the idea that topics covered in sociology cannot be clearly defined in one or two simple sentences. The mass media as a topic is no exception to this.

There are a number of ways of defining the mass media. Some see them in evolutionary terms as a form of *communication* beyond the face-to-face conversation. Such an approach involves an idea of

In Focus

◆

Definitions

❖ A *medium* (plural = *media*) is a means of communication such as the printed word, radio or television.

❖ The *mass media* are defined as large-scale organizations which use one or more of these technologies to communicate with large numbers of people ('mass communication').

Source: adapted from Marshall (1994)

❖ Activity 3 ❖

Write down in two or three sentences what you understand by the 'mass media'. Compare this to the descriptions written by others.

- What common themes can you identify?
- Are there any clear differences or controversial areas?

❖ Activity 4 ❖

Briefly list some ways that modern media audiences can answer back.

Mills' definition saw the form of communication as a one-way process. This chapter will examine how far this is true today.

The sociological view sees the mass media as a particularly twentieth-century phenomenon associated with industrialization and the spread of education throughout society: the media are institutions and organizations sending powerful messages to the masses. Along with this is the idea of ownership and control of the media by an élite or powerful few, who have the capacity to propagate their views of the world to a comparatively powerless majority. The media can be state owned, which is often associated with repressive or totalitarian societies, or they can be owned by individuals or small groups, whom Marxists see in terms of a capitalist or ruling class.

physical distance between those communicating. So, in the past and in present non-industrial societies, means of communication such as drums, conch shells, Viking horns, town criers and smoke signals could be seen as early forms of mass media.

Smoke signals: an early form of mass communication, but not one capable of conveying complex ideas

This idea of the *technology* of communication eventually develops into the newspaper and the television as forms of media which have dominated the twentieth century. In the later part of the century, the computer has become another form of technology which is revolutionizing the development of the media into forms that were unimaginable in earlier times.

The late C. Wright Mills, an American sociologist, pointed out that the mass media have two important sociological characteristics (Wright Mills 1956):

❖ Very few people can communicate to a great number.

❖ The audience has no effective way of answering back.

From modern to postmodern

Many commentators talk of the change from modern societies with mass media to postmodern societies with diverse, fragmented, computerized media offering limitless choice to consumers and individuals.

In earlier times there were few newspapers and one or two TV channels that most people read or watched, so such media were experienced by the mass of the population. Everyday conversations in the 1960s and 1970s often involved what was read in the papers or what was watched on television the previous evening.

The present

All of the media listed in Table 12.1 are still dominant. However, the advent of the video machine has meant that programmes can be deferred to a later date when there is often nobody to discuss this with beyond

Table 12.1 Mass media and mass audiences

The mass media in modern societies consists of:	*Mass audiences can be segmented along lines of:*
• the Press: national and local newspapers • magazines • books • radio • television	• age • ethnicity • gender • social class

immediate family members. Developments in computer technology are leading to dramatic changes in the nature of media. Multimedia systems, CD-ROM, interactive programmes, electronic mail, the internet, digital, cable and satellite broadcasting are all part of a dramatic expansion of choice of media and an increase in consumer power. Many of these, however, increasingly isolate individuals rather than act as common or mass forms of communication.

The future

Forecasts include the end of the written word obtained through books, magazines and newspapers and far-reaching changes in workplaces as more people work from home communicating via e-mail and the internet (see Chapter 5). The boundaries between work and leisure will become increasingly blurred and the newer forms of media are a key aspect of this. For example, someone busy climbing a mountain as a leisure activity, may still be contacted on a mobile phone to discuss business.

Postmodernism points to the way time and space boundaries have been altered via communications technology. We can send an e-mail to Japan in the same way we might write a note to the milkman for an extra pint of milk.

❖ Activity 5 ❖

Predict the implications of such changes for education and being a student in the twenty-first century.

What are the arguments for and against the replacement of books and newspapers by newer forms of electronic media?

People have developed positive and negative attitudes to the mass media, summarized in Table 12.2. Despite the negative views, the mass media are here to stay.

Table 12.2 Attitudes to the mass media

Positive	*Negative*
Educational	Diversion from serious pursuits
Informative 'window on the world'	Simplistic trivialization
Part of family/household life	Discourages conversation
Cheap mass entertainment	Inferior quality
Truth about world	Lies/distortion
Exposes corruption and wrongdoing (in the public interest)	Covers up, distracts from the main issue
Creates interest in cultural pursuits – brings culture to the masses	Discourages active reading/participation in cultural pursuits

A short history of the mass media

Some of the earlier forms of media were referred to in the previous section. In our society, when considering ways in which news and information were communicated in the past, we often think of the town crier: a colourful figure with a bell and an extremely loud voice (see the photo on the right). This form of communication was oral because the majority of the population was uneducated and could not read.

The rise of the printed media

The implementation of the 1870 Education Act led to the provision of mass education for all. Within a short period of time, the majority of the population could read. The nineteenth century saw the development of established newspapers, some for the upper ranks of society such as *The Times* and *The Observer*. Eventually newspapers aimed at the working classes spread. The *Daily Mirror* was first published in 1903. These were often advertised by dramatic billboards and news vendors whose loud voices proclaimed the latest sordid details of 'foul and grisly murders', as had the town criers in previous times. Early magazines and comics, nicknamed 'Penny Dreadfuls' became increasingly popular. Famous writers such as Arthur Conan Doyle first established themselves by having short stories and serialized versions of what were to become their novels published in such media.

The twentieth century saw the development and spread of what is now known as the newspaper industry – almost every adult member of the population reads a daily paper in one form or another. Britain now has the highest per capita newspaper readership in the Western world. However, there are some signs that such a high readership may be changing as more instantaneous forms of communicating news, such as radio and TV, become the main sources of such information. This has led in the past ten years to a shift in newspapers' focus on solely news and current affairs items to their becoming another form of entertainment, featuring the private lives of the Royals, popular stars, and sportsmen and women.

Today the press is divided into the tabloid press and the broadsheet press. Some of the tabloids, notably *The Sun*, are looked down on by the middle classes. Examples of broadsheet or 'quality' newspapers aimed at more middle class readers are *The Times* and *The Guardian*. Somewhere in between the two are newspapers such as the *Daily Mail* and *The Express*.

It is clear from Table 12.3 that far more people read the tabloid papers than the broadsheets. Sociologically it is possible to summarize readership in class and educational terms. As a general rule the working classes read the tabloids and the more highly educated middle classes read the broadsheets.

Table 12.3 National newspaper circulations, 1965 to 1996

		1965	1975	1985	1990	1996	change*
Dailies							
1	Sun	1,361,000	3,477,000	4,065,000	3,936,000	4,048,815	−0.75%
2	Daily Mirror	4,957,000	3,943,000	3,253,000	3,907,000	2,474,536	−17.0%
3	Daily Mail	2,425,000	1,725,000	1,828,000	1,669,000	2,057,593	+15.1%
4	Daily Express	3,981,000	2,798,000	1,875,000	1,560,000	1,244,749	−2.69%
5	Telegraph	1,351,000	1,323,000	1,221,000	1,086,000	1,043,677	−2.13%
6	Daily Star	–	–	1,434,000	919,000	755,489	+2.31%
7	Times	258,000	315,000	480,000	432,000	684,605	+5.86%
8	Today				closed on 17 November 1995		
9	Guardian	276,000	315,000	487,000	431,000	398,057	−0.41%
10	Financial Times	152,000	180,000	229,000	288,000	301,961	+2.63%
11	Independent	–	–	–	414,000	279,473	−5.05%
Sundays							
1	News of the World	6,175,000	5,646,000	4,787,000	5,038,000	4,607,799	+2.86%
2	Sunday Mirror	5,022,000	4,284,000	3,211,000	2,911,000	2,426,431	−5.21%
3	People	5,509,000	4,218,000	3,090,000	2,589,000	2,049,306	−0.83%
4	Mail on Sunday	–	–	1,605,000	1,890,000	2,108,298	+7.64%
5	Sunday Express	4,187,000	3,786,000	2,405,000	1,729,000	1,259,046	−10.27%
6	Sunday Times	1,275,000	1,396,000	1,258,000	1,187,000	1,298,998	+3.67%
7	Sunday Telegraph	662,000	757,000	690,000	592,000	666,938	−3.69%
8	Observer	829,000	761,000	746,000	568,000	453,415	−2.18%
9	Ind. on Sunday	–	–	–	363,000	303,801	−7.2%

*Percentage change in circulation since January–June 1995

❖ Activity 6 ❖

1 Referring to Table 12.3, compare the proportion of people who read the tabloids to those who read broadsheets.

2 How would you characterize the types of people (age group, occupation, education, life style, social class, gender, ethnicity, political views) who would read the following newspapers:

The Daily Mirror, The Financial Times, The Daily Mail, The Guardian, The Sun, The Times.

3 Collect examples of each of these newspapers and identify what types of people the editors of the different newspapers are aiming at.

Compare and discuss your findings with others.

The rise of broadcasting

Until the 1960s, the radio was the most popular and available form of broadcast medium, occupying a similar place in most households to the television today. Families from the 1930s through to the 1950s would gather round large bulky radio sets listening to the latest news and popular light entertainment programmes. Some famous stars of that era, such as the comedian Tony Hancock, were able to make the transition from radio to television. Others did not and their popularity declined.

In 1936 the BBC was the first public television station in the world to broadcast programmes. A television set was then very much a luxury item available to a rich minority. The postwar period from the 1950s on became known as the 'Television Age' as television sets became relatively cheaper and available to increased numbers. In 1951 approximately 1 per cent of the population watched television regularly. For many commentators, 1953 was the turning point for the attraction of mass TV audiences – the year in which the first televised coronation (of the present queen) took place. Until the 1950s the BBC was the only television station. In 1955 ITV broadcast its first programmes and by 1956 approximately 12 per cent of the population watched television. From the early 1960s, television spread to the mass of the population.

The early TV channels could be associated with social class. The audience for BBC1 and BBC2 was mainly middle class with ITV catering for the working class. This was reflected in programming for the supposedly different tastes, with early ITV programmes offering American-style giveaway quiz programmes and soap operas, and the BBC offering documentaries and serious drama. Even news programmes reflected social class, with the middle classes opting for BBC news and the working classes for ITN.

From the late 1960s, ownership increased until there was eventually a television set in virtually every household.

Mass audiences for popular programmes such as soap operas, game shows such as *Blind Date*, drama and comedy meant that they became focal talking points in workplaces and school playgrounds to the extent that 'what was on TV last night' was more talked about than the weather. In the late 1990s, despite the increased choice in viewing and the ability to defer viewing via the video, there are still mass audiences for prime-time TV programmes such as soap operas, the serialization of Jane Austen's novels, the comedy series *Absolutely Fabulous* and crime drama series such as *Prime Suspect*.

In December 1996 the final programme of the long-running comedy *Only Fools and Horses* attracted an audience of 24 million – almost half the UK population. Today, the tiny minority who do not own a set probably do so out of choice rather than poverty. An example would be an 'intellectual or academic' household who are critical of television as a trivial, diversionary leisure pursuit.

❖ Activity 7 ❖

Do you know anyone without a television? What are their reasons for not having one?

Despite high per capita viewing figures, Britain has fewer available channels than other industrialized countries. From 1997 the majority of households will have access to five main TV channels. Satellite and cable TV, offering a much greater number of channels, have become available since the early 1990s, although the take-up has not been as great as expected. One company, BSkyB, owned by the newspaper and publishing magnate Rupert Murdoch, is now available to about a quarter of British TV households. There has been some indication in the late 1990s that in high-tech countries such as the USA, mass TV audience numbers are falling. This could well be a reflection of a wider range of home entertainment, notably the advent of the video and multimedia technology, which has enabled people to become more selective in their viewing. Such developments feature in debates about the fragmentation of audiences which are now more segmented along lines of age, class, gender and ethnicity than in the earlier days of broadcasting. This is seen by some as a healthy trend offering a much wider choice to an increasingly informed audience. The advent of digital technology will expand such options even more, leading some to question whether there will be such a thing as a 'mass' audience for TV in the twenty-first century. Some see this is as empowerment and increased democratization for audiences who will be able to tailor their viewing to their needs. Others envisage increased scope for newer forms of social control and media tycoons making massive profits on a global basis. Such issues will be addressed in more detail toward the end of this chapter.

Explaining the media – early approaches

As the media became established as a mass audience phenomenon in the twentieth century, they increasingly became the focus of attention of academic researchers in the behavioural and social sciences. Early approaches tended to come from psychology and social psychology. These tended to concentrate on the effects of the mass media on the individual. The assumption was that the media were powerful and persuasive forms of communications and that individuals were powerless, absorbing media messages like sponges.

Such communication was seen as a *one-way process* and has been summarized as the hypodermic syringe model, i.e. the individual is 'injected' with the messages supplied by the media. This analogy can be pushed further, as the contents of the 'syringe' can be likened to a powerful drug which can anaesthetize the recipient, induce hallucinations or delusions, or, from a more optimistic angle, provide joy and pleasure.

Although seen as clearly deficient by modern academic researchers, the hypodermic syringe model still seems to be the dominant view adopted in current times. It influences debates about the impact of the media on individuals, particularly children and young people, with regard to violence, sex and drug abuse (see *In Focus* on the next page).

❖ Activity 8 ❖

In two or three sentences, explain why the hypodermic syringe model might be the dominant view. Give examples to back up your explanation.

A common-sense view on this is that if TV does not affect behaviour why do advertisers and party political broadcasters continue to spend huge sums of money on it? A debate aired in *The Observer* in 1996 between Martin Barker of the University of the West of England and two of the Glasgow Media Group (GMG) brought an academic dimension to this. Barker believes that newspapers have wildly exaggerated the dangers of television in corrupting the young and have contributed to a moral

The hypodermic syringe model...

In Focus

◆

Sex and violence, and the effects of the media on children

Empirical research on the effects of the portrayal of sex and violence on TV has been carried out for many years. Much of the work, even the most recent, works within the hypodermic frame of reference seeing the television in particular as an important agency in most children's socialization. This has led to moral panics about the amount of time American children spend watching TV, which is now more than the time spent in school. Initially, researchers thought that the TV had an imitative dimension, i.e. children copied what they saw. However, further research began to conclude that this was not the case for the 'normal' child brought up in stable family circumstances, but was often the case for the unstable child who was unable to distinguish between fact and fictionalized violence. Other early media research, such as that carried out by Hilde Himmelweit (1958), pointed to the *drip effect* of prolonged exposure to programmes portraying violence. She accepted that viewing one programme was not going to affect behaviour in all but the most disturbed, but saw that exposure to violence over the long term in the early socialization years might well set the agenda, giving children role models for solving conflicts. The most recent supporter of this view is Elizabeth Newson (1994) who has pointed to a wealth of American empirical research backing the idea that constant and prolonged exposure to violence on TV can be correlated with aggressive behaviour in children. However, she admitted that a correlation does not prove causality, so the debate continues.

panic. Miller and Philo of the GMG dispute the idea that television has no power and said that such views might as well say that parents have no power to influence their children's behaviour. They say that questions of television and violence have been ignored and played down. They point out that advertising relies on persuading people to buy a product. Studies of both TV news and fiction have shown how perceptions can be distorted. In reply Barker says, 'People enjoy the media, they fantasize about the media, but they understand the genre.'

Such views continue to the present with tragedies, such as the shootings in Dunblane in Scotland and Port Arthur in Australia, which involved mass killing by deranged gunmen, leading to political and media analysis evoking the hypodermic approach and the drip effect highlighting the harmfulness of media violence. In 1994 the judge in the James Bulger murder trial involving two 10-year-old boys speculated about the role played by video nasties, despite police statements that there was no evidence that either boy had seen one particular video nasty highlighted in the tabloid press (the film *Child's Play* – see p. 527).

In the early 1990s, members of the Policy Studies Institute surveyed recent work on the effects of violence on television and found that existing research findings were equivocal about its effects on young people. They compared young offenders and non-offender schoolchildren and found little difference between viewing habits. They concluded that 'considerable doubt must be cast upon claims of some direct causal connection or correlation between television and anti-social behaviour' (Newburn and Hagell 1995).

❖ Activity 9 ❖

1. Look up the words 'correlation' and 'causality' in your dictionary and explain the difference using TV violence and children's behaviour as an example.

2. Explain Barker's final quote. What do you think about such arguments?

   Compare your experience with other people's.

Figure 12.1
Diagram of the two-step flow model.

The two-step flow

Katz and Lazersfeld (1955) within a social psychological small group perspective saw the media–user dimension in a more complex manner than the hypodermic syringe model. They saw such communication as a *two-step flow* where there were intermediaries between the medium and the recipient (see Fig. 12.1). These intermediaries, sometimes referred to as *opinion formers/leaders*, act as go-betweens, interpreting and informing users as to the key messages to be ascertained from information given. Examples of such go-betweens are group leaders and those whose views are respected, ranging from politicians and doctors, to the pub know-all. As with the hypodermic syringe model, there is the implication of powerlessness on the part of the user. This has been seen to be inadequate by more recent researchers.

In modern marketing and advertising, this model applies where products are endorsed by the 'opinion leaders' or heroes/heroines from the entertainment and sports world.

Uses and gratifications

Another early approach was that of *uses* and *gratifications*. Katz (1959) shifted away from previous approaches which looked at what the media do to individuals and preferred to examine what people do with the media. He suggested that the same programme or media item could have a range of responses in terms of what is gained from it. For example, the same advert for crisps or beer may amuse some because it is highly entertaining, others may be encouraged to buy the product,

others may take the opportunity to make a cup of tea during the programme break.

It is worth noting at this stage that this type of uses and gratifications model, recognizing the complex dynamics behind people's relationship to the media, has similarities to the interpretive approach dealt with later in this chapter.

McQuail (1972) identifies a number of types of uses and gratifications:

❖ *Diversion* – Where the media help us to escape from daily reality.

❖ *Personal relationships* – Where the media may involve us in a community setting where there are relationships and moral dilemmas with which we identify. Soap operas are a good example of this. In the 1990s, such programmes dealt with a wide range of relationship issues including AIDS, incest, sexuality and abuse as well as the more familiar ones of marital breakdown and personal and family crises.

❖ *Personal identity* – Where the media are used to cement our sense of identity. There are many examples of this in programmes aimed at various age groups, such as gardening for the middle-aged, cookery programmes and youth programmes emphasizing rebelliousness and having fun.

❖ *Surveillance* – Where the media provide a window to the world and keep us informed of what is going on. News programmes and documentaries can provide this.

More recent work by Lull (1990) has followed this approach, pointing to how the media can act as:

❖ background noise

❖ a focal point for domestic interaction, communication and conversation

❖ companionship

❖ entertainment.

❖ Activity 11 ❖

Select several of McQuail and Lull's types of uses and gratifications and explain (in up to 200 words) how they apply in a typical household. Can you add any more?

Name the theoretical approach in sociology which might draw up such purposes for the media.

The models or approaches considered so far focus on the micro or small-scale dimension of how the media affect individuals and households. The more macro or societal dimension has also to be considered addressing such questions as:

❖ How does the way society is structured and organized affect the role of the media?

❖ What effects does the media's role in society have on people?

❖ What relation does the ownership and control of the media have to their content and the way this affects people?

Clearly such questions can be related to the structural approach in sociology seeing the media as a reflection of society.

Marxist-influenced approaches to the media

Marxist approaches highlight the national press in Britain which in political terms is predominantly Conservative. The *Daily Mirror* is the only mass-circulation newspaper that consistently supports the Labour party, so that at election times, with one or two exceptions, there is a clear message from most of daily newspapers to vote for the Conservative party. The decision of the *Sun* to back Tony Blair's Labour party in the 1997 general election was all the more remarkable considering the strong anti-Labour approach it took in the previous general election in 1992, when it fantasized about a nightmare situation of Labour winning (see headlines below).

Even if some of our papers advocated voting Labour or Liberal Democrat, for Marxists there is little difference, as they are all pro-capitalist parties. At its simplest, this could be summed up in the statement that

Nightmare on Kinnock Street

Would the last one to leave Britain please put the lights out...

'the media are capitalist media'. However, beyond this there are differences in the interpretation and detail in Marxist explanations of how the media work to serve capitalist interests.

Ownership and control of the media

There is fairly common agreement that there is an identifiable capitalist or ruling class. Marx (1845) pointed out that the capitalist or ruling class own the means of material production and therefore also control the means of mental production. Their ruling ideas or ways of looking at the world filter down to the rest of society. This notion of a dominant capitalist ideology is explained in other chapters of this book, notably Chapter 4, *Education and training* and Chapter 14, *Religion*.

Marx's original view has been developed by neo-Marxists such as Hall *et al.* (1978) examining the late-twentieth-century role of the mass media. They offer an explanation in terms of the way the powerful ruling class 'set the agenda' for their dominant ideas and directly and indirectly control and influence the content of the mass media. To put it another way, capitalists and the mass media are seen as having common interests to preserve the status quo. Hall showed how the sources of information coming from the

police and legal authorities in relation to the crime of 'mugging' in the 1970s acted as 'primary definers' for media personnel such as journalists. They present a biased view of the world as fair and just when in fact it is founded on inequality and injustice. So, big business and the profit motive are presented uncritically as working in the best interests of the whole of society. Any challenges or threats to this are focused on as deviant, as for example in the case of striking workers.

More recently neo-Marxists have pointed out that not only do the media reflect capitalist ideology, values and interests but such media themselves become capitalist enterprises and a means of making vast profits. They highlight the neo-capitalist owners of global media enterprises such as

---

In Focus

◆

News International

News International is the British arm of Australia's News Corporation, owning 40 per cent of BSkyB. Benefiting from nerve, ruthlessness and Tory government support in his empire-building, Rupert Murdoch now controls 38 per cent of the UK national press and enjoys complete hegemony in British pay-TV.

Interests

❖ four newspapers (*Sun, News of the World, Times, Sunday Times*)

❖ four *Times* supplements

❖ HarperCollins Publishers

❖ Digi-Media Vision (digital technology)

❖ BSkyB: 10 satellite channels (more in multichannel package)

❖ Germany: stakes in Vox, Premiere channels

❖ Holland: Sky radio

Connections and partners

❖ Granada in BSkyB

❖ Leo Kirch (the uncrowned head of the German media industry) in Premiere.

Source: adapted from The Guardian, 8 July 1996

Rupert Murdoch and Richard Branson, colourful figures who have become household names. Their organizations have become increasingly large as a result of takeovers of a wide variety of companies, some in the media field, such as newspapers, magazines, television and film. They have also diversified into a wide range of fields, some in entertainment and leisure such as travel companies, and others in non-related fields such as personal banking and insurance.

There are two distinguishable approaches to explaining the role of the media in society from a Marxist perspective: the manipulative and the hegemonic models. These broadly reflect the changes in Marxist theorizing through the twentieth century, with the former being seen as rooted in Marxist economic orthodoxy and the latter in more recent humanist reworkings of original Marxism.

The manipulative model

This emphasizes that the mass media are capitalist in the traditional Marxist sense. The owners of the means of production, the capitalist or ruling class influence, control or own the mass media in ways to protect their interests and keep the proletariat in their exploited, subservient position in society. Control of the media through ownership of newspapers can be used to disseminate the owner's political views even when the daily running of the paper is taken up by one of the employees. A famous example of this is the late Robert Maxwell who owned the Mirror Group newspapers and insisted that he saw the main articles and leading columns every day before production was allowed to proceed. This process can work in more indirect and subtle ways where a loss-making newspaper or venture is taken on in order to present the owner's views or the owner as respectable pillar of the local community.

In recent times, much media publicity has been given to football clubs which have been bought up by people who present themselves as 'one of the ordinary people', concerned to make a success of the local team. Sometimes the capitalist interests can be followed directly, as when a team is successful and becomes a money-making concern in its own right. Good examples of this in the late 1990s are Manchester United and Newcastle United, both owned by millionaire 'local boys made good'. Such clubs have made millions of pounds via the merchandising and skilful marketing of club-related products (shirts, scarves, hats and mascots, etc.) in addition to money generated from gate receipts.

In Focus
◆
Jack Walker

Jack Walker, one of two Blackburn brothers, made a fortune when his local firm Walkers' Steel was bought out by British Steel for around £300 million in the late 1980s. In the 1970s the firm, which was then managed and controlled directly by the brothers in a traditional capitalist style, was involved in a long and protracted dispute resulting in pickets outside the firm's gates. Workers accused Walkers' of acting in a dictatorial manner when they sacked and locked out union activists and workers pressing for higher wages.

With a proportion of his money from the buy-out, Walker, who has been a loyal fan since childhood, bought a controlling interest in and became club president of Blackburn Rovers which had been a struggling Second Division club for many years. His money helped to buy players which gained the team promotion to the Premier League and in 1995 they became Premier League Champions with Britain's most expensive team. Jack Walker was fêted as a local folk hero and nicknamed 'Uncle Jack'. Rovers' supporters described themselves as 'Uncle Jack's Barmy Army'. The days of the protracted industrial dispute at Walkers' Steel in the 1970s are long forgotten in Blackburn by the working-class football fans.

❖ Activity 12 ❖

- Are there similar examples to that of Jack Walker in your local area?
- How have they made their money?
- How are they seen by local people?
- Do they illustrate the Marxist view that such capitalists control and use the media in ways to promote their interests?

The hegemonic model

The hegemonic view is most commonly associated with the work of Antonio Gramsci (1971), an Italian Marxist who was imprisoned during Fascist rule in Italy in the 1930s. Gramsci saw traditional Marxist accounts of the direct way the capitalist or ruling class use their power to control and influence as inadequate. He described this process in terms of the concept of *hegemony*, which can be defined as control by means of dominant ideas and beliefs, rather than by direct or repressive means as in a slavery society. Put another way, traditional Marxists tend to emphasize the coercive nature of power and influence by capitalists ('This is all I am going to pay you – if you don't like it you can leave'), whereas hegemony emphasizes the ideological nature of power and influence ('I have no alternative to working for such wages in order to support my family').

Neo-Marxists examining the role of the mass media have used the hegemonic approach to explain how the ruling class can in a sense be distanced or detached from the direct influence of the coercive view referred to above. The key people in the media are the professional broadcasters and newspaper editors and journalists. It is they who are involved in the daily output and content of television and the press. Such professionals are paid salaries (admittedly large for the top people) as are other working people. Sometimes media tycoons such as Robert Maxwell do directly control and influence the content of their enter-

prises. But this is probably unusual; the owners and the capitalist class in general leave the daily operations to the experts. The point about the hegemonic view is that these experts present a view of the world which is very much that of the capitalist status quo. Ideologically, they are on the same side. To explain further, top media people are usually middle-class and university educated and can earn in excess of £100,000 a year. Their life style and standard of living is such that they see little wrong with society and rarely adopt a critical stance – certainly they do not adopt a Marxist position and advocate the overthrow of capitalism. So, the picture is one of shadowy figures in the capitalist or ruling class owning business and industry. They feel little sense of threat from the mass media and professional broadcasters and journalists who are portrayed as 'objective', impartial purveyors of the news of the day in an unbiased, professional way. Marxists diasagree and say the news is presented through pro-capitalist eyes.

❖ Activity 13 ❖

As an illustration of the 'shadowy', background role of capitalists try to name ten leading industrialists. Then try to name ten leading media professionals.

How does your answer relate to the neo-Marxist hegemonic model?

Connected with setting the agenda for media content, media professionals are referred to as 'gatekeepers', as they make decisions about what to feature as news and how to present it. The Marxist view sees this gatekeeping role as one that preserves and protects the capitalist system. Non-Marxists and media professionals themselves point to the variety of views that are offered and the way some programmes and newspapers criticize the establishment, which could threaten the status quo. So, in-depth news analysis programmes such as the BBC's *Panorama* can expose government incompetence or shady dealings in the arms industry, and consumer 'watchdog' programmes can make things difficult for manufacturers and producers of goods and services bought by the public.

Neo-Marxists answer such views by saying that despite such media criticism, the fundamental nature of capitalist society is rarely attacked head-on, and certainly alternative forms of society such as communism or socialism are never presented as a solution to the problems exposed. Rather, the media follow Winston Churchill's line that capitalist democracy could be seen as a mess until you consider the alternatives.

A further point made by neo-Marxists is that the minority of critical programmes help to foster the view that we live in an open, democratic society where there is a wide range of views offered. They see this as a form of illusion which is a more effective method of undermining opposition than open coercion and repression using force of arms. To paraphrase Marx, the media help to place imaginary flowers in our chains.

The debate between the manipulative and hegemonic positions is not as 'either/or' as it may appear. In some cases and contexts, elements of the manipulative view may apply such as Maxwell's direct involvement in the content of his newspapers. In other situations, the hegemonic model could apply, where the capitalist or ruling class are in the main left alone and the establishment is rarely threatened.

The Glasgow University Media Group (1985)

From a critical perspective which is not directly Marxist, a team of researchers at Glasgow University examined bias in TV news stories throughout the 1980s. Most people, if asked, will acknowledge and recognize that newspapers are politically biased. A common view is that while papers are biased, the TV news is impartial and factual. The Glasgow group decided to examine this by means of content analysis of videos of news broadcasts. They selected a number of case studies to examine in

detail how news stories are presented in terms of explanation and possible bias. Three of the major political events of the 1980s were the miners' strike, the Falklands War and sectarian violence in Northern Ireland. The Glasgow Group found clear evidence of bias in the way the stories about these situations were presented.

The miners' strike was presented from the viewpoint of the coal board and the Conservative government of Margaret Thatcher. There was an emphasis on picket-line violence, the 'heroism' of strikebreaking miners braving this violence and abuse, and the inconvenience to the public when electricity prices rose as a result of a shortage of coal. The striking miners were rarely given an opportunity to put their case.

During the Falklands War there was blatant censorship, distortion and false reporting as in an ITN broadcast with accompanying illustrative graphics which headlined the 'successful' RAF bombing raid on Port Stanley airfield. This supposedly destroyed the runway and several Argentinian planes. It was later revealed in a documentary on the army's role in the Falklands at the time, that the RAF had in fact missed the target and Argentinian planes continued to use Port Stanley airfield throughout the War.

In the reporting of events in Northern Ireland there have been many examples of censorship and distortion. A BBC *Panorama* programme, dramas and plays from a Republican perspective have been withdrawn and The Pogues, an Irish group, had a pro-Republican song banned from *Top of the Pops*. In 1995, the Government admitted that it had been engaged in secret discussions with Sinn Fein, the Republican Party, for several years, despite publicly banning them from broadcasting and criticizing their IRA sympathies in the media at every opportunity.

Evaluation

It is clear that the Glasgow Group originally offered a powerful corrective to such views as 'the camera can't lie' and that TV news is a more 'factual' method of reporting news than the press. They were among the first media sociologists to make links with *semiology* or *semiotics*. Semiotics is the study of visual symbols and imagery which points out that pictures and films can be constructed to support a variety of stances or viewpoints. From the Glasgow Group perspective, an example of this in the reporting of industrial disputes is that the employers and managers are often interviewed in offices with desks, computers and telephones. Managers are allowed to present their case in a reasonable manner. Striking workers may be interviewed but it is often in a crowd context, for example on a picket line, giving the impression of a disorderly rabble. The semiotic presentation is of employer/manager reasonableness and worker unreasonableness. Another dimension is to interview an inconvenienced member of the public which adds to the antistriking worker perspective given by the report.

> ## ❖ Activity 14 ❖
>
> Using a similar approach to the Glasgow Group, present a tabular report on the main TV news programmes for a week. You could choose a 'headline' story and follow it through to see if there is evidence to support their analysis.

Critics of the Glasgow Group have focused on the problems of investigating bias from what may be seen as another form of left-wing, biased perspective. Surveys indicate that the public are against strikes and industrial disruption, so reports focusing on such matters are a reflection of the reality and are not biased as such. The debate about where such antistrike views are fostered continues as Marxists' rejoinders would focus on ideological dominance in the media and the fostering of 'false consciousness' in the public at large. The most recent work by

the Glasgow researchers (1993) has adopted a more multimethod approach to investigate in a more in-depth manner focusing on ideological dimensions and the discourse of news reporting.

The pluralist model

Until the 1980s, the main opposition to Marxist analysis of the mass media came from what has been described as the pluralist model. There are a number of terms in this area including the liberal democratic, market and laissez-faire approaches, but broadly they analyse the media in similar ways. Sociologically, the theoretical link is with functionalism, which sees the media as operating in the context of a relatively stable society which is broadly based on consensus. The media help to reinforce this consensus, very much as did religion in earlier times (see Chapter 14). In the twentieth century, the mass media have contributed to social cohesion by giving people a sense of belonging to society. There may be trouble and turmoil in the world but the media can help people to cope with this by presenting an image of social harmony as a whole.

> ## ❖ Activity 15 ❖
>
> List some of the ways the press and television can contribute or have contributed to 'social harmony'.

The 'market' dimension of the pluralist model can be described as 'we get the media we deserve'. People are free to choose what they read or view. Here must be added 'within reason' as sometimes underlined by the law which applies to a number of areas such as pornography, racism, violence and paedophilia.

The market for the mass media involves people using their money to buy the newspapers, magazines, books and television channels and videos they wish. There is a

In Focus

◆

Censorship

There is a position, known as *libertarianism*, which states that people should be free to read or watch what they like. This may be prefaced by 'so long as it does no harm to others' but not always. In this view, no clearcut or concrete definitions can be offered on what it is that should be censored. Libertarians see censorship as unjust and full of problems concerning the restriction of individual liberties and the problem of defining what is to be censored or banned. If people want to read or watch something, they should be free to do so.

Functionalists would say that censorship reflects the consensus or commonly agreed views of the majority of people. There are certainly problems of uneven application of censorship. For example:

❖ Religion – UK blasphemy laws only apply to the Protestant Christian religion in England and not to other faiths. In the early 1990s, *The Last Temptation of Christ*, a controversial film about Jesus' life was banned in many cinemas. Not long after this, many Muslim groups demonstrated and felt a sense of injustice when Salman Rushdie's novel, *Satanic Verses*, containing passages which offended their religion, was published and became available in many bookshops.

❖ Pornography – What is pornography? Some people would classify pictures of topless women in the tabloid newsapers as pornographic. Some feminists see pornography as the degradation and exploitation of women, while moral campaigners focus on the depiction of sex. In 1996, a ruling was passed that a bra advert displaying a woman's cleavage was permissible whereas an advert for male underwear featuring a male model wearing underpants with the caption 'Loin King' was banned because of its portrayal of clothed male genitalia.

❖ Activity 16 ❖

What would you censor and why? Discuss and compare your views with others.

❖ Activity 17 ❖

Coursework suggestion

Within reason, taking into account ethical guidelines, think about conducting a survey on attitudes to censorship. The sociological dimension could be provided by sampling as wide a range of people as possible, covering social class, gender, ethnicity, age groups and so on.

wide variety of choice available, covering a range of political views, hobbies and interests. The liberal democratic dimension sees this wide choice reflecting an open, democratic society. Our situation is compared to repressive, totalitarian societies where there is state control of the media and the people have little choice in what they read and view.

Evaluation of the pluralist view

Sceptics point out that our supposed freedom to view and read what we like is illusory. As well as the types of censorship outlined above, there are numerous examples of political censorship. Under the Official Secrets Act, for example, the government can put a 'D-Notice' on a document that it wants to be confidential so it is illegal to publicize it. More indirect forms of control of what we read and watch comes in the form of lack of publicity for certain events such as the Liverpool Dockers' strike which started in 1995 and still continues in 1997. The journalist

Jonathan Pilger suggested that there is deliberate right-wing bias on the part of the mass media (*The Guardian*, 23 November 1996). Sometimes demonstrations and marches involving large numbers of people are either trivialized or go unreported, causing organizers to wonder why they get such low priority. The final comment is that our bewildering array of choice, while giving the impression of freedom, in fact is dominated by the lowest common denominator of trivia, sensationalism and escapism with no available serious critical or alternative viewpoints to the dominant ideology.

❖ Activity 18 ❖

Visit a large newsagent in a city or town and survey the 'serious', i.e. political and economic magazines and journals. What is available? Can you find out the political stance of what is offered? Compare this to the volume of popular, entertainment type of magazines. What sort of things are offered?

Write a short essay (500 words) addressing the question: 'Is the wide choice of magazines and journals in our newsagents a reflection of our freedom to read what we like?'

Recent sociological explanations of the media

Most of the previous sociological perspectives on the role of the mass media in society were dominant in the 1970s and 1980s. Surprisingly, most of such work paid little attention to conventional sociological categories of social class. Newer issues of age, gender and ethnicity were largely ignored. The assumption seemed to be that media users were in some senses sociologically neutral. Since then, a variety of approaches has developed, some as part of wider developments in theorizing and analysing society, such as feminism and anti-racist perspectives. Other developments have occurred as a result of the cross-fertilization of ideas and approaches from other discipline areas such as cultural studies, art and literary criticism, semiology, linguistics and media studies. More recent methodological approaches, which are critical of some of the underlying assumptions of much of the work on the media, will also be examined in the final sections of the chapter.

Gender and the mass media

Early approaches in this field were dominated by the feminist view, which highlighted the role of the media in the oppression of women. By now you should be familiar with feminist theories and concepts and the way in which the position of women in society has been analysed. Early feminist approaches to the media emphasized that the mass media were in essence patriarchal in structure, form and ideology. They concentrated on the following issues:

❖ Men dominate and are dominant throughout the media.

❖ Very little media time is devoted to women's issues.

❖ Women are portrayed in a stereotyped and sexist way in the written and broadcast media.

❖ There is trivialization and ghettoization of the important female concerns in soap operas and romance.

Underlying such approaches was a similar view to that of the hypodermic one examined earlier. The recipient of the media messages is powerless in the face of the ability of the media to affect behaviour. Such views have been challenged by more recent approaches which emphasize the more interactive relationship between the media and user and the changed nature of society which has changed media content. Is it true that the portrayal of women as attractive, unintelligent bimbos has changed from the 1950s? The readership of magazines is massive. What changes have occurred in these since then?

Another development has been to look closely at issues of gender in the use of the mass media, including such issues as:

❖ Do men and women use the media differently?

❖ What are the differences in the structure and content of media aimed expressly for female, as compared to male, consumption?

❖ What is the role of the media in domestic interaction – what David Morley (1986) has referred to as 'the politics of the living room' (see below)?

❖ How is masculinity portrayed in the media?

Recently Bev Skeggs (1994) has examined masculinity and the media. Skeggs has looked at the example of 'buddies' in war films such as *Platoon* and *Full Metal Jacket*. Men do cry, hug and touch each other, but in very prescribed circumstances, such as after an act of heroism or when a close friend is dying. In other contexts, crying, hugging and touching between men is disapproved of. A careful homophobic path is being trodden here.

❖ Activity 19 ❖

Look for examples of how masculinity and male emotions are portrayed in recent films about the Vietnam War.

In Focus

◆

Del girl wows football talent scout

'A football talent scout's excitement at discovering a "boy wonder" on a school playing field has collapsed – after the player turned out to be a girl.

Cheered on by supporters' yells of "Go, Del!", the slim midfielder with closely-plaited hair caught the eye of Leeds United staffer Ces Podd as she left rival players standing in a primary school derby in the city's Chapeltown area.

The name and the 10-year-old player's gutsy tackling, meant Mr Podd, United's community affairs officer, never considered that gender might be a barrier. He was about to offer the player a trial at the Leeds youth advanced centre, when a teacher at Leopold primary school said "Oh yes, Delana Morton. She's excellent".

"I was really shocked when I found out that Del was a girl," said Mr Podd. "She looked like a boy and her movements certainly didn't betray that she was a girl – and she was very good compared with the others." It was footwork and tactics which impressed Mr Podd, rather than the hugging and kissing techniques familiar when modern players score goals.

Delana's mother said: "I am very proud of her – I think she'd like to be a professional, but I'm not sure there's much chance of that." Delana may still get a chance to shine in the Premiership, though, if women's gradual progress in the world of soccer continues. Although banned from the boys-only centre at Elland Road, she has now taken up Mr Podd's offer of a place at Leeds United's new centre of excellence for girls.'

Source: adapted from
The Guardian, 26 November 1996

❖ Activity 20 ❖

Think about the media treatment given to Delana, the girl footballer (see *In Focus*). How would Delana have featured if she were male?

Early approaches deriving from feminism

These can be summed up as taking a view of the mass media as patriarchal: reflecting the disproportionate amount of power men enjoy throughout society. Early feminists argued that men were invariably portrayed as dominant and in control, women as dependent and not in control without a man's presence. Women were featured in sexist and stereotyped ways. Meehan (1983) identified several stereotyes in American drama serials including:

❖ the imp

❖ the good wife

❖ the harpy

❖ the bitch

❖ the witch

❖ the victim.

Most of these stereotypes display negativity about women, or, if seen as strong characters such as the witch, always have to depend on a man when things get too much out of control.

Trowler (1996) identifies some differences in earlier feminist approaches between three broad perspectives (i.e. liberal, radical and socialist feminist):

❖ *Liberal feminists* tended to offer an optimistic account focusing on the changing nature of the media in relation to women. In the past, there was male domination, sexism and stereotyping, but this was seen as gradually changing. More women were being featured in the media as newscasters and presenters. In the 1970s, television started to portray strong female lead characters in previously male-only domains, such as police and detective series. Soap operas became established as prime-time programmes and these featured strong female leads such as Ena Sharples in the early days of *Coronation Street*. Equal opportunities through legislation and an increased sensitivity to women's rights made the liberal feminist position optimistic about the future, which they saw as a more equal one for men and women.

❖ **Activity 21** ❖

- Do you consider the optimism of the liberal feminists to be justified?
- Is the situation of women in the media much improved and is the future going to improve more?

Provide evidence on current trends using examples from television.

❖ *Radical feminists* strongly disagreed with the liberal position, seeing little change in the situation of women in the media through time. They argued that patriarchy was still pervasive throughout society; the media were no exception and if anything, contributed to the continuing subordinate position of women, by acting in a reinforcing role. Advertising that features women in domestic roles provides the housewife as a model for *all* women despite the increased numbers of working women since the 1950s. Very few adverts had a working mother as a key character. Women are constantly devalued and treated as sex objects through pornographic representation. The text below accompanied a topless photo in a *Sun* 'exposé'.

Bruce's TV girl has got a great couple of aces!

PICTURE EXCLUSIVE

★ *Play Your Cards Right* beauty Debbie Flett shows off her stunning full deck in an eye-popping poolside snap.

★ Debbie, 23 – a new hostess on Bruce Forsyth's ITV card game show – posed for this saucy photo at just 19.

★ Snapper, David Muscroft said: "She's a natural in front of a lens." There's no doubt Debbie suits Brucie. And, with those aces, she'll always come up trumps.

❖ Activity 22 ❖

Look for evidence to support the radical feminist view in current advertising.

❖ *Socialist feminists* can be linked with the Marxist position described above. They view women's inferior position in society as serving the interests of capitalism, as women provide unpaid support for male wage-slaves and are themselves a source of exploited labour in part time work. The mass media reflect and reinforce this situation, because they are controlled by men (patriarchy) and owned by the rich and powerful (capitalism) who are also men. Featuring women as housewives and mothers doing domestic labour, and as cooperative and cheerful exploited workers, helps to convey the message to all women that this is their lot. Women's bodies and pornography can be used to make profits for the owners of the media that feature them.

❖ Activity 23 ❖

Look for evidence to support the views of socialist feminists from current television, radio, newspapers or magazines. Which of the three feminist approaches do you find the most convincing, and why?

Evaluation of feminist approaches

Trowler acknowledges that the boundaries between the three types of feminism are not always clear-cut as there is overlap and broad areas of agreement. For example, none of the approaches would reject the view that changes have occurred in the way the media represent and feature women. Liberal feminists would agree that there are still examples of the exploitation and oppression of women as indicated by the other approaches. The key disagreement is about the cause of this and whether fundamental change is possible within existing social structures.

Signs of change or new versions of old themes? Zoe Heyes as Sub Officer Carole Webb in LWT's *London's Burning*

In Focus

◆

The media construction of sex offenders

A study by Grover and Soothill (1995) of press portrayals of sex offenders adds another dimension to radical and socialist feminist views. They see the media construction of sex offenders as misleading and dangerous. Because it focuses on factors external to men and on minority ethnic men, it fails to confront the nature and reality of sexual violence which is most often enacted in household settings by 'normal' men, rather than the crazed 'sex beasts' of media headlines. The reasons for this are:

❖ To report the routine nature of sexual violence embedded within the social fabric of society would, by definition, not be sensational. This sensationalism keeps sales high.

❖ The challenge to the construction of masculinity which a full explanation of sexual violence involves would alienate the male component of the tabloid readership.

Source: adapted from Sociology Review, 4(3), February 1995

The current picture is complicated. There are examples to support any of the three positions above. For liberal feminists there are many female role models who work in the media as newspaper editors, journalists, sports writers, television newscasters, and TV and film producers. Dramas do feature women in lead roles as independent and heroic, as the picture on the previous page shows.

Radical and socialist feminists see such changes as largely cosmetic. There are still many examples of women being stereotyped as they always were. Women might be newscasters and journalists but in the former case they are in a minority still and in the latter they are often ghettoized into 'women's areas', as Agony Aunts and so on. When women do make it into male 'domains' of the media they are treated differently. Kate Adie achieved prominence as a BBC correspondent covering hazardous situations. During her time covering the 1990-91 Gulf War, some of the tabloid newspapers gleefully featured her 'problem' of a lack of toilet facilities in the male army camps.

Economic inequalities between women and men in the media still exist. In 1996, a female TV breakfast show presenter objected when she discovered that her male co-star received a higher salary. The female stars of the hit sitcom *Men Behaving Badly* also objected when they found that their male co-stars were paid more. Such persistent inequalities would be used by radical and socialist feminists as examples of continued exploitation.

❖ Activity 24 ❖

Write two short newspaper articles (100 to 200 words):

- one featuring a man newly appointed as a war correspondent, referred to in a degrading or trivializing way similar to that often used with Kate Adie
- the other a woman treated in a serious 'male' vein.

Morley's study of family viewing patterns

Some studies have started to examine the context of the media, notably television which has become an integral part of domestic life and routines. Gender differences emerge in what Morley (1986) has called the 'politics of the living room'. He conducted an empirical study using interviews with 18 families and examined their viewing habits focusing on gender differences (see *In Focus* below for a sample of his findings).

In Focus ◆ **Viewing behaviour**	*Husband:*	'I like all documentaries ... I like watching stuff like that. I can watch fiction but I am not a great lover of it.'
	Wife:	'He don't like a lot of serials.'
	Husband:	'It's not my type of stuff. I do like the news, current affairs, all that type of stuff.'
	Wife:	'Me and the girls love our serials.'
	Husband:	'I watch the news all the time, I like the news, current affairs and all that.'
	Wife:	'I don't like it so much.'
	Husband:	'I watch the news every time, 5.40 p.m., 6 p.m., 9 p.m., 10 p.m., I try to watch.'
	Wife:	'I just watch the main news so I know what's going on. Once is enough. Then I'm not interested in it.'

Source: Morley (1986, p. 82)

❖ Activity 25 ❖

How does this account of viewing compare to that in your household?

Discuss and compare results with others. In a paragraph summarize issues of gender inequalities raised in this interview.

Morley found eight key areas of distinction between females and males:

❖ *Power and control over programme choice –* This often rests with the man. The TV remote control is an item of technology that is often on father's chair arm for him to use as he pleases. Comments such as 'this is a load of rubbish' and flicking between channels is a common male activity. On Saturday nights in many households *Match of the Day* prevails. Other female-interest programmes are videoed for a later viewing.

> Husband: 'I like to watch it without aggravation. I'd rather watch on my own. ... I like to watch everything with no talking at all.'

> Wife: 'Every now and again he says, "Ssshh shut up". It's terrible. He comes in from a pool match and he'll say, "Shut up, please shut up!"'
> (Morley 1986, p. 156)

❖ *Styles of viewing –* Morley noted that men are more likely to watch a programme in silence without interruption (but is this true of sports programmes?) whereas women interact with the programme and make comments to other females in the household about what aspects they like or dislike.

> Husband: 'It really amazes me that this lot [his wife and daughters] can talk and do things and still pick up what's going on. To my mind it's not very good if you can do that.'

> Wife: 'Because we have it on all the time, it's like second nature. We watch, and chat at the same time.'
> (Morley 1986, p. 131)

❖ *Planned vs spasmodic viewing –* Men tend to be more systematic about planning their viewing, consulting newspapers and teletext, compared to women who 'take it as it comes' except when favourite soap operas are on.

❖ *Talking about television –* Women are happy to talk and admit to television viewing. Men are more dismissive – e.g. 'What a load of rubbish last night'.

❖ *Technology –* As well as men's possession of the remote control, there are differences in the operation and programming of video recorders, with men playing the dominant role.

> Wife: 'I can't use the video. I tried to tape *Widows* for him and I done it wrong. He went barmy. I don't know what went wrong. I always ask him to do it for me because I can't. I always do it wrong. I've never bothered with it.' (Morley 1986)

❖ *Watching alone and guilty pleasure –* Women admit to watching 'a good weepie' on their own and, like eating chocolate, see it as a guilty, secret pleasure.

> Wife: 'That's one thing we don't have on when he's here, we don't have the games programmes on because he hates them. If we women are here on our own I love it. I think they're lovely. If I'm here alone, I try to get something a bit mushy and then I sit here and have a cry, if I'm here on my own. It's not often, but I enjoy that.' (Morley 1986, p. 135)

❖ *Fact and fiction* – As a general rule, men express preference for factual, 'real life' programmes, such as documentaries, news and sport, women for the more fictional areas such as dramas and soap operas.

❖ *News* – Women watch the national news but tend to prefer local news. It is the other way round for men.

❖ Activity 26 ❖

1 Morley interviewed 18 families in his research and did not isolate individual members. What methodological criticisms can be made?

Which stereotypical family type did Morley base his research on?

If you were conducting similar research, how would you go about it? (Consult the methods sections in Chapter 7.)

2 Take each of the above explanations of gender differences and evaluate them in the light of:

• your own household circumstances

• those of others.

Discuss your ideas and make notes with fellow students.

3 Write a short essay (500 to 600 words): 'The study of the ways women and men use television tells us much about power and inequality in households.' Discuss.

Evaluation of approaches to gender in the mass media

There has been a change in recent years from focusing solely on how the mass media portray and affect women to general issues of gender, both male and female, in analysing the media. Clearly women are still portrayed in stereotypical and sexist ways – a glance at your newsagent's shelves will confirm that. There are continuing debates about the amount of changes toward non-stereotypical and equal treatment of women. More radical and socialist feminists tend to see such issues as very much with us and deeply embedded in patriarchal and capitalist economic and social structures. From a liberal perspective dramatic changes have occurred. There are far more women in influential positions in all kinds of media and there is greater awareness, sometimes backed by legislation, of avoiding stereotypical and sexist portrayals of women.

A different version of equality is the increased use of male models in similar ways to female models involving beauty and near nudity. Is this seen as a step towards equality or an increase in pornographic-style advertising, or a postfeminist 'anything goes' view incorporating choice, fragmentation, differing interpretations and unpredictability? Postmodernists may see it in this way, but more traditional sociological approaches would see such changes as trivial. The dominant themes of exploitation still persist whether women's and/or men's bodies are used to sell goods and services for profit.

This image from a men's aftershave advertisement is typical of the increased use by the mass media of erotic images of men

❖ Activity 27 ❖

1 Working if possible within a group, collect a range of daily newspapers, tabloid and broadsheet if possible, and construct a table to depict main themes of stories and the amount of content devoted to women and men. Compare and contrast women's and men's treatment in the papers. Also look at who is writing articles and whether there are differences in topics between male and female journalists? What proportion of articles are written by each?

2 Collect adverts from newspapers and popular magazines and also note the details of television adverts to illustrate the use of men to sell products. In what ways are they presented? Are men used in similar or different ways to women?

3 Write an essay or present a class group report (ideally with visual displays/sample adverts/posters, etc.) addressing whether women and men's portrayal and position in the mass media has changed in the direction of equality.

Ethnicity and the media

The term ethnicity covers a diverse range of sociological issues concerning identity ('I am half Norwegian'), which can be linked to nationality ('I am Italian'), birthplace ('I was born in Islamabad'), residence ('I have lived in England for most of my life'), skin colour ('I am black'), religion ('I am Muslim'), migration ('I am an immigrant'), political repression ('I am a refugee'), or mixtures of several of the above. An examination of the way the media deal with ethnicity reveals similarities to the situation regarding gender in the previous section, particularly in areas such as negative stereotyping, which presents certain people in derogatory ways. Examples include emphasizing supposed physical peculiarities, lack of intelligence, unusual accents, and difference and

strangeness compared to the dominant group. In Britain, the dominant group is white, so skin colour has often been a focus for stereotyping in the media. Other factors such as immigration, the Irish situation, non-Christian religions, the Celtic fringes of the British Isles have also featured at one time or another in recent history. This section will examine whether such issues are changing for the better and if so, what role the media have played in such changes.

Media portrayals of ethnicity: positive views

More positive views of recent portrayals of ethnicity are linked to the pluralist and liberal approaches outlined earlier. With regard to television such approaches point back to the 'bad old days' of appalling racial stereotypes of 1950s and 1960s TV programmes such as *The Black and White Minstrel Show*. This featured white singers and dancers 'blacked up' to appear as negro minstrels singing in exaggerated 'funny' accents. In the 1970s, there was a storm of protest about a comedy series *Mind Your Language* featuring a white language teacher with a class of students covering every racial stereotype. It highlighted their strange accents, large families and claiming of state benefits as targets for 'humour'. This series was eventually withdrawn. At about the same time, the hit series *It Ain't Half Hot Mum* about a World War Two concert party featured white actors made up to be Indian servants with the inevitable 'funny' accents (note the subservient social position as well as the racial stereotype). The *In Focus* on the next page explores other television influences.

❖ Activity 28 ❖

Identify a current TV programme featuring some aspect of ethnicity, e.g. a main character is black. Describe how three viewers (one racist, one liberal and one antiracist) might may offer different interpretations of this programme.

In Focus

◆

TV influences

In the 1960s *Till Death Us Do Part* became a hit comedy series. It featured the character Alf Garnett, portrayed as a racist bigot. Johnny Speight, a socialist, who wrote the series wanted to present a character so over the top that the audience would laugh at his stupidity, thus undermining racism. Critics pointed out that this did not work as Speight intended, for example, 'Alf's' use of derogatory racial terms served to legitimize such language for some viewers of the show. This raises interesting issues concerning more recent work on media audiences and the way a diversity of messages can be interpreted by viewers, listeners and readers. Ellis Cashmore (1994) pointed out that when this show, renamed *All in the Family*, was adapted for the USA, the main character became a mouthpiece for patriotic identification with American national identity, thus in a sense legitimizing his racist commentary. The optimistic view points out that such programmes have disappeared and there are no 'Alf Garnett' racist words and far fewer examples of racist programmes. A developing theme in recent years has been to challenge racism. In the popular police series *The Bill* several episodes featured racist police officers being exposed and taken to task by fellow police officers and superiors.

In the 1960s, one early breakthrough programme in challenging racial stereotypes was *Star Trek*. This has now developed a cult following. The programme-makers' early aims were to portray all ethnic groups and women in positive ways. Key characters featured were black, Chinese and Scottish (but note, as was pointed out by critics, the commander Captain Kirk was a white 'All-American boy'). Not only were there positive portrayals of women and ethnicity by means of the main characters, but several of the episodes had a profeminist and antiracist theme. An example of the latter was an episode featuring a planet where the inhabitants were split into two warring groups who bitterly hated each other. In appearance each group had half black and half white bodies: one group was white on the left side and black on the right side, while the other group was the mirror image. The clear aim of this episode was to expose the irrationality of prejudice.

The Voice, one of Britain's most popular newpapers aimed at a black readership

As well as improvements in the portrayal of ethnic groups in television programmes, optimists point to dramatic changes in employment patterns of media personnel. In the past, the dominant figures in broadcast and print media journalism were invariably male and white. This is not so today. Black and Asian people regularly feature in a wide range of TV programmes, some becoming top news presenters such as Moira Stewart, Trevor McDonald and Zeinab Badawi. There is a range of black and Asian interest programmes and they feature as lead characters in drama, comedy and soap operas in positive, non-stereotyped roles. There are newspapers and magazines written by black and Asian journalists aimed at ethnic minority audiences.

Media portrayals of ethnicity: negative views

Negative views question how much has changed in real terms. Sociologically, conflict-structural theories would see the oppression of ethnic minority groups continuing in the mass media, as elsewhere, despite the superficial and cosmetic changes outlined above. This is because the structural causes of this oppression have not been changed. Trevor McDonald may be ITN's top news presenter, but he is a minority and token figure in a total picture which is still discriminatory. Another dimension of this view is that, when a black or Asian person does make it, they take on aspects of white identity. McDonald's impeccable middle-class speech has been used as an example of this.

Three areas are particularly relevant here:

❖ *Employment of media professionals* – The methodology of this type of analysis uses statistics of the numbers of ethnic groups who feature in key programmes and are journalists in top magazines and newspapers. They point to the continuing under-representation of such groups as evidence for the of discrimination. This reflects similar findings in the wider field of job opportunities and ethnic representation in the professions (see also Chapter 5).

❖ *Ethnic minority programmes* – The existence of programmes specifically aimed at minority ethnic groups may be seen as a positive thing, but from a conflict perspective, it is another example of tokenism. Black and Asian programmes are ghettoized into awkward viewing time slots on minority channels, which gives the appearance of catering for 'minority' tastes. The 'mainstream' prime-time viewing still underrepresents ethnic groups.

❖ *Continuing prejudice* – While television may have made attempts to clear out racism from its programming, there is much less evidence of this in other areas of the media. An example of this is the British tabloid press, notably *The Sun* which takes delight in whipping up intolerance in a laddish, 'only joking' style. Campaigns against the French featuring 'Hop Off You Frogs' headlines have appeared in recent years.

Sport is often a focus for xenophobic and stereotyped portrayals of foreigners. During the 1996 European Football Championships, the *Daily Mirror* launched an anti-German campaign featuring all the worst World War Two stereotypes and derogatory names such as 'Fritz' and 'Kraut'. In response to protests, the newspaper's editor expressed surprise that people should take seriously what he had thought was 'harmless fun'. Such examples are interesting in that, while there is careful avoidance of blatant racism against black people (as this would contravene antiracism laws), the newspaper felt able to indulge in name-calling and lampooning of French, Italian and Spanish people as strange, lazy, cheating or deviant. It is only a small step to extending this approach to all groups, some of whom are black or Asian (see *In Focus*).

In covering international news, portrayals of black nations in Africa and elsewhere often focus on their poverty related to frequent famines, AIDS and other disease epidemics, tribal warfare and occasional climatic disasters. As with Muslim nations, it is rare to see or hear strongly positive images and stories.

The highly successful American TV series *The Cosby Show* has attracted a range of interpretations of its portrayal of a black family. Some, such as Downing (1988), see the series in a positive light presenting an 'ordinary' family with all the usual complications of family life who just happen to be black. Others, such as Jhally and Lewis

❖ Activity 29 ❖

1 First, read the *In Focus* on the following page. Collect news stories, both national and international, that feature ethnic groups and the other countries mentioned in the *In Focus*. What are the common themes in the stories?

2 Watch the main TV news for one week and conduct a similar exercise. Do you agree that in general ethnic groups are presented in negative ways?

Prejudice against Muslims is more indirect than in the 1970s and 1980s when news stories regularly featured alleged 'scroungers' on state benefits who often happened to be 'immigrants'. Today, stereotypes tend to be in terms of Asian shopkeepers, taxi drivers and owners of other small businesses, occasional demonstrations and riots in deprived inner-city areas, troublesome young males rebelling against their elders, victims of racist attacks and arranged marriages. None of these are blatantly racist, but there are few stories featuring more positive examples of Muslim and Asian achievements and success in business, professional life and sport.

The Muslim background of the boxing champion Naseem Hamed is rarely featured and he is presented as a true British hero with the Union Jack as a backdrop to emphasize this. Internationally, the world news focus on Muslim nations is invariably in terms of unbalanced warmongering leaders such as the ayatollahs in Iran, Saddam Hussein in Iraq and Colonel Gaddafi in Libya. The association with terrorism is often made with portrayals of wild-eyed, fanatical fundamentalists who are beyond rational Western reasoning and understanding. In short, the current media association with Islam is Muslim fundamantalism and a sense of threat.

(1992), see the show as portraying an unrepresentative black family which is far removed from the everyday circumstances of racism, poverty and discrimination experienced by many black people.

Stuart Hall's 'white eye' view

Stuart Hall (1990) identifies three characteristics associated with the portrayal of ethnic groups:

❖ 'the slave' – imagery and themes revolving around relationships of subordination and domination

❖ 'the native' – stereotypes grouped around 'superior' and 'inferior' peoples

❖ 'the entertainer' – members of minority ethnic groups described in relation to assumptions about their nature as gregarious, outgoing and cheerful

Hall talks about the 'grammar of race' with an audience viewing with a 'white eye':

'One noticeable fact about these images is their deep ambivalence – the double vision of the white eye through which they are seen. The primitive nobility of the ageing tribeman ... the native's rhythmic grace always contain both a nostalgia for an innocence lost forever to the civilized, and the threat of civilization being over-run by the recurrence of savagery ... or by an untutored sexuality, threatening to "break out".' (Hall 1990, p. 16)

Portrayal of Robinson Crusoe meeting 'Man Friday' – a typical depiction of racial stereotypes

❖ Activity 30 ❖

Do you agree with Hall's analysis of the media portrayal of black people? Watch TV programmes for one week and note examples to support Hall's case and those that challenge it.

Can his approach be applied to other ethnic groups such as Asians? Explain with appropriate examples and suggest other stereotypes.

In Focus

◆

**Lenny
Henry**

Lenny Henry started his career as a comedian in working men's clubs in the Midlands in the 1970s. In a recent interview he recounted how his agent had been pleased to have a black artist on his books who could tell racist gags. At that time another black club comedian, Chalky White (!), used to tell hecklers: 'I'll move in next door to you and play my drums all night!' This is the sort of material that Lenny Henry was expected to produce for his white, working-class audiences. He established himself on TV in a prime-time series *The Comedians* which reproduced the club acts with a live audience.

His success led to a realization that this was not what he wanted, as he was reinforcing black stereotypes and legit-imizing racism, not, as some advocated, defusing it. The rise of alternative comedy in the 1980s, which challenged conven-tional comedic stereotypes enabled him to rethink his approach and develop an act that aimed to avoid racist stereotypes. However, critics have pointed out that his portrayals of a drug-befuddled Rasta, an

African tribal leader and the sex-stud soul singer (see photo) perpetuated negative imagery of black people. In more recent TV programmes he has avoided some of the more extreme stereotypes, but he will probably always face difficulties which are not experienced by white comedians.

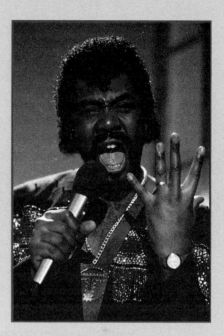

The example of Lenny Henry (see *In Focus*) shows the dilemma faced by people from ethnic minorities in developing a career in a predominantly white society.

Age and the media

The mass media present stereotypes of different age groups.

❖ Activity 31 ❖

1 Explore some of the issues raised by Lenny Henry's approach. Look at films and TV with black and Asian comedians and comedy actors to see if racial stereotypes are being reinforced or challenged.

2 Do you think black comedians and actors have a responsibility to portray positive role models? If so, why should they have this duty any more than white comedians or actors?

❖ Activity 32 ❖

What stereotypes do you think the media present of the following:

• boys and girls under 10 years old

• male and female teenagers

• middle-aged men and women

• elderly men and women?

Use appropriate examples from current televison programmes. Compare these images to those presented in the national and local press.

Childhood and the media

Phillipe Ariès's (1960) conception of the social construction of childhood as a twentieth-century phenomenon has already been mentioned (see pp. 69–70). The mass media treatment of childhood can be seen in two ways:

❖ as *reflecting* historical and cultural changes affecting childhood

❖ as *creating* images of childhood.

In the former area, prolonged compulsory schooling and the banning of child labour emphasized the separateness of childhood from the wider society and also the dimension of protectiveness towards it. The media build up images of childhood helplessness, dependency and vulnerability through a variety of imagery, most notably in adverts. One of the earliest examples of this is the 'Miss Pears' soap adverts dating from early in the twentieth century (see illustration) – an annual competition was begun to recruit an appropriate child model (usually blonde, blue-eyed and white).

Exaggerated images of children with large round eyes and chubby cheeks in various poses of helplessness have dominated the twentieth-century media, which certainly seems to support Ariès's case.

Medved (1992) suggests that this protectiveness has resulted in the presentation of children as full of wisdom, sanity and sensitivity where the adult world of parents, notably fathers, teachers and other authority figures, is portrayed as useless and stupid. Children are engaged in a struggle against such adult incompetence from which they usually emerge as winners. Popular TV cartoons such as *The Simpsons* often have this stress on adult incompetence and child superiority. Critics of Medved may suggest this is simply because the real world of childhood experience is one of 'losing' to adult power and dominance, so it is not surprising that portrayals of a reversal of this are popular.

Other critics have pointed to a more complex picture of representations of childhood. These can range from the 'little angel', to 'the mischievous scamp', to 'the

'*Pears*' is as British as the National Flag, as pure and dainty as babyhood, and for young and old alike forms the most perfect and most economical means of ensuring the health and beauty of the skin.

little devil' and 'the little monster'. Synott (1988) says that this complexity involves five beliefs about and representations of childhood:

❖ Children can be noble or savage.

❖ Children are sinful and need to be restrained and punished.

❖ Children are unformed in terms of character and personality. Adult influence shapes them.

❖ Children have an inborn nature which is not easy to change.

❖ Children are naturally good.

Recent media portrayals of children have certainly reflected some of these images. There is often ambivalence and polarized compartmentalization. This veers between 'good and innocent' children who are subject to sexual perverts, molesters and physical and sexual abuse; and 'bad and uncontrollable' children who are violent, delinquent and disruptive in school. The former type of child has an assumed 'good, loving, normal family', while the latter type of child draws in notions of 'bad parenting' and 'disruptive, dysfunctional families'.

❖ Activity 33 ❖

Select a range of media sources such as TV, newspapers, magazines and comics and find examples of how children are portrayed which support the above. What is the most prevalent belief?

Childhood culture

James and Prout (1990) take issue with previous assumptions about childhood which see children as underdeveloped adults who are evolving from simple, immature forms into complex, mature adults in a straightforward linear way. They offer a more postmodernist, interpretive view which sees childhood as not purely an adult-created phenomenon. Rather, children are active agents in creating their own social world and culture. This may or may not be antagonistic to the adult social world but it is often separate and self-contained. There are a variety of possible childhood cultures and subcultures and these can sometimes be influenced by gender, ethnic and class variables. In some respects, the mass media, notably television, have recognized this through time as programmes have shifted in emphasis from the avuncular, adult's view of what children want, to a more child-centred focus. *Blue Peter* on BBC TV might be seen as an example of this: programmes of several years ago had presenters who might be the children's uncles and aunts, whereas today they are more like (slightly) older brothers and sisters.

Youth culture and the media

Issues of youth and identity have been dealt with elsewhere in this book (see Chapter 3). As with childhood, media representations of youth emphasize difference and often conflictual aspects. Assumptions about the existence of a former golden age when young people 'behaved themselves' have existed in adult minds for centuries, as Geoffrey Pearson (1983) has pointed out from his historical study of concerns about delinquency. The mass media have often reinforced such views with a predominant focus on the 'problems' of youth, ranging from drug abuse to vandalism, violence, crime and various other forms of perceived threats to social order. There are two dimensions to the representation of young people in the media:

❖ The media reflect changes in the role of young people in society, such as extended dependency through lack of work and prolonged full time education.

❖ The media help to create images of what young people are like – through music, fashion and a host of forms of presentation of self and associated imagery.

Moral panics and deviance amplification

A number of historical studies such as Pearson's have shown that concerns about youth, particularly young men, are not new. One of the earliest sociological studies specifically examining the role of the media was

❖ Activity 34 ❖

1 Do you agree with the view that the media now show a more child-centred approach? Conduct a survey of current popular TV programmes for children. Are the programmes immersed in 'childhood culture' or are they adult versions of what childhood is like? Ask older adult relatives and friends what TV programmes were like when they were children.

2 What about comics? Have they always been directly related to childhood culture and offered a separate world from that of adults?

carried out by Stan Cohen (1980) in the early 1960s. Two opposing youth groups, the Mods and the Rockers, were involved in clashes and skirmishes in a number of seaside towns on a bank holiday. These events were seized on by the press in a quiet news period and publicized in a sensationalized and exaggerated manner. Cohen closely examined the more sober accounts in the local press, particularly the court reports, and interviewed some of the young participants. He concluded that rather than large-scale riots and a wholesale breakdown of public order, as featured in the national press headlines, what actually happened was a number of fairly minor crimes, such as the Mod who squirted an off-duty policeman with a soda syphon. There was in fact no major difference to the situation in any town or city centre on any Saturday night.

Moral panic, as used in Cohen's book title, has now become a term in everyday usage. His work developed into studies of the role of the mass media in *deviance amplification,* which looks at the way the media sieze on, exaggerate and sensationalize issues out of all proportion, as Cohen demonstrated.

As the previous section noted, the notion of moral panics has now extended to childhood with recent concerns echoing those that were once only applied to adolescents.

Old age and the mass media

'Coffin dodger', 'Silly old git' are terms of abuse used by the young against the old. What role do media representations play in such derogatory views? Clearly, getting old involves a physical and biological process where our bodies become weaker and more frail and our minds are not as sharp as they once were. Do the media reinforce this with their dominant images of the elderly?

❖ Activity 35 ❖

Draw up three or four examples of recent moral panics about young people and explain the role of the press or TV in creating or adding to these.

Paul Whitehouse, from BBC's *Fast Show*
Do the media reinforce stereotyped images of the elderly?

In Focus

◆

Alcopops: a justifiable moral panic?

In 1995, media attention turned to the increased availability of sweet, brightly coloured drinks that were strong in alcoholic content. Critics and anti-alcohol campaigners saw such drinks as deliberately aimed at young children, some investigations revealing that alcohol consumption can begin at 8 years or younger. The manufacturers responded that they were catering for a market of young people, aged 18 plus, who wanted 'fun' drinks. Pressure mounted via media campaigners and politicians who claimed that children were being enticed into alcohol abuse at too young an age. The manufacturers eventually agreed to tone down the fun element in their advertising and to change the names of some drinks from comic book terms to more adult ones.

The evidence is somewhat mixed. In some respects, the imagery of doddery old age is certainly evident, particularly in comedy and cartoon representations. However, the content of the media often focuses on older people as characters, programme presenters and as prominent people in the news. This can be negative, as in the 'interfering busybody' in soap operas and the comparison of 76-year-old Bob Dole campaigning against the 'youthful' 50-year-old President Bill Clinton in the 1996 American election. Nevertheless, there are often portrayals emphasizing the wisdom and positive qualities of being old. Many programmes are presented by older people and aimed at the older audience.

Another recent image is that of rebellious character in a struggle for freedom against various forms of bureaucratic and repressive officialdom and social expectations, as in the character of Victor Meldrew (BBC TV's *One Foot in the Grave*) or Diana and Tom, the irrepressible residents of Bay View Retirement Home in BBC TV's *Waiting for God*. It is worth noting that such characters are portrayed in a similar vein to the earlier representations of the rebellious teenager engaged in the youthful struggle against repressive adult society. There are similarities in that both groups are free from the constraints of jobs, mortgages and family responsibilities.

Biggs (1993) summarizes five trends in the representation of ageing:

❖ Significant numbers of middle-aged and older people appear in prime-time soap operas.

❖ Sitcoms in particular feature negative portrayals of 'doddery' old age.

❖ Reverse stereotyping can occur where an exception to the rule is featured, such as Victor Meldrew.

❖ More recent representations have shifted towards a more active view of older people.

❖ The problems of age and ageing, such as ill-health and poverty, do not tend to receive regular or prominent attention

(although there may already be discernible changes, as the ageing population increases and such concerns become increasingly visible).

❖ Activity 36 ❖

Take each of the above points and decide how they may apply to recent television programmes.

Gender and ageing

There are clear differences between how the mass media depict ageing men and women. As in all age groups, women are assessed on the criteria of beauty and sex appeal and older women do not escape this. Stars such as Tina Turner and Joan Collins are admired for their ability to retain youthful looks and bodies which belie their years. As Sontag (1978) pointed out, this does not apply in the same way to older men, who are more likely to be portrayed as possessing wisdom as world leaders and senior figures in all walks of life. The feminist writer and journalist Suzanne Moore (1993) compared the appearance of male newscasters with grey hair and wrinkled faces to older female newscasters who have to conform to a beauty ideal. Older female actresses complain about the lack of parts for older women in comparison with older men. In opera, Luciano Pavarotti can still play young romantic heroes in his sixties, despite his age and physical appearance. Would a woman of similar age and physique be cast as a young heroine?

When the soap opera genre is examined (Brian Longhurst 1987), a somewhat different picture emerges. Most soaps feature strong older women and, if anything, older men are often portrayed as weak and ineffectual. Might this be because the majority of viewers of soap operas are women?

❖ Activity 37 ❖

- Is the picture of strong women and weak men still applicable to soap operas?
- Besides soap operas, what other categories of programmes portray women in positive ways? Explain why you think this is.

Social class in the media

The press

The social class dimension of the press has already been referred to. In general the tabloid press is read by the working class, whilst the broadsheets are read by the middle classes.

❖ Activity 38 ❖

Do you think that it is still true that the British press broadly reflects the class structure of the nation? Explain your view.

Television

In comparison with the press, it is often assumed that television is relatively classless. Certainly the previously mentioned, clear distinction between the early BBC (middle-class viewers) and ITV (working-class viewers) is not so straight-forward today. The battle for audience

ratings has meant that large viewing targets have increasingly been cutting across class boundaries. However, reflections of the class structure remain:

❖ Opera, classical music, ballet, etc., have a predominantly middle-class audience.

❖ Soap operas, quiz and game shows appeal to a more working-class audience.

Class stereotyping

As with ethnicity and gender, negative stereotypes of working-class people can be identified through portrayals of them as unintelligent and badly behaved. However, it is not always correspondingly the case that the middle classes are presented positively. In the 1960s, it became 'trendy' to have a broad regional accent (The Beatles capitalized on this). Programmes for younger people still reflect this 'backlash', with figures such as Andy Kershaw presenting programmes in a broad Rochdale accent. However, it is still possible to distinguish the class bias in the presentation of serious programmes such as the news, where there is less evidence of working-class speech than in other areas of programming.

Radio broadcasting could be seen to reflect class imagery more than television, with the audiences being more segmented. Using BBC Radio as an example, clear class lines can be identified with audiences for the classical music programme Radio 3 being upper-middle-class, Radio 4 more mainstream middle-class, Radio 2 older lower-middle-class and working-class, and Radio 1 younger working-class. Local radio tends to have an older working-class audience.

In Focus

◆

The battle for listeners

In 1995, a row broke out when it was announced that former Radio 1 disc jockey, Paul Gambaccini, was to present a morning classical music programme on Radio 3. The aim was to provide lighter, more popular music to draw listeners away from the highly successful rival radio station, Classic FM. Indignant Radio 3 listeners wrote letters of protest to *The Times* and other broadsheets expressing concern about the DJ-style presentation of Gambaccini and his 'lowbrow' choice of music. Eventually Paul Gambaccini 'left' the slot, but Radio 3 is still looking for ways it can widen its appeal from its narrow upper-middle-class clientèle.

Interpretive approaches

Explanations of the media have changed from emphasizing *monosemic* communication to *polysemic* forms (see Fig. 12.2 for definitions). Most recent work has changed from an 'any reading of a text is possible' to a recognition that while there may be a number of possible readings a 'preferred reading' is dominant. Paul Trowler (1996) summarizes the changes in theories and research focus in Fig. 12.2.

❖ Activity 39 ❖

Give a monosemic reading and polysemic readings of a person wearing a red poppy. Which is the preferred or dominant reading? Explain your answer.

Such explanations can coexist with hegemonic structural theories as espoused by the Glasgow Media Group.

Previous sections of this chapter have focused on structural analyses of the media and their relation to recipients. Such approaches imply the *passivity* of the reader or viewer of media messages and the power of the media to affect behaviour. Recent developments linked with interpretive sociology have extended the earlier uses and gratifications approach, stressing the active and organic relationship between the media and consumer. The audience uses the media in complex ways involving a variety of meanings and interpretations of the same media messages. In this sense, the user is more powerful and the media less powerful than has often been supposed. However, it can be noted that structural views are not static – there is recognition that cultural and social change has occurred, for example in the portrayals of ethnicity and women outlined in previous sections. There is also increased recognition of the complexity of the interaction between media and audiences. There are two dimensions to the strengthening of the interpretative approach in recent years:

❖ *A more active audience* – It is recognized that people interact with the media and are not passive recipients. They are aware of bias and discount or ridicule a range of views. Think of the attitude towards party political broadcasts. Have you ever met anyone who believes them, even when they are by the party they support?

❖ *Changes in technology* – The advent of the video first extended people's ability to

---

Figure 12.2
Summary of changes in theoretical and research focus

Hypodermic approach: media strong	**Normative approach:** media weak	**Structured interpretation model:** media relatively strong
General direction of theoretical development →		
Monosemy: Only one message is read by the audience – mass media texts reproduce ideology.	*Semiotic democracy:* The text can be read in an unlimited number of ways.	*Polysemy with preferred reading:* The text can be read in multiple ways, but one is dominant.
Research implications: Study the message and the people who produce it.	*Research implications:* Study the audience.	*Research implications:* Study both the audience and the message.

interact with the media: you can watch when you want, freeze-frame shots, fast forward, rewind and skip the adverts. This has now extended massively via computers which means that the interactivity dimension has reached another level. We now have technology that enables the user of media to create their own viewing and/or listening. One example is interactive CD-ROM music fed through a computer; users can add, heighten or withdraw voices and musical instruments to tailor to their preference. Another example is a computer-generated novel where the reader can interact with the plot and tailor different outcomes to their preference. Does the hero/heroine die tragically or live happily ever after? The choice is yours! The newer technology means that you can now visit the Louvre and examine the paintings without leaving your front room. Such developments mean that you may know someone in Melbourne more intimately than your next-door neighbour.

There is now debate about whether the completely relative 'anything goes' in terms of interpretations and meanings is too open-ended. David Morley (1992) has developed a *structured interpretation* model which focuses on the preferred reading or dominant message. This takes into account criticisms of relativism that see a failure to address structural issues such as power and ideology. People's reading of media messages has to be located in their social context. They belong to social groups and subcultures, as well as the wider society, which is bound to affect their interpretation of the media. This recognizes issues of age groups, social class, ethnicity, gender as part of the social world of interaction with the media.

Ang (1991) criticizes approaches which use the idea of media audiences as an asocial, undifferentiated mass. She is also critical of overly concentrating on social divisions such as age, gender and class. Her preference is to advocate the empirical study, in an ethnographic manner, of the way people interact with the media in concrete situations. Such a study was carried out by Bob Mullan and Laurie Taylor (1986) in the 1980s to see how people interact with television. They found that contrary to the usual view that people are passive viewers of television as in the earlier hypodermic syringe model, they are in fact often active and doing a number of things while viewing. On gender, it was notable that women watch television while carrying out a range of tasks such as ironing and childcare. It is no accident that ITV companies should choose to schedule the omnibus edition of *Coronation Street* for early Sunday evening, when it is highly likely that many working wives and mothers are doing the ironing in preparation for the week ahead. Some people watch and comment on TV programmes while simultaneously reading the paper or listening to music through stereo headphones.

Radical critics, however, point out that such studies tend to be lacking a structural context which focuses on power and social control. Working in a neo-Marxist hegemonic frame of reference, Stuart Hall (1988) offers a view of a dominant ideology that is not necessarily coercive or manipulative but is part of the way we decode and encode messages which fit in with the views of the powerful.

❖ Activity 40 ❖

In the light of much negative publicity about the royal family in the 1990s, provide an explanation of how they are 'read' by the majority of people. Draw on the idea of a preferred reading and dominant ideology. From this, is it possible to say the monarchy is under threat? (Hint: you may find it useful to compare 'readings' of the institution of the monarchy as compared to 'readings' of the behaviour of individual members.)

Radical feminists point out that there needs to be a greater concentration in interpretive approaches on the different usage and access to the media of women compared to men, which can often reflect the exploitative and repressive nature of the relationship between men and women in society. Morley's work on family viewing cited earlier (see p. 548) goes some way towards this.

The uses and gratifications approach highlighted the way people are freer than traditionally thought to gain a variety of messages from the same media source. Watching a popular programme such as *Blind Date* can involve a range of interpretations and reactions. A young woman or man may watch purely to spot which date they would prefer or to try and guess which person will be chosen. This will be discussed with their friends. An older person may watch and comment on the suitability of choices made and in the follow-up hope that love has blossomed and marriage becomes a possibility.

Critics of this approach point to the somewhat asocial picture of the media user. The range of choices and interpretations is open-ended and is not linked to structural forces that may shape responses such as class and gender. There is, therefore, little attention paid to why people seek to gratify particular needs and where their choices derive from.

Early versions of the interpretive approach examined the way people use television. More recently, there has been a focus on the variety of *texts* which the consumer is capable of reading in a number of ways and to a quite sophisticated level. Fiske (1988) points to our ability to relate texts to other texts both within and outside the medium itself. So a death of a character in a soap opera can be read as part of the story but also as the actor having a row with the producer and their character being written out. Other texts can be gained from wider media sources, such as newspapers, or from what you have been told by a friend or workmate. Buckingham (1993) points to the varying degrees of media literacy as a factor. Media literacy can range from high to low: an example of the former would be wide reading of messages drawing from a range of sources, the latter would be believing that a character who dies is really dead and sending a card of condolence.

Discourse/thematic analysis

'Discourse comes from studies of linguistics and can mean a specialized form of language. It is taken to be the spoken expression of ideologies, or a form of speech used in an attempt to achieve social, personal or political power.' (Price 1993)

A key dimension of the way we interact with and interpret the world is language. The social sciences now use the term *discourse*. Foucault (1972) pointed to the way language and words are part of a structural context of discourse that communicates a 'taken-for-granted' or 'common-sense' view of the social world. The term originated from linguistics and was developed by Foucault into a wider, more social-structural term used to explain power and social control in modern societies.

Foucault believed that power and control in modern societies permeates everyday social life by means of discourses, rather than by emanating from grand-scale social institutions and organizations. He criticized this latter, dominant view in sociological theorizing about power and social control in society. While he did not write specifically about the mass media, it is clear from his work that the media are a vital aspect of discourse. He stated that 'knowledge is power' and if people gain knowledge from the mass media, as they clearly do, the mass media are in Foucault's terms 'powerful'.

In line with postmodern thinking, Foucault denied that you could ever have absolute truth: knowledge is what a group of people get together and decide is true. As well as physical force to control people, there is mental force which is exerted by a powerful minority who are able to impose their idea of the right, or the true, on the majority. This does not sound very different from a Marxist view, but Foucault went further and showed the importance of language or discourse in presenting knowledge which is powerful.

As well as describing, analysing and explaining human behaviour, a key feature of sociology and other social sciences is defining aspects of human beings. Most chapters of this book illustrate this in their introductory sections where definitional issues related to the topic are raised. People can be defined in terms of gender, social class, ethnicity, educational achievement, job, religion and so on. Another aspect is the categorization of people into normal and abnormal, which is a central mechanism of the social sciences. Most of Foucault's studies were of institutions and organizations such as mental hospitals, prisons and medical clinics, with 'experts' employed in them who engage in the discourse and knowledge of the abnormal and the normal. The dominant focus is on the abnormal and knowledge of its definition. For Foucault this is important, as knowledge of the 'abnormal' such as madness, criminality, sexual perversion and illness gives us an idea of the 'normal'. Our understanding of the 'normal' comes from defining what is 'abnormal'. The relevance to society is clear. Order and stability come from focusing on the abnormal to enable us to judge the

normal. So the single-parent family is 'abnormal' compared to the 'normal' stereotypical family; homosexuality is 'abnormal', heterosexuality is 'normal' and so on.

It is straightforward to apply Foucault's analysis to the mass media. The media through discourse (often involving 'experts' from institutions that Foucault studied) play a key role in disseminating knowledge, which is power, by defining and concentrating on the abnormal rather than the normal. This challenges the idea put by some critics that the media have a choice in whether to present good or bad news or focus on the normal rather than the abnormal. Such critics as the TV news presenter Martyn Lewis started a campaign in 1993 to focus on good rather than bad news. This would be seen by Foucault and others as naive and missing the point about how the media are a vital dimension of discourse concerning abnormality. By definition, according to this view, the media are bound to focus on abnormality and bad news, as these are a key dimension of human communication. In other, everyday

Cartoon by
Jacky Fleming
(from *Hello Boys*)

forms of communication, such as gossip, we also engage in talking about the abnormal, which helps to clarify the normal. Note how close this is to Durkheim's functional analysis of the *collective conscience*.

Another aspect of Foucault's detailed historical studies is that definitions of abnormality can change through time. Take the example of madness. In previous centuries 'mad' people lived in communities and were not segregated; there was acceptance of their situation. Today, the conception of madness is that it is threatening, so the 'mad' are shut away and kept separate from the 'normal' society. This shifting definition of 'abnormality' through time is reflected in the mass media. For example, homosexuality has recently been portrayed as *less* 'abnormal' or deviant. Educational programmes and newspaper and magazine articles explore issues associated with homosexuality, while same-sex relationships and kisses feature in prime-time soap operas. However, in 1996 this was strongly criticized by moralists who objected to the depiction of homosexuality as 'normal'. Clearly, such groups want to shift the clock

back to a time when the 'abnormality' dimension of homosexuality was stressed. Similarly, for the disabled, well-publicized events such as the Paralympics helps to lessen notions of 'abnormality'.

Figure 12.3
Coverage of topics in national and regional daily newspapers.

❖ Activity 41 ❖

1 Look at Fig. 12.3. Take each of the headings in turn and explain, giving appropriate examples, whether the dominant focus in the news is on the abnormal or the normal.

2 Look at TV news programmes and a range of newspapers and magazines for examples of definitions of 'the abnormal' in relation to crime, sexuality, marriage, the family, education, children, youth and drugs.

3 Make a list of 'experts' who appear, and describe how they are used to disseminate knowledge. Does this support a Foucauldian perspective?

4 Provide more examples of how the media have altered their perspective on 'abnormal' groups.

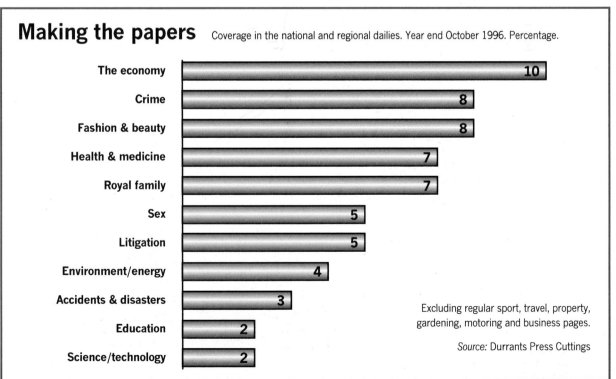

Making the papers
Coverage in the national and regional dailies. Year end October 1996. Percentage.

Topic	Percentage
The economy	10
Crime	8
Fashion & beauty	8
Health & medicine	7
Royal family	7
Sex	5
Litigation	5
Environment/energy	4
Accidents & disasters	3
Education	2
Science/technology	2

Excluding regular sport, travel, property, gardening, motoring and business pages.

Source: Durrants Press Cuttings

Potter and Wetherell (1987) use discourse analysis to examine the role of the media in presenting stories concerning terrorism. Such accounts involve words and phrases such as 'hijacking', 'bombs', 'gunman', 'innocent victims', 'negotiations', 'authorities' and 'resolute'. On their own, such terms can be neutral, but in a feature on terrorism the context stimulates the imagery for the words. So taking the word 'gunman', we immediately have a negative picture involving a wild-eyed fanatic waving a pistol in the face of a screaming mother and child. On the other hand, the police 'gunman' becomes a 'marksman' who is cool, calm and collected as well as 'normal' in appearance.

Norman Fairclough (1989) examined the discourse associated with Thatcherism in the media in the 1980s. He found this covered terms such as the nanny state, free-market economics, tax cuts to provide incentives for the wealth creators, freedom of choice, as well as her use of 'we' and 'the enemy within', which set the agenda for 'normal' and 'abnormal'. Such discourses are not simple representations of reality, they actually create reality for the reader, viewer or listener.

In Focus

◆

Judge Dredd and its 'awkward' audiences

Martin Barker (ATSS Lecture, 8 September 1996) in his earlier work on video nasties, challenged conventional accounts concerning their harmfulness, particularly to children, in the way they legitimate violence and 'desensitize' children to it. He linked such concerns to Cohen's ideas on moral panics (see p. 558) and saw no evidence that media violence causes real violence. He argues that such views misunderstand the nature of audiences and their divergent responses and motivations when viewing films and television. He develops this further in his more recent work, using the film of the 2001 AD comic book character 'Judge Dredd', starring Sylvester Stallone, as a case study. Baker sees children and young people as audiences who are 'knowing' and sophisticated – not vulnerable, as proponents of moral panics suggest. In this respect there is commonality with James and Prout's (1990) notion of a childhood culture which is separate from the adult world. A key aspect of viewing films such as 'Judge Dredd' is reinforcement through talk with friends and peers. There are deep cultural meanings embedded in how audiences respond to films. The variety of responses can range from 'The action is too slow', to a comparison with similar films, to 'I talk to my friends about it', to 'I liked it when Stallone came on', to 'a shiver went down my spine as it started, to 'I'd been waiting ages for a film of Judge Dredd'.

Another aspect is the response to viewers who take such films seriously, who are described as 'sad'. Barker stresses the idea of 'situated responses', which has links to the French sociologist Pierre Bourdieu's (1993) 'cultural field' and 'audience habitus'. This highlights the way viewers of media have complex sophisticated understandings within their own milieu. To see such complexities in terms of audience 'vulnerability' and panics about violence is to misunderstand the nature of audiences and the world they inhabit.

Barker's study raises methodological problems in terms of how to research such issues as the complexity of audience responses. A questionnaire could elicit one view of what the viewer is getting from a particular film, whereas in other contexts, such as the peer group, a different range of responses might be forthcoming. The methodological problem is which is the 'correct' version. Traditional debates between positivist and interpretive approaches tended to focus on the shortcomings of quantitative and qualitative approaches, each assuming they are better at gaining the truth. Barker's work suggests that there may be a number of versions of 'truth', each appropriate for a particular context and audience. This clearly has links with postmodern approaches and relativism where truth and reality are not fixed and are constantly shifting.

Globalization and the media

Ulrich Beck (1992) adds another dimension when he examines the role of television in developing individualization. He describes how social institutions such as television help to mould our biographies and life situations in ways which can be hidden. An example would be people who say: 'I can remember exactly what I was doing on the day the news about Dunblane came through.' Foucault would emphasize the role of discourse in this. Beck suggests that:

'Television isolates *and* standardizes. On the one hand, it removes people from traditionally shaped and bounded contexts of conversation, experience and life. At the same time, however, everyone is in a similar position: they all consume institutionally produced television programmes, from Honolulu to Moscow and Singapore. Everyone sits isolated even in the family and gapes at the set.'

He refers to the global dimension where people meet at the 'village green of television' and consume the news. We can be consuming a meal in Britain while simultaneously watching and hearing about civil wars and famine thousands of miles away. He describes this in terms of *individual and institutional schizophrenia*. With no sense of contradiction or irony, we can watch people bathing in bathfuls of baked beans to raise money for starving people in the Third World. Beck sees new opportunities for control and influence in television in the way it impacts on the daily and weekly schedule of the family.

❖ Activity 42 ❖

Explain the way television affects you and your family's daily and weekly schedule. Do you agree with Beck's view that when watching television 'Everyone sits isolated even in the family'? Explain.

With reference to Beck's idea of the 'village green of television', explain the impact of globalization on the mass media, particularly television?

Methodological criticisms of media research

Ray Pawson (1995) developed a methodological critique which raises questions about much research on the media. He distinguishes between three main approaches:

❖ formal content analysis

❖ thematic analysis

❖ textual analysis.

Formal content analysis

One of the most well-known examples of this is contained in the earlier work of the Glasgow Media Group who combined quantitative and qualitative techniques in their research. Content analysis seeks to be objective, systematic and quantitative in its description of the manifest content of communication. For example, if you are researching women's magazines, you could identify objective issues such as articles on housework, recipes, fashion and cosmetics. You would be systematic in choosing as wide a range of magazines as possible to avoid selective sampling which might reflect your own bias. The quantitative dimension is the numerical representation for purposes of comparison. So, you could count the number of articles and column inches on the issues chosen and compare them between different magazines. The most contentious aspect of content analysis is that it takes text and meaning at face value, the words are taken to mean exactly what they say. This can be a problem as much media content involves innuendo, metaphor, irony, symbolism, parody and so on. Popular newspapers such as *The Sun* are full of these linguistic devices: 'Reds Slaughter Dons' is not about socialists murdering lecturers on a university campus but about a football match between Liverpool and Wimbledon.

Qualitative critics of such an approach argue that there is no such thing as the manifest meaning of a text (i.e. one that is the same for everyone). For Stuart Hall *et al.* (1981), meaning is a process involving the encoding and decoding activities of writer and reader, producer and audience, broadcaster and listener. It is incorrect to assume that the same utterance or piece of text means the same to everyone. To take the 'Reds Slaughter Dons' headline further, if you were not a football fan all three words would be meaningless to you because your reading is not placed in a context of a 'knowing' reader. The difficulty for content analysis is that it cannot explain the values involved in media communication which is a weakness more qualitative media research attempts to redress.

❖ Activity 43 ❖

Collect similar headlines from newspapers and explain a range of meanings that could be associated with them by different readers.

Thematic analysis

This approach concerns itself with examining the underlying ideology and intentions of the producers of the mass media. Once this has been described and identified, the next stage is to explain it. We have already encountered two models associated with this – the manipulative and the hegemonic, which are rooted in Marxist theory. The former uses the *dominant ideology* thesis which sees the ruling or capitalist class as strongly involved in directing and influencing media production and content. This in turn filters down to the masses and is used to explain their subservience and conservatism. The latter uses the idea of *professional ideology* and

news values on the part of media personnel who reflect the values of the establishment. The task of researchers using this approach is to unmask the underlying ideology by deciphering the presentational style of the producer.

Pawson uses a study by Soothill and Walby (1991) of the portrayal of 'sex crimes' in the newspapers. They identify a highly selective process which is sensationalist and focuses on the multiple 'sex beast' who is demonized in terms of depravity, wickedness and lunacy. There are messages about the dangers to women alone in public places. The feminist view on rape as part of the domination of women by men and the high incidence of domestic rape is not addressed. The dominant portrayal of rape as committed by a crazed 'sex beast' on a woman alone in a public place is constantly reinforced and research such as Soothill and Walby's uses lots of examples to illustrate this. Pawson's criticisms of such research are as follows:

❖ There is a lack of objective sampling of illustrative material, so it is likely that the most sensationalized examples are chosen and ones that do not fit with the thesis are ignored.

❖ The examples are selectively chosen to illustrate bias, e. g. that rape is a rare event committed by a deviant madman, whereas the researchers themselves have a superior version which is that rape is more common and occurs more in households where husbands and partners rape their wives and partners. However, this version is also selective, so the result is that researchers say, 'My selective account is better than yours, which needs clearer evidence to support it'. Another way of looking at it is that the exposure of patriarchal ideology in the press is replaced by another ideology, feminism.

❖ Another problem is with the assumption that readers take at face value what is read, when there is much evidence from interpretive studies of reader resistance and scepticism. So the supposedly 'dominated' are not necessarily so by the 'dominant ideology'.

❖ The way researchers read is not the way reading usually occurs, i.e. searching text for appropriate examples to illustrate the ideology. So again there are questions about how powerful the daily dose of ideology is to the consumer.

Textual analysis

This is an attempt to redress some of the failings of thematic analysis. Textual analysis involves examining texts as linguistic devices within the documents in order to show how texts can be influential in encouraging a particular interpretation. Trew (1979) used the term 'consistency rule' to describe the device used to get a message across. Headlines in newspapers are not purely descriptive, they contain words or phrases that are used to trigger an explanation or interpretation of an event. A common one concerns cases of women subjected to violent attacks. The idea of an innocent victim is heightened by descriptive terms such as shy, schoolgirl, daughter, girl guide, friendly and so on.

Textual analysis also examines visual imagery in picture and film to unearth 'preferred readings' as in the semiotic analysis of the Glasgow Media Group referred to earlier (see p. 541).

Where thematic analysis involves examining broad stereotypes, textual analysis involves looking at clichés which reflect the wider ideology.

Pawson's criticisms of textual analysis are similar to his criticisms of thematic analysis. The researchers may well be putting their own 'preferred reading' into their examples, which is different from the way consumers may interpret and use the material. Closely examining every word in a headline or scrutinizing an advertising picture is very different to the way many people glance quickly at such material. Another criticism of content, thematic and textual analysis is that the idea of 'preferred reading' is somewhat monosemic (see p. 561) which is what earlier approaches were criticized for. Most recent work suggests polysemic readings covering a range of possible interpretations. Texts do not carry their own meaning.

❖ Activity 44 ❖

Collect newspaper headlines similar to those mentioned in the *In Focus* and explain which words or phrases convey the imagery required.

Find other examples of imagery through words about the following: strikes, homosexuality, young people, single-parent families, disability.

In Focus
◆
Media portrayals of victims

In the 1980s, there was a furore over press reportage of the victims of the notorious 'Yorkshire Ripper'. He had killed 8 prostitutes mainly in the red light districts of Bradford and Leeds. It wasn't until his ninth victim, a sales assistant who had been taking a short cut through part of such an area, that prominent attention was given to his murderous activities. There were protests about the way previous victims were not given as highly sympathetic a portrayal as his 'innocent' victim, suggesting overtones of 'deserving' and 'undeserving' victims. Consider the following headline featuring a later victim: 'Sunday School Teacher Jacqueline Hill is 13th Ripper Victim'. Jacqueline was a Leeds University student but her role as a Sunday school teacher clearly conveys the imagery that such headlines are after. We read such headlines and immediately recognize such imagery as part of a context of 'innocent victim' much more strongly than if it had been 'Leeds Woman is 13th Ripper Victim'.

how texts are actually produced. Audience research aims to unearth comprehension and decoding in terms of what people make of programmes and newspapers. The theoretical input is interpretive as there is an emphasis on meaning and how this is negotiated by the consumer in an active rather than a passive manner. The negotiation can range from 'acceptance' to 'indifference' to 'opposition'. Research investigates the nature and patterning of such responses.

Pawson (1995) sees problems with this, as such investigation adds another dimension to the response process. Being asked what you are understanding by a particular media item creates a self-consciousness or awareness which is different from normal viewing, listening or reading circumstances. We do not normally ask ourselves when using the media, 'What am I understanding by this?' If asked by a researcher, we may well say what we think the researcher wants to hear. Note how similar this is to methodological criticisms of quantitative research such as interviews and questionnaires.

Morley's research on *Nationwide* (an early evening magazine-style programme that was prime viewing in the 1970s) audiences is a good example of audience research. In his early work (1980), he used a multi-method approach which included panel viewing and group discussion with a wide range of people. He concluded that there was a huge and systematic fragmentation of audience response along educational and social class lines. He classified audience modes of comprehension as dominant, negotiated and oppositional. These were ascribed to the social backgrounds of his subjects. He found that shop stewards and black students were oppositional, and apprentices and bank managers were dominant comprehensions:

❖ 'I don't think you can take *Nationwide* in isolation ... add the *Sun*, the *Mirror*, and the *Daily Express* to it, it's all the same heap of crap... all saying to the unions "you're ruining the country"...' (oppositional)

❖ Activity 45 ❖

What imagery do the pictures in these adverts placed by charities portray of children and homelessness?

Briefly describe the 'preferred readings' of the audience for such advertising.

Audience research

Recent work has recognized that concentrating on the text alone is insufficient and does not encapsulate every aspect of the mass media and their effects. Ang's (1991) advocacy of ethnographic research to examine in detail how people use the media is an example of newer developments. Similar ethnographic work on the production processes of the media in newsrooms and TV studios aims to discover

❖ '*Nationwide* gets down into detail ... they go into the background ... down further into it ... they say it and then repeat it ...' (dominant)

Morley's work was praised for being the first substantial demonstration of the diversity of audience comprehension. However, there were criticisms. Turner (1990) points to the 'artificial research setting' which does not correspond with the 'mundane everyday viewing' of the average viewer watching after a day's work surrounded by family. It is perhaps not surprising that panel discussions engendered 'serious' responses whereas in the home responses may be much more diverse and trivial, 'I don't like that tie' or 'When's *Top of the Pops* on?'

In more recent work (1992), Morley has accepted criticisms that his *Nationwide* research was monosemic (a single way of reading a text). For example, viewers were assumed to think in terms of the programme as middle class or pro-Labour or anti-union, when their attitudes were in fact more fragmented and sometimes inconsistent. This is now referred to as *polysemic* (several ways of reading a text). Morley sums this up:

'What is involved is a set of processes – of attentiveness, recognition of relevance, of comprehension, and of interpretation and response – *all* of which may be involved for the single audience member in front of the screen.' (1992, p. 121)

Kitzinger's News Game (1990, 1993)

Pawson (1995) sees Kitzinger's approach as going some way to addressing the methodological criticisms he raises of much media research. She investigated audience perception of media messages on AIDS by means of a game or simulation. She worked with small, socially diverse groups of three people each being given a set of pictures taken from television news and documentary reports on AIDS. Examples included photographs of a woman holding a child, a crowded street scene, and a picture of a sick man in bed. The groups were asked to play the role of a TV production team and develop a script, action scenes, location, voice-overs, etc., appropriate to the scenes given. The results showed a remarkable similarity between such lay understanding of themes associated with AIDS and those of professional media presenters. For example, the photographs of the woman holding a baby drew the following AIDS related interpretations:

❖ from retired people: 'This unfortunate woman's baby was infected with the AIDS virus when the virus was passed to her from her husband who caught it while away on a business trip abroad.'

❖ from school students: 'This is the wife and kid who both contracted AIDS through the husband and now tragically both have AIDS.'

A crowd scene evoked the following 'voice-overs':

❖ from prisoners: 'Anyone in that photo could be an AIDS victim and you wouldn't know.'

❖ from schoolchildren: 'Can you spot the AIDS victim in this group of people? No.'

This research demonstrates the similarity between such perceptions and the dominant media presentation of 'innocent victims' and the 'hidden risks' associated with AIDS. However, what was displayed is not what the people concerned actually believed about AIDS, but that they can easily recognize media responses. In her follow-up group discussions, Kitzinger identified a considerable discrepancy between 'comprehension' and 'response'. An example of this was the pensioners group who recognized media presentation of 'innocent victims' but who themselves saw the transmission of AIDS as being due to 'irresponsible' people.

Such a point is similar to the familiar methodological debate which is often applied to research using such quantitative techniques as interviews. Critics say that answers are often 'approved of' responses to the interview situation, rather than the real or actual views of the respondent (see Chapter 7).

The future of the media

Aspects of the 'future of the media' are already with us, particularly in relation to technological developments associated with computers. Clearly, the twenty-first century will see a massive expansion in *choice*. In the late 1990s, digital television is seen as a key factor in this. Mathew Horsman a media research director for a city firm sees the future in terms of 'narrowcasting to defined, niche audiences, not broadcasting to all and sundry' (*New Statesman*, 15 November 1996). He envisages a market for the new services which is global, not regional or national. There are three models for the way things might develop in regard to this:

1 *Global dominance* – Here he cites Rupert Murdoch and the way he has built up an enormous global business empire founded on media, publishing and entertainment. The most recent successes have been in digital television with the fast growing 'pay-per-view' as potentially an enormously profitable venture. This opens up the possibility of users watching what they want (major sports events, top ten films) whenever they like and making vast profits for the few owners. Sociologically this can be linked to a traditional Marxist approach.

2 *Global village* – The 'global village' as originally devised by McLuhan is where the media act to draw people together in a global community rather than atomized individuals 'doing their own thing' as in 1 above. There are moralistic overtones to this view and questions about who controls output. Critics see this as already in place and dominated by an American form of cultural imperialism. Sociologically, communitarianism and functionalism can be seen in this view. The hegemonic approach can be detected in the criticisms.

3 *Global democracy* – This is the approach typified by Ako Morita the co-founder of Sony Corporation responsible for the Walkman. Here the idea is to make 'hardware' available to all through cheapness and accessibility, so that we all have the means of receiving or playing any form of content. We can choose what we want to consume, preserving our cultural identity by means of selection. Sociologically the pluralist approach, focusing on the market demands, applies. Critics see capitalist influence lying behind such apparent 'freedom' of choice.

In just over fifty years in the twentieth century, mass media have evolved from a few daily newspapers, magazines, television channels and radio stations used by the majority, to a multiplicity of choice and variety of forms. These are spread among a population which is segmented and diverse. The media have a major role in cultural consumption and lifestyle choices where ideas of self and identity are shaped (see Chapter 2). Postmodernists suggest that such forces now cut across conventional sociological categories of class, ethnicity and gender while introducing other aspects of stratification, such as sexuality and disability. Any examination of the future of the media must focus on postmodernist approaches.

Postmodernist approaches

'Postmodernism tries to come to terms with and understand a media-saturated society. The mass media, for example, were once thought of as holding up a mirror to, and thereby reflecting, a wider social reality. Now that reality is only definable in terms of the surface reflection of that mirror.' (Strinati 1992)

Trowler (1996) identifies two key themes that can be associated with postmodernism. One is that of a society that has come after modern societies which is ' … information-rich, global and composed of a great many sub-groups and subcultures'. The second theme sees postmodernism 'as a way of knowing the world, one which questions the nature of "truth", "reason" and even "reality"' (p. 102). This is the relativist position which denies that there are absolutes in any area of human knowledge. Following the phenomenological tradition in sociology, knowledge is socially constructed and reflects the social position of the informer and the informed.

Both postmodern themes are clearly relevant to the mass media:

❖ If society is 'information-rich', the majority of this information comes from the media.

❖ The media are a key factor in the spread of 'global' ideas and information. Critics point to the United States as the main producer, which has led to a form of cultural imperialism in the late twentieth century. A. Gunder Frank (1967) referred to 'Coca-Colonization' and Ritzer (1993) to the 'MacDonaldization' of the world to illustrate this.

❖ A response to the bewildering array of choice and diversity is to 'pick and mix' to suit subgroup and subcultural identities. So, young Japanese people may drive 1950s American cars, dance in the park to early rock and roll music and have elaborate Elvis Presley quiff hairstyles, while at the same time adhering to many aspects of Japanese culture and style.

❖ The media contribute to our knowledge of the world. Some of the approaches examined in this chapter see this as absolute knowledge, which can be capitalist from a Marxist perspective, or

❖ Activity 46 ❖

List and explain three further examples of American globalization. Are there any other countries which are now involved in a similar role? Explain with examples.

patriarchal from a feminist perspective. More recent approaches, including those of postmodernists, disagree and see the knowledge imparted by the media as fragmented, confused and overwhelming, stressing its relative nature. So, a tabloid newspaper such as *The Sun* can have a lead article attacking the role of pornography in the aftermath of a brutal sex crime, opposite a 'page 3 lovely' baring all.

Politicians are also contributors to the 'moral confusion'. In 1997, John Major greeted the return to politics of the self-confessed adulterer and serial philanderer Alan Clark in terms of the need for such 'characters' in public life. Such politicians can, in other contexts, condemn single mothers and assert the need for 'family values' to be the basis for an orderly society. Absolutists condemn this as hypocrisy, while relativists see this as the way of the modern media and political life. Moralists have attacked all kinds of media, including the BBC, for contributing to 'falling standards' by not giving firm guidelines on right and wrong. Postmodernists would see this as naive.

❖ Activity 51 ❖

1 Which of the following would you place under the heading of 'popular culture' and which under 'high culture':

football	soap opera	ballet	Radio 1
opera	poetry	rock music	classical music
horse racing	pop music	art	Radio 5 live

2 What makes something 'high' or 'popular' culture?

3 Are there any that are difficult to place or may have changed? Explain.

Popular and 'high' culture

'It has teenage suicide, murder, illicit drugs, rioting, holy desecration, teenage sex, homosexuality, cross-dressing, feuding families and young love. And, of course, it has great dialogue.' (Filmmaker Baz Luhrmann on his 1997 film Shakespeare's *Romeo and Juliet*)

In 1997, the leader of the schools' inspection agency, Ofsted, raised the issue of the distinction and value of different levels of culture when he criticized the mass viewing audience for *Only Fools and Horses*. He saw this as a symptom of a trivialized culture which has turned away from 'serious' cultural pursuits, such as Shakespeare and opera. Postmodernists would disagree that it is possible to make such a distinction between two 'cultures'. Cultural choices and styles are constantly changing, so what was once regarded as 'high culture' has now become 'popular' and vice versa. Football can be referred to as an 'art form' and has changed from a male, working-class activity to attract a more middle-class and female following since the 1980s. It is possible to buy opera on bestselling CD compilations. Opera stars record with rock stars and appear in concerts to celebrate the final of the football World Cup or at Olympic Games ceremonies.

'Cross over': a postmodernist phenomenon? Rock star Freddie Mercury and opera diva Monserrat Caballé sing their worldwide hit *Barcelona!* at the spectacular opening ceremony of the 1992 Olympic Games

The boundary between popular and classical chart listings has become increasingly confused as classical artists become more like pop stars (and vice versa – see photo) and modern film scores are seen as 'classical' music. Advertisements for cars and beer attract top graphic designers and video producers. Soap operas are 'deconstructed' and analysed by cultural theorists in the same way that Shakespeare's plays are examined by literary critics. Another dimension of postmodernism is that time and space are transformed. People all over the world can simultaneously watch major world sporting events and rock concerts, and have 'on the spot' news of the latest natural disasters or human tragedies from around the world.

Manning (1996) identifies two stances arising from postmodernist accounts of the media: an optimistic and a pessimistic view:

The optimistic view

The optimists see postmodern identities as diverse, pluralistic, sensitive to irony and parody in cultural production, capable of deploying sophisticated decoding skills as consumers of commodities and media, and able to construct subcultural identities.

Fiske (1989) sees popular culture as a culture of conflict reflecting postmodernism:

'It always involves the struggle to make social meanings that are in the interests of the subordinate and that are not those preferred by the dominant ideology.' (p. 2)

Hebdige (1990) and Chen (1992) have identified the ways social groups can mount localized resistance to dominant codes. This was exemplified in 1997 when motorway protestors attracted world media headlines by a new form of protest. They dug a network of tunnels under the site for a new road and barricaded themselves in. They gradually emerged to be arrested, on condition that each time they could have a press conference. The final protestor, Swampy, came out after eight days underground. In response to a reporter's question, 'Why did you do it? ', he grinned and replied, 'To get you and all the world's media here to publicize our case. It's worked hasn't it?'.

The pessimistic view

The pessimistic view, as espoused by Jameson (1991), doubts whether sustained political opposition to the dominant cultural codes is possible. To take the above example, road protestors get arrested and moved on, motorways and airport runways still get built, albeit at greater cost. Capitalists continue to make enormous profits by encouraging rapid change in consumption and cultural styles. The media play a key part in this. Kellner (1989) uses the term 'massification' to describe how mass audiences and homogeneous patterns of consumption merge together. It becomes impossible to untangle the commercial imperatives of the media from the mass appetites of audiences for entertainment and spectacle. Political and other forms of resistance get sucked in to this and undermined in a welter of everchanging images and information. A good example is the 'hero' of the tunnelling protest, Swampy, who was paid by a national daily to be photographed in Armani clothes rather than his normal crusty grunge gear. No doubt Swampy was satisfied by the fee paid so he could continue to finance his protest movement and so were the press who could feature a postmodern 'human interest' parody story to sell newspapers.

Evaluation of postmodernist approaches

Manning (1996) points out that several of the themes of postmodernism have echoes of older debates in the social sciences such as that surrounding 'the end of ideology', which centred around the work of the American sociologist Daniel Bell (1961) in the 1950s. The German sociologist Habermas (1976) predicted similar problems for capitalism, which he deemed the 'legitimation crisis'. There are echoes of manipulation theory of the Frankfurt school in the 1960s in views of the power of media and advertising to control and influence consumers. Critical sociologists, such as Marxists and feminists, would stress the continuing structural issues of power and inequality in the context of capitalism and patriarchy: the 'choice' and 'diversity' as presented are illusory, as there are still material constraints. You need money and a job to participate in postmodern media.

Nevertheless, postmodernists have highlighted significant qualitative change in cultural trends and the mass media. In terms of access, they point to technological developments that make the media relatively inexpensive once the basic hardware has been installed. It was probably unthinkable at the founding of the BBC over 60 years ago, that by the end of the century virtually every UK household would possess a large colour television set with five available channels, and a quarter of households would have access to many more via cable or satellite.

A final point is that the media as a social phenomenon now overlap with so many areas of life as covered in the topics in this book. With specific relation to the future of work, Angela McRobbie (*New Statesman*,

---

In Focus

◆

The 'haves' and 'have nots'

Doreen Massey (1993), a geographer, highlights the stark global contrasts between the 'haves' and 'have nots' in the following quotes:

'... the jet-setters, the ones sending and receiving the faxes and the e-mail, holding the international conference calls, the ones distributing the films, controlling the news, organizing the investments and the international currency transactions. '

as compared to:

'The refugees from El Salvador or Guatemala and the undocumented migrant workers from Michoacan in Mexico crowding into Tijuana to make perhaps a fatal dash for it across the border into the USA to grab a chance of a new life. Here the experience of movement, and indeed of a confusing plurality of cultures, is very different.'

1 February 1997) reminds us that various sociologists, including Beck and Giddens, talk frequently about 'uncertain futures', 'capital without work' and the growth of 'abnormal work'. She says: 'In this sense the cultural and media industries in Britain today are experiments in working, as well as living.' This, for better or worse, is the role that the media are increasingly going to play in the future.

Chapter summary

❖ This chapter has examined the development of the mass media through the twentieth century into a powerful and influential global social institution.

❖ Various explanations of the effects and role of the media in society have been covered. Earlier psychologically influenced studies focusing on individuals and their apparent powerlessness in relation to media messages were seen to be inadequate.

❖ Structural theories, influenced by Marxism and feminism, highlight the role played by the media in contributing to inequality and exploitation of less powerful groups in society.

❖ Such conflict views are opposed by pluralist approaches which emphasize market forces, and choice and variety so that 'we get the media we deserve'.

❖ The way the media portray and represent different groups, such as women, ethnic and age groups is examined in the context of change in such areas. We also consider whether such changes are beneficial to the groups concerned.

❖ In the later sections we look at more recent developments, such as interpretive approaches which highlight meaning and understanding and the way we interact with and use media.

❖ Discourse or thematic analysis of the content of the media are now important features of media debates.

❖ Behind all these studies and approaches are methods of gathering information; Pawson's critical appraisal of this area is also examined.

❖ Finally, the future of the media is considered against the backdrop of postmodernism and globalization. If the twenty-first century is going to witness an explosion of variety and choice, as developments such as digital broadcasting open up the possibility of tailoring media-use to individual preferences, then the media will no longer be 'mass'. Others doubt this and see a continuing role for the mass media as a key aspect of society and the way people interact and communicate in their daily lives.

Stimulus-response question

Item A

Share of total audience: January* 1996

BBC1	32.4%
BBC2	11.2%
ITV	36.6%
C4/SC4	10.7%
Satellite/cable, etc.	9.1%

*January is when hours of viewing are highest, so these figures give the best snapshot of TV viewing habits.

Source: Media Guide 1997, p.143

Item B

'You start with artists. They need the best recording studios, so you build them. They need videos, so you set up a video company. They also need overseas companies to promote them. Ditto. They need more outlets to expand the market for their products, so you open more shops and so on.' (Richard Branson, quoted in *The Guardian*, 11 October 1991)

Item C

EUREKA BUILT-IN VACUUM SYSTEMS
Get the Dirt Out Of Your House Once And For All

Clean Less Often - No recycled dust or odours.

Easy to Install - In just a few hours - no fuss - no mess.

Powerful And Quiet - High performance power unit mounted away from the living area.

Versatile - Lightweight, crushproof hose tackles ground-in carpet dirt and pet hairs.

Why you should own a Eureka built-in vacuum system:

- Permanent self cleaning filter - No bags
- A full line of power units to ensure an exact match to the needs of your home
- A choice of accessory kits with a full compliment of cleaning tools
- Five year limited warranty
- Nationwide service and parts availability
- The stability of the worlds largest manufacturer of vacuum cleaners

Unit 1 Ashley Hall Farm, Inglewhite Road, Longridge, Preston, Lancs. PR3 2EB
Telephone: 01772 786 336.

Questions

1 Which channel has:
(a) the largest and
(b) the smallest audience share?
(1 mark)

2 Briefly explain the different types of audience for each of the five channels in Item A. *(5 marks)*

3 In what ways do adverts such as the one in Item C reinforce stereotypes? *(4 marks)*

4 Evaluate the role of the media in reinforcing two stereotypes other than gender. *(7 marks)*

5 How would sociologists explain the role of Richard Branson quoted in Item B? *(8 marks)*

Essay questions

1 Assess the view that the mass media are the major source of stereotypes of ethnic minorities. Illustrate your answer with reference to sociological evidence. (AEB, June 1996)

2 'The selection and presentation of the news depends more on practical issues than on cultural influences.' Critically discuss the arguments for and against this view. (AEB, June 1996)

3 'Any adequate theory of the influence of the mass media on their audiences must consider the social context in which the messages are received and interpreted.' Assess this view in the light of sociological evidence and arguments. (AEB, AS, June 1996)

4 Evaluate the usefulness of interpretive approaches to a sociological understanding of the mass media.

5 Assess the role of the mass media in representations of any two of the following: age, ethnicity, gender, social class.

6 'The diversity and range of opinions represented in our mass media reflects the power of consumer choice in a modern society.' Discuss.

7 Examine the view that the ability to choose the subject, time and place for using a wide range of media means that it is no longer possible to talk in terms of the mass media in current society.

Further reading

Eldridge, J. (ed.) (1993) *Getting the Message: News, Truth and Power*, London: Routledge.

A collection of articles from the Glasgow University Media Group which conveys their recent multimethod work on analysing news, developed from their earlier classic studies of the 1980s.

McQuail, D. (1987) *Mass Communication Theory* (2nd edn), London: Sage.

A demanding blockbuster text by a leading figure, covering media theories in a detailed manner. Requires concentrated study but worth the effort.

McRobbie, A. (1991) *Feminism and Youth Culture*, London: Macmillan.

McRobbie was one of the first researchers to study girls' teenage magazines from a feminist perspective. Note particularly the section on 'Romantic individualism and the teenage girl', which is a clear and well-written account relevant to the media and gender issues.

McRobbie, A. (1994) *Postmodernism and Popular Culture*, London: Routledge.

A critical look at issues arising from postmodernist accounts of developments in the media in relation to popular culture.

Peak, S. and **Fisher, P.** (eds) (1997) *The Media Guide 1997*, London: Fourth Estate.

A very useful, annually published source book packed with information on all aspects of the media in Britain. Of particular sociological interest are sections on ownership, readership, viewing audiences and current developments such as digital broadcasting.

Trowler, P. (1996) *Investigating Mass Media* (2nd edn), London: Collins Educational.

A very thorough and accessible coverage of the topic, full of activities and ideas for coursework.

It is also useful to subscribe to the quarterly journal *Sociology Review* which has frequent up-to-date articles on all aspects of the media and related areas. Your teacher can arrange an individual subscription.

Chapter 13

Power and politics

❖ Preview

In this chapter we shall be looking at:

- ❖ traditional theories of power and how they are undermined by the postmodern condition

- ❖ the shift from class-based politics to a 'new' politics

- ❖ the nature of modernity and postmodernity – the breakdown of 'grand narratives' and the dissolution of the social

- ❖ identity politics and trust – with reference to the work of Heller and Feher and Bauman

- ❖ reflexive modernization in the work of Giddens and Beck

- ❖ the nature of polyarchy, the 'pure' relationship and democracy – the shift from emancipatory politics to life politics

- ❖ the political impact of globalization and individualization – including the reflexive nature of the self

- ❖ new social movements – looking at the work of Habermas, Giddens, Diani, McAllister-Groves and Bagguley – and the distinction with old social movements

- ❖ communitarianism – with reference to the work of Giddens, Etzioni and Macmurray with critiques from Sennett and Campbell

- ❖ the effects of the postmodern condition upon class, gender and voting behaviour.

❖ Introduction

Was the 1997 general election irrelevant? Do political parties and political leaders make a difference in the world? What is *politics* about now? Most people would argue that in the 1990s the world became a much more uncertain and dangerous place. What are the forces and factors which brought about this uncertainty and danger? Many commentators have suggested that the political uncertainty is part of a *postmodern* condition, in which we feel as if the *social* aspects of life are dissolving. The bonds which held together communities do not have the same force which they once had. Individuals have to create their own bonds of community, often based on style or life-style choice.

In this chapter we shall discuss the question of what postmodern politics actually is. In terms of politics and political activism, postmodernism does not involve campaigning for a new set of truth claims. In that sense it is very different from Marxism, feminism or forms of political correctness. In the 'new' politics, activism is all important, the only means by which people can change social reality. Every aspect of human existence is a human creation and individuals have to build their own 'social constructions', such as ideas, beliefs and ideologies, to reassure themselves that life has some order and meaning. Life without order and meaning has been said to produce 'ontological insecurity' – in other words, individual people are unsure of what reality consists of, so that life becomes full of meaning-lessness and dread. In the postmodern condition, people have to create meaning out of meaninglessness by their own activity. New social movements have been created as a way for people to come together to change the world and give it meaning.

In this chapter we will look at the nature of modernity and postmodernity, and the ways in which individual people cope with the consequences of these factors in their everyday lives. We shall also look at the global nature of modernity and some of the political issues raised by processes of global-ization, most notably attempts by politicians to enhance or recreate the bonds of *community* with the political ideology known as 'communitarianism'. Most of these issues have been investigated by Anthony Giddens and we shall use his work as a guide to understanding the complex range of factors which now make up the political world.

Sociological theories of power

Max Weber

Most sociologists would probably agree with Weber's view of power, which clearly states that power is the ability to make somebody do something which you want them to do.

Max Weber was one of the founders of sociology and one of his many contribu-tions to the sociology of politics was his three ideal types of legitimate rule:

❖ *Charismatic authority* – This refers to a political system upheld by the strength of its leader's character. Charismatic leaders are often believed to have almost supernatural qualities.

❖ *Traditional authority* – This is a political system which is upheld by continual reference to customs and traditions.

❖ *Rational legal authority* – A political system may be regarded as legitimate in the eyes of the population because it is thought to be 'legal' and built upon rational processes; the ideal type discussed by Weber is the bureaucracy.

Saddam Hussein, authoritarian ruler of Iraq

❖ Activity 1 ❖

Weber suggests that the bureaucracy is the most efficient form of administration.

- Do you agree with this view?
- What benefits do you think that a bureaucracy may have over other forms of administration?

In Focus

◆

**In Focus:
Max Weber's
ideal type of
bureaucracy**

An ideal type is a useful model by which to measure other forms of administration. This model includes the following features:

❖ The organization is in the form of a hierarchy – a structure in the shape of a pyramid with a small group of people at the top enjoying most of the power and a large group of people at the bottom holding limited power.

❖ Its procedures are directed by a system of theoretical or abstract rules.

❖ The ideal official behaves without friendship or favour to any clients.

❖ All bureaucrats have a rigid number of recorded duties.

❖ Employment in a bureaucracy is by appointment based upon qualifications, not by election.

❖ As a form of administration, the bureaucracy has the highest degree of efficiency.

Within the bureaucracy, officials hold a set of convictions or a code of principles, which Weber termed its *Amtsehre* and this includes:

❖ a recognition of the importance of their office

❖ a belief in the supremacy of their own qualifications and ability

❖ the opinion that the legislature or parliament is merely a talking shop

❖ the belief that bureaucrats are above party politics

❖ the belief that bureaucrats are the true interpreters of the national interest

❖ bureaucrats have their own interests which Weber terms their *Staatsraison*.

In Weber's view, modern government always results in government by bureaucracy. Hence, there is a need, he claimed, for a strong parliament as a guarantor of individual rights and independence. Weber was always in favour of political democratization, and that included supporting the case in favour of votes for women. Weak parliaments generate fanatical divisions between the parties, which Weber termed 'negative politics', because it was little more than an ideological masquerade, with the important decisions taken by the state bureaucracy (see *In Focus* above).

In Weber's view, the bureaucracy is clearly defined, soulless and machine-like. It is a technical mechanism for accomplishing preconceived, or pre-thought out, objectives. However, bureaucracy has an instinctive bias to exceed its purpose, and to become an independent force within society.

The origin of bureaucratic power is knowledge, by which Weber meant the technical ability to make use of information which is protected by secrecy.

❖ Activity 2 ❖

In Weber's view, all bureaucratic structures make use of secrecy. What value do you think a bureaucracy can gain from secrecy?

Many of Weber's critics neglect the nature of the ideal type as a research tool. The ideal type is a *model*, put together from a list of features which the researcher believes are the most important. By creating an ideal type as a model, the researcher builds on what Weber termed *value relevance*, – the informed personal feelings of the researcher. This is the starting point from which the researcher goes on to consider real bureaucracies. Weber's critics assume that the ideal type is the end point of the research process. It is not – it is the start.

Steven Lukes argues that Weber's conceptions of power, authority and legitimacy are too restricted in their focus. In contrast, Lukes (1974) argues that power has three dimensions, and Weber is solely concerned with the first. Lukes' three dimensions are:

1 *decision-making* – the actions of the decision-makers

2 *non-decision-making* – the way in which power is applied to restrict the scope of the decisions that the so-called decision-makers can select from

3 *shaping desires* – the extent to which individuals may have their attitudes and beliefs directed by others, so as to agree to a decision which may not be in their own interests.

Elite theory

Elite theorists argue that power is concentrated in the hands of a small minority: an élite. Elite theory developed originally as a response to Marxism which claims that true democracy is only possible under socialism. Elite theories reject democracy and assume that in any political system, a few will lead the majority. In other words, there will always be a small, self-conscious élite with power, and a large mass which has very little power.

All societies generally have a social structure, where *oligarchy* (the rule of the few) is inescapable. In addition, most classical élite theorists assume that the masses are psychologically inadequate and therefore unable to hold power. They also believe that the mass of people have an instinctual need to be dominated. Only the élite can satisfy that need. Robert Michels (1949) has termed this 'the iron law of oligarchy'. From this perspective, democracy is not a realistic choice for any political system.

Classical élite theory is associated with two Italian sociologists, Vilfredo Pareto and Gaetano Mosca.

Vilfredo Pareto (1847–1939)

Pareto (1935) begins his analysis with a theory of non-logical actions, arguing that all individuals have six basic instincts, which he terms '*residues*' (see Table 13.1). These residues are manipulated by the élite via the use of four political procedures which Pareto names '*derivations*'.

Table 13.1 Pareto's residues and derivations

Residues:		*Derivations:*	
• Residues of combination	All human beings have an instinct to live together in groups.	• Simple assertion	The élite directly pronounces that something is correct, and this is accepted as an adequate explanation.
• Persistence of aggregates	Once a group is set up, that community will have an instinctual need to preserve it.	• Authority	The mass agree to what they are told by the élite because they believe that élite power is legitimate.
• Sentiments of activity	Individuals strengthen the bonds which hold groups together by forming ceremonies.		
• Residues of sociality	All people have an instinctual hostility towards outsiders and a need for uniformity.	• Sentiments or principles	The mass embrace élite decisions because they believe such decisions are in agreement with widely held public feelings.
• Self-preservation	All people have an instinct to preserve their own safety, possessions and social standing.	• Verbal proofs	The mass are convinced by the persuasive reasoning of the élite.
• Sexuality	Sexuality has a part to play in sustaining the social control within society.		

For Pareto, the élite can choose to rule by cunning or by the use of force, conducting themselves either as 'foxes' or 'lions'.

Mosca

Gaetano Mosca (1858–1911), also antidemocratic, argued that society should be separated into a small, well-organized élite with its own collective aspirations, and a large mass, which would have no structure and no common aims or aspirations. Mosca (1939) outlines several types of élite group: military, priestly, wealthy and landowners. Although the élite would have a control of lawful violence, it would not keep its position by use of violence alone, but would strive to maintain its rule by use of political opinions, regarded by the mass as common sense or just. It is this manipulation of the ideas of the mass which would provide the élite with its source of legitimacy.

In Mosca's view, élites are fundamental for the continuance of the civilized world. The élite holds back social forces which can destroy civilization. Within any society there are a number of conflicting and competing social forces, and the stability of a community can be measured by the competence of the élite to restrain these social forces. The élite attempts to do this by imposing a 'political formula' – a set of doctrines which, if established, should bring about political stability. In Britain, the political formula would include the principle of 'government by due process of law'.

Mills and the power élite theory

Power élite theory is associated with C. Wright Mills (1956). According to Mills, élite rule emerged in the USA in the mid-nineteenth century. In his research, Mills identified three key institutions as the centre of power in the USA:

❖ the federal government

❖ the major corporations

❖ the military.

Mills argued that the top positions in these three institutions constituted the élite. According to Mills, the three élites were closely connected through education, kinship, origin and intertwined interests, and in reality were not separate, but formed a single *power élite*.

Evaluation of élite theory

Pareto does not clearly define his key terms: for example, a residue can be a sentiment, an instinct or a principle. The theory of non-logical actions is diminished by this inability to be clear on these terms. In addition, he provides no picture of the structure of institutions, and very few practical political situations are discussed.

Mosca is also unclear about many of his key terms, e.g. the idea of a social force. He too does not give many examples from everyday practical politics. However, what many people find offensive about élite theory is that it has been used as a justification for fascism.

Research evidence demonstrates that those people who occupy élite positions do indeed tend to come from particular backgrounds and, as Mills argued, there are strong social networks between the various élites. Marxists would argue that the evidence indicates a ruling class based on economic power.

Senior boys, 'Pops', at Eton College

❖ Activity 3 ❖

1 Is there evidence of a political élite in Britain? Find out how many members of the current Cabinet received a public school education and/or went to Oxford or Cambridge University.

2 Is the figure significantly different when a Conservative or Labour government is in power? Why might this be the case?

Marxist theories of power

Elite theory assumes that power rests with those who occupy key positions in the state. Marxists and neo-Marxists, however, see power as emanating from an economic base. From the Marxist viewpoint, if a group possess the means of production, not only do they have economic power, they also possess *political* power. The state, therefore, tries to organize capitalist society in the best interests of the capitalists.

The legitimacy of the capitalist system is maintained by ideology. In other words, working-class people are said to have ideas and beliefs which are not in their own economic interests. The working class are ideologically manipulated – through institutions such as the media, schools and religion.

Ralph Miliband (1973) argued that the state in Britain is made up of the following institutions:

❖ the police

❖ the judiciary

❖ the military

❖ local government

❖ central government.

Miliband argues that there is a well-organized capitalist class, occupying the top posts in all these institutions. Most of these people were educated in top private schools before going on to Oxford or Cambridge. This narrow group of individuals uses the state as an *instrument* for its own lasting capitalist supremacy. This theory has been called the *instrumentalist theory of the state*.

Nicos Poulantzas (1973), in contrast, argues that the class background of people in the highest governmental posts is unimportant. The organization of society is capitalist, and the role of the state is to sustain capitalism. The state must have a significant degree of *autonomy*, or independence, from separate capitalists, in order to choose between the rival requirements for state action that various capitalist interests demand. The state, in other words, is always necessary for satisfying or fulfilling the wants and needs of capital, even though individual members of top public organizations may not be from the highest-class backgrounds.

❖ Activity 4 ❖

For Marxists, economic factors determine the nature of political activity in what is termed 'economic determinism'. Discuss with other sociology students what you believe is the significance of gender and race in the political system.

What other divisions between people do you think are significant within any political system?

Antonio Gramsci (1971) abandoned the 'economic determinism' contained in the type of Marxist analysis that Poulantzas is suggesting. Working from his prison cell in the 1930s, Gramsci suggested a division between two parts of the state:

❖ *political* society, which included all the oppressive governmental organizations such as the police and the military

❖ *civil* society, which consisted of all the organizations which were involved in the production and distribution of ideology, i.e. were attempting to manipulate people's ideas and beliefs.

The capitalist state rules by consensus, but has the capability to use violence if required. Nevertheless, the state would always want to deal with others by using bargaining skills to bring forward a settlement. The state strives to form a historic bloc, which entails striking a balance with distinct groups, in an attempt to preserve society-wide feelings of togetherness. Agreement is sustained by hegemony. This is Gramsci's reformulation of the Marxian notion of ideology, a core of belief which becomes a key component of our consciousness and which we interpret as legitimate. Capitalism can only be removed by challenging and replacing hegemony with a new historic bloc.

In contrast, Abercrombie *et al.* (1981) reject approaches which stress the ideological appearance of state power. There are many studies, they suggest, which demonstrate that working-class people discard a dominant ideology: Paul Willis's study *Learning to Labour* (1977), for example, which clearly demonstrates how a group of working-class lads make an effort to introduce masculine shop-floor culture into their school and renounce the pro-school beliefs that the teachers seek to impose on all school-children. Abercrombie and his colleagues, argue that financial considerations, such as anxiety about unemployment, are more important factors in sustaining inequalities within capitalism. Before studying Table 13.2, answer the questions in Activity 5.

❖ Activity 5 ❖

1 What is the role of violence in the political system: for Marxists? for élite theorists?

2 What are the *differences* between Marxism and élite theory? (Many students wrongly assume that they are one and the same.)

3 Outline what you consider to be the *similarities* between the Marxist and élite theories of power?

Table 13.2 Elite theory and Marxism: comparison

Similarities

- Both Marxism and élite theory have a small ruling class which holds power, and a large group of powerless individuals.

- Both Marxism and élite theory are zero-sum conceptions of power; in other words they presume that there is an unchanging quantity of power in society.

- Both Marxism and élite theory presume that the ruling class sustains its power by manipulating the thoughts and ideas of the powerless.

Differences:

- In the Marxist analysis, the dominant class is invariably an economic class; in élite theory this is not the case.

- Marxism has a very promising view of the future – the powerless will one day arise from their exploitation and take power. In élite theory, oligarchy (the rule of the few) is inescapable – the mass will never rise up and take power.

- In the Marxist analysis, the connection between the bourgeoisie and the proletariat is always based on economic exploitation. In élite theory, by contrast, the masses have a psychological compulsion to be dominated.

- Marxism provides a political defence for socialism. In contrast, élite theory is used as a political apology for fascism.

State-centred theories

In state-centred explanations, the state is considered the most powerful organization in society. It is believed to have interests of its own and to behave in ways that promote these interests. The modern state is, therefore, not the product of capitalism or of class relations. There is no power in society pushing the state in any specific direction. Michael Mann (1993) suggests that there are several sources of social power:

❖ the economic

❖ the political

❖ the military

❖ ideological.

Military dangers from the outside world are one of the most important considerations in any theory of state formation.

Is the honours system open to manipulation?

contracts with private companies to persuade people to accept its policies and programmes

❖ making use of the state's assets to overcome opponents, e.g. the increased use of government advertising in Britain since 1979

❖ changing policy.

One of the most persuasive state-centred theorists is Theda Skocpol (1979) who describes a number of states behaving independently to fulfil their own interests. As with Gramsci, she suggests that whether a state matures into a powerful independent body or not depends upon how well-organized other interests are in society. In contrast to the Marxist analysis, states do not have to represent the interests of the bourgeoisie. A powerful state can shape the action of *all* classes, including the bourgeoisie.

However, state-centred theorists are often vague about the theoretical assumptions on which their analysis is based. Although they are critical of the assumptions of Marxists, pluralists and élite theorists, they do not make clear their own assumptions about the links between the state and society. At times they are neo-Weberian in nature, at times neo-Marxist.

The state is the only organization which can exercise power in a centralized territorial manner. Eric Nordlinger (1981) argues that the state can expand the degree of independence from other groups within the nation by:

❖ the use of concealed methods of decision-making

❖ manipulation of the honours system, to provide employment or government

 What is postmodernism?

❖ Activity 6 ❖

Read the descriptions of modernity and postmodernity (see *In Focus* on the next page). Spend a few minutes thinking about the following questions. If possible, discuss them with other sociology students:

1 What do you understand by the term *social*?

2 How would you explain the concept of the 'grand narrative' to a friend who was not a sociology student?

Within modernity, individuals relate to each other in rational ways. This is most clearly seen in the way people relate to each other in Weber's ideal type of bureaucracy. Moreover, because of the processes of globalization, rationality is said to be common across the world. From a postmodern perspective, the foundations of rationality are said to be undermined and people have to invent new ways of relating to each other. This means new forms of politics.

In Focus

◆

Modernity and post-modernity

*M*odernity: This term means the modern world, and according to Anthony Giddens (1985) modernity contains a number of institutional characteristics:

❖ capitalism

❖ industrialism

❖ centralized administrative power, which makes use of surveillance

❖ centralized control of military power.

For Zygmunt Bauman, within modernity there is a movement by the state towards the uniformity of its residents, achieved through erasing differences between individuals and imposing an approved identity upon them. Bauman terms this the *state-administered universal identity*, the outcome of a planned, managed and rational set of state actions:

> 'The imparting of beliefs, attitudes and behavioural patterns has to be problematized and structured as *education* (and, more generally, culture), run by the expert agents appointed and empowered by the state.' (Bauman 1992a, p. 99)

*P*ostmodernism: In contrast, postmodernism can be viewed as the culture of postmodernity, both of which come *after modernity*. Postmodernism exists in the same way that we could say that the 'Renaissance' existed in the fifteenth to seventeenth centuries. Postmodernism is a way of making sense of the world which is distinctly different from *modernist* political theories such as Marxism, élite theory and Weberian analyses. Within the postmodern culture, there are a range of life-style choices and social identities from which an individual can choose.

In his book *The Postmodern Condition*, Lyotard (1984) was highly critical of what he called the *grand narratives*. These were *myths*, or popular stories, of the modern world which provided legitimacy to both institutions and activities. Grand narratives outline the criteria of what to do, in what situation and for what reason. They include ideologies such as socialism, communism and feminism. In other words, grand narratives have a *universal* element and, moreover, need no proof or justification. In the postmodern condition these grand narratives are dissolved.

The 'new' politics

The 'new' politics involves a number of major shifts in how we view the political relationships in the world:

❖ a *new foundation for authority* and a need to re-evaluate the established sociological theories of authority such as those of Weber

❖ a shift away from *class-based* politics to *identity* politics

❖ a shift of support from *old social movements* such as political parties to *new social movements*

❖ the declining significance of the nation state in the face of *globalization*

❖ a loss of faith in grand narratives, or big ideologies, such as socialism.

This situation can bring with it new forms of community, which may well be very rewarding and very fulfilling for individuals. However, this condition can also generate new forms of hostility towards individuals or groups seen as outsiders. Because human behaviour is free from rationality, the scope for misunderstanding human behaviour and intentions is almost infinite.

In Chapter 2 we said that issues of culture and identity are central in defining:

❖ who we are as *individuals*

❖ who we are as *communities*

❖ whom we do *not accept* as part of 'us'.

Within the 'new' politics of the postmodern condition, these issues of identity have replaced class consciousness.

They have shifted the focus of politics away from material issues, such as the redistribution of wealth, to issues about who we are as people and whom we can trust.

We can say then, that postmodern politics is a non-institutional, *participatory* politics outside the established political institutions. It is not motivated by working-class people struggling to improve their economic situation, but by people concerned with issues of identity and culture.

The great danger is that this form of politics can become a politics without rules and without morality, in which people are capable of acts of great cruelty.

Within postmodernity, individuals are unable to tell the difference between the *morality* of something and the *appearance* of something. Morally, anything goes. This is what theorists call the *aestheticization of life*. As there is no coherent moral code, there is nothing to prevent individuals from becoming involved in acts such as ethnic cleansing – the extermination of people who are regarded as 'not one of us'.

Mike Featherstone suggests that, postmodernism:

'... has to be understood against the background of a long-term process involving the growth of a consumer culture and expansion in the number of specialists and intermediaries engaged in the production and circulation of symbolic goals. It draws on tendencies in consumer culture which favour the aestheticization of life, the assumption that the aesthetic life is the ethically good life and that there is no human nature or true self; with the goal of life an endless pursuit of new experiences, values and vocabularies.' (Featherstone 1991, p. 126)

It has been suggested that politics in the postmodern world is *neo-medieval* in nature – suggesting a return to the characteristics of the political system within medieval Europe:

❖ no nation state

❖ no democracy

❖ violent challenge to the power of the central authority (the king at that time) from various sources

❖ conflict between very different belief systems: church ideology vs secular ideology

❖ tension between the major institutions of the day: king vs church

❖ individuals unclear about their identity

❖ a politics without established rules

❖ resort to violence to resolve issues.

The coronation of Edward II in 1308, an era when the monarch enjoyed absolute power – although not without (often violent) struggle. Edward was murdered in 1327.

❖ Activity 7 ❖

Outline in a short paragraph, why a world with no moral code might be a place of great cruelty.

Jean-François Lyotard (1984) explores the idea of a postmodern world in which individuals have lost faith in grand narratives. These once gave reassurance and a feeling of 'ontological security' – the feeling that we know the world and how it works. Socialism and feminism, for example, as grand narratives no longer have anything relevant to say about people's lives. The postmodern world is highly *pluralistic*: power is widely shared and no one is completely powerless. In addition, postmodern politics is not about class-based issues, but about the single issue campaigns of 'new' social movements. This has great significance for political parties, which in Britain are mainly class-based, and which in the postmodern condition become increasingly irrelevant.

Habermas (1987) makes a similar analysis of the decline of 'old politics', which is concerned with the economic issues, such as debates about the social security system and who gets what within it. In contrast, Habermas outlines a 'new politics' which is concerned with issues such as identity politics and human rights. Habermas draws parallels between the 'new social movements' and what he terms the 'social-romantic' movements from the nineteenth century which rejected modern rational capitalism. These included groups

Environmental protester, 'Swampy', in the entrance to his tunnel at the 'Sir Cliff Richard Vegan Revolution' camp at Manchester Airport.

❖ Activity 8 ❖

1 Do any of the political parties have anything relevant to say about your life?

2 Does feminism have anything relevant to say about your life?

3 Does socialism have anything relevant to say about your life?

of craftsmen and 'escapist' movements, often supported by middle-class people.

Political life is becoming more 'decentered'. The suggestion is that 'the state' is no longer the primary focus of political activity. There is a wide range of political visions: a 'micro-politics' of mini public spheres each with its own new social movement, its own language and its own demands upon the individuals within their locality. The 'micro' political bonds are the strongest political bonds that individuals feel and it is for this reason that 'new' social movements are concerned with 'identity politics'. This politics assumes that the personal and interpersonal realms are of great significance in power relationships. Joining with others who share a common identity is a new departure for the politics.

Postmodern politics is then about the redefinition of the nature of social solidarity. In his essay 'Solidarity', Richard Rorty (1989) argues that bonds of solidarity are strongest within collectivities which are small and local. This is in stark contrast to critics such as Gellner (who argues that postmodernism cannot provide any foundation for political action or belief) and to critics who present postmodernism as a

---

In Focus

◆

The postmodernization of public life

We could argue that there has been a twofold postmodernization of public life:

❖ The proliferation of various peoples means that there is a decline of class-based politics and the politics of other

grand narratives, such as feminism, which tell large groups of people what to think.

❖ The breaking down of rigid barriers between political and private life allows the emergence of 'identity politics'.

terrifying vision of a 'non-society devoid of cohesive relations, social meaning and collective political struggle' (Best and Kellner 1997).

Rorty (1991) attempts to provide a distinctly postmodern notion of rights not built on grand narratives or similar universal criteria. In Rorty's view, all human beings need emotional attachment and feel sympathy for others. In addition, by education, we can reinforce individuals' identification with others, so that we view all individuals as fully and truly human. His foundation for human rights assumes that the human body is delicate and that some bodies are much weaker than others. All of us have a feeling to protect bodies which are weaker than others. This makes Rorty's theory of human rights one of a collective, shared compassion for other human individuals.

This suggests that the politics of the new social movements has more meaning for the *individual* than does the politics of the class-based political parties. There are similarities here with the 'postmaterialist' thesis of

❖ **Activity 9** ❖

Do you feel sympathy, and other forms of emotional attachment, for people who are weaker than you? Suggest some reasons for your answer.

In your view, does this provide a sound foundation for a theory of 'rights'?

Ronald Inglehart, who argues that the political changes in advanced societies can be tracked back to a transformation in 'the values of Western publics ... [from] an overwhelming emphasis on material well-being and physical security towards greater emphasis on the quality of life' (1990, p. 3).

Inglehart also argues that this change has resulted in a decline of the left/right social-class division and a rise in new social movements together with a greater emphasis on life-style problems, individual freedom and liberty.

Two views of politics in an uncertain world

Postmodern politics: Heller and Feher, and Bauman

The Postmodern Political Condition by Agnes Heller and Ferenc Feher (1988) defines postmodernity as:

> '... the private-collective time and space, within the wider time space of modernity, by those who want to take it to task ... the very foundation of postmodernity consists of viewing the world as a plurality of heterogeneous spaces and temporalities.'

In other words, from this point of view, modernity and postmodernity coexist. Postmoderns are people described as being *after the grand narrative*. In other words, postmoderns are people who choose not to make use of grand narratives to make sense of the world. Moreover, their world view

can be described as *post-historic*. In addition, Heller and Feher argue that poststructuralism has a specific meaning within postmodernity:

> 'It indicates the social and political prevalence of the functional over the structural, the gradual weakening if not total disappearance of a politics based solely on class interests and class perceptions.'

New social movements appear 'which are the epitomes of functionalist-postmodern politics'.

The breakdown of grand narratives has a number of consequences:

❖ The postmodern political condition becomes *pluralistic* in nature, with a plurality of 'cultures and discourses' each with its own 'small narrative', which may be local, cultural, ethnic,

In Focus

◆

Jürgen Habermas: NSMs and communicative competence

New social movements attempt to defend the quality of life of people by becoming concerned with issues of personal and collective achievement which the process of rationalization is taking away from them – issues such as equality, self-realization, participation and human rights. These may take the form of *particularistic* concerns, i.e. concerns specific to followers of a NSM rather than the wider society.

However, social movements are also concerned with re-establishing a *communicative ethic*, which is about the sharing of the same community norms. Although new social movements may have differences of opinion and be in conflict over a range of issues, any dispute can only be resolved if each movement is able and willing to listen to the other. This is what Habermas (1987) termed the *ideal speech situation* – a form of shared communication between people who want to resolve their differences.

religious or ideological in nature, living alongside each other.

❖ A foundation for what Habermas (1987) termed 'domination-free' discourse becomes possible – people can talk to each other free from ideology, with what Habermas terms *'communicative competence'*.

❖ The replacement of the state as a 'class agency'. Class politics was always rational and calculable because it was based upon economic interests. However, without the economic interests of classes, politics becomes *irrational* and *unpredictable*.

❖ Politics loses its sense of 'taboo'. Racism becomes politicized within a form of 'moral relativism' in which 'even the assessment of a mass deportation and genocide becomes a matter of taste' (Heller and Feher 1988, p. 9).

In contrast to Featherstone (see p. 588), Heller and Feher argue that from the arguments and debates about the postmodern condition, certain moral principles of democratic politics can be extracted. This is possible because, without direct financial economic reward as the sole measure of success and wellbeing, the postmodern condition promotes various *non-economic forms of satisfaction* which can be incorporated into an individual or collective life style. The postmodern political ethos is therefore said to be democratic in nature. With the decline in the grand narratives, there is a greater emphasis on the individual person actively making choices, rather than being pushed about by forces outside their control. It is this which upholds the postmodern democracy.

According to Zygmunt Bauman (see *In Focus*), postmodern politics has four characteristics:

In Focus

◆

Zygmunt Bauman

According to Anthony Giddens, Zygmunt Bauman is *the* theorist of postmodernism. Born in Poland, he taught sociology in a number of universities, including Tel Aviv, before becoming Professor of Sociology at Leeds University in 1970. He is at this time Emeritus Professor of Sociology at Leeds University. Now in his seventies, he continues to write books, articles and

reviews. His books include *Modernity and Ambivalence* (1991), *Intimations of Postmodernity* (1992), *Mortality, Immortality and Other Life Strategies* (1992), *Postmodern Ethics* (1993), *Life in Fragments* (1995) and *Postmodernity and Its Discontents* (1997). In addition, he has also written about freedom, culture, thinking sociologically and the holocaust.

❖ *Tribal* politics – Individuals come together with others whom they feel share a similar identity. Often these communities are nationalistic in nature and are referred to as 'tribes' or 'imagined communities'.

❖ Politics of *desire* – Individuals need to obtain tribal tokens to show that they are part of the community. Tokens could be as trivial as wearing the right kind of clothes, or as serious and unpleasant as involvement in ethnic cleansing.

❖ Politics of *fear* – This is concerned with avoidance of potentially harmful effects. New political issues emerge which have nothing to do with social class, for example the possible link between BSE and CJD.

❖ Politics of *certainty* – We have a need for expert advice, but in the postmodern condition we are unwilling to place our trust in experts. Loss of trust becomes a major political issue.

In short, postmodern politics is much more irrational and emotional than the politics which went before it.

The politics of fear: the awful reality of the programme of mass slaughter of cattle infected with BSE. Has this created new political aware-ness that cuts across social and political loyalties?

❖ Activity 10 ❖

How are 'newcomers' treated where you live? Is their treatment 'tribal' in any way?

You could attempt to outline and evaluate the values of people in your neighbourhood who behave or think in a tribal fashion. Could this be an element of the postmodern condition?

Anthony Giddens the politics of 'reflexive modernization'

Anthony Giddens has a very different view of politics in an uncertain world. For Giddens, nation states are *polyarchic* in nature, in other words they are highly pluralistic, i.e. power is widely shared and politics is based on shared rules. Individuals enjoy a number of citizenship rights which have been won by participation in forms of 'emancipatory politics'. Within the nation states, democracy is moving towards a *'dialogic democracy'* which is similar in many respects to the 'pure relationship' (see p. 594). As Giddens explains:

> 'There is a close tie between the pure relationship and dialogic democracy. Dialogue, between individuals who approach one another as equals, is a transactional quality central to their mutuality. There are remarkable parallels between what a good relationship looks like, as developed in the literature of marital and sexual therapy, and formal mechanisms of political democracy. Both depend on the development of ... a principle of autonomy.' (Giddens 1994, pp. 118–19)

As suggested above, pluralism describes a condition within a community in which power is widely shared amongst a multiplicity of groups and organizations, all of whom have their own sectional interests. The state is seen as the rule-maker or umpire, the 'honest broker' that attempts to balance opinions within the community.

Polyarchy

The most well-developed form of pluralism is known as *polyarchy*. According to Robert Dahl (1971), polyarchy is 'the government of a state or city by many: contrasted with monarchy'. Polyarchy includes a set of authoritative rules assigned in response to the citizens' wishes. This is necessary for the democratic process to work. The rules guarantee our civil and political rights, which according to Lindblom (1977) include:

- ❖ freedom to form and join organizations
- ❖ freedom of expression
- ❖ right to vote
- ❖ eligibility for public office
- ❖ right of political leaders to compete for support
- ❖ right of political leaders to compete for votes
- ❖ free and fair elections (open, honestly conducted, one person one vote), which will decide who is to hold the top authority
- ❖ alternative sources of information
- ❖ institutions for making government policies which depend upon votes and other expressions of preference.

These rules are based upon *volitions*. Volitions are choices which are created by the citizens themselves in consultation with each other. According to Lindblom, within polyarchy there is a common core of volitions:

- ❖ *Simple preference* – A person holds a view without the need for calculated thought or reason.
- ❖ *Complex judgement* – An individual holds a view after some consideration and analysis.
- ❖ *Moral or ethical rules* – An individual chooses a view on the basis of a moral code.
- ❖ *Simple preference between complex judgements* – An individual chooses between a range of complex judgements with little calculated thought. Lindblom gives the example of a person saying: 'No, I don't believe in foreign aid, but don't ask me why.' (1977, p. 135)

According to Giddens, all nation states have a tendency towards polyarchy. Robert Dahl argues that polyarchy is both a product of the democratizing of nation states and a type of régime. There is a high tolerance of opposition and widespread opportunity for participating in influencing the conduct of government. The institutions

within polyarchy have evolved in an effort to help democratize the political process.

However, there are a number of criticisms of pluralism and polyarchy:

- ❖ Researchers are only concerned with decision-making and they ignore the idea of non-decision-making.
- ❖ Pluralists do not take into account the fact that individuals may have their ideas, termed volitions, manipulated by others more powerful than themselves, e.g. capitalists or the mass media.
- ❖ Dahl has had to accept that the unequal distribution of wealth can sustain an unequal division of political power.
- ❖ There is a problem of unrepresented or under-represented interests.

In Giddens' view, we need to have a theory of democratization which takes into account both everyday life and globalizing systems. To this end, Giddens develops his notion of 'dialogic democracy' which stands in opposition to all forms of fundamentalism and attempts to 'create active trust through an appreciation of the integrity of the other. Trust is a means of ordering social relations across time and space' (Giddens 1994, p. 116). We attempt to live with others in a relation of 'mutual tolerance'. As Giddens suggests, our political relationships take on many of the characteristics of the 'pure' relationship. Read the *In Focus* on the next page before answering Activity 11.

❖ Activity 11 ❖

1 Do you strive for a 'pure' relationship?
2 What benefit or value do you think an individual will get from a 'pure' relationship?
3 Could you outline, in your own words, the link between the 'pure' relationship and political relationships?

In Focus

◆

**Giddens'
'pure'
relationship**

In Giddens' analysis, all individuals strive for a 'pure' relationship – one based solely on trust, which cannot be underpinned by any guarantee. In previous ages, it was possible to trust an individual in an intimate relationship because of their family or professional background. This guarantee of trust can no longer be given in the 'new times' of reflexive modernization.

The 'pure' relationship expresses a prime difference between the traditional and present-day marriage. Marriage has now become a signifier of commitment; when two people commit themselves to each other, this provides meaning, stability and security in day-to-day life. The marriage contract, with the 'pure' relationship, has taken the form of a 'Bill of Rights': an ethical framework for a personal democratic order, an intimacy based on autonomy and democracy.

Autonomy brings with it the successful realization of the 'reflexive project of self' – the ability of individual people to create and recreate themselves in any way they choose. Autonomy gives people opportunities to seek out ways of avoiding meaninglessness and dread which are common in the lives of people living in the modern world.

Giddens suggests that all relationships can become democratic – even the relationship between parent and young child. For Giddens, it is the right of a child to be treated as the equal of an adult. If it is not possible to negotiate with a child because he or she is too young to understand the issues in question, then the adult should provide counterfactual justifications. In other words, the adult should provide the child with hypothetical examples which draw on the child's experience.

In terms of politics, the significance of these developments is that within modernity we have moved from 'emancipatory politics' – which is itself a product of modernity – to 'life politics'. This is the key factor pushing new social movements to campaign for a form of politics which is on the far side of modernity (Giddens dislikes the term postmodernity and prefers the term 'reflexive modernization').

Reflexive modernization

The world is no longer so clearly defined in terms of modernity and tradition in the way that Durkheim, Weber and Tonnies described it at the turn of the century. In Giddens' analysis, for example, modernity is essentially a post-traditional order which brings with it the threat of personal meaninglessness. The self has to become *reflexive*: in other words, as individuals, we have to make a variety of life-style choices in an effort to avoid the new forms of risk

that we have to live with in the modern world. We have to ensure the self-organization and self-monitoring of life narratives when faced with what appear to be unlimited life-style choices. As individuals, we should feel free from structures.

Modernity has, as Giddens explains, an intrinsic reflexivity at an institutional level, i.e. a tendency to reflect upon itself. This means that not only are individuals constantly changing, but institutions are also constantly changing. In the modern world, we have overcome the dogma of tradition. This does not mean that tradition has no place in the modern world, rather that traditions need to be justified before they are acceptable to individuals. This brings with it new problems, as Giddens explains:

> 'The reflexivity of modernity actually undermines the certainty of knowledge, even in the core domains of natural science.' (Giddens 1994, p. 294)

There is also a significant shift in trust relations. Because of the notion of reflexivity, trust is no longer a matter of individual people interacting with each other face to face; trust is now much more likely to make use of expert systems. For example, I trust that the fund manager who looks after my endowment mortgage will generate sufficient money to pay for the cost of my home in twenty-five years time. As we all know, however, people make mistakes.

❖ Activity 12 ❖

1 Do you trust the government?
2 In 1996, the British Government told the public that British beef was safe to eat. Did you trust the government's advice on BSE? Outline the reasons for your answer.
3 Make a list of a number of people or organizations whom you trust – give some reasons why you trust them.

According to Giddens, in traditional cultures, the risk environment was dominated by the hazards of the physical world. Infant mortality was high, death of women in childbirth was high, life expectancy was low, and rates of chronic illness and infectious disease were high. In the modern world, however, we have a new risk profile which has its origins not in nature, but in the 'outcome of socially organized knowledge' – a *manufactured uncertainty*. By this, Giddens means uncertainties created by people, the like of which have never been seen before and which cannot be easily calculated, e.g. the effects of global warming or nuclear power. Individuals may find this situation *existentially troubling*. Existentialism is the attempt to make sense of the world which appears to be meaningless. Giddens' discussion is similar in a number of important respects to the discussion of risk in the work of Ulrich Beck (1992) (see pp. 599–600).

Reflexive modernization is made up of two processes: *individualization* and *globalization*.

What is individualization ?

A key element in any fully developed modernity is the single person, cut loose from previously supportive social forms, such as social class or fixed gender roles. According to Beck, this is a 'new mode of societalization' involving a redefinition of the relationship between the individual and society. On the one hand, Beck outlines an abstract or 'ahistorical model of individualization' which involves three components:

❖ The *liberating dimension* or disembedding – This involves the breaking down of socially and historically prescribed commitments. In other words, the individual person is free from any commitments.

❖ The *disenchantment dimension* or loss of traditional security – This refers to the breaking down of 'practical knowledge, faith and guiding norms' (Beck 1992, p. 128). Individual people have to live their lives without the reassurance provided by widely accepted norms or faith.

❖ The *control/reintegration dimension* or re-embedding – This involves the creation of new forms of social commitment. Individuals have to search for or create their own forms of rules, norms or commitments in an effort to give their life meaning again.

In Beck's view, individualization:

'... means that each person's biography is removed from given determinations and placed in his or her hands ... biographies become self-reflexive, socially prescribed biography is transformed into biography that is self-produced and continues to be produced.' (Beck 1992, p. 135)

What Beck is saying here is that individual people are not pushed about by forces outside their control as, for example, individual people are in a Marxist or feminist analysis.

In order to understand fully what Giddens understands by 'individualization', we need to have a clear outline of what he understands by 'the self'.

❖ Activity 13 ❖

- Do you accept Beck's view of individualization, given on the previous page?
- Outline a list of factors which you think may determine how you behave.
- Ask other sociology students whether they agree with your list and reasons.

❖ Activity 14 ❖

The world today has been described as 'post-human': individuals do not matter or make a difference in the world.

- What is a person, human agent or self?
- What does it mean to be a person?

These may seem like impossible questions; however, if we believe in human rights and personal freedom, we need to have a clear idea in our own mind of what it is we are arguing for.

Anthony Giddens discusses the notion of self under the concept of *self-identity*, and this is made up of three elements:

1 The *unconscious* – This concept, derived from Freud, refers to those elements of our self which we are not fully in control of, beyond our immediate intentions.

2 The *practical consciousness* – This is a concept derived from Harold Garfinkel to explain that human action is not pushed about, or determined, by forces outside the individual. Giddens also accepts, as suggested by Garfinkel, that individuals have the ability to establish rules and routines for themselves.

3 The *discursive consciousness* – This term is imported from Alfred Schutz to suggest that individuals reflect upon their social actions to make sense of these actions.

Why are individual selves reflexive in modernity?

To be reflexive is to have a *life narrative*: to choose our character, mould our personal identity and decide upon the moral and rational organizing principles that we use to make sense of our subjective experience. This narrative is what we use to define our selves as a self. Individuals then, have to create and constantly recreate themselves, choosing from life-style resources to develop and monitor their chosen life narrative.

In Giddens' analysis however, individuals have become reflexive in order to compensate for the breaking down of the basic security system of customs and traditions within local communities, brought about by the advancement of modernity.

This is a situation which individuals may again find existentially troubling, because this protective framework gave psychological support and without it individuals may feel the ontological insecurity of personal meaninglessness and dread. As Giddens makes clear (1992):

'The self today is for everyone a reflexive project – a more or less continuous interrogation of past, present and future. It is a project carried on amid a profusion of reflexive resources: therapy and self-help manuals of all kinds, television programmes and magazine articles.' (Giddens 1992, p. 30)

For Giddens then, individuals are reflexive for reasons of basic security. Individuals change in order to make themselves feel an enhanced sense of 'ontological security'.

❖ Activity 15 ❖

The human agent is reflexive for a variety of reasons.

1 Identify the reasons why people are reflexive, according to Giddens.

2 Reflecting on your answer above, outline the reasons why *you* are reflexive.

3 Compare your answers with those of other sociology students in your group.

Globalization is the idea that the whole world is becoming a single place. As a process, globalization directly affects the lives of all the people in the world. Drugs, cheap tourism, technology, manufacture of cheap goods, wider choice of (exotic) foods – all have a global dimension to them. As Roland Robertson has made clear:

> 'The fact and the perception of ever increasing inter-dependence at the global level, the rising concern about the fate of the world as a whole and of the human species (particularly because of the threats of ecological degradation, nuclear disaster and AIDS), and the colonization of the local by global life (not least via the mass media) facilitate massive processes of relativization of cultures, doctrines, ideologies and cognitive frames of reference.' (Robertson 1994, p. 87)

Arjun Appadurai (1990) explains that the notion of globalization is brought about by a number of flows:

❖ ethnoscapes – the flow of people, tourists, immigrants, refugees, exiles and guest workers

❖ technoscapes – the movement of technology

❖ finanscapes – the rapid movement of money via money markets and stock exchanges

❖ mediascapes – information and images generated and distributed by film, television, newspapers and magazines

❖ ideoscapes – the movement of political ideas and ideologies.

Leslie Sklair (1993) outlined a number of different models of globalization:

1 There is a world system model which is Marxist in orientation, as put forward by Immanuel Wallerstein. In this model there is an international division of labour within the world economy. A nation's economy is linked in a number of ways to the international economy and can be either at its core, semi-periphery or periphery. Those nations which are at the periphery are much more likely to be in poverty. However, this model is said to be too determined by economic factors and ignores cultural factors.

2 The second model is one of '*cultural imperialism*', in which local or traditional cultures are destroyed by the cultural products of multinational corporations in the advanced countries. Ulf Hannerz outlines a number of possible types of cultural unification, one of which is 'global homogenization'. This suggests complete domination in the world by 'lowbrow' Western life styles, Western products in the shops, Western cars in the streets, Western films at the cinema, Western soaps on television, etc. This spread involves *Dynasty* rather than Shakespeare.

3 The third model is Sklair's own model, which is that the global system is built upon *transnational* practices. These practices are formed by transnational corporations and they allow economic, political and cultural or ideological practices, like consumerism, to travel across state borders.

According to David Held (1991), governments find it difficult to regulate their own economies as global financial dealings can diminish the worth of a country's money. Environmental issues also cross national boundaries. Although transnational governmental organizations, such as the European Union, NATO and the International Monetary Fund (IMF), have expanded their influence in the world, it is still the case that bringing people together from diverse cultures can increase the chances of conflict between people of different ethnic identities. Globalization can diminish what were commonly accepted political and economic structures without inevitably leading to the foundation of new systems. Globalization can then generate nationalist conflict in the world, because political decisions are no longer taken by governments within nation states. It can also destroy a person's cultural identity and people have to fight to protect their local ways of living. Although there is no one acceptable definition of nationalism from this perspective, it is a counter-politics of the local.

Giddens' view of the world order

According to Giddens, there are two common explanations about the character of the world order:

❖ The first is Marxist in nature, where nation states are perceived as instruments of class domination. From this perspective, the world capitalist economy was brought about by the use of force.

❖ The second Giddens calls 'international relations'. In this perspective, states are viewed as social actors, with their own intentions and ways of behaving. Unlike the Marxist analysis, in the 'international relations' perspective, internal struggles within states are not regarded as significant.

Giddens rejects both of these perspectives. In his view, the world system has been influenced by several primary sets of processes: '... associated with the nation state system, coordinated through global networks of information exchange, the world capitalist economy and the world military order' (Giddens 1985, p. 290).

Nation states do appear to be like human individuals, because in the modern world they have become 'bounded administrative unities'. All states reflexively negotiate with each other. However, the human qualities of the modern nation state have to be explained by looking at the internal characteristics of states. For Giddens, the human qualities of nation states can not be treated as 'given'. They are created via a process of *structuration*: individual people, as human agents, create the structures of the world that we live in. These in turn develop a rule-like nature and affect the way we behave in the future.

In *The Nation State and Violence* (1985) Giddens explains that both the traditional imperialist state – such as the Ottoman Empire – and tribal societies, have either become assimilated into more global units or have disappeared altogether. This is because of two processes:

❖ the global incorporation of industrial capitalism

❖ the global domination of the nation state.

In Focus
◆
Giddens on the world system

The world system is characterized by Giddens as a transfer of the four institutional clusterings of modernity:

❖ industrialized economy

❖ capitalistic production

❖ political integration

❖ military rule.

These are linked to the global setting, in the way shown below.

So, modernity for Giddens is essentially 'globalizing' in nature but as he explains:

'Globalization is not a single process but a complex mixture of processes, which often act in contradictory ways, producing conflicts, disjunctions and new forms of stratification. Thus, for instance, the revival of local nationalisms, and an accentuating of local identities, are directly bound up with globalizing influences, to which they stand in opposition.' (Giddens 1994, p. 5)

❖ symbolic orders/modes of discourse ⏩	global information systems
❖ political institutions ⏩	nation-state system
❖ economic institutions ⏩	world capitalist economy
❖ law/modes of sanction ⏩	world military order

❖ Activity 16 ❖

For Giddens, globalization can bring about a local reaction, in which people are opposed to the way in which local cultures are destroyed.

Think of your local culture, would you prefer:

- a drink that was produced locally or a coke?
- a television programme produced locally or an American film or television programme?
- local folk music or some international superstar?

Do your answers to the above questions support or detract from Giddens' argument? Give reasons for your answer.

For Giddens, globalization consists of a large number of linkages and interconnections that exceed or transcend individual nation states. Globalization explains a process by which circumstances, opinions and actions in one part of the world can have important consequences for individuals and communities in quite distant parts of the world, a point which Giddens and colleagues expand in *Reflexive Modernisation* (Giddens *et al.* 1994).

Globalization then, involves more 'than a diffusion of Western institutions across the world, in which other cultures are crushed'. It involves 'a process of uneven development that fragments as it coordinates' (Giddens 1990, p. 175). The major

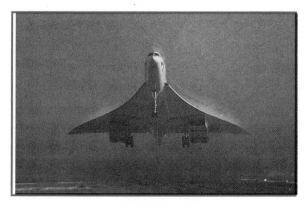

Concorde: helping to compress the world

feature of globalization for Giddens is the compression of the world. This is the profound reordering of time and space in social life, what Giddens terms 'time-space distanciation'.

Time–space distanciation

One of the central concerns for Giddens in his theory of structuration is with how social systems *bind* time and space. In Giddens' view, the 'problem of order' is the problem of time. His key concept is 'time–space distanciation', which is the condition by which society is 'stretched' across lengths of time and space. In simple societies, there is a low level of time-space distanciation, as almost all communication is face to face; little if any interaction takes place with people who are physically separated. Any time-consciousness that does exist is maintained by tradition. Kin relationships maintain a link between the living and dead. In modern societies, individuals interact with each other often over great distances of both time and space.

Moreover, in modern societies time becomes 'commodified' time, that is time of a measured duration with distinct differences between work time and non-work time. Giddens argues that the emergence of a distinct linear time-consciousness, with time moving in a progressive fashion from one point away to another, probably has its origins in the development of writing, which gave people the opportunity to organize their activities and have them organized. This is how we experience the day – individuals making their way through 'time space paths' of work time and non-work time. For Giddens, the control of time is a major resource in the structures of power and domination.

Beck's risk society

Both individualization and globalization are tendencies important for the reflexive project of self. For Ulrich Beck, *reflexive* in this sense means 'self-confrontation', rather than reflection. Individuals are expected: '... to live with a broad variety of different, mutually contradictory, global and personal risks' (Beck 1994 , p. 7). This means that we as individuals have to recognize the unpredictability of the modern world. In order to cope with these 'risky opportunities', the self becomes fragmented into a number of 'contradictory discourses' of the self. Modernity, as a social form, was brought about by the success of capitalism, which has changed industrial society into a much more radicalized form of modernity, which Beck terms 'the risk society'.

Ulrich Beck, therefore, argues that we are in transition from an industrial society to a risk society. This means that we are moving from a social situation in which political conflicts and divisions are based upon the distribution of an economic surplus to a situation in which conflicts are becoming defined by the attempts by people to avoid the distribution of hazards and risks.

The risk society is not a class society, as both rich and poor are subject to ecological risks. In place of the class vs class division of the industrial society, the risk society places sector in conflict with sector, with some sectors becoming 'risk winners', e.g. chemicals, biotechnology and the nuclear industry, while others may become 'risk losers', e.g. the food industry, tourism and fisheries. The risk society knows no national boundaries. For example, the effects of Chernobyl are said to have increased the number of cases of childhood leukemia in the North of England, although it is usually the poor, most notably in the Third World who are more likely to be adversely affected.

To summarize:

❖ 'Risks' become the most important principle of social organization; risk is becoming an essential element in the way we organize our society.

❖ 'Risks' take on a form which is incalculable, uncompensatable, unlimited and unaccountable.

This comes about because in such societies compensation is impossible. We are facing irreparable damage, while accountability for ecological catastrophes is limited because of the difficulty of enforcing the 'polluter pays' principle.

In Giddens' view, the transition from modernity to whatever is beyond is primarily brought about by new social movements.

The distinction between OSMs and NSMs

Unlike old social movements (OSMs), which tend to be class-based movements and focus on the state as the target for their collective activities, new social movements (NSMs) are said not to be class-based movements and not to direct their activities towards the state alone.

The distinction between OSMs and NSMs has been clearly outlined by Paul Bagguley (1995) . He explains that OSMs are influenced by economic factors which directly affect their members' future economic advancement, e.g. wages, job security and issues related to control at work. In contrast, NSMs are said to be 'post-materialist', concerned with issues that do not directly affect the members' economic position, such as peace, the environment and human rights. Alternatively, a significant number of NSMs are primarily concerned with what might be termed 'identity politics', issues about personal identity rather than ownership of the means of production. Gay and lesbian groups such as Stonewall or Outrage are examples.

The support for OSMs was mainly from working-class people; NSMs are said to be mainly drawn from the new middle classes, in particular from public sector white-collar employees. The organizational structures of the OSMs were built upon a central bureaucracy with a national committee structure. NSMs are built upon 'networks' which are largely informal, or *polycephalus* in nature, which means that they rely upon participation rather than representation. OSMs are motivated by influencing significant people who have been elected or by

laristic interests. This is because, universalistic interests rest upon grand narratives which postmodern writers have so strongly rejected. In contrast, Jürgen Habermas (1987) argues that the lifeworld, or world of lived experience, is in danger of being destroyed by the rational bureaucratic systems similar to those outlined by Weber, in his concept of rational-legal authority. This process of rationalization destroys local cultures and local processes of socialization. Habermas terms this invasion of local communities by processes of rationalization the 'colonization of the lifeworld'. NSMs fight back against this process in the interests of local communities everywhere.

influencing some group which is powerful within a corporate structure. In contrast, NSMs are concerned with direct action, often involving symbolic protests, such as climbing trees to prevent motorways from being built.

A key issue about new social movements (NSMs) is whether they express *particularistic* or *universalistic* values. In other words, do NSMs advance the values and interests of *small sections of the population* against the values and interests of the wider population? Or do they advance the cause of democracy and therefore improve the prospects for emancipation for *all oppressed groups* within the population?

Postmodernists, particularly, hold the view in favour of NSMs furthering particu-

Classification of NSMs: Mario Diani

Mario Diani has attempted to pull together much of the relevant research and theories in the area and to produce a clear view of the nature of the new social movements. Diani identifies four main trends within new social movement analysis:

1 *Collective behaviour approaches*, e.g. the work of Turner and Killian – They define a new social movement as 'a collectivity acting with some continuity to promote or resist a change in the society or organization of which it is part' (Diani 1992, p. 4). These groups do not have a clearly defined membership or leadership and their actions and views are determined by informal responses of the current supporters rather than by any formal management plan. In other words, this approach suggests that NSMs are networks of communication and action rather than formal organizations.

❖ Activity 17 ❖

Draw up a table in which you outline the characteristics of NSMs and compare them with the characteristics of OSMs.

In Focus

◆

Lifeworld

'Lifeworld' is a key term used mainly by phenomenological sociologists. It means 'the world of lived experience', the world we take for granted and understand through our everyday, common-sense assumptions that we share with others in our communities. You could describe 'lifeworld' as the assumptions you had about the world before starting to study sociology.

2 *Resource mobilization theory*, e.g. the work of Zald and McCarthy – They place much more attention on the role of the organizational factors within NSMs which they define as:

'... a set of opinions and beliefs which represents preferences for changing some elements of the social structure and/or reward distribution of a society. A counter movement is a set of opinions and beliefs in a population opposed to a social movement.' (McCarthy and Zald quoted in Diani 1992, p. 4)

This approach suggests that NSMs attempt to draw together resources in an effort to change some aspect of society.

3 *Political process approaches*, as in the work of Tilly – He associates the development of NSMs with the exclusion of individuals' interests from the established political processes and political channels. NSMs are a product of social unrest amongst people with a shared identity who are ignored by traditional political parties. He defined NSMs as a:

'... sustained series of interactions between power holders and persons successfully claiming to speak on behalf of a constituency lacking formal representation, in the course of which those persons make publicly visible demands for changes in the distribution or exercise of power, and back those demands with public demonstrations of support.' (Tilly quoted in Diani 1992, p. 5)

In other words, this approach suggests that NSMs are groups which are made up of individuals who are ignored by the major political parties.

4 *New social movement approaches*, as in the work of both Touraine and Melucci – This approach attempts to link the rise of NSMs to wider structural and cultural changes within society. NSMs emerge as a consequence of the new contradictions which replace the class conflict – between the bourgeoisie and the proletariat – that we find with modern, organized capitalism, as this form of society gives way to a post-industrial society. Touraine views the NSM as a: 'combination of a principle of identity, a principle of opposition and a principle of totality' (Touraine quoted in Diani 1992, p. 6). In other words, in the post-industrial society, individual people develop their own view of the world, their rivals and the winnings that can be gained from any conflict. NSMs are a product of the rise of a post-industrial society.

In summary, for Mario Diani a new social movement is not an organization, but is:

❖ a network of informal interaction involving links between a number of individuals, groups and organizations

❖ a form of solidarity built upon shared beliefs

❖ a form of collective action outside the traditional political institutions, promoting or resisting social change

❖ a basis for a collective identity.

If new social movements are not class-based movements, then what holds the group together? According to Julian McAllister-Groves, NSMs are held together by emotional factors.

New social movements: emotional recruitment

There is an emotional aspect to NSM recruitment which we do not find in the recruitment to class-based movements or traditional political parties. McAllister-Groves outlines what he calls the 'emotions approach to social movement recruitment'. Traditionally, it was asserted by functionalists such as Neil Smelser (1963), that people joined social movements because they had a grievance, brought about by some form of frustration, relative deprivation or other psychological condition caused by 'strains' within the social system. In contrast, McAllister-Groves explains that the most recent contributions to understanding NSM recruitment builds upon the work of Erving Goffman, and is concerned with how NSMs attract people to their cause by 'framing'.

What is 'framing'?

Goffman's book *Frame Analysis: An Essay on the Organization of Experience* (1974) is concerned with how people make sense of their personal experiences, as Goffman explained:

> 'I assume that definitions of the situation are built up in accordance with principles of organization which govern events – at least social ones – and our subjective involvement in them; frame is the word I use to refer to such of these basic elements as I am able to identify. That is the definition of frame. My phrase 'frame analysis' is a slogan to refer to the examination in these terms of the organization of experience.' (Goffman 1974, pp. 10–11)

Definitions of the situation can be viewed as informal rules or ways of behaving within a group; 'frameworks' are viewed as *schemata of interpretation*, organizing principles that people use to give their life and actions meaning. In some cases, such organizing principles have no apparent shape, but all provide the individual and the group with a perspective. The frame not only organizes meaning for the individual, it also helps to organize involvement. NSMs therefore are involved in 'constructing sets of beliefs that encourage potential recruits to act because their beliefs appeal to them' (McAllister-Groves 1995, p. 436).

McAllister-Groves goes on to explain that NSMs:

- ❖ are involved in providing a code that characterizes which emotions are common and acceptable for an ordinary person in any given situation
- ❖ clarify and brand sentiments according to the NSMs' own cultural categories
- ❖ provide a place to avoid 'emotional deviance'.

'The animal rights activists that I studied experienced affection and empathy for the animals portrayed in animal rights literature as helpless victims of cruelty.

Most of them, however, were attracted to the movement because of its ability to legitimate their affection and empathy for animals in a way that reduced difficult interactions with outsiders who viewed them as being too emotional and therefore irrational.' (McAllister-Groves 1995, p. 438)

This was particularly true for men who joined NSMs who are said to be embarrassed and unwilling to show emotion outside such a group. In other words, the NSM provided people, both male and female, with a legitimate opportunity to share their emotions about an issue with other, like-minded people. Such shows of emotion to non-activists would make a person feel great embarrassment or 'emotional deviance'.

In contrast to this emotional position, Day and Robbins suggest that middle-class people who joined CND and the Peace Movement in the 1980s did so, not out of any emotional attachment to 'peace', but out of economic self-interest. As they explain:

> 'The mobilization of welfare professionals must be seen in the context of the crises of social democracy and the sharpening of conflicts within the British state, between its repressive and productive arms. There has been a shift of resources from welfare services to the police and the military, and an accompanying tendency to legitimate the role of the state in terms of 'law and order' rather than social welfare. In the face of this material and ideological threat it is hardly surprising that the Peace Movement provides an avenue of mobilization that is particularly attractive to members of the caring professions.' (Day and Robbins 1987, p. 232)

In other words, for Day and Robbins, the rise of NSMs is seen as directly linked to the economic interests of their members; the activity of the peace movement can be viewed as a form of institutionalized class action.

Table 13.3 A simple categorization of NSMs

1. Movements which are principally organized to promote the defence of a natural or social environment that is perceived to be under threat.

   Examples:
   - animal rights groups
   - environmental groups
   - anti-nuclear groups

2. Movements which are organized for the purpose of extending the provision of social rights to constituencies in society where the state is seen as denying, limiting or repressing them.

   Examples:
   - feminist movements
   - anti-racist movements
   - gay and lesbian rights movements
   - civil rights organizations

❖ Activity 18 ❖

In your view, did people join the peace movement for 'emotional' reasons or did people join the peace movement to defend their economic interests?

In comparison, postmodernists who take an interest in NSMs, point to the variety of skirmishes and conflicts in the world which have little or no direct relationship to class divisions. They also point to the rich diversity of groupings that are attempting to impose their own view of how to organize society upon us all. As Paul Bagguley suggests:

> 'New social movements have been characterized as postmodern because they reject modernist political discourses and class identities.' (Bagguley 1995, p. 606)

According to Alain Touraine (1992), people are involved with a new social movement if they clearly characterize:

- ❖ an adversary – something or somebody they are in conflict with
- ❖ the prize of the struggle – arguments not just over different ways of solving the problem

- ❖ the actors themselves – in whose name they are fighting.

The views of the participants in these movements, on issues such as the nature and distribution of power, have a great deal in common with postmodern issues and concerns. New social movements are said to enhance participatory pluralistic democracy. As Boris Frankel (1994) has commented, the theory of new social movements is said to replace class theory and class politics, as new social movements are concerned with issues that affect all social classes and draw members and supporters from all social classes. These movements are seen as the carriers of future social change.

Modern states are shaped by new social movements which operate with all four of the dimensions of modernity that Giddens outlines. In his analysis, social movements have a key role to play in the transition from 'reflexive modernity' to 'postmodernity'. However, unlike most of the writers who consider the nature of postmodernity, Giddens views postmodernity as a form of 'utopian realism'. It is at the far side of modernity and has institutional dimensions which have been changed by the activities of social movements. Not only do social movements have opportunities to exercise countervailing powers within society, but their activities have moved the 'overall trajectory of development of modernity'

(Giddens 1992, p. 59) towards a 'radical democratization' within which all people have greater opportunities to exercise power within society. Giddens provides us with a 'conceptual map' in which social movements are placed within the four dimensions of modernity, and are actively engaged in forms of struggle with the institutions that operate there. Social movements attempt to enhance the citizenship rights of individuals within each of the dimensions of modernity, and bring about significant change.

In the 1990s, Giddens has argued that NSMs have important democratic qualities: they 'open up spaces for public dialogue in respect of the issues with which they are concerned' (Giddens 1994, p. 17). NSMs give people opportunities to discuss issues which were undiscussed by traditional political parties, including such issues as how people live their lives and the choices they make about any activity they choose to be involved in. As we suggested above, Giddens refers to this as *dialogic democracy* – an attempt by people to talk to each other in an effort to create active trust with others in order to further what Giddens calls *life politics*, the politics of self-actualization or self-creation. However, along with many other writers, Giddens argues that NSMs cannot be viewed as 'socialist' in nature. In contrast to the class-based issues of socialism, NSMs '... have a deep involvement ... with the arenas of emotional democracy in personal life' (Giddens 1994, p. 121). See *In Focus* below for a more detailed exposition of Giddens' views of new social movements.

In Focus

Giddens on new social movements

'New forms of social movement mark an attempt at a collective reappropriation of institutionally repressed areas of life. Recent religious movements have to be numbered among these, although of course there is great variability in the sects and cults which have developed. But several other new social movements are particularly important and mark sustained reactions to basic institutional dimensions of modern social life. Although – and in some part because – it addresses questions which antedate the impact of modernity, the feminist movement is one major example. In its early phase, the movement was pre-eminently concerned with securing equal political and social rights between women and men. In its current stage, however, it addresses elemental features of existence and creates pressures towards social transformations of a radical nature. The ecological and peace movements are also part of this new sensibility to late modernity, as are some kinds of movements for human rights. Such movements, internally diverse as they are, effectively challenge some of the basic presuppositions and organizing principles which fuel modernity's juggernaut.' (Giddens 1991, pp. 208–9)

'New social movements cannot readily be claimed for socialism. While the aspirations of some such movements stand close to socialist ideals, their objectives are disparate and sometimes actively opposed to one another. With the possible exception of some sections of the green movement, the new social movements are not 'totalizing' in the way socialism is (or was), promising a new 'stage' of social development beyond the existing order. Some versions of feminist thought, for example, are as radical as anything that went under the name of socialism. Yet they don't envisage seizing control of the future in the way the more ambitious versions of socialism have done.' (Giddens 1994, p. 3)

Table 13.4 From modernity to postmodernity

Institutional complexes of modernity	Types of social movement	Objectives of new order	Institutional elements 'beyond modernity'
Capitalism	labour	socialized economic organization	postscarcity system
Industrialism	ecological (counter-cultural)	system of planetary care	humanization of technology
Administrative power	civil and human rights	coordinated global order	multilayered democratic participation
Military power	peace	transcendence of war	demilitarization

Source: Held (1992, p. 34)

David Held makes a number of critical points about Giddens' analysis of new social movements. In particular, Held suggests that a number of social movements are excluded from Giddens' analysis, notably the feminist movement and religious groups. According to Held these groups: '... have no role in Giddens's scheme suggesting ... that his conceptual framework may not make adequate allowance for some of the key pressure points in contemporary culture and politics' (Held 1992, p. 37). However, in his book *The Nation State and Violence* (1985), Giddens does discuss both the women's movement and religious movements. He explains that these movements can still be placed upon his 'conceptual map' or 'scheme', because these groups are concerned with the expansion of democratic rights, and therefore, clearly concerned with issues of surveillance and governability.

From emancipatory politics to life politics

'Life politics is a politics, not of life chances, but of life style. It concerns disputes and struggles about how (as individuals and as collective humanity) we should live in a world where what used to be fixed either by nature or tradition is now subject to human decisions.' (Giddens 1994, pp. 14–15)

Life politics emerges from emancipatory politics and is the politics of self-actualization. In other words, life politics 'concerns debates and contestations deriving from the reflexive project of the self' (Giddens 1991, p. 215). Emancipatory politics has two main elements:

❖ an effort to break free from the shackles of the past

❖ overcoming illegitimate domination, which adversely affects the life chances of individuals.

Moreover, as we have suggested, its central principle is that of enhancing personal independence, by moving away from all forms of exploitation, inequality and oppression, while promoting justice, equality and participation. Ultimately, individuals have greater control over their own circumstances. Life politics recognizes that nation states have very limited effectiveness in areas which are significant to individuals. Giddens gives the example of IVF research or nuclear power. If any nation state were to ban research in these areas, it would have limited significance on global scientific developments.

Giddens adopts a rather optimistic view of these issues which emerge with globalization:

'Unpredictability, manufactured uncertainty, fragmentation: these are only one side of the coin of a globalizing order. On the reverse side are the shared values that come from a situation of global interdependence, organized via the cosmopolitan acceptance of difference.' (Giddens 1994, p. 253)

As suggested above, by 'manufactured uncertainty', Giddens means uncertainties created by people which have no real precedents, e.g. global warming or nuclear power.

❖ **Activity 19** ❖

1 Why does Giddens believe that NSMs are not socialist in nature? Write a paragraph in which you make use of his notion of life politics and his notion of dialogic democracy.

2 Would you suggest the NSMs in Giddens' view have particular or universal motives? Suggest a number of reasons for your answer.

❖ **Activity 20** ❖

Spend a few minutes thinking about the following questions. If possible, discuss them with other sociology students:

1 What do you think Giddens understands by 'community'?

2 According to Giddens, individuals seek a 'pure relationship' and this could provide the model for a new form of solidarity which he terms 'dialogic democracy'. Does Giddens' notion of solidarity based upon 'dialogic democracy' rest upon a solid ethical or sociological basis?

Communitarianism

'What was strong then is fragile now.'

Tony Blair, Labour Party Conference 1996

'I feel your pain.'

Bill Clinton, elected US President in 1992 and 1996

In an effort to make the world a more certain place, a number of politicians (e.g. in Britain, Tony Blair and David Willits and in the United States, Al Gore and Jack Kemp) have attempted to develop an approach to politics which enhances the bonds of community. This is known as *communitarianism*.

In Britain, the Labour Party moved towards a much more 'communitarian' stance under the leadership of Tony Blair. This is most clearly seen in the change made to Clause Four of the Labour Party Constitution which, before Blair's leadership, committed the party to public ownership. Communitarianism is said to be neither left-wing nor right-wing in nature. It is concerned with the responsibility of the individual to the community. Most notably, the community should become a 'stake-holder' in all its children. At the moment, the decision to have a child is a highly personal act, of no concern to anyone other than the prospective parents. In addition, in recent years divorce laws have become more liberal, making divorce much easier to obtain. Add to this the fact that in the 1990s, parents have to spend much more time at work, then for communitarians, the consequence is that many parents neglect their duties as parents. This argument has been most fully developed by the sociologist Amitai Etzioni.

According to Etzioni, communitarianism:

'[is] dedicated to the betterment of our moral, social and political environment ... and [is] dedicated to working with ... fellow citizens to bring about the changes in values, habits, and public policies that will allow us to do for society what the environmental movement seeks to do for nature: to safeguard and enhance our future.' (Etzioni 1993, pp. 2–4)

Sociologically, the notion of communitarianism can be seen as an attempt to rebuild the idea of 'the community' within a postmodern world where cultures appear to be fragmented, where individuals can select identities and where ideas of belonging to a neighbourhood are not accepted without question.

We could argue that both Etzioni and Giddens make impractical assumptions about the character of moral and ethical ideals within a society. In contrast, postmodern individuals have no sense of community.

In addition, both Etzioni and Giddens assume that 'the self' or the 'human agent' is a unified whole – that people have one solid identity and are clear about their role in the world and their place within it. In the postmodern condition, political identity is often multiple, fragile and incomplete. How such postmodern or reflexive selves could form a political community is problematic. Giddens and Etzioni are unclear as to what the bonds are that bind people together into such communities. Tony Blair himself has argued that his account of communitarianism has been in large part affected by the philosopher John Macmurray (1961), with whom Blair first came into contact during his time at Oxford University.

In Focus
◆
Communitarianism

'By and large, citizens like the idea of the welfare state to be there if they fall on hard times. But, increasingly, governments everywhere are realizing that the public purse cannot afford it at present levels.

Right-wingers say that health, education and social security should be cut because they induce a dependency culture and sap individual initiative. But social ills are not merely the product of moral turpitude. Left-wingers say that if unemployment were reduced then governments would have extra taxation income to pay for existing levels of payments. But nobody is simply a helpless victim – everybody has some contribution to make.

A midway position is quite possible, however. Some services now provided by the welfare state should and could be undertaken by people on their own. At the same time, society must continue to share the burdens.

Communitarians propose a principle of subsidiary in which the primary responsibility belongs to the individuals nearest the problem; if a solution cannot be found, then the responsibility moves to the family; if there is still no solution, then to the community; then and only then, when no solution is possible at all, should the state be involved.'

Source: Habitats-mini articles 1997

Both Etzioni and Giddens assume that in the postmodern world individuals are privatized. In other words, individuals break from traditional working-class or middle-class outlooks, lose their traditional attitudes and loyalties and are motivated by developing life styles for themselves which they find satisfying, unhindered by any notion of morality.

Are postmodern individuals irretrievably privatized?

John Macmurray

A community is a group of persons, each one a 'human agent' able of shaping some aspect of the world. For Macmurray, human beings should always think 'from the stand-point of action': when we carry out a social action, we bring about a change in the world and all social action involves choice. Before we make our choice, we have to take into account the possible repercussions of our actions, which will be either 'good' or 'bad'. This is important because action is unchangeable; we cannot undo a social action. To conduct oneself in a moral fashion involves doing 'good', while at the same time knowing that we have the freedom to act otherwise.

The agents who form a community are united in a common life, built upon common purpose, love and actions, motivated by thought for creating the common life:

'If we call the harmonious interrelation of agents their 'community', we may say that a morally right action is an action which intends community.' (Macmurray 1961, p. 119)

This consciousness is to be found in all personal associations within a community.

This interdependence of persons, for Macmurray, is the foundation for morality and has three modes:

❖ The *communal* mode – a 'positive' form of morality based upon actions which benefit others without benefiting oneself. This communal way of behaving reinforces the bonds of community. Therefore, to act in a communal way is regarded as 'good' because it involves actively bringing about a change for the better.

❖ The *contemplative* mode – a 'negative' mode of morality, based upon 'fitting in' to the ways of behaving which are seen as acceptable within the community. This contemplative mode is regarded as 'good' because it involves not acting in a way which may be seen to disadvantage the community.

❖ The *pragmatic* mode – based upon obedience or self-control. Individuals limit their own independence for the benefit of the community.

Clause Four of the Labour Party Constitution now states that:

'... by the strength of our common endeavour we achieve more than we achieve alone, so as to create for each of us the means to realize our true potential and for all of us a community in which power, wealth and opportunity are in the hands of the many, not the few, where the rights we enjoy reflect the duties we owe, and where we live together, freely, in a spirit of solidarity, tolerance and respect.'

Can you identify any communitarian assumptions within the new Clause Four?

'Amitai Etzioni's book *The Spirit of Community* ... says that about 20 years ago mothers did what men did: they ran away from their children by going out to get paid work. Their children were abandoned, as Etzioni puts it, to "the drinks cabinet and the television". ... But is it true?

We need to test the hypothesis. The most substantive work on what parents actually do in their everyday life has been researched in Britain by Jonathan Gershuny at the Centre for Micro-Social Research at Essex. Mapping, hour by hour, the activities of parenting and household responsibilities, he has come up with a very different picture from the one painted by Etzioni.

The work of parenting and housework has indeed changed. In 1961 women spent an average of 217 minutes a day and men 17 minutes a day on housework. In 1985 women spent 162 minutes a day and men something like double their previous figure – considerably more than they did, but considerably less than women.

The important thing here is the relationship between routine housework and routine parenting and *dedicated* parenting. How much time do parents spend eye-ball to eye-ball with their children? The average mother now with a full-time job spends more dedicated time with her children than the average homemaker of 30 years ago...

She may have been permanently present but she was also probably permanently "absent". Mothers were not people you played with or had conversations with. You played with and produced your culture with other children, your own generation... Parenting has indeed been refashioned... the kind of mother who is lodged in the nostalgic crusade of the communitarians didn't exist.'

Source: adapted from Campbell (1996)

❖ Activity 23 ❖

1 In your own words, write a paragraph which outlines Beatrix Campbell's critique of communitarianism.

2 The research which Campbell reviews on parenting provides us with information from 1961 and 1985. Discuss with other sociology students in your class what the current figures might be. This may involve recording how much time your parents or the parents of people you know spend on various activities including 'parenting'.

3 Do you agree that the 'normal' mother today has more 'dedicated time' with her children than parents in the past?

Although we looked at the nature of communitarianism and some of the criticisms of it, it is worth looking at the evaluation of Etzioni's work by Richard Sennett.

Sennett (1997) views communitarians as trying to keep a balance between individual rights and coercive conservatism, described through the metaphor of trying to ride a bicycle. In his review of Etzioni's *The New Golden Rule*, Sennett argues that:

'[Etzioni] ... thinks the "moral infrastructure" of society resembles a "Chinese nesting box" beginning with families, around which there are schools, then communities proper ("peer groups, voluntary associations, places of worship, community spaces") and, the biggest box of all, "the community of communities" (society at large). Everything falls nicely into place: strong family values are necessary to behave well in schools, firm rules in school make for sociable adults, and sociable adults make for good citizens. Bicycling through the boxes (the mixed metaphor is inescapable), a human being helps soften the rigour of rules by communicating his or her needs for autonomy, while the selfish or egoistic propensities of the self are softened by group firmness.' (Sennett 1997, p. 3)

Sennett goes on to make a number of critical points about Etzioni's work:

❖ There is no discussion of either political or economic power.

❖ Etzioni ignores Durkheim's argument that 'the stronger the social interaction between people, the more differentiated they become; shared values are easier for people who have a cooler, more distant relation to one another'.

❖ Bonds are often created by people who do not share the same values.

❖ Etzioni 'wants more agreement on "core" values without discouraging disagreement'.

❖ Etzioni's work does not adequately deal with 'commitment'.

❖ Activity 24 ❖

According to Richard Sennett: '... people may fall off their bikes for the sake of their beliefs' (Sennett 1997, p.3).

What do you think Sennett means by this critical remark about communitarianism?

 Voting behaviour

Table 13.5 Votes recorded in parliamentary general elections: by party, 1979–1992

	Votes recorded by party (%)			
	General election 3 May 1979	General election 6 June 1983	General election 11 June 1987	General election 10 April 1992
Conservative	43.9	42.4	42.3	41.8
Labour	36.9	27.6	30.8	35.2
Liberal Democrats	13.8	13.7	12.8	17.0
SDP	—	11.6	9.7	—
Plaid Cymru	0.4	0.4	0.4	0.4
Scottish National Party	1.6	1.1	1.3	1.9
Northern Ireland Parties	2.2	2.5	2.2	2.1
Green Party	0.1	0.2	0.3	0.6
Others	1.1	0.5	0.2	1.1
Turnout (%)	**76.1**	**72.7**	**75.3**	**76.3**
All (000s)	**31,221**	**30,671**	**32,530**	**33,275**

Source: Social Trends (1996)

As Johnston *et al.* make clear in *A Nation Dividing* (1988):

'People are socialized into particular sets of political attitudes that reflect their occupational class origins and local contexts within which they learn the political meanings of their class positions. This produces the general pattern of voting by occupational class that is known as the class cleavage. That cleavage is far from complete, because of a variety of other influences, but it remains the single most important influence on the development of political attitudes and the identification of voters with particular political parties that follows.' (Johnston *et al.* 1988, p. 269)

For many political scientists, the era 1945 to 1970 was one of two-party supremacy and class voting. However, since 1970 there has been escalating electoral volatility and, above all, class dealignment. The connection between an individual's social-class position and voting intention, based traditionally on working-class people voting Labour and middle-class people voting Conservative, has been broken. With class dealignment, class-based voting was said to be steadfastly breaking down. Indeed, by 1983 social class could 'correctly' be used to predict the votes of less than half of the British electorate. Voters were said to be leaving the 'natural' political party of their class.

For Ivor Crewe (1992), transformation of the social structure, and the growth of a 'new' working class, associated with the growth of working-class home ownership, produced a declining class consciousness. Working-class people were losing the taste for class-based politics.

More working-class people were finding themselves under cross-class tensions because they had diverse class character-istics. For example, home owners with manual occupations had children with ambitions to study at university. According to Ivor Crewe, this 'new' working class was likely to expand in future years. In Crewe's view, since 1970, the party choices of

working-class people have become more closely associated with their positions on a range of issues. As we shall discuss below, voters are now said to be *rational voters*. Individuals use their vote in the same way that consumers use their money in the supermarket: to get maximum benefit for minimum cost.

However, some criticism can be made of the way in which Crewe defines social class, which is called the 'social grade schema'. The origins of the social grade schema are found in the Annual Report of the Registrar General (1911) which consisted of five hierarchical grades. Under the influence of Research Services Limited in the 1950s, this was modified into a six-fold catego-rization of occupations (A, B, C1, C2, D, and E). The categories ran from unskilled manual workers in group E, to professionals in group A. This way of defining 'class' takes the family as its unit of analysis, not the individual; the occupation of the head of household is used as the indicator of the class position of all family members. This is a respectful way of saying that the social grade schema disregards women, presuming that all people in the household have the same social class position as the oldest male. Not only is this sexist, but it ignores the fact that, according to Marshall *et al.* (1988), up to 50 per cent of people live in cross-class marriages. In other words, half of married people have a spouse with an occupation in a different social class.

No valid sociological research has been conducted to show whether Crewe's conception of class reflects the structure of classes in society. Critics could call them 'arbitrary market research categories', rather than a class system. Outside the area of voting behaviour, the social grade schema is not used by any reputable social scientist (see Chapter 6).

Political scientists who make use of the social grade schema have left themselves open to the allegation that the class dealignment thesis is a product of attempts to measure the relationship between voting and class with defective measurement

Table 13.6 Voting behaviour of the 'new' and 'traditional' working class, 1992

The new working-class voter

	Lives in South	Owner-occupier	Non-union member	Works in private sector
Conservative	40%	40%	37%	32%
Labour	38%	41%	46%	50%
Liberal Democrat	23%	19%	17%	18%
Majority in 1992	Con + 2%	Lab + 1%	Lab + 9%	Lab +18%
Majority in 1987	Con + 18%	Con + 12%	Con +2%	Lab +1%
Swing to Labour 1987 to 1992	+ 8%	+ 6.5%	+5.5%	+ 8.5%

The traditional working-class voter

	Lives in Scotland or North	Council tenant	Union member	Works in public sector
Conservative	26%	22%	29%	36%
Labour	59%	64%	55%	48%
Liberal Democrat	15%	13%	16%	16%
Majority in 1992	Lab + 33%	Lab + 42%	Lab + 26%	Lab +12%
Majority in 1987	Lab + 28%	Lab + 32%	Lab +18%	Lab +17%
Swing to Labour 1987 to 1992	+ 2.5%	+ 5%	+ 4%	− 2.5% (to Con)

Source: Crewe (1992)

devices. However, Ivor Crewe's view that people no longer vote on the basis of social class, but on the basis of 'issues', is now the accepted view within the social sciences.

One problem for this type of rational analysis is in trying to explain why people vote for parties when it is not in their economic benefit to do so. For example, why do working-class people vote Conservative when that party has a policy of raising money from VAT rather than income tax?

Another significant issue with this type of investigation is *rational abstention*. In other words, the rational voter will understand that the significance of one vote is very small, and the cost of going to vote will always exceed the advantage gained from voting. In other words, it is always rational for the rational voter *not to vote*. One vote will not determine the outcome of an election and it is rational to let other people bear the cost of voting.

In the 1980s, Heath *et al.* (1985, 1991) carried out the British Election Surveys and attempted to demonstrate that social class continued to be the most significant determinant in explaining how people vote. Taking their starting point from the research of John Goldthorpe (1980), they redefined social class and asserted that the working class made up about 34 per cent of the

In Focus

◆

Assumptions on which the issue voting model is built

We might want to cast doubt upon some of the assumptions upon which 'issue voting' models are based. It is assumed that the issue voter is a rational voter, who attempts to get maximum personal benefit for minimum cost. In other words, the rational voter is a 'rational utility maximizer'. According to Anthony Downes (1957), rational individuals have a number of characteristics:

❖ A person can always make a decision when given a range of alternatives.

❖ A person can rank alternatives in order of preference.

❖ The preferences are logically consistent.

❖ The choice is always from the highest preference available.

❖ The person will always make the same decision when confronted with the same alternatives.

---

electorate. In addition, they made an important separation between two forms of class voting: *absolute class voting* and *relative class voting*.

❖ Absolute class voting is the total number of working-class people voting Labour, and this declined at each election from 1964 to 1983, with a slight increase in 1987, 1992 and 1997.

❖ Relative class voting is the strength of Labour support within the working class.

Absolute class voting has decreased, but relative class voting has shown 'trendless fluctuation'. This is because the sum total of people who could be called 'working-class' is getting smaller at each election. However, the remaining working-class people remain loyal to Labour. Heath *et al.* argue that this means there has been no significant class dealignment taking place.

All of the theories of voting behaviour assume that people are pushed about by forces outside their control, e.g. by social class factors or rationality. If we accept that individuals live within a postmodern condition, then we could argue that people's behaviour is not determined; voting is rather a question of personal, non-rational and total choice.

Women in politics

'Women are notably absent from what is conventionally seen as 'politics' in Britain … Women are assumed to be less able at carrying out political tasks than men and less interested in politics.' (Abbott and Wallace 1990, p. 184)

In the formal political arena, few political positions are occupied by women. In 1979 Margaret Thatcher became the first female prime minister, but during her period of office there were no female cabinet members. In John Major's 1997 cabinet of 24 members, there were just two women. Feminist sociologists have put forward a number of explanations for this situation:

❖ Women's traditional domestic responsibilities mean that they have less time than men to participate in formal political activities. Political institutions have been organized for the convenience of men – working hours give little regard for the needs of women members.

❖ Traditionally, politics has been dominated by men and male patterns of behaviour. The 'old boy' network has discouraged and disadvantaged women (the House of Commons has been described as 'the best men's club in Europe').

❖ 'Female' issues such as childcare facilities and care of elderly relatives are given little air time, and many women are left feeling that the political agenda is set by men and for men.

However, women are becoming more active in politics as the barriers to their participation are gradually dismantled.

Making it in a man's world: Glenda Jackson, Virginia Bottomley, front bench spokeswomen for, respectively, the Labour and Conservative parties

Table 13.7   Women's participation in parliamentary politics

	Candidates (%)	MPs (%)
Conservative		
1979	5.0	2.3
1983	6.3	3.3
1987	7.3	4.5
1992	9.8	6.0
Labour		
1979	8.3	4.1
1983	12.3	4.8
1987	14.5	9.2
1992	21.3	13.0

Source: adapted from Lovenduski and Randall (1993, p.156)

It would appear that more recent research demonstrates an increasing participation of women. Table 13.7 shows an increase in the number of women MPs in both the major parties from 1979 to 1992. Lovenduski and Randall (1993) argue that women are increasingly participating in

❖ Activity 25 ❖

1   Table 13.7 compares the percentage of woman candidates and MPs in the Conservative and Labour parties over a period of time. What explanations could you provide for the differences between the percentage of prospective candidates and actual MPs in 1992?

2   Compare the percentage of women MPs in the UK with the percentage in other Western European countries, as shown in Table 13.8. What explanations can you provide for the relatively low percentage of women MPs in the United Kingdom compared to Finland and Sweden?

In Focus

◆

Female MPs

Emma Nicholson, a Liberal Democrat MP up to 1997, argued that Parliament needs to do more to accommodate women's commitments to family life: 'In order to attract more women, there will have to be an improvement in the hours, so that work does not demolish family life, and a more welcoming approach from the men instead of sexist comments.'

Labour MP, Janet Anderson won her seat in 1992. She had fought for six years to win a seat and has three children. In order to finance her struggle to become an MP, she had to take out a second mortgage. 'Money is the biggest hurdle for female candidates. It is for men, too. But women have to think about getting childcare and cleaning, and are more concerned about using valuable housekeeping money for travel expenses and accommodation', she says.

Source: adapted from Roberts (1995)

Table 13.8 Proportion of women MPs, 1992

	Women MPs(%)
Finland	38.5
Sweden	38.0
Norway	35.8
Denmark	32.9
Netherlands	26.0
Germany	25.9
Switzerland	13.4
Italy	12.9
Eire	8.4
United Kingdom	6.8
Belgium	5.7
France	5.7

Source: The Independent, 17 March 1992

or 5.9 per cent of the total population of England and Wales. Despite this, only six black or Asian MPs were elected to parliament in 1992, i.e. less than one per cent of MPs. Before 1987 there had not been a black MP since 1924. The ethnic minorities are better represented in local government, where there are around 350 ethnic minority councillors out of a total of just over 21,000. As with MPs, most of these councillors are in London (57 per cent as opposed to an ethnic minority population of 40 per cent in London).

❖ **Activity 26** ❖

1 Find out how many MPs from black and ethnic minorities were elected to Parliament at the 1997 general election.

2 What sociological explanation can you give for the under-representation of black MPs in Parliament?

traditional political institutions, partly because the barriers to participation in political parties and trade unions have declined. A contributory factor is the success of the women's movement in campaigning for the removal of barriers such as the timing and location of meetings.

Ethnicity and politics

According to the 1991 census, the ethnic minority population is just over 3 million,

Table 13.9 MPs from ethnic minorities, 1992–97

Name	Constituency	Party	Elected
Diane Abbott	Hackney North & Stoke Newington	Labour	1987
Paul Boateng	Brent South	Labour	1987
Nirj Deva	Brentford & Isleworth	Conservative	1992
Bernie Grant	Tottenham	Labour	1987
Piara Khabra	Ealing Southall	Labour	1992
Keith Vaz	Leicester East	Labour	1987

Paul Boateng

Diane Abbott

The role of the media

We suggested earlier that voters' party loyalty is not as strong today as it was in the past and that a significant proportion of the electorate can be influenced to change its vote. In this respect, the influence of the mass media has been seen as important, particularly during election campaigns. In the 1992 general election, the *Sun* (the newspaper with the largest circulation in Britain) firmly backed the Conservative campaign of John Major and on the day following the Conservative victory led with the headline: 'It's the Sun wot won it!' On 17 March 1997, the day on which the date of the 1997 election was announced, the *Sun* declared that it was backing the Labour leader, Tony Blair. This was seen as a great coup by the Labour Party, but, as seen in Chapter 12, *Mass media*, there are many variables which intervene between the media and its audience. The role and influence of the media are dealt with fully in that chapter.

Chapter summary

❖ Modernity is said to be giving way to a *postmodern* condition, in which there are no *grand narratives*, such as socialism or feminism, and no enforced identity.

❖ The postmodern condition undermines traditional theories of power because they undervalue the role of the individual human agent, and assume that individuals are pushed about by forces beyond their control.

❖ Within the postmodern condition there is a 'new' politics, which is uncertain and based on issues of identity which individual people often construct within new social movements.

❖ Politics within the postmodern condition can be very cruel and often tribal in nature. This form of politics has been described as *neo-medieval*.

❖ Anthony Giddens argues that we do not yet live in a postmodern society, but within a 'reflexive modernity', in which there has been a shift from 'emancipatory politics' to 'life politics'. The self is highly reflexive and involved in a 'dialogic democracy', which is similar to the 'pure' relationship, a love relationship based upon trust between equals.

❖ In Giddens' analysis, all nation states have a tendency towards 'polyarchy'. The nation state is diminishing in significance because of processes of globalization compressing both time and space.

❖ Giddens' analysis shares a great deal in common with the analysis of Ulrich Beck who argues that 'reflexive modernization' is part of a 'risk society'.

❖ According to Giddens and Beck, social class has declined in significance with people joining *new social movements*, in which the bonds are emotional rather than economic.

❖ In order to resolve many of the problems of the 'new' politics, a number of politicians have suggested that politics should become *communitarian* in nature.

❖ The postmodern condition undermines theories of voting which assume that voters are *rational* and undermines *class-based voting*. These theories play down the role of the individual human agent and assume that people are pushed about by forces beyond their control, such as rationality and class.

Essay questions

1 Critically examine the usefulness of pluralist theories to an understanding of the relationship between power and the state in modern societies. (AEB Summer 1994)

2 Evaluate the contribution of élite theory to an understanding of the nature and distribution of political power in Britain. (AEB Winter 1993)

3 Evaluate the claim made by some sociologists that there is a 'dominant ideology' in modern capitalist societies. (AEB Summer 1995)

4 Examine sociological contributions to an understanding of the ideological differences between political parties. (AEB Winter 1991)

5 Critically assess the argument put forward by the New Right that the role of the state in society should be minimal. (AEB Winter 1995)

6 To what extent do sociological evidence and arguments support the claim that there has been a realignment of voting behaviour in Britain? (AEB Summer 1994)

Coursework

Every community and locality has a 'politics' – you could research the politics of your city, town, village or neighbourhood.

There is clearly much more to politics than politicians on the television and the established political parties. You could investigate who makes the decisions which directly affect your life, your school or college or your street.

Select a decision which you feel has directly affected you and try to build up a case study of that decision:

❖ Who made the decision and why?

❖ What were the other options?

❖ Sociologically, what factors were significant in influencing the decision?

❖ Who benefited and who lost out because of that decision?

Another possibility is to examine a political conflict, which could be local, national or international. You could investigate the role, purpose and organization of a new social movement. For example, do NSMs in your locality favour 'direct action', such as climbing trees or hiding in tunnels in an effort to stop a road development from going forward? If not, why not? Is this form of direct action ever likely to be successful?

Such questions lend themselves to a variety of different research methods depending on your interests and expertise:

❖ a content analysis of local and national newspapers

❖ a series of interviews

❖ observations of local groups

❖ a participant observation.

How are 'newcomers' treated where you live? Is their treatment 'tribal' in any way? You could attempt to outline and evaluate the values of people in your neighbourhood who behave or think in a tribal fashion. Could this be an element of the postmodern condition?

Further reading

Kirby, M. (1995) *Investigating Political Sociology*, London: Collins Educational.

Best, S. (1997) *Power and Politics*, London: Macmillan.

Chapter 14

Religion

❖ Preview

In this chapter we shall be looking at:

- ❖ how sociologists have defined religion and how useful these definitions have been

- ❖ sociologists' attempts to assess the extent to which people are religious by asking them about their religious practice and their religious beliefs

- ❖ the variety of religious organizations including churches, denominations, sects and cults

- ❖ ways in which religion is involved in social change

- ❖ the debate about the decline in religion (called 'secularization') and the views of Durkheim, Marx, Weber and Freud on that process

- ❖ the development of new religious movements (NRMs) and how popular they are

- ❖ the growth of fundamentalism in both the religious and the political spheres

- ❖ issues surrounding gender and religion

- ❖ the roles that religions play in a multiracial society

- ❖ social functions of religion.

❖ Introduction

We live in a society in which there are religious people, rationalists who say that science has replaced religious belief and people who are indifferent to religion. Most sociologists recognize that the first group is declining in size and that this is largely due to an increase in indifference to religion. There are also tensions and disagreement between those who are religious and those who say they are not, for example, over issues like birth control, abortion and the validity of the theory of evolution.

In Focus

◆

The Butler Act

In the USA, the Butler Act forbade the teaching of the theory of evolution in publicly funded schools because it contradicted what the Bible said about creation. The Act was not repealed until 1967 and even now evolutionism can only be taught as a theory but not as a fact.

In addition, we can see that there are conflicts between religion and the state, for example, the criticisms which the Church of England's 'Faith in the City' initiative drew from politicians. All of this means that religion is an important issue for sociologists and one which can tell us a good deal about how societies work.

Bryan Turner (1983) argues that the study of religion is extremely important for sociologists; not only are many people religious but many of the people who began to develop sociology as a discipline in the nineteenth and twentieth centuries had strong views on what religion was, what it was for and what future it had. Many of them thought it would decline and would have been surprised by the expansion of Islam, the rise of religious fundamentalism in the USA and the growth of new religious movements such as the Unification Church, the Children of God and the Solar Temple.

As sociologists, it is important to remember what we are doing in studying religion. We are looking at:

❖ *what* people believe, e.g. in God

❖ *why* people believe these things, e.g. how far religious belief helps them decide how to behave

❖ the organizational context of these beliefs, e.g. *churches* and *sects*

❖ how religion influences what they do, e.g. how it affects their work lives.

We might not believe in or practise a religion ourselves but our lack of such commitment should not lead us to treat religious belief and practice as odd or stupid. As sociologists, we are not interested in the validity of religious beliefs and it is not our job either to deny or to support those belief systems. Religious people, however, may find our accounts odd and perhaps argue that sociologists are unfair to believers; they may say that treating religion sociologically takes something important from it – its spirituality, its mystery, its ritual. As we will see later, some of the first sociological studies of religion, for example, by the Frenchman, Emile Durkheim and the German, Karl Marx, did tend to do this by arguing that religious behaviour was not really about gods and suchlike but about social factors, including social rules and systems of inequality. For Durkheim and Marx, therefore, when people say they are practising religion they are, in fact, doing something else.

You do not have to be religious to study religion sociologically, but neither does having a religious faith and commitment bar you from studying religion from a

Table 14.1 Church membership in the UK

Churches	Adult active members (in millions)		
Trinitarian churches	*1970*	*1980*	*1992*
Anglican	2.55	2.18	1.81
Presbyterian	1.81	1.51	1.24
Methodist	0.69	0.54	0.46
Baptist	0.30	0.24	0.23
Other Free Churches	0.53	0.52	0.66
Roman Catholic	2.71	2.34	2.04
Orthodox	0.19	0.20	0.28
All Trinitarian churches	8.78	7.53	6.72
Non-Trinitarian churches			
Mormons	0.09	0.11	0.15
Jehovah's Witnesses	0.06	0.08	0.13
Spiritualists	0.05	0.05	0.04
Other Non-Trinitarian	0.08	0.11	0.14
All Non-Trinitarian churches	0.28	0.35	0.46
Other Religions			
Muslims	0.25	0.31	0.52
Sikhs	0.08	0.15	0.27
Hindus	0.05	0.12	0.14
Jews	0.11	0.11	0.11
Others	0.05	0.05	0.08
All other religions	0.54	0.74	1.12

Source: Christian Research Association in *Social Trends* (1995)

sociological perspective. Indeed, many sociologists who have studied religion have been religious by commitment – Peter Berger and David Martin being two of the most notable examples.

Defining religion

As Steve Bruce (1995, p. viii-ix) suggests, sociologists have provided two types of definition of religion. One definition relates to what religion *does*, that is, to its *functions*. These functions might include answering fundamental questions – 'Why do people die?', 'Why are people poor and oppressed?', 'Why do they get ill?', 'What happens after death?'. Also, religion may provide guidance on how to behave – 'What does a good person do?', 'What should be done about those who do not behave in this way?'. In doing these things, religion may be contributing to social order and stability. The other definition – called *substantive* – says what religion *is* rather than what it does. For example, a substantive definition might say that religion comprises beliefs and practices which involve Gods and other supernatural beings.

These definitions can, of course, be combined: religion as a set of beliefs and practices which refer to God *and* which answer fundamental questions. This is close to the definition provided by Emile Durkheim:

'A unified system of beliefs and practices relative to sacred things, that is, things set apart and forbidden which unite into one single moral community – called a church – all those who adhere to them.' (Durkheim 1912)

So, for Durkheim, religion is about believing *and* practising something and this functions to unite people into communities. Collective worship draws attention to, and celebrates, shared values. This collective worship always involves some dealing with the sacred, which is both powerful and dangerous. The sacred objects of any religion are special to believers and can only be approached with great care and reverence. There are a number of important elements to this definition:

❖ Durkheim sees religion as a combination of belief *and* practice. This implies that religiosity would not be present where people just believed religious things but did not become involved in some form of religious practice.

❖ Durkheim also stresses the central role of the sacred as something which makes religion special and unlike everyday, mundane activities. While many religious people will recognize what 'sacred' means and will identify elements of their religion which are sacred – the Qu'ran for Muslims, the communion for Roman Catholics, the Torah for Jews – sociologists will draw attention to the things that people treat as sacred which do not seem to involve religious beliefs. For example, many people will put up the

Lenin's tomb in Moscow

Stars and Stripes outside their homes in the morning and take it down at night; Lenin's tomb in the Kremlin (see photo above) which, at least up to *Glasnost*, was regularly visited by 'worshippers' who treated it with great reverence.

❖ The community basis for religion which Durkheim emphasizes implies the possibility of communal conflicts between different religious communities with their own distinct beliefs and practices. In other words, religion can unite people and also divide them, as in Northern Ireland where many social divisions are associated with religious differences between Roman Catholics and Protestants.

Other sociologists, including the German, Max Weber (1864–1920) (see Weber 1920/1963) and Peter Berger (1967), provide definitions which go beyond the division between the functional and the substantive. For Weber in particular, religion deals with what he calls the 'problem of theodicy'. The problem of theodicy is, in fact, a very simple one: how do people come to see the world, with all its dangers, problems and nastiness, as meaningful? Religions therefore answer very practical questions such as 'Why am I poor?', 'Why are my relatives ill?', 'Why is my community oppressed?' They often do this in the context of a puzzle: if God is good then why do unpleasant things happen? Religions provide what Stark and Bainbridge (1985) call 'compensators'. For Berger, this process provides a sacred canopy in which these issues are made meaningful and understandable. For Weber, there are a number of distinct ways of dealing with these issues which characterize different religions. In some, including many Western religions, there is a belief that suffering in this life will bring its rewards in the next. So suffering becomes a test of faith and if you pass that test you will enter heaven. Included here can be a belief that physical suffering is a road to salvation. Some Eastern religions, including Hinduism, believe that living in the right way in this life can lead to a better life on earth in the future through reincarnation.

Other religions include a belief that the world is made up of two opposed forces – good and evil – which are constantly battling with each other. Only in the long-term will good triumph. In the meantime, believers can expect many of the malign effects of evil. Some religious theodicies include the belief that people's fate is sealed in advance – they are predestined either to be damned or saved – and there is little that can be done about that, either by the individual, the church or the priest. In this case, as we will see later in the chapter, success in this world gives people the psychological boost they need to combat the bleakness of the idea that there is nothing you can do to enhance your chances of salvation.

All these ways of dealing with the problem of theodicy have social consequences. We will explore the role that the belief in predestination had, according to Weber, in the development of modern, capitalist societies. In the case of Islam, a belief that suffering plays a crucial role in entry to heaven has important consequences for how Islamic fundamentalists react to opposition from Western governments. This opposition may, as in the case of Iraq, actually serve to strengthen the power of political and religious leaders because the suffering which results from trade sanctions feeds into the idea that this suffering is a means to religious salvation. In other words, religious beliefs are not just beliefs, but affect how people behave more generally; religions have profound and widespread social consequences, even when, for the outsider, these beliefs look unconvincing. Put another way, we can say, as the American philosopher W.I. Thomas put it: 'If men define situations as real, they are real in their consequences.' (Thomas 1928)

As with all definitions, the functional and the substantive have major limitations and raise difficult problems. First, functional definitions may include things which many people would not regard as religions, for example nationalism and other political ideologies which also offer answers to some of the fundamental questions. As we will see, this has led sociologists to say that things like nationalism are religious *surrogates* which perform religious functions whilst not actually being religions. Second, there is considerable debate and disagreement about what a fundamental question is – is the question 'Why am I poor?' fundamental? – and why religion should be uniquely cast in the role of being able to answer these questions. As Bruce and

others stress (Bruce 1995, p. ix; McIntyre 1971), there are always going to be fundamental questions that need to be answered so, in that sense, all societies need religion. From a functionalist point of view, therefore, it is difficult even to ask the question: 'Is a society without religion possible?'.

❖ Activity 2 ❖

'In the past, religion helped people negotiate times of chaotic change, but we have lost touch with that tradition. Our social networks, families and the associations that held civil society together, have been fragmented almost beyond recovery. This is fertile ground for false prophets of all kinds, evangelical or secular.' (McWhirter 1995)

1 Can we have a society without religion?

2 Are there any examples of societies which do not have religious belief and practice?

3 What problems arise in societies with religious belief and practice?

Substantive definitions are also not without their difficulties. As soon as we identify an essential feature of religion – let us say, a belief in God – then we may exclude things which believers themselves call religion. This would apply to Confucianists. We may also have problems with those religions that have many Gods. It is significant that the majority of sociological approaches to religion were developed in the context of Western religions which all have a belief in one god; that is, they are *monotheistic*. Many religions, however, believe in many gods; that is, they are *polytheistic*. Most of the religions of the Western world are monotheistic and, across the world, most people who are believers adhere to monotheistic religions.

Finally in this section, we can say what the social roles of religion are according to three of the sociological perspectives identified in Chapter 7, *Theory and methods*. These are summarized in Table 14.2.

Table 14.2 Sociological perspectives on social roles of religion

Functionalist e.g. Durkheim	• preserving social order • integrating people into community/society • maintaining value consensus
Conflict theory e.g. Marx	• hiding social problems and conflict • hiding exploitation • keeping people in order by hiding conflict and exploitation
Interactionism/ Phenomenology e.g. Weber	• providing answers to fundamental questions • making the world meaningful

❖ Activity 3 ❖

1 Look again at Activity 1. Would you modify your definition of religion at all? If so, how would you modify it?

2 Do you now have a different view on why people might accept or reject religion? What are these differences of view?

Measuring religion

Measurement and the production of statistics is one of the central aims of sociology; sociological data are often statistical and the production of such data is important for sociologists drawing any conclusions about social life. The study of religion is no less concerned with measurement than other areas of sociology. Sociologists have tended, therefore, to measure two things: how much religious *practice* there is and how much religious *belief* there is. A combination of these things will give us some measure of the extent of what is called *religiosity*; a measurement of how religious a society is. It will also help to tell us whether, over time, religion is becoming more or less important and whether the nature of religious behaviour and belief is changing.

This, of course, all seems very straightforward: ask people questions, add up the answers and there we have statistics about religion and we know if the society we are studying is one in which religion is important. However, there are major problems in asking these questions and in interpreting the answers.

❖ Activity 4 ❖

Identify:
- three questions to assess how much people *practise* religion
- three questions to assess whether they have religious *beliefs*.

The results of this activity are likely to have raised the following problems:

❖ The questions we ask will depend on how we define religion. If we define religion as dealing with fundamental questions, then our questions will be about these things. Other sociologists might have different definitions and will therefore ask different questions and obtain different statistics.

❖ When we ask about practice, we are likely to ask questions about going to church and about being a member of a church. If someone says that they go to church once a week, we might say they are religious. But what about people who only go at Christmas and Easter? What about *why* people go? If they only go because it is expected socially, then is this religious behaviour?

❖ Membership figures are difficult to interpret because some churches ask you to sign up if you want to be considered a member whilst others assume you are a member if you live in a particular community. In other words, membership figures might not tell us about how religious a society is.

❖ When we ask about belief, we again have problems that relate to definitions of religion. When asked, people regularly say they believe in God which is for them a sure sign that they are religious. However, is the belief in God without the practice enough to count as being religious? Do you have to believe in God *and* go to church to count as religious?

❖ Equally difficult when we look at beliefs is what we do with the significant numbers of people who believe in flying saucers, in ghosts and in mystical powers. Are these, as the Church of England has argued, signs of an increase in paganism or are they religious beliefs?

There are a number of conclusions here:

❖ Asking questions about religious belief

and practice is difficult if you want accurate measures of religiosity.

❖ More people are likely to say they have religious beliefs than say that they practice a religion on a regular basis.

❖ Many people seem to be religious even though their beliefs do not always fit into the doctrines of established churches like the Church of England and Islam.

Figure 14.1
Adult church attendance, Britain 1851–1989
Sources: Brierley and Macdonald (1985), Brierley (1991b), British Parliamentary Papers (1854, 1970)

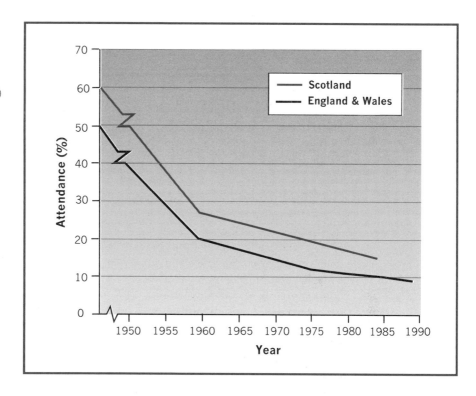

Table 14.3 Church of England Membership, 1900–90

Year	Members (000s)	Ratio (base-line 100)	% of adult population
1900	2, 800	100	13.5
1930	3, 100	131	12.8
1950	3, 000	106	9.2
1970	2, 600	92	7.2
1990	1, 500	55	3.9

Source: Brierley (1989)

Table 14.4 Methodist Membership, England 1900–90

Year	Members (000s)	Ratio (base-line 100)	% of adult population
1900	727	100	3.1
1930	788	109	2.5
1950	682	97	2.0
1970	572	80	1.5
1990	416	57	1.0

Source: Brierley (1989)

❖ Activity 5 ❖

1 Look at Fig. 14.1 and Tables 14.3 to 14.6. What do they tell us about religious practice and religious belief?

2 From what you have read, decide how religious you think people are.

Table 14.5 Religious beliefs and observances

% believing in**	Britain	USA	Eire	N Ireland
God	69	94	95	95
That God is concerned personally with people*	37	77	77	80
Life after death	55	78	80	78
Heaven	54	86	87	90
Religious miracles	45	73	73	77
Hell	28	71	53	74
The devil	28	47	49	69
The bible as being the 'actual' or inspired word of God	44	83	78	81
Affiliated with a denomination	64	93	98	92
Attend service 2/3 times a month	16	43	78	58
Have had intense religious experience	28	33	22	24

* percentages show those 'agreeing and strongly agreeing'.
** percentages are those 'definitely and probably believing'.

Source: Greeley (1992)

Table 14.6 Religious beliefs and observances in Britain

% believing in	All	C of E	RC	Pres.	Free church	Other prot.	No religion
God	69	84	92	88	91	89	28
Life after death	55	57	78	67	77	66	35
Religious miracles	45	49	80	46	78	61	22
Pray weekly	27	30	52	30	38	52	8
Attend service 2/3 times a month	16	14	36	25	31	49	1
Intense experience	28	27	32	29	51	42	19
Feel close to God	46	51	72	60	71	69	18

Source: Greeley (1992)

Table 14.7 Beliefs, Britain 1957–91 (%)

	1957	1981	1987	1991
Sin	–	69	51	–
Soul	–	59	50	–
Heaven	–	57	48	46
Life after death	54	45	43	27
Devil	34	30	31	24
Hell	–	27	29	24

Source: Gallup (1976), Gerard (1985), Svennevig *et al.* (1989), British Social Attitudes Survey (1991)

Table 14.8 Superstitions, Britain 1991 (%)

Propositions	*'Definitely' and 'Probably' true*	*'Probably' and 'Definitely' false*	*'I can't choose' and 'No answer'*
Good luck charms sometimes do bring good luck	22	72	6
Some fortune-tellers really can foresee the future	40	53	8
Some faith-healers really do have God-given healing powers	45	45	10
A person's star sign at birth, or horoscope', can affect the course of their future	28	64	9

Source: British Social Attitudes Survey (1991)

❖ Activity 6 ❖

1 Look at Tables 14.7 and 14.8. Are the beliefs listed in them religious?
2 Take one example from Table 14.7 and one from Table 14.8 and discuss what role these beliefs are playing for the believers.

The lesson here for sociologists is that the collection and interpretation of statistics is neither an easy nor a neutral thing.

Sociologists have not found it easy to interpret statistics on religiosity, in part because they do not all work with similar definitions of religion. Once they have produced statistics and these have entered the public, non-sociological domain, they have often been interpreted in ways the sociologists would find unacceptable. Neither of these issues should lead you to deny the usefulness of statistical information, but what you need to remember is that statistics only give an approximate idea of what things are like and that their interpretation is often a political issue.

Religious organizations

Like other forms of social behaviour, religions exist as a variety of social organizations. Many sociologists have identified four social organizations of religion: the church, the denomination, the sect and the cult.

The word church is, of course, used by all these religious organizations: hence, the Unification church (for sociologists, a sect); the Methodist church (for sociologists, a denomination); and the Roman Catholic church (for sociologists, a church).

Religions are social organizations with their own specific structure. The most common distinction is the one originally developed by Troeltsch (1931) and Weber (1920/1963) between *churches* and *sects*. Their features are summarized in Table 14.9.

The church/sect dichotomy

Churches can often be large in terms of membership. This is partly because they often assume people are members if, for example, their parents were members. In a sense, you do not have to join actively to count as a member. Sects, on the other hand, require people to join actively, perhaps by a conversion experience, or by paying a member's fee and filling in a membership form. This tends, therefore, to make churches inclusive and sects exclusive. If you have not actively joined the sect and given a commitment, you cannot count as a member.

Churches only require partial commitment and often allow people considerable freedom in their dealing with non-members and in how they live their lives. This does not, of course, prevent churches from setting rules which have profound effects on people's lives – rules about what you can eat, who you can marry, what, if any, form of contraception you can use. However, sects tend to require a total commitment to their beliefs and practices and to require separation from ties, including the family, that people had before they became members. This is especially the case with those sects that reject the wider society (see below).

Churches are more likely to accept the existing political order of things and are often state religions; as such they are often conservative forces. Sects, on the other

Table 14.9 Distinction between churches and sects (Troeltsch and Weber)

Church	*Sect*
large membership	small membership
inclusive, i.e. open to everyone	exclusive, i.e. open to the few
involuntary membership	voluntary membership;
membership by birth	conversion
professional clergy	no professional clergy
partial commitment	total commitment
linked with wider society	separation from society
acceptance of the world	rejection of the world
often linked to the state	often separate from, and opposing, the state
monopoly of truth	monopoly of truth
bureaucratic	charismatic
asceticism as a preparation for the afterlife	asceticism as a means to gain direct contact with God

hand, are more likely to oppose the existing order of things and therefore to find themselves in conflict with the state. Finally, we can say that churches tend to be bureaucratic and hierarchical, with a professional clergy who are the real experts in religious belief and practice. Sects lack that hierarchy although they will often have a leader whom members see as charismatic (this idea is developed later in the chapter). In addition, sects tend to recruit from particular groups of people who are materially underprivileged, who suffer poverty, material deprivation and discrimination.

The church

In the UK there is a wide variety of churches, that is, large-scale religious organizations which are frequently inclusive in that they will accept anyone as a member. These include the Roman Catholic, Anglican and Eastern Orthodox churches, Judaism, Islam and Hinduism. Although each of these may produce sects which break away, the central church organization and belief is maintained and keeps the allegiance of the majority of members.

In terms of membership and religious practice in the UK, churches are far more important than sects. Whereas the Children of God, a religious sect, is estimated to have

500 members, the Anglican church has 1.8 million, the Roman Catholic church has 1.9 million, Islam 900,000, and Hinduism 150,000. In other words, on a religious holy day there are large numbers worshipping within the major church religions, and small numbers celebrating within sects. These figures, however, disguise a trend for many churches – those that are Protestant – to be losing support whilst others – for example, Islam, are gaining support.

Although these figures might not tell us a great deal about how religious people are or about why they are religious, they do indicate that the attention given to sects in both the media and by many sociologists lacks balance. Stressing sect membership does not give an accurate picture of how religious people in the UK are.

The sect

Sects are, however, especially interesting organizations. They often emerge when churches are in conflict over some issue of doctrine and may develop when a new doctrine is sponsored by a small group or individual within a church. Sects seem to develop in response to some group's material underprivilege: poverty, unemployment, racial discrimination and so on. Sect membership provides solutions to underprivilege in terms of theodicies which see underprivilege as a sign of worth. They also give people status, as sect members, which is denied in the wider society. We will explore this issue when we look at religion and social change later in the chapter. Sects are also interesting because many of the new religious movements of the late twentieth century – for example, Scientology, the Unification Church, the Children of God – are sects.

Wilson (1982) and Wallis (1976) show that sects often have major conflicts with the wider society, basically because they claim to have access to the truth which non-members do not have. They will, therefore, often avoid or actively reject that wider society and its rules of behaviour.

Mosque in West London

Photo © George Montgomery/Photofusion

Conversionist
Example:
the Salvation Army

As their name implies, these sects actively seek to convert people. This is an obvious way of increasing membership but also brings the sect into conflict with both other religions and those who are not religious. Early Christianity was conversionist and, like many conversionist sects, rapidly became a church with a more formal structure and a claim to inclusive, rather than exclusive, membership. Contemporary conversionist sects emphasize religious revival in a world in which religion has become less important; this revival is centred on preaching the original, fundamental message. There is believed to be a strong personal relationship between the believer and the saviour, and conversion is rapid.

Revolutionist
Examples:
Christadelphians,
Jehovah's Witnesses

These usually emphasize conversion but take a more radical stance towards the wider society. They are more likely to portray that society as evil and dangerous and wish for the overthrow of the existing order of things. When the world is overturned, the sect members will become powerful. Therefore membership of the sect guarantees salvation. These sects are hostile to social reform through religion and believe in a slow, rather than a rapid, conversion to sect beliefs. This slow conversion also involves strict tests of membership and a stress on the purity and sacredness of sect beliefs. Predictions about the future and about imminent salvation are related to contemporary events which are seen as signs that change is just around the corner. The view of god in these sects is of an autocratic dictator who controls the universe and is not open to control by the sect.

Introversionist
Example: Pietism

These are sects that withdraw from the world and are indifferent to social reform and to conversion. Rather than trying to change things, members aim for a deeper spiritual experience and for inner change; there is a strong element of self-mastery and self-discipline. Ideas of god do not include the idea of a personal god who can be influenced but some sort of holy spirit.

Manipulationist
Examples:
Christian Science,
Scientology

These sects believe that members can have access to some special knowledge or technique which can achieve social ends. Individuals can use this knowledge or technique and they do not need a special relationship with the movement, a god or saviour. Where the members do come together, they do so as a way to claim status and prestige and to show how successful the sect is in improving people's status in the wider society. Anyone can learn the knowledge and techniques if they are willing to undergo what is often a long and expensive training. There is no belief in a personal god or saviour and the sect's beliefs are often a mix of religious and non-religious traditions. Where they make claims to deal with illness, they come into conflict with medicine, for example over opposition to the use of blood transfusions. These are the least religious looking of the sects and have been called *cults* (see below).

Thaumaturgical
Example:
Spiritualism

Their belief is that the supernatural can be experienced in daily life and can produce extraordinary effects, for example miracles, cures, messages from the dead and so on. As such, they believe that the normal processes of life, ageing and death can be suspended. They are very pragmatic in that they offer practical and personal solutions to problems, in particular in helping people to deal with loss. There is no real requirement to believe something if you want to join and no test of membership. The community is rudimentary; the audience at a seance is the typical community.

Reformist
Example:
Quakers

These are often the result of failures of revolutionist and introversionist sects. They follow from the failure of a revolutionist sect to bring about change in the short-term and the problem that introversionist sects have in maintaining a community of people all of whom are concerned primarily with mastery of the self. The typical reformist sect acts as a social conscience and specializes in doing good deeds. The members aim to be untainted by the wider world because that world is the source of evil and unhappiness, whilst doing good. Such sects have an undeveloped idea of god or saviour.

Utopian
Examples:
Amish,
Mennonites,
Shakers,
Oneida community

Utopian sects are more radically opposed to the world than reformist sects, less violent than revolutionist sects, and more interested in social change than conversionist sects. They stress social reconstruction on community lines, where communities are often based on some model from the past. As such, members often oppose or avoid many of the features of the modern world – cars, televisions, cinema – in pursuit of a simpler, less urban lifestyle. They form religious communities and will not try to convert many people. They have typically developed in the USA as a way of opposing the assimilation of immigrant groups; the community becomes a way of maintaining a distinct way of life.

Because of these conflicts, and as a sign of commitment, members will often be asked to reject past social ties to friends and family and to give themselves wholeheartedly to the sect. Wilson (see Bocock and Thompson 1985), proposed a complex typology of sects which is based upon the interrelationships between the sect and the wider society (see *In Focus* opposite).

In common with many classifications in sociology, this one is based upon Western religions and there is the question of whether this classification applies equally well to non-Western religions. Wilson's classification proposes that sects do not remain permanently in one category. For example, a revolutionist sect which wants to change the world may, if it fails to do this, become utopian. In effect, therefore, the fate of the sects is tied closely to the stance it adopts towards the wider world and how that wider world reacts to what the sect does.

What is clear is that all religions have the potential to develop sectarian break away. This happens, in part, because the church is seen by particular group of people not to offer answers to fundamental questions. This takes us back to Weber's view that churches are more likely to represent those with material privilege and status, and sects are more likely to appeal to the underprivileged.

❖ Activity 7 ❖

Using a CD Rom in your local library, look through the newspapers to research one example of a sectarian break-away. Write short notes on your findings.

The denomination

Somewhere in the middle in organizational terms is the *denomination*; examples of which include the Methodist and Baptist movements. Unlike the church and the sect, the denomination does not claim a monopoly of truth but recognizes that there are many religions each with its own truth. In a sense, the denomination is likely to be a common organizational form in a complex society where there are a variety of belief systems because, in such a society, it is very difficult for *one* organization to claim a monopoly of the truth as the church did in the past.

Three things characterize the denomination:

❖ It asks for a low level of commitment, particularly when compared with the sect.

❖ It is tolerant and open and therefore rarely seeks to convert people.

❖ It is often difficult to distinguish denominations from other, similar groups.

The cult

The final religious organization is the *cult* which has a rather shadowy role to play in sociology. It is common, for example, for the phrase 'sects and cults' to be used, thus suggesting that they are similar forms of organization. It is also noticeable that, in popular discussions of religious movements, some which sociologists would call sects are labelled cults. This has particularly been the case with some of the more sensational media portrayals of sects/cults, for example the Waco Siege (see p. 636). In popular discussion, the term 'cult' is loaded with negative connotations of extremism, madness and sexual exploitation. This denial of the validity of some sects and cults has also been extended to non-Western religions. In the past, for example, Islam was portrayed negatively and its prophet – Mohammed – was called a sexual libertine. Similar negative images of Islam are found in contemporary discussions of fundamentalism.

There is, in fact, no general agreement about how to characterize a cult. Sociologists distinguish between the denomination, which is a sect which has become institutionalized and acceptable and does little in the way of protest; and the cult – for example, astrology, transcendental meditation – which is a loosely structured movement which may not last. Rather than joining a cult, people follow some philosophy or theory which the cult is advocating, which is generally about how to live your life better. Cults do not usually require people to give up existing religious commitments. Stark and Bainbridge (1985) take a slightly different position and argue that the sect is an offshoot of an existing religion and a cult involves a mixture of imported religions and some cultural innovation. They classify cults into three types:

❖ audience cults

❖ client cults

❖ cult movements.

The first is highly individualistic, involves little organization and is often sustained through the mass media. An example is astrology. Client cults have a higher degree of organization and offer services to members, for example the contact with the dead which spiritualism offers. Cult movements are more organized and offer members a wide range of things including the more religious activities of worship and spiritual support. In this classification, the Unification Church would be identified as a cult.

Table 14.10 Wallis' summary of religious organizations

External conception	Respectable	Deviant
Uniquely legitimate	Church (Catholic church)	Sect (Mormons)
Pluralistically legitimate	Denomination (Methodism)	Cult (Scientology)

There are two problems with this classification.

❖ There seem to be no good sociological reasons why movements which import other religious traditions should not be termed sects. We have already noticed the focus within the sociology of religion on western religions. This classification of cults merely maintains this and portrays movements which mix traditions as in some ways unusual. As we saw in Chapter 1, the mixing of traditions is one of the main characteristics of post-modern societies and may, therefore, be an important aspect of religions in increasingly global and post-modern societies.

❖ This classification means we have to define most new religious movements (NRMs) as cults even though they look, in the context of most sociological explanation, like sects. A solution here might be to reserve the term cult for small scale, individualistic movements which offer immediate and pragmatic solutions to people, e.g. astrology.

There are two crucial issues here:

❖ How does the religious organization regard its own beliefs in comparison with other religious organizations (the internal conception)?

❖ How is it regarded by the wider society (the external conception)?

Both church and sect claim they have the unique and true message; the difference between them is that the church is generally seen as legitimate, even by non-believers, whereas the sect is usually seen as deviant. What the cult and the denomination have in common is that both recognize that there are a variety of beliefs; however, the denomination is generally seen as legitimate and the cult as deviant.

Religion and social change

Many people think that religious organizations are conservative and support the status quo. However, there are at least two indications that things might not be as simple as this and they are both rooted in ideas developed by Max Weber (1904/74).

Religion and capitalism

Weber asked a very simple question: noticing that modern forms of economic activity, sometimes called capitalism (see Chapter 7 for definitions of capitalism and of modernity), developed first in certain parts of Europe, he asked if religion had any part to play. His conclusion was that there was a relationship between capitalism and forms of religion called Lutheranism and Calvinism.

Lutheranism

Lutherans believe that any form of social activity can be of religious significance, even things that appear to be non-religious, for example, coal mining, rearing children, fishing. So, religion is more than going to church on a Sunday; it is a lifelong *vocation* which can be revealed in the most mundane duties which people have to perform. In performing those duties people are being religious as much as when they go to church. For Luther this idea was part of a battle between Protestantism and Roman Catholicism; in the latter, only some forms of activity count as religious activity. As we shall see, this religious battle came to have a wider social significance.

Calvinism

Calvinists believe that you cannot, as a religious person, know whether you are damned or saved and that religious people – priests and clergy – cannot tell you or make it more likely that you will be saved. You are *predestined* to either heaven or hell.

❖ Activity 8 ❖

You are a religious person and discover that there is nothing you can do to improve your chances of salvation. How might this effect the way you behave and what you do?

For Weber these two combined to support *the spirit of capitalism* – careful, planned acquisition – and to favour the development of capitalism as an economic system – one in which there was inequality and people could legitimately make profits and wealth. Lutheranism allowed people to work and earn money, of course without self-indulgence, and this would count as religious activity which God wanted. What made this activity religious was that it was *ascetic* and avoided pleasures. Calvinism made people work hard in the belief that success would be a sign to others that they might be saved even though the individuals could not actually know. Taken together, the spirit of capitalism and Calvinism suggest that religion had a major part to play in the social change from pre-industrial to

In Focus
◆
Religion and capitalism today

 eber's views have been criticized, partly by those who have thought his argument implied a causal link between religion and capitalism. What is clear is that religion stills plays an important part in how industrial and other organizations work.

Schools in Britain still have predominantly Christian worship; the Houses of Parliament have Church of England services. There are also religious organizations with an overtly capitalist message, for example, the Fellowship of Companies for Christ International.

industrial society. It was not, therefore, a conservative force even though, as Marx argued, it did become one of the major justifications for capitalism once it had developed. For Weber, religion was not a *cause* of capitalism and Weber was not trying to develop a causal model for the social sciences. Calvinism and Lutheranism were developed as religious ideas which then came to have an affinity with forms of economic activity crucial to capitalism

Religion and charisma

There is a second link between religion and social change and that has to do with how sects develop and change. Two factors help in the development of sects:

❖ A group of people find that their existing religion is not dealing with their needs.

❖ A leader claims to have a new answer. This leader can be called *charismatic.*

Charisma has two features: people with charisma have some special features ascribed to them by followers. These features may well include special personality characteristics, for example powerful oratory or magical powers to heal. These powers are what link the leaders to their followers. Second, the charisma is particular to the individual person; it is unique.

There are three interesting issues here:

1 Charisma is now used very widely to describe a wide range of people – politicians, rap artists, actors, teachers, sports stars.

2 Charisma is often seen as dangerous in that a leader can motivate people to do things that they would not, normally, do. This is, of course, partly rooted in an interpretation of what Adolf Hitler did in Nazi Germany, and similar fears are expressed about those new religious movements which have powerful leaders.

3 Because charisma is unique to the leader and his or her small band of followers, there are problems maintaining the charisma. Weber talked about the routinization of charisma. If the movement is to have a wide impact, then a structure will need to be established to take the message to a wider public. This means that movements dominated by charisma often become *bureaucratic.* There is also a particular problem of who is to succeed the leader when he or she dies. This problem of succession is acute precisely because the charisma *is* unique, so no one can inherit it as it stands. In practice, movements will develop methods of dealing with this. The charisma may become hereditary, or attached to the office of the person. In this process, the magic of charisma is increasingly lost. In many cases – for example, Christianity, Rastafarianism – believers argue that the leader has not really died, so someone else can take the message forward in the leader's place, acting as his or her representative.

Adolf Hitler reviewing the Nazi Labour Party with a march past of 40,000 men, Nuremberg 1938

Photo © Hulton Deutsch Collection Limited

❖ Activity 9 ❖

Make a list of charismatic figures. What do they have in common?

The point for the discussion of social change is simple: charisma makes sects develop and break away from churches but it cannot last as the leader is unique. So, many sects turn back into churches and then, later, sects break away again. Charisma, here, becomes a major motor of social change. In extending the term charisma to other areas of social life, particularly the political, we have a term which may also serve to explain how political movements develop and change.

New religious movements (NRMs)

Wallis (1984) argues that what we have seen, particularly in the USA, UK and Western Europe in the last 30 years, is the growth of *new religious movements* (NRMs). Such movements are developing precisely in those societies where the power of the established churches seems, with a few notable exceptions, to be in decline. Wallis identifies three types of NRM (see Fig. 14.2). One group – the world-rejecting – are the most sect like and have many things in common with the sects discussed by Weber and Troeltsch (see p. 628). They oppose the wider world, see it as evil and debased and often ask members to separate from that world. Examples include the Children of God and the People's Temple. Another group – the world accommodating – are like denominations and stress that religion is more a personal matter than a social one. Examples include Subud and neo-Pentacostalism. Finally, we have world-affirming movements. These often do not look like religious movements at all and make claims that membership will improve your chances of being a successful person. Sociologists – Wallis, for example – have termed these movements cults. Examples include Scientology and Erhard Seminar Training (EST).

We need to look at a number of issues in considering NRMs and we will concentrate on the world-rejecting and world-affirming movements.

World-rejecting movements

A typical example here is the Unification Church, popularly called the 'Moonies' after its leader Sun Myung Moon. What is noticeable about the church is that it holds what most people would recognize as religious beliefs – in heaven, god, the spirit

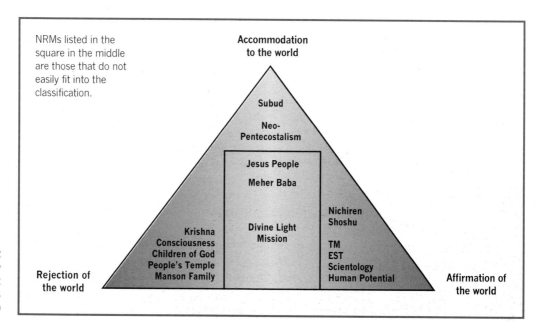

Figure 14.2
Types of new religious movement
Source: Wallis (1984)

The siege of the headquarters of the Branch-Davidian sect in Waco provides an interesting example of the dynamics of the world-rejecting movements. The sect predicted the end of the world and separated itself from the wider society. Its leader, David Koresh, was seen to be charismatic. Membership included whole families as well as people who had left their families to join. The wider society's view was that Koresh had captured and indoctrinated people and was sexually abusing them. In addition, the sect armed itself in preparation for the end. This heady mixture of charisma, arms, fears of abuse and indoctrination became the basis for the involvement of the US police and military. The Waco siege ended in the death by fire of most members in 1993 (see photo below). Those that remained were divided. One camp sought a successor to David Koresh, others looked to George Rodin, the original leader whom Koresh ousted in 1987. Many, however, still believe in the veracity of Koresh's message and trust that he will return.

and suchlike. It asks for a rejection of a world which is seen as evil and degraded and, therefore, requires people to give a commitment to the church and to undergo a conversion experience. This means that members will have to leave their former social ties and commit their lives – including their wealth – to the movement.

In common with many religious movements, there is a belief in the importance of a leader who is charismatic. Members subordinate themselves to the leader. This has lead to public fears that such movements control and brainwash members. This contrasts with the reality that world-rejecting movements usually have very small memberships, characterized by a small hard-core of support and a larger group which is less committed and likely to leave the movement.

World-affirming movements

Scientology is a typical world-affirming movement. It holds that the world is one of opportunity and that all that holds people back is some form of restriction or repression. The movement seeks to give people a way to become better. As Wallis (1976) suggests, many Scientologists joined in order to become better people: better teachers, better at social relationships and so on, and Scientology played on this desire for improvement. In this sense, world-affirming movements often do not look like religious movements at all.

Scientology's history is interesting. Established by the science fiction writer Lafayette Ron Hubbard in the form of Dianetics, it claimed to deal with psychiatric problems. This brought it into conflict with the medical profession and so the movement began to develop a more religious stance, including a belief in the soul and reincarnation; this included the development of a belief in spirits and in the immortality of the soul. The sect has, in fact, fluctuated between phases of world rejection and world affirmation; in the former phases, small groups of committed followers withdraw from the world and seek spiritual renewal. World affirmation includes many basically financial activities including followers making a financial commitment to a long and expensive series of levels of training.

Themes

Beliefs

Both world-rejecting and world-affirming movements have similar characteristics in that they combine different beliefs in the same movement. So the Unification Church combines Christianity and eastern religions; Scientology combines eastern religions and psychotherapy. In addition, as we have seen, Scientology started out as a form of therapy and only later took on some of the elements of a religious belief system.

This raises a major problem for the sociologist concerning how we are to deal with unusual beliefs. Sociologists would generally take a stance towards such beliefs based upon *relativism* and *tolerance*. Relativism involves a commitment to seeing others' beliefs in their own context and accepting that the social context explains why people believe things that appear, on the surface, not to make sense. Therefore, all beliefs make sense in their social context. Tolerance towards other people's beliefs follows from this. There is, of course, a problem about how far you go in tolerating the beliefs of others. What the sociologist tries to do is to explain why people believe what they do without justifying it.

Membership

World-rejecting movements tend to have more restricted memberships than do the world-affirming ones. In part, this is because the former cast their nets much less widely. In both, there are likely to be hard-core members – *believers* – and those who exist on the fringe of the movement – *consumers*. World-rejecting movements are more likely to seek to control members in what they do and believe.

Popularly, there is often fear of both world-affirming and world-rejecting movements. The fear that people are

In Focus

◆

Eileen Barker and cult-watching

'Inform was launched last week as Britain's first objective and officially supported group of cult-watchers. Information Network Focus on Religious Movements promises to conduct research, amass a computerized data bank with world-wide sources, and give out information, advice and counselling to cult-recruits and their parents in a country-wide network in conjunction with churches and, where appropriate, psychiatrists.

Inform was launched at the London School of Economics, whose formidable guru on new religions, the sociologist Eileen Barker, had conceived the idea.

'I realized that cults can give rise to a lot of anguish and even tragedy, and objective, value-free science is not going to help if it isn't made available,' Dr Barker said.

Some of the best-known cults like the Moonies, the sexually liberated followers of Bagwan Rajneesh (the man with the fleet of Rolls-Royces who was hounded out of the US by tax men), the Children of God and others have faded from the headlines. Moonies have stopped mass recruiting, Bagwan followers and the Children of God have largely retreated from Europe.

But Scientologists still claim hundreds of recruits a month for their costly, pseudo-scientific self-improvement 'courses' for which students often abandon regular studies. And Dr Barker says hundreds of new, lesser-known or unknown cults are claiming converts and causing, at best, mystification for parents.

Dr Barker interprets cults as the price we pay for a pluralistic society. 'We are bound to get highly dubious efforts to provide one single truth. So much is offered, we don't look at the contract...'

Now, thanks to Dr Barker's diplomacy, government, churches and academics can act together and settle down to some serious cult-watching and counselling, but with no overtones of cult-bashing.'

Source: The Guardian, 16 September 1987

controlled, brainwashed and so on is contradicted by the reality of membership. As Barker shows (1984, p. 146), the Unification Church was very unsuccessful in keeping members. Only 7 per cent of people who attended initial workshops were still affiliated to the church after one year; this declined to 5 per cent after two years and to 3.5 per cent after five years. The Moonies also recruited a distinct type of person – particularly middle class, educated men who had parents who were teachers, doctors, nurses and in the armed forces and the police. Despite the distinct and transitory membership, the fear of control still exists and has lead to the development of groups of professional 'deprogrammers' who seek to recapture members and return them to their families.

There are age differences in membership: the world-rejecting movements are more likely to appeal to the young and the world-affirming ones to those who are somewhat older (see next section). This begins to explain the greater public hostility to world-rejecting movements from parents – it is their children who are being 'captured'.

However, membership is typically from those who are relatively affluent. In this sense, the views of Weber and Troeltsch that what they call religious sects appeal to the materially underprivileged may need modifying.

New age movements

As Bruce suggests (1995), the major sociological explanation of new religious movements developed in the context of movements that were emerging in the 1970s and early 1980s. These were the ones studied by Wallis and Barker, containing a mixture of sects and cults. The 1980s and 1990s has seen further developments in what he calls 'new age movements', the majority of which are cults, based on a whole range of things such as spiritual healing, paganism and elements of the ecology movement. These comprise two of the three types of cult discussed on p. 632: client cults where there is an individual relationship between a consumer and someone who is selling something; and audience cults where there is a mass distribution of the message.

Centrally, in common with many new religious movements, the ideas and beliefs are hybrids, taking elements from many different beliefs systems. Many of these

---

In Focus

◆

The 'Bishop of Cyberspace'

Enter the virtual bishop

'Cyberspace now has its own bishop. Jacques Gaillot, the "Red Cleric" who was sacked by the Vatican for his liberal views, now has a "virtual diocese"; the world-wide Web. In his first pastoral letter, Gaillot, former bishop of Evreux, northern France, says: "Getting on to the Internet is a dream for me, a dream of a child who walks along the shore of a sandy beach and looks at the ocean. Suddenly a desire grows in him to get into contact and to talk with all the people of the earth who live on distant shores." Gaillot's site is called Partenia after the diocese of the ruined city in the Sahara desert which the Pope gave him as a punishment. Gaillot now wants virtual Partenia to be a meeting place for all.

All the major religions face fierce competition on the Internet from alternatives, including Satanism and Paganism. However, the Universal Life Church may well be more in tune with Net culture.

According to Brother Daniel, the church's Net Representative, the ULC has only two tenets: "the absolute right of freedom of religion and to do that which is right." Anything else, within the law, is up to the individual. This means you can subscribe to another religion at the same time.'

Source: Jack Schofield, *The Guardian*, 25 January 1996

movements use and rely on the mass media for dissemination of their ideas and for linking 'members'. As such, there is really no community of believers; we have, in effect, moved from religious organizations to a religious *milieu*.

> ### ❖ Activity 10 ❖
>
> 1 Think about how you would normally define a 'church'; considering, for example, its physical structure, its congregational make-up, etc.
> 2 How far do you think Partenia can be described as a 'church'? How does this affect your definition of what a 'church' is? Do you need to reconsider your definition?

The appeal of new religious movements

For sociologists, one of the most interesting questions is why people join and support new religious movements. As we have already seen with Scientology, the motivations are often very pragmatic – success, security, job enhancement. These motives are not ones that many religious people would recognize and this is probably one of the main reasons why the religious nature of many new religious movements is questioned.

However, we can suggest reasons for the support for new religious movements. First, given the decline in the importance of religion, there is a niche in the market for belief systems which explain the world and its difficulties.

More specifically, new religious movements appeal to particular groups of people. Earlier we mentioned that world-rejecting movements appeal more to young people, in particular those who are no longer children but are also not yet adults, that is, not yet married, with a job and children; world-affirming sects appeal to those who are more likely to have finished education, be married and have children and mortgages. These groups have different issues and problems to deal with which NRMs seek to address.

World-rejecting movements and the young unattached

Being unattached is part of the increasing gap between childhood and adulthood. It is to these unattached groups that world-rejecting movements appeal. They try to provide some certainty within a community of people who face similar problems and difficulties. What seems to be particularly appealing is that the movement offers radical and imminent solutions to social and personal problems.

The particular appeal to certain age groups explains the rapid turnover of membership of world-rejecting movements. Once you are older, have dependants, have a job, the reason for membership has gone. There are, however, other reasons for this turnover: these include the public hostility to such movements which may frighten people away; and the likely failure of any religious message which predicts imminent changes. If these changes do not occur, then the movement is likely to enter a period of crisis and lose members.

A niche in the market for belief systems...

World-affirming movements and the older attached

There are two issues in the modern world that suggests the appeal of world-affirming movements. First, as Weber had suggested, the modern world is one in which rationality dominates – that is, one in which magical, unpredictable and ecstatic experiences are uncommon. Furthermore, in the modern world there is tremendous pressure on people, for example through advertising, to be successful and to become better and better people.

World-affirming sects simultaneously do three things:

❖ provide some spiritual component in an increasingly rationalized world – this is part of the appeal of new age movements

❖ provide techniques and knowledge to help people become wealthy, powerful and successful

❖ provide techniques and knowledge to allow people to work on themselves – this is the appeal of an enormous number of movements which claim to facilitate personal growth.

This has led Paul Heelas (1992) to argue that what we have here are *self-religions* which act as *cults for capitalism* (see *In Focus*).

In some ways there are common motivations at work here. Both the young- and older-attached groups live in societies where there is great pressure to succeed and therefore great fear of failure. Religious movements can, therefore, provide both communities of the like-minded and, in some case, some guarantee of success. Scientology provides its own community of successful people; that is, those who are better trained and understand the movements better; these people gain status and prestige as they gain understanding.

Finally, it is important to reiterate the point that new religious movements have many fewer devotees than the traditional religions. In addition, there are things happening with established religions that are important – these include movements to *revitalize* a particular religion (the 'House church' movement and the 'Nine o'clock service' movement); and movements to unite different religions, that is, *ecumenicalism*.

In Focus

◆

'New agers'

Heelas notes that, in the USA, there are 10 to 12 million people who claim to be new agers who are variously committed to astrology, crystals, Gaia and so on; many of these are what he calls new age professionals who are looking for more from their work than simply money.

'The key to the matter lies in the meanings which are attributed to work. In a broadly similar fashion to the capitalists discussed by Weber... who did not work hard merely to become wealthy but treated work as a way to the end of obtaining a 'sign' that they were of the elect – self-religionists... believe that work caters for something much more important than wealth creation alone. Essentially work is understood to be a spiritual discipline.' (Heelas 1992, p. 157).

Many committed to self-religions, that is movements which claim to have a way of making people better people, work in large corporations where there is considerable stress and anxiety. The movements they are committed to, which include a whole range of training systems – Erhard Seminar Training, Exegesis – do two major things: they claim to humanize large organizations and make better use of people in them; and they claim that you can endlessly improve yourself. Heelas provides some strange, but interesting examples of the mix of religion and economic success – Zen and the art of telephoning; a book entitled *How to Be Chic, Fabulous and Live Forever*. These seem odd but show how religious ideas can be linked to ideas about how organizations can be made more human.

Source: Heelas (1992)

Extended holy family sees chance of profit in unity

'Britain's Protestants, for centuries divided by history, doctrine and practice, are finally seeing the advantages of working together. In the face of dwindling congregations, cash crises and underused church buildings, denominational leaders are now talking about formal unity.

Many churches recognize that they have more chance of surviving with other denominations than without them. "There is a groundswell at the moment," said the Rev Duncan McClements, convener of the Church of Scotland's ecumenical affairs committee. "It would undoubtedly strengthen the mission of the Church if we could have one voice instead of competing with different brand names."

This week, leading ministers in the United Reformed Church, a 20-year-old union of the Congregational and Presbyterian Churches, will meet for private talks with senior Church of England figures. This follows successful talks between the Church of England and the Methodist Church two months ago.

"Economics may be contributing to ecumenics," said Martin Reardon of Churches Together in England and Wales, a council which promotes unity among the 22 different denominations in membership. "But the main factor is a genuine desire for unity."

Nowhere is the problem starker than in Wales, where the Presbyterian Church, whose membership has fallen since the war from 200,000 to 56,000 last year, has voted to close a third of its 1,000 chapels, converting most to housing. Its senior ministers have opened discussions on sharing buildings with the Anglican Church in Wales, the United Reformed Church, the Baptists and the Roman Catholic Church.

Formal church unions may take years of negotiations, but at local level many people are simply getting on with it. There are now 800 local ecumenical projects where members of different churches have pooled resources and are working together under one roof.'

Source: Martin Wroe, *The Observer*, 28 May 1995

The decline in religion

Defining and measuring secularization

In an earlier chapter you will have looked at some of the people who developed sociology in the nineteenth and early twentieth centuries. Many of them – Durkheim, Marx, Weber, Freud – had theories about religion and how it would develop or, alternatively, decline. This idea that religion may decline and become less socially significant is what sociologists call *secularization*.

Durkheim

For Durkheim, religion was about celebrating the rules of your society and making people keep to those rules. In other words, religion makes communities. As societies become more complex, religion is less and less likely to do this. What happens is that religion becomes one of many belief systems and finds it more and more difficult to represent everyone in a complex society. In order to appeal to a wide range of different social groups, religions have to become less prescriptive and specific in what they say. In doing this, they increase the number of potential followers but also look less and less specifically religious.

Marx

For Marx, religion is about providing people with an explanation of their suffering and a way of coming to terms with that suffering. People's real suffering comes from the social system – from the powerful oppressing the powerless; as such, religion is an illusion and will be superseded by more scientific explanations of suffering.

Freud

For the Austrian, Sigmund Freud (1856–1939) religion is again an illusion in which people fail to give up their infantile attachment to their parents; God takes the place of parents. The solution is to find more rational and perceptive ways of dealing with day-to-day problems.

All the above, and Weber, were atheists, opposed to religion. Durkheim, Marx and Freud all said that when people were practising religion they were really doing something else; they were not being religious and, in the extreme, they didn't really know what they were doing.

Weber

Weber's views are slightly different. Religion, he claims, is about fundamental issues: 'Why do I die?', 'Why do I suffer?', 'Why am I powerless?' He is interested in taking people's religious practice at face value and looking at the effects of that practice. Weber's view on the future of religion was of its steady erosion and the replacement of 'mystical' ideas with scientific ones. He suspected that people might not like that change and could find scientific answers unsatisfying. Furthermore, in Weber's opinion, the development of Calvinism and Lutheranism were themselves contributing to the decline in religion: the former said that priests and prophets had no role to play and that god could not be influenced; the latter said that *everything* is religious, which is not far from saying that nothing is! In other words, for Luther, religion was nothing special, it was not only about the sacred.

Weber's view that there is a process of secularization happening *within* religion allows us to understand the idea that people can be religious without going to church. For Weber, Protestantism sanctioned this. Calvinism, in reducing the role of priests, made it possible, for example, for people to worship at home. An interesting modern example here would be the house church movement which, according to Abercrombie and Warde (1994, p. 463), increased the

---

Bell, book and scandal

'Modern Anglican faith is riddled with philosophical doubt. Virgin birth, the Crucifixion, even Heaven and Hell have been downgraded to the status of metaphor. When the future head of the Church of England is an adulterer, it is difficult to accept the denouncement of adultery from the pulpit because of a commandment that huge numbers of the population will never have actually read for themselves. "Bishops care more about global warming than adultery", proclaim the headlines, suggesting that the Church is reflecting a contemporary agenda rather than leading it. Our demands are somewhat contradictory. The Church, if it is to be about anything, must be about eternal truths; but the Church knows that if it doesn't move with the times, it will have no one to whom to preach these truths.'

Source: Suzanne Moore, *The Guardian*, 15 February 1996

❖ Activity 11 ❖

Read the text about the Church of England (see *In Focus*, p. 642) and then answer the following questions:

1   In what ways does this passage reflect Weber's views?

2   Think of examples, other than adultery, which show changing attitudes within the Church of England, Catholic Church or other faiths.

3   Discuss the following question with other sociology students: How far do you think the Church should 'move with the times'?

number attending services by 144 per cent between 1979 and 1989.

Deriving from the ideas of Durkheim, Marx, Freud and Weber comes a complex set of ideas about what a religious society would look like and what a secular society would be like. These include ideas about disengagement; differentiation; pluralism and disenchantment.

Disengagement

If we see the true religion as one which involves itself in all of social life, then any religion which disengages from some of social life – let's say from politics – would be a sign of secularization. To that extent, then, the Church of England's recent interventions in political debates about poverty and the inner city would be a sign of a thriving, non-secular, society. Two things are interesting here:

❖ Politicians were highly critical of the church's intervention in political issues.

❖ Some state religions (e.g. Islam in Iran and Pakistan) take a stance that religion must never disengage from other aspects of social life.

Differentiation

Sociologists often characterize the modern world as one in which institutions become more specialized in what they do. In the case of religion, this process of differentiation and specialization means that religions have less links with other social institutions. This has an implication for religious beliefs in that they become more generalized in the attempt to maintain the link between religious beliefs and other beliefs. Some sociologists, for example Parsons (1951), argue that this is not, in fact, a sign of secularization.

❖ Activity 12 ❖

A survey published by the General Synod in 1996, emphasized the Church's central role in providing general moral guidance. How valid do you think this is and how far could or should this moral concern affect the Church's right to intervene in politics?

Discuss this question with other sociology students.

Pluralism

The issue here is that religion in the modern world ceases to claim that it represents the only truth. Instead it comes to recognize that other religions, and other belief systems, have legitimate truth claims. This is what happens as denominations develop, and it means that religion no longer serves to maintain social solidarity. Whilst this is part of secularization, the process of *ecumenicalism* may reverse this trend as a number of religions get together and recognize a common truth.

Disenchantment

Finally, we can argue, as Max Weber did, that the modern world is one in which the magical and mystical elements of life, which religion celebrated, have declined in significance, and have been replaced by the world of scientific calculation in which natural and social behaviour is predictable. We can also argue that people might not find such a rationalist approach to social life satisfying and that this is one of the reasons for the increasing support for NRMs.

If we go back to the start of this chapter, we can see that measuring secularization is related to how we define religion. Secularization could be measured by looking at practice or belief; if fewer people go to church regularly, or fewer people believe in God, then we have a more secular society.

❖ Activity 13 ❖

What is the religious history of your family? Are your parents religious and were their parents religious? Which religions did they accept? Is your family now less religious than it used to be?

Measuring the extent of secularization is, therefore, a very complicated thing:

❖ There is some evidence that religion was in the past more significant to individuals and social groups than it is now, i.e. that there was some sort of 'golden age' of religion. Significant numbers of people believed in heaven and hell and feared the supernatural. They also feared the clergy who were in fact very powerful. It is now the case that religion has less of a role in social control than in the past and is less significant in determining how people live their daily lives.

❖ There is the problem of unusual beliefs – e.g. in witches, ghosts, horoscopes – and whether such beliefs are religious.

❖ Activity 14 ❖

Do you, your relatives and friends believe in any of the following: ghosts, witches, flying saucers, faith healing? Why do you believe in these and are these beliefs religious?

❖ There are problems, for example in Latin America, where the clergy get involved in political activity and are told by the church that that is not religious behaviour (see *In Focus* below).

❖ There are social processes which are seeing religion decline in significance, including the emergence of a variety of belief systems challenging the dominance of religion. At the same time there are processes within religion which take away some of its religious elements, such as the process at the heart of Protestantism and Calvinism which reduced the significance of church worship and priests.

❖ In all modern societies religions are in decline, but rates of decline are different and in some societies – the USA and Australia for example – rates of decline seem to be slowing down. Where there is an expansion in religious faith and observance, this is often the result of migration and subsequent birth patterns, as with the expansion of Islam in Britain. We need, therefore, to be careful in linking increases in religious observance to arguments that the decline in religions has been halted or indeed reversed.

In Focus

◆

Liberation theology

Liberation theology developed primarily within the Roman Catholic church in Latin America in response to problems of poverty and oppression. The important point is that, for many priests in Latin America, there is a religious justification for fighting against oppression – they have a 'religious duty' to oppose what is happening to the majority of poor people. Put another way, there is a link between theology, religious practice and politics; religion is not neutral in the world of politics. There have, in consequence, been conflicts between the Vatican and priests in Latin America over their left-wing political involvements. For the Vatican, religious activity is distinct from and superior to political activity. Priests should not, therefore, work in the realm of politics.

Table 14.12 Areas of growth in religion

Religion	Number of places of worship in the UK	Areas of growth
Islam	c. 600 mosques	The Mohammedi Park Masjid Complex is currently being completed by Dawoodi Bohras Muslims in Northolt, London. Recent development has also taken place in Leicester, Birmingham, Glasgow and Blackburn.
Hinduism	c. 120 temples	Many of the traditional temples are to be found in London and Leicester. The most recent development is the marble temple of the Swaminarayan Hindu Mission, completed in Neasden, London in 1995. Another temple in Ealing is currently at planning stage.
Judaism	c. 350 synagogues	Over half of all Jewish synagogues are in London. Numbers rose by 30 over the 1980s as new communities began to grow in East Anglia, Kent and the south coast.
Christianity	c. 49,850 churches	The fastest growing denominations are evangelical New Churches which have opened up to 1,900 churches since 1980. The Baptists have opened 439 and Pentecostalists 419.

Source: adapted from Bunting (1996)

❖ More people go to church at crucial times of status passage – birth, marriage, death – than are regular attenders and practitioners. This raises the question of what counts as a religious person's regular or irregular attendance. In addition, it seems that both regular attendance and attendance associated with status passage are *both* declining, even though the latter started from a higher base.

We can say with some certainty that religion in a society like ours *is* in a new position: one in which it has to *compete with other belief systems.*

❖ Activity 15 ❖

Make a list of the belief systems with which religions have to compete. How do they compete with these and are they successful?

In Focus
◆
Rites of passage

Rituals that deal with status passage (called *'rites de passage'*) are common in both premodern and modern societies, although they have much greater social significance in the premodern ones. In such small-scale societies, the ritual usually includes a period of total isolation from society and an often painful ritual to signal that the person has reached the new status (say, moving from being a child to an adult). In modern societies we still have rituals – marriage, funerals and so on – but they are less elaborate, rarely involve periods of separation from everyday life and rarely involve the deliberate inflicting of pain.

Surrogate religions

As we said earlier, functional definitions of religion make it likely that we will find many sets of beliefs and practices that perform religious functions but don't look like religions. We can include nationalism here. Many nationalisms answer fundamental questions – e.g. 'Why are we powerless and oppressed?' – and have elements of the sacred, e.g. the flag. And yet, nationalism is not, for most people, a religion. Bellah (1970) has developed some of these ideas and claimed that in the USA there is a form of civil religion which includes ideas like freedom, justice and quality. These have a sacred significance, serve to unite people of different ethnic, class and cultural backgrounds and therefore play a key role in maintaining social solidarity.

> ❖ **Activity 16** ❖
>
> Do you think the American flags flanking the picture below are suggestive? In the light of the above, what might their symbolic role be?

Signs of a surrogate religion? American President, Bill Clinton at the signing of the Crime Bill 1994

There are also a number of candidates for systems of belief and practice which have replaced religion: these include science, medicine and psychotherapy.

Science

There is a commonly held view that it is science which has replaced religion because of the factual nature of its explanations. In fact, it seems that this is not the case. The majority of the population who are indifferent to religion are also indifferent to science. In addition, the conflict between science and religion is easy to exaggerate. Important scientific innovators from Isaac Newton to Steven Hawking have also been convinced that god has a role to play in the development of the laws of physics.

Science often provides *different* answers to questions. If, for example, a brick falls on my head when I walk near a building site, the scientist will be able to tell me how fast it falls and the sort of damage that may happen to my head. A religious explanation may add to this *why* it fell on *my* head. The religious explanation may be more satisfying even if it is scientifically wrong. This is the point behind Weber's idea that the modern world is disenchanted; this is a world dominated by bureaucracy, so that more and more of life becomes predictable. For many individuals this robs the world of magic and mystery, and they seek these things in, amongst other things, religion.

> ❖ **Activity 17** ❖
>
> Read the *In Focus* on the next page.
>
> 1 What are Watts, and Dawkins and Crick disagreeing about?
>
> 2 Summarize your own view about the relationship between science and religion, and the relative merits of each.

Medicine

Bryan Turner (1983) argues that, whereas in the past religion had the power over life and death (people were born into a religion and had religious rituals when they died), now this power has passed to medicine and the medical profession. The problems of theodicy have been medicalized in that medicine tells us when we are ill, why we

Crusade against God

'Two of the world's most prominent biologists, Richard Dawkins and Francis Crick, are today accused of conducting an anti-religious crusade that has no basis in scientific research.

Fraser Watts, who last year became Britain's first full-time lecturer in science and religion at Cambridge, is to say in the Starbridge Lecture tonight, that the ideas of the socio-biologist Dr Dawkins and the neuroscientist Dr Crick are 'really incidental to serious scientific work in their fields. They have no proper basis in scientific research.'

Dr Crick, who won the Nobel Prize for his joint discovery of the structure of DNA, argued in his book *The Astonishing Hypothesis* that human feelings are no more than the behaviour of nerve cells.

Dr Watts will say that such ideologies 'clash with religion, not because they are scientific, but because they are really quasi-religious ideas that have taken an anti-religious turn and infiltrated the scientific enterprise.'

Dr Dawkins, Reader in Zoology at New College, Oxford, is one of Britain's most polemical atheists, and said recently that theology was no longer a respectable subject for academics.'

Source: W. Schwartz, *The Guardian*, 7 November (1994)

are ill and what to do about it. The answers given are primarily scientific. However, unlike many other explanations of illness – for example, those which blame illness on how you live your life or on malign people who don't like you – medical answers rarely provide satisfying solutions to the acute problems of infant death or death from AIDS.

Psychotherapy

Both Christopher Lasch (1980) and Ernest Gelner (1985) argue that many of the ways of dealing with problems of unhappiness and misery have been taken over by various forms of psychotherapy which claim to diagnose social ills and cure them. They do this in a particular way by telling people that there is something wrong with their psyche, their identity. For most psychother-apies – psychoanalysis, group therapy, family therapy – many of these difficulties developed in early life, that is, in relationships with parents and guardians. If this is put right they will become better, happier, people. These therapies emphasize a principle of working very hard on your self and, in so doing, trying to make it a better

self; there are therapies of personal growth which often have very practical aims.

Probably the best way to conclude this section is to say that, in the modern world, religion is still important but that it has taken on new organizational forms and new beliefs. In particular, established religions have to compete in a market for believers and, increasingly, behave like large corporations; they advertise on television, they become involved in politics and so on (see *In Focus* on the following page).

Fundamentalism

There is a related feature of religion in the contemporary world besides the development of NRMs and religious surrogates and that is the growth of *fundamentalism*. We need to contrast the stereotype of fundamentalism with the reality. Whilst the stereotype emphasizes the violent, dangerous, ecstatic and irrational elements of fundamentalism happening outside the modern world (e.g. in Iran), the reality is a little different. Fundamentalism is common at the heart of modern societies – at the heart of US politics, for example.

Advertising God is effective

'Christian advertising succeeds in making people think about their religious beliefs, reveals the first survey into its effectiveness. A third of 404 people questioned in Birmingham and the West Midlands believed such advertising could encourage church attendance; 52 per cent said it made them think about their view of religion; and 70 per cent believed advertising was appropriate to communicate the Christian message.

The survey was conducted following a controversial Easter campaign with the message: "'Surprise!' said Jesus to his friends three days after they buried him... to be continued in a church near you this Easter."'

Source: Madeleine Bunting,
The Guardian, 3 October 1995

It is noticeable that in the last 15 to 20 years a form of fundamentalist Christianity has come to play a central role in American politics. Although fundamentalist religious movements have a long history in America, their recent political role is particularly significant and has a number of features:

❖ the link between *fundamentalism in religion* and *fundamentalism in politics*

This includes the opposition to a whole series of liberal political ideas – equal rights for minorities, government involvement in what states do, government involvement in life-politics, e.g. abortion, the teaching of evolution in schools. Fundamentalists oppose all these on the grounds that they go against religion and go against certain basic rights that people have always had. So, for religious reasons, fundamentalists oppose evolutionism and for political reasons, they oppose central government's powers.

❖ the link between *fundamentalism* and *the media*

One of the most noticeable feature of all religions in the USA, but especially those aspects of fundamentalism which seek to have political influence, is that they use the media very effectively. As Steve Bruce (1993) suggests, in America we have the era of PrayTV. The media is used in two ways: to lobby for particular political positions and to carry out religious worship. Both of these also allow religious movements to gain large amounts of financial sponsorship, which is especially valuable as religious movements have tax exempt status in the USA.

❖ the desire in fundamentalism *to sanctify politics*

Central to fundamentalism in American society is the desire to give religious justification to political programmes and particularly to programmes which are politically of the right.

As Bruce (1993) and Davie suggest (1995), it is in fact debatable whether the protestant fundamentalists in the USA could sanctify politics and the extent of their influence may be exaggerated. They face a problem common to religion in modern societies, that is that religion has become a private rather than a public matter. It is difficult for fundamentalists to turn back to a time when religion was a public issue, particularly given that most religious fundamentalism in the USA is Protestant fundamentalism. It therefore has great difficulty appealing to both non-fundamentalist protestants and other religious groups. However, fundamentalism may serve to maintain a deep-seated conservatism in voters rather than creating such conservatism.

What then do the various fundamentalist movements have in common?

❖ the call for a return to tradition: *tradition vs modernity*

Fundamentalists regard the modern world as problematic because traditional ways of doing things have been forgotten. This loss of tradition then allows them to explain all social ills. The solution is a return to tradition and traditional ways of life. This idea is contained in John Major's short-lived 'back to basics' initiative. Importantly, when sociologists explore this call, it is always unclear what these traditions were and whether they were anything more than the basics for only a small section of the population.

❖ the call for a return to certainty: *absolutism vs relativism*

The loss of tradition includes a move from a world in which things were certain to one in which values, morals and beliefs are relative to the society in which they have arisen. Put in the language of sociology beliefs and values are *socially constructed*. What fundamentalists want is to return to a time when answers to questions like 'How should I behave?' or 'What should we do about crime?' were straightforward and not open to discussion and debate.

❖ the call for a return to community: *community vs alienation*

Finally, most fundamentalists argue that the causes of the collapse of tradition and the relativism of values is the collapse of the community as the structure in which we live our lives. Returning to community therefore becomes a condition for the return to tradition and to certainty.

This is what most fundamentalists believe and the programme they argue is necessary for social improvement. We can, however, be highly critical of the idea that in the past there was certainty and people lived in peaceful communities with each other. There was the dark side of community life which involved the exclusion of outsiders. What fundamentalists seem to be doing is seeking a recreation of what Benedict Anderson (1983) calls *imagined communities*.

❖ Activity 18 ❖

Give four examples of fundamentalist movements. What do they have in common?

In Focus

◆

Media portrayals of funda-mentalism

 edia portrayals of fundamentalism are usually negative, presenting fundamentalists as anti-modern, anti-democratic and violent. This is particularly clear in portrayals of Islam. Islam is presented as a danger from outside – Saddam Hussein in Iraq, Islam in Iran – and a danger from within – opposition to Islamic worship in schools and to separate Muslim schools. A lot of this negative portrayal does not correspond to the realities of Islam as it is practised by believers.

Gender and religion

In Focus

◆

God a woman?

Face to Faith: Wisdom that is Woman

'George Austen, Archdeacon of York, is upset. The 600-year-old cycle of Mystery Plays is this year introducing an unwelcome innovation: the part of God is to be played by a woman. "This," he said, "is political correctness gone mad." For him, as for many other faithful churchgoers, the image of God is incontrovertibly masculine.'

Source: Jeremy Goring, *The Guardian*, 2 March 1996

Within any population there are variations in religious belief and practice; for example, there are variations in belief and attendance related to age and social class. One of the most notable features of religion in Britain is that women are more likely to *attend* church services than are men. In 1991, 63 per cent of frequent attenders were women compared with 37 per cent for men, and 65 per cent of regular attenders were women, compared with 35 for men (Jowell *et al.* 1992). There are few available statistical sources which indicate whether men and women differ in the nature and extent of their religious *beliefs*.

❖ Activity 19 ❖

In small groups decide why women might attend church more than men do.
Are women more religious than men and, if so, why?

Max Weber was one of the first sociologists to address the issue of women's role in religion and why religion might appeal to women more than to men. In an article first published in 1922 under the rather off-putting title *The Soteriology of the Underprivileged* (soteriology means 'doctrine of salvation'), he argued two important things (Weber 1922/1978):

❖ that religious sects appeal to those who are underprivileged because they offer salvation from real suffering

❖ that women have an important and central role to play in such religious sects, in part because they are themselves underprivileged – the Seventh Day Adventists and the Christian Science movement are examples of this.

As we saw in the chapter on religious organizations, sects are unstable and often, through a process of becoming more and more bureaucratic, will develop into churches. This has two effects: the church becomes less and less concerned with the underprivileged and, in so doing, the central role that women play in sects declines. The typical church – the Church of England for example – gives a very marginal role to women.

In many churches, women have low status. In the Church of England until 1992, for example, women could not perform the religious rituals that male clergy did. This provides a series of interesting contrasts. Sects usually give a central role to women. Denominations gave a central role to women as clergy before most churches. Some churches – the Church of Scotland, for example – ordained women before others; in this case, in the 1960s. As Bruce notes (1995, p. 15), there are further complexities here. For example, the sister churches of denominations which were in former colonies tended to accept

A woman priest breaks the bread during a Eucharist service

women as clergy before the same denominations in Britain.

The ordination of women has proved very contentious. It has led to male clergy leaving the Anglican church and to prominent supporters of the Anglican church converting to other religions. The ordination of women is, in part, to do with theological issues, issues which have a long history. It is significant that, in the past, male Christian theologians have felt comfortable in debating whether women have souls and what is the significance of the notion that Eve was born from the rib of Adam! The ordination of women is also part of the process of extending rights to women – the right to vote, to have equal pay and to not be discriminated against in employment.

The greater religiosity of women needs explaining. If we go back to the Weber article mentioned above, it is clear that women have a high status and central role in particular types of sect, that is, those which stress inspiration, charisma and pacifity. In other words, there is a link between those features which many people – including feminist theorists – say are normal and natural for women and their role in religious sects and new age movements. The emphasis on feeling, cooperation and caring are part of many new age movements and of many religious sects of the past and are, at the same time, seen as gender-specific attributes.

There is, in fact, a divergence within theories of gender. We can sum this up by saying that some argue that most, if not all, of the differences between men and women are a result of socialization. This would mean that the greater religiosity of women and their important role in sects and new age movements would, itself, be a result of that process of socialization. Other feminist theorists argue that women and men are fundamentally different and these differences are not simply a result of learning. In this case, sects and new age movements appeal to something that is basic and essential to women and has little to do with socialization.

The appeal of many new age movements to women may have another stimulus. We have already seen that part of the debate about secularization is about the extent to which religion becomes more and more a matter of personal choice and the private sphere; that is, religion becomes less and less important in economic and political life. As Bruce (1995) and others argue, the religiosity of women and the role of religion in the private, family sphere are linked and support each other. Women are still seen as the guardians of the private sphere of family life and, to the extent that it is that area which is the sphere of religion, women are likely to have high levels of religious commitment.

In the next section we will look at the role of religions in multiracial Britain. There is, however, one other gender-related issue which is important and interesting: the debate about the role of women in Islam. The popular image of Islam is of a fundamentalist religion which, amongst other things, oppresses women. Part of that oppression involves women veiling themselves in public. Opposed to this popular view is that of many Muslim women that the veil is liberating and allows women to participate in the public sphere. There is, in Islam, a theological justification

Veiled Muslim
women

Western notions of liberation and freedom which may not apply in other cultures. This may be one of the reasons why many Western people have difficulties when Muslim women say that the veil is not oppressive:

'There are lots of other kinds of advantages to wearing the veil... I find it easier to mix and get around in public and not to be bothered by lecherous stares or worse. But these are just advantages of a certain style of dress which doesn't draw attention to the body or fit the Western stereotypes of sexy clothes. They don't have anything specific to do with Islam, they have more to do with being female in a sexist and male dominated society where women are judged by how they look.' (Watson 1994, p. 149)

This is the view of an educated, young British-Asian woman. Essentially, there are a number of motivations behind veiling, only some of which are religious. For some women the veil is a sign of religious faith; for others it provides a way of working in an environment which is sexist and racist; for others, it is a way of making a statement about moral values or it may involve a combination of all these.

for veiling which is to do with modesty (*hijab*), a modesty which both men and women are encouraged to develop. In such situations veiling may become a means by which men control women, but there is more to it than oppression and control.

There is the issue of how one society understands another. The popular image of the oppressed Muslim woman is based upon

 ## Religion in a multiracial society

There are a wide variety of religions in the UK and that is partly because the UK is a multicultural and multiracial society. It has been multicultural for a considerable period of time; arguably, it has always been multicultural. It is not surprising, therefore, that we find a multiplicity of religious faiths and movements in Britain.

What is noticeable is that not only are there many religious faiths in Britain, but many of them have nothing at all to do with Christianity and this is despite the fact that many people think of Britain as Christian. The range is very great: Judaism, Islam, Sikhism, Buddhism, Confucianism, Hinduism, Taoism. In addition, there is a large number of faiths which have Christian origins: these include Pentacostalism and Methodism. This list does not include the large number of new religious movements we studied earlier, nor new age religions which include what some people would call paganism. We can look at some of these in more detail.

❖ Activity 20 ❖

Carry out a religious census of your locality. How many different religious faiths are there in that locality?

Portraits of religious diversity

There are two issues which we should consider before we provide a brief portrait of some of the major religions in multiracial Britain:

❖ These portraits will be drawn by a socio-logist who is, in this case, not a religious person; they are a non-believer's and an outsider's view. For believers, they will not, therefore, be entirely accurate or fair.

❖ As suggested when we discussed fundamentalism, there are lots of negative images of minority religious faiths which, to believers, are misleading and offensive.

There is a group of monotheistic religions all of which originated in the Near East and which have had important influences on each other – see *In Focus* below for a summary of these religions.

In Focus

◆

Summary of religions

Islam

Islam originated in the near East and is now a powerful religious force in many countries: Iran, Iraq, Pakistan. There is a central group of beliefs and practices – professing one's faith, daily prayer, giving of charity, pilgrimage to Mecca and fasting. There are two main traditions: *Sunni*, the majority in the UK, and *Shi'a*, the minority in the UK. The latter see a much stronger relationship between religion and politics than do the former. Both, in the UK, emphasize the important relationships between religion and cultural and political identity. In addition, there are mystical groups within Islam including Suffis.

For Islam, there is a close interrelationship between religious and other aspects of life; as such, there is no separation between church and state. Religious leaders are experts in the interpretation of the Qu'ran, the revelations of the prophet Mohammed, and the application of the Qu'ran to daily life.

Judaism

Judaism is at least 2500 years old and was originally the religion of groups of nomadic peoples who lived in areas where the dominant religious tradition was polytheistic. There is a strong emphasis on the importance of religious texts and on strict moral codes of behaviour which influence all aspects of life, be it marriage, work or diet, for example. These codes derive from the Torah, consisting of the books of the Old Testament, and the Talmud, which contains interpretations of the Torah. Religious leaders – rabbis – are experts in interpreting the Torah and Talmud. There is an important element of diaspora in Judaism, that is, a view that the Jewish peoples have been dispersed about the world and now, following the establishment of the state of Israel in 1948, there is a need to come together again in a particular territory.

As with many other religions, there are distinct sub-groupings. Whereas most Jews believe in the eventual return of the Messiah who will redeem his people, few believe that this coming is imminent. Some sects – for example, the Lubavitch – do believe in imminent salvation. There are also divisions between orthodox and assimilated Jews.

Christianity

In terms of belief and organization, Christianity is diverse – Roman Catholicism, Protestantism and Eastern Orthodoxy are its main components. In all there is recognition of the importance of Jesus Christ as the founder of the church. Pentacostalism is basically rooted in Christianity and developed as a major religious tradition in the Caribbean and is now particularly important in black communities. There is a strong emphasis on salvation and more 'ecstatic' forms of worship.

In many senses, Christianity is the dominant religion in Britain. The monarch is the head of the Church of England; religious services in the House of

In Focus

◆

Summary of religions

Commons are Christian ones; religious worship in schools is still predominantly Christian.

Islam, Judaism and Christianity have become, at various times, state religions. Christianity and Islam in particular have often been committed to conversion. However, they have all seen the development of sectarian breakaways from the central church and divisions and conflicts between those who wish to maintain the original message and those who wish to change it, that is, a distinction between fundamentalists and reformers.

There is also a group of religions which developed outside Western Europe, predominantly in the Far East; most of these are polytheistic. These are now important religions in the UK and Western Europe.

Hinduism

Hinduism has existed for more than 6000 years. It is very diverse, with many local variants and has a large number of religious books – the Vedas, Ramayana, Mahabharata; Bhagavad-Gita; none of these claims to provide the truth. What links all Hindus is the caste system, a system of hereditary ranking. Traditionally there are four castes: Brahmans (priests and intellectuals), Kshatriyas (administrators and the military), Vaishyas (merchants and agriculturalists) and Sudras (workers); these have numerous occupational sub-divisions. Outside these are whole groups of untouchables. Each caste is to carry out its duties (*darma*), to carry out appropriate economic behaviour (*artha*) and pursue love and pleasure (*kama*). To the extent that people realize these responsibilities, they can move up the cycle of rebirth until finally they are released from the process itself.

Recently in India, more fundamentalist variants of Hinduism have developed, which strongly oppose other religions, especially Islam and Sikhism.

Buddhism

Buddhism was derived from Hinduism by Siddhartha Gautama. There is a stress on self-discipline, meditation and the renunciation of desire. This emphasis is orientated towards the attainment of *nirvana*, that is complete spiritual fulfilment. Buddhism is very tolerant of diverse traditions.

Within the sociology of religion there has been a major debate over whether Buddhism is a religion or simply a guide to living an ethically correct life. In Britain, Buddhism is increasingly appealing to people who have no past allegiance to it and do not come from the traditional Buddhist cultural background.

Confucianism

Confucianism was established in the 6th century BC. Confucius was a teacher, not a prophet, and developed a belief system which emphasizes wisdom and adjustment in human behaviour, so that life develops a natural harmony. In addition, there is a belief in the importance of ancestors. Again, there is a sense in which Confucianism is an ethical system, rather than a religion.

Sikhism

Sikhism was established in the 15th century in the Punjab in India. It shares many of the ideas of Hinduism – for example, reincarnation and karma – but is monotheistic in the sense that Sikhs believe that there is one god with many different names.

In practice, Sikhs accept the caste system. Sikhs are organized in caste associations which they tend to marry within; they will also share rituals with Hindus of the same caste. Orthodox Sikhs are committed to, and wear, five symbols of their religion: uncut hair in a turban; the small comb in the hair; a steel bracelet; knee length undergarments; a dagger. They worship in a *Gurdwara* which is – as with the Islamic mosque and the Hindu temple – a religious centre and a centre for the community.

Religions and community solidarity

It is noticeable that many communities that were formed relatively recently as a result of patterns of migration from Europe, the Caribbean, Africa and Asia, place a greater emphasis on religion than do indigenous white populations. This is for a number of reasons.

❖ People had high levels of religious mobilization before migration.

❖ Religion becomes a basis for building new communities in potentially or actually hostile social circumstances.

❖ Religion therefore performs the functions that Durkheim emphasized of building and maintaining social solidarity.

However, what is also clear is that religion has become a basis for conflict between cultures. These conflicts are, in part, a result of changes within minority communities, for example where younger people feel less allegiance to religion than do their parents. However, such conflicts also result from pressures on minorities to assimilate, changing your religious allegiance being a sign of that assimilation. Religious mobilization for minorities therefore becomes a way of resisting pressures to assimilate by, for example, maintaining traditional forms of worship.

The conflict between what is a dominant culture and one that is subordinate is an unequal one, particularly given the tendency for minority cultures to be seen in a negative light. As an example we can take attitudes to arranged marriages, which have a religious justification for Muslims. Politicians have sometimes taken the attitude that insisting on an arranged marriage is itself a sign of an unwillingness to assimilate – indeed, of racism – whereas many Muslims see it as essential to maintaining their cultural identity. Similar difficulties have arisen where Sikhs have argued that their religious tradition demands that they wear turbans and not, for example, crash helmets or police helmets. The conflict between religious traditions is therefore a highly politicized one and also one that has fuelled the debate about immigration, immigration control and the identification of British culture.

Different religions and the education system

The debate about religious education, in particular the role of multifaith worship in schools and the possibility of separate schools for religious minorities, is a complex and unresolved one. It is a debate that tells us a lot about British culture and the ideas of tolerance. We can take as examples here the issues of separate Muslim schools and the role that non-Christian worship has in state schools.

Muslim schools

The history of British education has seen most schools separating from the link they had to the church in the eighteenth and nineteenth centuries. However, some schools are directly funded by the government but still controlled by religious organizations. These include Roman Catholic schools which, although they may recruit non-believers, remain church schools.

This is not the case for Muslims, which raises a number of issues:

❖ the perceived unfairness of government funding not being available for Muslim schools

❖ concern amongst some Muslim parents over the education of girls in mixed-sex schools

❖ a concern among Muslim parents that important aspects of their religious tradition are lost in mainstream schools, even in schools with many Islamic pupils.

The demand for Muslim schools is, then, a demand for equal treatment and recognition for Islam, for the maintenance of a cultural tradition, and for proper education for boys and girls. These demands are complex and relate to many areas

The debate about religious education and Britishness relates to the different policies which exist for dealing with ethnic diversity, including:

❖ *Assimilationism* – which asks minorities to give up their culture and way of life

❖ *Integrationism* – which permits some measure of cultural self-determination

❖ *Pluralism* – which calls for considerable self-determination

❖ *Separatism*.

For a minority, the demand for separatism – say for separate education – is often the result of concern over what happens when assimilationism and integrationism occur.

already covered including family, gender and identity (see Chapters 2 and 3). They are also demands which are opposed, in part, on the grounds that some form of assimilation, by Muslims in particular and minorities in general, is the best way to become British. This idea of Britishness here is, of course, very narrow and excludes many religious traditions.

Multifaith worship

What is permitted in state schools is forms of multifaith worship which will include aspects of other religious traditions. Although these are often opposed by both those committed to Christian worship in schools and by those from other traditions, the idea behind such worship is to introduce pupils to a variety of faiths as a way of helping them to accept differences of view and to seeing other views as having validity. This is also, of course, part of the aim of multicultural education (see Chapter 4) which includes the view that if people learn about other's cultures they will be less likely to discriminate against those people.

The debate about the variety of religious faith in Britain and, in particular, its role in the education system, tells us a great deal about the nature of British society, and about democracy and tolerance:

❖ The debate emphasizes that the issue of culture is not uncontested; in part, the resistance to separate Muslim schools is based on a desire to simplify what is meant by British culture.

❖ The debate raises issues about identity (see Chapter 2) and about the right to be different and to have those differences recognized and accepted.

❖ The debate gives us an interesting perspective on the widely held idea that we are a tolerant people. Tolerance is widely seen as a feature of British culture, but the word itself has two meanings: one about recognizing and

❖ Activity 21 ❖

1 Are you familiar with multifaith worship? From your own experience, what happens in a session of worship?

2 In the light of the above, consider the arguments for and against segregated religious education.

3 The 1944 Education Act made religious instruction a legal requirement, although parents could withdraw their children from RE if they so wished. The 1988 Education Act changed the word 'instruction' to 'education', thereby paving the way for multifaith teaching. However, schools are encouraged to look particularly at Christianity and the law requires that the whole school meet every day for worship 'wholly or mainly of a Christian character'. From your reading in this chapter, discuss whether you think the law needs to be changed and, if so, in what ways?

Keeping the Faith: Muslims set schools spiritual test

'In our education supermarket, religions are laid out like so many brands of washing powder. You can pick as you like.

Or so Mohamed Mukadam parent-governor of a Birmingham primary school where 500 Muslim children have been withdrawn from mainstream religious education perceives. He argues that the multifaith religious education enshrined in the national curriculum has bred an objective rather than spiritual approach to religion.

"Multifaith education nurtures a spectator approach to all religion. It teaches you about religion but doesn't teach you faith," he says. "If you believe in all religions, you end up believing in none."

Muslim parents have campaigned for segregated religious education at Birchfield Community School in Birmingham for three years. Seventy per cent of the children at Birchfield are Muslim. Two years ago they won the right to a separate act of worship. Now they have won an even more significant battle. Imran Mogra, a trained teacher and Islamic scholar, will take one hour a week of segregated religious education.

Mr Mukadam believes segregated education is necessary to stop young Muslims drifting away from the faith. "We have no doubt that if we don't act to preserve our traditional faith it will be diluted, as the Christian faith has been."

Fundamentalist Christians could also jump on the bandwagon. "Christian parents can be expected to ask for Christian religious education in primary schools," said Richard Wilkins, general secretary of the 2,800-strong Association of Christian Teachers. "The Muslims have shown what is possible under the law."

This dissatisfaction has created some strange alliances, with fundamentalists, traditionalists and progressives finding common cause. Next month the Third Sector Schools Alliance, which brings together new Christian, Muslim, Steiner and Human Scale Education schools will be launched in Parliament. The groups are united by dissatisfaction with the "constraints" of the national curriculum and the lack of a "spiritual dimension" in state education.'

Source: Natasha Narayan, *The Observer*, 25 February 1996

accepting other people's ways of life; the other about putting up with those who have different ways of life. There is a strong element of the latter in the sort of paternalism that helps parents put up with children!

The social functions of religion

Earlier in this chapter we suggested that religion has a number of social functions, depending on the theoretical perspective you adopt. The sorts of question we need to answer include:

❖ What roles does religion play in society?

❖ If religion is important, then what are the implications of any decline in religious belief and practice?

❖ Are people right in accusing religions and religious leaders of giving up on key issues like right and wrong, morality and so on?

We can contrast those views which see religion as a conservative force in society, that, is as preserving the status quo, the accepted order of things; and those which see religion as a force for social change.

Religion as a conservative force

Despite the major differences in their views, Marx and Durkheim both see religion as performing a predominantly conservative and stabilizing role. For Durkheim religion integrates people by promoting a sense of group identity, both in terms of beliefs and practice. This is what makes social solidarity possible. Marx also identifies the stabilizing role of religion, but in his case the society being stabilized is based on fundamental inequalities. In this case religion makes it less likely that people will challenge inequality and provides beliefs which justify acceptance of that inequality. This is what Marx meant when he referred to religion as both the opium of the people and the heart of a heartless world.

What we mean by the word conservative is, of course, complicated. From one point of view, religion supports the status quo; in that sense, it is likely to support the basic institutions of society. However, religion may be conservative in a slightly different sense, that is, in opposing some aspects of social change. This is the case with the Roman Catholic church's opposition to birth control and abortion. Finally, as with religious fundamentalism, the church may support traditional values as a way of opposing wider social changes. In the case of the 1979 Islamic revolution in Iran, part of what was going on was opposition to Westernization. In this last case, religion is both conservative and radical: supporting social change in the name of a return to traditional ways of doing things.

Religion as a force for change

Whereas most functionalists argue that religion plays a mainly conservative and stabilizing role, there is considerable evidence that religions have some role to play in social change; that is, they do not just inhibit social change (see *In Focus* below for a discussion of what this means).

One of the major aims of Max Weber's study of Protestantism (1904/1974) was to suggest that religion has some role to play in the growth of capitalism, in that a form of religion did *not* act as a brake on capitalist development. We have already seen that what Weber calls the Protestant ethic was important in the development of modern, capitalist societies. Historians have made similar claims, for example concerning the role that Methodism played in the development of the labour movement in Britain. Indeed, it is now suggested by researchers that one of the reasons for the decline of the Methodist church is the fragmentation of the working classes.

In Focus

◆

Defining social change

Sociologists are not agreed about what is meant by social change. What is clear is that many of them see change being about major changes in the structure of society. This is what Marx talks about when he discusses the change from feudalism to capitalism, and what Durkheim is interested in when discussing the change from mechanical to organic solidarity. However, there is clearly more to change than this and change occurs more often and at a more micro-level than the major changes which Marx and Durkheim discuss. For example, changes in church attendance and the development of religious sects suggests that there are many real and significant changes occurring in religious belief and practice in modern societies which are not, at the same time, producing a different type of society. There are, therefore large-scale *system* changes as well as frequent and more small-scale *social* changes.

Nelson Mandela, leader of opposition to Apartheid and South Africa's first black president

- ❖ the Islamic revolution in Iran in 1979
- ❖ the fall of communism in Poland in the late 1980s and the Roman Catholic church's support for democracy
- ❖ the organization of black opposition to apartheid in South Africa.

There are two lessons for sociologists here:

- ❖ Religions are too diverse in terms of belief, practice and social location to make any simple generalization along the lines that religion makes a conservative or radical force sustainable.
- ❖ Social change is, in itself, very complex and is concerned with much more than the large-scale changes of social systems which many of the founders of sociology were interested in.

We can broaden our discussion here and suggest a number of situations in which religious belief and practice were crucial in challenging the power of the state and in helping to initiate social change, e.g.:

In Focus

◆

Evangelism

Evangelists 'used as right-wing force'

'Fast-growing Christian movements in developing countries are acting as agents of right-wing repression, according to officials of Christian Aid and the Catholic Institute for International Relations in London.

At a conference organized by the two groups at the weekend, a spokesman said such movements provided a "moral underpinning for grossly unjust forms of ordering civil society in repressive states". Affected areas included Latin America, South Africa and the Philippines.

Mr Ian Linden, the institute's general secretary, said that one interpretation of Christianity, as participation in the suffering and struggle of the people, was being "calculatedly countered" by another, in a "deliberate misuse of religion by the West."

Professor Michael Dodson, of Texas Christian University, said that every hour, 100 Latin Americans convert to the Pentecostals, who had grown from 12 million, in a traditionally Roman Catholic region, in 1968 to 55 million in 1988.

While Roman Catholicism had "turned left" in the region, "the pre-millennialist outlook in Protestant fundamentalism had the effect of discouraging believers from taking an active part in political life." In the Pentecostal sect "one draws closer to God not by creating His kingdom on earth, but by renouncing material benefits," said Prof. Dodson.

"In the Philippines, evangelical churches had made 500,000 converts between 1984 and 1988," said Mrs Sheila Coronel of the Philippines Centre for Investigative Journalism. She said evangelical sects gave material gifts to the poor, "but instead of conscienticizing and empowering communities so they could confront the roots of their poverty, these projects only reinforce the fatalism of the poor."

She said aid projects were also used for political mobilization. A Baptist sect, organized from the US, had children at a political rally wearing T-shirts marked "No to Communism, Yes to Jesus".'

Source: Walter Schwarz, *The Guardian,* 30 October 1989

❖ Activity 22 ❖

1 Read the text on evangelism (see *In Focus*). Explain in your own words how religion is being used to create a conservative force.

2 Is religion the only force acting? Consider the other social, economic or political factors that might need to be taken into account.

Chapter summary

Religion is clearly still an important social phenomenon today, despite those factors which are favouring secularization. Not only the founders of sociology but many contemporary sociologists find religion a fascinating subject for study. There are some crucial points to remember from this chapter:

❖ It is not the role of sociologists to decide whether religion is good or bad.

❖ Definitions of religion and measurements of religion and secularization are problematic.

❖ In the modern world religion has taken on distinct forms – NRMs, established

religions using the media and marketing – that indicate the changing nature of religiosity but perhaps do not indicate a uniform process of secularization.

❖ Fundamentalism is not a marginal pre-modern phenomenon, but a perspective on the social world which is common in modern capitalist societies.

❖ Because the UK is multiracial, it is also multireligious.

❖ Issues of religious diversity are social and political ones, and ask profound questions about culture and democracy.

Coursework

There are many possibilities for coursework based on the sociology of religion. This can include both quantitative and qualitative work. There is a great deal of information on religious beliefs in *British Social Attitudes* which comes out every year and so allows you to look at changes over time. Data on membership and attendance can be found in Brierley (1989 and 1991a, 1991b) and in several publications available from the Christian Research Association, formerly known as MARC (4 Footscray Road, Eltham, London, SE11 4BT). There is less material on non-Christian religions, although Badham (1989) is useful. The lack of overall

material on minority ethnic religions is itself indicative of the stress in studies of religion in the UK on what are seen as 'indigenous' religions (Christianity, Roman Catholicism, Judaism and so on).

As with all projects it is important to chose a topic which is doable and manageable. There is a lot you could do by involving people you know in your area: asking them if they go to church, why they go, if they want their children to go and so on. You could also do your own mini-census of religion in your area or you could look at the sorts of religious activity within your school or college.

Stimulus-response question

Using the information from this chapter and the stimulus items below, answer the following questions:

1 Why has attendance at churches declined and support for new religious movements increased?

2 What is a 'world-rejecting sect'?

3 Do the stimulus items suggest that there has been a process of secularization?

4 Why have the numbers of Muslims and Hindus increased in Britain?

Item A Church of England membership

Year	Members (000s)	% of adult population
1900	2,800	13.5
1950	3,000	9.2
1990	1,500	3.9

Source: Brierley (1989)

Item B The significance of new religious movements

How important were the new religious movements as cultural innovations? Though exotic and always good for a tabloid horror story, the world-rejecting ones were numerically insignificant... In 1989 the Unification Church claimed only 350 full-time core members, a further 100 'practising' members, and only about 8,000 'associates' (and less than one in ten of these had any continuing contact with the organization) There were about 150 Emissaries of Divine Light, sixty of whom live in their Cotswold community. There were only some 300 full-time devotees of the hare Krishna movement. Set against the shrinkage of the Christian denominations and sects, such figures are trivial... It is obvious that only a minute proportion of those who are free to do so have taken the opportunity to explore radically different forms of spirituality.

Source: Bruce (1995, pp. 101–2)

Item C Churches in Britain

'Christian churches in Britain have lost half a million members in five years, while Muslims have increased by more than a third to 852,000. Muslims now outnumber the combined strength of Methodists and Baptists by 152,00 according to figures for last year... Christian church membership declined to just under 7 million last year compared with nearly 7.5 million in 1980 and 8.5 million in 1970. The number of mosques increased from four in 1960 to 314 last year. In the five years to 1985, 750 churches closed and there were 1500 fewer Christian ministers. In the same five years, Sikhs increased from 100,000 to 180,000, Hindus went up by a third to 30,000 and Buddhists increased by 35 per cent to 23,000.'

Source: 'Muslims flourish, Christians decline', *The Guardian*

Essay questions

For essays and coursework you can get lots of basic data from CD-Roms *(Encarta*, the Hutchinson *Encyclopedia)*.

1 How useful is Wallis's idea of new religious movements for describing religion in Britain today.

2 Assess the view that we now live in a secular society.

3 Does religion favour or hinder social change?

4 What roles does religion play in a multiracial society?

5 Do sociological studies of religion suggest that women are more religious than men?

Further reading

Bruce, S. (1995) *Religion in Modern Britain*, London: Oxford University Press.

Bruce, S. (1993) *PrayTV*, London: Routledge.

Barker, E. (1984) *The Making of a Moonie*: *Choice and Brainwashing*, London: Blackwell.

Wallis, R. (1984) *Elementary Forms of the New Religious Life*, London: Routledge.

References

Abbott, P. and Wallace, C. (1992) *The Family and the New Right*, London: Pluto Press.

Abbott, P. and Wallace, C. (1996) *An Introduction to Sociology: A Feminist Perspective* London: Routledge.

Abercrombie, N. and Warde, A. (1992) *Social Change in Contemporary Britain*, London: Polity.

Abercrombie, N. and Warde, A. with Soothill, K., Urry, J. and Walby, S. (1994) *Contemporary British Society: A New Introduction To Sociology*, London: Polity.

Abercrombie, N., Hill, N. and Turner, B.S. (1980) *The Dominant Ideology Thesis*, London: Allen & Unwin.

Aberle, D. (1966) *The Peyote Religion among the Navaho*, Chicago: Aldine Press.

Adam, C. (1990) *The Sexual Politics of Meat*, Cambridge: Polity.

Adler, F. (1975) *Sisters in Crime*, New York: McGraw Hill.

Ahmed, A. and Donnan, H. (1994) *Islam, Globalization and Postmodernity*, London: Routledge.

Allied Dunbar National Fitness Survey (1992) quoted in *Focus on Healthy Ageing*, Research into Ageing, Baird House, 15–17 St. Cross Street, London.

Althusser, L. (1969) *For Marx*, London: Allen Lane.

Anderson, B. (1983) *Imagined Communities*, London: Verso.

Anderson, M. (1980) *Approaches to the History of the Western Family*, London: Macmillan.

Anderson, M. (1981) *Family Structure in 19th Century Lancashire*, Cambridge: Cambridge University Press.

Ang, I. (1991) *Desperately Seeking the Audience*, London: Routledge.

Appadurai, A. (1990) 'Disjunction and difference in the global cultural economy', in *Theory Culture and Society*, 7, pp. 295-310.

Arber, S. and Ginn, J. (1991) 'The invisibility of age: gender and class in later life', *Sociological Review*, 39(2), p. 260.

Arber, S. and Ginn, J. (1993) 'The gendered resource triangle: health and resources in later life', in S. Platt, H. Thomas, S. Scott and G. Williams (eds) *Locating Health: Sociological and Historical Explorations*, Aldershot: Avebury.

Archbishop's Commission on Urban Priority Areas (1985) *Faith in the City*, London: ACUPA.

Ariès, P. (1960/1973) *Centuries of Childhood*, Harmondsworth: Penguin.

Atkinson, J. (1978) 'Societal reactions to suicide', in S. Cohen, *Discovering Suicide*, London: Macmillan.

Atkinson, P., Davies, B. and Delamont, S. (eds) (1994) *Discourse and Reproduction: Essays for Basil Bernstein*, New York: Hamton Press.

Back, L. (1993) 'Race, identity and nation within an adolescent community in South London', *New Community*, 19(2), pp. 217–33.

Back, L. (1996) *New Ethnicities and Urban Culture: Racisms and Multiculture in Young Lives*, London: UCL Press.

Backhurst, D. and Sypnowich, C. (1995) *The Social Self*, London: Sage.

Badham, P. (1989) *Religion, State and Society in Modern Britain*, Lampeter: Edwin Mellen.

Bagguley, P. (1993) 'Urban Sociology', in *Developments in Sociology*, 9, pp. 121–38.

Bagguley, P. (1995) 'Protest, poverty and power: a case study of the anti-poll tax movement', *The Sociological Review*, 43(4), pp. 693–719.

Ball, S.J. (1981) *Beachside Comprehensive*, Cambridge: Cambridge University Press.

Ball, S.J. (1990) *Politics and Policymaking in Education*, London: Routledge.

Ball, S.J. (1994a) *Education Reform: A Critical and Post-structural Approach*, Buckingham: Open University Press.

Ball, S.J. (1994b) 'Some reflections on policy theory: a brief response to Hatcher and Troyna', *Journal of Education Policy*, 9(2), pp. 171–82.

Barash B. (1979) *The Whisperings Within*, New York: Harper and Row.

Barber, M. (1994) *The Making of the 1944 Education Act*, London: Cassell.

Barker, E. (1984) *The Making of a Moonie: choice and brainwashing*, London/Oxford: Blackwell.

Barker, M. (1981) *New Racism*, London: Junction Books.

Barker, M. (1996) *Ill Effects*.

Barnett, A. (1988) *Sociology of Development*, London: Hutchinson.

Barrett, M. (1980) *Women's Oppression Today*, London: Verso.

Barrett, M. and McIntosh, M. (1982) *The Anti-Social Family*, London: Verso.

Barron, R. and Norris, G. (1976) 'Sexual divisions and the dual labour market', in D. Barker and S. Allen (eds) *Dependence and Exploitation in Work and Marriage*, London: Longman.

Barthes, R. (1972) *Mythologies*, London: Cape.

Basset, K., Boddy, M., Harloe, M. and Lovering, J (1995) 'Economic and social change in Swindon', in J. Anderson and M. Ricci (eds) *Society and Science: A Reader*, Milton Keynes: Open University Press.

Bates, I. (1988) 'No bleeding, whining minnies: some perspectives on the role of YTS in class and gender reproduction', *British Journal of Education and Work*, 3(2), pp. 90–110.

Bates, I. (1989) 'No roughs and no really brainy ones: the interaction between family background, gender and vocational training on a BTEC fashion design course', *British Journal of Education and Work*, 4(1), pp. 79–90.

Bates, I. and Riseborough, G. (eds) (1993) *Youth and Inequality*, Milton Keynes: Open University Press.

Batteson, C. and Ball, S.J. (1995) 'Autobiographies and interviews as means of "access" to elite policy making in education', *British Journal of Educational Studies*, 43(2), pp. 201–16.

Baudrillard, J. (1988) *Selected Writings*, Cambridge: Polity.

Bauman, Z. (1989) *Modernity and the Holocaust*, Cambridge: Polity.

Bauman, Z. (1992) *Intimations of Postmodernity*, London: Routledge.

Beck, U. (1992) *The Risk Society*, London: Sage.

Beck, U. (1994) *Organised Irresponsibility*, Cambridge: Polity.

Becker, H. (1963) *Outsiders*, Glencoe: Free Press.

Becker, H. (1967) 'Whose side are we on?', *Social Problems*, 14(3), pp. 239–47.

Becker, H. (1976) *Sociological Work*, New York: Transaction Books.

Beechey, V. (1982) 'The sexual division of labour and the labour process', in S. Wood (ed.) *The Degradation of Work? Deskilling and the Labour Process*, London: Macmillan.

Bell, C. and Newby, H. (1976) *Community Studies*, London: Allen and Unwin.

Bell, D. (1961) *The End of Ideology*, London: Collier-Macmillan.

Bellah, R. (1950) *Through Values to Social Interpretation*, Durham, North Carolina: Duke University Press.

Bellah, R. (1970) *Beyond Belief*, New York: Harper & Row.

Berger, B. (1993) 'The bourgeois family and modern society', in J. Davies (ed.) *The Family: Is It Just Another Lifestyle Choice?*, London: IEA.

Berger, B. and Berger, P. (1983) *The War Over the Family*, London: Hutchinson.

Berger, P. (1967) *The Social Reality of Religion*, Harmondsworth: Penguin.

Berger, P. and Kellner, H. (1964, reprinted 1977) 'Marriage and the construction of reality', reprinted 1980 in M. Anderson (ed.) *Approaches to the History of the Western Family*, London: Macmillan.

Bernstein, B. (1975) *Class, Codes and Control*, Vols 1 to 3, London: Routledge.

Bernstein, B. (1990) *Class, Codes and Control: Vol. 4*, London: Routledge.

Best, S. and Kellner, D. (1997) *The Postmodern Adventure*, http://ccwf.cc.utexas.edu/~panicbuy/HaTeMail/marxtopomo.htm

Beveridge, W. (1942) *Social Insurance and Allied Services*, CMD 6404, London: HMSO.

Beynon, H. (1973, 1975) *Working for Ford*, Harmondsworth: Allen Lane.

Beynon, H., Hudson, R., Lewis, J., Sadler, D. and Townsend, A. (1989) '"It's all falling apart here": coming to terms with the future in Teesside', in P. Cooke (ed.) *Localities: The Changing Face of Modern Britain*, London: Unwin Hyman.

Biggs, S. (1993) *Understanding Ageism*, Milton Keynes: Open University Press.

Billig, M., Condor, S., Edwards, D., Gane, M., Middleton, D., and Radley, A. (1988) *Ideological Dilemmas*, London: Sage.

Bilton A., Bonnett, K., Jones, P., Skinner, D., Stanworth, M. and Webster, A. (1996) *Introductory Sociology*, London: Macmillan.

Blackwell, T. and Seabrook, J. (1996) *Talking Work: An Oral History*, London: Faber & Faber.

Blakenhorn, D. (1995) *Fatherless America*, New York: Basic Books.

Blane, D., Davey Smith, G., Filakti, H., Bethune, A. and Harding, S. (1994) 'Social patterning of medical mortality in youth and early adulthood', *Social Science and Medicine*, 39(3), pp. 361–66.

Blau, P. (1955) *The Dynamics of Bureaucracy*, Chicago: University of Chicago Press.

Blauner, R. (1964) *Alienation and Freedom*, Chicago: University of Chicago Press.

Blaxter, M. (1990) *Health and Lifestyles*, London: Routledge.

Blaxter, M. and Patterson, E. (1982) *Mothers and Daughters: a Three Generational Study of Health, Attitudes and Behaviour*, London: Heinemann.

Bleier, R, (1984) *Science and Gender*, New York: Pergamon Press.

Bocock, R. and Thompson, K. (1985) *Sociology and Religion*, Manchester: Manchester University Press.

Bottomore, T. and Rubel, M. (1956) *Karl Marx, Selected Writings*, London: Watts & Co.

Bourdieu, P. (1977) *Reproduction in Education, Society and Culture*, London: Sage.

Bourdieu, P. (edited by J.B. Thompson) (1977) *Symbolic Power*, London: Polity.

Bourdieu, P. (1984) *Distinction: A Social Critique of the Judgement of Taste*, London: Routledge.

Bourdieu, P. (1993) *Sociology in Question*, London: Sage.

Bourdieu, P. and Passeron, J.C. (1990) *Reproduction in Education, Society and Culture*, London: Sage.

Bowlby, J. (1971) *Attachment, Separation and Loss*, Vol. 1, *Attachment*, Harmondsworth: Penguin.

Bradley, H. (1996) *Fractured Identities: Changing Patterns of Inequality*, Cambridge: Polity.

Brake, M. (1980) *Sociology of Youth Culture and Youth Sub-cultures*, London: Routledge, Kegan & Paul.

Braverman, H. (1974) *Labour and Monopoly Capital: The Degradation of Work in the Twentieth Century*, London: Monthly Review Press.

Bridges, D. and McLaughlin, T.H. (eds) (1994) *Education and the Market-Place*, London: Falmer Press.

Brierley, P. (1980) *Prospects for the Eighties: From a Census of the Churches in 1979*, London: Bible Society.

Brierley, P. (1989) *A Century of British Christianity: Historical Statistics 1900–1985 with Projections to 2000*, Research Monograph 14, London: MARC Europe.

Brierley, P. (1991a) *'Christian' England: What the English Church Census Reveals*, London: MARC Europe.

Brierley, P. (1991b) *Prospects for the Nineties: Trends and Tables from the English Church Census*, London: MARC Europe.

Brierley, P. and Macdonald, F. (1985) *Prospects for Scotland: From a Census of the Churches in 1984*, Edinburgh: Bible Society of Scotland.

British Crime Survey, see Hough and Mayhew.

British Parliamentary Papers (1851/1970) *1851 Census, Great Britain, Report and Tables on Religious Worship 1852–3*, repr. Irish University Press (1970).

British Parliamentary Papers (1854) *Religious Worship and Education, Scotland, Report and Tables*, London: HMSO.

Brittan, A. (1989) *Masculinity and Power*, Oxford: Blackwell.

Broadbent, G. (1985) 'Estates of an outer realm', *New Society*, 14 June 1985.

Brown, P. and Scase, R. (1995) *Higher Education and Corporate Realities: Class Culture and the Decline of Graduate Careers*, London: UCL Press.

Bruce, S. (1992) 'The twilight of the gods: religion in modern Britain', *Sociology Review*, 2(2), pp. 11–17.

Bruce, S. (1993) *PrayTV*, London: Routledge.

Bruce, S. (1995) *Religion in Modern Britain*, London: Oxford University Press.

Bruegel, I. (1979) 'Women as a reserve army of labour: a note on recent British experience', *Feminist Review*, 3.

Bryce, C., Curtis, S. and Mohan, J. (1994) 'Coronary heart disease: trends in spatial inequalities and implications for health care planning in England', *Social Science and Medicine*, 38(5), pp. 677–90.

Bryman, A. (1991) 'Charisma and leadership', *Sociology Review*, 1(1), pp. 10–13.

Bryman, A., Blytheway, B., Allatt, P. and Keil, T. (eds) (1987) *Re-thinking the Life Cycle*, London: Macmillan.

Buckingham, D. (1993) (ed.) *Reading Audiences: Young People and the Media*, Manchester: Manchester University Press.

Bumiller, E. (1991) *May You Be the Mother of a Hundred Sons: A Journey among the Women of India*: Harmondsworth: Penguin Books.

Bunting, M. 'Minarets and domes rise among the warehouses', *The Guardian*, 20 March 1996.

Burgess, R. (1983) *Experiencing Comprehensive Education: A Study of Bishop McGregor School*, London: Methuen.

Burke, P. (1988) *Popular Culture in Early Modern Europe*, London: Wildwood Press.

Burnham, J. (1943) *The Managerial Revolution*, London: Putnam.

Burns, T. and Stalker, G. (1961) *The Management of Innovation*, London: Tavistock.

Bush, A. and Coleman, M. (1992) *The Financial Implications of Mass Opting Out*, Leicester: Educational Management Unit, University of Leicester.

Byron, M. (1994) 'Labour migration from the Caribbean', *Geography Review*, 7(5), p. 18.

Cain, M. (1989) *Growing Up Good*, London: Sage.

Campbell, A. (1984) *The Girls in the Gang*, Oxford: Blackwell.

Campbell, A. (1986) 'Self-report of fighting by females', *British Journal of Criminology*, 2.

Campbell, B. (1996) *The Dangers of New Labour's Communitarian Ideas*, http//www.democraticleft.org.uk/redkite/bea.htm

Carlen, P. (1988) *Women, Crime and Poverty*, Milton Keynes: Open University Press.

Carlen, P. *et al.* (1985) *Criminal Women*, London: Blackwell.

Carter, H. (1990) *Urban and Rural Settlements*, Harlow: Longman.

Cartwright, A. and O'Brien, M. (1976) 'Social class variations in health care. The sociology of the NHS', *Sociology Review* (monograph).

Casey, C. (1995) *Work, Self and Society: After Industrialism*, London: Routledge.

Cashmore, E. (1982) *Black Sportsmen*, London: Routledge.

Cashmore, E. (1994) *And There Was Television*, London: Routledge.

Castells, M. (1977) *The Urban Question*, London: Arnold.

Castells, M. (1983) *The City and the Grass Roots*, London: Arnold.

Castles, S. and Kosack, G. (1973) *Immigrant Workers and Class Structure in Western Europe*, Oxford: Oxford University Press.

Champion, A. (1993) 'Census of Britain 1991: population distribution and change since 1981', *Geography Review*, 7(1), September 1993, p. 10.

Chandler, J. (1991) *Women without Husbands*, London: Macmillan.

Charles, N. (1993) *Gender Divisions and Social Change*, Hemel Hempstead: Harvester Wheatsheaf.

Charles, N. and Kerr, M. (1988) *Women, Food and Families*, Manchester: Manchester University Press.

Chen, K. (1992) 'Post-Marxism: critical postmodernism and cultural studies', in *Culture and Power*.

Chester, R. (1985) 'The rise of the neo-conventional family', *New Society*, 9 May 1985.

Chignell, H. and Abbott, D. (1995) 'An interview with Anthony Giddens', *Sociological Review*, November 1995, p. 11.

Child Poverty Action Group (1992) *Poverty in Black and White*, London: CPAG.

Christman, H. (ed.) (1987) *Essential works of Lenin*, London: Constable & Co.

Cicourel, A.V. (1976) *The Social Organisation of Juvenile Justice*, London: Heinemann.

Cicourel, A.V. and Kitsuse, J.I. (1963) *The Educational Decision Makers*, Indianapolis: Bobbs-Merrill.

Clark, S. (1994) 'Heartbreaking truth about women and the "man's disease"', *Sunday Times*, 27 November 1994.

Clarke, J. and Critcher, C. (1985) *The Devil Makes Work: Leisure in Capitalist Britain*, London: Macmillan.

Clarke, J. and Saunders, C. (1991) 'Who are you and so what?', *Sociology Review*, 1(1), September 1991, pp. 17–21.

Cloward, R.A. and Ohlin, L.E. (1961) *Delinquency and Opportunity*, Glencoe: Free Press.

Coard, B. (1971) *How the West Indian Child is Made Educationally Sub-normal*, London: New Beacon Books.

Cockburn, C. (1991) *In the Way of Woman*, Basingstoke: Macmillan.

Cockett, M. and Tripp, J. (1994) 'Children living in re-ordered families', *Social Policy Findings*, 45, York: JRF.

Cohen, A.K. (1955) *Delinquent Boys: The Culture of the Gang*, New York: Free Press.

Cohen, A.K. (1966) *Deviance and Control*, Englewood Cliffs: Prentice-Hall.

Cohen, A.K. (1985) *The Symbolic Construction of Community*, Chichester: Ellis Horwood.

Cohen, S. (1980) *Folk Devils and Moral Panics* (2nd edn), Oxford: Martin Robertson.

Coleman, D. and Salt, J. (1992) *The British Population*, Oxford: Oxford University Press.

Commission for Racial Equality (1988) *Learning in Terror: A Survey of Racial Harassment in Schools and Colleges*, London: Commission for Racial Equality.

Connell, R. (1987) *Gender and Power*, Cambridge: Polity.

Connell, R. (1996) *Masculinities*, Cambridge, Polity.

Cooke, P. (1989) *Localities: The Changing Face of Urban Britain*, London: Unwin Hyman.

Cooley, C. (1969) *Sociological Thought and Social Research*, New York: Wiley.

Cooper, D. (1972) *The Death of the Family*, Harmondsworth: Penguin.

Cowen, H. (1990) 'Regency icons: marketing Cheltenham's built environment', in M. Harloe, C. Pickvance and J. Urry (1990) *Place, Policy and Politics*, London: Unwin Hyman.

Craib, I. (1994) 'Going to pieces or getting it together: Giddens and the sociology of the self', *Sociology Review*, November, pp. 12–15.

Crawford, A., Jones, T., Woodhouse, T. and Young, J. (1990) *Second Islington Crime Survey*, Middlesex University Centre for Criminology.

Crewe, I. (1992) 'Why did Labour lose (yet again)?', *Politics Review*, September 1992.

Crompton, R. (1997) 'Gender and employment', *Social Science Teacher*, 26(2), Spring 1997, pp. 2–7.

Crompton, R. and Jones, G. (1984) *White-Collar Proletariat: Deskilling and Gender in Clerical Work*, London: Macmillan.

Crompton, R. and Mann, M. (1986) *Gender and Stratification*, Cambridge: Polity.

Crook, S., Paluski, J. and Waters, M. (1992) *Postmodernisation: Change in Advanced Society*, London: Sage.

D'Houtaud, A. and Field, M. (1984) 'The image of health: variations in perceptions by social class in a French population', *Sociology of Health and Illness*, 6(1), pp. 30–60.

Dahl, R. (1971) *Polyarchy*, Yale: Yale University Press.

Dalton, K. (1961) 'Menstruation and crime', *British Medical Journal*, 2.

Davidson, B. (1984) *The Story of Africa*, London: Mitchell Beazley.

Davie, G. (1995) 'Competing fundamentalisms', *Sociology Review*, 4(4), pp. 2–7.

Davies, B. and Anderson, L. (1992) *Opting for Self-Management*, London: Routledge.

Davies, T. (1995) 'Homosexuality: sexual deviance or sexual diversity?', *Sociology Review*, 5(2), November.

Davis, K. and Moore, W.E. (1945) 'Some principles of social stratification', *American Sociological Review*, Vol. X, pp. 242–54.

Davis, M. (1990) *City of Quartz*, London: Vintage Books.

Day, G. (1995) 'Community, locality and social identity', in *Developments in Sociology*, 12, Ormskirk: Causeway Press.

Day, G. and Murdock J. (1993) 'Locality and community: coming to terms with place', *Sociological Review*, 41(1), pp. 82–111.

Day, G. and Robbins, D. (1987) 'Activists for peace: the social basis of a local peace movement', in C. Creighton and M. Shaw (eds) *The Sociology of War and Peace*, London: Macmillan.

Day, P. and Klein, R. (1991) 'Britain's health care experiment', in B. Davey, A. Gray and C. Seale (eds) (1995) *Health and Disease: A Reader*, Buckingham: Open University Press.

Dean, H. (1991) 'In search of the Underclass' in Brown and Scase (1991).

Deem, R. (1984) 'The politics of women's leisure', *Leisure Studies*, 1(1).

Deem, R. (1990) 'Work and leisure: all work and no play?', *Social Studies Review*, 5(4), March 1990.

Dennis, N. (1993) *Rising Crime and the Dismembered Family*, London: IEA.

Dennis, N., Henriques, F. and Slaughter, C. (1956) *Coal Is Our Life*, London: Eyre & Spottiswoode.

Denzin, N. (1987) 'Postmodern children', *Society*, 24.

Department of Health and Social Security (1980), *Inequalities in Health: Report of a Research Working Group Chaired by Sir Douglas Black*, London: DHSS.

Department of Health and Social Security (1993) *The Health of the Nation: Variations in Health. What Can the Department of Health and the NHS Do? Variations Subgroup of the Chief Medical Officers*, London: Health of the Nation Working Group, DHSS.

Desai, M. (1986) 'Drawing the line', in P. Golding (ed.) *Excluding the Poor*, London: Child Poverty Action Group.

Devine, F. (1992) *Affluent Workers Revisited*, Edinburgh: Edinburgh University Press.

Diani, M. (1992) 'The concept of social movements', *The Sociological Review*, 40(1), pp. 1–25.

Dickens, P. (1993) 'Society and nature', *Developments in Sociology*, 9, pp. 141–64.

Dillon, T. (1973) *The Irish in Leeds 1851–1861*, Publications of the Thorseby Society, 54.

Dobash, R. and Dobash, R. (1979) *Violence against Wives*, Wells: Open Books.

Donzelot, J. (1980) *The Policing of Families*, London: Hutchinson.

Douglas, J.D. (1967) *The Social Meaning of Suicide*, New York: Princeton University Press.

Douglas, J.W.B. (1967) *The Home and The School*, London: Panther Books.

Douglas, M. (1966) *Purity and Danger: An Analysis of Concepts of Pollution and Taboo*, London: Routledge.

Downes, A. (1957) *Economic Theory of Democracy*, New York: Harper & Row.

Downes, D. and Rock, P. (1988) *Understanding Deviance* (2nd edn), Oxford: Clarendon Press.

Downing, J. (1988) 'The Cosby Show and American racial discourse', in G. Smitherman-Donaldson and T. van Dijk (eds) *Discourse and Discrimination*, Michigan: Wayne State University Press.

Duncan, C., Jones, K. and Moon G. (1993) 'Do places matter? A multi-level analysis of regional variations in health related behaviour in Britain', *Social Science and Medicine*, 37, pp. 725–33.

Duncombe, J. and Marsden, D. (1995) 'Women's triple shift', *Sociology Review*, 4(4), pp. 30–3.

Durkheim, E. (1893, reprinted 1947/1960) *The Division of Labour in Society*, New York: Free Press.

Durkheim, E. (1895, reprinted 1938) *The Rules of Sociological Method*, New York: Free Press.

Durkheim, E. (1897, reprinted 1952) *Suicide: A Study in Sociology*, London: Routledge.

Durkheim, E. (1903, reprinted 1956) *Education and Sociology*, New York: Free Press.

Durkheim, E. (1912, reprinted 1961) *The Elementary Forms of the Religious Life*, London: Allen and Unwin.

Durkheim, E. (1961) *Moral Education*, Glencoe: Free Press.

Eichler, M. (1988) *Non-sexist Research Methods: A Practical Guide*, London: Unwin.

Elias, N. (1978/1994) *The Civilising Process 1: the History of Manners*, Oxford: Blackwell.

Elston, M. (1980) 'Medicine: half our future doctors?', in R. Silverstone and A. Ward (eds) *Careers of Professional Women*, London: Croom Helm.

Engel, G.L. (1977) 'The need for a new medical model: a challenge for biomedicine', *Science*, 196, pp. 129–36.

Engels, F. (1844, reprinted 1973) *The Condition of the Working Class in England in 1844*, Moscow: Progress.

Engels, F. (1884, reprinted 1985) *The Origin of the Family, Private Property and the State*, Harmondsworth: Penguin.

Erikson, K.J. (1966) *Wayward Puritans*, New York: Wiley.

Etzioni, A. (1995) *The Spirit of Community*, London: Fontana.

Evans, K. and Heinz, W.R. (1994) *Becoming Adult in England and Germany*, London: Anglo-German Foundation for the Study of Industrial Society.

Evans-Pritchard, E.E. (1980) *Witchcraft, Oracles and Magic among the Azande*, Oxford: Clarendon Press.

Eysenck, H.J. (1970) *Crime and Personality*, London: Paladin.

Fairclough, N. (1989) *Language and Power*, London: Longman.

Faulkner, W. (1930) *As I Lay Dying*.

Featherstone, M. (1991) *Consumer Culture and Postmodernism*, London: Sage.

Featherstone, M. (1995) (ed.) *Global Culture: Nationalism, Globalization and Modernity*, London: Sage.

Ferrie, J.E., Shipley, M.J., Marmot, M.G., Stansfield, S. and Davey Smith, G. (1995) 'Health effects of anticipation of job change and non-employment: longitudinal data from the Whitehall II Study', *British Medical Journal*, 311, pp. 1264–9.

Fillingham, L.A. (1993) *Foucault for Beginners*, London: Writers and Readers.

Finch, J. and Mason, J. (1993) *Negotiating Family Responsibilities*, London: Routledge.

Firestone, S. (1971) *The Dialectic of Sex*, London: Jonathan Cape.

Fischer, P. and Warde, A. (1994) 'Complementary Medicine in Europe', *British Medical Journal*, 309, pp. 107–11.

Fiske, J. (1988) *Television Culture*, London: Methuen.

Fiske, J. (1989) *Understanding Popular Culture*, Boston: Unwin Hyman.

Fitz, J., Halpin, D. and Power, S.(1993) *Grant Maintained Schools*, London: Kogan Page.

Fitz-Gibbon, S. (1996) *Not Mentioned in Despatches*, Cambridge: Lutterworth Press.

Fleming, S. (1993) 'Schooling, sport and ethnicity: a case study', *Sociology Review*, 3(1), Sept. 1993.

Fletcher, R. (1966) *The Family and Marriage in Britain*, Harmondsworth: Penguin.

Foskett, R. and Foskett, N. (1992) 'Villages and rural areas', *Geography Review*, 5(5), pp. 9–10.

Foster-Carter, A. (1984) *The Sociology of Development*, London: Macmillan.

Foster-Carter, A. (1992) 'Development', in M. Haralambos (ed.) *Developments in Sociology*, Vol. 9, Ormskirk: Causeway Press.

Foucault, M. (1971) *Madness and Civilisation: A History of Insanity in the Age of Reason*, London: Tavistock Publications.

Foucault, M. (1972) *The Archaeology of Knowledge*, New York: Pantheon.

Foucault, M. (1973) *I, Pierre Rivière, Having Killed My Mother, My Sister and My Brother: A Case Study of 19th Century Parricide*, Harmondsworth: Peregrine.

Foucault, M. (1976) *The History of Sexuality*, Vol. 1, Harmondsworth: Penguin.

Foucault, M. (1977, 1979) *Discipline and Punish: The Birth of the Prison*, New York: Vintage.

Foucault, M. (1980) *Herculine Barbin: Being the Recently Discovered Memoirs of a Nineteenth Century French Hermaphrodite*, London: Harvester Press.

Foucault, M. (1983) 'Social security', Reproduced in L.K. Kritzman, (ed.) (1988) *Politics, Philosophy, Culture* (trans. A. Sheridan), New York: Routledge.

Fox, N.J. (1993) *Postmodernism, sociology and health*, Buckingham: Open University Press.

Fox, R. (1967) *Kinship*, Harmondsworth: Penguin.

Frank, A.G. (1967) *Capitalism and Underdevelopment in Latin America*, New York: Monthly Review Press.

Frank, A.G. (1981) *Crisis: In the Third World*, London: Heinemann.

Frankel, B. (1994) 'Class, environmental and social movements', in *The Polity Reader in Social Theory*, Cambridge: Polity.

Frayman, H. (1991) *Breadline Britain 1990s*, Domino Films/LWT.

Freud, S. (1905, reprinted 1977) 'Three essays on the theory of sexuality', in *On Sexuality*, Penguin Freud Library, Vol. 7, Harmondsworth: Penguin.

Freud, S. (1930, reprinted 1985) 'Civilisation and its discontents', in *Civilisation, Society and Religion*, Penguin Freud Library, Vol. 12, Harmondsworth: Penguin.

Froebel, F., Kreye, J. and Heinrichs, O. (1980) *The New International Division of Labour*, Cambridge: Cambridge University Press.

Frow, M. (1996) *Roots of the Future: Ethnic Diversity in the Making of Britain*, London: Commission for Racial Equality.

Fryer, P. (1984) *Staying Power: The History of Black People in Britain*, London: Pluto Press.

Fukuyama, F. (1995) *Trust: The Social Virtues and the Creation of Prosperity*, London: Hamilton.

Fussell, S. (1991) *Muscle: Confessions of an Unlikely Bodybuilder*, London: Abacus.

Gallie, D. (1978) *In Search of the New Working Class*, Cambridge: Cambridge University Press.

Gallie, D. (1994) 'Social consequences of long-term unemployment in Britain', in O. Benoit-Guilbot and D. Gallie (eds) *Long Term Unemployment*, London: Pinter.

Gallup, G.H. (ed.) (1976) *The Gallup International Public Opinion Polls: Great Britain 1937–75*, New York: Random House.

Gans, H. (1962) *The Urban Villagers*, New York: The Free Press.

Garfinkel, H. (1984) *Studies in Ethnomethodology*, Cambridge: Polity.

Geertz, C. (1975) *The Interpretation of Cultures*, New York: London: Hutchinson.

Gelner, E. (1985) *The Psychoanalytic Movement*, London: Paladin.

George, S. (1993) 'The debt boomerang', *New Internationalist*, May 1993.

Gerard, D. (1985) 'Religious attitudes and values', in M. Abrams, D. Gerard and N. Timms *Values and Social Change in Britain*, London: Macmillan.

Gershuny, J. (1992) 'Changes in the domestic division of labour 1975–1987', in N. Abercrombie and A. Warde (eds) *Social Change in Contemporary Britain*, Cambridge: Polity.

Gershuny, J. in *The Observer*, 19 Jan. 1997.

Gewirtz, S., Ball, S.J. and Bowe, R. (1995) *Markets, Choice and Equity in Education*, Buckingham: Open University Press.

Giddens, A. (1976) *The New Rules of Sociological Methods*, London: Hutchinson.

Giddens, A. (1984) *The Constitution of Society*, Cambridge: Polity.

Giddens, A. (1985) *The Nation State and Violence*, Cambridge: Polity.

Giddens, A. (1990) *The Consequences of Modernity*, Cambridge: Polity.

Giddens, A. (1991) *Modernity and Self Identity*, Cambridge: Polity.

Giddens, A. (1992) *Human Societies*, Cambridge: Polity.

Giddens, A. (1992b) *The Transformation of Intimacy*, Cambridge: Polity.

Giddens, A. (1993/5) *Sociology* (2nd edn), Cambridge: Polity.

Giddens, A. (1994) *Beyond Right and Left*, Cambridge: Polity.

Giddens, A., *et al.* (1994) *Reflexive Modernisation*, Cambridge: Polity.

Giles, G. and Johnson, P. (1994) 'Taxes reform in the UK and changes in the progressivity of the tax system, 1985–94', *Fiscal Studies Review*, 15(3), pp. 64–86.

Gill, D., Mayor, B. and Blair, M. (eds) (1992) *Racism and Education: Structures and Strategies*, London: Sage.

Gillborn, D. (1990) *Race, Ethnicity and Education*, London: Unwin.

Gilroy, P. (1987) *There Ain't No Black in the Union Jack*, London: Hutchinson.

Gilroy, P. (1993) *The Black Atlantic: Modernity and Double Consciousness*, London: Verso.

Glaser, B.G. and Strauss, A.L. (1967) *The Discovery of Grounded Theory*, Chicago: Aldine.

Glasgow Media Group (1985) *War and Peace News*, Milton Keynes: Open University Press.

Glasgow Media Group with Eldridge, J. (ed.) (1993) *Getting the Message: News, Truth and Power*, London: Routledge.

Glass, D. (1954) *Social Mobility in Britain*, London: Routledge, Kegan and Paul.

Glassner, B. (1989) 'Fitness and the postmodern self', *Journal of Health and Social Behaviour*, 30 June, pp. 180–91.

Goffman, E. (1961, 1968) *Asylums: Essays on the Social Situation of Mental Patients and Other Inmates*, Harmondsworth: Penguin.

Goffman, E. (1969) *The Presentation of Self in Everyday Life*, Harmondsworth: Penguin.

Goffman, E. (1970) *Stigma: Notes on the Management of Spoiled Identities*, Harmondsworth: Penguin.

Goffman, E. (1971) *Relations in Public*, London: Allen Lane.

Goffman, E. (1974) *Frame Analysis: An Essay on the Organization of Experience*, Harmondsworth: Pelican.

Goldstein, H. (1995) *Multi-Level Statistical Models*, London: Edward Arnold.

Goldthorpe, J.H. and Hope, K. (1974) *The Social Grading of Occupations: a New Approach and Scale*, Oxford: Clarendon Press.

Goldthorpe, J.H. and Payne, C. (1987) 'The class mobility of women', in Goldthorpe *et al.* (1987), pp. 277–301.

Goldthorpe, J.H., Llewellyn, C. and Payne, C. (1980, 1st edn; 1987, 2nd edn) *Social Mobility and Class Structure in Modern Britain*, Oxford: Oxford University Press.

Goldthorpe, J.H., Lockwood, D., Bechhofer, F. and Platt, J. (1968, 1969) *The Affluent Worker* (3 Vols), Cambridge: Cambridge University Press.

Goode, W.J. (1963) *World Revolution and Family Patterns*, New York: The Free Press.

Goode, W.J. (1993) *World Changes in Divorce Patterns*, Yale: Yale University Press.

Goschel, A. *et al.* (1982) 'Infrastructural inequality and segregation', *International Journal of Urban and Regional Research*, 6.

Gottman, J. (1961) *Megalopolis: The Urbanised North-Eastern Seaboard of the United States*, New York: Twentieth Century Fund.

Gough, I. (1979) *The Political Economy of the Welfare State*, London: Macmillan.

Gouldner, A. (1971) *The Coming Crisis of Western Sociology*, London: Heinemann.

Graham, H. (1994) 'Gender and class as dimensions of smoking behaviour in Britain: insights from a survey of mothers', *Social Science and Medicine*, 38(5), pp. 691–8.

Gramsci, A. (1971) *Selections from the Prison Notebooks*, London: Lawrence & Wishart.

Greeley (1992) 'Who says the nation is on its feet?' *The Guardian*, 18 October 1992.

Grint, K. (1991) *The Sociology of Work: An Introduction*, Cambridge: Polity.

Grint, K. (1992) 'The sociology of work', in M. Haralambos (ed.) *Developments in Sociology*, Vol. 8.

Grover, C. and Soothill, K. (1995) 'The social construction of sex offenders', *Sociology Review*, 4(3), Feb. 1995.

Gunder Frank, A. *see* Frank, A.G.

Habermas, J. (1976) *Legitimation Crisis*, London: Heinemann.

Habermas, J. (1987) *The Theory of Communicative Action*, Cambridge: Polity.

Habitas-mini articles (1997) http://www.on-the-net.com/interskills/minis/habitat.htm#comm

Hacker, R. and Troyna, B. (1994) 'The 'Policy Cycle': a ball-by-ball account', *Journal of Education Policy*, 9(2), pp. 155–70.

Hacking, A. (1995) 'Why multiple personality tells us nothing about the self/mind/person/subject/soul', in D. Backhurst and C. Sypnowich *The Social Self*, London: Sage.

Hakim, C. (1995) 'Five feminist myths about women's employment', *British Journal of Sociology*, 46(3), pp. 429–55.

Hall, P. (1981) *The Inner City in Context*, London: Heinemann.

Hall, S. (1988) 'The toad in the garden: Thatcherism among the theorists', in C. Nelson and L. Grossberg (eds) *Marxism and the Interpretation of Culture*, Urbana: University of Illinois Press.

Hall, S. (1989) 'New ethnicities', in K. Mercer *Black Film, Black Cinema*, ICA Document 7, London: Institute of Contemporary Arts.

Hall, S. (1990) 'The whites of their eyes', in M. Alvarado and J. O'Thompson (eds) *The Media Reader*, London: BFI.

Hall, S. (1992a) 'The question of cultural identity', in S. Hall, D. Held and T. Mcgrew (eds) *Modernity and Its Futures*, Cambridge: Polity.

Hall, S. (1992b) 'Our mongrel selves', *New Statesman*, Supplement: 'Borderlands', 19 July 1992, pp. 18–19.

Hall, S. (1992c) 'The West and the rest: discourse and power', in Hall and Gieben (1992) *Formations of Modernity*, Cambridge: Polity.

Hall, S. (1996) 'Introduction: who needs "identity"?', in S. Hall and P. Du Gay *Questions of Cultural Identity*, London: Sage.

Hall, S. and Du Gay, P. (1996) *Questions of Cultural Identity*, London: Sage.

Hall, S. *et al.* (1981) *Culture, Media and Language*, London: Hutchinson.

Hall, S., Critcher, C., Jefferson, T., Clarke, J. and Roberts, B. (1979) *Policing the Crisis: Mugging, the State, and Law and Order*, London: Macmillan.

Hall, S., Held, D. and McGrew, T. (eds) (1992) *Modernity and its Futures*: Milton Keynes: Open University Press.

Halpin, D. and Troyna, B. (eds) (1994) *Researching Education Policy*, London: Falmer Press.

Halpin, D., Fitz, J. and Power, S. (1993) *The Early Impact and Long-term Implications of the Grant-Maintained Schools Policy*, Stoke-on-Trent: Trentham Books.

Halsey, A.H. (1992) Foreword to N. Dennis and G. Erdos *Families without Fatherhood*, London: Institute of Economic Affairs.

Halsey, A.H., Floud, J. and Anderson C.A. (eds) (1961) *Education, Economy and Society*, Glencoe, Illinois: Free Press.

Halsey, A.H., Heath, A. and Ridge J.M. (1980) *Origins and Destinations*, Clarendon Press, Oxford.

Handy, C. (1984) *The Future of Work*, Oxford: Blackwell.

Hannerz, U. (1969) *Soulside: Inquiries into Ghetto Culture and Community*, New York: Columbia University Press.

Hardyment, C. (1990) 'Squaring the Family Circle', *Weekend Guardian*, 16–17 June 1990.

Hareven, T.K. (1994) 'Recent research on the history of the family' in M. Drake (ed.) *Time, Family and Community*, Oxford: Blackwell.

Hargreaves, D. (1967) *Social Relations in a Secondary School*, London: Routledge.

Hargreaves, D., Hestar, S. and Mellor, F. (1975) *Deviance in Classrooms*, London: Routledge.

Harrington, M. (1962) *The Other America: Poverty in the United States*, Harmondsworth: Penguin.

Harris, C.C. (1983) *The Family and Industrial Society*, London: Allen & Unwin.

Harris, N. (1987) *The End of the Third World: Newly Industrialized Countries and the Decline of an Ideology*, Harmondsworth: Penguin.

Harrison, P. (1983) *Inside the Inner City*, Harmondsworth: Penguin.

Hart, N. (1976) *When Marriage Ends: A Study in Status Passage*, London: Tavistock.

Hartmann, H. (1981) The unhappy marriage of Marxism and feminism: toward a more progressive union', in L. Sargent (ed.) *The Unhappy Marriage of Marxism and Feminism*, London: Pluto.

Hartmann, H. (1982) 'Capitalism, patriarchy and job segregation by sex', reprinted in A. Giddens and D. Held (eds) *Classes, Power and Conflict*, Basingstoke: Macmillan.

Harvey, D. (1973) *Social Justice in the City*, London: Arnold.

Heath, A., Curtice, J., Evans, G., Jowell, R., Field, J. and Witherspoon, S. (1991) *Understanding Political Change*, Oxford: Pergamon.

Heath, A., Jowell, R. and Curtice, J. (1985) *How Britain Votes*, Oxford: Pergamon.

Hebdige, D. (1979) *Subcultures: the Meaning of Style*, London: Methuen.

Hebdige, D. (1990) *Hiding in the Light*, London: Comedia.

Heelas, P. (1992) 'Sacralization of self and new age capitalism', in N. Abercrombie and A. Warde, *Social Change in Contemporary Britain*, London: Polity.

Heidensohn, F. (1985) *Women and Crime*, London: Macmillan.

Held, D. (1991) *Political Theory Today*, Cambridge: Polity.

Held, D. (1992) in Hall, *et al.* (eds) *Modernity and Its Futures*, Cambridge: Polity.

Heller, A. and Feher, F. (1988) *The Postmodern Political Condition*, Cambridge: Polity.

Helman, C.G. (1990) *Culture, Health and Illness*, London: Butterworth.

Henderson, J. and Karn, V. (1987) *Race, Class and State Housing*, London: Gower.

Henwood, M. (1987) *Inside the Family*, London: Family Policy Studies Centre.

Heron, L. (1985) *Truth, Dare or Promise: Girls Growing up in the Fifties*, London: Virago.

Hickox, M. (1995) 'Situating Vocationalism', *British Journal of Sociology of Education*, 16(2), pp. 153–62.

Hides, S. (1995) 'Consuming identities', *Sociology Review*, November, pp. 30–3.

Himmelweit, H. (1958) *Television and the Child*, Oxford: Oxford University Press.

Hindess (1973) *The Uses of Official Statistics in Sociology: A Critique of Positivism and Ethnomethodology*, London: Macmillan.

Hollinger, F. and Haller, M. (1990) 'Kinships and social networks in modern societies: a cross-cultural comparison among seven nations', *European Sociological Review*, 6.

Holme, A. (1985) 'Family and homes in East London', *New Society*, 12 July 1985.

Hough, M. and Mayhew, P. (1983) *The First British Crime Survey*, HMSO.

Hudson, M. (1994) *Coming back Broken*, London: Jonathan Cape.

Humphreys, L. (1970) *The Tea Room Trade*, London: Duckworth.

Hunt, S. (1995) 'The Race and Health Inequalities Debate', *Sociology Review*, 5(1), Sept. 1995.

Hyman, R. (1984) *Strikes* (3rd edn), London: Fontana.

Illich, I. (1976) *Medical Nemesis: Limits to Medicine*, London: Boyars.

Independence Educational Publishers (1993) *The Poverty Trap Issues for the Nineties*, Cambridge: IEP.

Independent Commission on Population and Quality of Life (1996) *Caring for the Future*, Oxford: Oxford University Press.

Inglehart, R. (1990) 'Values, ideology and cognitive mobilisation in New Social Movements', in R.J. Dalton *et al. Challenging the Political Order*, Cambridge: Polity 1990.

Jackson, B. and Marsden, D. (1962) *Education and the Working Class*, London: Routledge.

Jacobson, *et al.* (1991) *The Nation's Health*.

James, A. and Prout, A. (1990) *Constructing and Reconstructing Childhood*, Lewes: Falmer Press.

Jameson, F. (1991) *Postmodernism or the Cultural Logic of Late Capitalism*, London: Verso.

Jary, D. and Jary, J. (1991) *Dictionary of Sociology*, London: HarperCollins.

Jenkins, R. (1986) *Racism and Recruitment: Managers, Organisations and Equal Opportunity*, Cambridge: Cambridge University Press.

Jewson, N. (1991) 'The development of cities in capitalist society', *Sociology Review*, 1(2), pp. 6–10.

Jewson, N. (1994) 'Family values and relationships', *Sociology Review*, 3(3), pp. 2–5.

Jhally, S. and Lewis, J. (1992) *Enlightened Racism: The Cosby Show, Audiences and the Myth of the American Dream*, Oxford: Westview Press.

Johnston, R.J., *et al.* (1988) *A Nation Dividing*, London: Longman.

Jonathon, R. (1990) 'State education service or prisoner's dilemma: the 'hidden hand' as source of education policy', *Educational Philosophy and Theory*, 22(1), pp. 16–24.

Jones, R.B. (1971) *Economic and Social History of England*, Harlow: Longman.

Jones, S. (1996) *In the Blood: God, Genes and Destiny*, London: Harper Collins.

Jones, T. (1993) *Britain's Ethnic Minorities*, London: Policy Studies Institute.

Jones, T., MacLean, B., and Young, J. (1986) *The Islington Crime Survey*, Aldershot: Gower.

Jordan, B. (1987) *Rethinking Welfare*, Oxford: Blackwell.

Jordan, W. (1989) 'Face-to-face', *Social Studies Review*, 5(2), p. 56.

Jorgensen, N. (1995) *Investigating Families and Households*, London: Collins Educational.

Jowell, R., Brook, L., Prior, G. and Taylor, B. (eds) *British Social Attitudes Survey*, published annually, Aldershot: Dartmouth Publishing.

Katz, E. (1959) 'Mass communications research and the study of popular culture' in *Studies in Public Communication*, 2.

Katz, E. and Lazersfeld, P. (1955) *Personal Influence*, New York: Free Press.

Kay, T. (1989) 'Unemployment', in M. Haralambos (ed.) *Developments in Sociology*, Vol. 5.

Keddie, N. (1971) 'Classroom Knowledge' in M.F.D. Young (ed.) *Knowledge and Control*, London: Routledge.

Keith, M. and Pile, S. (1993) *Place and the Politics of Identity*, London: Routledge.

Kellner, D. (1989) *Jean Baudrillard: From Marxism to Postmodernism and Beyond*, Cambridge: Polity.

Kennedy, P. (1996) 'Forecast: global gales ahead', *New Statesman and Society*, 31 May 1996.

Kerlinger, F.N. and Pedhazur, E.J. (1982) *Multiple Regressions Analysis in Behavioural Research*, London: Holt Rhinehart & Winston.

Kerr, C., Dunlop, J.T., Harbison, F.H. and Myers, C.A. (1962) *Industrialism and Industrial Man*, London: Heinemann.

Kessler, S. J. and McKenna, W. (1978) *Gender: An Ethnomethodological Approach*, New York: Wiley.

Kettle, M. and Hodges, L. (1982) *Uprising: The Police, the People and the Riots in Britain's Cities*, London: Pan.

Kinsey, R. (1985) *The Merseyside Crime Survey*, Merseyside Police Authority.

Kirby, M., Koubel, F. and Madry, N. (1993) *Sociology: Developing Skills through Structured Questions*, London: Collins.

Kitzinger, J. (1990) 'Audience understanding of AIDS media messages', in *Sociology of Health and Illness*, 12(3), pp. 36–50.

Kitzinger, J. (1993) 'Understanding AIDS – media mssages and what peole know', in J. Eldridge (ed.) *Getting the Message Across*, London: Routledge.

Knox, P. (1992) *Urban Social Geography: An Introduction*, Singapore: Longman.

Kuhn, T. (1962) *The Structure of Scientific Revolutions*, Chicago: University of Chicago Press.

Labov, W. (1973) 'The Logic of Non-standard English' in N. Keddie (ed.) *Tinker Taylor...*, Harmondsworth: Penguin.

Laclau, E. (1971) 'Imperialism in Latin America', *New Left Review*, 67.

Laing, R.D. and Esterson, A. (1970) *Sanity, Madness and the Family*, Harmondsworth: Penguin.

Lane, D. (1970) *Politics and Society in the USSR*, London: Weidenfeld & Nicolson.

Lasch, C. (1980) *The Culture of Narcissism: American Life in an Age of Diminishing Expectations*, London: Abacus.

Lash, S. and Urry, J. (1994) *Economies of Signs and Space*, London: Sage.

Laslett, P. (1972) *Household and Family in Past Time*, Cambridge: Cambridge University Press.

Laslett, P. (1979) *The World We Have Lost*, London: Methuen.

Le Grand, J. (1982) *The Strategy of Equality*, London: Allen & Unwin.

Lea, J. and Young, J. (1984) *What is to be Done about Law and Order*, Harmondsworth: Penguin.

Lemert, E. M. (1972) *Human Deviance, Social Problems and Social Control* (2nd edn), Eaglewood Cliffs: Prentice-Hall.

Leslie (1980) quoted in S. Curtis and A. Taket (1996) *Health and Societies: Changing Perspectives*, London: Arnold.

Leslie, G.R. and Korman, S.K. (1989) *The Family in Social Context* (7th edn), Oxford: Oxford University Press.

Levi-Strauss, C. (1968) *Structural Anthropology*, London: Allen Lane.

Lewis O. (1959) *Five Families*, New York: Basic Books.

Lewis, G. (1985) 'From deepest Kilburn', in L. Heron, *Truth, Dare or Promise: girls growing up in the 50s*, London: Virago; 213-236.

Lewis, O. (1961) *The Children of Sanchez*, Random House: New York.

Liebow, E. (1967) *Tally's Corner*, Boston: Little Brown.

Lindblom, C. (1977) *Politics and Markets*, New York: Basic Books.

Lockwood, D. (1958) *The Black Coated Worker*, London: Allen & Unwin.

Lombroso, C. (1897) *The Criminal Man*, Putnam.

Lombroso, C. and Ferrero, W. (1895) *The Female Offender*, London: T. Fisher Unwin.

Longhurst, B. (1987) 'Realism and naturalism in television soap opera', *Theory, Culture and Society*, 4(4).

Lovenduski, J. and Randall, V. (1993) *Contemporary Feminist Politics*, Oxford: Oxford University Press.

Lukes, S. (1974) *Power: A Radical View*, London: Macmillan.

Lull, J. (1990) *Inside Family Viewing: Ethnographic Research on Television's Audiences*, London: Routledge.

Lyon, D. (1994) *The Electronic Eye: The Rise of Surveillance Society*, Cambridge: Polity.

Lyotard, J.-F. (1984) *The Postmodern Condition: A Report on Knowledge*, Manchester: Manchester University Press.

Mac an Ghaill, M. (1988) *Young, Gifted and Black: Student–Teacher Relations in the Schooling of Black Youth*, Milton Keynes: Open University Press.

McAllister-Groves, J. (1995) 'Learning to feel: the neglected sociology of social movements', *The Sociological Review*, 43(3), pp. 435–61.

Macdonald, I., Bhavnani, T., Khan, L. and John, B. (1989) *Murder in the Playground: The Report of the Macdonald Enquiry into Racism and Racist Violence in Manchester Schools*, London: Longsight Press.

MacFarlane, A. (1978) *The Origins of English Individualism*, Oxford: Blackwell.

MacGregor, M. and Pimlott, B. (1991) *Tackling the Inner Cities: The 1980's Reviewed. Prospects for the 1990's*, Oxford: Clarendon.

McIntyre, A. (1971) *Against the Self-Images of the Age*, London: Duckworth.

Macintyre, S. (1996) *The Black Report and Beyond: What Are the Issues?*, MRC Medical Sociology Unit Glasgow.

Mack, J. and Lansey, S. (1985, 1st edn; 1993, 2nd edn) *Poor Britain*, London: Allen & Unwin.

Mack, J. and Lansey, S. (1992) *Breadline Britain 1990s: The Findings of the London Weekend Television Series*, London: LWT.

McKenzie, K. and Crowfoot, N. (1994) 'Race, Ethnicity, Culture and Science', *British Medical Journal*, 309, pp. 286–7.

McKeown, T. (1976) *The Role of Medicine: Dream, Mirage or Nemesis?*, Oxford: Basil Blackwell.

Maclean, C. (1977) *The Wolf Children*, Harmondsworth: Allen Lane.

McLoone, P. and Boddy, F. (1994) 'Deprivation and mortality in Scotland, 1981 and 1991', *British Medical Journal*, 309, pp. 1465–70.

McLuhan, M. (1964) *Understanding Media*, quoted in Cohen, J.M. and Cohen, M.J. (1985) *Penguin Dictionary of Modern Quotations*, p. 218.

Macmurray, J. (1961) *Self as Agent*, London: Faber and Faber.

McNay, L. (1994) *Foucault: A Critical Introduction*, London: Polity.

McQuail, D. (1972) *The Sociology of Mass Communications*, Harmondsworth: Penguin.

McRobbie, A. and Garber, J. (1976) 'Girls and Subculture', in S. Hall and T. Jefferson *Resistance Through Rituals*, London: Hutchinson.

McWhirter, I. 'When false prophecy usurps faulty politics', *The Observer*, 3 September 1995.

Maguire, M., Morgan, R. and Reiner, R. (1994) *The Oxford Handbook of Criminology*, Oxford: Clarendon Press.

Mair, L. (1971) *Marriage*, Harmondsworth: Penguin.

Malinowski, B. (1932) *The Sexual Life of Savages in North-Western Melanesia*, London: Routledge.

Mallet, S. (1963) *The New Working Class*, London: Spokesman.

Malson, L and Itard, J. (1972) *Wolf Children: The Wild Boy of Aveyron*, London: New Left Books.

Mann, M. (1993) *The Sources of Social Power*, Cambridge: Cambridge University Press.

Manning, P. (1996) 'Postmodernism and the mass media', *Social Science Teacher*, 25(3), Summer 1996.

Mansfield, P. and Collard, J. (1988) *The Beginning of the Rest of Your Life?*, Basingstoke: Macmillan.

Marcuse, H. (1964) *One Dimensional Man*, London: Routledge.

Marmot, M.G., Davey Smith, G., Stansfield, S., Patel, C., North, F., Head, J., White, I., Brunner, E. and Feeney, A. (1991) 'Health Inequalities among British Civil Servants: The Whitehall II Study', *Lancet*, 337, pp. 1387–93.

Marshall, G. (ed.) (1994) *The Concise Oxford Dictionary of Sociology*, Oxford: Oxford University Press.

Marshall, G., Newby, H., Rose, D. and Vogler, C. (1988) *Social Class in Modern Britain*, London: Hutchinson.

Marshall, T.H. (1954) *Citizenship and Social Class*, Cambridge: Cambridge University Press.

Marsland, D. (1989) 'Face-to-face', *Social Studies Review*, 5(2), p. 55.

Marx, K. (1845, reprinted 1970) *The German Ideology*, London: Lawrence & Wishart

Marx, K. (1859, reprinted 1956) *Karl Marx: Selected Writings in Sociology and Social Philosophy* (ed & trans T.B. Bottomore and M. Rubel), London: Watts & Co.

Marx, K. (1859, reprinted 1956) Preface to *The Critique of Political Economy* (translated Bottomore and Rubel 1956).

Marx, K. (1867, reprinted 1970) *Capital*, Harmondsworth: Penguin.

Marx, K. and Engels, F. (1844/1955) *On Religion*, Moscow: Foreign Language Press.

Marx, K. and Engels, F. (1848, reprinted 1967) *The Communist Manifesto*, Harmondsworth: Penguin.

Massey, D. (1991) 'A global sense of place', *Marxism Today*, June 1991.

Massey, D. (1993) 'Power geometry and a progressive sense of place', in J. Bird *et al.* (eds) *Mapping the Future: Local Cultures, Global Change*, London: Routledge.

Matza, D. (1964) *Delinquency and Drift*, New York: Wiley.

Mead, G.H. (1934) *Mind, Self and Society*, Chicago: University of Chicago Press.

Medved, M. (1992) *Hollywood versus America*, London: HarperCollins.

Meehan, D. (1983) *Ladies of the Evening: Women Characters of Prime Time Television*, New York: Scarecrow Press.

Merson, M. (1995) 'Political explanations for economic decline in Britain (and their relationship to policies for education and training)', *Journal of Education Policy*, 10(3), pp. 303–15.

Merton, R K. (1957, 1968) *Social Theory and Social Structure*, Glencoe: Free Press.

Michels, R. (1949) *Political Parties*, New York: Free Press.

Miliband, R. (1973) *The State in Capitalist Society*, London: Quartet.

Millett, K. (1971) *Sexual Politics*, London: Sphere Books.

Mills, C.W. (1956) *The Power Elite*, Oxford: Oxford University Press.

Mills, C.W. (1963, 1970) *The Sociological Imagination*, Harmondsworth: Penguin.

Mirza, H. (1992) *Young, Female and Black*, London: Routledge.

Mohan, J. (1988) 'Restructuring privatization and the geography of health care provision in England, 1983–1987', *Trans. Institute of British Geographers*, 13(14), pp. 449–65.

Moore, S. (1988) 'Getting a bit of the other: the pimps of postmodernism' in R. Chapman and J. Rutherford (1988) (eds) (1988) *Male Order: Unwrapping Masculinity*, London: Lawrence and Wishart.

Moore, S. (1993) 'A certain ageism', *The Guardian*, 13 August 1993.

Morgan, D.H.J. (1985) *The Family, Politics and Social Theory*, London: Routledge.

Morgan, D.H.J. (1991) 'The family', in M. Haralambos (ed.) *Developments in Sociology*, Vol. 7, Ormskirk: Causeway Press.

Morgan, L. H. (1963) *Ancient Society*, New York: Meridian.

Morley, D. (1980) *The Nationwide Audience*, London: BFI.

Morley, D. (1986) *Family Television: Cultural Power and Domestic Leisure*, London: Comedia.

Morley, D. (1992) *Television Audiences and Cultural Studies*, London: Routledge.

Mosca, G. (1939) *The Ruling Class*, New York: McGraw-Hill.

Mott, P. (1983) *Home Office Adult Prisons and Prisoners in England in Wales*, Home Office Research Study, 1970–82, London: HMSO.

Moxnes, K. (1989) 'Women after divorce: the Vienna Centre Project', in J. Brannen *et al.* (eds) *Cross-National Studies of Household Resources After Divorce*, Aston: Aston Modern Languages Club, Aston University.

Moynihan, D.P. (1967) 'The negro family, the case for national action', in L. Rainwater and W.L. Yancy (eds) (1967) *On Understanding Poverty*, New York: Basic Books.

Mullan, B. and Taylor, L. (1986) *Uninvited Guests: Intimate Secrets of Television and Radio*, London: Chatto & Windus.

Murdock, G.P. (1949) *Social Structure*, New York: Macmillan.

Murray, C. (1984) *Losing Ground*, New York: Basic Books.

Murray, C. (1990) *The Emerging British Underclass*, London: IEA.

Murray, C. (1994) 'The New Victorians and the New Rabble', *Sunday Times*, 29 May 1994, pp. 1.12–13.

Myers, N. (ed.) (1994) *Sickness and Stress: The Gaia Atlas of Planet Management*, London: Gaia Books.

Naughton, J. (1994) 'Britain's cities may be dysfunctional planning disasters. But is that any reason to live in the country?' *The Observer*, 7 August 1994.

Navarro, V. (1978) *Class Struggle, the State and Medicine*, London: Martin Robinson.

Newburn, T. and Hagell, A. (1995) 'Violence on screen', *Sociology Review*, 4(3), Feb. 1995, pp. 7–10.

Newby, H. (1980a) *Community*, Milton Keynes: Open University Press.

Newby, H. (1980b) 'Urbanization and the rural class structure', in H. Newby and F. Buttell *The Rural Sociology of Advanced Societies*, London: Mountclaire.

Newson, E. (1994) *Video Violence and the Protection of Children* (1994 Report), London: Broadcasting Standards Research Monograph.

Nichols, T. and Beynon, H. (1977) *Living with Capitalism*, London: Routledge & Kegan Paul.

Nordlinger, E. (1981) *The Autonomy of the Democratic State*, Cambridge, Massachusetts: Harvard University Press.

Oakley, A. (1972/7) *Sex, Gender and Society*, London: Temple Smith.

Oakley, A. (1974/5) *The Sociology of Housework*, Oxford: Martin Robertson.

O'Brien, M. and Jones, D. (1996) 'Revisiting family and kinship', *Sociology Review*, pp. 19–22.

O'Donnell, M. (1993) *A New Introductory Reader in Sociology*, London, Nelson.

Office of Population Censuses and Surveys (1995) *Health Survey for England 1993*, London: HMSO.

Oppenheim, C. and Harker, L. (1996) *Poverty: The Facts*, London: Child Poverty Action Group.

Orbach, S. (1989) *Fed up and Hungry*, London: Women's Press.

O'Rourke, P.K. (1994) *All the Trouble in the World: the Lighter Side of Famine, Pestilence, Destruction and Death*, London: Picador.

Oxford English Dictionary (1970) Volume 5, Oxford: Clarendon Press.

Pahl, R. (1965) *Urbs in Rure*, London: Weidenfield and Nicholson.

Pahl, R. (1968) *Readings In Urban Sociology*, Oxford: Pergamon.

Pahl, R. (1984) *Divisions of Labour*, Oxford: Blackwell.

Pahl, R. and Gershuny, J. (1980) 'Britain in the decade of three economies', *New Society*, 3 January 1980.

Pahl, R. and Winkler, J. (1974) 'The economic élite: theory and practice' in P. Stanworth and A. Giddens (eds) *Elites and Power in British Society*, Cambridge: Cambridge University Press.

Pareto, V. (1935) *The Mind and Society*, London: Cape.

Park, R.E. (1950) *Race and Culture*, Glencoe: Free Press.

Parker, J. and Dugmore, K. (1977/78) 'Race and the allocation of public housing: a GLC survey', *New Community*, 6, pp. 27–40.

Parker, S. (1971) *The Future of Work and Leisure*, London: McGibbon & Kee.

Parker, S. (1976) *The Sociology of Leisure*, London: Allen & Unwin.

Parker, S. (1983) *Leisure and Work*, London: Allen & Unwin.

Parkin, F. (1971) *Class Inequality and Political Order*, London: McGibbon and Kee.

Parlee (1982) article in *The Psychology of Women Quarterly*, 7(2), p. 119.

Parsons, T. (1951) *The Social System*, New York: Free Press.

Parsons, T. (1959) 'The social structure of the family', in R.N. Anshen (ed.) *The Family, its Functions and Destiny*, New York: Harper Row.

Parsons, T. (1969) *Politics and Social Structure*, New York: The Free Press.

Patrick, D.L. and Scramble, G. (1986) *Sociology as Applied to Medicine*, London: Ballière Tindall.

Patrick, J. (1973) *A Glasgow Gang Observed*, London: Eyre Methuen.

Pawson, R. (1995) 'Methods of content/document/media analysis', in M. Haralambos (ed.) *Developments in Sociology*, Vol. 11, Ormskirk: Causeway.

Payne, G. (1994) 'Community and community studies', *Sociology Review*, 4(1), September, pp. 16–19.

Pearce, F. (1976) *Crimes of the Powerful*, London: Pluto Press.

Pearson, G. (1983) *In Search of the Hooligan Solution: A History of Respectable Fears*, London: Macmillan.

Penn, R. (1984) *Skilled Workers in the Class Structure*, Cambridge: Cambridge University Press.

Perks, R. (1992) 'Managing a school and developing a grant-maintained ethos', in B. Davies and L. Anderson *Opting for Self-Management*, London: Routledge.

Pfeffer, N. (1987) 'Artificial insemination, in vitro fertilisation and the stigma of infertility', in M. Stanworth (ed.) *Reproductive Technologies: Gender, Motherhood and Medicine*, Cambridge: Polity.

Phillimore, P. and Morris, D. (1991) 'Discrepant legacies, premature mortality in two industrial towns', *Social Science and Medicine*, 33(2), pp. 139–152.

Phillimore, P., Beattie, A. and Townsend, P. (1994) 'Widening inequality of health in Northern England, 1981–91', *British Medical Journal*, 308, pp. 1125–28.

Phillips, T. (1995) 'Constructing vocational identities', *The Vocational Aspect of Education*, 47(1), pp. 5–19.

Piachaud, D. (1981) 'Peter Townsend and the Holy Grail', *New Society*, 10 September.

Piore, M. and Sabel, C. (1984) *The Second Industrial Divide: Prospects for Prosperity*, New York: Basic Books.

Plummer, K. (1979) 'Misunderstanding labelling perspectives', in D. Downes and P. Rock (eds) *Deviant Interpretations*, London: Martin Robertson.

Polsky, N. (1967) *Hustlers, Beats and Others*, New York: Aldine.

Popper, K. (1959) *The Logic of Scientific Discovery*, London: Hutchinson.

Porter, R. (1986) *Patients and Practitioners: Lay Perceptions of Medicine in Pre-industrial Society*, Cambridge: Cambridge University Press.

Postiglione, G.A. (ed.) (1991) *Education and society in Hong Kong*, Hong Kong: ME Sharpe Inc.

Potter, J. and Wetherell, M. (1987) *Discourse and Social Psychology*, London: Sage.

Poulantzas, N. (1973) *Political Power and Social Classes*, London: Verso.

Power, C., Manor, O. and Fox, J. (1991) *Health and Class: the Early Years*, London: Chapman Hall.

Price, S. (1993) *Media Studies*, London: Pitman.

Pryce, K. (1979) *Endless Pressure*, Harmondsworth: Penguin.

Pyle, G. (1990) 'Regional inequalities in infant mortality within North Carolina, USA', *Espace, Populations, Sociétiés*, 3, pp. 439–45.

Rahkonen, O., Arber, S. and Lahelma, E. (1995) 'Health inequalities in early adulthood: a comparison of young men and women in Britain and Finland, *Social Science and Medicine*, 41(2), pp. 161–71.

Raleigh, V., and Balarajan, R. (1994) 'Public health and the 1991 Census: non-random under-enumeration complicates interpretation', *British Medical Journal*, 309, pp. 287–8.

Rapoport, R. and Rapoport, R.N. (1975) *Leisure and the Family Life-Cycle*, London: Routledge.

Registrar General (1911) *Annual Report of the Registrar General*, London: HMSO.

Renner, K. (1953) *Wandlungen der Modernen Gesellschaft: Zwei Abhundlungen über die Probleme der Nachkriegszeit*, Vienna: Wiener Volksbuchhandlung.

Rex, J. and Moore, R. (1967) *Race, Community and Conflict*, London: Oxford University Press.

Rex, J. and Tomlinson, S. (1979) *Colonial Immigrants in a British City*, London: Routledge & Kegan Paul.

Ritzer, G. (1993) *The MacDonaldisation of Society*, Thousand Oaks: Pine Forge Press.

Roberts, D. (1995) *British Politics in Focus*, Ormskirk: Causeway Press.

Roberts, H. and Woodward, D. (1981) 'Changing patterns of women's employment in sociology', *British Journal of Sociology*, 32.

Roberts, K. (1986) 'Leisure', in M. Haralambos (ed.) *Developments in Sociology*, Vol. 2.

Roberts, K. (1995) *Youth and Employment in Modern Britain*, Oxford: Oxford University Press.

Roberts, K., Campbell, R. and Furlong, A. (1990) 'Class and gender divisions among young adults at leisure', in C. Wallace and M. Cross *Youth in Transition*, London: Falmer.

Robertson, R. (1994) *Globalisation*, London: Sage.

Robinson, V. (1994) 'The geography of ethnic minorities', *Geography Review*, 7(4), pp. 10–15.

Robson *et al.* (1994) quoted in *The Guardian*, 6 March 1994.

Rojek, C. (1993) *Ways of Escape*, London: Macmillan.

Rorty, R. (1989) *Contingency, Irony and Solidarity*, Cambridge: Cambridge University Press.

Rorty, R. (1991) *Essays on Heidegger and Others*, Cambridge: Cambridge University Press.

Rosen, H. (1974) *Language and Social Class* (3rd edn), Bristol: Falling Wall Press.

Rosenhan, D.L. (1975) 'On being sane in insane places', *Journal of Abnormal Psychology*, 84(5), pp. 462–74.

Rostow, W. (1960) *The Stages of Economic Growth*, Cambridge: Cambridge University Press.

Rowntree, S. (1901) *Poverty: A Study of Town Life*, London: Macmillan.

Rowntree, S. (1941) *Poverty and Progress*, London: Longman.

Rowntree, S. and Lavers, G. (1951) *Poverty and the Welfare State*, London: Longman.

Rutter, M. and Madge, N. (1976) *Cycles of Disadvantage: A Review of Research*, London: Heinemann.

Said, E. (1985) *Orientalism*, Harmondsworth: Penguin.

Sainsbury, P. (1955) *Suicide in London: An Ethnomethodological Study*, London: Chapman.

Sainsbury, P. and Barraclough, B. (1968) 'Differences between suicide rates', *Nature*, 220.

Salter, B. and Tapper, E.R. (1988) 'The politics of reversing the ratchet in secondary education, 1969–1986', *Journal of Education Administration and History*, 20(2), July 1988, pp. 57–70.

Saunders, P. (1983) *Urban Politics: A Sociological Interpretation*, London: Hutchinson.

Saunders, P. (1990) *Social Class and Stratification*, London: Routledge.

Schaefer, R.T. and Lamm, R.P. (1994) *Sociology: A Brief Introduction*, New York: McGraw-Hill.

Schutz, A. (1932/1972) *The Phenomenology of the Lifeworld*, London: Heinemann.

Scott, H. (1976) *Women and Socialism*, London: Allison & Busby.

Scott, J. (1986) 'The debate on ownership and control', in *Social Studies Review*, Jan. 1986.

Scraton, P. (1991) 'Recent developments in criminology: a critical overview', in M. Haralambos (ed.) *Developments in Sociology*, Vol. 7, Ormskirk: Causeway.

Scraton, S. (1992) 'Leisure', in M. Haralambos (ed.) *Developments in Sociology*, Vol. 8, Ormskirk: Causeway.

Scraton, S. and Bramham, P. (1995) 'Leisure and postmodernity', in M. Haralambos (ed.) *Developments in Sociology*, Vol. 11, Ormskirk: Causeway.

Secombe, W. (1992) *A Millennium of Family Change*, London: Verso.

Sen, A.K. (1985) 'Poor relatively speaking', *Oxford Economic Papers*.

Senior, M. (1996) 'Health, illness and postmodernism', *Sociology Review*, 6(1), September 1996.

Sennett, R. (1997) 'Drowning in syrup', *Times Literary Supplement*, February.

Sharma, V. (1992) *Complementary Medicine Today*, London: Routledge.

Sharpe, S. (1976, 2nd edn 1994) *Just Like a Girl: How Girls Learn to be Women*, Harmondsworth: Penguin.

Sheeran, Y. (1995) 'Sociology, biology and health: is illness only a social construction?', *Sociology Review*, 4(4), April 1995.

Sheldon, T. and Parker, H. (1992) 'Race and ethnicity in health research', *Journal of public health medicine*, 14(2), pp. 104–16.

Shields, R. (ed) (1992) *Lifestyle Shopping: The Subject of Consumption*, London: Routledge.

Showalter, E. (1991) *The Female Malady: Women, Madness and English Culture 1830–1980*, London: Virago.

Simmel, G. (1903/50) 'The metropolis and mental life', in Wolff, K. (ed.) *The Sociology of George Simmel*, Glencoe: Free Press.

Simon, B. (1994) *The State and Educational Change*, London: Lawrence & Wishart.

Skeggs, B. (1994) 'Masculinity in war films', 1994 Updates Conference lecture in Manchester.

Skellington, R. and Morris, P. (1992) *Race in Britain Today*, London: Sage.

Sklair, L. (1991) *Sociology of the Global System*: London: Harvester/ Wheatsheaf.

Sklair, L. (1993) 'Going global: competing models of globalisation', *Sociology Review*, November.

Skocpol, T. (1979) *States and Social Revolutions*, Cambridge: Cambridge University Press.

Slattery, M. (1990) 'Urban Sociology', in M. Haralambos (ed.) *Sociology New Directions*, Ormskirk: Causeway Press.

Smart, C. (1976) *Women, Crime and Criminality*, London: RKP.

Smelser, N. (1963) *Theory of Collective Behaviour*, New York: Free Press.

Smith, A. (1776/1991) *The Wealth of Nations*, London: Everyman.

Smith, A.D. (1995) 'The dark side of nationalism: the revival of nationalism in late twentieth-century Europe', in L. Cheles (ed.) *The Far Right in Western and Eastern Europe*, London: Longman.

Smith, A.D. (1995b) 'Towards a global culture?', in M. Featherstone (ed.) *Global Culture*, London: Sage.

Smith, D. (1989) 'Exploring the city: the Chicago School', *Sociology Review*, 4(4), pp. 164–7.

Smith, D. (1990) *Stepmothering*, London: Harvester.

Smith, D.J. and Tomlinson, S. (1989) *The School Effect: A Study of Multiracial Comprehensives*, London: Policy Studies Institute.

Snider, L. (1993) 'The politics of corporate crime control', in F. Pearce and M. Woodiwiss, *Global Crime Connections*, Basingstoke: Macmillan.

Social Trends, Annual publication, published by the Office for National Statistics, http://www.ons.gov.uk/ welcome.htm

Sontag, S. (1978) 'The double standard of ageing', in V. Carver and P. Liddiard (eds) *An Ageing Population*, London: Hodder & Stoughton.

Soothill, K. and Walby, S. (1991) *Sex Crime in the News*, London: Routledge.

Sorokin, P.I. (1959) *Cultural and Social Mobility*, Glencoe, Illinois: Free Press.

Spender, D. (1983) *Invisible Women*, London: Women's Press.

Stacey, J. (1993) 'Untangling feminist theory', in D. Richardson and V. Robertson (eds) *Introducing Women's Studies*, London: Macmillan.

Stainton Rogers, W. (1991) *Explaining Health and Illness: An exploration of Diversity*, Hemel Hempstead: Harvester/Wheatsheaf.

Stanworth, M. (1983) *Gender and Schooling*, London: Hutchinson.

Stanworth, M. (1984) 'Women and class analysis: a reply to John Goldthorpe', *Sociology*, 18.

Stanworth, M. (1987) *Reproductive Technologies*, Cambridge: Polity.

Stark, R. and Bainbridge, W. (1985) *The Future of Religion*, Berkeley: University of California Press.

Strauss, A. Erlich, D., Bucher, R., Sabschin, M. and Schatzman, L. (1978) 'The hospital and its negotiated order' in P. Worsley *et al.* (eds) *Modern Sociology*, Harmondsworth: Penguin.

Strinati, D. (1992) 'Postmodernism and popular culture', *Sociology Review*, 11(4), April 1992.

Sugrue, B. and Taylor, C. (1996a) 'Cultures and identities', *Sociology Review*, 5(3), pp. 10–13.

Sugrue, B. and Taylor, C. (1996b) 'From Marx to Man. City: sociology and popular culture', *Sociology Review*, 6(1), pp. 2–6.

Svennevig, M., Haldan, I., Speirs, S. and Gunter, B. (1989) *Godwatching: Viewers, Religion and Television*, London: John Libbey/IBA.

Sweeting, H. and West, P. (1994) 'The patterning of the events in mid to late adolescence: markers for the future?', *Journal of Adolescence*, 17, pp. 283–304.

Sweeting, H. and West, P. (1995) 'Family life and health in adolescence: a role for culture and the health inequalities debate', *Social Science and Medicine*, 40(2), pp. 163–75.

Synott, A. (1988) 'Little angels, little devils', in G. Handel (ed.) *Childhood Socialisation*, Aldine de Gruyter, New York: Hawthorne.

Szasz, T.S. (1974) *The Myth of Mental Illness*, New York: Harper and Row.

Taylor F.W. (1947) *Scientific Management*, New York: Harper & Row.

Taylor, I., Walton, P. and Young, J. (1973) *The New Criminology*, London: RKP.

Taylor, L. (1971) *Deviance and Society*, London: Michael Joseph.

Taylor, S. (1988) *The Sociology of Suicide*, London: Longman.

Taylor, S. (1990) 'Beyond Durkheim: sociology and suicide', *Social Studies Review*, November.

Teague, A. (1993) 'Ethnic group: first results of the 1991 Census', *OPCS Population Trends*, 72, Summer, pp. 12–17.

Thomas, W.I. (1928) *The Child in America*, New York: Knopf.

Thompson, E.P. (1986) 'Work', in M. Haralambos (ed) *Developments in Sociology*, Vol. 2.

Tierney, J. (1996) *Criminology: Theory and Context*, Hemel Hempstead: Prentice Hall/Harvester Wheatsheaf.

Timms, D.W.G. (1976) 'Social bases to social areas', in P. Knox (1992) *Urban Social Geography: An Introduction*, London: Longman.

Tonnies, F. (1957) *Community and Society*, New York: Harper & Row.

Touraine, A. (1992) 'Beyond social movements', *Theory, Culture and Society*, 9, pp. 125–45.

Townsend, P. (1979) *Poverty in the UK*, Berkeley: University of California Press.

Townsend, P. (1993) *The International Analysis of Poverty*, Hemel Hempstead: Harvester.

Townsend, P., Phillimore, P. and Beattie, A. (1988) *Health and Deprivation: Inequality and the North*, London: Croom Helm.

Trew, T. (1979) 'What the papers say', in R. Fowler (ed.) *Language and Control*, London: Routledge.

Troeltsch, E. (1931) *The Social Teachings of the Christian Churches*, London: Allen & Unwin.

Trowler, P. (1995) *Investigating Education and Training*, London: Collins Educational.

Trowler, P. (1996) *Investigating Mass Media* (2nd edn), London: Collins Educational.

Troyna, B. (1993) 'Can you see the join? An historical analysis of multicultural and antiracist education policies' in D. Gill *et al.* (eds) (1992) *Racism and Education: Structures and Strategies*, London: Sage.

Troyna, B. and Carrington, B. (1990) *Education, Racism and Reform*, London: Routledge.

Tuckett, D. and Kaufert, J.M. (eds) (1978) *Basic Readings in Medical Sociology*, London: Tavistock.

Tudor-Hart, J. (1971) 'The Inverse Care Law', *Lancet*, (27 Feb), pp. 405–12.

Tumin, M. (1953) 'Some principles of social stratification: a critical analysis', *American Sociological Review*, 18.

Tunstall, J. (1962) *The Fisherman*, London: McGibbon & Kee.

Turner, B. (1983) *Religion and Social Theory*, London: Gower.

Turner, G. (1990) *British Cultural Studies*, London: Unwin Hyman.

UNESCO (1995) *World Education Report 1995*, Paris: UNESCO.

Urry, J. (1990) *The Tourist Gaze*, London: Sage.

Useem, M. (1984) *The Inner Circle: Large Corporations and the Rise of Business Political Activity in the United States and the United Kingdom*, Oxford: Oxford University Press.

Van Dalen, H., Williams, A. and Gudex, C. (1994) 'Lay people's evaluation of health: are there variations between different subgroups?', *Journal of Epidemiology and community health*, 48, pp. 248–53.

Veal, A. (1993) 'The concept of lifestyle: a review', *Leisure Studies*, Vol. 12, pp. 230–52.

Waddington, D., Wykes, M. and Critcher, C. (1991) *Split at the Seams? Community, Continuity and Change after the 1984–5 Coal Dispute*, Milton Keynes: Open University Press.

Walby, S. (1990) *Theorizing Patriarchy*, Oxford, Basil Blackwell.

Walker, C. and Walker, A. (1995) 'Poverty and the Poor', *Developments in Sociology*, Vol. 10, Lancaster: Causeway Press.

Walklate, S. (1994) 'Crime victims: another "ology"?', *Sociology Review*, 3(3).

Walklate, S. (1995) *Gender and Crime*, Hemel Hempstead: Prentice Hall/Harvester Wheatsheaf.

Wallerstein, I. (1995) 'Culture as the ideological battleground of the modern world-system', in M. Featherstone (ed.) *Global Culture*, London: Sage.

Wallis, R. (1976) *The Road to Total Freedom*, London: Heinemann.

Wallis, R. (1984) *The Elementary Forms of the New Religious Life*, London: Routledge.

Ward, D. (1980) 'Environs and neighbours in the "Two Nations": residential differentiation in Leeds', *Journal of Historical Geography*, 6.

Warde, A. and Abercrombie, A. (1994) *Family, Households and the Life Course*, Lancaster, Framework Press.

Warren, W. (1981) *Imperialism Pioneer of Capitalism*, London: Verso.

Waters, M. (1995) *Globalization*: London: Routledge.

Watson, H. (1994) 'Women and the Veil: personal responses to global process', in A.S. Ahmed and H. Donnan *Islam, Globalization and Postmodernity*, London: Routledge.

Waugh, D. (1990) *Geography: An Integrated Approach*, Hong Kong: Nelson.

Weber, M. (1904, reprinted 1974) *The Protestant Ethic and the Spirit of Capitalism*, London: Unwin.

Weber, M. (1919, reprinted 1970) 'Politics as a vocation', in H. Gerth and C.W. Mills *From Max Weber*, London: Routledge.

Weber, M. (1920/63) *The Sociology of Religion*, Boston: Beacon.

Weber, M. (1922/1978) 'The soteriology of the underprivileged', from W.G. Runciman (1978) *Weber: Selections in Translation*, London: Cambridge University Press.

Weber, M. (1948) in H.H. Gerth and C.W. Mills (eds) *Max Weber: Essays in Sociology*, London: Routledge & Kegan Paul.

Weber, M. (1978) *Economy and Society: An Outline of Interpretive Sociology*, 2 Volumes, Berkeley: University of California Press.

Webster, A. (1984) *Introduction to the Sociology of Development*, London: Macmillan.

Webster, P. (1996) 'Sociology and the genes debate', *Sociology Review*, 6(1), September, pp. 7–10.

Wedderburn, D. and Crompton, R. (1976) *Workers' Attitudes and Technology*, Cambridge: Cambridge University Press.

Weeks, J. (1986) *Sexuality*, London: Tavistock.

Whillock, R. and Slayden, D. (1995) *Hate Speech*, London: Sage.

Whitehead, M. (1987) *The Health Divide: Social Inequalities in Health*, Health Education Council.

Whitty, G. (1989) 'The New Right and the National Curriculum: state control or market forces', *Journal of Education Policy*, 4(4), pp. 329–41.

WHO/EURO (1984) 'Summary report of the working group on concepts and principles of health promotion', reproduced in T. Abelin (1987) *Measurement in Health Promotion and Protection*, Copenhagen, WHO.

Whyte, W.F. (1955) *Street Corner Society* (2nd edn), Chicago: University of Chicago Press.

Wickman, P.M. (1991) *Encyclopaedic Dictionary of Sociology*, Guilford, Connecticut: Dushkin.

Wilkinson, R. (1993) 'The impact of income distribution and life expectancy', in S. Platt, H. Thomas, S. Scott, and G. Williams (eds.), *Locating Health: Sociological and Historical Explorations*, Aldershot: Avebury.

Williams, A. (ed.) (1989) *Issues in Physical Education for the Primary Years*, London: Falmer Press.

Williams, J. (1995) *FA Premier League Fan Survey 1994–95*, Leicester: University of Leicester.

Williams, R. (1973) *The Country and the City*, London: Chatto & Windus.

Willis, P. (1977) *Learning to Labour*, London: Saxon House.

Willis, P. (1990) *Common Culture: Symbolic Work at Play in the Everyday Lives of the Young*, Milton Keynes: Open University Press.

Willmott, P. (1963) *The Evolution of Community: A Study of Dagenham after Forty Years*, London: Routledge & Kegan Paul.

Willmott, P. and Young, M. (1961) *Family and Kinship in East London*, Harmondsworth: Penguin.

Wilson, B. (1982) *Religion in Sociological Perspective*, London: Oxford University Press.

Wilson, E.O. (1975) *Socio-biology: the New Synthesis*, Cambridge, Massachusetts: Harvard University Press.

Wilson, J.Q. (1977) *Thinking About Crime*, New York: Vintage Books.

Wilson, J.Q. and Herrnstein, R.J. (1985) *Crime and Human Nature*, New York: Touchstone.

Wilson, W.J. (1987) *The Truly Disadvantaged*, Chicago: University of Chicago Press.

Woodward, M., Shewry, M., Smith, W.G. and Tunstall Pedoe, H. (1990) 'Coronary heart disease and socio-economic factors in Edinburgh and north Glasgow', *The Statistician*, 39, pp. 319–29.

Wright Mills, C. *see* Mills, C.W.

Young, J. (1971) *The Drugtakers*, London: McGibbon & Key.

Young, J. (1988) 'Recent developments in criminology', in M. Haralambos (ed.) *Developments in Sociology*, Vol. 4, Ormskirk: Causeway Press.

Young, J. and Matthews, R. (1992) *Rethinking Criminology: The Realist Debate*, London: Sage.

Young, M. (1961) *The Rise of the Meritocracy*, Harmondsworth: Penguin.

Young, M. and Willmott, P. (1957) *Family and Kinship in East London*, Harmondsworth: Penguin.

Young, M. and Willmott, P. (1975) *The Symmetrical Family*, Harmondsworth: Penguin.

Young, M. and Willmott, P. (1986) *Social Networks, Informal Care and Public Policy*, London: Policy Studies Institute.

Young, M.F.D. (ed.) (1971) *Knowledge and Control*, London: Routledge.

Index

reproductive technology 120
residues 582
reskilling 181
rewards 229–31
rights, civil and political 593
risk 57, 401, 423, 595, 599–600
risk society 600
rites of passage (*rites de passage*) 248, 645
romantic love 102
Rowntree, Seebohm 460–1
rural life 357–65
 changes in 373
 compared with urban life 358–9
 conflict in 369, 372–5
 effect of newcomers on 373
 Fearnbeg study 374
 hunting 374
 move towards 370–6
 oppression in 375
 social class and 369, 372
rural–urban continuum 376

S

sabotage, industrial 184
Said, Edward 52
Saunders, Peter 230–1
Saussure, Ferdinand de 290
scars 28
schizophrenia, individual and institutional 567
schools 125
 church 126
 competition between 155, 160
 comprehensive 127, 129–30
 counsellors in 138
 grammar 126, 161
 grant-maintained 155, 158, 159–61
 interaction with home culture 136
 labelling of pupils 138–9, 140
 local authorities and 126–7, 129, 155, 159–60
 organization of 132
 performance of 145–6
 selection of pupils 161
 staying-on rate 155
 types of 159
Schutz, Alfred 287–8
Scientology 636, 637
Scraton, Phil 502–3
Secombe, Wally 71
sects 628–31
 Branch-Davidian 141
 conflict with society 629, 631
 conversionist 630

differences from cults 631–2
 introversionist 630
 manipulationalist 630
 origin of 629, 631
 reformist 630
 revolutionist 630, 631
 state and 629
 thaumaturgical 630
 typology of 630
 utopian 630, 631
secularization 11–12, 641, 642–4
 measuring 644
self
 defensive 51
 ideal 422
 projects of 47–50
 reflexive 594, 596, 599
 work and 50–1
self-identity 222, 596
 ethnicity and 242
self-image 231
semiotics 542
Sen, Amartya 459
Sennett, Richard 610–11
sex 23
 ambiguous 26
 changing 26
 determination of 25–6
 interaction with gender 24–5
 legal definition 26
 number of 26
 Olympic definition 25–6
 society and 90
sexism, avoiding 95
sexual dysfunction 89
sexuality 89–90, 284–5
 biological rules 24
 diversity 24
 non-normative 26
 pathological 24
 repressed 285
shareholding 176
Sharpe, Sue 148–9
Shields, Rob 46
shopping 45–6, 211–12
 lifestyle 45
shopping malls *see* malls
sickle-cell anaemia 438
sickness *see* illness
significant others 23
Sikhism 654
Simmel, Georg 4, 359–60, 366
single parents 95, 96–7, 112–13
 women 112–13
skill polarization 182

skills
 file organization 12
 note-taking 10–12
 reading 10
 sociological 7–8
 study 10–12
 transferable 8
Sklair, Leslie 329–30
Skocpol, Theda 586
slavery 321
social action 282, 609
 affective 282
 focus on 287–9
 goal-oriented 282
 traditional 282
 value-oriented 282
social anthropology 5, 24
social behaviour 3
social change
 convergence theory 318
 defining 658
 development theories 317–18
 evolutionary theories 317–19
 modernization theories 317–18
 revolutionary 287
 theories 316–22
 underdevelopment theory 319–22
 see also development
social class 51, 280–1
 determined by health 431
 stereotyping 560
social constructionists 24–5
social control
 agencies of 484–5
 family and 484
 in the home 513
 law and 484
 media and 484
 police and 484
 religion and 484
 schools and 484
 sociological perspectives on 484
 of women 513
 work and 484, 513
social determinism 178–80
 variations in 179–80
social differentiation 30
social facts 278
social grade schema 612–13
social inequalities 282, 286
socialism, irrelevance in postmodern society 588–9
socialist feminism *see* feminism, socialist
socialization 36–9, 124
 change and 37–8

Permissions

The Publisher, authors and editors would like to thank the organizations listed below for permission to reproduce material from their publications. (Sources for all extracts are given on the relevant pages and full bibliographic information is given in the References on pp. 663–678.)

page

63	Kidscape
64	McGraw-Hill Inc
68	Penguin Books Ltd
183	*Lancashire Evening Telegraph*
185	*The Blackburn Citizen*
193	Employment News
194	Faber & Faber Ltd
217	The California Council for Social Studies (*Social Studies Review*)
218	*OPCS Monitor*
223	Polity Press
256	Oxford University Press
320	Mitchell Beazley
331	Oxford University Press
343	Penguin Books Ltd
346	ME Sharpe Inc.
418	The Consumers Association
418	*Glasgow Evening Times*
433	Ballère Tindall
445	Croom Helm
446	OPCS Monitor
459	Causeway Press
461	Child Poverty Action Group
462	Peter Townsend *Poverty in the United Kingdom: A Survey of Household Resources and Standards of Living* Copyright (c) 1979 Peter Townsend. University of California Press
463	Domino Films/London Weekend Television
464	Independent Educational Publishers
465	Child Poverty Action Group
466	Parliamentary copyright material from Hansard is reproduced with the permission of the Controller of Her Majesty's Stationery Office on behalf of Parliament.
466	Child Poverty Action Group
471	The California Council for Social Studies (*Social Studies Review*)
532	Media Guide
552	*The Voice*
576	Media Guide
605	Polity Press.
606	Polity Press.
613	Phillip Allan Publishers Ltd (*Politics Review*)
615	Causeway Press Ltd
615	Oxford University Press

Particular thanks are extended to the following organizations who have allowed us to quote extensively from their publications:

❖ Central Office for Statistics, for tables taken from *Social Trends* (see website information on p. 198)

❖ the following newspapers and journals: *The Guardian, The Independent, The Observer, The Sunday Mirror, The Sunday Times, The Mail on Sunday, The Citizen, Community Care, Sociology Review.*

Every effort has been made to contact copyright holders, but if any has been inadvertently overlooked, the Publisher will be pleased to make the necessary arrangements at the first opportunity.

Photographs